W9-BJD-084

To Order a Copy of This Book, Please Mail To:
MICHAEL A BLAUGHER   Author / Publisher
124 EAST FOSTER PARKWAY
FORT WAYNE, IN 46806-1730
(260) 744-1020
e-mail: airmuseums@aol.com,
www.aircraftmuseums.com

Museum Codes:

AFB	=	Air Force Base	Dr	=	Drive	P	=	Restoration Project	
Adm	=	Admission	E	=	Easter	PA	=	Public Affairs	
ANG	=	Air National Guard	Exec	=	Executive	POB	=	Post Office Box	
Appt	=	Appointment	Intl	=	International	Pres	=	President	
ARB	=	Air Reserve Base	Jr	=	Junior	Rep	=	Replica	
Ave	=	Avenue	L	=	Labor (Sept 1)	RoY	=	Rest of Year	
Blvd	=	Boulevard	M	=	Memorial	Snrs	=	Senior Citizen	
C	=	Christmas	Mi	=	Miles	S	=	Static Indoor Display	
CAF	=	Commemorative Air Force	Mncpl	=	Municipal	St	=	Street	
D	=	Day	N	=	New Years	T	=	Thanksgiving	
Dir	=	Director	NAS	=	Naval Air Station				

All aircraft are stated by their Type, Model and Series For sorting purpose in the Aircraft Alphabetical section of this book. All aircraft in this book are listed with one letter with the full any addition letters name in parentheses. **Example U H - 1A is listed as H - 1A (U H)**

Due to constant changes any information in this book may not be correct. For current information contact the museum. Some Military Bases may not allow civilians on the base unless you get a pass. Check ahead for the bases you plan to visit.

Other Items Available by Author - Contact the Author above for information
- **Get this 24th Edition Book on CD in PDF Format**
- **Advertise in the next edition** (Artwork to have embedded fonts, 0.125 Bleed Off, jpg, tiff, pdf)
- **Mailing List on CD in MS Excel format to Aircraft Museum Gift Shops in this book.**

Advertisers Index:	Page		
		Marfa Gliders	132
Aero-Grafix	132A	Military Magazine	100
Flight Journal Magazine	132B	TMC Pacific Modelworks	132D

Feature Photos		Page	Feature Photos	Page
Cavanaugh Flight Museum - Addison, TX		Front Cover /	Bomber Restaurant, Milwaukee, WI - 132D	
US Midway Museum - San Diego, CA		Front Cover /	Willow Grove NAS Museum, PA - 132D	
Pacific Aviation Museum, Honolulu, HI		Back Cover		

Publication Yearly,	1 st Ed Published May 1987	ISBN 0-9749772-1-7
	24 th Ed Published June 2007	ISBN 0-9749772-2-5

ALABAMA

Ardmore - Alabama Welcome Center, 26865 I-65, 35739, (256) 423-3891, AL / TN Border, Saturn I Apollo

Birmingham - Southern Museum of Flight, 4343 73rd St N, 35206-3642, (205) 833-8226, Fax 836-2439, Tue-Sat 9:30-4:30, Sun 1-4:30, Adm Adult $5, Snrs & Child $4 Under 4 Free, Exec Dir Wayne, Library, Gift Shop, Restoration Facility and Theater. www.southernmuseumofflight.org, (AP)=Air Park, (EB)=Engineering Bldg, (EA)=Early Aviation Hanger, (GA)=General Aviation Hanger, (L)=On Loan, (MG)=Museum Grounds, (R)=Restoration Bldg, (SW)=South Wing

A-4J(TA) Cockpit	(SW)(L)	F-86F	(SW)(L)	Piel-Emeraude	(GA)
A-7E	(MG)(L)	F-100C	(AP)(L)	Pitts Special	(GA)
A-12	(AP)(S L)	F-101	(SW)(L)	PL-4A	(GA)
AT-6G	(SW)	F-102A(TF)	(AP)(L)	PT-19 Project	(SW)
Aero Commander 680	(AP)	F-104	(AP)(L)	R4D-6Q	(AP)
Aeronca 11AC	(SW)	F-105F	(AP) L)	Rand KR-1	(GA)
Aeronca K	(R)	F-106	(SW)(L)	RC-3	(SW)
B-25C	(SW)	F-111A	(AP)	Ross Seabird	(GA)
B-26(A-26C)	(EB)(L)	Foker D.VII	(EA)	Rotorway Helicopter	(GA)
BD-4	(GA)	Follant Gnat		Rutan Vari-Eze	(GA)
BD-5B	(GA)	Forney Ercoupe F-1	(SW)	S2F-1(TS-2A)	(AP)
Beagle B.206	(AP)	Glassair II-FT	(GA)	Sport Fury	(GA)
Beech Starship	(AP)	H-1(AH)	(L)	Starduster	(GA)
Bell Model 47(H-13)	(SW)	H-1(UH)	(MG)(L)	Stearman Cropduster	(R)
Bensen Gyrocopter	(GA)	H-6(OH)	(GA)(L)	Stinson SR-5	(R)
BT-13B	(SW)(L)	H-54B(CH)	(AP)(L)	Stinson 10-A	(R)
Bushby Mustang II	(GA)	Harrison Mini-Mack	(GA)	T-2C	(AP)(L)
C-45 Fuse	(EB)	Heath Super Parasol	(GA)	T-28	(AP)(L)
Cessna 310A	(AP)	Huff-Daland Duster	(EA)(L)	T-33A	(EB)(L)
Cessna 337A	(AP)(L)	J-3 Project	(S L)	T-33A	(SW)(L)
Culver Cadet	(SW)	L-39C	(AP)	T-34B	(R)
Cumulus Glider	(GA)	Link Trainer	(GA)	T-37B	(AP)(L)
Curtiss D.5 Rep	(EH)	Longwing Eaglerock	(EA)	T-38	(AP)(L)
Davis DA-2	(GA)	MiG-15	(SW)(L)	T-39	(AP)(L)
Decathlon	(SW)	MiG-21	(AP)(L)	TG-4A	(SW)
F-4N	(MG)(L)	Mitchell B-10 Buzzard	(GA)	Vari-Viggen	(GA)
F-14	(AP)(L)	Monerai S Glider	(GA)	Wright Flyer Replica	(EA)(L)
F-84F	(AP)	Mooney Mite M.18	(SW)		
F-84F	(R)(L)	NE-1	(EB)(L)		

Huntsville - Alabama Space & Rocket Center, 1 Tranquility Base, Off I-565 Between I-65 and US 231, 35805-3371, (800) 633-7280, (256) 837-3400, Daily 9-5 Except: Memorial-Labor Day, Daily 9-5, Closed TD, CE, CD, NE, ND, Adm Adult $16, Child 6-12 $11, www.spacecamp.com/museum   Quick 1910,   A-12,   V-1 & V-2 Rockets Spacecraft

Aviation Challenge, 1 Tranquility Base, 35805-3371, (888) 364-3483, Aviation Camps for Grades 4-12 & Adult, One Week of: Land/Water Survival, Principals and Simulator Flight Basics

www.dogfite.com	F-4	F-111	YAV-8B Harrier II
AH-1	F-14	MiG-17	

U.S. Space Camp, 1 Tranquility Base, 35805-3371, (800) 637-7223, Space Camp for Grades 4-12 & Adult, One Week of: Space Training & Missions, www.spacecamp.com Static Displays Include: SR-71, Apollo 16, Saturn V, Space Shuttle,

Redstone Arsenal, Gate 9, Martin Rd and Mills Rd, Base Pass Needed

ACH-47A	AH-1F	AH-64A	UH-1M

Maxwell AFB, Chennault Circle, 36112-5000, (334) 293-2017, Air University, Daily 7-6, Free Adm

B-25J"Poopsie"	F-86L"Chris"	F-105D
B-52D	F-100C	T-38A
F-4C	F-101C(RF)	T-38A

ALABAMA

Mobile - Battleship Memorial Park, 2703 Battleship Parkway, 36601, Between
Exit 27&30, Mail: POB 65, (251) 433-2703, Oct-March 8-4, April-Sept, 8-6, Closed CD,
Adm Adult $12, Child 6-11 $6, Under 6 Free, Gift Shop, Breakfast $14-18,
Lunch $16-18, Dinner $24-27, www.ussalabama.com

A-12 Cygnus 938	F-86L	KA-6D	M-26 Tank
A-4L	F-8G(RF)	OS2U	M-48AL Tank
B-25J	F-105B-IRE	P-51D(F)	M-42A1 Tank
B-52D	F4B-4 Rep	SH-2F	M-60A1 Tank
C-47D(VC)	F4U-7	YF-17(F/A-18)	T-55 Tank Iraqi
CH-21B	F8G(RF)	USS ALABAMA	PBR Gun Boat
F-4C	F9F-5P	USS DRUM	ICBM
F-14A	HH-52A	M-75 APC	
F-16A(GF)	HU-16E	M-4 Tank	

Montgomery - Gunter AFB, 36114, (334) 279-1110, Mon-Fri 8-4, Closed Holidays, C-47B, GAM-72

Ozark - Alabama Aviation & Technical College, US Hwy 231S, 36361, (334) 774-5113, Lear Jet 25

US Army Aviation Museum, Fort Rucker, Bldg 617, POB 620610, 36362-0610, (334) 598-2508,
Mon-Fri 9-4,Sat-Sun 12-4 Free Adm, Closed TD, CE, CD, NE, ND, Gift Shop 598-9465,
www.armyavnmuseum.org,

Bldg 600[ ]		Bldg 600 [ ]		Bldg 600 [ ]		Bldg 600 [ ]	
AX-6	[13]	H-23B(OH)	[0]	L-13A	[7]	RU-8D	[0]
Bell 207	[0]	H-23C(OH)	[7]	L-15A(YL)	[9]	S-60	[13]
C-7A(YC)	[0]	H-23F(OH)	[9]	L-16A	[0]	SE-5A	
C-45H	[C]	H-25A	[0]	L-17A	[7]	T-28A	[9]
C-45J(UC)	[C]	H-26A(XH)	[0]	L-17B		T-34A(YT)	[S]
C-47A	[0]	H-30(YH)	[8]	L-18C	[7]	T-37A	
C-121A(VC)	[C]	H-32(YH)	[7]	L-19A	[7,S]	T-39A	[S]
C-126(LC)	[0]	H-34A(CH)	[0]	L-19D(TL)		T-41B	[7]
CL-475	[8]	H-34A(VCH)	[8]	L-20A	[7]	T-42	[C]
DH 1A	[0]	H-37B(CH)	[0]	L-21A(TL)	[8]	TG-3	[13]
E-5A(YE)	[7]	H-39A(XH)	[8]	L-200A	[9]	U-1A	[9]
F-51D	[9]	H-40H(XH)	[7]	Lockheed Aquilla [0]		U-3A	[S]
Fairchild Dragonfly [13]		H-41A(YH)	[7]	Lockheed Test Bed [13]		U-4A	[S]
H-1	[77]	H-47A(ACH)		MI-4	[S]	U-6A(YU)	[0]
H-1F (AH)		H-51A(XH)		MDouglas Mark II		U-8A	[S]
H-1G (AH)	[0]	H-55A(TH)	[7]	Nieuport 28C-1		U-8G	[S]
H-1J (AH)		H-56A(AH)	[0]	N.V. [0]		U-9A	[C]
H-1B (UH)	[GG]	H-58A(OH)	[GG]	O-3G1(XAO)[13]		U-9A(YU)	[S]
H-1H (UH)	[8]	H-61 (UH)	[13]	O-3A(YO)	[0]	U-9D(NRU)	[C]
H-1M (UH)	[G]	H-61A(YUH)		O-3BR(YHO) [0]		U-10(YU)	[8]
H-1D(YUH)	[0]	H-63 (YAH)		OV-1A(YO)	[9]	U-10A	[S]
H-4A (OH)	[8]	H-64 (AH)		OV-1B	[C]	U-21(YU)	[9]
H-5A (OH)	[7]	H-64A(YAH) [0]		OV-1C	[C]	V-1 (XV)	[9]
H-6A (OH)	[78]	H-347(CH)	[S]	P-2E (AP)	[C]	V-3A (XV)	
H-6A(YOH)	[0]	J-3	[0]	P-9 (AO)	[9]	V-5B (XV)	[S]
H-13B(OH)	[77]	JN-4D		P-51		V-6A (XV)	
H-13E(OH)	[0]	L-1A	[9]	Philco-Ford Prairie II 0		VZ-3RY	[9]
H-13T(TH)	[0]	L-2A	[9]	PT-17		VZ-ZAP	[0]
H-18 (XH)	[7]	L-3A	[7]	QH-50C	[13]	X-14	[7]
H-19C	[0]	L-4B	[0,7]	QQ-50	[13]	X-26B	[9]
H-19D(UH)	[9]	L-5	[0]	R-4B	[0]	XROE-1	[0]
H-21C(CH)	[0]	L-5G	[0]	R-5	[9]		
H-23A(OH)	[0]	L-6	[7]	R-9B (XR)	[8]		

Tuskegee - General Daniel "Chappie" James Airman's & Industrial Museum, Modem Field,
2307 Dr Lincoln Ragsdale Dr, Daily 9-5, Free Adm, Gift Shop, 36083-2813, (334) 724-0602, F9F, PT-17

Tuskegee Airmen National Historic Site, 1616 Chappie James Ave, 36803, I-85 exit 38,
Daily 9-4:30, Free Adm, (334) 724-0922, www.nps.gov/tuai, Artifacts

ALASKA

Anchorage - Alaska Aviation Heritage Museum, 4721 Aircraft Dr, 99502, (907) 248-5325, Fax 248-6391, May 15-Sept 15, Daily 9-5, RoY Wed-Sun 9-5, Adm Adult $10, Snrs &Child 13-17 $8, Child 5-12 $6, Flight Simulator, Theater, Gift Shop, Library, Banquet facility, Project=(P), www.alaskaairmuseum.org

American Pilgram 100B	Grumman G-44 Widgeon	Stearman C2B
AT-19	Hamilton Metalplane H47	Stinson 108
Bellanca Sr Pacemaker Fus	J2F-6	Stinson SR-9 CM
Bellanca Pacemaker CH-300	K1-84 Keystone Loening	Stinson SR
C-45H	L-5 Stinson Sentinel	Stinson A Trimotor
C-45F(UC)	Noordyn Norseman	T-50
Curtiss Robin	P-40E	Travelair S6000B Floats (P)
DWC	PBY-5A	UH-1H
Fairchild FC2W Frame	S-43 (Nose Only)	Waco UIC
Fairchild 24G	Spartan Executive	Waco YKC Floats
Ford 5-AT Wreckage	Spencer Aircar	

Kulis ANG Base Museum, 6000 Air Guard Rd, 99502-1998, (907) 249-1176,

AT-6D	C-123J	F-86A
C-47A	F-80	T-33A

Elmendorf AFB, 3rd Wing Grp Info Mana, HQ 21ST TFW/PA 99506, (907) 552-5755,

F-4C	F-102A	P-38G	T-33A

Fairbanks - Pioneer Air Museum, 2300 Airport Way, 99701, (907) 451-0037, 452-2969, Mail: Interior & Arctic Alaska Aeronautical Museum, POB 70437, 99707-0437, Memorial-Labor Day, Daily 11-9, Open Holidays, Adm $2

B-10	HO45	Rutan Vari-eze
Baking Duce II (F.M.1)	MX Quicksilver	Stinson SR-5 Jr
C-45F(UC)	Pereira S.P. 3	UH-1
C-64A Mk.IV	PT-22 (ST3KR)	V-77
Fairchild 24J	Raven S-50	
Fokker Super Universal Frame	Rotorway 133	

Healy - Denali Wings, Box 254, 99743, (907) 683-2245,   Ford Tri-Motor

Wasilla - Museum of Alaska Transportation & Industry, 99687, POB 870646, 99687 (907) 376-1211, Mem - Labor Day Mon-Sat 10-6, Winter Tue-Sat 8-4, Adm Adult $3, Student $1.50, Family $7, Gift Shop, Train Museum, www.museumofalaska.org

Bowers Model A	F-102A	JB-2	Waco
C-47A	H-1(UH)	K-84	
C-123J	H-5(HH)	L-6A	
D.W.C.	H-21B(CH)	Stinson SR	

Whitehorse - Yukon Transportation Museums, 30 Electra Cresent, Y1A-6E6, (867) 668-4792, Fax 633-5547, May 14-Aug 31 Tue-Sun 10-5, Adm Adult $4.25, Senior(55+)$3.25, Student $3.25, Child(6-12)$2, Family $9, Gift Shop, DC-3

ARIZONA

Casa Grande - Goss Hawk Unlimited (Restoration Facility), 3184 N Rockwell Ave, 85222 (520) 423-2622, Mail: POB 12040, 85230, www.gosshawkunlimited.com,

Projects: Ki-43	P-51	T-28	V-77

Ft Huachuca - Huachuca Museum Society, Boyd & Grierson St, POB 12766, 85670-2766, (520) 458-4716, Mon-Fri 9-4, Sat-Sun 1-4,Free Adm, Dir Tim Phillips, Gift Shop Beth Banister,

OV-1D,	RC-121G

Gila Bend - Gila Bend AF AUX, (520) 683-6200,   F-105D   T-33A

ARIZONA

Grand Canyon - Planes of Fame, Grand Canyon Valle-Williams Airport, 755 Mustang Way, 86046, (928) 635-1000, Hwy 64 & 180 Junction, Mail: HCR 34 Box B, Valle Williams, AZ, 86046, Daily 9-5, Closed TD, CD, Adm Adult $5.95, Child 5-12 $1.95, Under 5 Free, Constellation Tour $3.00, Gift Shop, www.planesoffame.org

AD-4N	(F)	F11F-1	(S)	Mooney Mite	(S)
B-26C(RB)	(F)	F3F-2	(F)	MXY-7 Yokosuka Ohka 11	(S)
Baby Great Lakes	(S)	F-84B	(S)	Pitts S-2	(F)
BD-5V	(S)	F-86L Sabre Cockpit	(S)	PT-17	(F)
Bristol F2b	(Rep)	Ford 5-AT Trimotor	(F)	Rutan Long-Easy	(S)
BT-15	(F)	Hawker Hunter Mk 58	(F)	Schmidt Commuter Helicopter	(S)
C-121A	(F)	J-1	(S)	Siemens-Schukert D.IV	(Rep)
Curtiss Model 50 Robin	(F)	J2F-6	(F)	Sorta Baby Lakes	(S)
D4Y Yokosuka Suiseu	(S)	L-19	(F)	T-28B	(F)
DD-1Lew Ann	(S)	L-29	(S)	T-28C	(F)
DH 100 Mk III	(S)	Me-109G-10/U4 Gustov	(S)	T-33	(S)
F-105B Fuselage	(S)	MiG-15	(S)	T-6G/SNJ-4	(F)

Williams AFB, 85240-5000, PA: (520) 635-8200, 82 FTW/DOOB

F-86E	P-80A	T-33A	T-38A(QT)

Mesa - CAF - Arizona Wing & Museum, 2017 N Greenfield Rd, Falcon Field Airport, 85215 (480) 924-1940, Oct 15-May 14 Daily 10-4, May 15-Oct 14 9-3, Adm Adult $7, Child 6-13 $3 Child Under 6 Free, Gift Shop, Restoration Facility, Meeting Facility, www.arizonawingcaf.com

A-26C	F-4N	P-47 ½ Scale
AF2S	Fokker D.III Replica	SE-5A
B-17G (Rides Available)	L-16	SNJ (Rides Available)
B-25J	MiG-15bis	T-33
Bleriot XI 5 Replica	MiG-21	
C-45 (Rides Available)	N2S	

Marsh Aviation Co, 5060 Falcon Dr, 85215, (480) 832-3770, Fax: 985-2840, Firefighting Fleet of S-2F1T & S2R Air Tankers

Luke AFB(afres), 85309-5000, PA: (623) 856-6011, Daily 7:30-4, Tours Fri 9-1,

AT-6	F- 84F	F-102A	HU-16E
F- 4N	F- 86F	F-104C	T-33A
F-15B	F-100C	HH-34J	

Prescott - Embry-Riddle Aeronautical University, 3700 Willow Creek Rd, 86301-3720, (928) 777-6600, www.erau.edu   F-104 (North of Bookstore)

Quartzsite - W.A.S.P. Museum, (Opens Fall 2007), 1555 Dome Rock Rd, POB 6, 85346, (928) 927-5555, DH-18H (2ea), F9F, Cougar (Not the Jet), www.waspmuseum.com

Sahuarita- Titan Missile Museum, 1580 W Duval Mine Rd, 85714, I-19 Exit 69, Daily 9-5, Last Tour 4pm Closed TD, CD, (520) 625-7736,791-2929, Adm Adult $8.50, Snrs & Military $7.50, Child 7-112 $5, Under 7 Free, www.pimaair.org, Titan II Missile Silo # 571-7,   UH-1F

Tucson - AMARC=Aerospace Maintenance and Regeneration Center (Boneyard) Tours Only, Contact: Lynda McWilliams at Pima Air & Space Museum: (520) 574-0462 48 Hours Prior, Tickets & Departure at Pima Air Museum, Gift Shop(9:30, 11, 12:30, 2, 3:30), Closed Major Holidays, Adm Adult $5, Snrs/Mil $3.50, 17 & Under $3, Schools $2, Photo ID Required, Containing of 4926 Aircraft in 2600 Acres of Outdoor Storage,

426 Cargo Planes	2087 Jet Fighter	570 Trainers
1142 Ground Attack Jets	139 Patrol Planes	

ARIZONA

Tucson - 390th Memorial Museum, 6000 E Valencia Rd, on the grounds of Pima Air & Space Museum
POB 15087, 85708-0087, (520) 574-0462, 574-0287, 9-5 Daily, Closed CD, ND, Admission Charged
www.390th.org   B-17G

Davis-Monthan AFB, NCOIC, Public Affairs, 836 AD/PA, 85707-5000, (520) 228-4717, Appt Only

A-7D	C-130A	F-86	O-1G
A-10A	CH-3C	F-100F	OV-10A
B-52D	F-4N	F-105D	U-2C

Hamilton Aviation, 6901 S Park Ave, 85706, (520) 294-3481, Convair 580 (2 each) Outside Airport

Pima Air & Space Museum, 6000 E. Valencia Rd, 85706, (520) 574-0462, 574-9658,
Daily 9-5, No Adm After 4pm, Jun-Oct: Adm Adult $11.75, Sr $9.75, Child 7-12 $8, Under 7 Free,
Nov-May Adm Adult $11.75, Sr $9.75, Child 7-12 $8, Closed CD, Snack Bar, Gift Shop 618-4815,
www.pimaair.org/,

A-4C	B-58A	CG-4A	FJ-4B(AF-1E)
A-6E	B-66D(WB)	CT-39A	Flagor SkyScooter
A-7D (LTV)	BC-12D	D-16	Fleet Model 2
A-7E	Bede 4	D-21	FM-2
A-10A	Bede 5	DC-7B	Fw 44-J
A-20G	Bede 5J	E-1B	GNAT T-185
A-26C	Beech D-18S	Ercoupe 415-C	H-1S(AH)
A3D-1(YEA-3A)	Beechcraft 2000A	F-4C	H-1F(UH)
A4D-2N	Bellanca 14-13-2	F-4E(NF)	H-1H(UH)
AD-5N1(EA-1F)	BGM 109G	F-4N(NF)	H-1M(UH)
ADM-20C	Bonanza N-35	F-4J(YF)	H-3F(HH)
Aerosport Quail	Bowers Fly Baby	F-5B	H-5G(R-5)
AEW Mk 3	Brewster Bermuda	F-9J(RF)	H-13N(TH)
AF-2S	BT-13A	F-14A	H-19B(UH)
AGM-12	C-14(YC)	F-15A	H-21C
AGM-28A 2ea	C-45J(VC)	F-84C	H-34C(VH)
AIM-4	C-46D 2ea	F-84F	H-37B(CH)
AIM-21A-1M	C-47	F-84F(RF)	H-43F(HH)
AP-2H	C-47D	F-86H	H-52(HH) (S-62)
AQM-34L Drone	C-54D(DC-4)	F-86L	H-52A(HH)
AT-6B	C-69 (L-049)	F-89J	H-54A(CH)
AT-7	C-78B(UC)	F-84F	HO3S-1G
AT-9A	C-82A	F-94C	HTL-2(TH-13N)
AT-11	C-97G(KC)	F-100C	HU-16A (SA-16)
AV-8C	C-97G	F-101B	HUM-1
B-10	C-117D (R4D-8)	F-101C(RF)	HUP-2 2ea
B-17G(PB-1G)	C-118A(VC)	F-101H(RF)	HUP-3 (H-25A)
B-18B	C-119J	F-102A(TF)	Icarus Hg
B-23(UC-67)	C-119 Fire Fight	F-102A	Il-2M3
B-24J	C-121A	F-104D	J-2
B-25J	C-121T(RC)	F-105D	J-4A
B-26B(EDB)	C-123B	F-105G	J4F-2
B-26K	C-123K Fire Fight	F-106A	J-6A
B-29A(TB)	C-123K	F-107A	JRS-1/S-43
B-36J	C-124C	F-111E	KD6G-2
B-377SG 201	C-130A	F11F-1A (F-11A)	L-2M
B-45A	C-130D	F3D-2 (TF-10B)	L-3B
B-47A	C-131F 2ea	F3H-2 (F-3B)	L-5B
B-47E(EB)	C-133B	F4D-1(F-6A)	L-23D (U-8)
B-50J(KB)	C-135J(EC)	F4U-4	Lark 95
B-52A	C-135A(KC)	F7F-3N	Learjet 23
B-52D	C-141B	F8U-1 (F-8A)	LCM-25C
B-52G	Cassutt Racer	F9F-4	Long EZ
B-52A(NB)	Cessna 120	F9F-8	Martin 404
B-57E	Cessna 150L	Falcon II	MC-4C(J-2)
B-57F(WB)	Cessna 310C	FireFly 7 Balloon	**Continued Next Page**Ã

From Previous Page	P-40N	RB-1	TH-55A
MiG-15 bis	P-47	RNF	TV-2(T-33B)
MiG-15 UTI	P-47D	S-1C	U-3A(L-27A)
MiG-17 F	P-63E	S-43	U-8D
MiG-17 PF	P-80B	S2F-1 (2 ea)	U-11A(UO-1)
MiG-21 PF 2ea	P2V	SBD-5	UC-36(L-10A)
MM-2 Mustang II	P2V-7 (AP-2H)	SE-210	UH-12C
MQM-33	P.Airwave 69 Kiss	SHK-1	VC-137B
MQM-57 Drone	PBM-5A	SNB-5(UC-45J)	VC-140B
MS-500	Pentecost Hoppicopter	Spad XIII Rep7/8	Vickers 744
N22B Nomad	PGM-17(DSV-2C)	SR-71A	VP-1
N3N	Pitts Special S1	Star Bumble Bee	VT-29B
NA-64(BT-14)	PQ-14 Drone	Swallow A	Waco ZKS-6
O-2A	PT-17	T-2C	Waco UPF-7
O-52	PT-19A	T-28C	Wright Flyer Rep
OA-10A	PT-22	T-33A	X-15A-2
OH-43D	PT-26	T-37B	XJL-1
OQ-3 Drone	PV-2	T-38	YC-125A
Osprey 2	QH-50C/DSN-3	T2V (T-1A)	YO-3A
OV-1C	Quickie	TBM-3E	YQM-98A Drone
OV-10D	R-4B	TF-9J	Zuzvogel III-B
P-39	R5O-5	TG-3A 2ea	
P-40K	RA-5C	TG-6A	

Tucson ANG, Tucson Int'l Airport, 85734, (520) 573-2210, HU-16 (2ea)

A-7D	F-84F	F-100D	F-102A

Winslow - Meteor Crater, (928) 289-2362, (800) 289-5898, I-40 Exit 233, 86047,
Mail: Meteor Crater Enterprises, Inc, POB 30940,Flagstaff, 86002-0940, (May 15 -Sept 15) 7-7,
RoY 8-5, Adm Adult $9, Sr $8, Child 6-17 $5, Under 6 Free, 71 Space RV Park, 928-289-4002,
Gift Shop, Cafe, www.meteorcrater.com, 1 Mile Wide Crater, Apollo Space Capsule

Yuma - Marine Corps Air Station, 85369-5001, (928) 341-2011, A-4,   F-4,   F-5E,   AV/8A

US Army Proving Grounds, 85365, SW Gate, AH-1F

ARKANSAS

Eureka Springs - Aviation Cadet Museum, 542 Cr 2073 72632, (479) 253-5008, Wed-Sat 10-5,
1½ Hr Tours, Adm Adult $10, Child 5-12 $6, Under 5 Free, Pres Errol Sever, Gift Shop, Library,
www.aviationcadet.com, F-100F,   F-105 Cockpit,   F-105G,   F-5,   Aero Commander Quail

Fayetteville - Arkansas Air Museum, 4290 S School St, Drake Field, 72701, (479) 521-4947,
Mon-Fri, Sun 11-4:30,Sat 10-4:30, Sun 11-4:30, Closed TD, CD, ND, Adm Adult $4, Child 6-12 $2,
Under 6 Free, Restoration Viewing, Gift Shop, Theater, www.arkairmuseum.org

A-4C	DGA 6	H-1H(UH)	PT-17
American Eaglet 230	DGA 11	L-16	SE.5A (2/3 Scale)
BC-12D Taylorcraft	DGA 18K	LearJet 23	Stinson Junior S
Curtiss CW-1	Globe Swift	Luscombe 8E	T-34B
DC-3 Cockpit Proj	H-1S(AH)	Mini-500	TravelAir 4000

Fort Smith - Ebing ANG Base, 188TH TFG, Ft Smith Municipal Airport, 72906, (479) 648-5271,

F-4	RF-84

Little Rock - Aerospace Education Center, 3301 E. Roosevelt Rd, 72206, (501) 371-0331,
376-4232 Gift Shop, IMAX Theater, www.aerospaced.org,

Adventura	Bell Eagle Eye	Headwind JD-HWL-7	Sopwith Camel F-1
Apollo CM	Command Aire 5-C-3	Link	Wright Flyer

All Flags Heritage Park, Camp Robinson Army Reserve Base,
PA: Lt Col Lashbrook , (501) 212-5020, F-104, USAF & Army Aircraft Displayed

ARKANSAS

Little Rock - Little Rock AFB, 314 TAW /HO, 72099-5000, (501) 988-3131, Hist: Sgt. John G Schmidl

B-47E	C-119J	F-4C(RF)	H-1M(UH)
B-57C	C-131A(HC)	F-84(RF)	M-60 Tank
C-47	C-130A	F-101C(RF)	T-33A

Pine Bluff - Razorback EAA 1388, 619 Hangar Row, 71601, Contact CM Rittlemeyer

Aeronca Chief	BT-13	L-3	SNJ
AT-6	Cessna 172	Navion	Stearman
Beech 18	Cessna 182	Piper Apache	
Bosbok	EAA Biplane	RV4	

Springdale - Ozark Military Museum, 4360 S School Ave, 72701, (479) 587-1941, Fax 587-0848, Sun-Fri 10-4:30, Sat 10-4:30, Adm Adult $4, Child 6-12 $2, Under 6 Free, Curator Mike Eckles, Library, Theater, Restoration Facility, www.ozarkmilitarymuseum.org

A-7C	H-1S(AH)	H-21	NE-1
Beech 3NM (Flyable)	H-1H(UH)	JRB (Project)	SNJ
DH 82	H-1M(UH)	L-13 (Project)	T-2
H-1(AH)	H-1S(UH)	L-3 (Flyable)	T-33

Walnut Ridge - Walnut Ridge Army Flying School Museum, 2 Sky Watch Dr, Walnut Ridge, AR 72476, (870) 886-7357 or 886-3859, www.walnutridge-aaf.com/museum.htm,

H-1(AH),	Link Trainer,	SNB/JNB Trainer

CALIFORNIA

Alameda Point - Alameda Naval Air Museum, 2151 Ferry Pt, Bldg 77, Mail: POB 1769, 94501, (510) 522-4262, Sat-Sun 10-4, www.alamedanavalairmuseum.org, A-4, A-7

USS Hornet Museum, Pier 3, Mail: POB 460, 94501, (510) 521-8448, Fax 521-8327, Daily 10-4, Closed TD, CD, ND, Adm Adult $14 Snrs 65 & Mil $12, Child 5-17 $6, Under 5 Free, Gift Shop, Facility Rental, www.uss-hornet.org,

A-7	FJ-2	S-2B(US)
A-4J(TA)	FM-2	SBD
F-4	H-2(SH)	TBM-3
F-7U3 (Project)	H-3H(SH)	Apollo Lunar Lander
F-14A	H-34(UH)	BP1102A
F8U-1(F-8A)	HUP-1	MQU-004 (Apollo14)

Atwater - (See Next Page)

Boron - Saxon Aerospace Museum, 26922 Twenty Mule Team Rd, 93516, (760) 762-6600 Daily 10-4, Closed TD, CD, ND, www.saxonaerospacemuseum.org,

F-4D-31-MC,	X-25A,	Eugene Turner Experimental

Burbank - Producers Air Force, 1 Orange Grove Terrace, 91501,Contact: Chuck Hood, (818) 845-5970 Fax 845-4033, www.producersairforce.com   Replica's From Movies For Sale:

AV-8,	F-5,	F-15,	F-16,	F-18,	F-22,	Cockpits

Camarillo - WWII Aviation Museum, CAF Southern California Wing, Camarillo Airport, 455 Aviation Dr, 93010, (805) 482-0064, Formerly Oxnard AFB, Daily 10-4, Closed CD, ND, Adm Adult $5, Child 7-16 $2, Under 7 Free, Gift Shop, Library, All Aircraft Flying, www.orgsites.com/ca/caf-socal

A6M-3 (Project)	F4F(FM-2)	SNJ-4 (Project)
B-25J(PBJ-1J) (Project)	F6F-5	SNJ-5
C-46F	F8F-2	Spitfire Mk.XIVe (Project)
C-61K(VC)	Fairchild 24	T-34B (Member Owned)
C-131(VC) (T-29)	P-38	YAK-3

CALIFORNIA

Atwater - Aviation Challenge, 3600 B St, 95301, 888-MACHONE, (209) 726-0156, Located at Castle AFB, Aviation Camps for Grades 4-12 & Adult, One Week of: Land/Water Survival, Principals and Simulator Flight Basics, From $399-899, www.aviationchallenge.net

Castle Air Museum, 5050 Santa Fe, 95301, (209) 723-2178, May 1-Sept 30 Daily 9-5, RoY 10-4, Closed: ES, TD, CD, ND, Adm Adult $8, Snrs & Child 6-17 $6, Child Under 6 Free, Open Cockpit Day Adult $10, Snrs & Child 12-17 $8, 6-11 $4, Under 6 Free, Gift Shop 723-2182, Restaurant 723-2177, Curator Jack R Gotcher, www.elite.net/castle-air, (S) = Storage

A-4L	BT-13	F-86H	PT-17 (S)
A-26B	C-45A	F-89J	PT-22
AGM-28B	C-46D	F-100	PT-23 (S)
AT-6	C-47A	F-101B	O-2A
B.2 Avro Vulcan	C-54E(R5D)(S)	F-104D	SA-16 (S)
B-17G	C-56 C-60B(L-18C)(S)	F-105B	SR-71A
B-18A	C-78(VC) (S)	F-106	T-33A
B-23	C-119C	F-111A(FB)	T-34(YT)
B-24M	C-123K	GAM-63	TG-3
B-25J	C-131A(HC)	HH-43B	U-3A
B-26B (S)	C-135A(KC)	HU-16B	UC-78
B-29A(B-50)	CG-4 (S)	L-4 (S)	WB-50D
B-36H(RB)	F-4	L-5E (S)	VH-13H (S)
B-45A	F-14	L-13 (S)	U-6A(L-20A)(S)
B-47E	F-15A	L-21A (S)	
B-52D	F-80B	KAQ-1	
B-57E(EB)	F-84F	KC-97L	

Chino - Yanks Air Museum, Chino Airport West Side, 7000 Merrill Ave, Hangar A207, Box 35, 91710, (909) 597-1734, Tue-Fri 8:30-3:30, Sat 8:30-2, Adm Adult $8, Snr $7, Student $5, (R) = Restoration; (A) = Awaiting Restoration; (S) = Storage; www.yanksair.com

A-3(KA) (S)	F-80C (A)	O-52	YPT-9B Cloudboy
A-4B (A)	F-84 (A)	Ohka 11 (A)	Cockpits:A-10
A-4C	F-86E (S)	OS2U-3 (A)	A-6B
A-4E	F-100C	P-38L/F5G	A-7B
A-6E	F-105D	P-39N-0	B-52
A-7B	F-106B	P-40E-1	F-111D
American Eagle A-1 (S)	F-111 (S)	P-47D (A)	F-14
AQM-37A Drone	F4U-4B	P-47M	Martin 404
B1 Mahoney Ryan (R)	F6F-5	P-51A-1	T-37
B-25J (R)	F6F-5 (A)	P-51D-10	T-7
Bell 47D-1	F9F-2 (A)	P-63C	Drones:
BQM-126A Drone	FJ-1 (A)	PB4Y-2	AGM-45A
BT-13B	FM-2	PBY-5A (A)	AGM-141
Bruner-Winkle Bird (S)	G-1B(YG)	PT-26 (A)	AIM-7
C-2 (S)	G-44 (A)	R-4Y/C-131F	AQM-37A
C-40A/12A	H-3C(CH)	S-58B/H-34 (A)	Brave 300
C-43(UC)/D-17S (S)	H-52(HH)	SB2C-3	BQM-126A
C-46	HU-1B (A)	SBD-4	KDB-1/MQM-39A
C-121T(EC) (S)	HUP-2 (A)	Schultz Glider (A)	KD6G-2/MQM-40
Cessna AW	J-1 Curtiss (A)	SNJ-5 (S)	M-41
CG-4A (R)	J-1 Standard	Stearman 4D JR	Maxi-Decoy
CL-13B Mk VI	JN-4D (A)	Swallow TP (A)	MQM-107
Curtiss Robin C-1	JN-4D	T-33A (A)	SM-1
C-47A	KD-1A	T-37A (A)	YCGM-121
C-121T(EC)	L-5 (A)	T-38	Vehicles:
DH 60GM (S)	Lear Jet 23 (S)	T-38A (A)	M3
Double Eagle (S)	LP-3	T-50 (UC-78)	M3A
E-2C	MC-4C/YH-30 (A)	TBF-1C	M35
Ercoupe 415-D (A)	Mig 27 Drone	TDU-25B Drone	M106
F-4C (A)	M.S 230	TG-3A (A)	M113
F-4S	N3N-3	Thomas Pidgeon (A)	HUMVEE
F-14A	N3N-3 (A)	Waco UEC	

CALIFORNIA - **Chino** - The Air Museum "Planes of Fame", 7000 Merrill Ave, 91710, (909) 597-3722, Daily 9-5, Closed TD, CD, Adm Adult $11, Child 5-12 $4, Under 5 Free, Gift Shop, Restoration Facility, Curator Ed Maloney, (F)=Flying, (R)=Restoration, (Rep)=Replica, (S)=Static Display www.planesoffame.org,

#35 Racer	(S)	F-86F	(S)	P-26A	(F)
1903 Wright Flyer	(Rep)	F-86H(QF) Drone	(S)	P-38J	(F)
A-36	(R)	F8F-1	(R)	P-39N	(S)
A-37	(S)	F8F-2	(F)	P-40N	(F)
A-4B	(S)	F8U-1	(S)	P-47G	(F)
A6M5	(F)	F9F-5P	(S)	P-51A	(R)
Aichi D3A2	(R)	Fiesler Storch	(R)	P-51D	(R)
Alpha	(S)	FJ-3 Fury	(S)	P-51D	(F)
AN-2	(F)	Fokker DR-1	(R)	P-51D	(F)
AT-12	(F)	Folland Gnat MK.1	(F)	P-51D(TF)	(F)
AT-6G Harvard Mk IV	(F)	Formula 1 Racer	(S)	P-59(YP)	(R)
B-17G (F)	(R)	G4M1 Betty	(S)	P-80	(S)
B-25J	(F)	Gee Bee R-1 Racer	(Rep)	PQ-14/TDC-2	(F)
B-50A Fuselage	(S)	Gloster Meteor MK IV	(S)	PT-17	(F)
Ba-349	(Rep)	H-23 Helicopter	(S)	PT-19 Cornell Cockpit	(S)
Beechcraft Baron	(F)	H-34 Sea Bat	(S)	R3C-2	(Rep)
Benson Gyrocopter	(S)	HA-1112-MIL	(R)	RF-84K	(S)
Blaty Orion Homebuilt	(S)	HD-1 Scout	(S)	Rick Jet RJ-4	(S)
Bristol F2b	(Rep)	He-100	(Rep)	Rider R-4 Racer	(S)
C-60	(S)	He-162A-1	(S)	Rider R-8 Racer	(S)
Cessna 210	(F)	Horten Ho-IV Glider	(S)	Rutan Quickie II	(S)
Chanute Glider	(R)	Howard 250	(F)	SBD-5	(F)
Convair 240	(R)	Hurricane Mk X	(F)	Schupal & Nylaner	(S)
Convair 240 Cockpit	(S)	J2M3 Raiden	(S)	SNJ-5 Texan	(F)
Curtiss 1910 Pusher	(Rep)	J8M1 Shusui	(S)	Sopwith Pup	(Rep)
D-558-II Skyrocket	(S)	L-13A Grasshopper	(F)	Spitfire Mk IXe	(F)
DC-3	(F)	L-18 Lodestar	(S)	Spitfire Mk XIV	(F)
Deperdussen Racer	(Rep)	L-5G Sentinel	(F)	Supermarine S6B Racer	(Rep)
DGA-5 Racer	(Rep)	Luscombe Silvaire 8A	(F)	T-2A Buckeye	(S)
DH-100 Mk IV	(F)	M-39 Racer	(Rep)	T-33 Shooting Star	(S)
F+W C-3605 Schlepp	(F)	MC-12	(S)	T-33/TV-2	(F)
F-100D	(S)	Me-163 Komet	(Rep)	TBM-3 Avenger	(F)
F-104G	(S)	MiG-15	(F)	TG-4A/LK-10 Glider	(S)
F3F-2 (F)	(F)	MiG-15	(S)	TS-11 Iskra (Spark)	(F)
F4F/FM-2	(F)	MiG-17	(S)	UC-45 Expeditor	(S)
F4U-1A	(F)	MiG-21	(S)	Williams W-7 Racer	(S)
F6F-3	(F)	Miles & Atwood Racer	(Rep)	X-2	(Rep)
F7F-3N	(S)	N9MB (F) Wing	(F)	Yak-11	(S)
F-84F	(S)	O-1E (L-19E)	(R)	Yak-18	(S)
F-86F	(F)	P-12E	(F)	Yak-3	(R)

Chico - Chico Air Museum, 170 Convair Court, Chico Mncpl Airport, 95973, (530) 345-6468, Sat 10-4, www.chicoairmuseum.org,   AN-2   Howard Super Ventura   Yak-52

China Lake - US Naval Musem of Armament & Technology , Blandy Ave, 93555, Mail: POB 217, Ridgecrest, 93556-0217, Mon-Fri 10-4, Closed Holidays, (760) 939-3105, Gift Shop, (S)=Storage

A-4F(NA)	F-86(QF) (S)	**Missiles:**	AIM-54
A-6E (S)	F-111B	AGM-45A	BLU-80/B
A-7C(S)	F11F-1	AGM-65	BLU-97
AV-8A (S)	F/A-18 (S)	AGM-83	BGM-109
F-4B(RF) (S)	H-1(UH) 3ea	AGM-88	CBU-59
F-4D-1(XF)	H-1K(HH)	AIM-7	CBU-72
F-8L(DF) (S)	RA-5C (S)	AIM-9	UGM-27

Compton - Tomorrow's Aeronautical Museum, 961 West Alondra Blvd, 90220, Compton Airport (877) 999-2099, (310) 618-1155, Daily 8-8, Gift Shop, www.tamuseum.org,   UH-1   OH-6A

Coronado - North Island NAS, C-2, S-3, SH36,   SH60,   SH2F

CALIFORNIA

El Cajon -San Diego Air & Space Museum, Gillespie Field Annex, 335 Kenney St, 92020, (619) 234-8291, Mon, Wed, Thur, Fri 8-3, Free Adm, Gift Shop, Restoration Facility, www.sandiegoairandspace.org/gillespie/index.html

A-4C	F-14A	MiG-21	Shoestring	
A-6E	F-16N	Pietenpol Air Camper	Sonerai Two	
A-7B	F-86F	Pitts S-1-S	Stinson Detroiter	
AV-8A	F-102A	Primary Glider	T-18	
B-52E Nose	F4B-4	PT-22	**Missiles:**	
Bee Honey Bee	H-13D	Ryan 147T Drone	AGM-129	
F-8J	L-19	Ryan NYP (Rep)	Atlas	

El Cajon - CAF Air Grp 1, Flying Field Museum, Gillespie Field, 1860 Joe Crosson Dr, Ste B, 92020, (619) 448-4505, Wed-Sat 10-3, Free Adm, www.cafairgroup1.org, L-5,   SNJ-5

Warbirds West Air museum, 1942 B Joe Crosson Dr, 92020, Mail: 7918 N, El Cajon, CA 91941, (619) 449-1504, Sat 9-4, 1st Sun Monthly 11:30-4, www.wwam.org
AD-1H, L-29C, O-2A, T-28C, T-34A

El Centro - El Centro Naval Air Facility, 92243-5000, (760) 339-2519, 8 Miles W of City, N of I-8, www.nafec.navy.mil/index.htm, A-4, A-7D, F-4, F-11, F-18A,

Fairfield - Travis Air Museum, 461 Burgan Blvd, Bldg 80, Mail: 400 Brennan Circle, 4535-5000, (707) 424-5605, Mon-Sat 9-4, Closed Federal Holidays, Adm Free,
Airpark Open Daily, Dawn till Dusk, Gift Shop, www.travisairmuseum.org, Indoor Museum = *

A-26C	C-56	F-4C	Gonzales *	O-2A
AT-11 (P)*	C-118A(C-54Q)	F-84F	H-21B	PT-19 *
B-29 *	C-119	F-86L	H-34(VC)	T-28 *
B-52D	C-124C	F-101B	L-4 *	T-39A
BT-13 *	C-131E	F-102A	L-5 *	U-3A
C-45H	C-140A	F-104A	LC-126A	
C-47	CT-39A	F-105D	Link Trainer *	

Firebaugh - Central California Historical Military Museum, 11100 West Eagle Field Rd, 93622, (209) 392-8264, www.eaglefield.org   PT-22   Stearman UH-1

Heritage Eagles Museum, 11163 North Eagle Ave, Eagle Field, 93622, Sat-Sun, (209) 392-8264, www.b25.net   B-25J

Fresno - Fresno ANG, Fresno Air Terminal, 93727-2199, (559) 454-5100, 26th NORAD Region & Air Div; 194th FIS, 144th FIW,

F-86A	F-4	F-106A	T-33A
F-86L	F-102A	P-51D	

Fullerton - Air Combat USA, 230 N Dale Pl, Mail: POB 2726, 92833-2524, (800)522-7590 (714) 522-7590, Fly Laser Dog Fights in the SIAI Marchetti SF260, $695 Phase I/II, $1295 Full Day Training & 2 Flight Missions & G-1 Jacket,

Hayward - Vintage Air Museum, Field Bud Aviation, 22005 Skywest Dr, 94541, (510) 782-9063

C-3 (2ea)	Cessna 180	DH 89 Project
PA-12	PA-23-250	Ryan STA
Stearman 4CM-1	Stearman Stock	Travel Air 4000

Hemet - Ryan School of Aeronautics Museum, 4280 Waldon Weaver Rd,
Mail: 5001 W Florida Ave # 176, 92545-3823, (909) 658-2716, Thur-Sun 10-3
Closed Major Holidays, Free Adm, Gift Shop, Theater, Artifacts

Hemet Air Attack Base Fire Station, 4710 West Stetson Ave, (530) 477-0641, Hemet Ryan Airport, S-2, C-130A

CALIFORNIA

Imperial - Pioneer's Museum, 373 E Aten Rd, 92251, (760) 352-3211 or 1165,
June-Aug Tue-Sat 10-4, Sun 12-5, Adm Adult $4, Child $0.50, Gift Shop, Library, F-14A, M-60 Tank

Constellation Historical Society, 104 East Ave, K4 Suite G, 93535, (760) 945-2093, Fax 945-7055,
C-121C

Poncho Barnes Aviation, 4555 W Ave G, 93536, (760) 948-4048, Travel Air Mystery NR-613K

Lancaster - Jethawks (Lancaster Municipal Stadium), 2400 W Ave I, 93536, (661) 726-5400, F/A-18

Lemoore - Leemore Naval Air Station, 93245, (559) 998-4045, www.lemoore.navy.mil,

A-1	A-4	A-7E	F-18

Los Alamitos - Naval Air Station, US 405&605, 90720-5001, (562) 795-2000, 2533, UH-1, XFV-1

Los Angeles - California Science Center, 700 State Dr, 90037, Exposition Park,
(323) 724-3623, 7547, Daily 10-5, Closed TD, CD, ND, Free Adm, $6 Parking,
Space Shuttle Cargo Bay, www.casciencectr.com

A-12	F-104D	Wright Glider
Bell 47G-5	Gemini 11 Capsule	X-1
Comet Glider	Mercury MR-2 Capsule	
DC-8-52	T-38	
F-20	Velie Monocoupe 70	

The Cockpit, 7510 Melrose Ave, 90046, (323) 782-0617, Mon-Sat 10-6, Sun 12-5,
Aviation Clothing (WWI-Today Military & Civilian), P-51 Suspended From Ceiling

Flight Path Learning Center of Southern California, 6661 W Imperial Highway, LAX Imperial Terminal,
Mail: POB 90234, 90009, (310) 215-5291, Tue-Sat 10-3, Free Adm, Artifacts, www.flightpath.us

Marysville - Beale AFB, 9SRW/CCX, 95903-5000, (530) 634-2038, Mon-Fri 10-4,
Closed Holidays, Free Adm, BIG RED 1 Reenactment Grp.

A-26	C-97L(KC)	SR-71A	U-2R

Forgotten Warriors Museum, 5865 A Rd, 95901, (530) 742-3090, Thur 7-10pm,
1st Sat Each Month 10-4,Open Memorial / Veterans Day, Free Adm   H-1H(UH)   H-6(OH)

Mather(Sacramento) - Military Hospital, Mather AFB, 10535 Hospital Rd, 95655,
(916) 364-2177,   F-105G   H-1H(UH)   H-58(OH)

McClellan - Aerospace Museum of California, 3200 Freedom Park Dr, 95652, (916) 643-3192,
Fax: 643-0389, Tue-Sat 9-5, Sun 10-5, Closed Mondays, Adm Adult $9, Snrs 60 & Child 13-18 $7,
Chlid 6-12 $5, Under 6 Free, Gift Shop, www.aerospacemuseumofcalifornia.org

A-1E	C-53D	F-86L	HU-16B
A-7D	C-54D	F-100D	L-2M
A-10A	CH-3E	F-101B	MiG-17PF
AT-6G	F-4C	F-102A	MiG-21F
C-119G	F-14	F-104B	T-28B
C-121T(EC)	F-80B	F-105D	T-33A
C-131D(VC)	F-84F	FB-111A	T-39A
C-45HJ(UC)	F-86F	CH-21C(CH)	

Modesto - CAF Central California Valley Squadron, County Harry Sham Airport, (209) 577-5318,
www.cafvalleysquadron.org   L-5E

Hillier Air Museum, 700 Tioga Dr, Hangar 7, 95354, (209) 526-8297, 2nd Sat Montly,
Free Adm, Library, www.hillierairmuseum.com

Beech D-17S	Cessna 140	J-2	PT-22
Beechcraft 35	Globe GC-1B	N2S-2	RC-3

CALIFORNIA

Mt View - Moffett Field Museum, Bldg 126, Mail: MFHS, POB 16, 94305-0016, (650) 603-4024,
Wed-Sat 10-2, 1st & 3rd Sun 12-2, Free Adm, Gift Shop, www.moffettfieldmuseum.org/

F-104	Mercury Space Capsule	U-2
HiMAT	P2V	Space Shuttle 1/3 Scale

U.S. Space Camp, Moffett Federal Airfield, P.O. Box 6, 94035, (800) 637-7223,
(650) 603-8902, Space Camp for Grades 4-12 & Adult, One Week of: Space Training
& Missions From $399-799. www.spacecampecalifornia.com.

Murrieta - Wings and Rotors Air Museum, 37552 Winchester Rd, Hangar 2D, Murrieta Executive Air
Park, 92563, (951) 662-5653, Mon-Fri 6:30am-3pm, Adm Adult $3 Donation, Gift Shop,
www.wingsandrotors.org

F-4H-1	UH-1B	T-41
OH-58	UH-1H	TH-55

Oakland - CAF Golden Gate Wing, Oakland Int'l Airport, 94601, Mail: POB 6056, 94603
(510) 568-7708, www.goldengatewing.org   SNJ   T-33A

Museum Department of History, 1000 Oak St, 94607, (510) 238-3842, Wed-Sat 10-5, Sun 12-7,
Closed July 4, TD, CD, ND, Adm Adult $8, Snrs 65 & Child $5, Under 6 Free,
www.museumca.org, 1919 Meteor.

Oakland Aviation Museum, Oakland Int'l Airport, 8260 Boeing St, Bldg 621,
North Field, Across From Hangar 6, Mail: POB 14264, 94614-4264, (510) 638-7100, Fax 6530,
Wed-Sun 10-4, Adm Adult $9, Snrs $8, Active Mil $7, 6-12 $5, Under6 Free, Gift Shop, Library,
Short Solent Tour $3, www.westernaerospacemuseum.org

A-3B(KA)(A3D)	Bede BD-5B	Glasair	PT-13
A-4M	Curtiss Robin	Ikarus Aero 3A	Short Solent Mk.3
A-6D(KA)	F-14	Link Trainer	TBM-3
A-7E	F-86H	Lockheed 10-A	Wright EX Vin Fiz
Arrow Sport F	Funk Model B	MiG-15	
AV-8A(TAV)	GAM-72	Monocoupe 110	

Palm Springs - Palm Springs Air Museum, 745 N Gene Autry Trail, Palm Springs Regional Airport,
92262-6603, (760) 778-6262, Daily 10-5, Closed TD, CD, Adm Adult $10, Snrs 65 /Mil $8.50,
Child 6-12 $5, Child Under 6 Free, Dir: Fritz Frauchiger 778-6262, www.palmspringsairmuseum.org

A-4J	F6F-5K	JD-1	SBD-5
A-6	F7F-3	N2S-3	Spitfire Mk.XIV
A-26C	F8F	N2S-5	T-28
AT-6G (SNJ)	F-16N	P-40N	T-34B
B-17G	F-18	P-47D	TBM-3E
B-25J	FG-1D	P-51D 2ea	Wright Flyer ½ Scale
C-1A(S-2)	FM-2	P-63A	
C-47B	G-21(OA-13)	PT-17	
F-14	J-3C	PT-22	

Palmdale - Blackbird Airpark, Edwards AF Production Flight Test Installation, (661) 272-6718,
Fri-Sun 11-4,

A-12	SR-71A	U-2D

Palmdale Plant 42 Heritage Park, 2001 E Ave P, Mail: 38300 Sierra Hwy, Ste A, 93550,
(661) 267-5155, Fri-Sun 11-4, Guided Tours 7am-11am, www.palmdaleairpark.com

A-4F(TA)	C-140A	F-86A	F-105D
A-7C(TA)	F-4E	F-100D	T-38A
B-2 (1/8 Scale)	F-5	F-101	Triumph
B-52	F-14	F-104	

CALIFORNIA

Paso Robles - Estrella Warbird Museum, 4251 Dry Creek Rd, 93446, Recording (805) 227-0440, Voice & Fax 238-9317, Sat 10-4, Sun 12-3, Free Adm, Gift Shop, * = Privately Owned, www.ewarbirds.org

A-4A	F-8G(RF)	Morrissey 2000C	x J-47 Engine
A-6E	F-86F(QF)	S-2D	x J-79 Engine
A-7C	H-1(UH)	Stinson V-77	x T-53 Engine
AT-11 *	JN-4D *	T-28B	x TF-30 Engine
F-104G(TF)	L-5E	T-33A	
F-4D	L-17A	Titan II	
F-14	L-16A	x Allison 250-C18 Engine	

Point Mugu - Point Mugu Missile Park, SR 1 & Pacific Ave, (805) 989-1110

F-4	F6F	F-14	Missiles

Port Hueneme - Channel Island ANGB, 146th AW, Mail: POB 4001, 93041-4001,   F-86A

Ramona - Classic Rotors, 2898 Montecito Rd, Hangar G, (760) 803-0244, Mon, Wed, Fri-Sun 10-4, www.rotors.org

Adams Wilson Hobbycopter	H-26(XH)	KA-26
AeroLIft Cyclocxrane X.2	H-30	Mil-2
Allied Aerospace UAV	H-31(YH)	MonteCopter Model 10
Bell 47-B3	H-32	MonteCopter Model 12
Benson Gyrocopter	H-32	Rotary Rocket
Bolkow 102	H-32	Rotorway Exec 90
Brantly B-305	H-34	Rotorway Scorpion 1
Goodyear GA-400	H-43A	Rotorway Scorpion 133
H-13	H-46F Maintenance Trainer	Sud SA-341G
H-18	H-55(TH)	SUD Ouese Djinn
H-19B(UH)	H-67(TH)	SUD SA.341G
H-19D	Hiller CAMEL	V-44
H-21B	HUK	Westland WASP
H-23B	HUP-1	XA-6 American Helicopter
H-25A	J-2 McCulloch	

Rialto - Westpac Restorations,(Formerly Klaers Aviation), 1462 N Fitzgerald Ave, L67, Art Scholl Field, 92376-8621, (909) 874-9108

B-25J	F7F-3E	P-38F-5 (P)	P-47D (P)
P-47D	P-38J-15 (P)	P-47D-11-RE (P)	P-47D-2-RE (P)

Riverside -March Field Air Museum, 22550 Van Buren, Off I-215, 92518-6463, (951) 697-6602 Fax 697-6605, Mail: POB 6463, Daily 9-4, Closed CD,TD,ND,ED, Gift Shop, 697-6603, Library 697-6604, Theater, Restoration Facility, Adm Adult $7, Child 5-11 $3, Under 5 Free, www.marchairmuseum.com,

A-4J(TA)	C-119F	F-105D	P-39Q
A-7D	C-123K	FB-111A	P-6E Hawk
A-9A(YA)	C-131D	FO-141	P-40 Replica
AN-2 Colt	C-135A(KC)	H-1(AH)	P-59A
A-26C	C-141B	H-1F(UH)	PT-6A
B-8M Bensnon	D3A Val	H-13A(VH)	PT-13D
B-17G	F-4C(RF)	H-21B(UH)	PT-19B
B-25J	F-14	HU-16E(SA-16)	R50-5(C-60)
B-29A	F-84C	L-5	SNJ-4
B-47E	F-84F	LGM-30 Minuteman II	SR-71A
B-52D(GB)	F-86H	MiG-19	T-33A
B-57(EB)	F-89J	MiG-21F13	T-37B
BT-13A (2ea)	F-100C	MiG-23 BN	T-38A
C-45F(JRB-4)	F-101B	Nieuport II Rep	T-39A
C-47A(VC)	F-102A	O-2B	TG-2
C-54D	F-104	OH-6A	U-9A(YU)
C-97L(KC)	F-105B	OH-58A	

CALIFORNIA
Riverside
CAF Inland Empire Squadron, 6936 Flight Rd, Riverside Municipal, 92504-1967, (951) 354-7954,
www.inlandempirewingcaf.org, L-4F   PT-22   C-53D

P-38 National Assoc,(At March Field Air Museum), Mail: POB 6453, March ARB, 92518,
www.p38assn.org, P-38 Replica

475th Fighter Group Historical Foundation, March AFB, Mail: POB 6463, 92518-0394,
Next to the P-38 National Assoc, www.475thfghf.org, Artifacts

Rosamond - Edwards AFB, NASA Ames-Dryden Visitor Center, POB 273, 93523-0273,
(661) 276-5247, Gift Shop, www.dfrc.nasa.gov/Dryden/tour.html,
SR-71   X-1E   X-15   X-29

Edwards AFB, Air Force Flight Test Center Museum, 95ABW/MU, 405 S Rosamond Blvd,
Bldg 7211, 93524-1850, (661) 277-8050, Fax 277-8051, Tours Only 1st and 2nd Fri Weekly,
TD, CD, ND, Free Adm, Gift Shop 277-6500, INC = incomplete, OD = On Display,
OS = Off Station, R = Restoration, S = Storage, AT = Awaiting Transportation, NS = Non Standard;

A-3D-1	S	C-135A	S	F-100A	INC	NF-11(TT-20)	OD
A-7D(Y)	R	C-140A	S	F-100A	OS/AT	P-59B(XP)	OD
A-7F(Y)	R	C-141A(NC)	R	F-100A(YF)	R	PA-48	R
A-9A(YF)	S	CH-3E	OD	F-100A(YF)	S	PGM-17A	OD
A-10B(Y)	R	CT-39A	OD	F-101B	OD	Rutan 354	S
A-37B(NA)	OD	D-21	OD	F-102A(TF)	S	SR-71	OD
AQM-34	OD	F-4C(NF)	OD	F-104A	OD	T-28B	OD
AT3	R	F-4C(RF)	R	F-104A	OD	T-33A	OD
B-26B(T)	R	F-4E(YF)	R	F-104A(NF)	OD	T-33A	OD
B-47B	INC	F-8G(RF)	S	F-105D	R	T-38A	OD
B-52D	OD	F-10B	R	F-106B	R	T-46A	S
B-57B	R	F-16B	OD	F-111A(N)	R	Titan Missile	
B-58A(N)	INC	F-16B	OD	F-111A	OD	U-2D	OD
BQM-34A	S	F-20	S	H-21C	S	X-1	
C-7B	S	F-80A(EF)	R/OS	H-34C(VH)	S	X-4	R
C-45J(U)	OD	F-84F	OD	H-34G(SH)	OD	X-21A	INC
C-53	R	F-86F	OD	HL-10		X-25B	OD
C-119B	S	F-89D	S	HUP-2	S	X-36-2	
C-123K	S	F-94A(YF)	R	MMC-845	S		

Jet Engines: J35, J47, J57, J79, J85, YJ93, YF101, F-109;
Rocket Engines: XLR-8, XLR-11, XLR-99, LR-121

San Carlos - Hiller Aviation Museum, 601 Skyway Rd, 94070, (650) 654-0200,
Fax 654-0220, Daily 10-5, Adm Adult $9, Snrs & Child 8-17 $6, Under 5 Free,
Gift Shop, Library, Theater, Restoration Viewing, (P) = Project, www.hiller.org

Avitor Hermes, Jr	Gonzales Tractor	Montgomery "Santa Clara"
Boeing 747-100 Cockpit (P)	H-12L(UH) Model 360	Nasa Swing Wing
Boeing 2707-300 Fuse	H-23B(OH)	Pietenpol Aircamper
Boeing Condor	H-32(YH) Hornet	RC-3 Seabee
Boeing T-3	H-44(XH)	Stearman Hammond YS-1
Christen Eagle	HOE-1(H J-1)	Stinson Detroiter
Curtiss D	J-10-Jet	VXT-8
Diamond (P)	JN-4D	VZ1 Hiller 1031
Fairchild 22	"Little Looper" Aerobatics	Waco 10
Fairchild 24C8C	Monocoupe Model 70	Wright Brothers B
FH-1099 CAMEL	Montgomery "Gull Glider"	XROE
Fowler-Gage Panama	Montgomery "Evergreen"	YO3A

San Diego - San Diego Flight Museum, 1424 Continental St, Hangar #8, Brownfield Airport, 92154
(619) 661-2516, www.sandiegoflightmuseum.org

Folland Gnat	Frati Falco	MiG-21U-600	PT-19
Founja CM-170	Long-Eze	PL-2	

CALIFORNIA

San Diego - San Diego Air & Space Museum, Inc, 2001 Pan American Plaza, Balboa Park, 92101,
(619) 234-8291, Daily 10-4, Summer 10-5, Closed TD, CD, ND, Adm Adult $10, Snrs 65 $8,
Child 6-17 $5, Under 5 Free, Theater, Restoration Facility,Gift Shop 234-8291 Ext 31,
See also El Cajon, CA Restoration Facility, www.sandiegoairandspace.org, GF=Gildred Flight Rotunda,
EC=East Concourse, SC=South Concourse, W C=W est Concourse, CY=Court Yard, FY=Front Yard,
S=Storage,

A-4B	EC	F-86F	EC	OQ-2	SC
A-6	S	F8U	GF	Ornithopter	W C
A-7	S	Fleet 2	SC	P-40E	EC
A-12	FY	Fokker DR.I (R)	W C	P-51D	GF
A6M7	EC	Fokker E III (R)		PBY-5A	CY
Albatross D-Va (R)	W C	Ford 5-AT-B P	S	PCI-1A	EC
Am Eagle A-1	GF	Gemini	EC	Pitts S-L-S	EC
Apollo Capsule	EC	GPS-12 Satelite		PT-1	S
ASG-21	S	H-1E(AH)	GF	PT-22	
B-5	SC	H-1B(UH)	GF	Quicksilver	S
Bf-109G(Mock-Up)	EC	J-1	SC	Rearwin Cloudster	GF
Bleriot XI	W C	J2F-6	EC	RQ-1K	
Bowers Flybaby 1A	GF	J-3	SC	RV-4	EC
Bowlus Albatross	EC	JN-4D	W C	Ryan STA	SC
BQM-34F		Jungster VI		S-4C	W C
Brunner Bird BK	GF	Lilienthal Glider	W C	SBD-4	EC
C-3	W C	Link Trainer		SG-1 Racer (Gillespie Field)	
Cayley Glider	W C	M-1	W C	SPAD VII	W C
Curtiss A-1 Traid	GF	Mercury Air Racer	EC	Spitfire Mk 16	EC
Curtiss B-1 Robin	SC	Mercury Capsule	EC	Sundancer I Racer	EC
Curtiss L. Looper	W C	MiG-15	EC	Swallow TP	SC
CW-1	W C	MiG-17	CY	W aco YKS-7	SC
Deperdussin C	W C	Montgolfiere	W C	W ee Bee	EC
DH 2		Montgomery	W C	W right EX Vin Fiz	W C
DH 60-M	SC	MS-230	GF	W right Flyer	W C
F4B-4	SC	N2S-3	SC	X-13	
F4F-3A (P)	EC	Nieuport 11 (R)	W C	YF2Y-1	FY
F-4S	CY	Nieuport 28	W C		
F6F-3	EC	NYP	GF		

San Diego Aircraft Carrier Museum, 910 N Harbor Dr, 92101, (619) 544-9600, Daily 10-5,
Adm Adult $15, Snrs 62 /Mil/ $10, Child 6-17 $8, Under 6 Free, Cafe, Gift Shop, www.midway.org

A-3B(EK)	E-2C	F/A-18	SH-2F
A-4F	F-4N	H-1(UH)	SNJ-7
A-4C	F-4S	H-3(SH)	T-2C
A-6E	F-8	H-34(UH)	T-34
A-7B	F-9F-5	H-46(CH)	TBM-3 (2ea)
A-24	F-9F-8P	RA-5C	
AD-1	F-9J(TF)	S-3A	
C-1	F-14A	SBD-1	

San Diego - Miramar - Flying Leatherneck Aviation Museum, Bldg 4203 Anderson Ave,
MCAS Miramar, Mail: POB 45316, 92145-0316, (858) 693-1723, Tue-Sun 9-3:30, Free Adm,
W ed-Sun 10-4, Restoration Facility, Gift Shop 693-1791, www.flyingleathernecks.org,
S=Storage, P=Project, PX=at PX, L=On Loan to Pensacola W ings of Gold TV Series,

A-4C	F/A-18A (2ea)	HOK-1(HH-34D)	R4Q-2(C-119)
A-4M	F2H-2(F9F-2)	HRS-3(H-19)	R5D-2Z(C-54)
A-6E	F3D-2(EF-10)	HTL4(S)	RF-4B
AH-1	F4D (P)	HUP-2(H-25)	RF-8G(F8U-1P)
AH-1J	F4U-5N	HUS(UH-34)	SNJ-5 (S)
B-25(PBJ)	F8E	MiG-15	TA4 (S)
Bell 214	F9F-8P	OV-10D	TBM-3E(TBF)
CH-46	FJ-3	OY-1(L-5) (S)	TO-1 (S)
CH-53A	FM-2(S)	R4D-8(C-117)	

CALIFORNIA

San Francisco - Crissy Field Aviation Museums Assoc, Pier One, Ft Mason, Mail: POB 210671 94121, (415) 602-8625, Appt Only, www.crissyfieldaviation.org,   DH-4 Project

The Exploratorium, 3601 Lyon St, 94123, (415) 563-7337, Sun-Wed 1-5, Free Adm,
Glider   Spacecraft

San Luis Obispo - O'Sullivan AAF, Camp San Luis Obispo, Cal Rt 1, Officers Club, (805) 541-6168,

H-13(OH)	H-47(CH)	H-19(CH)	O-1
H-23(OH)	U-6	H-34(CH)	

San Martin - Wings of History Air Museum, S County Airport, 12777, Murphy Ave, Off Hwy 101
Just North of Gilroy, POB 495, 95046-0495, (408) 683-2290, Fax 683-2291, Sat-Sun 11-4
Airshow Memorial Day, Restoration Facility, Gift Shop, Restaurant, www.wingsofhistory.org

Alexander Primary Glider	EAA Biplane	Security Airster (P)
American Eagle A-101	Link Trainer	Sopwith Pup Rep
AT-11	LNE-1	Spad VII (P)
Avro 595 (P)	Marske Pioneer II	Stahltaube 3/4 Scale
Beech 23	Mitchell Wing	Stan Hall Cherokee II
Bensen B.8M	Nelson Glider	Stan Hall Safari
Bowlus Albatross	Nieuport 11 Rep	Stinson 10A
Bowlus Baby Albatross	P-51	Stolp 7/8 Scale
Bowlus Flybaby	Peel Glider Boat	Taylor Titsch
Bowlus Super Albatross	Penguin Trainer	VJ-21
Culver Cadet (P)	Pietenpohl Air Camper (P)	Waco 10
DH 88 Rep	Rutan Quickie	Wright Flyer Rep

San Pedro - Ft MacArthur Museum, 3601 S Gaffey St, 90731, (310) 548-2631, Nike Ajax SAM

Santa Maria - Santa Maria Museum of Flight, 3015 Airpark Dr, 93455, (805) 922-8758
Fax 922-8958, Fri-Sun 10-4, Closed Holidays, Donations Requested, Gift Shop, Library,
Banquet Facility, Dir: Michael Geddry Sr, www.smmof.org

A-4L	F-86	H-1 Rep	Parker Sailplane
Bowers Fly Baby	Fleet II	KR-2	Stinson Reliant
F-4S	Great Lakes 2T-1A	P-38 (1/2 Scale)	Wright Glider

Santa Paula - Aviation Museum of Santa Paula, 824 E Santa Maria St, 93060, Mail: POB 908, 93061,
(805) 525-1109, 1st Sun Monthly 10-3, Gift Shop, www.amszp.org

Beech D17S	Fairchild F-24	Howard DGA

Santa Rosa - Pacific Coast Air Museum, Sonoma County Airport, 2230 Becker Blvd, 95403
(707) 575-7900, Fax 545-2813, Tue,Thur, Sat-Sun 10-4, $5 Donation, Child Under 13 Free
Gift Shop, Restoration Facility, Pres: Don Doherty, Airshow 3rd Weekend Aug,
3rd Weekend Climb In Museum Aircraft Monthly, www.Pacificcoastairmuseum.org,

A-4E	F-14A	HU-16A & (P)	T-28B
A-6E	F-16N(FC)	IL-14P	T-28C (P)
A-26 (P)	F-84F(P)	L-3 (P)	T-33
BD-5	F-86F(RF)	MiG-15 (P)	T-37
Broussard MH.1512	F-86H	Nanchang CJ-6 2ea	T-38
C-118(DC-6)	F-105F	P-51D	YAK 52
F-4C	F-106	PA-22	
F-8U	H-1H(UH)	PA-23(U-11A)	

Shafter - Minter Field Air Museum, 401 Vultee Ave, Shafter Airport, Mail: POB 445, 93263,
(661) 393-0291, Fax 393-3296, Fri-Sat 10-4, Airshow in April, www.minterfieldairmuseum.com

AT-6	L-5	T-33	PT-17
F-80 Mockup	Link Trainer	BT-13	PT-26
L-3	PT-17	P-51 (2ea)	T-50

Simi Valley - Ronald Regan Presidential Library and Museum, 40 Presidential Dr, 93065,
(800) 410-8354, Daily 10-5, Adm Adult 18-61 $12, 62+ $9, Child 11-17 $3, Under 11 Free, Cafe,
www.reaganlibrary.com, Boeing 707 Air Force 1,   VH-3,   F-14D   BGM-109   **17**

CALIFORNIA

South El Monte - American Society of Military History Museum, 1918 N Rosemead Blvd
91733, (626) 422-1776, Fax 443-1776, Fri-Sun 10-4:30, H-1C/M(UH),
Tanks: M4A3, M47, M48, M60, M551

Torrance - Western Museum of Flight, 3315 Airport Dr, Red Baron # 3, 90505,
(310) 326-9544, Fax 326-9556, www.wmof.com   OL = On Loan

A-4A (OL)	F-5A (OL)	JB-1	**Engines:**
AT-6E(XA) (OL)	F-86	P-51	A-1020
DH 82 (OL)	Gyrocopter (OL)	Radioplane RP-5A (OL)	GR-1820-G205
F-14A (OL)	JB-1	Radioplane RP-76 (OL)	J-79-GE-3A
F-17(YF) (OL)	Montgomery Glider (OL)	Rogallo Wing (OL)	R-985-AN-1
F-20 Fuse (OL)	Northrop KD2R-5 (OL)	Sierra Sue	T-51R-5190
F-23(YF) (OL)	O-3A(YO) (OL)		V-12

Twentynine - Twentynine Palms Marine Corps Air-Ground Combat Center, Box 788100
92278-8100, (760) 830-6000,   A-4

Upland - CAF 3rd Pursuit Squadron, 1749 W 13th St, Cable Airport, 91786, (909) 751-1131
3rd Sat Monthly 5:30, www.3rdpursuit.com

AN-2	FM-2	PT-22	T-34
AT-6	I-16	SNJ	

Van Nuys - Main Gate, F-104C

Whittier - Whittier Museum, 6755 S Newlin Ave, 90601, (562) 945-3871, 1949 Miller Special JM-101

Yorba Linda - Richard Nixon Library & Birthplace, 18001 Yorba Linda Blvd, 92886, (714) 993-5075
528-0544 Fax, Mon-Sat 10-5, Sun 11-5, Adm Adult $7.95, 62+ $5.95, Child 7-11 $4, Under 7 Free
www.nixonlibrary.org   H-3A(VH) Sea King

COLORADO

Aurora - Colorado ANG/PA, Buckley ANGB/STOP # 24, 140 TFG, 80011-9599, (303) 366-5363

DHC-2	F-100A	F-86D	F-86F(RF)	T-6A

Colorado Springs - Fort Carson, Butts Airfield, Free Adm, OH-6, OH-13, Many Tanks
US Air Force Academy/PA, 80840-5151, (719) 472-2025, 472-2555,

B-52D	F-104A	Minuteman II	X-4
F-4C	F-105D	SV5-J	
F-16	GF-16A	T-38A	

Peterson Air & Space Museum, Peterson AFB, 150 E Ent Ave, Bldg 981, 80914-1303,
(719) 556-4915, Tue-Sat 10-4, Closed Holidays, Free Adm, Gift Shop,
www.petemuseum.org, (P = Project)

Air-2A Genie Replica	F-4C	F-102A	P-40E Replica
CF-100	F-15A	F-104C	P-47N (P)
CF-101B	F-86L	F-106A (P)	T-33A
CIM-10A (P)	F-89J	Hawk	Vela Satellite
EB-57E	F-94C	Nike Ajax	
EC-121T (P)	F-101B	Nike Hercules	

Denver - J W Duff Aircraft Salvage, 8131 E. 40th Ave, 80207, (303) 399-6010, Mon-Fri 8-4:30,
Aircraft Fuselage & Wings, Some Full Aircraft, www.jwduffaircraft.com/index.html

Aero Commander 100	Cessna 305A	Noorduyn Norseman	SNJ-4
BC-12-65	Fairchild F-24	O-2	T-37
Brantley 305	J-4 (2ea)	PA-15	U-6A
Cessna 120 (2ea)	H-1H(UH)	PA-22-108	U-8G (2ea)
Cessna 140A	L-18C	PA-28-140	Young Turbo Cruiser
Cessna 150	LA-4-200	PT-26	
Cessna 172	Mooney M20	Ryan Aeronautical	
Cessna 172F	Navious 2	S-1A	

COLORADO

Denver - The 69th Battalion, POB 24286, 80224,
E-mail: robert@carik.com, Pyro/Special Effects Contractor, Flying:

A1-D	A-37	O1-A	O-2A	OV-1D	UV-18A

Wings Over the Rockies Air & Space Museum, Lowry AFB, 7711 E Academy Blvd,
80230-6929, (303) 360-5360, Fax: 360-5328, Mon-Sat 10-5, Sun 12-5, Closed: ED, TD, CD, ND,
Adm Adult $7, Snrs $6, Child 4-12 $5, Under 4 Free, Pres Greg Anderson, Gift Shop, 360-8535,
Library, Restoration Facility, www.wingsmuseum.org,

A-7D	Christen Eagle	F-101B	J-3
Alexander Eagle Rock	der Kricket	F-102A	Kit Fox
B-1A	F-4E	F-104C	Moni Glider
B-18A	F-14A	F-105D	Nord 3202
B-52B(GB)	F-84K(RF)	F-111A	T-33A
B-57E	F-86H	FG-1D	U-3A
C-45	F-100D(GF)	H-21C	Woody Pusher

Fruita - Western Slope Vietnam War Memorial Park - I-70 Exit, Mail: PO Box 340, 81521,
(970) 242-0073, UH-1

Ft Lupton - CAF - Mile High Wing, Front Range Airport, 7607 County Rd 39, 80034-0528,
Mail: POB 471596, Aurora, CO, 80047-1596, (303) 851-1499, Info (303) 841-3004,
3rd Sat Monthly 10am, www.milehighcaf.org, C-60A (Rides Available)

Vintage Aero Flying Museum, Lafayette Foundation, 7507 County Rd 39, 80621-8515
Platte Valley Airport (18V), (303) 668-8044, Sat 10-4, www.lafayettefoundation.org

BT-13A	Fokker D-VIII (Project)	Spad VII (Project)
Fokker DR-I	SE-5a American 7/8	Great Lakes (Project)
Fokker D-VII	SE-5a British 7/8	

Grand Junction - CAF - Rocky Mountain Wing, 780 Heritage Way, Walker Field, 81506,
(970) 256-0693, Mail: POB 4125, 81501, Sat 9-4, Gift Shop, www.rockymountainwingcaf.org,

DHC-1	J-3	SNJ	TBM-3E

Lafayette - The Spirit of Flight Center, 1208 Commerce Ct, Ste 3, 80026, (303) 460-1156 Ext 21
New Facility at Denver, CO Late 2007, Mon-Fri 10-2, Sat by Appt, Adm $2 Donation, Facility Rental,
Gift Shop, Theater, Restoration Facility, www.spiritofflight.com

AT-6	Culver Dart	P-51D Project
Bf-109 (3ea) Project	MiG-21	

Pueblo - Pueblo Weisbord Aircraft Museum, 31001 Magnuson Ave, 81001, (719) 948-9219
Fax 948-2437, Mon-Sat 10-4, Adm Adult $6, Under 10 Free, Sit In A Cockpit, Quarterly,
Different Aircraft Each Quarter, Gift Shop, www.pwam.org

A4D-2	F-6A	F-101A	PT-17
A-26C	F8	F-104A	RA-5C
B-29A	F9F-8	H-1(UH)	RB-37
B-47E	F11F-1	HC-21B	T-28C
Bell H47G	F-80	H-34J(SH)	T-33B
C-47	F-84G	HC-131A	T-34B
C-119	F-100D	P2V-5	T-37B

CONNECTICUT

Hartford - Prop-Liners of America, 58 Lindbergh Dr, 06114, (860) 684-4988,
www.propliners.com/index.html, Convair 240 Restoration

Stratford - National Helicopter Museum, 2480 Main St, 06615, (203) 767-1123,
May-Oct Wed-Sun 1-4, Free Adm, Gift Shop, Contact Igor Sikorsky Jr (Son of the Pioneer),
www.nationalhelicoptermuseum.org, S-76 Cockpit

Windsor Locks - Air National Guard, Bradley Airport, A-10, F-105, F-106

CONNECTICUT

Windsor Locks - New England Air Museum, Bradley Int'l Airport, 36 Perimeter Rd, 06096, Exit 40(I-91) (860) 623-3305, Fax 627-2820, Daily 10-5, Closed TD, CD, NY, Adm Adult $9, Snrs 60 $8.00, Child 6-11 $5, Under 6 Free, Gift Shop, Theater, Restoration, www.neam.org,

A-3B	F4D-1	MC200
A-4A	F4U-4(XF)	Mead Rhone Ranger
A-10A	F6F-5K	MiG-15
A-26C	F9F-2	Monerai S Sailplane
AD-4N	FJ-1	Mosquito H. Glider
AEW 3	FM-2	NIK2-J
AT-6	Fokker DR.1	Nixon Special
B-25H	Gee Bee Model E	OH-23G
B-29A	Gee Bee R-1	OH-50C
B-57A(RB)	Gee Bee Model A	P-47D
Bell 47D-1	Goodyear ZNP	P-51D
Bensen B-8M	Great Lakes 2T-1A	Pioneer Flightstar
Blanchard	H-5H	Pratt-Read Line-1
Bleriot X1	Hanson-M. Quickie	PT-23A
BT-13	Heath Parasol	R-3(M-B)
C-7A	H-1(AH)	R-4B
C-50	H-1(UH)	Rearwin Cloudster
CBY-3	H-6A(OH)	Republic Seabee
CH-54B	H-23G(OH)	Rutan Quickie
Chanute Glider	H-54B(CH)	Rutan Vari-eze
Corben Jr Ace	HH-43F	S-39
Curtiss Pusher	HH-52A	S-60
D-558-11	HRP-1	S-51
DC-3	HU-16E	SP-2E
Dyndiuk Sport	HUP-1	SR 71 Engine Only
E-1B	HUP-2(H-25)	Stinson Detroiter
F-4A	J-3	SUD VI-R
F-4B	JB-2	T-28C
F-8K LTV	K-225	T-33A
F-14B	K-16 V-STOL	TV-2
F-86	Laird Solution	U-6A
F-89J	LH-34D	UH-1B
F-94C	Link ANT-18	Viking Kittyhawk
F-100 Cockpit	Lockheed 10A	VS-44A Sikorski Flying Boat
F-100A	Lockheed 12	XF15C-1
F-104C	Lockheed 14	Zephyr
F-105B	Marcoux-Bromberg	

Delaware

Dover AFB - Air Mobility Command Museum, 1301 Heritage Rd, 19902-8001, (302) 677-5938 Fax 677-5940, Tue-Sun 9-4, Free Adm, Gift Shop, Restoration Facility, Curator: Jim Leech www.amcmuseum.org/ email: museum@dover.af.mil

B-17G	C-119G	C-141A	H-43(HH)
BT-13	C-121	C-141B	Link Trainer
C-7A	C-123K	CG-4A Project	PT-17
C-9	C-124A	F-101B	T-33A
C-45G	C-130	F-106	TG-4A
C-47A	C-131D	F-106 Simulator	
C-54M	C-133	H-1(UH)	
C-97(KC)			

Georgetown - Delaware Aviation Museum, 21513 Rudder Ln, Sussex County Airport, (302) 854-0244, Sat-Sun 10-4, May-Oct Fri 10-4, Free Adm, Gift Shop, Library (4,000 Books),

B-25	L-16	PT-26	Yak-52
C-78B(UC)	MiG-15	Su-25K	
CJ6	MiG-17 (2ea)	Yak-3	
Iskra Jet	MiG-21	Yak-9	

D.C.

Anacostia NAS, SE Wahsington D.C. Off Route 295 and Potomac River, T-28

Bolling AFB, 20332-5000, (202) 545-6700, 1100th ABG/CC, F-105D

National Postal Museum, 2 Massachusetts Ave, 20002, (202) 633-5555, Daily 10-5:30, Closed CD, Free Adm, www.postalmuseum.si.edu/, DH 4   SR-10F   Weisman Cook

US Soldiers and Airmens Home, 3700 N Capital St, (800) 422-9988, F-86, M60 Tank

National Air & Space Museum, Smithsonian Institution, Independence Ave SW, 20560, (202) 633-1000, Daily 10-5:30, Closed CD, Free Adm, Gift Shop, Chairman - Dept of Aeronautics: Dr Thomas Crouch, www.nasm.si.edu

Gallery Number	206 FH-1	209 P-59A(XP)
203 A4D-2N(A-4C)	20x Fi-103	206 P-80(XP)
205 A6M5	209 Fokker D.VII	202 PA-5
209 Albatross D.Va	202 Ford 5-AT	206 Pfalz D.XII
205 B-26B	202 G-21	208 R3C-2
205 Bf 109G	204 G-22	213 Rockwell HiMAT
207 Bleriot XI	207 Gallaudet Hydro-Kite	LOB Rutan Voyager
200 Boeing 247D	208 Gossamer Condor	203 SBD-6
Boeing 747 Fuse	205 H-1	202 Sopwith Snipe
205 C-17L	209 Hawker Siddeley Kestrel	205 Spitfire Mk.VII
207 Curtiss D	205 J-1	208 T-2(F.IV)
202 DC-3	207 Lilienthal	206 Voisin Model 8
202 DC-7 Fuse	208 Lockheed 5B Vega	205 Wittman
210 DH 4	209 Lockheed 5C Vega	200 Wright Kitty Hawk
ESC D-558-2	208 Lockheed 8 Sirius	208 Wright EX Vin Fiz
208 DWC-2	205 MC-202	209 Spad XIII
207 Ecker Flying Boat	206 Me 262A	210 U-2C
206 Explorer II	202 Northrop 4A Alpha	207 Wright Military Flyer
203 F4B-4	205 Northrop Gama	200 X-1
203 F4F-4(FM-1)	214 Northrop M2-F3	200 X-15A-1
ESC F-104A	200 NYP	213 X-29
202 FC-2	204 P-26A	
206 FE-8	205 P-51D	

FLORIDA

Cocoa Beach - US Air Force Space Museum Cape Canaveral, AF Station, 32925, (321) 867-7110, Daily 9-3, Free Adm, 80 Spacecraft, Rockets & Missiles

Astronaut Memorial Planetarium and Observatory, Brevard Community College 1519 Clearlake Rd, 32922, (321) 634-3732, 631-7889

Daytona Beach - Embry-Riddle Aeronautical Univ, 32114, (386) 226-6175
Aircraft Here Are For Training Purpose Only,

Aerospatial Tampico	Beechcraft Dutchess	C-172Q	Mooney M.18
American General Tiger	C-303	C-303	PA-44
Beechcraft 35	C-172	C-182RG	Piper Cadet

Wright Flyer Replica In Front Of School For Public Viewing.

DeLand - CAF-Florida Wing, 2302 Old Daytona Beach Rd, Deland Mcpl Airport, 32720 Mamil: PO Box 1944, 32721-1944, http://caffl.org,   L-17B

Deland Naval Air Station Museum, 910 Biscayne Blvd, 32724, Tue-Sat 12-4, (386) 738-4149, www.delandnavalairstation.org, Bell 47   F-14B   TBM-3 Project

Fernandina Beach - Amelia Island: Island Aerial Tours, 1600 Airport, 32034-0204, 35 Mi S of Jacksonville, (904) 261-7890, J-3   Waco Model 10

FLORIDA

Ft. Lauderdale - The Discovery Center, 231 SW 2nd Ave, 33301-1892, Space Artifacts

World Jet Aircraft Int'l Sales & Leasing, 1710 W Cypress Creek Rd,
33309-1806, (954) 776-6477, Planes May Be Sold, Check Ahead

Me-109	Nord	P-51	TBM

Ft. Myers - Southwest Florida Museum of History, 2300 Peck St, 33901, (239) 332-5955,
Tue-Sat10-5, Sun 12-4, Adm Adult $9.50, Child $8.50, Under 12 $4, Grp $7.50 ea,
www.citymyers.com/museum, AT-6, P-39 Parts, Railroad Caboose

Homestead - AFB, 33039-5000, (305) 257-8011,   F-4D   F-100D

Indian Rocks Beach - Florida Aviation Historical Society, POB 127, 33535, Ford Flivver

Jacksonville - Commanding Officer Naval Reserve Officer Training Corps Jacksonville
University NROTC, 2800 University Blvd North, 32211-3394, (904) 745-7480,
Daily 8-4:30, JU Pub Affairs: Doris Barletta, By Direction: SL Vencel,
A-7E (In Front of NROTC Building)

Jacksonville ANG, Int'l Airport, (904) 741-4902, F-106A   T-33A

MCAS New River, Heros Park, Off Hwy 17 S of City, AH-1W, CH-34, CH-53E, MV-22, UH-1

Naval Air Station Jacksonville, 32212-5000, 14 Mi SW of Jacksonville, I-10 & Whitehouse Exit,
S on Chaffe Rd to Normandy then R, Passes at Bldg 327 Main Gate, Daily 7:30-2pm,
(904) 542-2345/4011, Aircraft Inside Main Gate, www.nasjax.navy.mil

A-4C	F-14A	P-3A	S-3A
A-7E	F/A-18A	P2V-5	SH-3H(HS-7)
F-8U-1	N2S-4	PBY-5A	TBM-3E

Key West - Naval Air Station Key West, (305) 293-3700, A-4E, A-5, F-4, F-14B
EA-6A

Conch Republic Trading Company, 725 Duvall St, 33040, (305) 292-9002, Fax 292-0270
1946 Sea-Bee

HT Chittum & Co Sport Clothing Store, 725 Duval St, (305) 292-9002, RC-3

Kissimmee - Howard Johnson Lodge, Fountain Park Plaza Hotel & Conference Center
5150 W Space Coast Pkwy, (800) 432-0763, Titan I Missile

Warbird Adventures, Adjacent to Flying Tigers Warbird Air Museum, 233 N Hoagland, 34741,
(800) 386-1593, (727) -870-7366, Daily 9-5, warbirdadventures.com, AT-6 Flights, H-13(UH)

White 1 Foundation Inc, 233 N Hoagland Blvd, 34741, Inside Warbird Adventures Hangar
(727) 365-1713, Daily 9-5, Gift Shop, www.white1foundation.org, Restoring FW-190 F8, P-51

Lakeland - Explorations V Children's Museum, 109 N Kentucky Ave, S, (863) 687-3869, Small Plane
Cockpit

FLORIDA

Lakeland - Florida Air Museum, 4175 Medulla Rd, Lakeland - Linder Regional Airport, Mail: POB 7670, 33807, I-4 Exit 25, (863) 644-0741, Mon-Fri 9-5, Sat 10-4, Sun 12-4, Closed CE, CD, ND, Adm Adult $8, Seniors $6, Child 8-12 $4, Gift Shop, Theater, Dir: Gregory Harbaugh, www.sun-n-fun.org

AT-11	Ercoupe 415-C	Q-200 Quickie
Aeronca C-3	Evans VP-1	Ranchero
Aeronca LB	F-14	Rand KR-1
Aerosport Scamp	Flying Flea	Rans S-9
American Eaglet	FP-303	Revolution Mini 500
Anderson Kingfisher	Glassair R6	Russ Ritter Special
Anglin Spacewalker II	G-44A	Rutan Vari-eze
Auster AOP-9 XN-408	Hawker Tempst Mk II	Rutan Variviggen
B-17 Ball Turret	Heath Super Parasol	SE5A
B-29 Nose	J2F6	Smyth Sidewinder
Barracuda	Kit-Fox Model #1	Stits Playmate
Bede BD-4	Laird Baby	Sunshine Clipper
Bede BD-5	Lazair	Super Lancer Hang Glider
Bellanca 14-9	Loving's Love	T-33A
Bensen B.8M	Lysander	Taylorcraft BL-65
Bowers Fly Baby	Mitchell P-38	Taylorcraft E-2
Brokaw Bullet	Monnet Moni	Travelair
Chief Oshkosh	Mooney M.18L Mite	Vangrunsven RV-3
Command-Aire	OQ-19(KD2R-3)	VJ-24
CP-65 Project	P-51D	VP-1
Cricket MC-10	P-63	Woody Pusher
DGA 1-A	Pitts Special	XFV-1 VTO
EAA Acro-Sport	Q-1 Quickie	YF2Y-1
Emeraude		

Mary Esthler - Hurlburt Field Memorial Air Park, 1 SOW/HO, 131 Bartley St, Suite 246, 32544-5000, (850) 884-6507, Off Highway 98, www2.hurlburt.af.mil/library

A-1E	C-46D	C-130A(AC)	O-2A
A-37B(OA)	C-47A(AC)	H-3E(HH)	OV-10A(NH)
B-25N	C-119G(AC)	H-1P(UH)	T-28D(AT)
B-26K	C-123K(UC)	O-1E	U-10A

Melbourne - FIT Aviation, LLC, Melbourne Airport, 640 Harry Sutton Rd, 32901-1885 (321) 674-6500, Mon-Fri 9-5, Temporary Stationed until 2008 are: British Canberra TT18, Jet Provost T5A

Merritt Island - Brevard Veterans Memorial Center Museum, 400 S Sykes Creek Pkwy, 32952 (321) 453-4526, Mon-Fri 8:30-4:30, Adm Free, Meeting Room, Curator Alex Terrero, AH-1, UH-1

NASA Kennedy Space Center, 32899, (321) 452-2121, Daily 9-5:30, Closed CD, Adult $38, Child 3-11 $28, Gift Shop, Restaurant, 3-D IMAX Theater, www.kennedyspacecenter.com,

Apollo II	Space Shuttle	Saturn V	Missiles	Launch Vehicles

Miami - George T Baker Aviation School, 3275 NW 42nd Ave, 33142, (305) 871-3143 Ext 300 www.universities.com/Schools/G/George_T_Baker_Aviation_School.asp

A-4	Boeing 707	Martin 4-0-4
Beech D18S	F-86	T-33

Miami - Wings Over Miami Museum, 14710 SW 128th St, Kendall-Tamiami Airport SW of Miami, 33196, (321) 449-4444, Thur-Sun 10-5:30, Adm Adult $9.95, Snrs & Child Under 12 $5.95, Gift Shop, www.wingsovermiami.com

A-26C	F-86F	PBY-5A
British Provost	Fairchild 24R	PT-17
CJ6A Nanchang (2ea)	Folland Gnat	PT-22
Davis DI-W	Fouga Magister	SNJ-6
DH-82	Ikarus	TBM-3
F-14	L-29	YAK-52

FLORIDA

Orlando - Church Street Station, 129 W. Church St, 32801, (407) 422-2434,
Commander Ragtimes, Fokker D.VII   Fokker DR.1   SE-5A

Helicopter Inc, 240 N Crystal Lake Dr, 32803, (407) 894-7428,Owner: Fred Clark,
Curtiss Robin B   Paramount Cabinaair

John Young Museum & Planetarium, 810 E Rollings St, 32803,
(305) 896-7151, Daily 10-5, Free Adm,   Spacecraft

Panama City - (See Next Page)

Pensacola - National Museum of Naval Aviation,1750 Radford Blvd, 32508-5402, (850) 452-3604,
Exit 7 (I-10), (850) 452-3604, Mail: NAM Foundation, Box 33104, Daily 9-5, Closed: TD, CD, ND
Free Adm, Gift Shop, Cafe, Library, IMAX Theater, Restoration Facility, Dir: Bob Rasmussen,
SW = South Wing, WW = West Wing, AD = Antrium Display, OD = Outside Display, IS = Inside
Storage, OS = Outside, www.navalaviationmuseum.org,

A-1 (TRIAD)	SW	F2H-2P	WW	NT-1	SW
A-4A(A4D-1)	IS	F2H-4	SW	HU-1B	OD
A-4E (2ea)	IS	F3D-2(F-10B)	OD	OE-1	
AD A-4F (3ea)		F3F-2	SW	OS2U-3	WW
A-6E	SW	F4D-1(F-6A)	SW	OY-1	SW
A-7E	SW	F4F-3 (3ea)	SW	P-3A	OD
A3D-1(A3A-1)	OD	F4U-4(2ea)	WW	P-40C	WW
A6M-2B	WW	F6C-1	SW	P-80A	WW
AD-5Q(EA-1F)	OD	F6F-3	WW	P2V-1(XP)	OD
AD-6(A-1H)	WW	F6F-5	SW	P2V-7	OD
AF-2S	WW	F7C-1	SW	P5M	OD
AH-1J	SW	F7F-3	WW	PB2Y-5R	OD
AJ-2	OD	F7U-3M	SW	PB4Y-2	OD
AM-1	WW	F8F-2	WW	PBY-5	WW
AQM-37A		F8U-1(F-8A)	SW	PS-2	
Arado AR 196A		F8U-1P(RF-8G)	OS	R4D-5	OD
AV-8C	SW	F9C-2	WW	RA-5C	OD
B-25		F9F-2	WW	RR-5	SW
BFC-2	OS	F9F-5P	IS	S-4C	SW
Bleroit XI		F9F-6	SW	S2F-3	OD
C-1A	OD	FF-1	SW	SB2U	IS
C-46(R5C)	OD	FG-1D(F4U)	WW	SBD-2	WW
C-47H(R4D-5)	OD	FH-1	WW	SBD-3	WW
C-117D(R4D-6)	OD	FJ-1	WW	SBD-4	WW
C-118B(R6D-1)	OD	FJ-2	SW	SH-3G	OD
C-121K(EC)(WV-2)	OD	FJ-3M	IS	SNB-5P	OD
C-130	OD	FJ-4(F-1E)	SW	SNC-1	WW
C-131F(R4Y-2)		FM-2(F4F)2ea	WW	SNJ-5C	AD
Cessna 180F		Fokker D-VII	SW	SNV-1	WW
H-19(HRS-2)		GB-2	SW	Sopwith Camel	SW
CH-19E(HRS-3)	OS	GK-1	IS	T-2C	
CH-37C(HR2S-1)	OD	H-1K(HH)	SW	T-28B	SW
CH-53A	OD	H-2D(HH)	IS	T-34B	AD
Command Module	SW	H-3F(HH) OD		TBM-3E	WW
D-558-1	IS	H-3 (VH)		TD2C-1	WW
E-1B(WF-2)	OD	H-13M(TH)	SW	TDD-1	WW
E-2B	OD	H-52A(HH)	SW	TDD-2	WW
F-4N(F4H)	SW	H-57C(TH)	SW	TDR-1	WW
F-11A(F11F-1)	SW	HD-1	SW	TS-1	SW
F-14A (2ea)	OD	HNS-1	WW	YRON-1	SW
F/A-18(YF-18)		HO-49	SW	ZPG Rudder	WW

Pensacola - Memorial Park, Bay Front Av e at 9th Ave, Next to Gulf Power
Building, Mail: Vietnam Veterans Wall South Foundation POB 17886
32522-7886, (904) 433-8200, UH-1M, The Wall South - 58,204 American Names

FLORIDA

Panama City - Vets Memorial Park, Civic Center Marina, 1 Harrison Ave, 32401, (850) 872-7272
F-101B,   F-15C

Gulf Coast Community College, Hwy 98 E, 12 Miles E of Gulf Coast Community College
F-101B (½ Mile East of Hathaway Bridge),   F-15C

Tyndall AFB, 325 TTW/MAM, 32403, (850) 283-1113, At Flag Park,
F-4C/D   F-15   F-86D   F-106

Polk City - Fantasy of Flight, 1400 Broadway Blvd SE, I-4, Exit 21 N to SR 559 E,
33868-1200, 863-984-3500, Fax 984-9506, Daily 9-5, Adm To All Exhibits,
Adm Adult 13-59 $24.95, 60+ $21.95, Child 5-12 $13.95, Under 5 Free,
Year Pass $59.95, Limited Time Simulator $3.25, Compass Rose Restaurant 8-4,
Gift Shop, Owner: Kermit Weeks, Marketing Dir: Debra Johnson Ext 221,
www.fantasyofflight.com,

A-1	E-1 Standard	Norde Stampe
A-20	F4U-4	NYP
A.V. Roe 504J	F6F	P-35A
A6M5	F7F	P-38
AN-2	Fi-156	P-39
AT-6D	FM-2	P-40N
B-17G (2ea)	Ford 5-AT-34-B	P-47
B-23	FW-44J	P-51C
B-24J	Gee Bee Model Z	SBD
B-25	Hawker Hurricane	Short Sunderland Mk.V
B-26	HOE-1	Spitfire Mk.XVI
Ba 349	J-1 Standard	SV-4C
Beech D-17S	J2F	TBM
Bell 47G	JN-4D	Thomas-Morse T4M
Bristol Bolingbroke	JU-52	Travel Air B-4000
BT-15	Ki-61	Trautman Road Air #1
Bu 133	L-1 (2ea)	Valkyrie Replica
Bu 181	L-4	Week Solution
Curtiss Jr CW-1	Lockheed Vega 5A/5C	Wright Flyer Replica
Curtiss Pusher D	Morane Saulnier 230	
DH 98	Neuport 17	

Pompano Air Center, 305-943-6050, Dir: Brian Becker, PT-13 Model 75

Sanford - Vertical Aviation Technology, Inc, Sanford Orlando Airport, 1642 Hanger Rd, (407) 322-9488,
Fax 330-2647, Owner: Brad Clark, Restores Sikorsky S-55 Helicopters

Shalimar - Air Force Armament Museum, 100 Museum Dr, Eglin AFB, 32542-5000,
(850) 651-1808, Daily 9:00-4:30, Closed Holidays, Theater, Gift Shop, (ID = Inside Display)
www.destin-ation.com/airforcearmamentmuseum/

A-10A	C-131B	F-86J	MIG-21
Apollo Module	C-47A(AC)	F-100C	O-2A
B-17G	C-130(AC)	F-101C	P-47N (ID)
B-47N(RB)	F-4C(RF)	F-104D(TF	P-51D-11 (ID)
B-25J	F-15A	F-105D (ID)	SR-71A
B-52G	F-16	F-111E	T-33A
B-57B	F-80-1D (ID)	GAM-77/AGM-28	TM-76
BQM-34F	F-84F	IM-99 Bomarc	UH-1H
BQM-34A	F-89D	MGM-13A	V-1

St. Petersburg - St Petersburg Historical & Flight One Museum, 335 Second Ave NE, 33712
(727) 894-1052, Mon, Tue-Sat 10-5, Except Holidays, Adm Adult $6, Snr 60 $5
Child 7-17 $4, Under 7 Free, Gift Shop, Theater, www.spmoh.org,
Benoist Airboat 1914 Replica, Ford Flivver Replica

FLORIDA

Starke - Camp Blanding Museums and Memorial Park, 5629 SR 16 W, 32091, (904) 682-3196
Daily 12-4, Adm Adult $, Gift Shop, www.30thinfantry.org

A-6A	C-47	M4 Tank
A-7	OH-13	M60 Tank
Bell 206	UH-1 (2ea)	

Tampa - McDill AFB, 56 CSG/CC, 33608-5000, (813) 830-1110, B-50J(KB)   F-4E   F-15

Veterans Memorial Museum & Park, 3601 Highway 301 N, 33619, Hillsborough County, (814) 744-5502, Park Daily 10-5:30, Museum Sat-Sun 10-3, Free Adm, www.dhr.do.state.us/wwii/sites.cfm?PR_ID=115

AH-1	OH-6	OH-58	UH-1H

Tarpon Springs - Starfighters, Inc, 1608 North Jasmine Ave, 34689, (727) 452-8817, www.starfighters.net   CF-104   CF-104D Both Flown at Airshows

Titusville -Astronaut Hall of Fame, 6225 Vectorspace Blvd, 32780, (321) 449-4444, www.spacewalkoffame.org, Mercury Space Capsule   Space Shuttle Simulator

U.S. Space Camp, 6225 Vectorspace Blvd, 32780, (800)637-7223, (321) 267-3184, Space Camp for Grades 4-12 & Adult, One Week of: Space Training & Missions, From $300-875

Valiant Air Command Warbird Museum, Space Center Executive Airport, 6600 Tico Rd 32780-8009, (321) 268-1941, Fax 268-5969, Daily 9-5 Closed TD, CD, ND, Adm Adult $12.00 Mil/Snr $10, Child 12-4 $5, Under 4 Free, Gift Shop, Restoration Facility, www.vacwarbirds.org
F = Flyable, O = Outside, R = Restoration, P = Partial Aircraft, X = Periodic Display

A-6E	F-14A	L-4J	S2F
A-7A	F-84F Project	Link Trainer	SM8Z (X)
AN-2 (X)	F-86F (P)	Me-208 (R)	T-28D (F)(X)
AT-6(SNJ)(X)	F-101B-115-MC(D)	MiG-17 (O)	T-33A
C-45 (X)	F-105D (O)	OV-1D (O)	TBM-3E (R)
C-47A (R)	F-106 Simulator	OV-1 Simulator	UH-1A (O)
F-4J (O)	F4U-1 1/2 Scale(X)	P-51 3/4 Scale	UTVA-66 (F)
F-8K	FM-1	PT-17 (X)	2B13 Mult Eng Sim
F9F-5 (R)	HA 200A (X)	Rutan Variviggen	

Wauchula - Wauchula Municipal Airport, 33873, (863) 773-9300, Mail: POB 891, 33873
Adm Adult $2, Child $1, Sat 10-3,

Aero Commander	Beechcraft 35	Grand Commander	Missiles
AG-CAT	C-45	HH-3F	PA-23
Beech D18S	F-86L	Lake Buccaneer	UH-1H

West Melbourne - Air America Foundation, 1589 S Wickham Rd, 32904, (321) 725-4043, Fax 725-4047, www.airamfoundation.org, C-123 (2ea)

Whiting - Naval Air Station, (904) 623-7011, HU-57   SNJ-5C   SNJ-6   T-34C

GEORGIA

Atlanta - Delta Air Transport Heritage Museum, 1060 Delta Blvd, Bldg B, Dept 914, Hartsfield Atlanta Int'l Airport, 30354, Mail: POB 20585, 30320-2585, (404) 773-1219, Mon-Fri 9-4, Cafe, Gift Shop, Library,Restoration Facility, www.deltamuseum.org

Boeing 767	L-1011 Cockpit & Fuse	Travel Air S-6000B
DC-3	Stinson Reliant SE	

Fernbank Science Center, 156 Heaton Park Dr NE, 30307, (678) 874-7102, Mon-Fri 8:30-5, Sat 10-5, Sun 1-5, Free Adm, www.fernbank.edu   Apollo Space Capsule

Augusta - ATZH-DPM, Bldg 36305, 37th St, 2 Mi Inside Gate 5, Ft Gordon, 30905-5020, (706) 791-2818, 780-2818, Mon-Fri 8-4, Sat-Sun 12-5, CLosed ES, TD, CD, ND, Independencs Day, Free Adm,   USD-4   USD-5

GEORGIA

Calhoun - World Aircraft Museum, Mercer Air Field, Hangar 411, Mail POB 638, 30703-0368
Daily 8-5, Free Adm,

F-84F	F-86C	H-34 2ea	T-29(VT)	T-33A

Cordele - Georgia Veterans Memorial State Park & Gen Courtney Hodges Museum, Rte 3,
9 Mi W of City on US 280, Mail: Box 382, 31015, (229) 276-2371,
Museum Daily 8-4:30, Park Daily 7am-10pm, Free Adm,

B-29	LTV	T-33A	Patton Tank
FJ4B	F-84F	German Tank	Stewart Tank

Ft. Benning - Army Ft Benning National Infantry Museum, Bldg 396, Baltzell Ave, 31905,
(706) 687-3297,   CG-4A (Storage)   C-119

Griffin - Alexander Aeroplane Co, Spalding County Airport, 118 Huff Daland Cir,
30223, (770) 228-3901, (800)831-2949, DC-3 (2 Hour Flights), T-33

Curtiss Hawk Factory,   P-36   P-40E   P-40K   P-40N

Hampton - Army Aviation Heritage Foundation, Clayton County Airport, Tara Field,
506 Speedway Blvd, 30228, (770) 897-0444, Fax 897-0066, Appt Only, Pres: Mike Brady
www.armyav.org, email: skippowell@aol.com,

DH CV-2B	H-1P(TAH)	L-4B	T-42A (2 ea)
H-1F(AH) (11 ea)	H-13T(TH) Project	OH-6A	U-8F Project
H-1G(AH)	H-23	OH-23B	U-21G
H-1H(UH) (5 ea)	L-17	OV-1B	
H-1M(UH)	L-19A Project	OV-1D	
H-1S(UH) (2 ea)	L-19D Project	T-41B	

Kennesaw - Atlanta FAA ARTC, McCollum Airport, 30144, (770) 422-2500,   F-100C

Macon - Macon ANG, Cocran Field, (912) 788-3423, F-86L

Marietta - Cobb County Youth Museum, 649 Cheatham Hill Dr, 30064, Mail POB 78, 30061,
(770) 427-2563, Mon-Fri 8:30-1:30, Adm $7, Curator: Anita S Barton,   F-84F

Dobbins AFB ANG, 14th AF, 94th TAW, 30069-5000, PA: (770) 421-5055,

B-29	F-84F	F-105G
F-4C	F-100D	OV-1

Lockheed Plant, Dobbins AFB, Building L 22, F-22 ½ Scale Model

NAS Atlanta, Dobbins AFB, 1000 Halsey Avenue, Marietta, GA 30060-5099
(770) 919-6392, http://www.nasatlanta.navy.mil/

A-6	AT-11	F-14	T-33
A-7E	E-2C	F-18	

Peachtree City - CAF - Dixie Wing, 1200 Echo Ct, 30269, 30144, (678) 364-1110, Daily 9-4,
www.dixiewing.org,

AT-6	L-16 Project	P-63 Project	SNJ (2ea)
C-45	LT-6	PT-22	Soko 522
Fw-149	OV-1	SBD	
Havard	P-51		

Pooler - Mighty Eighth Air Force Heritage Museum, 175 Bourne Ave, I-95 & US 80
Exit 18, 31322, Mail: POB 1992, Savannah 31402-1992, (800) 421-9428, (912) 748-8888,
Fax 748-0209; Daily 9-5, Adm Adult $10, Snrs $9, Child 6-12 $6, Under 6 Free, Gift Shop;
Canteen, Library, Mission Experience Theater, WWII Flight Simulation,
www.mightyeighth.org; O=Outdoors / Rest Inside

B-24 Nose Section	F-4C (O)	MiG-21 Cockpit	PT-17
B-47 (O)	Me-163	P-51 Replica	
Bf-109 Replica	MiG-17A (O)		

GEORGIA

Savannah - Savannah ANG, 165 TAG/MA, Savannah Int'l Airport, 31402, (912) 964-1941,
165th TAG   F-84D   F-86L

Savannah State College, 31404, (912) 356-2186, PR Office, 356-2191, A-4L

Sparta - Georgia State Military Academy, National Guard Academy Off Hwy 16 South
H-54D(CH)   OV-1D

Warner Robins - Warner Robins AFB, Museum of Aviation 78ABW/MU, 1942 Heritage Blvd,
31098-2442 Hwy 41/129 South, (478) 926-6870, 926-4242, Mail: POB 2469, 310, Gift Shop, I-75,
Exit 126 East to Hwy 247, South 2 Mi, Daily 9-5, Closed TD, CD, ND, Free Adm, H=Hangar 01,
C=Century of Flight Building, E=Eagle Building, P=Project, S=Storage, www.museumofaviation.org

A-37A [C]	C-47J	F-105D	RB-57F
AC-47	C-54G	F-105G	RB-69A
AC-130 [E]	C-60A	F-106A	RF-101C
Aeronca Champ 7AC	C-119B	F-111E [C]	SR-71A [C]
AGM-136A [S]	C-124C	HH-3E [C]	T-28A [H]
AIM 4D-G [S]	C-103A	HH-19D [H]	T-33A
AIM 9J [S]	C-141B	HH-34J	T-37B
AIM-26A [S]	CH-3E	HH-43A [H]	T-39A [C]
AIR-2A [S]	CH-21B [H]	HH-43F [C]	TG-4A [E]
AQM-34V [C]	Chanute Glider [E]	HU-16B [C]	TH-13M [P]
AT-6G [S]	D-21 Drone	KC-97L	TM-61A
AT-11	EC-121K [E]	L-19A/O-2A [H]	U-2D [C]
B-1B	Epp's Monoplane	MGM-13A	U-3B [C]
B-25J [C]	F-4C	MGM-107B	U-4B [C]
B-26C	F-15A [E]	MiG-17	U-6A [C]
B-29B-55 [C]	F-80C [H]	O-1E [H]	U-10D [C]
B-52D	F-84E [E]	O-2A [H]	UC-78 [P]
B-66D(WB)	F-84F(RF)	OH-23C	UC-123K
Bae Mk.53	F-84F [H]	OH-50C	UH-IF [H]
Bensen X-25A	F-86H	P-40N	UH-1P
BQM-34F	F-89J	P-51D	UH-13P
BT-13A [H]	F-100C	PT-17D [E]	VC-140B [C]
C-7A [C]	F-101F	PT-19A [H]	X-25
C-45G	F-102A	PT-22 [C]	YCGM-121B
C-46D	F-104A	RB-57A	YMC-130H

Williamson - Canler Field Museum, (Opens Fall 2007), Peachstate Aerodrom,
401 Jonathan's Roost Rd, 30292, (770) 467-9490, Gift Shop, Cafe, Library, Restoration Facility
Contact Ron Alexander ronalexander@mindspring.com wwwww.peachstateaero.org

C-3B	DC-3A	PT-17
Curtiss Robin	JN-4	Waco CSO

Woodstock - Air Acres Museum, 376 Air Acres Way, 30188, (770) 517-6090,
Tue-Sat 8-4, Contact Liz Porter (678) 491-5843

Cessna 172	J-5	L-17	Navion

Warbirds of America Sq 17, 455 Air Acres Way, 30188
(770) 928-9042, All are Projects in Process, except (X = Pending)

Ag Cat (X)	Cessna 182	Loehle 5151 Mustang	PT-17 (X)
Bob Cat Kit	Cessna 180	Pietenpol Aerial	Stinson 108-3
C-45J(RC) (X)	L-2M (2ea) (X)	PT-17	

HAWAII

Honolulu - Hickam AFB, 15 ABW PA, (808) 449-2490, Tours only Wed 10-11,
F-4C, F-15A, F-86E, MiG-15 O'at Malley Blvd, F-102A (2ea) at Bas Op, Vickers & O'Malley
F-4C (2ea) at Hickman AFB Firefighting Unit , RB-26C at Scott Circle

Hawaiian ANG, F-4C,   F-86E,   F-86L,   F-106

Pacific Aviation Museum - Pearl Habor, 319 Lexington Blvd, Forld Island, 96818, (808) 441-1000,
Fax: 441-1019, Daily 9-5, Closed TD, CD, ND, Adm Adult $14, Child $7, Gift Shop, Café,
Flight Simulator, Theater, (note1 Wreckage from Pearl Harbor Attack), (note2 Flown during attack)
www.pacificaviationmuseum.org

A6M2-21 (note1)	F-14D	H-1S(AH) (Storage)	N2S-3
Aeronca 65TC (note2)	F-15A	H-1H(UH) (Storage)	SBD Rep
B-25J	F4B-4J Rep at Airport	H-3H(UH) (Storage)	SNJ-5B (Storage)
B-52 (Nose)(Storage)	F4F-3	P-40E Rep	

Kalaeloa
Naval Air Museum Barbers Point, Bldg 1792 Midway Rd, Kalaeloa Airport, 96707, (808) 682-3982,
Mon-Fri 8:30-4:30, Adm Adult $5, Child Under 12 $2, www.nambarberspoint.org,

A-4E (3ea)	F6F Rep	P-3A(UP)	TBM-3E
C-47A	H-1H(UH)	SB2C Rep	
F-4N	H-3H(UH) (2ea)	SNJ-5B	
CH-53D	H-53D(CD)	TBF Rep	

Kaneohe - Kaneohe Bay MCAS Marine Base (North Shore) 96744,
CH-53D, F-4S, F-8J, P-3, P2V-5, S2

Waikiki - Fort DeRussy Army Museum, AH-1S

Wheeler AFB, 96854-5000, (808) 422-0531, Main Gate, P-40 Mock-Up
AH-1S,   OH-23G,   OH-58A,   UH-1H

IDAHO

Boise - Boise ANG, Gowen Field, 83707, (208) 385-5011, 124th TRG,   F-102A

Cadwell - Aeroplnes Over Idaho, 5017A Aviation Way, 83605, (208) 455-1708
www.aeroplanesoveridaho.org

A-4	Champ	L-5
AN-2	Formula 1	PA-23-160
Cessna 180	L-3	Yak-3U

Driggs - Teton Aviation Center. 675 Airport Rd, Off Hwy 33, Mail: POB 869, 83422
(800) 472-6382, (208) 354-3100, Fax 354-3200, Daily 8-5, Closed TD, CD, Free Adm
Curator: Rich Sugden, www.tetonaviation.com,All Aircraft Flyable, Rides Availabe

A-1 (Rides Availabe)	L-39	T-28
Aviat (Rides Availabe)	MiG-15	T2-B
Blanik Glider (Rides Availabe)	N3N	
HU-16	SNJ-5	

Idaho Falls - Pacific Fighters, Restoration Facility, POB 50218, 83405-0218, (208) 522-3502, Appt Only,

A2D-1(XA)	P-47	P-51C	TBM (2ea)
F-86D	P-51B	P-51D (2ea)	

Mountain Home - Mountain Home AFB, 83648, (208) 828-2111, F-84F, F-100C, F-111A(RF)

Nampa - Warhawk Air Museum, 201 Municipal Way, Nampa Municipal Airport, 83687,
(208) 465-6446, Fax 465-6232, April 1-Oct 15 Tue-Sat 10-5, Sun 10-4, Oct 15-March 31
Tue-Fri 10-4, Sat 10-5, Closed TD, CE, CD, NE, ND, Adm Adult $6, Snrs 65 $5, Child 4-10 $3
Under 4 Free, Gift Shop, Library, Restoration Facility, All Flyable, www.warhawkairmuseum.org,

DR-1	P-40N	P-51D
P-40E	P-51C (Project)	YAK-3

IDAHO

Rexburg - Legacy Flight Museum, 425 Kelly Johnson Way, Rexbug-Madison Airport,
Mail: POB 405, 83440, (208) 359-5905, Fax 356-7989, MD-LD Mon-Sat 9-6, RoY Sat 10-5,
Adm Adult $6, Snrs $5, Student $5, Child 6-12 $3, Under 6 Free, www.legacyflightmuseum.com,

A-1E	N2S-3	P-63A-6
D17S	P-51D	SNJ-3
L-39	P-51D(PF)	TBM-3E

Twin Falls - N W Warbirds Inc, POB 1945, 83303-1945, (208) 734-1941,
Twin Falls Airport, Mon-Fri 8-5, Manager: Rob Werner, N3N TBM

ILLINOIS

Aurora - Weary Warriors Squadron, B-25H

Belleville - Scott AFB, 62225-5000, (618) 256-1110, C-45J, T-39A , C-140(VC)

Bloomington - McLean County Historical Society, 200 N Main, 61701,
309-827-0428,   Tilbury Flash Racer

Prairie Aviation Museum, Bloomington-Normal Airport, 2929 E Empire St, 61704,
Mail POB 856, 61702, (309) 663-7632, Fax 663-8411, Tue-Sat 11-4, Sun 12-4, Adm Adult $4,
Child 6-11 $2, Under 6 Free, Charles Lindbergh's De Havilland Remains of
Mail Run Crash in the Area, DC-3 Rides $80, www.prairieaviationmuseum.org

A-4M	AH-1J	DC-3	T-33 (Project)
A-7A	Cessna 310B	F-14D	T-38

Cahokia - Saint Louis University Parks College, 62206, (618) 337-7500,
Mon-Fri 8-4:30, Dir of Public Relations: For Any Information

AT-6	H-1(AH)	T-33
Cessna 320	QU 22	T-39
Cessna 310	Short Skyvan	T-39A

Greater St Louis Air & Space Museum, St Louis Downtown-Parks Airport, 2300 Vector Dr
62206, (618) 332-3664, Wed-Sat 10-4, www.airandspacemuseum.org

Austria Sailplane	Meyers OTW	YAV-18 Full Scale Mock Up

Cary - Phoenix Restoration Group, Inc, 209 Cleveland, Unit E, 60013-2978
Mon-Fri 8-5, Sat Appt, Restoring Weeks Air Museum Aircraft

Chicago - CAF Great Lakes Wing, Gary Regional Airport, (847) 364-7232, www.greatlakeswing.org

C-47	Ju 52

Museum of Science & Industry, 57th St & S Lake Shore Dr, 60637-2093, (773) 684-1414
Summer Mon-Sat 9:30-5:30, Sun 11-5, Winter Mon-Sat 9:30-4, Sun 11-4, Closed CD,
Adm Adult $11, Snrs 65 $9.50, Child 3-11 $7, Free on Thursdays, Gift Shop, Parking $12
U-505 Adm $5, Museum & Omni Max Adm Ault $17, Snrs $14.50, Child $12, www.msichicago.org

Boeing 727	Spitfire Mk.1A	Apollo 8
Boeing B 40B-2 Mail	Texaco Mystery Ship	Mercury Aurora 7
JN-4D	Wright Flyer Rep	New York Central 999 Train
Ju 87B-2/Trop	Wright Redux Spirit of Glen Ellyn	Pioneer Zephyr Train
Piccard Stratospheric		U-505 Sub

Danville - Midwest Aviation Museum, Vermillion Co Airport, 22563 N Bowman Ave, Ste 1, 61834,
(217) 431-2924, (217) 1998, Fax 431-8989, Contact Butch Schroeder,

AT-6G	P-47D	P-51F-6	T-33
BT-13			

Elliott - Commanche Flyer Foundation, Inc, Gibson City Municipal Airport, RR1,
574 N 1000 E Rd, Box 31, 60936, (217) 749-2371, 749-8295
Piper Commanche 1959 World Flying Record, Owner: Schertz Richard 749-2293

ILLINOIS

Glenview - NAS Glenview Museum, 2040 Lehigh Ave, 60025, Mail POB 198, 60025-0198
www.hangarone.org, (847) 657-0000, Sat 10-6, Sun 11-5, Artifacts, TBM Engine Only

Von Maur - 1960 Tower Dr, 60023, (847) 724-4199, PT-17

Great Lakes - Great Lakes Naval Training Center, Main Entrance at Buckley & Sheridan Rd, A-4

Joliet - Replica Fighters Assoc, 2409 Cosmic Dr, 60435, 5/8 & 3/4 Scale
Aircraft Thru The US consisting of the Following Squadrons: 999th Sq, www.replicafighters.org

DH 98	F8F	Ju 87 Stuka	P-47
F-86	Fw 190	Me-109	P-51
F4U	Hawker FB.11	P-38	Spitfire
F6F	Hawker Tempest	P-40	

Lincoln - Heritage in Flight Museum, Logan County Airport, 1351 Airport Rd,
62656, (217) 732-3333, Sat-Sun 8-5, Free Adm, Donations Accepted,
Housed in WWII German P.O.W. Barracks, www.heritageinflight.org

A-7E	F-4B	H-13T(TH)	L-17
C-45	H-1H(UH)	L-16	T-33A

Marengo - B-17E Restoration Project, Contact Mike & Ken Kellner, 21010 Anthony Rd, 60152
(815) 568-9464, B-17E (XC-108) S/N 41-2595

Mascoutah Community Unit Museum, 1313 W Main St, 62258-1065
(815) 566-8523, Curator: John D Roy III, 8-3:30, Free Adm, Military, Artifacts

Paris - Heartland Antique Auto Museum, 1208 N Main, 61944, (217) 463-1834
Lincoln Page LP3A (Project), PT-22 (Project), Engines, Artillery, Antique Autos

Peoria - Peoria ANG, Greater Peoria Airport, 61607, (309) 697-6400, F-84F

Wheels of Time Museum, 11923 N Knoxville Ave, 61601, (309) 243-9020, May-Oct Wed-Sun 12-5,
www.wheelsoftime.org, Adm Adult $5, Child 3-11 $2.50, Under 3 Free, Fokker DR.III Replica

Poplar Grove - Vintage Wings & Wheels Museum, 11619 Route 76, Mail: POB 236
61065, (815) 547-3115, Sat 10-4, Free Adm, www.wingsandwheelsmuseum.org, Circa

Quincy - World Aerospace Museum, Quincy Regional Airport (UIN), N39-56.56, W091-11.67
62305, (217) 885-3800, Mon-Fri 9-4 by Appt Only, Free Adm, Contact Ellen, www.jet-warbirds.com

L-39C	L-39ZA	MiG-29
L-39MS	MiG-21	

Rantoul - Chanute Air Museum, 1011 Pacesetter Dr, 61866-0949, (217) 893-1613, Fax: 892-5774,
Mon-Sat 10-5, Sun 12-5, Closed: ND,ED,TD,CD, Adm Adult $7, Mil/Snrs 62 $6, 4-12 $4,
Under 4 Free, Gift Shop, Ntn'l Balloon Races, First Week-end in Aug, www.aeromuseum.org

A-4A	C-97G	F-100D	LGM-30A Minuteman I
A-7D	C-121K(EC)	F-101B	Mong Sport
Aeronca 65LB	C-130A	F-104A	O-2A
AGM-28	C-133A	F-105B	P-51H
American Eagle	Cessna 120	F-105F	PA-22
AT-6B-NT	Chanute Glider Rep	F-111A	Ryan NYP Rep
B-25J-25-NA	F-4C(RF)	Fokker DRI	T-33A
B-47E(B)	F-15A	Foose Tigercat	T-38A(F-5B)
B-52D Cockpit	F-84A	H-1B(UH)	CT-39A
B-58A	F-84F	HU-16B	Wright Flyer Rep
B-66B	F-86A	ICBM Silo(3Sections)	
C-47D(VC)	F-100C-5-NA	JN-4D Rep	

Rockford - Courtesy Aircraft Sales, 5233 Falcon Rd, 61109-2991, (815) 229-5112, Warbird Aircraft Sales,
www.courtesyaircraft.com

AT-6	P-51	T-28	Stearman 75

ILLINOIS

Russell - Russell Military Museum, 43363 Old Hwy 41, 60075, (847) 395-7020, Fax 395-7025
May-Sept Wed-Sun 9-5, Oct-April, Sat-Sun 12-5, Adm Adult $7.50, www.russellmilitarymuseum.com

A-7C(TA)	M-60 Tank	M-38A1
F-4 Cockpit	OV-1D (5ea)	M-41 Walker Bulldog Tank
H-1(UH) 3ea	T-33A-5-LO	M-42 Duster (2ea) Tank
H-6(OH)	M-2 Half Track	M-47 Patton (2ea) Tank
H-54(CH) (2ea)	M-3 Stuart Tank	M-151
H-58(OH)	M-4 Sherman Tank	PBR Vietnam River Boat
HH-3 (3ea)	M-5A Stuart Tank	U-9
Hiller Helicopter	M-7 Stuart Tank	
Hughes Helicopter	M-38	

Springfield - Air Combat Museum, 835 S Air port Dr, 62707, (217) 698-3990, Mon-Fri 9-4,
Closed LD, TD, CD, ND, Donations, Curator: Mike George

AeroCommander	FC-24 (Project)	MiG-15 Cockpit	Soko Galeb G-21
AT-11	Fleet Model 9	P-51D	T-34
Extra 300L	L-2B	PT-22	
F4U-5	L-2M (2ea)	R-44	

Springfield ANG, Capitol Airport, 62707, (217) 753-8850, 183rd TFG, F-4,   F-84

Army Reserve Center, 62708, (217) 785-3600, F-86F, Tank, M9 3" Gun,

Sugar Grove - Air Classics Museum of Aviation, Chicago/Aurora Airport,
Mail 43W636 US Rte 30, 60554, (630) 466-0888,Sat-Sun10-3, Mon-Fir by Appt,
Adm Adult $5, Snr $4, Child $3, Under 6 Free, Gift Shop, www.airclassicsmuseum.org

A-4J(TA)	F-86F(RF)	T-39A
A-7E	F-105	
F-4	H-1H(UH) 2ea	

Volo - Volo Auto Museum, 27582 Volo Village Rd, 60073, Off I-94, (815) 385-3644, Daily 10-5,
Adm Adult $9, Snrs $7, Child 5-12 $5, under 5 Free, Cafe, Gift Shop, 300 Classic Cars,
Pres Greg Grahms, www.volocars.com   H-1(UH) (2ea)

Waukegan - Warbird Heritage Foundation, 3000 Corporate Dr, 60087, (847) 244-8701, Fax 244-8703
By Appt Only, www.warbirdheritagefoundation.org

F-86F	L-39C	AT-6G	N2S-3
T-2B	T-28B	L-19A	

INDIANA

Anderson - Historical Military Armor Museum, 2330 Crystal St, (765) 649-8265, Tue, Thur, Sat 1-4
Adm Adult $3, Child under 6 Free, Banquet Facility, Dir Joseph McClain, AH-1, TH-55A, Tanks

Auburn - Auburn-Cord-Duesenburg Museum, 1600 S Wayne St, Mail POB 271, 46706-3509,
(260) 925-1444, Fax 925-6266, Daily 9-5, Closed TD, CD, ND, Adm Adult $8, Child $5
www.acdmuseum.org, Stinson 1911

Hoosier Warbirds, Inc, 2822 CR 62, SW Side of Airport, Mail: POB 87, 46706
(260) 927-0443, Mar 15-Dec 15, Mon-Sat 10-4, Sun 1-4, Adm $5, Child 6-18 $4, Under 6 Free
Gift Shop, Library, Banquet Facility, Pres Niles Walton, www.hoosierairmuseum.org

AT-11 On Loan	LNE-1	P-51 (7/10 Scale)	V-77 (Gullwing)
C-45	Mini Helicopter	Smith Mini Plane	WR-3 Lovings
H-1(AH)	Nieuport 11	Speedbird	
J-3	Nieuport 27	T-50 (UC-78)	

Bippus - Penn Aviation Company, 46713, (260) 344-1168, Dave Van Liere, AT-6D

Columbus - Atterbury-Bakalar Air Museum, 4742 Ray Boll Blvd, Columbus Mncpl
Airport, 47203, (812) 372-4356, Tue 10-12, Wed-Fri 10-2, Sat 10-4,
Donations Requested, Curator: Bob Henry, www.atterburybakalarairmuseum.org;
F-4, CG-4A Nose Project, TG-2A,

INDIANA

Crawfordsville - Ropkey Armor Museum, 5649 E 150N , 47933, (317) 295-9295,
Mail: 8608 Highwoods Ln, Indianapolis, IN 46278,Thur-Fri 10:30-4:30, Adm Donations
Pres Fred N Ropkey III, www.ropkeyarmormuseum.com

A-4B	PT-17	T-2	M26 Tank
AN-2	P2V-7	X-14	
O-1	T-11	M4A3 Tank	

Edinburg - Camp Atterbury Museum and Memorial Complex, Bldg 47 Egglestone,
Wed, Sat-Sun 1-4, Gift Shop, (812) 526-1744, www.campatterbury.org/museum.htm,
H-1M(UH), Tanks: M4A1 (2ea), M41, M42, M47, M50, M60

Elkhart - Northern Indiana Aviation Museum, 12264 County Rd 148, Ligonier, In 46767
Pres Steve Hay, (574) 642-4961, email: wawaseeaircraft@skyenet.com,

A-4J(TA)	NA-50	T-33A Project

Fort Wayne - Mercury, 4021 Air St, 46809, (260) 747-1565, Appt Only,
Owner of Aircraft: Dean Cutshall, F-5A, F-100F-16, GNAT

Lt Paul Baer Terminal Bldg, 2nd Floor, Ft Wayne Int'l Airport, 3421 Air St, Mail:
POB 9573, 46899, (260) 478-7146, Daily 7-7, Free Adm, Smith Aeroplane, Artifacts
www.fwairport.com/museum.html

Indiana ANG, 122nd TFW, Baer Field, Ft Wayne Municipal Airport,

46809-5000, (260) 478-3210, F-4	F-86	F-100

Kloffenstein Furniture, 6314 Lima Rd (Hwy 3), (260) 627-2115, 3/4 Scale P-51

Hagerstown - Wilbur Wright Birthplace Museum, 1525 CR 750E, 47346,
(765) 332-2495, April 1-Nov 1, Tue-Sat 10-5, Sun 1-5, Adm Adult $4, Snrs $3, Child $2
Family $10, www.wwbirthplace.com, F-84F, Wright Flyer Rep

Hobart - Richard A Boyd, 5253 S Liverpool Rd, 46342, (219) 942-8692,   T-33

Indianapolis - CAF Indiana Wing, Squadron Leader: Karl Franzman, 1045 North
Shore Dr, Martinsville, 46151, (317) 342-3257, www.indianawingcaf.org, PT-26

American Military Heritage Foundation, 1215 S Franklin, Post Air Hangar, Mail POB 29061
46229, (317) 335-2889, Mon-Sat 9-5, Gift Shop, www.amhf.org

BT-13A	PV-2	SNJ-5B

La Porte - LaPorte County Historical Society Museum, 2405 Indiana Ave, Suite 1, 46350
(219) 324-6767, Tue-Sat 10-4:30, Adm Adult $5, Child $3, Gift Shop, Theater,
 www.laportecountyhistory.org,

Chanute Glider 1896	Sonerai II
Clement-Bayard Demoiselle	Tri-Pacer Model 22-162
Pietenpol Air Camper	

Mentone - Lawrence D Bell Aircraft Museum, S Oak St, Mail: Box 411, 46539, US31 Exit N on
SR25, (574) 353-7296, June 1- Oct 1 Sun 1-5pm, Adult $1, Artifacts from Lawrence Bell
www.livingweblibrary.com/bell

H-13	UH-1H	UH-12

Muncie - Academy of Model Aeronautics / National Model Aviation Museum,
5151 E Memorial Dr, 47302, (765) 289-4236, Mon-Fri 8-5, Sat-Sun 10-4,
Closed Sun TD thru ED, Adm Adult $2, Child 7-17 $1, Gift Shop, Library, Theater
www.modelaircraft.org/museum   RC and Free Flight Model Airplanes

INDIANA

Peru - Grissom Air Museum, 1000 W Hoosier Blvd, 46970-3647, US 31,
(765) 689-8011, Fax 68-9288, Indoor Displays Adm Adult $4, Mil/Snrs 55/Child 7-18, $3
Under 7 Free, Tue-Sun 10-4, Extended Summer Hours, Closed TD, CD, ND, Holidays, Gift Shop,
Curator: Andrew Cougill, www.grissomairmuseum.com,

A-10A	C-119G	F-101B	T-37B
B-17G	C-135L(EC)	F-102A(TF)	T-41 (Storage)
B-25J	F-4C	F-105D	T-33A
B-47D	F-11F	H-1(UH)	U-3(A)
B-58A(TB)	F-14B	HUP-2 (Project)	YS-11
C-1	F-84F	J-3 (Project)	
C-47D	F-89 Project	O-2A	
C-97L(KC)	F-100C	T-2	

Richmond - Wayne County Historical Museum, 1150 N, A St, 47374, (765) 962-5756,
Mon-Fri 9-4, Sat-Sun 1-4, Adm Charged, Davis Aircraft 1929

Seymour - Freeman Army Air Field Museum, 1035 A Ave, Freeman Mncpl Airport, Mail: POB 702,
47274, (812) 522-2031, US 50 go S on S Airport Rd(1st Ave).
www.indianamilitary.org/FreemanAAF/; Parts from WWII Enemy Aircraft Stored There

South Bend - Jeep Acres - Contact: Charles R Dadlow 29430 SR2, 46624, (574) 654-8649, HRP-3

Terre Haute - Terre Haute ANG, Hulman Regional Airport, 47803, (812) 877-5210,

F-4C	F-84F	F-100D

Valparaiso - Indiana Aviation Museum, Porter County Municipal, 4601 Murvihill Rd,
46383, (219) 548-3123, May-Oct Sat 10-4, Sun 1-4, Adm Adult $5, Vet/Snr $4, Child Under 13 Free.
Curator: Jim Read, www.in-am.org, Rides Available = (Ride) $100 - $1,000

A-37	L-2	PT-17 (Ride)
AT-6G (Ride)	P-51D (Ride)	T-28B (Ride)
F4U-5N (Ride)	T-28B	T-34B (Ride)

Vincennes - Indiana Military Museum, 4305 Bruceville Rd, 47591, (812) 882-8668, 882-4002
Mail: POB 977, Adm Adult $3, Child 1-18 $1, April-Oct Daily 12-4, Nov-March Call (800) 886-6443,
Knox County & Visitors Bureau for Tour, www.vincennescvb.org/attractions.asp

C-47 Nose,	M3A1 Tank	M5A1 Tank	1/2 Track
H-1(UH)	M4A1E8 Tank	M-114	German PAK 40 Gun

IOWA

Altoona - Sam Wise Youth Camp, Veterans Memorial, 8th St, A-7D

Ankeny - Iowa Military Aviation Heritage Museum, Ankeny Regional Airport, I-35 & 80,
Mail: 3704 SE Convenience Blvd, 50021, (515) 964-2629 0r 8556, www.aviationiniowa.com

AT-6(SNJ-5)	F-84F	PT-19A
D-16A Twin Navion	N3N	

Davenport - CAF Hawkeye State Sq, T-28A

Council Bluffs - Great Plains Wing, 16803 McCandless Rd, 51503, (602) 322-2435
Mail: POB 68, Griswold, IA 51535, Wed 6-9, Sat 9-4, Sun 12-4, Adm Free, www.greatplainswing.org

L-3	L-5	P-51D

Des Moines - Iowa State Historical Society, 600 E Locust, 50319, (515) 281-5111,
Tue-Sat 9-4:30, Sun 12-4:30, Free Adm, Curator: William M Johnson,

Bleriot XI,	Curtiss Pusher	Quickie	Solbrig

Iowa National Guard, Beaver Dr, 50318, (515) 252-4236,

A-7	F-84	H-1(AH)	H-1(UH)	6 Tanks	7 Cannons

Ft. Dodge - Ft Dodge IA ANG, 133 TCF/CC, 50501, (515) 573-4311, 3611, F-84F

IOWA

Greenfield - Iowa Aviation Museum, 2251 Airport Rd, Greenfield Mncpl Airport,
Mail: POB 31, 50849-0031, (641) 343-7184, Mon-Fri 10-5, Oct 1-April 30 Sat 1-5, RoY Sat 10-5,
Sun 1-5, Closed E, TD, CE, CD, ND, Adm Adult $3, Sr $2.50, Child 5-12 $1.50, Under 4 Free,
Gift Shop, Library, www.flyingmuseum.com

A-7D	Easy Riser Glider	Pietenpol Rep
Aetna-Timm #4	J-2	Pitts S-1-S
AH-1	J-3	Schweitzer Secondary Glider
Curtiss Robin #6	Kari Keen	Stearman C3-R Mail Plane
DH 82C Australian	Mead Primary Glider	Taylorcraft BC-12
DH 82C Canadian	Northrup Primary Glider	

Grimes - Grimes ANG, Des Moines Municipal Airport, 50321, (515) 285-7182, F-84F

Hampton - Doyle W W I Aircraft Museum, Beeds Lake Airport, 903 2nd Ave SE, 50441-2733,
(515) 456-4512, Fokker DR-1 Rep,   Nieuport 28 Rep,   Sopwith Pup Rep

Indianola - US National Balloon Museum, 1601 N Jefferson St, Box 149, 50125-0149,
(515) 961-3714, Summer: Mon-Fri 9-4, Sat 10-4, Sun 1-4, Free Adm, Gift Shop, Library
www.nationalballoonmuseum.com   Helium and Hot Air Balloons

Johnston - Camp Dodge (HQ Iowa National Guard), NW Beaver Dr, Main Gate, A-7D, 2 Tanks

Marshalltown - Central IOWA All Veterans Memorial, American Legion
Post 46, 1301 S 6th St, Curator: Jeff Heiden, (641)752-0544, F-4C

Ottumwa - Airpower Museum, 22001 Bluegrass Rd, Antique Airfield, Route 2, Box 172,
52501-8569, (641)938-2773, Mon-Fri 9-5, Sat 10-5, Sun 1-5, www.aaa-apm.org

Aeronca K	BD-5	Kinner Sportster	Rearwind Skyranger 190F
Aeronca C-2	Bolkow Bo 208A-1 Jr	L-4	Rearwind Sportster
Aeronca C-3	Brewster B-1	LH-2	Ritz Ultrlight
Aeronca 65CA	CP-40 Porterfield	Luscombe 8F	Rose Parakeet A-1
Aeronca LA65	Culver LCA Cadet(LFA)	Monocoupe 90	Ryan STA
Aeronca 65TC	Culver Cadet PQ-14B	Monoprep	Stinson S Junior
Aeronca 7AC	DSA-1 Smith Miniplane	Mooney M-18 Mite	Stinson 10
Aeronca 11AC	Fairchild 22	Morrisey Bravo	Taylo-Young A
AmEagle Eaglet	Fairchild 71	Nesmith Cougar	VJ-23
Anderson Z	Fleet 7	Pietenpohl Sky Scout	VP-1 Evans Volksplane
Arrow F Sport	Funk Model B	PT-22 Ryan Recruit	Welch QW-8
Backstrom Plank	Great Lakes 2T-1A	Rearwind Cloudster	

Indian Hills Community College, 60 Aviation Program Center, 52501, (641)-683-5111, www.ihcc.cc.ia.us

C-45	Cessna 310	H-1H(UH)	T-39
Cessna 150	Cessna 421	PA-22	
Cessna 172	F-84	Piper Aztec	

Sioux City - Mid America Transportation & Aviation Museum, Sioux Gateway Airport,
6715 Harbor Dr, 51111, (712) 252-5300, Tue-Sun 9-5, Closed TD, CD, ND, Easter, Adm Adult $3,
Child 6-18 $1, Gift Shop, www.matamuseum.org

A-7D	Glider	T-18
A-6A	H-1B(UH)	T-33
CallAir Spray Plane	Hawker-Siddeley Argosy	Ultralight Snoopy's BobCat
F-84F	KR-2	

Sioux City ANG, Sioux City Mun Airport, 51110, (602) 255-3511,

A-7D	F-84F	F-84F Photo Recon
A-7K	F-100C	T-33

St Maries - David Freeman, Nicholas-Beazley Racer NR-1W

KANSAS

Ashland - Pioneer-Krier Museum, Clark County Historical Societ, 430 W 4th Hwy 160,
N of Route 160, 67831, (620) 635-2227, Mon-Fri 10-12 &1-5, Free Adm, Curatot Tony Lee Maphet
www.pioneer-krier.com, email pionees@ucom.net, Krier Kraft, DHC 1, Great Lakes Special

Augusta - Augusta Air Museum, 135 South Hwy 77, 67010, (316) 775-1425,
April-Sept Daily 1-5, Oct-March Sat-Sun 1-5, www.augustaairmuseum.com

Avid Flyer	H-1(UH)	Penguin	Volscraft
BD-5	H-58(OH)	Pizza Peddler HG	
Easy Riser	High Max	Quickie	

Coffeyville - Coffeyville Aviation Heritage Museum, 2002 N Buckeye St, 67337, (620) 515-0232
Sat 10-4, Sun 1-4, www.kansastravel.org/coffeyvilleaviationheritagemuseum.htm

Breezy	F-84	Funk Model B	Gyrocopter	Mitchell U-2

Hutchinson - Kansas Cosmosphere Museum, 1100 N Plum, 67501, (800) 397-0330,
(620) 662-2305, Mon-Thur 9-6, Fri-Sat 9-9, Sun 12-6, Adm Adult $8, Snrs 60+ or Child 5-12 $7.50,
Under 5 Free, Plus OMNIMAX & Planetarium Adm Adult $13, Snrs $12, Child $10.50, Gift Shop,
Cafe, Astronaut Training Programs Available, www.cosmo.org

Apollo 13	Gemini	Mercury 7	V-1 Rocket
F-1 Saturn V Engine	Lunar Rover	SR-71	V-2 Flying Bomb
F-104B	Lunar Lander	T-38	

Liberal - Mid-America Air Museum, 2000 W 2nd St, POB 2199, 67901-2199, (620) 624-5263,
Mon-Fri 8-5, Sat 10-5, Sun 1-5, Closed: TD, CD, ND, Adult $7, Snr $5, Child $3 (6-18)
5 Under Free, Gift Shop, Theater, Restoration Facility, Air Show In Mid Sept,
www.cityofliberal.com/airmuseum

A-4L	CW-1 Jr	KR-1	PT-19A
A-7E	D-16	L-2	PT-22
Aero Commander	Der Kricket	L-3B	PT-23
Aeronca 65C	Dragonfly	L-5	Quail 1969
Aeronca K	Ercoupe 415C	L-6	Rally 3
Aeronca 7AC/L-16	F-4D	L-9	Rearwin 8135
Aeronaut	F-8U-2N	L-17	Rearwin 7000
AT-19(V-77)	F-14A	LB-5	Rearwin Skyranger
Avid Flyer	F-80C	Luscombe 8A	RLU-1 Breezy
B-25J	F-86H	Luscombe T-8F	Rutan Vari-Eze
Baby Great Lakes	F-104C	Miller Fly Rod	Rutan Quickie
Beech 35	F-105	Moni Motor Glider	S2F-1
Beech 150	F4U-5	Mooney M.18C Mite	SA 102-5
Beech D17S	Fairchild 24-C8F	NW Porterfield	Scorpion 133
Bellanca 190	Fisher Koala 202	Nieuport II	Shober Willie II
BT-13A	Fly Baby 1A	O-2A	Skybolt
Bushby Mustang	Funk B-75	OH-6	T-18
C-45	Globe Swift GC-1B	OQ-19	T-37(XT)
Cessna 120	H-1S(AH)	OV-10	T-38
Cessna 140	H-1B(UH)	PA-22	T-50D
Cessna 145	H-13	PA-23	TBM-3
Cessna 165	Hawker Siddley Gnat	PA-24	Viking Dragonfly
Cessna 175	HUP-3	Phoenix Glider	X-28
Cessna 195	J-2	Pietenpol B4A	
Cessna 195A	J-3C	Pober Pixie P-9	
Culver V	J-4F	PT-17	

New Century - CAF Heart of America Wing, #3 Aero Plaza, 66031, (913) 397-6376, Mail:
15011 West 147th St, Olathe, KS 66062, www.kcghostsquadron.org

AT-6	L-2 2ea	PT-17
BT-13 3ea	L-39	PT-19 2ea
F4F-3	MiG-17	T-28

KANSAS

Topeka - Combat Air Museum, Forbes Field, Hangar 602 & 604, J St, Mail POB 19142, 66619-0142, (785) 862-3303, Fax 862-3304, Mon-Sat 9-4:30, Sun and Dec1-Feb 28 12-4:30, Closed: ES, TD, CD, ND, Adm Adult $6, Snrs 60 $5, Child 6-17 & Military $4
Under 6 Free, Curator: Danny J San Romani, E-mail CAMTopeka@aol.com
Hangar 602 = 2; Hangar 604 = 4; Outside Display = O, www.combatairmuseum.org/

A-4J(TA)	2	F-18		H-53A(NCH)		Nike Tartar	2
AT-6 Harvard Mk IV	2	F-84F(2ea)	4,0	H-54B(CH)	4	Nike Ajax	O
Bf-109 Rep Disa	4	F-86H	4	H-1H(UH)	2	O-47B	2
BT-13 Disa	4	F-105D		H-1M(UH)	4	RU-8D	4
C-47D (2ea)	4	F-101B	4	Honest John	O	S-2A(US)	4
C-121T(EC)	O	F11F-1	2	Little John	4	SNB-5	4
C-61K(UC)	4	F3D	2	JN-4D	2	T-33A	
Corporal M2 Missile	O	F4F-3		Meyers OTW	2	Tartar Navy Missile	
F-4D		F9F-5 Disa	4	MiG-15	2		
F-14A		H-23A(OH)		MiG-17	4		

Kansas Museum of History, 6425 SW 6th St, 66615-1099, (785) 272-8681, Tue-Sat 9-5, Sun 1-5, Adm Adult $5, Snrs $4, Child $3, Under 5 FreeDir: Robert J Keckeisen, www.kshs.org
Curtiss Pusher

Museum of Kansas National Guard, Forbes Field, 6700 S Topeka Blvd, 66619, (785) 862-1020, Tue-Sat 10-4, Theater, F-16 Model ½ Scale

H-1(AH)	H-1(UH)	H-6(OH)	H-54(CH)	H-58(OH)

Air Guard, 190th ARW, Forbes Field, 66619-5000, B-57, Helicopters, Tanks

American Flight Museum, Hangar 603, Forbes Field, Mail 2630 SE Bennett Dr, 66605, (785) 862-1234, www.squadron14.com, C-47(AC)

Wichita - Kansas Aviation Museum, 3350 George Washington Blvd, 67210, (316) 683-9242, Fax: 683-0573, Tue-Fri 9-5, Sat 1-5, Closed TD, CD, ND, TD, CD, Adm Adult $6, Snrs 62 $4 Child 6-11 $2, Under 6 Free, Gift Shop, www.kansasaviationmuseum.org,

American Eagle	Boeing 737-200	Lear 23	Stearman 4D
B-29	C-135E(KC)	Melton Bi Plane	Swallow 1927
BD-4	Cessna 206	Mooney Mite	Swallow C Coupe
B-52D	Cessna 310F	NS-1	T-33
Beech 75 Mentor	F-84F	Prescott Pusher	T-37
Beech Starship	Funk	O-2B	Travel Air 2000
Beechcraft B-35	J Craft Cygnet	Rawdon T-1	U-8
Boeing 727-100	Laird Swallow	Rearwin Speedster	Watkins Skylark

Kansas & Historical Air, McConnell AFB, 184th TFG, 2801 S Rock Rd, 672221-6225, (316) 652-3141

B-47E	F-80C	F-100C	T-33A-5-LO
F-4D	F-84C	F-105D	
F-16	F-86L-LO	F-105F	

CAF Jayhawk Wing, 2560 S Kessler St,67217, (316) 943-5510, Gift Shop
(Rides Available for $75), Contact Phyllis Sears, www.cafjayhawks.org (M) = Private Member Owned

AT-11(C-45G) (M)	L-3B (M)	PT-23 (Rides)	UC-78 (Rides)
L-2M (M)	PT-22 (M)	PT-26 (M)	

KENTUCKY

Fort Campbell - Don F Pratt Memorial Museum, 42223-5335, (720) 798-3215, Mon-Fri 12-4:30, Sat 10-4:30, Sun 12-4:30, Free Adm, Curator: Don Pratt, www.campbell.army.mil/pratt/index.htm

A-10	C-119	H-1(UH)
C-47	CG-4A	H-65(AH)

KENTUCKY

Fort Knox - Patton Museum of Calvary & Armor, 4554 Fayette Ave, POB 208, 40121-0208
(502) 624-3812, Mon-Fri 9-4:30, Sat-Sun 10-4:30, May-Sept Mon-Fri 9-4:30, Sat-Sun 10-6
Closed E, TD, CE, CD, Free Adm, Registrar: C Lemon, www.generalpatton.org
H-1B(UH)(2ea)   H-1G(AH)   H-13E(OH)   H-23B(OH)   L-19A M-75 Tank

Frankfort - Boone National Guard Center, 40601, (502) 564-8464, F-84F   F-101C(RF)

Lexington - Aviation Museum of Kentucky, 4316 Hangar Dr, Blue Grass Airport, Mail: POB 4118,
40544, (859) 231-1219, Gift Shop, Mon-Sat 10-5, Sun 1-5, Closed E,TD, CD, ND,
Adm Adult $7, Snrs 60 $5, Child 6-16 $3, Under 6 Free, www.aviationky.org/

A-4L	F-14	L-4B	Pulsar Ultralight
Aeronca Model K	H-1(AH)	L-10 Electra	Sellers Quadraplane
Cessna 150	H-1(UH)	Link Trainer	T-38B(AT)
Crosley Moonbeam	H-58A(OH)	LNE-1	Travel Air D4D
F-4S	Heath Center Wing	Nimbus II Glider	Youngsters Sim

Louisville - Bowman Field, 5 Mi SE of City, (502) 368-6524, AT-6, DC-3/C-47 Flights

Louisville ANG, Standford Field, 40213, (502) 364-9400, F-4C(RF), F-101H(RF)

LOUISIANA

Alexandria - England AFB, Flying Tiger Heritage Park, 23TFW/PA, 71311-5004,
(318) 448-2401, 1406 Van Gossen Ave 448-1083 Or 3908 Coliseum Blvd 448-0701,
A Sponsor or Escort & Public Affairs Office Is Required To Visit Museum,
A-7D   A-10   F-84F   F-86E   F-105G

Baton Rouge - USS Kidd & Nautical Center, 305 S River Rd, 70802-6220, (225) 342-1942
Daily 9-5, Closed TD, CD, Museum Adm: Adult $4, Child 5-12 $3, Under 5 Free
Ship & Museum Adm: Adult $7, Snr $6, Active Military $5, Child 5-12 $4, Under 4 Free,
www.usskidd.com A-7E, P-40E Replica, USS KIDD (Camping aboard available groups of 20)

Barksdale AFB - 8th AF Museum, Barksdale AFB (North Gate), 88 Shreveport Rd, 71110,
(318) 456-5553, POB 75, Daily 9:30-4, Closed TD, CD, ND, Gift Shop 752-0055, www.8afmuseum.net/

B-17G	B-52G	F-84F	T-33
B-24J	B-58A Rocket Sled Fuse	F-111(FB)	Vulcan B Mk.2
B-29	Beech 18	MiG-21	
B-47E	C-47A	P-51D	
B-52D	C-97L(KC)	SR-71	

Houma - Airborne Support Inc, 3626 Thunderbird Rd, Houma-Terrebonne Airport, 70363,
N29-33.9 W 090-39.63, (985) 8851-6391, Fax 851-6393, Pres Howard Barker,
www.houma-airport.com, C-47B (3ea),   C-54D/Q

Monroe - Aviation and Military Museum of Louisiana, 701 Kansas Lane, Monroe Regional Airport
(Formerly Selman Field), Mail POB 13113, 71213, (318) 362-5540, (800) 391-1493,
Mon-Fri 9-4:30, Sat 9-5, Sun 1-5, www.ammla.net, Artifacts

New Orleans - Belle Chase NAS, Alvin Callender Field, 70143, (504) 394-2818,
Inside Main Gate, A-7,   A-10,   AH-1,   F-15,   F-18,   P-3

National World War II Museum, 945 Magazine St, 70130, (504) 527-6012, Tue-Sun 9-5,
Adm Adult $14, Student & 65 $8, Child 5-17 $6, Under 5 Free, Gift Shop, Library, Theater,
Facility Rental, www.nationalww2museum.org

C-47	Spitfire Mk.VI	Higgins LCVP Boat	M3 Half Track
L-5	TBM	M4A3 Tank	

LOUISIANA

New Orleans - Jackson Barracks Military Museum, Jackson Barracks, 6400 St Claude Ave, Bldg 53, 70146-0330, (504) 278-8241, Mon-Fri 7:30-4:00, Free Adm, www.122nd.com, Closed from Hurricane Katrina, Temporary Contact Sherrie Pugh (318) 290-5201 sherrie.pug@us.army.mil, Mr Amerski (504) 417-1064

A-26	F-15	F-102(YF)	T-33A
AT-11	F-86D	H-23	
F-4C	F-100D	OH-58A	

Patterson - Wedell-Williams Memorial Aviation Museum, 394 Airport Circle, Off IA 182 Hwy, Mail: POB 655, 70392, (985) -399-1268, Tue-Sat 8:30-5, Adm Adult $2 Curator:Lisa Cotham, http://lsm.crt.state.la.us/aviation/wedwm.htm

Aero Commander 680	Farley Vincennt-Starflight	Stearman
Beech D17S	Replica P-47 (½ Scale)	Wedell-Williams Racer 44
Bf 109 (½ Scale)	PT-17	

Reserve - American Military Heritage Foundation Museum, St John Baptist Airport, 355 Airport Rd, 70084, (985) -536-1999

A-4	AT-6G (2ea)	H-6(OH)
A-7E	C-45	T-28 (2ea)

Ruston - LA Tech Univ ROTC, Det 305, (318) 257-4937, Col: Stamm,

T-33A	ICBM	Minuteman 1

MAINE

Auburn - US Airliner Industry Museum, 1649 Constellation Dr, Lewiston-Auburn Airport, 2355 Hotel Rd, 04210-8821, (207) 777-7077, By Appt Only, Contact: Maurice A Roundy, www.starliner.net, L-1649A (2ea)

Augusta - Maine Army National Guard, Camp Keyes Augusta State Airport, UH-1H

Bangor - Cole Transportation Museum, Mecaw & Perry Rd, (207) 990-3600, May-Nov Daily 9-5, Adm Adult $6, Snrs 62 $4, Child Under 19 Free, Gift Shop, Facility Rental, www.colemuseum.org

UH-1H	M-60 Tank

Maine ANG, 101st ARW, Bangor Int'l Airport, 04401-4393, (207) 947-0571,

F-89F-101B	CF-101B

Maine Air Museum (Maine Aviation Historical Society), 04901, Mail: POB 2641, 04402, (207) 941-6757, (800) 280-MAHS In State, www.maineairmuseum.org, email: townsend@acadia.net

F-89J	Luscombe 8A	UH-1H

Brunswick - Naval Air Station Brunswick, 010 Bath Rd, 04011-0010, (207) 921-1110, P-3A, P2V-5

Owls Head - Owls Head Transportation Museum, Box 277, 04854, (207) 594-4418, Fax 594-4410, March-Oct Daily 10-5, Nov-Feb Daily 10-4, Closed TD, CD, ND, Adm Adult $8, Snrs $7, Child 5-17 $5, Family $20, www.ohtm.org, email: ohtm@midcoast.com

Antoinette	Deperdussin	Milliken Special
Bellanca	Etrich Taube	Nieuport 28
Bleriot XI	FE8	Penaud Planaphore
Burgess-Wright F	Fokker C.IVa	S.E.5a
Cayley Glider	Fokker DR.I	Sopwith Pup
Chanute Glider	Henri Farman III	Spad XIIIc.1
Clark Bi Wing	J-1	Stearman A75N/1
Curtiss Pusher D	J-3C	Waco UBF-2
Domenjoz Sailing Glider	JN-4D	
DH 82	Lilienthal Glider	

Presque Isle - Presque Isle Air Museum, 650 Airport Rd, Suite 10, 04769-2088, (207) 764-2542 www.victorian.fortunecity.com/stanford/8505

MARYLAND

Aberdeen - US Army Ordnance Foundation, Aberdeen Proving Ground, Rt 715, POB 377, APG, MD, 21005-5201, (410) 272-3602, End of State Route 22, Daily 9-4:45, Closed Holidays Except Armed Forces, Memorial, Independence Day, Free Adm, Gift Shop 272-8442, Mon 12-4, Tue-Sun 10-4, (410) 272-8442, 225 Items of a 25 Acre Tank & Artillery Park, www.ordmusfound.org

Tanks:	German Panther	Japanese 94	M3A1 Medium
British WWI Wippet	German Jadgtiger	Japanese 97	M4A4
British WWI Mk IV	Italian 13/40	M1	M26
French 1935R	Italian L6/40	M2	M-60
French Char 35 SOMUA	Italian M14/41	M3A1 Light	V-2

Andrews AFB, 89th Airlift Wing/PA (MAC), 20331-5000, (301) 981-9111, www.andrews.af.mil
Open House May 22-23, F6F,   F-4,   F-18,   F-105D,   F-106,   H-1B(UH)

Annapolis - US Naval Academy Museum, 118 Maryland Ave, 21402-5034, (410) 293-2108, Mon-Sat 9-5, Sun 11-5, Curator James W Cheevers, Bookstore, www.nadn.navy.mil/Museum/
A-4A   F4F

Baltimore - Baltimore ANG, GL Martin Airfield, 212220-2899, (410) 687-6270,
F-86H   HU-16B   XF2Y-1

Baltimore Museum of Industry, 1415 Key Hwy, 21202, (410) 727-4808, www.thebmi.org
Martin 162A   PBM-1 2/3 Scale

Beltsville - Naval Reserve Center, 2600 Powdermill Rd, (301) 394-3966, Missle

College Park - College Park Aviation Museum, 1985 Corporal Frank Scott Dr, 20740, I-495, S on Kenilworth Ave,W on Paint Branch Pkwy, (301) 864-6029, Fax 927-6472, Daily 10-5, Closed Holidays, Adm Adult $4, Snrs $3, Child $2, Under 2 Free, Annual AirFair Sept, www.collegeparkaviationmuseum.com

Aeronca 65LA	J-2	Taylorcraft BL-65
Berliner 1924 Helio	JN-4D	Wright B Aeroplane
Bleriot XI	Monocoupe 110	
Ercoupe 415D	PT-17	

Ft Meade - National Vigilance Park, National Security Agency, East Off of I-95 on Route 32, Left on Colony 7 Rd After Passing Baltimore-Washington Parkway (Rt295),
C-130A,   EA-3B   RU-8D(L-23D)

Quest Masters, Box 131, 20755, Curator: Chris Van Valkenburgh, www.questmasters.us, All Projects in Storage, By Appt Only

B-24L (Fuselage)	PT-26A (Fuselage Frame)	SNJ-5B (Project)
CG-15A (Cockpit Frame)	P-61B (Nose)	M4 Tank
LNE-1 (Cockpit Frame)	UC-45F (Cockpit)	

Hagerstown - Washington County Regional Airport, Rt 12, Box 62, Off Rt 11 &
I-81, Dave Rider (301) 791-6231,   AT-6   DC-3   J-2

Hagerstown Aviation Museum, 101 West Washington St, 21740, Mail: 14235 Oak Springs Rd, 21742, (301) 733-8717, Tue-Sat 10-4, Sun 1-4, Closed All Holidays, Adm Adult $7, Snrs 55 $5, Child $6, Under 2 Free, Gift Shop, www.hagerstownaviationmuseum.org,
(NM) = For New Museum when Built

AT-6 (NM)	C-119 (NM)	KR-31	UC-61C
C-82	F-24W	PT-19	

MARYLAND

Lexington Park - Patuxent River Naval Air Test & Evaluation Museum,22156 Three Notch Rd, 20653, (301) 863-7418, Fax 342-7947, Tue-Sun 10-5, Closed ED, TD, CD, Free Adm, Gift Shop, www.paxmuseum.com

A-4M	F-6A(F4D-1)	Link Trainer	T-39D
A-6E	F9F-8B	Pioneer UAV	TH-1L
A-7A	F-14A (Storage)	QH-5D ASH	X-32B
AV-8B (Storgage)	F-14B	RA-5C	X-32C
E-2B	F/A-18A	S-2	X-47A UCAV-N
F4J	H-1J(AH) (Storage)	S-3	
F4 Cockpit	H-53A(CH)	SH-2G	

Middle River - Glenn L Martin Maryland Aviation Museum, 701 Wilson Point Rd, Martin State Airport, POB 5024, 21220, (410) 682-6122, Wed-Sat 11-3, Closed Holidays, Free Adm, Gift Shop, Mus Illustrator Rober Hanauer, (410) 252-4191, www.marylandaviationmuseum.org, S = Storage

A7D	F-84F(RF)	F-105G (S)	P&W R2800
B-57A(RB) (2ea)	F-100F (2ea)	F9F (S)	P6M Fuse/Tail (S)
F-4D	F-101B (S)	Martin 4-0-4	T-33

Suitland -NASM/ Paul E Garber Facility, (Closed to Public), 3904 Old Silver Hill Rd, 20746, (202) 357-1552, www.nasm.si.edu/museum/garber, All Aircraft to Be Sent to Udvar-Hazy Center.

Bldg		Bldg		Bldg	
22	A-1H		FJ-1	23	O-1A(L-19)
21	Abrams Explorer		Franklin Texaco		OA-1A
20	AN-2	07	Fw Ta-152H	06	Olmstead Pusher
	Applebay Zuni II	20	G4M3 Nose		P-56(XP)
22	Ar 196A		GC-1A	20	P-63A-10-BE
23	B-26(VB)	22	Goodyear Gondola	23	P-84(XP)Fuse
22	B-43 (XB)		H-1F(AH)	07	P1Y1-C
22	B-42A(XB)	22	HA-200B	23	PG-185B
22	B-17D	20	He 162A	23	PT-19A
0D	B-57B(EB)	20	Helio No. 1		PT-22
22	B6N2		Herring-Burgess		RA-5C
22	B7A2	24	Hiller 1031-A-1	21	RC-3
20	Bachem Ba 349	07	HJD-1(XHJD)		RQ-2A
	Beechcraft 35	22	Ho 229	21	Rutan Quickie
22	Beechcraft D18S	22	HRP-1(XHRP)		SB2C-5
	Bell 65		Huff-Daland Duster		Schempp-Hirth Nimbus II
23	Bellanca 14 -13 -2	23	HV-2A		Shoemaker-Cannonhouse
21	Bu 181B	03	Icarus I	23	SG. 38
22	BV-155B V2	21	J-1	23	SNJ-4A(AT-6)
07	C-8 Mk IV		J5N1	21	Stearman-Hammond Y
07	C-64(YC)	23	J-29	21	Stout Skycar
24	C-97L(KC) Cockpit	07	J7W 1		T-38
07	C6N1-S	20	JN-4D	20	TBF-1
20	CCW-1	23	JRS-1(S-43)	20	TD2C-1
23	Cessna 150L	20	Ju-388L	22	VZ-9V
22	Convair 240	21	Kasperwing 180B	23	VZ-2A
	Cosmos Phase II	07	Ki-115	09	Waco Primary Glider
22	Curtiss E Boat Fuse		Kikka	24	Waco UIC Cabin
22	CW 1 Junior	20	Laird LCDW 500Fus	24	Waco 9
23	CW X-100	07	Lippisch DM-1	22	Waterman Whatsit
	DH 98		M -1		Wills Wing Talon 150
21	Double Eagle II		M -2	23	Windecker Eagle I
20	Erco 415		MacCready Solar Challenger	22	XF2Y-1
23	F-5L	24	Martin, JV, K-III	22	XFY-1
24	F-100 Cockpit	22	Me 410A-3	07	XR-1
22	F-100D		MQ-12	23	XR-5(VS-317)
	F-101C(RF)		MXY7-K2	07	XR-8
22	F-105D		N1K1	23	XV-1
23	F9F-6	23	O-2	23	Yak-18
20	Fi 156	22	O-47A(RO)		YROE-1

MARYLAND

Suitland - Airmen Memorial Museum, 5211 Auth Rd, 20746, (800) 638-0594, Mon-Fri 8-5, www.afsahq.org/AMM/amm-htm/mwelcome.htm, Artifacts

Wallops Island - NASA/Goddard Visitor Center, Bldg J-17, 23337, (757) 824-1344
March-June Thru-Mon 104, July-August Daily 10-4, Sept-Nov Thur-Mon 10-4, Dec-Feb Mon-Fri 10-4
Free Adm, Tours on Thur at 2pm, 1.5 Hrs long, Gift Shop, Dir DeAnna Hickman 824-1148
www.wff.nasa.gov/vc; Rockets only

MASSACHUSETTS

Bedford - Hanscom AFB, 01731, (781) 861-4441, F-86H ?

Boston - Museum of Science Park, 02114-1099, (617) 589-0100, Daily 10-5,
Adm Adult $2, Child $.50   Five Spacecraft

Cape Cod - Coast Guard Air Station, Race Point Beach, End of Rte, HH-60,   HU-16E,   HU-25

Hq Massachusetts Military Reservation, 02542, (508) 968-1000, 7:30-4, T-33

Otis ANG, MASS ANG Museum, 02542-5001, (508) 968-4090, 102nd FIW,

F-84F	F-86	F-100D	T-33A

Chambridge - New England Escadrille, 26 Cambridge St, 01803-4604, Mail: POB 605,
Kendal Square Station, (617) 273-1916, 02142, By Appt Only

Stow - Bob Collings Foundation, 137 Barton Rd, 01775, POB 248, (978) 568-8924,
By Appt only, R=Restoration, All Flyable, www.collingsfoundation.org,

Bleriot	F4U-5	Fi-156	T-33
C-78(UC)	Foker DR-1 Rep	PT-17	Wright Ex Vin Fizz

Westfield - MA ANG, 104 TFG/CC, 01085, (413) 568-9151   F-100D

Pioneer Valley Military & Transportation Museum, (Expected Opening 2008), 20 Airport Rd,
Barnes Mcpl Airport, Mail POB 1332, 01086-1332, By Appt Only, www.pvmtm.org

AN-2	P.56 Provost	PT-23	M59 APC	M76 Full Track

MICHIGAN

Battle Creek - ANGB, 49015-1291, (269) 963-1596, A-10(Active),

A-37	F-100F	T-37B	UH-1B	Tank

Belleville - Yankee Air Museum, 2041 A St, Willow Run Airport - East, 48112-0590, Mail: POB 590,
48112-0590, (743) 483-4030, Fax 483-5076, Tue-Sat 10-4, Sun 12-4,Jan 1-Mar 1, Thur-Sat 10-4,
Sun 12-4, Adm Adult $7, Child 5-12 $3, 62+ Child 13-19 $5, Gift Shop Manager: Dale Worcester,
Restoration Facility, www.yankeeairmuseum.org,

A-4 Cockpit		B-52D	(O)(L)	H-1D(UH)		(O)
A-6A(EA)	(S)	B-57A(RB)	(O)(L)	Link Trainer		
A-7D Project	(L)	C-47B(TC)	(F)	P-51D	(F)	
A-10 Cocpit		CG-4A	(P)	PB4Y-2G		(O)
A-W 650-101	(O)	DC-6B(C-118)	(O)	PT-19A :Leslie Day	(F)	
Argosy		F-4C	(L)	SA-300 Starduster Too	(D)	
AT-6D :Yankee Flyers	(F)	F-4 Cockpit		T-28A :Yankee Flyers	(F)	
AT-6D :Max Holman	(F)	F-84F	(S)(L)	T-28C :Stu Dingman		(F)
AT-6D :Jack Rouch	(F)	F-84F(RF)(3ea)	(O)(L)	T-33A (2ea)		(O)
AT-11	(S)	F-86D	(O)	T-33A :Connie Katitta		
AT-19(V-77)	(F)	F-101B(NF)	(O)(L)	TS-11 :Yankee Spark Flyers	(F)	
B-17G	(F)	F-102A(TF)	(O)(L)	Wallis Model 3 1976		(D)
B-25D	(F)(P)	F-102 Cockpit				

MICHIGAN

Belleville - Divisions of the Yankee Air Force are at the following locations:
NE = North-East Division, Sussex Airport, POB 1729, Fairfield, NJ, 07007-1729
SAG = Saginaw Valley, Michigan - Harry Browne Airport, Saginaw, MI
WUR = Wurtsmith, Michigan - Oscoda County Airport, Division - Oscoda, MI

Charlotte - North American Air Museum, 9854 Curtis Rd, Charlotte Airport, Nashville, 49073
www.northamericanairmuseum.org

Dearborn - Henry Ford Museum, 20900 Oakwood Blvd, POB 1970, 48121-4088,
(313) 982-6100, Daily 9:30-5, Sun 12-5, Closed TD, CD, Adm Adult $14, Snr $13, Child 5-12 $10
Under 5 Free, Gift Shop, www.thehenryford.org/museum/heroes/theplanes/default.asp

Bleriot XI	Ford Flivver	Pitcairn Autogyro
Boeing 40-B2	JN-4D	Stinson SM-1
DC-3	Laird LC-D W500	VS-3000A
Fokker F.VIIa	Lockheed Vega	Wright Flyer
Ford 4-AT-15	NYP	Wright RB-1

Detroit - The National Museum of Tuskegee Airmen, 6325 W. Jefferson Ave, 48209, Mail POB 9166
Arlington, VA, 22219-1166, (313) 297-9360, Wed-Sun 9-5, Artifacts Only, www.tuskegeeairmen.org

Farmington Hills - Marvin's Marvelous Mechanical Museum, 31005 Orchard Lake Rd, 48334,
(248) 626-5020, 100 Model Airplanes suspended on Conveyor Line, www.marvin3m.com

Frankenmuth - Michigan's Own, Inc, Military & Space Museum, 1250 Weiss St, 48734,
(989) 652-8005, March-Dec Mon-Fri 10-5, Sun 12-5, Adm Adult $5, Snrs 65 $4, Child 6-18 $2,
Under 6 Free, www.mmm.com, email michown@ejourney.com, F-86

Gwinn - KI Sawyer Heritage Air Museum, KI Sawyer AFB, 301 A Ave, 49843, (906) 346-6511,
www.kishamuseum.org, B-52D   F-101B (2ea)

Grand Haven - Grand Haven Memorial Airpark, Gate Entrance, 49417, (616) 842-4430, F-100

Grand Rapids - CAF West Michigan Wing, Wing Leader: Shirley A. Schouw, 19788 92nd
St, Byron Center, 49315, (616) 878-9145, AT-11

Gerald R. Ford Museum, 303 Pearl St, NW, Off US 131 Exit 85B, 49501, (616) 451-9263
Mon-Sta 9-4:45, Sun 12-4:45, Closed ND, TD, CD, Adm Adult $2, Snr $1.50, Child
Under 16 Free,   UH-1

Greenville - Fighting Falcon Military Museum of the Flat River Historical Museum,
516 W Cass St, 48838, (616) 225-1940, Sun 2-4, www.thefightingfalcon.org CG-4A Project

Jackson - EAA Chapter 304, Jackson County Airport, 49202, www.eaa304.org, T-33

Kalamazoo - (See Next Page)

Lake Orion - Canterbury Village Toy Shop, 2369 Joslyn Ct, 48361, SE-5A Replica

Lansing - Michigan Historical Museum, 702 Kalamazoo St, 48918, (517) 373-3559
Mon-Fri 9-4:30, Sat 10-4:30, Sun 1-5, Free Adm, Gift Shop, B-24 Nose Section

Lapeer - Yankee Air Force Mid-Michigan 3rd Division, Lapeer Airport, 1232 Roods
Lake Rd, 48446-8366, (810) 664-6966, These Aircraft Are In Storage:
A-6   F-84K   F-84F(RF)   Stinson Model 10A   UH-1D

MICHIGAN

Kalamazoo - Air Zoo, 6151 Portage Rd, 49002-1700, (269) 382-6555, (866) 524-7966,
Fax: 382-1813,Mon-Sat 9-5, Sun 12-5, Closed TD, CE, CD, Adm Adult $19.50, Snrs 60 $17.50,
Child 5-15 $15.50 and Under 5 Free, Simulator Rides F4U Corsair, Ford Trimotor Ride, Cafe,
Gift Shop, 3D & 4D Theater, Daily Plane Flights, May-Oct, Wed, Sat-Sun, www.airzoo.org

A4D-2(A-4B)	Fokker DR.1 (3/4 Scale Rep)	P-51 (Winter Only)
AD-4NA	Ford Tri-Motor 5-AT	P-55-CS(XP)
Aeronca 65 CA	GH-2	P-80
Avid Flyer	Guff R/C	PT-13D-BW/N2S
B-25J	H-1J(AH)	PT-22
B-57B	H-23(UH-12)	PT-23HO
Boeing 727-25C	H-25(UH)	Renegade Spirit
BT-13	H-53(CH) Cockpit	Rotorway Exec 90 (Storage)
C-47	HA-1112-M1L	S-3B (Storage)
Christine Eagle II	Heath Parasol	SBD-3
CG-4A	HUP-3	SNJ-5 2ea
Curtiss Pusher	J-3C-65	Sopwith Camel
El Kabong Gemini Capsule	JN-4D (2/3 Scale)	SPad VII
F-4E	Lear-23	SR-71B
F-8J	Link Trainer	T-28 Cockpit
F-9J(TF)	L-3B	T-28B
F-14A	L-4H	T-33B(TV-2)
F-16 Cockpit	L-19	T-34B
F/A-18	LNS-1	TG-4A
F-84F-35RE	MiG-15	Travel Air Texaco Mystery Ship
F-86A	N2T-1	V-1 (Restoration)
F-104	N3N	Waco INF
F4U-4B 1/2 Scale	O-58B	Waco VPF-7
F6F-5K	OQ-2A (Project)	Wright Flyer Rep
F7F-3P	OV-1D	Wolf Boredom Fighter
F8F-1D	P-38J 2/3 Scale Rep	X-28
F11A-1	P-39Q-20BE(RP)	Zenair (Storage)
FG-1D	P-40N	
FM-2	P-47D	

Mt Clemens - Sefridge ANG Base Selfridge Military Air Museum, 127W G/MU, 27333 C St,
Bldg 1011, 48045, (586) 307-5035, Fax 307-6646, April-Oct, Sat-Sun 12-4:30, Adm Adult $4,
Child 4-12 $3, Under 4 Free, Gift Shop, Library, Restoration Facility, www.selfridgeairmuseum.org

A-4B	F-14A	F-102A(TF)	S-2A(US)
A-7D	F-16A	F-106A	SNB-5
B-26C(GB)	F-84F	FG-1D	T-33A
B-57A(RB)	F-84F(RF)	H-1F(AH)	U-3A
C-45B	F-86A	H-1H(UH)	Nike-Ajax & Hercules
C-130A	F-100D	HH-52A	
C-131D	F-100F	O-2A	
F-4C	F-101C(RF)	P-3B	

Nashville - North American Air Museum, 9854 Curtis Rd, 49073, 2nd Sat Monthly 9am
www.northamericanairmuseum.org Artifacts

Oscoda - Yankee Air Force Wurtsmith Division, Oscoda-Wurtsmith Airport, 3961 E Airport Dr,
Mail: POB 664, 48750, (989) 739-7555, Fax 739-1974, Mid May-Mid Oct Fri-Sun 11-3
Adm Adult 3, Uchild Under 12 $2, Gift Shop, Restoration Facility, Library
www.wurtsmith-yaf-museum.org, email: YAF@theenchantedforset.com,
(S) = Storage, (P) = Project, (O) = On Loan,

Baker Special Racer		DC-8-55JT	(O)	Sperry Messenger	(P)
Barracuda Homebuilt		H-1D(UH)-BF		T-33A-1-LA	(S)
Boeing 727		L-19A-CE	(P)	T-33A-5-LO	(P)
CG-4A	(P)	Link Trainer	(P)		

MICHIGAN

Saginaw - Yankee Air Force Saginaw Valley Division, Harry Browne Airport,
Airport Number (989) 754-2459, 4821 Jones St 48601, Not Available to Public
DC-65 (L-2B) Flyable   L-4 Replica Project

Sterling Heights - Freedom Hill McComb County Park, Metropolitan Parkway Between Schoenherr &
Utica Rds, F-4,   HU-1,   M60A1 Tank   US Navy Torpedo Mk.14

MINNESOTA

Alexandria - Alexandria Airport, Chandler Field, 2 Mi SW of City, 210 Nokomis St
56308, (320) 762-1544, 762-2111,   T-33

Blaine - American Wings Air Museum, Janes Field, NW Corner of Anoka County Airport, POB 49322,
 55449-0332, (763) 786-4146, Tue 6pm-9pm, Fri 12-5, Sat 8-5, Jan 5-April 8 , Fri-Sat 10-4,
Adm Adult $5, Family $12, Mil & Snrs 55 & Student $3, Under 6 Free, www.americanwings.org

AO-1A	H-34D(CH)	O-2	OV-1D
F-5E	L-2M	OV-1 Cockpit	S2F-1
JOV-1A	L-3B	OV-1B	
JOV-1C	O-1E(L-19)	OV-1C	

Golden Wings Flying Museum, 8891 Airport Rd, Anoka County Airport, C-6, 55449, (763) 786-5004
Greg Herrick's Collection, By Appt Only, www.goldenwingsmuseum.com, All Flying Except (R)=Restoration

Aero Car	Fairchild F-45 (R)	Paramount Cabinair (R)	Stearman C3B
Aeronca C-3	FC-2-W2	PT-6F	Stinson A Tri-Motor
Alliance Argo	Fleetwings Seabird	PT-19	Stinson Detroiter (R)
Arrow Sport M (R)	Ford 4-AT	PT-23A	Stinson SM-7A (R)
Avro Avian	Interstate S-1-A	PT-26 (2ea)	Travel Air A-6000-A
Bushmaster 2000	Keystone K-84 (R)	Sikorsky S-39-C (R)	Waco CUC-1
Buhl Sport Airsedan	Krutzer K-5	SM-6000-B	Waco UKC
Call-Air A-4 (R)	KR-34C (R)	Spartan C2-60	YPT-9

Chisholm - Minnesota Museum of Mining, (218) 254-5543, F-94C

CAF/Lake Superior Squadron 101, 4931 Airport Rd, Hangar S101, Duluth International Airport Duluth,
55811, (218) 733-0639, B-25 Simulator, Link Trainer, PBY-6A, PBY-6ACF

Eden Prairie - Wings of the North, 9960 Flying Cloud Dr, Suite 204, 55347, (952) 746-6100
http://www.wotn.org, email: info@wotn.org, AT-6

Marshall - Red Baron Museum, 1632 West College Dr, 56258, (507) 537-8909, Tue-Sat 10-5
Free Adm, Gift Shop, Theater, PT-17 (5ea), www.redbaron.com

Fountain - Fillmore County Museum, 202 County Rd 8, 55935, (507) 268-4449, Mon-Fri 9-4, Free Adm
Dir Jerry Henke, Pietenpohl Air Camper,   Pietenpohl Sky Scout

Minneapolis - Jim Johns, (612) 881-1797, 9108 Logan Ave, 55400
AT-6 Harvard   BT-13   L-13   TBM-3

South St Paul - CAF- Minnesota Wing, Fleming Field, 310 Airport Rd, Hangar #3,
55073, (651) 455-6942, Wed 10-6, Sat 10-5, Gift Shop, www.cafmn.org,

B-25J	Harvard Mk IV	P-51C	PBY-6A
BT-13A	L-5A	PBY	

St Paul - Minnesota Air Guard Museum, Minneapolis-St Paul Intl Airport, 1 Scanlan Plaza, 55111-0592,
POB 11598, (612) 713-2523, Tue-Sat 9-2, Donation Adm Adult $3, Family $5, Gift Shop,
www.mnangmuseum.org

BC-1A(AT-6)	C-131E	F-94C	JN-6H
C-45	Curtiss Oriole	F-101(Black)	MiG-15
C-97	F-4C(RF)	F-101B	P-51D
C-47B	F-4D	F-102A	T-33A
C-130A	F-89H	H-1H(UH)	

MINNESOTA

St Paul - Minneapolis/St.Paul Int'l Airport, Wold Chamberlin Field, 6 Mi SW of
City, Gate 12 West side of Main Lobby, (612) 726-5032,
Spirit of St Louis Replica,   Waco 125 Gate 15
Link Trainer at North West Air Lines Curtiss Pusher Gate 12

Minnesota Air & Space Museum, Holman Field Airport, POB 75654, 55175
(651) 291-7925,   Steco Aerohydro-Plane

Stewartville - Carr Care Center, 211 S Main St, 55976, (320) 533-8175, Culver Dart

Winoma - Winoma Technical Institute,

C-45	Erocoupe	Luscombe 8	Taylorcraft
Cessna 2ea	Hiller	PA-31	Unident Aztec
Colt	L-19	S-61	

MISSISSIPPI

Bay St Louis - NASA's National Space Technology Laboratories, Visitor Center Bldg,
1200, NSTL, 39529, (228) 688-2211

Biloxi - Keesler AFB, 39534-5000, (228) 377-1110

F-100(YF)	F-104C	T-28
F-101C(RF)	F-105D	T-33A

Columbus - Columbus AFB, 39701-5000, (662) 434-7322   T-37B   T-38A

Jackson - Jackson ANG, Jackson Municipal Airport, Allen C Thompson Field,
39208-0810, (601) 968-8321, 173rd TAG, A-26B   F-84F(RF)   F-101C(RF)

Jackson AFB Museum, Hawkins Field, 39201, (601) 373-1574, 965-5790

National Agricultural Aviation Museum / Jim Buch Ross Mississippi Ag &
Forestry Museum, 1150 Lakeland Dr,

CAF - Mississippi Wing, Wing Leader: Robert L Bates, POB 16907,
39236-6907, (601) 992-1074, www.mississippiwingcaf.org, C-45

Meridian - NAS, T-2A

Petal - M W Hamilton Machine Museum, 39465,
Aircraft Restorations - All Aircraft Semi-Restored

BT-13	DC-3	HUB-1
C-53D	F9F	PT-17

McLaurin - Armed Forces Museum at Camp Shelby, Bldg 850, 12 Mi S of Hattiesburg on Hwy 49
(601) 558-2757, Tue-Sa 9-4:30, Free Adm, www.armedforcesmuseum.org, CH-54

MISSOURI

Branson - Veterans Memorial Museum, 1250 W 76 Country Music Blvd, 65616, (417) 336-2300
Fax: 336-2301, Daily 8-9pm, Adm Adult $10, www.veteransmemorialbranson.com,   P-51

Kansas City - Airline History Museum Inc, 201 NW Lou Holland Dr, Hangar 9
64116, (816) 421-3401, 513-9484, Mon-Sat 10-4, Sun 11-5, Closed Holidays
Adm Adult $7, Snrs 65 $6, Child 6-13 $3, Under 6 Free, Gift Shop,
Restoration Facility, Dir: Ona Gieschen, www.airlinehistorymuseum.com
L-1049H,   Martin 404   DC-3

Knob Noster - Whiteman AFB, 351 CSG/DEER, 65305, (660) 687-1110,
B-29   B-52D   B-47B   C-97G(KC)   H-1F(UH)

MISSOURI

Maryland Heights - Historic Aircraft Restoration Museum, Dauster Flying Field, Creve Coeur Airport, 3127 Creve Coeur Mill Rd, 63146, (314) 434-3368, Fax 878-6453 Sat-Sun 10-4, By Appt, Adm Adult $10, Child 5-12 $5, Under 5 Free, Rides: SNJ $75, Stearman $50, www.historicaircraftrestorationmuseum.org

Aeronca C-3	JN-4D	Stinson SM.8A
AN-2	KR-31	Timm Collegiate
AT-6(SNJ)	KR-21	Travel Air 4000 (R)
C-2	Monocoupe Clipwing	Waco ARE
Curtiss Air Sedan	Monocoupe 90	Waco ATO
Culver Dart	Mooney Mite	Waco JWM
Curtiss Robin (R)	N3N-3	Waco QCF-2
DH-89	NB-8G	Waco UBA
Driggs Dart	Pietenpohl Air Camper	Waco VKS-6
Fairchild CBA	Piper Vegabond	Zenith Biplane (R)
Flagg	PT-22	
Hisso Standard	Stearman	

St Charles - CAF Missouri Wing Museum, St Charles County Smartt Field, Mail: POB 637, 63302 (636) 250-4515, 928-5687, Tue, Thur, Sat 10-2:30, Adm Adult $2, Child $1, Gift Shop, www.cafmo.org,

B-25J	L-3B	TBM-3E

St Louis - McDonnell Douglas Prologue Room, McDonnell Blvd, & Airport Rd, Lambert St Louis Airport, Box 516, 63166, (314) 232-5421, 10 Mi NW, June-August, Mon-Sat 9-4, Curator: Larry Merritt, Replica Gemini, Mercury Capsules

McDonnell Planetarium, 5100 Clayton Rd, 63110, (314) 535-5810, Daily 9-5, Adm Adult $1.25, Child $0.75, PGM-17 Spacecraft

National Personnel Records Center, 9700 Page Ave, (314) 538-4261 H-1B(UH) Bradley Fighting Vehicle WWII 8" Howitzer

Missouri History Museum, Forest Park, (314) 746-4599, Ryan NYP Replica

MO ANG St Louis, Lambert Field, 63145, (314) 263-6356, F-4E, F-15A, F-100D

Museum of Transportation, 3015 Barrett Station Rd, Lambert St Louis Int'l Airport, 63122-3398, (314) 965-7998, Labor Day-April 30 Tue-Sat 9-4, Sun 11-4, Summer Mon-Wed, Sat 9-5, Thur 9-7, Sun 11-5, Closed TD, CE&D, NE&D, Adm Adult $4 Child 5-12 & Snr 65 $2, Under 5 Free, Gift Shop 965-5709, Restoration Facility www.museumoftransport.org, C-47A(VC) T-33 Project

Ozark Airlines Museum, 638 Bellerive Estates Dr, 63141, (314) 576-1747, www.iidbs.com/ozmuseum.htm c47oami@aol.com C-47

St Joseph - National Military Heritage Museum, 701 Messanie, 64501, (816) 233-4321 Mon-Fri 9-5, Sat 9-4, Adm Adult $2, Child $0.50, Contact Frank, www.geocities.com/nmhm89/ H-1(AH) H-1(UH)

Springfield - Air & Military Museum of the Ozarks, CAF Ozark Mountain Squadron, Springfield Regional, 2305 E Kearney St, North off I-65, (417) 864-7997, Fax 882-0188, Tue-Sat 12-4, Adm Adult $5, Child 6-12 $3, Under 6 Free, www.ammomuseum.org, AH-1

MONTANA

Great Falls - Great Falls ANG, Great Falls Int'l Airport, Gore Hill, 59401-5000, (406) 727-4650,

F-16A	F-86A	F-89J	F-106A	T-33

Malmstrom AFB & Airpark, 2177 St North, Suite 144, 59402-5000, (406) -731-2705
Mon-Fri 10-4, Free Adm, www.malmstrom.af.mil/library/malstrommuseum/index.asp

B-25M	C-97L(KC)	F-101B	T-33A
B-57B(EB)	F-84F	H-1F(UH)	

Helena - Montana Historical Society's Museum, 225 north Roberts, Mail POB 201201, 59620-1201
(406) 444-2694, Summer Mon-Sat 9-5, Adm Adult $5, Child $1, DH 60 #179, UH-1

College of Technology, 2300 Poplar(Airport)Rd, 59601, (800) 241-4882, www.hct.umontana.edu/

EC-121	H-19(S-65)	T-39

Firefighting Training Center, Helena Municipal Airport, A-7D

Missoula - Museum of Mountain Flying, Missoula Int'l Airport, 713 S 3rd St West, 59801-2513,
(406) 555-5555, May-Oct Daily 10-5, Adm Adult $4, Snr/Mil $2,
Student $1, Gift Shop, Smokejumper & Parachutes Artifacts , www.museumofmountainflying.org

C-45	DH Moth	Youngster 2
C-47(DC-3)	J-3	F-89
Clark Special	N2S-3	F-102A

Smokejumper Center, Aerial Fire Depot,US Dept of Agriculture, 5765 W Broadway, 59808,
Airport Terminal, Box 6, 59801, (406) 329-4900, Fax 329-4955, Memorial Day - July 4th Mon-Fri
8:30-5, July 4th-Labor Day 8:30-5 Daily, Hourly Tours,

Beech 58P	DHC 6	DC-3
Cessna 206	Beech 99	Sherpa C203A

NEBRASKA

Ashland - Strategic Air and Space Museum, 28210 West Park Hwy, 68003, Exit 426, Off I-80,
Mail: POB 68508, (402) 944-3100, Daily 9-5, Closed ED, TD, CD, ND, Adm Adult $7, Sr $6,
5-12 $3, Under 5 Free, Store, Snack Bar, www.strategicairandspace.com

Atlas D	B-52B(RB)	F-102A	T-29A
A-26B	B-57E	F-105	T-33A
B-1A	B-58A	F-111A(FB)	T-39A
B-17G	C-47A	H-19B(UH)	U-2C
B-25N	C-54D	H-21B(CH)	Vulcan B-2 Mk.II
B-29(TB)	C-97G(KC)	HU-16B	XF-85
B-36J	C-135C(EC)	ICBM,Minuteman I	
B-45C(RB)	F-84F	MiG-21	
B-47E	F-86H	SR-71A	

Lexington - Heartland Museum of Military Vehicles, 606 Heartland Rd, 68850, (308) 324-6329
Mon-Sat 10-5, Sun 1-5, www.heartlandmuseum.com   H-1(AH)   H-1(UH) (3 ea)

Lincoln - Lincoln ANG, Lincoln Municipal Airport, 68524-1897, 402-473-1326, 155th TRG

F-4C(RF)	F-84F(RF)	F-86L	T-33A

Minden - Harold Warp Pioneer Village Foundation, POB 68, 68959-0068, 138 E Hwy 6,
(800)445-4447, 308-832-1181, Memorial Day-Labor Day Daily 8-6, Winter daily 9-4:30,
Closed CD, Adm Adult $9.50, Child (6-15) $3.50, Under 6 Free, Manager: Marvin Mangers,
Gift Shop, Cafe 832-1550, www.pioneervillage.org

Bensen B-6	Ercoupe 67	P-59	Swallow
Bensen B-7	Hartman	PA-23	Weed Hopper
Cessna	Heath Parasol 5	PCA-2	Wright Flyer
Curtiss JN9	J-2	Sikorsky	
Curtiss	JN-4D	Stinson Detroiter 30	

NEBRASKA

Omaha - Freedom Park, 2497 Freedom Park Rd, 68110, (402) 345-1959, From I-29 Go W on I-480 Then N on Freedom Park Rd, Apr 15-Oct 31, Daily, 10-5, Adm Adult $5, Snrs 65 $4, Child 6-12 $3, Under 6,

A-4D	USS Hazard AM-240 Mine Sweeper
A-7	USS Towers DDG-9 Captains Gig
H-1(UH)	USS Marlin SST-2 (Submarine)
SH-3	

Offutt AFB, 68113-5000, Hangar 20 E, 402-294-1110, 8 Mi S of Omaha,

B-17F	B-52D	C-135(KC)

S Sioux City - Martin Flying Service, W. Hwy 20, 68776, 402-494-3667, A-7D

NEVADA

Carson City - Yesterday's Flyers Ltd, Carson City Airport, 3 Mi NE of City, (775) 882-1551

Bellanca	Curtiss Robin	Pfalz D.XIII	Stinson SR-4E
BT-13	Depordussin	Starduster II	T-28
Curtiss Junior	N3N	Steen Skybolt	

Fallon - Naval Air Station Fallon, 4755 Pasture Rd, 2 Mi NE of City, 89496-5000 (775) 426-5161, AP = Air Park; CU = Credit Union; MG = Main Gate

A-4	MG	AD-4B	MG	F-16	AP	MiG-23	AP
A-4	AP	E-2C	AP	F-86	AP	RA-5C	CU
A-7	MG	F-4	AP	FA-18	AP	UH-1	MG
A-7E	AP	F-8	AP	MiG-15	AP		
A-6	AP	F-14	AP	MiG-17	AP		

Las Vegas - CAF Nevada Wing, Wing Leader: Lois Larson, POB 27476, 89126-1476, AT-19

McCarran Int'l Airport, 5757 Wayne Newton Blvd, 2nd Level Above Baggage Claim, Near Scenic Airlines, 89119, (775) 261-5192, POB 11005, 89111, Free Adm, Ford 5AT, Cessna 172,

Military Heritage Command, POB 12543, 89112-0543, (800)347-4385, Dir: Gen D Smith, P2V-7(SP2H)

Nellis AFB, 157 NFWW, 89191-5000, (702) 652-1110, MV=Missile Hevicle

F-4C	F-100D	SA-3 MV	T-72 MV
F-5E	F-111A	SA-8 MV	
F-86	F-117A	SU-7	
F-105G	MiG-17	T-62 Tank	

Air Force Thunderbird Museum, Nellis AFB, Las Vegas Blvd & Craig Rd, Tue & Thur 2pm, By Appt Only (702) 652-9902 / 652-4019, F-16

Reno - May ANG Base, Cannon Int'l Airport, 89502, (775) 788-4500, RF-101B

Nevada Aviation Historical Society, 3035 Slatter Court, 89503, (775) 747-3888, F-86D

NEW HAMPSHIRE

Danville - Atlantic Warbirds, 23 Pleasant St, 03819-3221, Mail: POB 715, 01845, North Andover, MA, (603) 382-3493, DC-4 (C-54)

Wolfeboro - Wright Museum of American Enterprise, 77 Center St, 03894, (603) 569-1212 Mon-Fri 9:30-5, Exec Dir Mark Foynes, Army Spotter Plane, 2 Tanks

NEW JERSEY

Fairfield - Yankee Air Force NE Division, Caldwell-Wright (Essex County) Airport
171 Passaic Ave, 07004-3502, Mail: POB 1729, 07007-1729, Not Open to Public
C.51 Pembroke (Storage)　　　DC-62 (L-2C)(Flyable)　L-13A (Storage)

Farmingdale - Berlin Airlift Historical Society, Mail To: POB 782, 07727
(732) 818-0034, www.spiritoffreedom.org,　C-54　　　C-97G

Ft Monmouth, US Army Communications-Electronics Museum, Kaplan Hall Bldg 275,
07703-5103, (732) 532-4390, 542-7267, Mon-Fri 12-4, Free Adm, ANTSC-54 Satellite

Lakehurst - Navy Lakehurst Historical Society, POB 328, 08733-0328, (732) 244-8861
fAX 244-8897, www.nlhs.com, Crash Site Tour & Artifacts from Hindenburg

Naval Air Engineering Center/Station,　　　A-7B　　　E-2B　　　F-14

Lumberton - Air Victory Museum, 68 Stacy Haines Rd, South Jersey Regional Airport,
08048, (609) 267-6268, Fax: 702-1852, Nov 1-March 31 Wed-Fri 10-3, Sat 10-4, Summer
Wed-Sat 10-4, Sun 11-4, Adm Adult $4, Snrs $3, Child 4-13 $2, Gift Shop,
www.airvictorymuseum.org/

A-4C	F-4A	F-104G
A-7B	F-14A	FP-404
E-2B	F-86L	H-53D(RH)

Millville - Millville Army Air Field Museum, Municipal Airport, 1 Leddon St, 08332, (856) 327-2347,
Tu-Sun 10-4, Closed Holidays, Free Adm, Gift Shop, www.p47millville.org

A-4	H-26(XH)	Link Trainer	O-46A	P-47

Pomona - Air National Guard - Atlantic City Int'l Airport, F-100F,　F-106B

Rio Grande - Naval Air Station Wildwood Aviation Museum, 500 Forrestal Rd, 08242,
(609) 886-8787, May-Sept: Mon-Sun 9-5, Oct-April Mon-Sat 9-4, Adm Adult $6, Child 3-12 $3
Under 3 Free, Gift Shop, www.usnasw.org

A-4	H-6(OH)	MiG-15	T-33 2Seater
F-14B	H-13G(OH)	PT-17	TBM
H-1(AH)	H-52A(HH)	T-28	Tomahawk
H-1(UH)	L-19	T-33	

Rockaway - Picatinny Arsenal Museum, 07801, Rt 15, Pitcatinny Base, Phipps Rd,
(973) 724-2797, Tue, Wed & Thur 9-3, Outdoor Displays Open Daily, Free Adm,

AGM-22	M3	M31	M51

Sea Girt - National Guard Militia Museum, P.O. Box 277, 08750, (732) 974-5966
Tue, Thur 10-3, Summer Daily 10-3, Free Adm, Gift Shop, Library, Artifacts

Teterboro - Aviation Hall Of Fame & Museum of New Jersey, 400 Fred Wehran Dr,
Teterboro Airport, 07608, (201) 288-6344, Fax 288-5666, Tue-Sun 10-4, Adm Adult $6
Mil/Snrs/Child $4, Under 2 Free, Gift Shop, www.njahof.org

H-1 (AH)	H-13	Martin 202 Airliner	Stinson Voyager
H-52A(HH)	Lockheed Bushmaster	OV-1D	

NAPC Trenton,　A-4B

Wrightstown - McGuire AFB Museum, 08562, 438 MAW/SEN,

C-118A	F-4	P-38L
C-141	F-84F	F-105B

NEW MEXICO

Alamogordo - Holloman AFB, 833 CSG/CD 88330-5000, (505) 479-6511,

F-4C	F-84F	F-100D	F-105D
F-80C	F-86E	F-104C	

New Mexico Museum of Space History, Top of Highway 2001, (505) 437-2840, (877) 333-6589, Mail: POB 5430, 88311-5430, Gift Shop, Restoration Facility, Daily 9-5, Closed TD, CD, Adm Adult $3, Snrs 60 $2.75, Child 4-12 $2.50, Under 4 Free, IMAX Theater, Shuttle Camp, www.nmspacemuseum.org Little Joe Rocket   Satellites,   Sonic Wind I Rocket Sled,

Albuquerque - New Mexico ANG Complex, Bldg 1055, 87100, (505) 678-3114, A-7D, F-100A
At Falcon Rd & Air Guard Rd - F-80, P-51
At 551st Op Sq, Bldg 4279, Frances St & Hercules Way SE - CH-3

Anderson/Abruzzo Int'l Balloon Museum, 9201 Balloon Museum Dr, NE, Mail POB 1293, 87103-1293 (505) 768-6020, Cafe 880-0500, Theater, Gift Shop, Facility Rental, Tue-Sat 9-5, Adm Adult $4, Snrs 65 $2, Child 4-12 $1, Under 4 Free, www.balloonmuseum.org Balloons

CAF Lobo Wing, Moriarty New Mexico Airport, PO Box 20576, www.lobowing.org , 87154-0576,

AT-11 Project	B-29 Tail	Link Trainer	PT-26

Kirtland AFB, 58th Special Ops, 87117-5000, Doris St & Aberdeen Ave, (505) 853-5856

CH-21B(2ea)	H-13E(OH)	H-5G	HU-16A
H-1F(UH)	H-43(HH)	H-19F(UH)	

National Atomic Museum, 1905 Mountain Rd NW, Mail: POB 5800, MS 1490, 87104, (505) 245-2137, Daily 9-5, Closed ED, TD, CD, ND, Adm Adult $5, Snrs 60 & Child 6-17 $4, Child Under 6 Free, Gift Shop 242-6083, www.atomicmuseum.com

A-7C(TA)	B-52B	F-105D	ICBM	SM-2
B-29	CIM-10A	MGM-13A	TM-61C	

Angel Fire - Vietnam Veterans National Memorial, NW of Angel Fire on US64, 28 Miles E of Taos on US64, Contact: David Westphall, POB 608, 87710, 505-377-6900, Fax: 377-3223,   UH-1H

Carlsbad - Carlsbad Museum & Art Center, 418 West Fox, 88220, (505) 887-0276, Mon-Sat 10-5, Free Adm, Artifacts

Clovis - Cannon AFB, Public Affairs, 27 FW/PA, Cannon Airpark, 88103-5000, (505) 784-4131, PA: Michael Pierson, 1Lt, Historian: 784-2460,www.cannon.af.mil

F-80B	F-86H	F-101A	T-33A
F-84C	F-100D	F-111A	

Hobbs - CAF New Mexico Wing, Flying Museum, POB 1260, Lea County Airport, (505) 395-2377, Daily 8-Sunset, Wing Leader: Philip L Ross

BT-14	C-45	Me-108	SNJ-4

National Soaring Foundation, 88241, (505) 392-6032,

Blanik L-13	Grob 103	Schweizer 1-26	Schweizer 2-33

Las Cruces - Southwest Aviation, Las Cruces Int'l A, 88000, (505) 524-8047, 7 Mi West of City,

A-26B	C-46	PV-2

White Sands Missile Range Museum & Park, Las Cruces or El Paso Gate, 88002-5047, (505) 678-2250, Mon-Fri 8-4, Sat-Sun 10-3, Free Adm, Gift Shop 678-8824, www.wsmr-history.org

C-6A(VC)	H-1M(UH)	V-2 Rocket	Over 60 Missiles

Melrose - Melrose Bombing Range, N of Hwy 84, In Town, (505) 784-6644, F-100

NEW MEXICO

Moriarty - US Southwest Soaring Museum, POB 3626, 87035, (505) 832-0755,
Daily 9-4, www.swsoaringmuseum.org

B-10	KA-6	TG-1
Hummingbird	MSK	TG-4A
KA-4	SG-1A	Zoegling Rep

Roswell - Int'l UFO Museum & Research Center, 114 N Main, 88202, (505) 625-9495,
Fax 625-1907, Daily 9-5, Adm Adult $5, Child $2, Gift Shop, Library, www.roswellufomuseum.com

Roswell Goddard Rocket Museum, 100 W Eleventh St, (505) 624-6744, Mon-Sat 9-5, Sun &
Holidays 1-5, Closed TD, CE, CD, Free Adm, Gift Shop, Planetarium, Contact Lori Roof
www.roswellmuseum.org   Rockets

UFO Enigma Museum, 6108 South Main, 88203-0828, Mon-Sat 9:30-5, Sun 12-5,
Adm Adult $1, Child $0.50

Santa Teresa - War Eagles Air Museum, 8012 Airport Rd, 88008, Santa Teresa Airport,
(505) 589-2000, Tue-Sun 10-4, Adm Adult $5, Snrs 65 & Mil $3, Child 5-12 $2, Under 5 Free,
Gift Shop, www.war-eagles-air-museum.com

A7-E	DH 82	J-3	PT-17
A-26C	F4U-4	L-13A	T-28B
AT-6F	F-84F	Link Trainer	T-33
AT-19	F-86 Mk VI	MiG-15UTi2Seater	T-38B
BT-13B	FJ-2	MiG-21PFM	Target Drone
C-5A Simulator	Fi-156	P-38L	TBM-3E
Cessna 140A	Globe Swift	P-40E	TU-2
CW Simulator	Great Lakes Sport	P-51D	
DC-3 (C-47A)	Hawker Sea Fury	P-51D(TF)	

NEW YORK

Albion - Vintage Aircraft Group, 4906 Pine Hill Rd, 14411, (585) 589-7758,
www.vintageaircraftgroup.org, Project Include: L-5G,   PT-19,   PT-26,   T-33

Bayport - Bayport Aerodome, Hangar 23 Vitamin Dr, POB 728, 11705, Jun-Sept Daily 10-4,
Adm Free, Gift Shop, www.bayportaerodrome.org

Aeronca C3	Fairchild F24	PT-19
Aeronca 7AC	Fleet 16B	PT-26
Aeronca 11AC	J-3Globe Swift	SE.5a
Auster AOP 6	N2S-3(V)	SVFC Ryershtahl
Brunner-Winkle Bird	N3N-3	Stearman
Cessna C-140	Nicholas-Beazley NB-86	Tiger Moth
Curtiss Robin	Piper Vagabond	Yak 12
DH 82C	PA-20	

Binghamton - Link Flight Simulation Corp, Colesville Rd, 13904, (607) 721-5465, Link Trainer

Brooklyn - Northeast Aircraft Restoration Facility & Museum, Floyd Bennett Field
(718) 338-3799, Mon, Thur & Sat 9-1,

A-4	DC-3	P2V
C-45	Fantasy Island Sea Plane	PBY
C-54	HU-16	SH-3A Helio

Buffalo - Amherst Museum, 3755 Towanda Rd, 14228, (716) 689-1440, Fax 689-1409, Aircraft

Buffalo & Erie County Historical Museum, 25 Nottingham Court, 14216, (716) 873-9644,
Tue-Sat 10-5, Sun 12-5, Adm Adult $6, Snrs 60 $5, Child $4, Under 6 Free, Gift Shop, Library,
www.bechs.org   J-1

NEW YORK

Buffalo & Erie County Naval & Military Park, 1 Naval Park Cove, 14202, (716) 847-1773,
Daily April 1-Oct 31 10-5, Nov Sat-Sun 10-4, Adm Adult $8.00, Snrs 60 & Child 6-16 $5,
www.buffalonavalpark.org,

F-101F	P-39Q "Snooks 2nd"	USS Little Rock (CLG-4)
FJ-4B	PTF-17 Boat	USS Croaker SSK-246
M-84 A.P.C.	UH-1H	USS Sullivans (DD-537)
M-41 Tank	X-RON 1	

Calverton - Grumman Memorial Park, I-495 Go W on Rte 25A(Edwards Ave)to Rte 25A,
Mail: POB 147, 11933, (631) 369-1826, Daily 9-5, Free ADm, Sec Patricia Wetering,
www.grummanpark.org, A-6E, F-14A

Coronia - New York Hall Of Science 47-01 111th St, 11368, (718) 699-0005,
Dir: Marily Hoyt, Atlas-Mercury Saturn V Boat Tail Titan II-Gemini

Elmira - National Soaring Museum, 51 Soaring Hill Dr, 14903-9204, (607) 734-3128,
Fax 732-6745, Daily 10-5, Adm Adult $6.50, Snrs 60 $5.50, Child 5-17 $4, Under 5 Free
Gift Shop, Sailplane Rides, www.soaringmuseum.org

Albatross	Hutter	SGS 1-19	Wright Glider #5
Baby Bowlus	Minimoa	SGS 26	
BG-12BD	Primary LNE-1	Teasdale	
CG-4A	Rigid Midget	TG-3A	

Farmingdale - American Airpower Museum, 1230 New Highway, (212) 843-8010
Thur-Sun 10:30-4, Adm Adult $9, Snr $6, Child $4, www.americanairpowermuseum.com

A6M	C-46	Me-109	PT-26
B-23	F-14	OH-13	SNJ
B-25	FG-1D	PBY-6A	TBM
B-29	I-16	PT-17	YO-55
C-45	L-2	PT-19	

Garden City - Cradle of Aviation Museum, Charles Lindbergh Ave, Mail: One Davis Ave, 11530,
(516) 572-4111, Fax 572-4065, Thue-Sun 9:30-5, Adm Adult $9, Snrs 62 & Child 2-12 $4, Cafe,
Gift Shop, IMAX Theater Adult $8.50, Snrs 62 & Child 2-14 $6.50, www.cradleofaviation.org

A-6F	F6F-5	TBM-3E
A-10A Cocpit	F9F-7	Veligdans Monerai
Aircraft Eng Co Ace	Fleet 2	Wright EX VinFiz
Bleriot-Queen XI	G-21	XRON-1
Boeing 707 Cockpit	G-63	Spacecraft, Missiles
Breese Penquin	Gyrodyne 2C	Convair/Sperry SAM-N-7
Brunner-Winkle Bird	JN-4	Douglas M-6 Nike Hercules
C-47 Simulator	Lilienthal	Fairchild Petrel
Cassutt B	Merlin Glider	Goddard A-Series Rocket
CG-4	NGT(T-46)	Grumman Missile Rigel
Commonwealth	OV-1B	Grumman Echo Cannister 7
Convertawings A	P-47N	Grumman AWS
Convair 340 Cockpit	Paramotor FX-1	Grumman LM Simulator
Curtiss Robin 50C	Peel Z-1 Glider	Grumman LM L-13, LTA-1
E-2C	QH-50C	Grumman LRV Molab
F-11A	RC-3	Grumman TBM
F-14A & Cockpit	Ryan B-1	Maxson AQM-37A Drone
F-84B	Ryan NYP	Maxson A6M-12C Bullpup
F-84F	S-56	Republic JB-2 Loon
F-105B	S2F & Cockpit	Republic Rocket Terrapin
F-105D Simulator	S4C	Rockwell Command Module
F3F	Sperry AT	Sperry SAM-N-7 Terrier
F4F-3	Sperry M1	Sputnik Satilite

NEW YORK

Geneseo - 1941 Historical Aircraft Group Museum, Geneseo Airport, 3489 Big Tree Lane, Mail: POB 185, 14454, (585) 243-2100, April-Sept Daily 10-4, Oct-March Mon, Wed, Fri 10-4, Closed TD, CD, ND, Adm Adult $4, Child 12 & Under $1, Restoration Facility, www.1941hag.org

AD-4W	C-47	L-16A	YO-55 (2ea)
AN-2 (2ea)	C-119G	L-17	
C-43	Ercoupe 415C	L-21B	
C-45H	L-2	Lancair Simulator	

Ghent - Parker-O' Malley Air Museum, 435 Old Rte 20, Columbia County Airport, Mail POB 216, 12075, (518) 392-7200, Fax 392-2408, By Appt only, Adm Adult $5, Child 5-12 $3, Under 5 Free, Contact James McMahon, www.parkeromalley.org

Fleet 2	Link Trainer	NE-1	Star Cavalier
Harvard IV	Me-108	PT-17 (Rides $75)	Travel Air 4000

Glenville - Empire State Aerosciences Museum,250 Rudy Chase Dr, Schenectady County Airport, 12302-4114, (518) 377-2191, Fax 377-1959, Fri-Sat- 10-4, Summer Same & Sun 12-4, Adm Adult $6, Snrs $5, Child 6-16 $2, Under 6 Free, Gift Shop, Library, Restoration Facility, O=Outdoors, D=Indoor Display, S=Storage, P=Project, www.esam.org,

A-4F	(O)	F-86D		MiG-21MF	(O)
A-6E	(O)	F-101F	(O)	Mooney Mite	(S)
A-7E	(P)	F-105G	(O)	RAND Kr-2	(S)
A-10	(O)	Fisher 303	(S)	RP-1	(D)
AKAGI Rep		GNAT	(O)	Sky Scooter Rep	(D)
C-47 (P)	(O)	H-1F(UH)	(O)	Sonerai II	(D)
C-123K	(O)	H-6A(LOH)		Starlite	(S)
Chanute Hang Glider(D)		Huntington Chum	(D)	Stits Skycoupe	(D)
Curtiss Pusher Rep (D)		J4 Javelin	(S)	STRAT M-21	(O)
F-4D II	(O)	L-3	(P)	T-38	
F-14A	(O)	Lockheed 10	(D)	AKAGI Aircraft Carrier Replica	
F-84F	(O)	MiG-17F	(O)		

Hammondsport - Curtiss Museum, 8419 Route 54, 14840, (607) 569-2160, Fax 569-2040, May 1-Oct 31 Mon-Sat 9-5, Sun 10-5, Nov 1-April 30, Mon-Sun 10-4, Closed ED, TD,CE,CD,ND, Adm Adult $7, Snrs 65 $4, Child 7-18 $4, Under 7 Free, Gift Shop, Library, Theater, Restoration Facility, www.glennhcurtissmuseum.org

AEA Glider	Curtiss E Boat	Doppelraab Glider	P-40 3/4 Scale
Baldwin Gondola	Curtiss June Bug	J-1	Silver Dart
C-46	Curtiss Oriole	JN-4D	Target Drone
Curtiss America	Curtiss Robin	Link Trainer (Proj) (2ea)	Travel Air D-4000
Curtiss A-1 Triad	Curtiss Seagull	Mercury S-1 Racer	OX-5 Engine
Curtiss D Pusher	Curtiss Wright Jr (2ea)	Mercury Chick	18 - Curtiss Motorcycles

Wings of Eagles Discovery Center, 17 Aviation Dr, Elmira-Corning Regional Airport, 14845, (607) 739-8200, Fax: 739-8374, Mon-Fri 10-4, Sat 10-4, Sun 12-4, Closed TD, CD, ND, Adm Adult $7, Snrs 65+ $5.50, Child 6-17 $4, Under 6 Free, Gift Shop, Snack Bar, Art Gallery, Theater, Restoration Facility, Airshow Third Weekend of September, www.wingsofeagles.com

A-7D	F-15B	H-1H(UH) 3ea	MiG 17
A-10A	F2H-2P	H-6A(OH)	MiG 21
A-37B	F4-B	HAR10	LNS-1(TG-2)
AIM/RIM-7	F9F-7	J-3C	OV-1C
AT-6D	F9F-BP	J-4B	PT-17(N2S-3)
B-26B	FH-1	L-3	PT-19B
B-57A(RB)	GAM77/AGM28	L-3B	R4D/C-47
BTD-1	H-1C(UH)	LNE-1(X)(HH-2)	TBM-3E
F-14A			

Jamestown - Lucille M Wright Air Museum, Airport, 14701, (716) 664-9500, Artifacts

Manhattan - Cockpit USA, 652 Broadway, 10012, (212) 254-4000, Mon-Sat 11-7:30, Sun 12-6:30 www.cockpitusa.com   C-45 Cockpit

NEW YORK

Mayville - Dart Airport, 6167 Plank Rd, POB 211, Route 430, 14757, (716) 753-2160,
Tue-Sun 10-Dusk, Free Adm, Gift Shop, Owner Bob Dart

Aeronca C-3	Ercoupe 415	J-3 (Rides Available)	SE-5a Replica
Bowlus Nelson Glider	Gyro Copter	Mead Primary	Swallow Monoplane
Curtiss Wright Jr	Heath Parasol	Pequin	Ultra Lights
Driggs Dart	Henderson Longster	Pou de Ceil	

w Windsor - Red Star Aviation Museum, 1188 First St, Bldg # 140, Stewart Int'l Airport, 12553
Mail: 8 Knollwood Rd, Hackettstown, NJ, 07840, General Inquiries: (908) 813-1398, www.redstaraviation.org

Casa	L-29	MiG-17	T-28
DH 100	L-39	MiG-21	T-33
Fouga	MiG-15	Provost Jet	Yak-52

New York City - Intrepid Sea-Air-Space Museum, **Closed until Fall 2008**, 1 Intrepid Plaza, Pier 86,
12th & 46th, 10036, (212) 245-0072, April 1-Sept 30 Mon-Fri 10-5, Sat-Sun 10-6, Oct 1-March 30
Tue-Sun 10-5, Closed TD, CD, ND, Adm Adult $10, Snr & Child 12-17 $7.50, 6-11 $5, 2-5 $1, Under 2 Free,
www.intrepidmuseum.org   OM = At Other Museum

A-3D	(OM)	F3D (TF-10B)		MiG-17	
A-4B		F6F-5 Rep	(OM)	M-42 Duster Tank	(OM)
A-4D		F9F		Neptune Submersible	(OM)
A-6A		FJ-3		RA-5C	(OM)
A-12		Gemini Capsule Rep		SB2C-4 Replica	(OM)
AH-1J		H-1A(UH)		S-2PE	(OM)
AV-8C		H-1M(UH)	(OM)	S-58D	(OM)
Apollo Capsule Rep	(OM)	H-3S(OH)	(OM)	SE5A	(OM)
Boeing 707 Cockpit	(OM)	H-19		Sea Hawk F.1	(OM)
Concorde		H-21C	(OM)	SP-2E	(OM)
Curtiss Pusher Rep	(OM)	H-34(UH)	(OM)	Supermarine Scimitar F1	
Demoiselle Rep	(OM)	H-52A(HH)		T-33A	(OM)
E-1B		HU-16E	(OM)	T-34	
F-3B		HUP-2		TS-2A	(OM)
F-3H		LEM Grumman	(OM)	TS-2E	
F-4N		Lunar Lander Rep	(OM)	TV-2	(OM)
F-14		H-13S(OH)		UH-340	(OM)
F-16		H-23(OH) (2 ea)	(OM)	Voisin Rep	
F-80F	(OM)	M-60 Patton Tank	(OM)	USS Intrepid	
F-84F	(OM)	Mercury Aurora7	(OM)	USS Growler	
F11F-1		MiG-15			

Niagara Falls - Niagara Aerospace Museum, 345 Third St, Mail POB 935, 14303,
(716) 278-0060, Fax 278-0257, Tue-Sun 10-4, Closed ND, TD, CD, ED, Adm Adult $7,
Snrs/Students $6, Child 5-18 $4, Under 5 Free, Gift Shop, Theater, Restoration Facility,
www.niagaramuseum.org

Bell 47B-3	F-94G	I-23	Pietenpol Air Camper
Bell 47H-1	GA-36	J-2	X-22A
Curtiss Robin	H-1F(AH)	JN-4D	
F-94A	H-1(UH)	P-39Q	

Niagara Falls ANG, Int'l Airport, 914 TAG/RMX, 14304-5000, (716) 236-2000

F-100D	F-101F	F-101C(RF)	F-4C

Plattsburg - Plattsburg AFB Military Museum, Route 22, 12901, (518) 565-5000, 565-5165,

B-47E	F-111

NEW YORK

Riverhead - Raceway Equipment, RD #2, BOX 92K, Horton Ave, 11901, (631) 727-6191,
Mon-Fri 8:30-4:30, Sat By Appt, President: Joe Gertler

Aeronca C-3	C-78(UC)	L-19	Taylorcraft BC-12D
Birdwing Imperial	Emigh Trojan	Luscombe 8E	
Bleriot Original	J-3	Nieuport 27	

Talmage Field Aircraft Collection, Friars Head Farm, 36 Sound Ave, (631) 727-0124, John Talmage

Aeronca Champ	Hispano-Suiza	Rearwin Cloudster	Curtiss J6-7
Burnner CK Bird	Hovercraft	Travel Air 4000	Curtiss OX5 Engine
Fokker D VII Project	Quick Kit Seaplane	Continental R670	Curtiss OXX6 Engine

Rhinebeck - Old Rhinebeck Aerodrome, 44 Stone Church Rd, Mail: BOX 229, 12572
(845) 752-3200, Fax: 758-6481, May 15-Oct31, Daily 10-5, Adm Adult $10, Snrs 65 & Child 13-17 $8
Child 6-10 $3, Under 6 Free, June 15-Oct 15 Sat-Sun Airshows 2pm, Adult $20, Snrs 65 &
Child 13-17 $15, Child 6-10 $5, Gift Shop, Cafe, Restoration Viewing,
1929 New Standard Biplane Rides 15 Min $50 Per Person, www.oldrhinebeck.org/,
(1)=Pioneer Bldg, (2)=WW I Bldg,(3)=Lindberg Era Bldg, (4)=New Bldg,
(F)=On Field, (EF)=EastSide of Field.

Aeromarine 39B	(Pieces)	Fleet Finch 16B	(F)	Nieuport 2N	(1)
Aeromarine Klemm	(3)	Fokker D.VIII	(F)	Passett Ornithopter	(1)
Aeronca C-3	(F)	Fokker D.VII (2ea)	(F)	PHSC Scout	
Albatross D-Va	(2)	Fokker Dr.I (3ea)	(2,F)	Pietenpol Air Camper	(F)
Albree Pigeon Fras.	(2)	FOkker E.III	(Stored)	Piper Vagabond	(EF)
American Eagle	(4)	Great Lakes T21MS	(F)	Pitcairn Mailwing	(3)
Ansaldo Ballila SVA-5	(2)	Gyrodyne 2B Chopper	(4)	Rabkaatsentein Glider	(2)
Avro 504-K	(F)	Handriot HD1	(F)	RAF FE.8	(2)
Bleriot XI (3ea)	(1,4,F)	Heath-Parasol LNA	(3)	RAF BE.2C (2ea)	(EF)
Boeing-Stearman	(F)	Howard DGA-15P	(EF)	Ryan NYP	(1)
Breguet 1911	(Pieces)	J-1	(Pieces)	Short S-29	(1)
Brunner Bird CK	(3)	J-2	(F)	Siemens-Schucker DIII	(2)
Bucker Jungmann		J-3	(EF)	Sopwith Camel	(2)
Caudron G.III	(F)	J-5A	(EF)	Sopwith Dolphin	(2)
Chanute Glider	(1)	JN-4D	(F)	Spad XIII C1	(4)
Curtiss Wright CW-1	(F)	Luscombe 8A	(EF)	Spartan C-3	(3)
Curtiss Pusher D (2ea)	(F)	Monocoupe 113	(3)	Stampe SV-4B	(F)
Curtiss Fledgling	(F)	Monocoupe 90	(3)	Taylor E-2	(Shop)
Davis DIW	(F)	Morane Saulnier MS130	(3)	Thomas Pusher E	(1)
Demoiselle (2ea)	(4F)	Morane Saulnier A-1	(4)	Thomas-Morse S4.B	(2)
Deperdussin (2ea)	(1)	Morane Saulnier N	(2)	Voisin 8 Bomber	(4)
DH-80A		New Standard D-25(4ea)	(F)	Waco 10	(3)
DH-82 (3ea)	(EF)	New Standard D-29(2ea)	(4F)	Waco 9	
Dickerson Glider	(3)	Nicholas Beasley	(3)	Wright Glider	(1)
Ercoupe	(EF)	Nieuport 11	(F)	Wright Flyer	(1)
Fairchild 24-C8F	(4)	Nieuport 10/83	(2)		

Rome - Griffiss AFB Museum, Mohawk Valley B-52 memorial, 13441-5000,
Contact: Henry P Smith Post 24, 325 Erie Vlvd W, 13440, (315) 336-2680,
www.borg.com/~post24/monument.html, B-52G

Shirley - Brookhaven L.I. Airport, Dwn Dr, 11967, (631) 281-5100

Convair 240	Me-109	Swift GC-1 Globe
Erocoupe F-1 (Fornaire)	SNJ-4	

Warbirds Over Long Island, Brookhaven Calabro Airport (HWV), 11967, Gift Shop,
www.warbirdsoverlongisland.com

P-40E	P-51D	PT-17	SNJ-5

National Aviation & Transportation Center, Dowling College Annex, Brookhaven Airport,
Pitts Special   PT-17   PT-26

NEW YORK

Syracuse - Syracuse ANGB, Hancock Field, 13211-7099, (315) 458-5500,

F-86H	F-94B	F-102A

Syracuse Airport Exhibit, I-81, Hancock Int'l Airport, Center Lobby Main Floor, Artifacts, Cafe

Williamsville - Niagara Frontier Aviation & Space Museum, 5583 Main St,
Municipal Bldg, 14221, (716) 631-3276, Vice Chairman: Jack Prior

NORTH CAROLINA

Asheboro - North Carolina Aviation Museum, 2222-G Pilots View Rd, 27204, Mail: POB 1814,
27204-1814, (336) 625-0170, Fax 625-2984, Mon-Sat 10-5, Sun 1-5, Adm Adult $5,
Students $3, Child Under 6 Free, Grp Rates, Gift Shop, Restoration Facility,
Airshow 1st Weekend in June, www.ncairmuseum.org

AT-6G	J-3 Flitfire	P-3 Pilatus	TBM-3E
BT-13A	L-4	PT-13D	
C-45H	L-19A	T-28B	
F-84F	O-2A 2ea	T-34A	

Candler - Enka Junior High School, 475 Enka Lake Rd, 28715, (828) 667-5421, F-84F(RF)

Charlotte - Carolinas Aviation Museum, 4108 Minuteman Way, Charlotte/Douglas Int'l Airport,
28208, (704) 359-8442, Fax 359-0057,
Tue-Sat 10-4, Sun 1-5, Adm Adult $3, Snrs $2, Gift Shop, Restoration Facility
www.carolinasaviation.org

A-4	F-14D	HOK-1	T-28 Cockpit
A-7E2	F-84G-30RE	J-3	T-28B
A-26C	F-86L	L-19	T-33 Cockpit
AV-8B-1	F-100D	Link Trainer	T-33A
Bellanca 14-9L	F-101B	Long Midget Mustang	T-33B
C-47 (2ea)	F-102(YF)	Mercury Capsule rep	Wright Glider (At Airport)
C-97(KC) Cockpit	Goodyear Racer	OV-1D (2ea)	
CG-15A	H-1H(UH)	P-80	**Missiles**:
DC-3	H-1J(AH)	PT-17(N2S)	AIM-54
Douglas D-558-1	H-34C(CH)	Hal Fogle V33 Skycat	MGR1B
Ercoupe 415-C	H-46E(QH)	Sikorsky Green Giant	SSM-N-8R egulasa
F-4S (Cockpit)	H-50C(QH)	SNJ-5C	TM-61C
F-4S	HO3S-1	T-2A	M551A Tank

Charlotte ANG, Charlotte/Douglas Municipal Airport, 28208, 145 TAG/CC
(704) 399-6363, 145th TAG,   F-86L

Cherry Point - Cherry Point Marine Base, Pres Edward Ellis, (252) 447-2346, F-4U   PBY

Dunn - General Williams C Lee Airborne Museum, 209 W Drive St, (910) 892-1947,
Mon-Fri 10-4, Sat 11-4, Free Adm, Artifacts, www.generalleeairbornemuseum.org

Fayetteville - 82nd Airborne Division War Memorial Museum, Fort Bragg, Bldg C-6841 Ardennes St
28307-0119, (910) 432-3443, Tue-Sun 10-4:30, Free Adm, Gift Shop 436-1735, Theater,
www.bragg.army.mil/18abn/museums.htm

C-7	C-47B	C-123K	CG-15A
C-46F	C-119L	C-130E	H-1A(UH)

Airborne & Special Operations Museum, 100 Bragg Blvd, From I-95, 28301, (866) 547-0649,
Tue-Sat 10-5, Sun 12-5, Closed ED, TD, CD, ND, Free Adm, www.asomf.org,

C-47A	CG-4A	H-6J(AH)	H-1(UH)	M551 Tank

NORTH CAROLINA

Fayetteville - John F Kennedy Special Warfare Museum, Ardennes & Marion St, Bldg D-2502, (910) 432-4272, Tue-Sun 11:30-4

Pope AFB, Main (Reilly Gate), 28308, (910) 394-0001, L= Located Off Hwy 23 FW Ramp

A-7D (L)	A-10A(OA) (L)	C-119	F-105D (L)
A-10A (L)	C-47B	C-123K	P-40

Goldsboro - Seymour Johnson AFB, 4th Wing HQ Wright Brothers Ave, 27531-5000, (919) 736-5400,

F-4C	F-15B/E	F-86H	F-105D
F-4E	F-15E	F-86E	P-51D

Havelock - Cherry Point Marine Corps Air Station, Hwy 70 & Cuningham Blvd, 28533-5001, 2 Hour Tour 1st & 3rd Thur ea Month at 8:45am, Adm Free, (252) 466-5895,   AV-8

Havelock Tourist Center, 202 Tourist Cntr Dr, 28532, (252) 444-6402, Mail: POB 368

A-4M	F4B-3	F9F-6P	RF-4B

Hendersonville - Western North Carolina Air Museum, 1340 Gilbert St, (828) 698-2482, Mail POB 2343, 28793, All Year Wed & Sun 12-5, April-Oct Sat 10-5, Nov-March 12-5, Free Adm, Gift Shop, Pres: Stuart W MacRoberts, www.wncairmuseum.com   Project=(P)

Aeronca C-3	Curtiss Robin 4C-1A	J-3C	SE-5
Aeronca 7DC Champ	E-2	J-5	SNJ-5
BC-12D Taylorcraft(P)	Ercoupe 415CD	L-2	Stearman N2S
Cessna 120	Heath Parasol (P)	Nieuport Bebe 11	Stearman N4S
Corbin Junior Ace	J-2	PA-12	Wittman Tailwind W-8

Hickory - Hickory Aviation Museum, 1301 9th Ave Dr NW, 28601, Tanya Sharp Airport, May-Oct Mon-Fir 9-4, (828) 328-4078, Pres Jeff Wooford, www.hickoryaviationmuseum.org

A-7A	F-4B	F-105B	HA-200(Me-200)
DH-100	F-14D	FJ-3M	T-33A

Kill Devil Hills - Wright Brothers National Memorial, Mile Post 7.5 US 158(Croaton Hwy) & E Ocean Bay Blvd, (252) 441-7430, Mail: POB 1903, 27948, Sept-May Daily 9-5, June-Aug 9-6 Adm Adult $4, Wright Brothers Landmark, www.nps.gov/wrbr/index.htm,

Kure - NC Military History Museum, NC National Guard Training Facility, 116 Air Force Way, 28449 (910) 251-7325, Fri-Sun 12-5, Closed Holidays, Adm Free, Gift Shop, UH-1, Tank, Howitzer

Manteo - Wright Brothers National Memorial, POB 457, 27954, Virginia Dare Trail-By Pass, (252) 441-4481, Daily 8-8, Free Adm, Wright Flyer, Glider

Maxton - Gulledge Aviation, Laurin-Maxton Airport, (910) 844-3601, Jetliner Salvage

Raleigh - North Carolina Museum of History, 5 E Edenton St, 27601-1011, Mail 4650 Mamil Service Center, 27699-4650, (919) 807-7900, Fax 733-8655, Tue-Sat 9-5, Sun 12-5, Free Adm, Gift Shop 807-7835, www.ncmuseumofhistory.org, B-8M Bensen Gyrocopter, Rogallo Wing, Wright Flyer Replica

Southern Pines - CAF - Carolinas Wing, Moore County Airport, Second Sun Monthly 1:00pm www.carolinaswing.org, AT-19

NORTH DAKOTA

Casselton - Aero Replicas, Casselton Regional Airport, 58012, (701) 347-4680, 2½ Mi S of City, Mail: POB 64, email: RJM1003@acol.com, Daily 8-5, Bf-109 Replica   F-4C   Pitts S-1-C

NORTH DAKOTA

Fargo - Fargo Air Museum, 1609 19th Ave N, 58109, (701) 293-8043, Fax 293-8103
Tue-Sat 9-5, Sun 12-4, Closed E, TD, CD, ND, Adm Adult $6, Snrs 60 & Mil $5, Child 5-12 $4,
Under 5 Free, Gift Shop, Restoration Facility, www.fargoairmuseum.org

A6M2 Model 21	F2G-1D	LNE-1	Standard
AT-6	F4U	P-40	T-28A
B-25	L-5	P-51D	TBM
Beech D17	L-6	PT-17	
DC-3	L-19A(O-1)	PT-19	

Fargo ANG, Hector Field, 58105-5536, (701) 237-6030,

C-45J	F-16A	F-101B	F-104C
C-47B	F-89J	F-101F	P-51D
F-4D	F-94C	F-102A	

Grand Forks - Center For Aerospace Sciences, Box 8216, Univ Station, 58202
(701) 777-2791, Project Officer: Lt Col Terry Young

Grand Forks AFB Heritage Center, Building 125, 58205, (701) 747-6924, 319BW

A-26C	F-101B	H-19D	Transporter Erector
B-25J	F-102A	Minuteman III	
B-52G	H-1F(U)		

Minot - Dakota Territory Air Museum, Minot Int'l Airport, Mail: POB 195, 58702-0195
(701) 852-8500, May-Oct Mon-Sat 10-5, Sun 1-5, Adm Adult $2, Child 6-17 $1
www.dakotaterritoryairmuseum.com, email fhg1961@minot.com

A-7	Ercoupe	Starduster Two
Arrow Sport	J-2	T-33
Arrow Monoplane	J-3	Taylorcraft
Breezy Open Cockpit	L-29	Travel-Aire 3000
Breezy RL-1	Monocoupe 110	Veri-ezee
C-47 Cockpit	P-40	Volks Plane
C-47	Pietenpol	Waco GXE
Cessna 195	SR-5A	Waco UPF-7

Minot AFB, 919 MW/CVS58705, (701) 727-4761,

F-102A	F-106A	H-1F(UH)	T-33A

Wahpeton - Tri State Aviation, Restoration & Serv ice of Military Aircraft, Wahpeton Airport,
(701) 642-5777, Mon-Fri 8-5, These are Past Project,

West Fargo - Eagles Air Museum, Bonanzaville USA, 1351 Main Ave W, 58078
(701) 282-2822, May Mon-Fri 9-5, June-Sept Mon-Sat 10-5, Sun 12-5, Closed Oct-May,
Adm Adult $6.50, Child 6-16 $3.50, Under 6 Free, Gift Shop, Facility Rental, www.bonanzaville.com
Over 40 Hisotic buildings or Museums in Area, Locomotive Train

A-26B	C-45H	Hawker Hunter Mk.51	Pitts S-1
BG-12	C-47	J-1	PRG-1
Bowers Fly Baby	Curtiss Pusher D III	J-3-F-65	PT-19A
Breeze	F-4C	McKinnie 165	Stits SA-3-B
BT-13	H-1(UH)	Pietenpol Air Camper	Swallow OX5

OHIO

Akron - Goodyear World of Rubber, 1144 E. Market St, 4th Floor, 44316, (330) 796-2121
Daily 8:30-4:30, Free Adm,   FG-1D Fuse

Alliance - Alliance High School, 400 Glamorgan St, 44601, (330) 821-2100, A-7

Batavia - Tri-State Warbird Museum, 4021 Borman Dr, 45103, (513) 735-4500, Fax 735-4333
Wed 4-7, Sat 10-3, www.tri-statewarbirdmuseum.org

AT-6D	FG-1D	P-40M	Stearman 75
B-25	Link ANT-18	P-51D	TBM-3

OHIO

Bryan - Military Heritage Museum, American Legion Post 284, 519 E. Butler St
43506, (419) 636-7354, By Appt, Artifacts all Wars

Carroll - Historical Aircraft Squadron, 3266 Old Columbus Dr, 43112, (740) 653-4778, Fax 653-2387
Wed, Sat 9-5, Gift Shop, Restoration Facility, www.historicalaircraftsquadron.com,
A-26 Project   BT-13 Project

Cincinnati - Blue Ash Airport, B-17E "My Gal Sal" Restoration from Greenland
Contact: Bob Ready, Exec Aviation, 4393 Glendale Milford Rd, 45242, (513) 984-3881,
www.ultimatesacrifice.com,   E-mail: bob_ready@hotmail.com

Cincinnati Warbirds EAA Squaron 18, 5823 Wooster Pike, 45227, First Thur Eve Monthly
N39-06.2, W084-2.12, www.cincinnatiwarbirds.org

AT-6	T-28	T-34B
L-17A	T-34A	TS-11

123rd Air Control Squadron, 10649 McKinley Rd, 45242, A-7D

Lunken Airport Benefit Assoc, 4510 Airport Rd, 45226-0156, Mail: POB 26156, (513) 321-4291, F-86H

Cleveland - Burke Lakefront Airport, Marjorie Rosenaum Plaza, 1501 Marginal Rd, 44100,
(216) 781-6411,   F-4J   F-4E

Frederick Crawford Auto-Aviation Museum, 10825 E Blvd, (216) 721-5722, Mon-Sat 10-5, Sun 12-5,
Adm Adult $8.50, Snrs $7.50, Child $5, Under 6 Free, Library, www.wrhs.org/crawford

Cessna 182P	DGA-3	Gee Bee R-1 Rep
Chester Special	DH-4	Great lakes 2T-1A
Curtiss Bumblebee	F2G-2D	P-51K
Curtiss MF	Fulton Airphibian	Weddell-Williams Special

International Women's Air & Space Museum, Inc, Burke Lakefront Airport, Room 165,
1501 N Marginal Rd, 44114, (216) 623-1111, Fax: 623-1113, Mon-Fri 10-4, Free Adm,
Gift Shop, www.iwasm.org, Smith Mini Plane, Artifacts

NASA John H Glen Research Center, 21000 Brookpark Rd, MS 8-1, 44135,
 (216) 433-4000, Mon-Fri 9-4, Sat 10-3, Sun 1-5, Free Adm,
www.nasa.gov/centers/glenn/about/visitgrc.html   Apollo Skylab III Command Module

Columbus - CAF - Ohio Valley Wing, 2000 Norton Rd, Bolton Field, 43228, Second Sun Monthly 2:00
www.cafohio.org, L-5(OY-2)

Center of Science & Industry, 333 W Broad St, 43215, (614) 221-2674,
Wed-Sat 10-5, Sun 12-6, Fri 10-9, Adm Adult $12.50, Snrs $10.50, Child 2-12 $7.50, Under 2 Free,
www.cosi.org PT-12   Mercury Capsule

Columbus DCSC, 3990 E Broad St, 43213, (614) 238-3131, www.dscc.dla.mil   F-100D

OHIO

Dayton - Carillon Historical Park, 1000 Carillon Blvd, 45409, (937) 293-2841, March 31-Oct 31
Mon-Sat 9:30-5, Sun 12-5, Closed TD, CE, CD, NE, ND, Adm Adult $8, Snrs $7, Child 3-17 $5,
Under 3 Free, www.carillonpark.org, Wright Flyer, Six Trains

Dayton Aviation Heritage National Historical Park, 22 S Williams St, 45407, (937) 225-7705
Daily 8:30-5, Closed TD, CD, ND, www.nps.gov/daav   Wright Flyer III

Museum of Pioneer Aviation and Wright Brother's Aeroplane Company, PO Box 204
45383, 4th & Ludlow St (Wilkies Bookstore), www.first-to-fly.com
Replica Wright Flyer 1 & 3

National Aviation Hall of Fame, 1100 Spaatz St, WPAFB, 45433,Mail: POB 31096,
45437, (937) 256-0944, Daily 9-5, Closed: TD, CD, ND, ED, Adm Free, www.nationalaviation.org
Artifacts

National Museum of the US Air Force, 1100 Spaatz St, Wright-Patterson AFB, 45433-7102,
(937) 255-3286, Daily 9-5, Closed TD, CD, ND, Free Adm, Annex Hours Daily 9:30-3,
IMAX Theater (937) 253-IMAX, Gift Shop, Library, www.nationalmuseum.af.mil,

(Gallery Aircraft is in it to the Left of the Aircraft Name)

A-10	Cold War	C-118A(VC)	Presidential
A-17	Early Years	C-119J	Air Park
A-1E	Modern Flight	C-121D(EC)	Modern Flight
A-1H	Storage	C-121E(VC)	Presidential
A-20G	Air Power	C-123K	Modern Flight
A-24B	Air Power	C-124C	Modern Flight
A-26A(K)	Modern Flight	C-125B(YC)	Air Park
A-26C	Modern Flight	C-130A(AC)	On Exhibit
A-36A	Air Power	C-130A(AC)	Cold War
A-37A(YA)	Modern Flight	C-131D	Air Park
A-48(PA)	R&D	C-133A	Cold War
A6M2	Air Power	C-135A(NKC)	Air Park
A-7D	Modern Flight	C-135E(EC)	Air Park
Albatros DVA Rep	Storage	C-137C(VC)	Presidential
Avro 504K Rep	Early Years	C-140B(VC)	Presidential
B-10	Early Years	C-141C	Air Park
B-17F	Restoration	C-142A(XC)	R&D
B-17G	Air Power	C-39	Storage
B-18A	Air Power	C-43(UC)	Air Power
B-1B	Cold War	C-45H	Presidential
B-2	Cold War	C-46D	Air Power
B-23	Storage	C-47D	Air Power
B-24D	Air Power	C-54C(VC)	Presidential
B-25D	Air Power	C-60A	Air Park
B-25D	Modern Flight	C-61J(UC)	Presidential
B-26G	Air Power	C-64A(UC)	Air Power
B-29	Air Power	C-6A(VC)	Presidential
B-36J	Cold War	C-78B(UC)	Air Power
B-45C	Modern Flight	C-7A	Modern Flight
B-47E	Storage	C-82A	Air Park
B-47H(RB)	Cold War	C-97L(KC)	Cold War
B-50D(WB)	Cold War	CA 36	Early Years
B-57B(EB)	Modern Flight	Camel F.1 Rep	Early Years
B-57D(RB)	Cold War	Casa 2.111H (He-111H)	Storage
B-58A	Cold War	Casa 352L (JU 52)	Air Park
B-66B(RB)	Modern Flight	CF-100 Mk.IV	Cold War
B-70A(XB)	R&D	Corben Super Ace	Storage
Beaufighter	Air Power	Curtiss Pusher Rep	Early Years
Bird of Prey	Modern Flight	DH-4B	Early Years
Bleriot	Early Years	DH-82A	Early Years

Aircraft	Category	Aircraft	Category
DH-89B	R&D	G-4A(CG)	Air Power
DH-98B	Air Power	G-4A(TG)	Air Power
Ercoupe 415	Storage	H-13J(UH)	Presidential
F-100D	Presidential	H-16B(UH)	Cold War
F-100F	Modern Flight	H-19B(UH)	Modern Flight
F-101B	Cold War	H-1F(GUH)	Storage
F-101C(RF)	Modern Flight	H-1P(UH)	Modern Flight
F-102A	Cold War	H-20(XH)	R&D
F-104A	Outdoors	H-21B(CH)	Cold War
F-104C	Cold War	H-26(XH)	Restoration
F-105D	Modern Flight	H-3E(CH)	Modern Flight
F-105G	Modern Flight	H-43F(HH)	Modern Flight
F-106A	Cold War	H-5A(YH)	Modern Flight
F-107A(YF)	R&D	Halberstadt CL IV	Early Years
F-111A(EF)	Cold War	Hurricane Mk.IIA	Early Years
F-111A(EF)	Modern Flight	J-1	Early Years
F-111F	Cold War	J-1	Early Years
F-117A(YF)	Cold War	J2F-6(OA-12)	Early Years
F-12A(YF)	R&D	J-3C-65-8	On Exhibit
F-15A	R&D	JN-4D	Early Years
F-15A	Cold War	JU-88D-1	Air Power
F-16A	Cold War	Kellett K-2	Early Years
F-16A(NF)	R&D	Kittyhawk	Air Power
F-22A(YF)	Modern Flight	L-17A	Modern Flight
F-23A(YF)	Storage	L-1A	Modern Flight
F-4C	Modern Flight	L-26C(U-4B)	Presidential
F-4C(RF)	Cold War	L-2M	Air Power
F-4D	Storage	L-3B	Air Power
F-4D	Storage	L-4A	Air Power
F-4E(YF)	R&D	L-5	Air Power
F-4G	Cold War	L-6	Air Power
F-5A(YF)	Modern Flight	LC-126	Cold War
F-80C	Modern Flight	Luscombe 8A	Storage
F-80R(XP)	R&D	MB-2 Rep	Early Years
F-81(ZXF)	Storage	MC 200	Air Power
F-81(ZXF)	Storage	Me-109G-10	Air Power
F-82B	Modern Flight	Me-163B	Air Power
F-84E	Modern Flight	Me-262A	Air Power
F-84F(YRF)	R&D	MiG-15	Modern Flight
F-84F(YRF)	Cold War	MiG-17C	Modern Flight
F-84H(XF)	R&D	MiG-19S	Cold War
F-84K(RF)	Cold War	MiG-21	Modern Flight
F-85(XF)	R&D	MiG-21F	Modern Flight
F-86 Parts	Storage	MiG-23	Cold War
F-86A	Modern Flight	MiG-23K	Cold War
F-86D	Cold War	MiG-25	Storage
F-86F(RF)	Cold War	MiG-29A	Restoration
F-86H	Cold War	MXY7-K1 (Ohka II)	Air Power
F-89J	Cold War	Mystere IV A	Storage
F-90(XF)	Storage	N1K2-J	Restoration
F-91(XF)	R&D	Nieuport 28 Rep	Early Years
F-92A(XF)	R&D	O-1G	Modern Flight
F-94A	Modern Flight	O-2A	Modern Flight
F-94C	Cold War	O-38F	Early Years
FA-330A-1	Air Power	O-46A	Storage
Fi-156	Air Power	O-47B	Early Years
Fokker DR-1 Rep	Early Years	O-52	Early Years
Fokker D-VII	Early Years	OV-10A	Modern Flight
FW-190D-9	Air Power	P-12E	Early Years
G-32(TG)	Storage	P-26A Rep	Early Years
G-3A(TG)	Air Power	P-35	Air Power
G-3A(TG)	Storage	P-36A	Air Power

P-38L	Air Power	U-6A	Cold War
P-39Q	Air Power	V-3A(XV)	Restoration
P-47D	Air Power	V-6A(XV)	R&D
P-47D	Air Power	Wright Flyer Rep	Early Years
P-51D	Air Power	Wright Model B	Modern Flight
P-59B	R&D	X-13	R&D
P-61C	Air Power	X-15A	Missile
P-63E	Air Power	X-19	Storage
P-6E	Early Years	X-1B	R&D
P-75A	Restoration	X-24A	Missile
Packard-Lepere Lusac	Early Years	X-25A	R&D
PBY-5A(OA-10)	Air Power	X-29A	R&D
Q-14B(PQ)	Modern Flight	X-3	R&D
R-4B	Air Power	X-32A	Storage
R-6A	Air Power	X-4	R&D
SE-5E	Early Years	X-5	R&D
Spad VII	Early Years		
Spad XIII	Early Years		
Spitfire Mk VC	Air Power	Aerojet Aerobee Rocket	
Spitfire Mk XI	Air Power	Agena Space Vehicle	
SR-71A	Cold War	Apollo 15 Command Module	
ST-1A(YPT-16)	Early Years	ASV-3 ASSET Lifting Body	
SU-22M4	Storage	Block IV Satellite	
SV-5J(X-24A)	Missile	Discoverer XIV Satellite	
T-1(PT)	Early Years	DSP Satellite	
T-10(AT)	Air Power	EROS Reflector Satellite	
T-11(AT)	Air Power	Excelsior Gondola	
T-13B(BT)	Air Power	Gemini Spacecraft	
T-13D(PT)	Air Power	LGM-30G Minuteman III	
T-19A(PT)	Early Years	LGM-118A Peacekeeper	
T-22(PT)	Air Power	LGM-30B Minuteman I	
T-26(PT)	Storage	LRSED Model Satellite	
T-28A(JT-28A)	Cold War	LTV ASAT Missile	
T-28B	M	Manhigh II Gondola	
T-33A	Cold War	Mercury Spacecraft	
T-33A(NT)	R&D	Northrop OV2-5 Space Satellite	
T-34A	Cold War	PGM-11A Redstone	
T-37B	Cold War	SM-68B/LGM-25C Titan II	
T-38B(AT)	Cold War	SM-65 Atlas	
T-39A	Presidential	SM-78/PGM-19A Jupiter	
T-41A	Cold War	SM-75/PGM-17A Thor	
T-46A	Storage	SM-68A/HGM-25A Titan I	
T-6D	Modern Flight	Stargazer Gondola	
T-9(AT)	Air Power	SV-5D PRIME Lifting Body	
T-9B(BT)	Early Years	TACSAT I Satellite	
Tacit Blue	R&D	Teal Ruby Satellite	
Thomas Morse S.4C	Early Years	Thor Agena A Missile	
Tornado GR1	Cold War	X-15A-2	
U-10D	Modern Flight	X-24B Martin	
U-2A	Cold War	X-24A Martin	
U-3A	Cold War	X-17 Lockheed	
		X-20A Dyna-Soar	

Elyria - CAF - Cleveland Wing, Lorain Cnty Reginal Airport, 44050 Russia Rd, 44035
(440) 323-8335, Sat 9:30-4, www.clevelandwing.org   SNJ-4

Fairborn - Wright-Patterson Material Command Headquarters, 4375 Chidlaw Rd, Bldg 262, 45433
F-15   F-16

OHIO

Groveport - Motts Military Museum, Inc, 5075 S Hamilton Rd, 43125, (614) 836-1500
Fax 836-5110, Tue-Sat 9-5, Sun 1-5, Adm Adult $5, Seniors $4, Student $3
www.mottsmilitarymuseum.org,

A-10	M42A1 Tankù	PA 36-7 Higgins Boat
H-1(AH)	M47 Tank	M110A2 Howitzer
Apollo 13 Module	M151 Jeep	105mm Iraq Cannon

Lockbourne - Rickenbacker ANGB, 7370 Minuteman Way, 43217-5875, 121st ARW/PA
(800) 377-5570, www.ohcolu.ang.af.mil

A-7D 2ea	F-14	F-100D	T-33A
C-131E(TC)	F-15A	O-2A	
F-4C(RF)	F-84F	P-80C	

Madison - Charles F Reed, 5782 Trask Rd, 44057, (440) 298-1314, Appt Only

Aeronca Champ (2 ea)	Fokker Dr.I	Piper J-5	Stinson 108
Bowers Flybaby	Luscombe	PT-22	
Fleet Model 2	OTK Myers	Smith Miniplane	

Miamisburg - Wright B Flyer Museum, 10550 Springboro Pike, Dayton- Wright Brothers Airport
(Dayton General Airport), 45342, (937) 885-2327, Tue,Thur,Sat 9-2:30,
Closed Holidays, www.wright-b-flyer.org, Wright B Flyer Flyable Rides for $150

Mansfield - Mansfield ANG, Mansfield Lahm Airport, 1947 Harrington Memorial Rd, 44903
(419) 520-6377, www.ohmans.ang.af.mil   F-84F

North Canton - Army Aviation Support Facility # 1, 5989 Airport Dr NW, 44720, AH-1S

Maps Air Museum, 2260 Int'l Pkwy, 44720, (330) 896-6332, Mon-Tue,Thur-Sat 9-4, Wed 9-9,
Closed Holidays, Adm Adult $7, Seniors 55 $6, Child Under 12 $4, Under 5 Free, Gift Shop,
www.mapsairmuseum.org,   (UR) = Under Restoration   (S) = Storage

A-7E	F-100D	L-2D	P-51
AT-19(V-77)	F-101B	L-17B	PT-19
B-26(UR)	F-102D	Link Trainer 2ea	S-2F
C-47B(UR)	F-105B	Martin Glider 1908	SBD-5 (UR)
F-4S	H-1B(UH) (S)	MiG-17F (UR)	SNB-5 (UR)
F-11	H-1S(AH)	O-2A	T-28S (S)
F-14B	H-58(OH)	P-39Q (2ea)(UR)(S)	

Norwalk - Firelands Museum of Military History, 4755 SR601, (419) 668-8161,
Mail: c/o Richard Rench, 202 Citizens Bank Bldg, 448547, www.huey.org
UH-1H,(Rides Available), AH-1A, Tanks: M-42, M-60; APC Fort T-16, Mark VII Ferrett
(UH-1H 2ea in Storage 961, 20 East Norwalk Airport)

Springfield - OH ANG, Springfield ANG, 178th FW, Springfield-Beckley Mncpl Airport,
706 Regula Ave, 45502-8783, (937) 327-2100, A-7D,   F-84C,   F-84F,   F-100D

Swanton - Toledo ANG, Toledo Express Airport, 2660 S Eber Rd, 43558, (419) 868-4180,
www.ohtole.ang.af.mil   F-84F F-100D

Trotwood - Wright Stuff Squadron - CAF, Dahio Airport (I44), 1334 N Lutheran Church Rd
45427, (937) 248-4777, Third Sat Monthly 12:00, www.wrightstuffsquadron.com, UC-78(T-50)

Troy - Waco Aircraft Museum & Aviation Learning Center, 105 S. Market St, 45373, Mail: POB 62
(937) 335-9226, May-Oct Sun 1-5, Gift Shop, www.wacoairmuseum.org, Junkin Brukner
Waco: CG-4A,   ATO,   CTO,   Glider,   UPF-7W,   YMF,

Wapakoneta - Armstrong Air & Space Museum, 500 S Apollo Dr, 43211, Mail: POB 1978,
45895-0978, (419) 738-8811, (800) 860-0142, Tue-Sat 9:30-5, Sun 12-5, Closed TD, CD, ND,
Adult $7, Child 6-12 $3, Under 6 Free, www.ohiohistory.org/places/armstron

Aerobat	F5D-1	Wright Model G
Aeronca 7AC	Gemini VIII	

OKLAHOMA

Altus - Altus AFB, 73523-5000, (580) 482-8100, 443rd MAW, 47th FTW, C-118B, T-34B

Bartlesville - Woolaroc Museum, 1925 Willow Rock Ranch Rd, Mail POB 1647,74005, (918) 336-0308, Wed-Sun 10-5, Adm Adult $8, 12 Under Free, www.woolaroc.org   Woolaroc Airplane

Vance AFB, 73705-5000, (580) 237-2121, 71st FTW, F-105D   T-28A   T-33A

Bethany - Oklahoma Museum of Flying, 7110 Millionaire Dr, 73008, AD-1,   L-39,   P-51

Fort Sill - US Army Field Artillery & Fort Sill Museum, 437 Quanah Rd, 73503-5100, (580) 422-5123, Tue-Sat 8:30-5:00, Closed TD, CD, ND, Free Adm, http://sill-www.army.mil/Museum/Home_Page.htm

H-1B(OH)	L-4	T-41B	
H-23F(OH)	L-19	Missile Park	

Guymon - CAF Cimarron Strip Wing, POB 64, 73942, (580) 338-7700, C-45

Lexington - Citizen Potawatomee Territory, Hwy 59 West, H-12

Oklahoma City - CAF Oklahoma Wing
  http://www.contrails.us/~oklahoma_wing/44.00_CAF_Oklahoma_Wing/index.htm   PT-19

FAA Aeronautical Center, Academy Building, Room 101, 6500 S. Mac Arthur Blvd, 73169, (405) 954-4709, POB 25082, AMG-400D, Librarian: Virginia C. Huges, Reference Material

45th Infantry Division Museum, 2145 NE 36th St, 73111, (405) 424-5313,
Tue-Fri 9-4:15, Sat 10-4:15, Sun 1-4:15, Free Adm,

A-7	H-6A (OH)	L-4B	T-33A
F-80C	H-13E(OH)	L-17A	
F-86L	H-23C(OH)	L-19	
H-1B(UH)	H-58(OH)	L-20	

Aerospace Museum, 6000 N Martin King Blvd, (405) 685-9546, Curtiss Pusher

Omniplex Science Museum, 2100 NE 52nd, 73111, (800)532-7652, (405) 427-5461,
Adm Adult 13-64 $13.50, Snrs & Child 3-12 $8.25, Under 3 Free, Mon-Fri 9-5, Sat 9-6, Sun 11-6,
Gift Shop, Cafe 425-7529, Omni Dome, Planetarium, Curator Suzette Ellison, www.omniplex.org

Apollo Command Capsule Replica	F-104	Parker Pusher
Bede BD-5	Fokker DR.1 (2 ea)	PT-22
Boeing Brave	Gemini Capsule	Schweitzer I-19 Glider
Bu.133	Gulfsteam Peregrine	Star Cavalier
Bunker 154	JP-51 Pierce Sawyer	Stinson Voyager
Cloud Cutter	Lone Star Helicopter	T-33A
Coffman Ranger Monplane	Lunar Module	V-2 Replica
Cricket	Mercury Capsule	Wiley Post
Curtiss Pusher D	Mitchell B-10 Wing	Woodstock Sailplane
Electra Flyer Cirrus 3 Glider	Mong Sport	
Experimental Sailplane	Nieuport XI Bebe	

Museum of Women Pilots, 4300 Amelia Earhart Rd, 73159, (405) 685-9990, Mon-Fri 9-4,
Sat 10-4, Adm Adult $5, Child 4-10 $3, Under 3 Free, www.museumofwomenpilots.com

Tinker AFB, 73145	B-29	B-52D	C-121K(EC)
(405) 734-7321	B-47(RB)	C-47(EB)	C-135(KC)

Tinker ANG, 3000 S, 73125, (405) 734-2778, F-105D,   F-86D,   T-33A

Tulsa - CAF - Spirit of Tulsa Squadron, POB 158, 74037-0158, www.caftulsa.org

Liberty Foundation,11564 E 7th St, 74128, (918) 340-0243, Gift Shop
www.libertyfoundation.org, AT-6   B-17(2ea)   C-47   P-40E

OKLAHOMA

Tulsa ANG, Tulsa Int'l Airport, 74115, (918) 832-5208, F-100D, F-86D

Tulsa Air & Space Center, Tulsa Int'l Airport, 3624 N 74th Ave, 74115, (918) 834-9900, Fax 834-6723,
Tue-Sat 10-5, Sun 1-5, Adm Adult $6, Snrs 62 & Students $5, Child 5-12 $4, Under 5 Free,
Gift Shop, Library, Closed ES, MD, July 4, LD, TD, CD, Space Artifacts,
www.tulsaairandspacemuseum.com

C-2	F-14A	Ranger 2000T-37
C-3	HK-47	

Weatherford - Stafford Air & Space Center, 3000 E Logon Rd, Stafford Airport, 73096,
(580) 772-5871, Mon-Sat 9-5, Sun 1-5, www.staffordspacecenter.com

Curtiss D	F-86	Ryan NYP Rep	Wright Flyer Rep
F-16	MiG 21	T-38	

OREGON

Clackmas - Clackmas ANG, 6950 SW Hampton, 97015, (503) 557-5368, F-86F(QF)

Cottage Grove - Oregon Aviation Historical Society, 2745 Jim Wright Way, Mail: POB 533
97424, (541) 942-2567, May-Sept Tue 9-4, Free Adm www.oregonaviationhistoricalsociety.com
Contact Wilbur Heath, Great Lakes 2T-1A,   Rupert Special,   Stinson SR-5E

Eugene - Oregon Air and Space Museum, 90377 Boeing Dr, 97402-9536, (541) 461-1101,
Wed-Sun 12-4, Adm Adult $5, Snrs 62+ $4, Child 13-18 $3, 6-10 $2, Under 6 Free, Gift Shop,
http://www.northernoregon.com/profiles/orspace.html

A-4	B-10 Mitchell Wing	Hobby Copter	RLU-1
A-6E	F-86	MiG-17	Smith Termite
A6M2 Rep	Fokker DR 1	Nieuport 17	T-18

Hillsboro - Classic Aircraft Aviation Museum, 3005 NE Cornell Rd, 97125, N45.53269, W122.95144
Mail: POB 91430, Portland, OR 97291-0430, (503) 693-1414, Mon-Fri 9-4, Free Adm,
Exec Dir Doug Donkel, www.classicaircraft.org   email doug@classicaircraft.org

A-26C Tanker 4	F-104G (2ea)	MiG-17F
A-26C Tanker 10	F-104G(TF)	MiG-21F-13
CL-13 Mk 6 (F-86E)	Provost Mk 3A	

Hood - Western Antique Aeroplane & Automobile Museum, 1600 Air Museum Rd, 97031,
(541) 308-1600, Fax 308-1601, April-Oct Tue-Sun 9-6, Nov-March Wed-Sun 10-4,
Closed TD, CD, ND, Adm Adult $8, Snrs 55 $6, Child 8-18 $5, Under 5 Free,
Gift Shop, Library, Restoration Facility, www.waaamuseum.org

Aeronca K (Project)	Fairchild 22-C7B	Stinson Model R (Project)
Aeronca LC	Franklin Sport 90	TG-6 (Project)
American Eagle 101	HE-1 / AE-1 (Project)	Travel Air 4000 (Project)
American Eaglet	Heath Super Parasol (Project)	Waco QCF-2 (Project)
Arrow Sport Pursuit	Henderson Longster	Waco GXE 10
Arrow F (Project)	J-2 (1936) (Project)	Waco GXE 10 (Project)
Beech D Super 18	J-3 1st Ed (1938)	Waco Primary Glider (Project)
Buhl Pup	J-3 (1946) (Project)	Waco INF (Project)
C-3 Aeronca (1931)	J-3P (1938)	
C-3 Aeronca (1932)	J-5 (1940) (Project)	**Engines On Next Page**
C-3 Aeronca (1931) (Project)	JN-4D	
C2-60 Spartan	L-2M	
Command-Aire 5-C-3 (Project)	L-4A	
Curtiss Junior Teal (Project)	L-4J	
Curtiss Pusher	LP–3	
Curtiss Pusher (Project)	NSN Seaplane	
Curtiss Robin	Pietenpol Sky Scout	
Curtiss Wright Junior	PT-22	
Curtiss Wright Travel Air 12-W	Rearwin Cloudster (Project)	
Davis D-1-K	Sperry Messenger (Project)	
E-2 (Project)	Stearman Model 70 (Project)	

ENGINES:

2 Cylinder Lawrence	Cirrus 95hp	O-145-B2 Lycoming
3 Cylinder Radial - Wright	E107 Aeronca	OX-5 Wright
4AC 150A Franklin	E113-A Aeronca	R-55 Kinner
5E Leblond	H-2 Wright	R-56 Kinner
5G Leblond	Henderson 4	R-670 Lycoming
A-40 Continental	J-6-7 R975-E3 Wright	R-670 Continental
A-50 Continental	K-5 Kinner	R1690 Hornet - Pratt&Whitney
A-55 Continental	L-3 Jacobs	Ranger 440
A-65 Continental	L-4 Jacobs	S-R-30 Szekely
A-70 Continental	L320 Gipsy - Wright	V-8 Ford
B-5 Kinner	Lycoming 225	Warner 110
C-4 Priate Menasco	M-50 Menasco	
	Merlin Packard from PT Boat	

OREGON

Hubbard - Lenair Corp, 29502 S Meridian Rd, 97032-9405, (503) 651-2187,
www.LenhardtAirpark.com, Restores CG-4A's

Klamath Falls - Kinsley Field Oregon ANG, Klamath Falls In't Airport,
F-4   F-15A   F-16A

McMinnville - Evergreen Aviation Museum, 500 NE Captain Michael King Smith Way,
97128, (503) 434-4180, Fax 434-4058, Daily 9-5, Closed ED, TD, CD, ND, Adm Adult $12,
Mil & 65+ $11, Child 3-18 $10, Under 3 Free, Café, Gift Shop, Theater, www.sprucegoose.org,
(F) Flayable, R=Restoration

A-4E	F-105 (Storage)	MiG-29
A-7E	F6F-3	OV-1D1
A-26C	FG-1D (F)	P-38L (F)
B-17G (F)	Ford 5-AT-B (F)	P-40N (F)
B-25J (F)	FP404	P-51D (F)
BD-5B	Glassair SHA	PT-13
Beechcraft D 17A	Granville E Sportster (F)	Republic Seebee
Beechcraft Starship 2000A	H-1H(UH)	RODA Homebuilt
Bf 109G-10 (F)	H-3	S-2B
Bonanza 35	H-12E(UH) 2ea (S&R)	S-51 (HO3S-1G)
C-47	H-13E(OH)	SGS 2-32
Christen Eagle II	H-19	SNJ-4(AT-6) (F)
Curtiss Headless Pusher Rep	H-23	Sopwith Camel F.1 Rep (F)
CW-A-22	H-4 Spruce Goose	Spitfire Mk.14 (F)
D-17A Staggerwing	HTL-3	T-28B
DC-3A	Hughes 500 Helicopter	T-33A-15-LO
DC-9 Fuse	J-3C-65	T-38A
DH-4M-1	JN-4	TBM-3E (F)
DH-100	Lancair 360	TH-55
F-4C	MiG 15 UTI 2ea (S&R)	Titan II Missile
F-14	MiG-17A	Wright Flyer
F-15A		YAK 50
F-102A		

Milwaukie - Wings of Freedom, 13515 SE. McLoughlin Blvd, Hwy 99E, 97222, (503) 654-6491,
 B-17G Fr-Sun 10-4, Free Adm, Banquet Facility (40 people), Gift Shop,
Restaruant (See Restaurant Section), www.thebomber.com   B-17G (Project)

Pendleton - Pendelton Air Museum, POB 639, 97801, (541) 566-3906,
www.pendletonairmuseum.org, B-25

Portland - OR ANG Portland, 142 FIG/MAW, Portland Int'l Airport, 97218-2797
(503) 288-5611   F-101B

UFO Museum, 1637 Sw Alder St, 97205, (503) 227-2975

OREGON

Tillamook - Tillamook Air Museum, 6030 Hangar Rd, 97141, (503) 842-1130, Fax 842-3054,
Day Daily 9-5, Closed TD, CD, Adm Adult $11, Snrs 65 $10, Child 6-17 $6.50, Under 6 Free,
Cafe, Gift Shop,Theater, www.tillamookair.com

A-4B	Bellanca 66-75	GK-1	P2V-7
A-7E	Bf-109	H-43B(HH)	PBY-5A
A-24	Boeing 377	J2F-6	PT-17
A-26	C-47	Ki-43	PV-2
AD-4W	Cessna 180	L-29 (2each)	Quickie
Alien Blimp	Chris-Teena Coupe	Nord 1101	Sopwith Spad XIII
AM-1	F-14A	Oscar	TBM-3E
AT-6	F4U-7	P-38	
Bell Helicopter	FM-2	P-51	

Tillamook County Pioneer Museum, 2106 Second St, 97141, (503) 842-4553, Tue-Sat 9-5, Sun 11-5
Adm Adult $3, Snrs 60 $2, Child 12-17 $0.50, Gift Shop, Library, www.tcpm.org, Artifacts

PENNSYLVANIA

Annville - Annville ANG, 17003, (717) 948-2200, F-102A(TF)

Beaver Falls - Air Heritage Museum, Inc, 35 Piper St, Beaver County Airport, 15010, (724) 843-2820
Mon-Sat 10-5, Sun 11-6, Free Adm, Restorations in Progress, Gift Shop, www.airheritage.org

A-20H	C-123K	H-1H(UH)	Nanchang CJ6A	P-39N
AT-19	Cessna 401	L-21B	OV-1D	T-28

Bethel - Golden Age Air Museum, 371 Airport Rd, 19507, (717) 933-9566, May-Oct Fri-Sat 10-5
Sun 11-5, RoY by Appt, Adm Adult $5, Child 6-12 $3, Under 6 Free, Gift Shop,
Restoration Facility, (UR)=Under Restoration, (AR)=Awaiting Restoration, (F)=Flyable,
www.GoldenAgeAir.org

Allison Sport (AR)	E-2 (F)	RLU-1 Breezy
NC-12D	Fleet Model 7	Rose Parrakeet
Bird CK (F)	Great Lakes (F)	Star Cavalier Model B (AR
C-3 (UR)	J-1 (UR)	Star Cavalier Model E (AR)
Cessna AW (AR)	JN4D (UR)	Travel Air 2000
Cessna 195 (F)	Link Trainer	Windstead Special (F)
Dormoy Bathtub (AR)	Monocoupe Model 90A (AR)	
DR.I (UR)	Pietenpol Air Camper (F)	

Eldred - Eldred W W II Museum, 201 Main St, Mail: POB 273, 16731, (814) 225-2220, Fax: 225-4407
Tue-Sat 10-4, Sun 1-4, Free Adm, http://www.eldredwwiimuseum.org , Artifacts

Greencastle - AR Johns Exper Aircraft, Johns Alvin R, 346 Frank Rd, 17225, (717) 597-2256
Homebuilts: Green Demon, Rason Warrior X-3 (5 Seater), Aero Sport, Tornado JV,

Harrisburg - State Museum of Pennsylvania, 300 North St, 17120-0024, (717) 787-4980,
Tue-Sat 9-5, Sun 12-5, Free Adm, www.statemuseumpa.org, J-3C   Jacobs   OX-5

Lock Haven - Piper Aviation Museum. One Piper Way, Mail: PO Box J-3,
17745-0052, (570) 748-8283, Mon-Fri 9-4, Sat 10-4, Sun 12-4, Adm Adult $6, Snrs 55 $5,
Child 7-15 $3, Under 7 Free, Gift Shop, www.pipermuseum.com,

J-2	Link Trainer	PA-23	Tomahawk Simulator
J-3	PA-11	PA-29	

Philadelphia - Franklin Institute, 222 North 20 th St, 19103-1194,
(215) 448-1200, 9:30-5 Mon, 9:30-9 Tue-Thur, Sun, 9:30-10 Fri, Sat, Adult $8.50,
Child 4-11 $7.50, Omniverse $7 & $6, Planetarium $6 & $5, www.fi.edu/wright

Quickie	PA-38-2	RB-1	T-33	Wright Brothers B

CAF - Delaware Valley Wing, Northeast Philadelphia Airport, Mail 325 Frankford Ave,
Blackwood, NJ 08012, www.delvalwing.org, L-6   Fi 156D

PENNSYLVANIA

Pittsburgh - Pittsburgh ANG, Greater Pittsburgh Int'l Airport, 300 Tanker Rd # 4200, 15108-4200, (412) 269-8350, www.papitt.ang.af.mil, F-84F   F-86L   F-102A

Reading - Mid Atlantic Air Museum, Reading Regional Airport, 11 Museum Dr, Rte 183 North Side of Airport, 19605, (610) 372-7333, Daily 9:30-4:00, Closed Major Holidays, Adm Adult $6, Child 6-12 $3, Gift Shop, Pres: Russ Strine, www.maam.org/

Aeronca Model K 3	Fairchild 24G	PT-13D
American Aerolites Double Eagle	H-21B	PT-19
Auster MKV J/1	Heath LNA-40	PT-19B
B-25J	HH-52A	PT-23
Bede 5B (2 ea)	Hild Marshonet No 17	PT-26
Beech G-18S	J-2	RC-3
Bensen B-8M	KD-1A Kellet	R4D
BG-12	Kinner Sportster B-1	Rearwin 8135 Cloudster
Brewster Fleet 7	L-21B	Reid Flying Submarine
Brunner Winkle Bird A-1	Martin 4-0-4	Rutan Vari-Eze
BT-13A	Mitchell Wing Ultrlight	SNJ-4B
C-3	N2S3	Spratt Control Wing
C-119F	N3N-3	Steen Skybolt
Cessna 150M	NE-1	Taylor Young Model A
Cessna 172	P-84B-35-RE	TBM-3
Commonwealth 185	P-61B-1	Troyer VX
Custer CCW-5	P2V-7	UC-78
D.H. 104	PA-22-125	UH-34D
Elias EC1 Aircoupe	PA-22-150	Vickers 745D Viscount
Erco 415G	PA-34-200	
F-86F-25	Pietenpol Aircamper	

Smethport - Allegheny Arms & Armor Museum, 505 - 1/2 W Mail St, 16749, Rte 46, (814) 887-0947, Fax 558-6112, Daily 10-6, Gift Shop, www.armormuseum.com, A-6, UH-1 (2ea), Coast Guard Boat, M-42, M-48A1, M-115,

Toughkenamon - Colonial Flying Corps Museum, New Garden Airport, Newark Rd, Mail: POB 171, 19374, (610) 268-2048, Airshow 2nd Sunday In June, Sat-Sun 12-5, Adm Adult $1, Child Under 12 50¢

Barlett M-8	FM-2	PT-19B
Bergfalke 11	L-2A	PT-26
C-3	Latter	Ryan ST-3KR
Cessna 185	Liverpuffin 11	SNJ
DH 82A	MPA	
DHC.	PT-19A	

West Chester - American Helicopter Museum, Brandywine Airport, 1220 American Blvd, 19380, (610) 436-9600, Fax 436-8642, Wed-Sat 10-5, Sun 12-5, Adm Adult $6, Snrs $5 Child 2-18 $4, Under 2 Free, Gift Shop, Library, Theater, www.helicoptermuseum.org

Air Command Autogyro	H-12D(UH)(H-23)	QH-50C
Bell 47B	H-21	S-51(R-5)
Bell 47D-1(H-13)	HRP-1	S-52(HO-55)
Bell 47H-1	HUP-2	S-61(HH-3A)
Bell Jet Ranger	MH-6 "Little Bird"	S-62(HH-52)
Benson Autogyro	OH-6A	TH-55
Boeing 360	Parsons Autogyro	V-22
Brantley B-2	PCA-1A Autogyro	VS-300 Cocpit
Enstrom F 28 A	Princeton Air Cycle	VZ-8P
Eurocpoter Djinn So 1221	Robinson R-22	XR-4 Cocpit
H-1(AH) Cockpit	Rotorway Scorpion	XRG-65
H-1L(TH)	Rotorway Scorpion II	
H-2D(HH)	RPV Rep	

West Mifflin - CAF - Keystone Wing, Allegheny Cnty Airport, Hangar #20, 15122, (412) 343-2152 www.c4ever.com/keystone, L-5   L-9B

PENNSYLVANIA

Willow Grove - DVHAA Wings of Freedom, NAS JRB, Bldg 2, 1155 Easton Rd (Rte 611), 19090-5010, (215) 443-6039, Fax 675-4005, Mon-Fri 10:30-3:00, Sat-Sun 10:30-4:00, Free Adm, ID=Indoors, www.dvhaa.org/

A-4M	F7U-3	H-1V(UH)	Me-262B1-A (ID)
C-1A	F8U-1	H-13 (ID)	P-3
F-14A	F9F-2	H-34D(UH)	P-80C(TV-1) (ID)
F-18	FJ-4B	HUP-3B	YF-2Y

RHODE ISLAND

North Kingstown - Quonset Air Museum, Quonset State Airport, 488 Eccleston Ave, I-95N Exit 8, Rte 4S & Quonset Point, Davisville Exit, Mail: POB 1571, 02852, (401) 294-9540, Daily 10-3, Closed ED, TD, CD, ND, Adm Adult $7, Child 6-12 $3, Under 6 Free, Gift Shop, www.theqam.org   Restoration Facility, (P) = Project

A4D-2N(A-4C)(P)	C-1A	H-1S(AH)	MiG-17F
A-4F	CW XF15C-1	H-1H(UH)	O-2A
A-4M	F3D-2 Project	H-1M(UH)	Stolp Starduster 2
A-6E	F6F-5 Project	H-3H(SH)	T-28S
A-7D	F-4A	H-6A(OH)	TBM-3E
Aero Commander 680	F-14	H-58A(OH)	

SOUTH CAROLINA

Beaufort - Marine Air Station, (843) 522-7100,

A-4L	F-4N	F-18 FJ-3	F8U-2

Charleston - Charleston AFB, 29404-5000, (843) 554-0230,

C-47D(VC)	C-124C	F-106A
C-121C	F-4C	T-33A

The Citadel, 171 Moultrie St, 29409, (843) 953-5000, www.citadel.edu/ginfo/tour/jet.html

AH-1	F-4C	M4A3 Tank	LVT-H-6	Redsotne Missile

Columbia - Ft Jackson Museum, UH-1B

South Carolina State Museum, 301 Gervais St, 29202-3107, (803) 737-4978, POB 100107, Tue-Sat 10-5, Sun 1-5, Open Mon May 31-Sept 6, Adm Adult $5, Child, Snr 62 & Military $4, Child 3-12 $3, Contact: Nat Pemdelton, www.museum.state.sc.us 1929 Clemson Plane   B-25C

McEntire - McEntire ANGB, Memorial Park, 29044-9690, (803) 776-5121,

A-7D	F-80H	F-102A	T-33A
F-4	F-86H & L	F-104C	

Mt Pleasant - Patriots Point Museum, 40 Patriots Point Rd, 29464, (866) 831-1720, (843) 884-2727, Daily 9-6:30, Closed CD, Adm Adult $15, Snr & Mil $13, Child 6-11 $8, Under 6 Free, Gift Shop, Snack Bar, www.patriotspoint.org

A-4 2ea	E-2C	F9F	UH-34
A-6	F-4J	FG-1D	UH-1H
A-6B(EA)	F-14	J-2	USCG Ingham
A-7E	F-18	H-3	USS Laffey
AD-4N	F11F-1	N2S	USS Yorktown
AH-1	F4F-3A	S-2E	USS Clamagore
B-25D-NC	F6F	SBD	MARK I Patrol Boat
E-1B	F8U	TBM-3E	Mercury Capsule Rep

Myrtle Beach - Myrtle Beach AFB, Air Base Redevelopment A, 1181 Shine Ave, F-100D

North Myrtle Beach - Mayday Miniature Golf, 715 Hwy 17N, 29582, (843) 280-3535, Daily 9am-10pm, Adm Adult $7.50, Child $6.50, Under 3 Free, www.maydaygolf.com, PV-2, UH-1

SOUTH DAKOTA

Sumter - Shaw AFB, 29152-5000, (803) 668-3621, Open House May, PA: Fran Hutchison

B-66C(RB)	F-16A	F-105	P-47D Replica
F-4C(RF)	F-101C(RF)	O-2A	

Ellsworth AFB - South Dakota Air & Space Museum, Ellsworth AFB, 2890 Davis Dr, 57706, (605) 385-5188, POB 871, Box Elder, 57719-0871, Exit 67 A/B Off I-90, Summer Hours Daily 8:30-6 Winter 8:30-4:30, Gift Shop: Beverly LeCates, Free Adm, Base & Minuteman Missile Silo Tours $6, Child Under 12 $4, www.ellsworth.af.mil/museum.asp N44 07.946, W103 04.348

A-7D	C-45	F-101B	O-2A
B-1B	C-47A	F-102 (Project)	Quail
B-25J(VB)	C-54	F-105B	T-33A
B-26K	C-131	FB-111A	T-38
B-29	C-135(EC)	H-13-H(OH)	Titan I (Project)
B-52D	F-84F	L-5	U-3A
B-57B(EB)	F-86H	Min. II	U-8D
BT-13A	F-100	Nike-Ajax	UH-1F

Mitchell - Soukup & Thomas Int'l Balloon & Airship Museum, 700 N Main St, 57301, (605) 996-2311, Memorial Day - Labor Day Daily 8-8, May, Sept-Nov Mon-Sat 9-5, Sun 1-5, Closed January, Feb-April Fri, Sat, Mon 9-5, Sun 1-5, Adm Adult $3, Sr $2.50, 13-19 $1.50, 6-16 $1, Under 6 Free, Gift Shop, Dir: Becky Pope, 1890's Charles Dolfus Balloon Baskets Shennandoa Gerders/Control Room Doors,

"Zanussi" Trans-Atlantic Capsule	Super Chicken Gondola 1st Non-Stop
Chesty (US Marine Bulldog)	Uncle Sam (100 Foot Tall)
Chic-I-Boom (Carmen Miranda)	US Aero Star Int'l
Hilda (13-Story Witch On A Broom)	WWI US Army Gas Balloon
Hindenburg (LZ-129) Dishes	WWI Paris Basket
HOT AIR BALLOONS:	WWI Observation Balloon Basket
Matrioshka Russian Nesting Doll	

Pierre - SD ANG Pierre, SDNG Museum, Dakota & Chapelle, POB 938, 57501-0938, (605) 224-9991,   A-7D

Sioux Falls - SD ANG Sioux Falls, Industrial & Algonquin, Box 5044, 57117-5044, (605) 333-5700,   A-7D   F-102A   T-33A

TENNESSEE

Arnold - Arnold AFS, 37389, (931) 454-3000, AEDC/DOPO, F-4C   F-105D

Athens - Swift Museum Foundation, Inc, McMinn County Airport, Hwy 30, Mail: POB 644, 37303-0644, (423) 745-9547, 744-9696, email: swiftlychs@aol.com, Swift Aircraft Displays

Caryville - Campbell County Military Display, I-75 Exit 134 & US 25W on Hwy 116(Old SR 9)
UH-1   M-60A3 Tank

Chattanooga - Chattanooga ANG, 37412, (423) 892-1366, F-101B   F-104C

Crossville - Cumberland High School, 660 Stanley St, 38555, (931) 484-6194
A-4   T-33A

Johnson City - Radio Controlled Flying Field, Contact: Vic Koening, 502 Steeple Chase Dr, 37601, T-33

Knoxville - Catalina Air Inc, 2221 Alcola Hwy, 37701-3162, (865) 984-4092   C-47A
Knoxville ANG, McGhee Tyson Airport, 37901, (865) 970-3077, 134th ARG, F-104C

Millington - NSA Memphis (NATTC), 38053, (901) 873-3033, A-4M   A-5 Outside Officers Club

TENNESSEE

Nashville - Nashville ANG, Nashville Metropolitan Airport, 37217-0267,
(615) 361-4600,   F-84F(RF)

Bristol Heritage Collection, 210 Club Parkway, 37221-1900, Mail: POB 210876, (615) 646-2473,
383-9090, Mon-Fri 9-5, Wetland Lysander MK111A, Fairey Swordfish, Bristol Beaufort, Bollingbroke

Pigeon Forge - Helicopter Headquarters Museum, 2491 Parkway, 37863, (865) 429-2929
Labor Day-Memorial Day Daily 10-6, RoY 9-9, Adm Adult $15, Child 5-11 $10, Under 5 Free
Gift Shop, Theatre, Café, Restoration Facility, www.helihq.com

H-1H(UH)	Bell 222-A "Airwolf"	Bell 47-G3B1
H-34C(S-58)	Hughes 269-A	Bell UH-A
H-58A(OH)	Rotorway Scorpion 1	
Hoplite MI-2	Revolution Mini 500	

Professor Hacker's Lost Treasure Golf, 3010 Parkway, 37863, (865) 453-0307, Beech D18S

Rossville - CAF - Tennessee Volunteer Squadron, Squadron Leader: Gene Johnson, 5917
Blackwell Bartlett, 38134, (901) 372-8162,

Sevierville - Tennessee Museum of Aviation, 135 Air Museum Way , 37862, Mail POB 37864-5587,
(866) 286-8738, (865) 908-0171, Fax 908-8421, Mon-Sat 10-6, Sun 1-6, Closed TD, CD,
Adm Adult $12.75, Snrs 65 $9.75, Child 6-12 $6.75, Under 6 Free, Gift Shop,
www.tnairmuseum.com , Flyable=(F)

AT-6D (F)	MiG 21	T-28B (F)	TBM-3E (F)
F-86	P-12B (3/4 Scale)	T-33-A-N (F)	
MiG 17(2ea)	P-47D-40 (2ea)(F)	T-33A	

Tullahoma - Staggerwing Museum, POB 550, Tullahoma Airport, 37388, (931) 455-1974,
Fax 455-1994, Take I-24, Exit 111, Hwy 55 S, Right 130 S, 3/4 Mi, March-Nov Mon-Fri 8:30-4:30
Sat-Sun 1-4, Dec-Feb by Appt, Closed All Holidays, Adm Adult $5, Gift Shop, www.staggerwing.com

Beech A17R	Beech 95-55	Beechcraft 2000A
Beech B17L	C-45H	Griffon Aerospace Lionheart
Beech C17L	C-45J(UC)	T-34
Beech D17S (2ea)	Beechcraft 35 (2ea)	Travel Air Mystery Ship
Beech E17B	Beechcraft A36	Travel Air 4000
Beech F17D	Beechcraft D-50	Travel Air 1000
Beech G17S	Beechcraft 55	V-35B
Beech E18S	Beechcraft V-109D	

TEXAS

Abilene - CAF - Big Country Squadron, 4886 Newman Rd,Abilene Mun. Airport, Hangar #2,
76601-6720, Mail:POB 6511, 79608, (915) 676-1944, Daily 9-5, Squadron Meetings
6:30 PM First Tue Monthly, C-94(UC)

Dyess Linear Air Park, Arnold Blvd, Dyess AFB, Mail: 7 WG/CVM 650, 2nd
St 9607-1960, (915) 793-2199, Need Free Pass at Visitor's Center, 696-2432, Daily 5:30-10pm

A-26C	C-7A(YC)	F-84F(RF)	O-2A
AGM-28A	C-47A	F-86L	T-28A
AT-6F	C-97L(KL)	F-89H	T-29C
B-17G(DB)	C-123K	F-100C	T-33A
B-47E(EB)	C-130A	F-101B	T-34B
B-52D	C-135A(KC)	F-104A	T-37B
B-57B(EB)	F-4D	F-105D	T-38A
B-66A(RB)	F-84F	HU-16E	T-39A

TEXAS

Addison - Cavanaugh Flight Museum, 4572 Claire Chennault, Addison Airport, 75001,
(972) 380-8800, Mon-Sat 9-5, Sun 11-5, Adm Adult $8.00, Child 6-12 $4.00,
Under 6 Free, All Aircraft Flown Regularly, Canteen Area, Gift Shop,
www.cavanaughflightmuseum.com   **(Front Cover Feature of this book)**

AT-6D (2ea)	F-105F	L-3B	P-51D
B-25J(TB)	FG-1C	L-4J	Pitts S-1-S
Bell 47	F9F-2B	Me-109G	PT-19A
C-47A	FM-2	MiG-15UTI	PT-22
Christen Eagle	Fokker DR.I	MiG-17	S-2F
DH 82	Fokker D.VIIa	MiG-21	Sopwith Camel
EC-120	H-13 (2ea)	N2S4	Spitfire Mk.VIII
F-86E	Hawker Sea Fury	OV-1D	T-28B
F-4C	He-111	P-40N	TBM-3E
F-104A	J-3	P-47N	TS-11

Amarillo - CAF - Dew Line Squadron, 903 S Carolina, Perry Lefors Field, 79103,
(806) 665-1881, Gift Shop, www.caf-dewline.org (note 1 at Guymon Hangar)

AT-6	C-45 (Project) (note 1)	L-16	PT-26 (P)
BT-13	L-5	PT-26	T-34

English Field Air & Space Museum, 2014 English Rd, Mail: POB 31535,
79120-1535, (806) 372-1812, Sun-Fri 12-5, Sat 10-5, Winter Sat-Sun 12-5, Free Adm,
Gift Shop, Restoration Facility, Annual Air Show, www.texasaviationmuseum.org

C-7A	F-105	OV-1B	Viking Mars Lander
F-84F			

Austin - Texas Military Forces Museum, Camp Mabry,2200 West 35th St, West of
Loop 1(MOPAC Blvd), Camp Mabry, (512) 782-5659, Wed 2-6, Sun 10-4, Closed Holidays,
Free Adm, www.texasmilitaryforcesmuseum.org

F-4C	M1	M60A1	M56
F-86D	M24	M60A3	M108
H-1H(UH)	M26	M7B1	M110A2
H-1M(UH)	M48	M42	
L-4	M60	M44	

Beaumont - Babe Didrikson Zaharious Memorial Park, Interstate Hwy 10,   RF-101

Beeville - Chase Field Naval Air Station, PA, (512) 354-5464,   A-4J(TA)

Big Spring - Hangar 25 Air Museum, 1911 Apron Dr, 79720, Mail POB 2925, 79721,
(432) 264-1999, Fax 466-0316, Mon-Fri 8-4, Sat 9-3, Closed Holidays,
Adm Donation, Gift Shop, www.hangar25airmuseum.com

A-10 Cockpit	B-52 Nose	T-28	T-37
AT-11	Harrier	T-33	T-38

Brownsville - CAF - Rio Grande Valley Wing Museum, 955 S Minnesota, 78521, (956) 541-8585,
Daily 9:30-3:30,Adm Adult $6, Snrs 55 $5, Child 12-18 $3, Under 12 Free, Barnstormers Lounge,
www.rgvwingcaf.com

BT-13(2ea)	J3C-65	Moth Minor	PT-26(2ea)
C-47 Project	L-2	P.H. 94 S	SNJ
C-54	L-3	PBY-5A Project	Swith Bi-Plane
CM-170R	L-4	PT-17	Train 2-4-2
Fleet Finch 16B	L-5	PT-19(2ea)	
FW-44	L-6	PT-22(2ea)	

TEXAS

Burnet - CAF - Highland Lakes Sq Air Museum (Hill County Squadron), 2402 S Water St,
Burnet City Airport (BMQ), S on US 281, (512) 756-2226, Mail: POB 866, 78611, Sat 9-5, Sun 12-5,
Adm Adult $5, Snrs/Military/Student $3, Child6-12 $1, Under 6 Free, Gift Shop,
www.highlandlakessquadron.com

A-7D	L-5	PT-17	T-38
C-47	L-17B	PT-19	
F-100F	PT-13	T-37	

College Station - George Bush Library Museum, 1000 George Bush Dr, 77845,
(979) 691-4000, Mon-Sat 9:30-5, Sun 12-5, Closed TD, CD, ND, Adm Adult $7,
Snr 62+ $5, Child 6-17 $2, Under 6 Free, Gift Shop (888) 388-2874, (979) 862-2874
www.bushlibrary.tamu.edu, TBM-3

Conroe - CAF -Big Thicket Squadron, Montgomery County Airport, BT-13A,   YO-55

Corpus Christi - CAF - Third Coast Wing, 1309 S Airport Rd, 78332, (361) 661-0321, Mail: POB 8192,
Corpus Christi, TX 78468-8192, Sat 9-5, Sun 9-12, Gift Shop, L-6, PT-17

Int'l Kite Museum, Best Western Sandy Shores Beach Hotel, Quarium
Village, 3200 Surfside, Mail: POB 839, 78403, (361) 883-7456, Daily 10-5, Free Adm.

Naval Air Station, 78419, (361) 961-2568,   A-4J(TA)   C-12B(UC)   T-28

USS Lexington Museum, 2914 Shoreline Dr, Mail: POB 23076, 78403-3076,
(361) 888-4873, MD-LD Daily 9-6, LD-MD Daily 9-5, Closed CD, Adm Adult $11.95, Snrs 60 $9.95,
Child 4-12 $6.95, Under 4 Free, Gift Shop, Cafe, Theater, Restoration Facility, www.usslexington.com

A-4B (2ea)	F-14A	L-4 Storage	T-34B
A-4J(TA) Trainer	F2H-2	N3N-3	T-6 Storage
A-6E	F9F-8T(TF-9J)	PV-2D	T2C
A-7B	GH-3	SBD-3	TBF-3E
DGA Storage	H-1S(AH)	SNJ-5	USS Lexington
F-4A	KA-3B(A3D)	T-28B	

Corsicana - Glen Cumbie Air Museum, 9000 Old Navarro Rd, 75109,
Corsicana Field Heritage Foundation, Hwy 287, Mon-Sum 9-5, Adm Free, (903) 654-4847, PT-19

Navarro College, 3200 West 7 th Ave, 75110, (800) 628-2776, PA: Linda Timmerman (903) 875-7594
F-4D

Dallas - Frontiers of Flight Museum, 6911 Lemmon Ave, Dallas Love Field, 75209,
Exit: Lemmon at University, (214) 350-3600, Fax (351) 0101, Mon-Sat 10-5, Sun 1-5,
Closed TD, CD, ND, Adm Adult $8, Snrs 65+ $6, Child 3-17 $5, Under 3 Free,
Gift Shop 350-1651, Airshow 2nd wknd In Sept, e-mail: fofm@iglobal.net, www.flightmuseum.com

A-7	D-21 Drone	Jupiter IRBM Missile	PT-22
AGM-136	DH-82	Lear 24D	Sopwith Pup
Apollo 7	F-4C	Learfan 2100	T-33A
AT-6G	F-8G(RF)	LTV(L-450)	T-38A
Aviat Christen Eagle	F-16B	Quicksilver MXL-II	Temple 1928
Beech Staggerwing	F-86L	Meyers "Lil Toot"	TH-1L
BGM-109C	F-105F	PA-18-125	TH-13T
Boeing 737 Nose	F-11F Escape Module	PA-22 Airframe Only	Thorp T-18
Culver Dart	Glasflugel BS-1	Pitts S-2B	Whitman Tailwind
Bu-133	H-1D(UH)	PQ-13	Wright Flyer

History of Aviation Collection, Univ of Texas at Dallas, Eugene McDermont Library, 2901 N Floyd Rd
75221, Mon-Thur 9-6, 9-5 Fri, Free Adm, James Doolittle Library, Artifacts, Glasflugel BS-1 Sailplane

Del Rio - Laughlin AFB, 78843-5000, (830) 298-5675, 47OSS/CC

AT-6	C-123K	T-33A	T-38
B-57B(EB)	F-84F	T-34B	U-2C
C-45J(UC)	T-28A	T-37A	

TEXAS

Del Valle - Del Valle High School 2454 Cardinal Loop, 78614, (512) 385-1921, F-4C(RF)

Denison - Perrin AFB Museum, 4575 Airport, Dr, Graysson Cnty/Perrin Airport, 75020
(903) 893-6900, Tue-Sat 10-4, Free Adm, Gift Shop, www.perrinfield.org, T-37

Denton - Hangar 10 Antique Airplane Museum, Denton Mncpl Airport, 1945 Matt Wright Ln
76207, (940) 565-1945, I-35E, West Oak Exit, R on Airport Rd, Mon-Sat 8:30-3,
Adm Donations, www.hangar10.org/   (P) = Project

Cessna 140	Cessna LC-126	J-3 (P)	Pitts S-1-S
Cessna 180	Howard DGA (P)	L-17A	
Cessna190 (P)	Interstate Cadet	Lancair Legacy	

Texas Women's Univ Library Blagg H, 76201, (940) 898-2665, WASP's Artifacts

Ellington - Ellington ANGB,TX 77034-5586, (821) 929-2892, 147 FIG/MA,

F-101F	F-102A	T-33A

Fort Bliss - Third Cavalry Regiment Museum, ATZC-DPT-MM, Forrest & Chaffee Rds,
Bldg 2407, 79916-5300, (915) 568-1922, Mon-Fri 9-4:30, Free Adm,

S-55	M-2 Half Track	M-4AS Sherman Tank	M-8 Armored Car

US Army Air-Defense Artillery Museum, Blvd 5000, Pleasonton Rd & Robert E Lee Blvd,
79916-5300, (915) 568-3390, Daily 9-4:30, Closed ES, TD, CD, ND, Free Adm,

AH-1F	M-60A3	Bofors 40mm	88mm German	Firebee	Nike Ajax
M-42	M-163	Gun	V-2	Hawk	Nike Hercules

Fort Worth - American Airlines C.R. Smith Museum, 4601 Texas Highway 360, 76155,
Mail POB 619617, MD 808 GSWFA, DFW Airport, 75261-9617, (817) 967-1560,
Tue-Sat 10-6, Adm Adult $4, Snrs 55 & Child 2-12 $2, Under 2 Free, Gift Shop 967-5922,
Theater, Facility Rental, www.crsmithmuseum.org, DC-3, Airline Cockpits: 757, 767, F-100

Forward Air Controller's Museum & OV-10 Bronco Assoc, 505 NW 38th St, Hangar 33s, 76106
Sat 10-5, Sun 12-5, Gift Shop, Library, Restoration Facility, www.ov-10bronco.net,
www.facmuseum.org

A-4C (P)	F-4S(QF)	F-14D	F-105 (P)	OV-10A (2ea)
A-7B (P)	F-5E	F-102(TF) (P)	O2-A (2ea)	

NAS Ft Worth Joint Reserve Base, Carswell Field, 76127, (817) 782-7815,

A-4M 2ea	F-4E	F-86L	H-34(UH)
A-4J(TA)	F-14A	F-105D	H-58(OH)
C-97L(KC)	F-16N	FA-18	
F-4D	F-80L	H-1(UH)	

Pate Museum of Transportation, 18501 Highway 377 S, 76035, Mail: POB 711, 76101,
(817) 332-1161, Tue-Sat 10-5, Sun 12-5, Except Holidays, Free Adm,

A-4	F-8A(F8U-1)	F-100	H-43B(HH)
BQM-34	F9F-6P	CF-101B	T-28
C-119	F-80	F-105	T-33A
C-47	F-84F(RF)	F-86H	UH-34
CH-21B	F-14	H-16B(HU)	
F-4D	F-16	H-23B(OH)(2ea)	

Vintage Flying Museum, 505 NW 38th St, Hangar 33 S, 76106, Meacham Airport (FTW),
(817) 624-1935, Fax 624-2840, Sat 10-5, Sun 12-5, Weekdays by Appt, Adm Adult $8, Snrs $5,
Child 6-12 $3, Under 6 Free, Gift Shop, www.vintageflyingmuseum.org

Aeronca Chief	Convair	L-5	PT-17
AT-6	Daphne 1	L-450	Stearman
B-17G	F-86	Morrisey 2000	Stinson V77
B-25	Knight Falcon	Piaggio Amphibian	18 Engines
Beech D18S (2ea)	L-3	Piaggio Royal Gull	

TEXAS

Fredericksburg - National Museum of the Pacific War, 340 E Main St, POB 777,
78624, (830) 997-4379, 7269, Daily 10-5, Closed CD, Adm Adult $7, Snrs 65 & Mil $6, Child $4,
Under 6 Free, www.nationalmuseumofthepacificwar.org

B-25J	M7 Priest Tank
D3A-1	MK3 Tank
FM-2	N1K-1
Japanese Midget Sub Type A	PT Boat
Japanese Tank Chi-ha	TBM-3E
LVT4	USS Pinato Conning Tower
M3 Tank	

Galveston - Lone Star Flight Museum, 2002 Terminal Pkwy, 77554, (409) 740-7722, Fax 740-7612
Mail POB 3099, 77552, Daily 9-5, Closed CD, Adm Adult $8, Snrs 65 & Child 5-17 $5
Under 5 free, Gift Shop, Library, Theater, Restoration Viewing,
All Aircraft Flyable, (Project = P), (Non Flayable = N), (Storage = S), www.lsfm.org

A-20G	DC-3A	Hawker Hurricane (P)	SBD-5(A-24B) (P)
AT-6A	DH-82A	L-5	Spitfire (P)
AT-11	F3F-2	Motor Glider (S)	T-34A
B-17G	F4U-5N	N3N-3	T-40 (N)
B-25	F6F-5K	P-47	T-50
Baby Great Lakes (N)	F8F-2	PB4Y-2 (P)	TBM-3E
Beech D18H4	FM-2	PBY-5A (N)	VP-1 (S)
C-1A Project (N)	Harvard Mk.IV	PV-2D	VP-1A (N)

Gilmer - Flight of the Phoenix Aviation Museum, Hangor One, Gilmer Airport, Mail: POB 610, 75644,
(903) 843-2457, Fax 843-3123, www.flightofthephoenix.org,

AT-6G	D.H.82A	J-3
Bu-131	D-18S	Great Lakes 2T-1A

Graham - CAF - Cactus Squadron, Robert E Richeson Memorial Museum, Graham Mncpl Airport,
POB 861, 76450, Thur 1-5, (866) 549-0401, SB2C

Hawkins - RRS Aviation (Restoration Facility), POB 233, 380 N Beaulah,
75765, (903) 769-2904, Pres Bob Schneider,

Bristol Beaufort	Hawker Hurricane	PBM
F9-5	P-40	TBM-3

Houston - CAF - Gulf Coast Wing, 8411 Nelm St, Hangar ER-7, (281) 484-0098
2nd Sat 9:30am Monthly, www.gulfcoastwing.org, A6M Rep, B5N Rep, B-17, BT-13, D3A Rep

CAF - West Houston Squadron, West Houston Airport, Hangar B-5, 18000 Groeschke Rd
77084, Hangar: (281) 578-1711, 3rd Sunday each Month, (Rides) Rides Available
(See Biplane & Warbird Rides Section for details)

AT-6D (Rides)	C-60A (Rides)	S-108 (Rides)	T-28 (2ea)
BT-13A (Rides)	N3N (Rides)	SNJ	T-34

1940 Air Terminal Museum, 8325 Travelair Rd, William P Hobby Airport, 77601, (713) 454-1940,
Tue-Sat 10-5, Sun 1-5, Adm Adult $2, Child $1, www.1940airterminal.org, D-185, C-60(L.18)

Houston Museum of Natural Science, One Hermann Circle Dr, 77030, (713) 639-4629,
Mon-Sun 9-5, Tue 9-9, Adm Adult $9, Child $6, Mercury 6 Spacecraft

Houston Space Academy, 403 NASA Rd 1, Ste 360, 77598, (281) 486-4446,
Summer Space Camps Ages 6-20, Astronaut Training, Rockets, Simulators

NASA Lyndon B Johnson Space Center, 2101 NASA Rd 1, 77058,
(281) 483-4321, Daily 9-4, Free Adm, PGM-11A Spacecraft

TEXAS

Houston - Space Center Houston at LBJ Space Center, 1601 NASA Rd 1, Off I-45, 77058
(281) 244-2100, (800) 972-0369, Memorial Day-Labor Day 9-7, Labor-Memorial Day
Mon-Fri 10-5, Sat-Sun 10-7, Closed CD, Adm Adult $18.95, Snrs $17.95, Child $14.95, Parking $5,
Gift Shop, www.spacecenter.org   Space Shuttle

Kerrville - Mooney Aircraft Factory, West Side of Louis Schreiner Field On Hwy 27,
(830) 996-6000, Mon-Fri, 1 Hour Tours at 10am.

Kingsbury - Pioneer Flight Museums part of Vintage Aviation Historical Foundation,
190 Pershing Ln, 78638, (830) 639-4162, Mon-Fri 9-4, ,
www.vintageaviation.org, (F) = Flyable , (P) = Project

Bleriot XI (F)	Fokker Dr.I (P)	Rearwin 2000C (P)
Bristol Fighter (P)Rep	Luscombe 8A (F)	SE-5a (P) Rep
Bristol Fighter (P)	Meyers OTW (F)	Thomas-Morse Scout (F)
Curtiss Canuck(P)	Pietenpol Sky Scout (F)	
Fokker D.VII (P)	Piper J-3 (P)	

Kingsville - Naval Air Station, Hwy 77 South of City, 1201 E Caesar Ave, 78363,
(361) 516-6200, A4D-2N

Lago Vista - Lago Vista Airpower Museum, Rusty Allen Airport, Flight Line Rd,
Hangar 9, Lago Vista Airport, 78645, (512) 267-7403, Sat-Sun 1-5, From I-35
Take F.M. 1431, R on Bar-K Ranch Rd, F-4C(RF),   F-100C,   L-4,   PT-13

Lancaster - CAF - Dallas / Ft. Worth Wing Museum, Lancaster Airport, Belt Line Rd, 75146
(972) 227-9119, 6 Mi East of I-35E in SE Dallas County, Sat 9-4, Adm $2, Aircraft Rides Available
www.dfwwing.com, (Rides) = Rides Available

BT-15 (Rides Available)	L-5 (Rides Available)	V-77
FG-1D	R4D-S (Rides Available)	

Cold War Air Museum, Lancaster Airport, (KLNC), www.coldwarairmuseum.com,

M-2 (4ea)	MiG-21	L-39 (Several)
M-24 (3 ea)	L-29	

Laredo - Airport, 3 Mi NE of City, (956) 795-2000,

Aero Commander	C-46	J-3	YS-11
Beech 35	Convair 340	Rotorway Exec 162F	
Bell 47	Convair 440 (2ea)	T-28	
C-45	DC-3 (3ea)	T-39 Parts	

Lubbock - Lubbock State School, 3401 N Univ & Loop 289, 79417, (806) 763-7041, T-33A

Science Center, 2579 S Loop 289, 79423, (806) 745-2525, T-28A

Silent Wings Museum, 6202 N Interstate Hwy, 1-27 Exit 29, 79403-9710, (806) 775-2047, Tue-Sat 10-6,
Sun 1-5, Closed TD, CD, ND, Adm Adult $4, Snrs 60 $3, Child Under 12 $2, GPS N 39.467' W 49.911',
www.silentwingsmuseum.org

C-47	Coffman Glider	L-4	PT-22A
CG-4A	Culver Cadet	Lyster 1943	

Marfa - Marfa Gliders, Texas Hwy 17, Mail POB 516, 79843, (800) 667-9464, Daily 11-4,
Free Adm, Glider Rides, Contact Burt Compton, www.flygliders.com **(See Classified Ad Section)**

Blanik L-23 (2ea)	Schempp-Hirth Cirrus (2ea)
Schweizer 1-36	Scheicher ASK-13

Marshall - CAF - Lone Star Wing, 2020 Warren, 75670, (903) 923-8335,
www.lonestarwing.org, PT-17 (2ea)

TEXAS

Midland - CAF - B-29/B-24 Squadron, www.cafb29b24.org, B-24   B-29

CAF - High Sky Wing, 9600 Wright Dr, Midland Int'l Airport, Mail: POB 61064,
79711-7064, (915) 563-5112, www.highskywing.org, C-61(UC)   SNJ-4

CAF - West Texas Wing, Municipal Airport, By Appt, Free Adm, Library (1,000 Books)
http://mywebpage.netscape.com/westtexaswing/Home+Page.htm,   Artifacts   SB2C-5

American Airpower Heritage Museum, 9600 Wright Dr, Midland Int'l Airport, POB 62000
79711-2000, (432) 563-1000, Fax 567-3047, Tue-Sat 9-5, Holidays 12-5, Closed ED, TD, CE, CD
Adm Adult $10, Child 13-18, 65+ $9, 6-12 $7, Under 6 Free, Airshow Dates: (800)CAF-SHOW
(Loan) = On Loan, www.airpowermuseum.org

A6M	F-14	L-2	PV-2D (Loan)
AT-11	F-100 (Loan)	Me-109B	SNJ
B-23	F-105 (Loan)	OH-13	TBM
B-25	F-111 (Loan)	O2-A	YO-55
Bu-133 (Loan)	Fokker DR1 (Loan)	P-82	M-4 Tank
C-45	H-1(UH) (Loan)	PT-17	M4-81 Half Track
C-46	I-16	PT-19	WC-46 Ambulance
C-78(UC)	JRB-4	PT-26	
F-4 (Loan)			

Odessa - CAF - Desert Squadron, Odessa-Schlemeyer Airport, (915) 335-3021, PT-13, T-33A

Pampa - Freedom Museum USA, 600 N. Hobart, 79065,
(806) 669-6066, Tue-Sat 12-4, Library, Gift Shop, www.freedommuseumusa.org
UH-1F   B-25(PBJ)   M110A2 Howitzer

Paris - Flying Tiger Airport, Hwy 82, 75461, (903) 784-3613,
Daily 8-6, Free Adm, A-4D   AT-6   F-86D   SAM

Pyote - Pyote Museum and Rattlesnake Bomber Base, 79777, 15 Mi W of Monahans,
On I-20, In Ward County Park (N Hwy 18), 79756, (432) 389-5660, Sat 9-6, Sun 2-6,
Artifacts of Former 19th B-17 Base.

Richardson - History of Aviation Collection, 2901 N Floyd Rd, Eugene McDermontt Library,
Special Collections, University of Dallas, 75083, POB 830643, 75083-0643, (972) 883-2570,
Fax: 883-4590, Mon-Fri 9-5, Free Adm, www.utdallas.edu/library
(Jimmy Doolittle and China Air Transport) Artifacts

San Angelo - Mathis Field Airport, 8618 Terminal Circle, Suite 101, 76903,
(915) 659-6409,   UH-1H   CAF Ft Concho Squadron Also There

Goodfellow AFB, 76908-5000, (915) 657-3231, 3480 ABG,
B-25N(TB)   F-4C(RF)   MiG-15   T-28A
BT-13A   F-100A   MiG-29

San Antonio - US Army Medical Dept Museum, Ft Sam Houston, 1210 Stanley Rd, Bldg 123,
Mail: POB 340244, 78234, Gift Shop 2310 Stanley Rd, (210) 221-6358, Wed-Sun 10-4
UH-1H,   H-13

Brooks Heritage Foundation, Brooks AFB, 8081 Inner Circle Rd, Bldg 671, 78235,
Mail: POB 35362, (210) 536-2203, Mon-Fri 8-4, Free Adm, Gift Shop 531-9767,
www.brooksheritage.org,   F-100D   JN-4

TEXAS

San Antonio - Lackland Static Airplane Display/Lackland AFB,78236-5218, (210) 671-3055, 0655,
Mon-Fri 8-4:45, Free Adm, Closed Holidays, Closed ED, TD, CD, ND, PA=Parade Airpark,
GA=Global Airpark, SAP=South Asia Airpark, A=Annex, HT=History & Traditions

A-7D (GA)	B-66(WB) (SAP)	F-82E(EF)(PA)	P-38L Rep (PA)
A-10A (GA)	C-47D (PA)	F-84B	P-47N (PA)
A-37	C-45J(UC)	F-86A (HT)	P-51H (PA)
AT-6D (PA)	C-118 (PA)	F-100A (SAP)	P-63G(RP) (PA)
B-17G(TB) (PA)	C-119C	F-101B (A)	SR-71A (GA)
B-24M Replica (PA)	C-121C(EC) (PA)	F-101F	T-28A(GT) (PA)
B-25H (PA)	C-123K (PA)	F-104C	T-29B(VT)
B-26C (PA)	F-4B (SAP)	F-104D(TF)(A)	T-34A (PA)
B-29A (PA)	F-5B (SAP)	F-105B(GF)(A)	T-38A
B-52D (SAP)	F-15A (GA)	F-105D (SAP)	
B-58(RB)(SAP)	F-16B (GA)	JN-4D (HT)	

Texas ANG, 149th Fighter Wing, Chappie James Way, Lackland AFB, F-4C, F-100D

Vigilance Memorial Park, Air Intelligence Agency, Lackland AFB,

AQM-34L	EC-47	O-2A	RF-4C

Kelly Field, Lackland AFB, 145 Duncan Dr, B-58   F-106B F-111A

Int'l Liaison Pilot & Aircraft Assn Museum, 16518 Ledgestone, 78232, (210) 490-4572

AE-1	L-2	L-4	L-6
L-1	L-3	L-5	L-8

Randolph AFB, 78150-5001, (210) 652-1110, ET=Located by East Tower,

AT-6D	T-29 (ET)	T-37B
T-11 (ET)	T-33A	T-38A
T-28A	T-34B	T-41

Texas Transportation Museum, 11731 Wetmore Rd, 78247, (210) 490-3554,
Thur-Fri 9-4, Sat-Sun 10-5, Adm Adult $6, Child Under 12 $4,
www.txtransportationmuseum.org   JN-4D   Trains

Texas Air Museum, 8535 Mission Rd, Stinson Mncpl Airport, 78214
(210) 977-9855, Fax 927-4447, Mon-Sat 11-5, Closed TD, CE, CD, NE, ND,
Adm Adult $4, Snrs 55 &Mil $3, Child 6-12 $2, Under 12 $1, Gift Shop,
www.texasairmuseum.org, AT-6,   Bleriot,   FW-190A-8

San Marcos - CAF - Centex Wing, 1841 Airport Dr, 77666, (512) 396-1943,
Mon,Wed,Fri-Sat 9-4, Adm $3, Gift Shop, All Aircraft Flyable, www.realtime.net/centex

AT-6 (2ea)	CJ-6 (3ea)	P-39Q	T-34A
B-25J	L-4	T-33	U-3A

Schulenburg - Stanzel Model Aircraft Museum, 311 Baumgarten St, 78956,
(979) 743-6559, Fax 743-2525, Mail POB 6, 78956, Mon, Wed, Fri-Sat 10:30-4:20, Sun 1:30-4:30,
Adm Adult $2, Senior $1, Under 12 Free, www.stanzelmuseum.org,
30 Static Model Displays

Slaton - Texas Air Museum, Caprock Chapter, Slaton Airport, Mail: POB 667,
79364, (806) 796-7618, Tue, Thur 11-3, Sat 9-4, Adm Adult $5 & Child $3, Gift Shop,
Restoration Facility, Contact: Mike De Lano 828-4334, Malcolm Laing 863-2118,
www.texasairmuseum.com

A-7B	F-4S	L-2M	M-16 Halftrack
AT-6G	F-14A	L-3J	M- 4 HS Tractor
AT-19	F-101	NA-64	M-59
Bf-108	F-105D	T-2	M- 2 Halftrack
Bf-109F-4	H-1(UH)	T-33	
DH-104	Ki-51		

TEXAS

Sweetwater - National Wasp WWII Museum, Avenger Field, 210 loop 170, Mail: POB 456, 79556, (254) 710-7202, Thur-Mon 1-5, Gift Shop, www.waspwwii.com, Artifacts

Terrell - British Flying Training School Museum, 119 Silent Wings Dr, Terrell Mncpl Airport, POB 1586, 75160, (972) 524-1714, Fri-Sat 10-5, Sun 1-5, Artifacts

Tyler - Historical Aviation Memorial Museum, 2198 Dixie Dr, Tyler Pounds Airport, 75704 Mail: 150 Airport Dr, (903) 526-1945, Fax 692-1202, Mon-Sat 10-4, Adm Adult $4, Child 6-18 $2, Under 6 Free, Gift Shop , Library, Theater, Restoration Facility, www.tylerhamm.com

TA-4J	F-105D	H-1H(UH)	T-2C
AD-5	F-111A	L-29	T-33
F-100	F4D	MiG-17F	
F-104A	FJ-4	Quail	

Uvalde - Aviation Museum, Garner Field Airport, Hangar 1, Sul Ross Blvd, 78802, Mail: POB 453, (830) 278-2552, Wed-Fri

L-4	PT-19 Project	Vari-Giggan

Waco - CAF - Ranger Wing, Waco Regional Airport, Mail: POB 8060, 76714-8060, www.rangerwingcaf.com,   A-26   T-37

Wharton - CAF - River Bend Squadron, Wharton Regional Airport, Rte 1 Box 660, Hwy 59, 1st Sat Monthly 2pm, BT-14,   www.riverbendsquadron.org

Wichita Falls - Sheppard AFB, 76311-5000, (940) 851-2511, STTC/XR

B-52D	F-4D	F-101C	T-29A
C-130A	F-4E	F-102A	T-29A(GT)
C-130E	F-5E	F-104C	T-33A
C-135	F-15A	F-105D	T-33A(QT)
F-4C	F-100D(GF)	F-111A	T-38A

UTAH

Bluffdale - Camp Williams, 17111 S Camp Williams Rd, 84065, 40.503142, -112.009227 (801) 254-9036, Mon-Fri 9-5, UH-1

Draper - Utah National Guard Headquarters, 12953 S Minuteman Dr, 84020-9286, F-86

Ft Douglas - Ft Douglas Military Museum, 32 Potter St, 84113-5046,(801) 581-1251, Tue-Sat 12-5, Free Adm, AH-1, OH-6, UH-1, Tanks (5ea)

Heber - Heber Valley Aero Museum, 2002 Airport Rd, Russ McDonald Field, SOAR Hangar, 84032-4026, Mail: POB 680405, Park City, UT, 84068, (435) 657-1826, Gift Shop , www.hebervalleyaeromuseum.org ,

Boeing Stearman	J-3	MiG-15	T-28

Ogden - (See Next page)

Salt Lake - CAF - Utah Wing, Wing Leader: Richard W Meyer, POB 26333, 84126, (801) 571-3610, www.cafutahwing.org   AT-19   F4U   PT-17

Salt Lake City ANG, Salt Lake City Int'l Airport, 84116, 151st ARG, F-86A   F-105B

Washington - Southern Utah Air Museum, 400 W Telegraph Rd, 84780 (435) 656-8292, www.suam.us Restoration of Nose Sections

Wendover - Historic Wendover Airfield, Inside Operations Bldg, 345 S Airport Apron Rd, 84083, (435) 665-2308, Office (801) 571-2907, Daily 8-6, Free Adm, Gift Shop www.wendoverairbase.com, Artifacts   T-28B   T-33 (2ea)

West Jordan - National Guard Armory, Salk Lake City Airport, 7602 S Airport Rd, UH-6,   UH-1

UTAH

Ogden - Hill Aerospace Museum, 75th ABW/MU, 7961 Wardleigh Rd, 84056-5842, (801) 777-6868
Exit #341 & I-15, Daily 9-4:30, Closed TD, CD, ND, Free Adm, Gift Shop, Theater,
www.hill.af.mil/museum/

A-1E	B-52G	F-15A	LGM-30A
A-7F(YA)	B-57A(RB)	F-16	LGM-30G
A-10A	BGM-109G	F-18A	LGM-118A (4ea)
A-26B	BOLT-117	F-80A Mock-Up	Link AN-T-18
ADM-20C	BT-13B	F-84F	MiG-17
AGM-45	Burgess-Wright Flyer	F-84F(RF)	MiG-21F
AGM-65A	C-7B	F-84G	O-2A
AGM-84L	C-45H	F-86F	OQ-2A
AGM-86	C-47D(VC)	F-86L	OV-10A
AGM-109	C-54G	F-89H	P-38J
AIM-4	C-119G	F-100A	P-40KT-37B
AIM-7	C-123K	F-101A(RF)	P-47D
AIM-9	C-124C	F-101B	P-51DT-38A
AIM-26	C-130B	F-102A	PT-17
AIM120	C-130B Simulator	F-105D	SR-71C
AQM-34L	C-131D	F-105G	T-28B
AIR-2A	C-140	F-106A	T-29C
A-26B	CBU Mk.20	F-111E	T-33A
AT-6	CH-3E	H-1(HH)	T-37B
B-1B	CIM-10A	H-3E(CH)	T-38A
B-17G	CIM-10B	H-13T(TH)	T-39A
B-24D Project	F-4C	H-21C(CH)	U-3A
B-25J	F-4C(RF) (2ea)	H-34J(HH)	V-1
B-26	F-4D	H-43B(HH)	Wright Flyer 3/4 Scale
B-29	F-4E	JN-4D	XSM-62A
B-47E(WB)	F-5E	L-4J	

VERMONT

Burlington - Burlington ANG, Burlington Int'l Airport, 05401, (802) 658-0770, 158 TFG

B-57B(EB)	F-4D	F-102A
C-45	F-89J	T-29
C-131	F-94C	T-33A

Post Mills - Experimental Balloon & Airship Museum, Post Mills Airport, Robinson
Hill Rd, Mail: POB 51, 05058, (802) 333-9254, Dir: Brian Boland, Apt Only,
Over 60 Balloons and Airships, 24 Other Vehicles.

VIRGINIA

Bealeton - Flying Circus Aerodrome, 15S. Route 17, BOX 99, 22712, (540) 439-8661,
Daily 11-Sunset, Adm Adult $10, Child $3, Under 3 Free, Airshow Every Sun at 2:30, May Thru Oct,
www.flyingcircusairshow.com   Rides Available   (See Biplane and Warbird Rides Section)

Corbin Jr Ace	Fokker D.VIII	PT-17	Waco UPF-7
Fleet Biplane	J-3 (2ea)	Stearman A-75 (8 ea)	

VIRGINIA

Chantilly - NASM/Udvar-Hazy Center, 14390 Air and Space Parkway, Washington Dulles Int'l Airport SE Corner, 20151, (202) 357-2700, Mail: NASM, Independence Ave at 6th St SW, Suite 3700, Washington, DC, 20560-0321, (202) 357-4487, Daily 10-5:30, Free Adm, Parking $12, 135 Spacecraft, www.nasm.si.edu/museum/udvarhazy/ (S) = Storage, Rest of Collection in Storage

A-1H (AD-6) (S)
A-6E
American Aerolights Double Eagle (gondola only)
Applebay Zuni II
Arado Ar 234B-2 Blitz (Lightning)
Aero Commander Shrike
Arlington 1A Sisu
Arrow Sport A2-60
Avro VZ-9AV Avrocar
B-17D (S)
B-25J (TB-25J-20) (S)
B-26B(VB) (S)
B-29-35-MO
Bachem Ba 349B-1 Natter (Snake) (S)
Baldwin Red Devil (S)
Balloon Basket USA WWI
Balloon Basket USMC WWI
Balloon Basket Wicker
BB-1
BD-5A/B
Beech D18S (S)
Beech 35 Bonanza (S)
Beech King Air
Beech King Air 65-90
Bell 47J (VH-13J)
Bell Model 30
Bell ATV (Air Test Vehicle) (S)
Bellanca CF
Bennett Phoenix Viper 175 Delta Wing
Bennett Phoenix Streak Delta Wing
Bennett Mariah M-9 Delta Wing
Bennett Phoenix 6 Delta Wing
Bennett Model 162 Delta Wing
Benoist-Korn
Bensen B-6 Gyroglider
Bensen B-8M Gyrocopter
Berliner 1924 Helicopter No.5 (S)
Boeing 727-100 (S)
Boeing 307 Stratoliner
Boeing 367-80
Bowlus BA-100 Baby Albatross
Bowlus-Du Pont Albatross
BT-13A
Bü-133C
Bü-181B (S)
C-2 Collegian (S)
C-35(AC)
C-121C
C-150L (S)
Caudron G.4
Cessna 180
Cessna Citation (S)
Concorde
Curtiss E Boat
Curtiss-Wright X-100 (S)
CW-1 Junior (S)
Dassault Cargo Fanjet Falcon 20C

DH-98 B/TT Mk.35
DHC.1A
Do-335A-1
Double Eagle Balloon Gondola (S)
DSI NASA Oblique Wing RPRV
Eipper-Formance Cumulus 10
Erco 415 Ercoupe (S)
Extra 260XP (S)
F-4S-44
F-14D
F-8G(RF)
F-100D (S)
F-105D (S)
F-86A
F4U-1D
F6C-4
F6F-3
F8F-2
F9C-2
F9F-6 (S)
Fa 330A-1 Bachstelze (S)
FA-3-101
Farman Sport
FB-5 Hawk
Felixstowe (NAF) F5L (S)
Fowler-Gage Tractor
Fw 190F-8/R1
G-21
G-22
G4M3 (nose section only) (S)
Gates Learjet 23
Gittens Ikenga 5302
Global Flyer
Gondola Balloon (Piccard)
Gondola (Raven)
Gondola (Strato-Jump III)
Goodyear K-Car (airship gondola) (S)
Goodyear (airship gondola) (S)
Gossamer Albatross
Grob 102 Standard Astir III
Grunau Baby lib
H-1H(UH)
H-13J(VH)
H-19A(YH)
H-34D(UH) (S)
Halberstadt CL.IV
Hawker Hurricane Mk.IIC
He 162A-2 (S)
He 219 Fuselage
He 219A-2
Helio No. 1
Hiller 1031-A-1 Flying Platform (VZ-1)
HM.14 Pou du Ciel
HOE-1
Horten IIIF
Horten IIIH
(Continued on Next Page)

(From Previous Page)

Horten VI-V2
Huff-Daland Duster
HV-2A (S)
Ilyushin IL-2 Sturmovik (S)
J-1 (S)
J-3 Cub
J1N1-S
JC-24C Windecker Eagle I (S)
JN-4D (S)
Ju 52/3m (CASA 352L)
Junkers 388L-1 (S)
Kaman K-225
Kaman K-228
Ki-43-IIb (S)
Ki-45
KR-34C
L-5
Langley Aerodrome A
Lockheed 5C Vega "Winnie Mae"
Loudenslager Laser 200
M-2 Douglas Mailplane
M-18C Mite
M6A1
Mahoney Sorceress
Manta Pterodactyl Fledgling
Martin, J.V., K-III Kitten (S)
Me 410A-3/U1 (S)
Me 163B-1a (S)
MIG-15bis
MIG-21F-13
Monnett Moni
Monocoupe 110 Special
Monocoupe 70 (S)
MXY7 Ohka 22
N-1M
N-9H
N1K2-Ja
N2S-5 Kaydet
NAF N3N-3
Nagler-Rolz NR 54 V2
Nemesis
Nieuport 28.C1
NLS-5
O-1A (L-19A) (S)
O-2A (S)
O-47A (S)
OS2U-3
P-26A Peashooter
P-38J-10-LO
P-39Q (S)
P-40E Warhawk
P-47D-30-RA
P-51C
P-61C-NO
P-63F (S)
PA-12 Super Cruiser (S)
PA-18 Super Cub

PA-23 Apache (S)
Pathefinder (Solar Power Wing)
Phoenix 6B
Pitcairn AC-35
Pitts Special S-1S
Pitts Special S-1C
PV-2 (2ea)
RC-3 (S)
PT-22
RF-8G
N.A. Rockwell Shrike Commander 500S
Robinson R-22
Robinson R-44
Rotorway Scorpion Too
RP-63A (S)
RT-14 Turner Meteor
Rutan Quickie (S)
Rutan VariEze
SB2C-5 Helldiver (S)
Schweizer 2-22 EK
SGU 2-22 EK
Sharp DR 90
SNJ-4 (AT-6) (S)
SPAD XVI
Sperry-Verville M-1
Sportwings Valkyrie
SR-71
Stanley Nomad
Stearman-Hammond Y (S)
Stout Skycar (S)
Su-26M
T-33A
Ta 152H-1 (S)
TBF-1C
TG-1A
Travel Air D4D Pepsi Skywriter
U-2
Ultraflight Lazair SS EC
VB-26B (S)
Verville Sport Trainer (S)
VZ-1 (S)
VZ-2A (S)
Waco 9 (S)
Waco UIC (S)
Waterman Aerobile
Westland Lysander IIIa
X-35
XH-44
XO-60
XP-84 (forward fuselage only) (S)
XR-4 (VS-316)
XR-5 (VS-317) (S)
XR-8 (S)
XV-1 (S)
XV-15
Yak-18 "Max" (S)
YROE-1

Franklin - CAF - Old Dominion Museum, Hampton Roads Executive Airport, Rte 58, (757) 481-1230, www.olddominionsquadron.org (Note1=Storage at Hampton Roads Exec Airport)

C-60A(L-18) (Note1)	L-5 Project	L-19	US-2B

VIRGINIA

Ft Eustis - US Army Transportation Museum, 300 Washington Blvd, Besson Hall,
23604-5260, (757) 878-1115, Tue-Sun 9-4:30, Free Adm, Gift Shop, Library, Theater
www.eustis.army.mil/dptmsec/museum.htm

Bell Rocket Belt	H-1B(UH)	H-25A(UH)	TH-55A
CH-47	H-1H(UH)	H-34C(CH)	U-8D
CV-2	H-13E	H-37B(CH)	U-6A
DeLacker Aerocycle	H-19C(UH)	H-54A(CH)	VZ-8P2
GEM X-2	H-21C(CH)	O-1A	VZ-4-DA
H-1A(UH)	H-23B(OH)	RU-8D	VZ-9V

Hampton - Air Power Park, 413 W Mercury Blvd Off Hwy 64 West, 23666,
(757) 727-1163, Daily 9-4:30, Free Adm,

A-7E	F-86L	Hawker P.1127	Polaris A-2
AIM 4	F-100D	MA14/LJ-5B	SM-78
Argo-D-4	F-105D	NIM-14	T-33A-1
Copral M2	F-89J50	NIM	V-6A(XV)
F-4C(RF)	F-101B	P-1127	

Virginia Air and Space Center, 600 Settlers Landing Rd, 23669-4033, (757) 727-0900,
(800) 296-0800, Sept-May Mon-Sat 10-5, Sun 12-5, May-Sept Mon-Wed 10-5, Thur-Sun 10-7
Closed CD, Adm Adult $9, Snr $8, Child 3-18 $7, Cafe, Gift Shop, IMAX, www.vasc.org

American AA-1	F-16A(YF)	H-1M(UH)	Rutan Vari-eze
A-6 Nose	F-18	J-3	Schleiche ASW-12
Apollo 12	F-104C	N2S-3	Wright Flyer
B-24 Nose	F-106B(NF)	P-39Q	XV-6A
DC-9	F-84F	Pershing II Missile	
F-16 Cockpit	F-4E	Pitts S-1-C	

Langley AFB, 23665-5548, (757) 764-2018, 1st FW/PA

B-52G	F-15A(YF)	F-16A	F-86H	F-105D

Manassas - CAF - National Capital Squadron, 12499 Beverly Ford Rd, Brandy Station, 22714
(540) 727-0018, Squadron Leader: Robert C Flint, BT-13, L-5(2)

Newport News - Virginia War Museum, 9285 Warwick Blvd (US 60), Huntington Park, 23609
(757) 247-8523, Mon-Sat 9-5, Sun 1-5, Closed TD, CD, Adm Adult $6, Snrs 62 $5, Child 7-18 $4,
Under 7 Free, Gift Shop, www.warmuseum.org, HH-52A

Norfolk - Naval Air Station, Eugene Ely Air Park

A-6	F-14	HSL-30	SH-2F
E-2C	H-53	HT-033	

Nauticus Maritime Museum, A-4

Oceana - Oceana Aviation Historical Park, Oceana NAS, (804) 433-3131, www.nasoceana.navy.mil
Gift Shop June-Sept, Contact PA Officer, 1750 Tomcat Blvd, Virginia Beach, VA 23460

A-4F	F-4B	F-18	F9F-2
A-6E	F-8A	F2H-3	
AD-1	F-14A(009)	F4D-1	

Richmond - Defense General Supply Center, 8100 Jefferson Davis Hwy, (804) 279-3861,

A-6	F-14	F-15	F/A-18	F-84F

VIRGINIA

Richmond - Virginia Aviation Museum, Richmond Int'l Airport, 5701 Huntsman Rd, 23250-2416,
Take Exit 197 South off I-64, (804) 236-3622, Mon-Sat 9:30-5, Sun 12-5, Closed TD, CD,
Adm Adult $6, Snrs 60 $5, Child 4-12 $4, Under 4 Free,Gift Shop, Theater,
Viewable Restoration Facility, www.vam.smv.org

A-4C	F-14	SPAD VII
A-7D	Fairchild 24G	SR-71
Aeronca C-2N	Fairchild FC-2W2	Standard E-1
Aeronca C-3	Flaggler Scooter	Stinson SR-10G
American Aerolight Eagle	Fleet Model	Taylorcraft E-2
Bellanca Skyrocket	H-1V(UH)	Travel Air B-2000
Bruner Winkle Bird	Heath Super Parasol	Vultee V-1AD
Bucker Jungmeister	J-3 Piper Cub	Waco YOK
Cirrus 2 Hang Glider	JN-4D	Wright Brothers 1900
Curtiss Robin J-1D	PietenpohlAir Camper	Wright Brothers 1901
Curtiss A-14	Pershing II Missile	Wright Brothers 1902
Eipper Quicksilver MX	Pitcairn PA-5	Wright Brothers 1903
Ercoupe 415-D	Quickie 200 Tri-Gear	WB Kite 1899

Sandston ANG, 192 TFG/CC, Byrd Int'l Airport, 23150, (804) 272-8884,
A-7D   F-84F   F-105D

Suffolk - Military Aviation Museum, Fighter Factory,1341 Princess Anne Rd, 23457,
Virginia Beach Airport, (757) 721-7767, Mail: Suite 500, 4455 S Blvd, Virginia Beach, VA 23452,
Daily 9-7, Pres Gerald Yagen, www.militaryaviationmuseum.org, email epy 1@aol.com

(P) = Project   (R) = Restoration   (S) = Storage Virginia Beach Facility

A-20 (R)	DHC-1	I-153	SNJ-2
A-26 (R)	F-86 (R)	Ki-61 (P)	SNJ-4
A-35A	FG-1D	L-5	Spitfire
AD-4	F4U-1D (P)	MiG-3	N2S-3
Albatross D.V	Fairey Firefly (P)	OS2U (R)	T-28D
B-25J (R)	Fi-156	P-38 (P)	T-34
Bf-108	Fiat G.55 (R)	P-39 (R)	TBM
Bf-109E-7(R)	Fleet 2 (P)	P-40E	V-1(Fi-103) (R)
Bf-109K	Fw-190A-8 (P)	P-51D	Wright Vin Fiz
Bf-208	Fw-190A-8N (P)	P-63E (P)	Yak-3M
Bu-133C	Hawker Hurricane(P)	PBY 5-A	Yak-18 (R)
CL-1V	Hughes 500	Po-2	Yak-55
DH-82A	I-16 (R)	R-6 (R)	Vultee Vergeance (P)
DH-98 (R)	I-152	Sea Fury FB.Mk.II	

Virginia Air National Guard, Camp Pendleton, 23458, (757) 437-4600, F-84F

Triangle- National Museum of the Marine Corps, 18900 Jefferson Davis Hwy, 22172,
(877) 653-1775, Daily 9-5, Closed CD, Free Adm, Cafe, Gift Shop, Library, Restoration Facility
Theater, (S) = Storage (LG) = Leatherneck Gallery, (LW) = Legacy Walk, (KG) = Korea Gallery,
(VNG) = Vietnam Gallery (WWIG) = WWII Gallery, (S) = Storage at Quantico Marine Corp Facility
www.usmcmuseum.org

A-4E (VNG)	H-46(CH) (VNG)	AV-8B Fuse (S)	S-4 (S)
AV-8B	HO3S-1 (KG)	F3D-2(EF-10B) (S)	SNJ-5 (S)
DH 4 (LW)	HRS-1 (LG)	F6C-4 Rep (S)	SBD-3 (S)
F4F-4 (WWIG)	JN-4D (LG)	F-4A (S)	OY-2 (S)
F4U-4 (LG)	MXY7 Oka Mod II (LW)	H-1J(AH) (S)	PV-1 (S)
F9F-2 (KG)	TBM-3E (WWIG)	H-34(VH) (HUS-Z) (S)	YRON-1 (S)
FG-1A (LG)	**Following at Quantico**	H-53A(CH) (S)	
H-1E(UH) (LW)	A-2 Curtiss (S)	HTL-4 (S)	

Wallops Island - NASA Wallops Visitor Center, Bldg J-17, 23337, (757) 824-2298,
Thur-Mon 10-4, Adm Free, Gift Shop, Rockets, www.wff.nasa.gov/vc/
Beech C23   Rockets: Little John, Nike-Cajun,

WASHINGTON

Arlington - Flying Heritage Collection, Bldg 17622, 51st St, (360) 435-2172, By Appt Thur 9-4
Fri-Sat 10-12 & 2-4, Adm Adult $20, Snrs $16, www.flyingheritage.com

A6M3-22	F-8	Hurricane Mk XIIb	P-38L
A6M5-52 (2ea)	F-84G	He-111H (2ea)	P-40C
AD-4N	F-86A	IL-2M-3	P-47D
B-17E	F-105G	Il-16	P-51D
B-25D	FG-1D	JN-4D	Spitfire Mk.Vc
B-25J	Fi-103/V-1	Ki-43-1b	U-2/PO-2
BAE/GR-3	Fi-103R	Me 163B	V-2
Bf 109E-3	Fi-156-C2	Me 262A-1a	Yak-3U
DH.98	FM-2	MiG-21	
F6F-5	FW 190A-5	P-38F	

Bellingham - Heritage Flight Museum, 42000W Bakerview, Ste B, Mail: 4152 Meridan St # 105-135
98226, (360) 733-4422, Fax 733-4423, 3rd Sat Monthly 12-4, www.heritageflight.org

A-1D	H-13	O-1	PT-13
AT-6D	L-13	O-2	PT-19
AT-6F	L-39	P-51D	SNJ-4

Everett - Future of Flight Aviation Center and Boeing Tour, POB 3707, m/s OE-44, 98124-2207,
(360) 756-0086, (800) 464-1476, www.futureofflight.org   Tours of the Boeing Plant

CAF - Evergreen Wing, Snohomish County (Paine Field), Wing Leader: Richard
Scarvie, 2110 S 300th St, Federal Way, 98003, (425) 839-8091, L-2

Museum of Flight Restoration Facility 2909 100th SW, Hangar C72, Everett, Wa 98204,
Tue-Thur 10-4, Sat 9-5, (360) 745-5150, Adm Free, www.museumofflight.org Project = (P)

Boeing 272 (P)	DH Comet (P)	FM-2 (P)	XF8U-1 (P)
Boeing 747	DGA 25	Heath Parasol	

The ME 262 Project, Paine Field (Snohomish County Airport, Bldg 221, (Next to Fire Station)
10727 36th Pl SW, 98204, (425) 290-7878, Mon-Fri 9-5, Contact: Jim Byron,
email: me262project@juno.com, www.stormbirds.com, Me-262 (5ea) Reproduction (3 for sale)

Ft. Lewis - Fort Lewis, 98433, (253) 967-0015, Exit 120, H-1B(UH), Nike Missile
Ajax Missile   Iraq Vehicle   Tanks Issaquah

Olympia - Olympic Flight Museum, 7637 A Old Highway 99 SE, 98501, (360) 705-3925,
Wed-Sun 11-5, Closed TD, CD, Adm Adult $5, Child 7-12 $3, Gift Shop,
www.olympicflightmuseum.com

A6M2	F-104A	H-1K(HH)	T-28
AT-6 (2ea)	FG-1D	Hawker Hunter	T-37B
BAC-167	FM-2L-2	L-39	TBM-3
BAE	H-1(AH)	P-51D	

Port Townsend - Port Townsend Aero Museum, Jefferson County Airport,
Mail: POB 101, Chimacum, 98325, (360) 531-0252, 437-0863, Wed-Sun 9-4,
Closed CD, Free Adm, Spruce Goose Cafe 385-3185, Restoration Facility,
www.ptaeromuseum.com, email: thuotte@waypoint.com, (F) = Flyable,(P) = Project

Aeronca 7AC (2ea)(F)	CW-1 (P)	Luscombe 8A (F)
Aeronca C-2 (P)	DH-82B (P)	Piper J-3 (F)
Aeronca C-3 (F)	Funk B75L (P)	Stinson SM8A (2ea)(F)
Aeronca L-3 (F)	Howard Racer Rep	Travel Air 2000
Corben Baby-Ace (F)	Irwin Meteorplane (P)	Travel Air 4000

WASHINGTON

Seattle - Museum of Flight, 9404 E Marginal Way S, King County Int'l Airport, 98108-4097,
(206) 764-5720, Daily 10-5, Adult $14, 65 Plus $13, Child 5-17 $7.50, Closed TD, CD
First Thur of ea Month Free from 5-9pm, Airpark 11-3:30, Gift Shop, Cafe, Theater,
Exec Dir: Ralph Bufano, S=Storage, P=Paine Field, R=Restoration Facility, www.museumofflight.org

Restoration Facility 2909 100th SW, Hangar C72, Everett, Wa 98204, Tue-Thur 10-4, Sat 9-5,
(206) 745-5150, Adm Free, I-5 Exit 189, W on Rte 526, Left on Airport Rd to Snohomish County Airport

A-4F	Durand Mk.V (R)	P-38
A-6E	Eipper Cumulus (R)	P-40N
A-12 Blackbird	Ercoupe 415-C (R)	P-47D-2 (5/8 Scale)
A-26	F-4C	P-51D Replica
AT-6D	F-5A(YF)	P-80C/TV-1 (R)
Aerocar III	F9F-8	P-86A (P)
Aeronca C-2	F-14A	Pfalz D-XII
Aero Sport Scamp 3	F-18L Mockup	PT-13A
Albatross D Va	F-86	Quickie Q.200
Alexander Eaglerock	F-104C	QH-50C
An-2 (S)	Fairchild F-24W	Resurs 500 Capsule
AV-8C (R)	Fiat G.91 PAN	RF-4D (R)
Aviatik D-I	FG-1D	Rotec Rally IIIB (S)
Bede BD-5B	Fokker D VII	Rotorway Scorpion Two
Bensen B-8M (R)	Fokker D VIII	Rutan Quickie (R)
Bf 109E (R)	Fokker E III	Rutan Vari-Eze (R)
Boeing 80-A	Fokker DR I	Rutan Vari Viggen (R)
Boeing 247-D (R)	FM-2 (R)	Rumpler Taube
Boeing 100	Gossamer Albatross II	SE-5A
Boeing 727-022 (R)	H-1H(UH) (R)	Sopwith F.1
Boeing 737-130	H-12(UH)	Sopwith Pup
Boeing 737-200	H-21B (R)	Sopwith 7F.1 Snipe
Boeing 747-121	H-32(YH)	Sopwith Triplane
B-17F (P) (R)	H-52(HH) (R)	Spad XIII
B-29	Heath Parasol (R)	Spitfire Mk IX
B-29 Nose	Huber 101-1 Aero (R)	Sorrell Bathtub Parasol (P)
B-47E (P) Boeing Field	Insitu Aerosonde	SR-71A Cockpit (P)
B-52G (R)	J-2 (R)	Stephens Akro (P)
BC-12 (R)	J-3C-65	Stinson 108 (P)
Bf-109E-3	JN-4D	Stinson SR Float
Boeing B&W Replica	Ki-43B	Swallow CAM 3
Bowers Flybaby BA-100 (R)	Kolb Ultralight (S)	T-33 (Project)
Bowlus BA-100 (P)	L-3B	T-33 Cockpit
C-1 Curtiss Robin	L-13B (CL-13B) (P)	Task Silhouette (S)
C-3B Stearman	L-106 Alcor Glider (P)	Taylorcraft A (R)
C-45	L-1049G	T-18 (P)
C-137B(VC) #970	Lear Fan 2100	Vickers Viscount 724
C-140 (S)	LF-107 (R)	Wickham B
CA-20	Lilienthal Glider	Yak-9
Cascade Kasperwing 180-B (S)	LNE-1 (PR-G1) (R)	XF8U-1 (R)
Chanute-Herring	M-1	XF2Y-1 (S)
CG-2 (P)	M-21	Wright Glider
Concorde	McAllister Yakima Clipper	AGM-86A
D-21B Drone	MiG-17	GAPA
da Vinci Uccello (R)	MiG-21 PFM	IM-99 Bomarc
DC-2 (S)	Monnett Monerai (S)	KD6C-2 Drone
DC-3	N-62 Sather RPV (DEX-1) (P)	Apollo Module
DGA-15P (R)	N1K2 (S)	Boeing Upper Stage
DH 4C Comet (R)	Nieuport 24 (S)	Hibex Nose Section
DH 4M	Nieuport 27	Mercury Capsule Replica
DH 100 (R)	Nieuport 28	Pterodactyl Ascender (R)
LNE-1	OMAC-1 (P)	Pterodactyl Ascender II (R)
Dornier DO.27 (R)	P-12	Sputnik

WASHINGTON

Seattle - Seattle Historical Society Museum of History & Industry, 98112, (206) 324-1125, 2700 24th Ave, Adm Adult $1.50, Child $0.50, Curator:William Standard, B-1 Flying Boat

Pacific Science Center, 200 Second Ave N, 98109, (206) 443-2001, June-Sept Mon-Fri 10-5, Sat-Sun 10-6, Adm Adult $10, Snrs 65 $ 8.50, Child 3-12 $7, Gift Shop, Theater, www.pacsci.org Gemini XI Mock Up

Spokane - Armed Forces and Aerospace Museum, Mail 5813 E 4th Ave, 99212-0308, (509) 244-0244 or 994-5272, www.armedforces-aerospacemus.org
All Aircraft at Fairchild AFB Airpark (Miliatry Access Only)

AJAX	F-86E	F-102	NIKE
B-52D	F-101 (2ea)	F-105	T-33A
C-47D	F-101	GAM 72	

Stevenson - Columbia Gorge Interpretive Center Museum, 990 SW Rock Creek Dr, Mail POB 396, 98648, (800) 991-2338, Daily 10-5, Closed TD, CD, Adm Adult $7, Snrs 60 & Student $6, Child 6-12 $5, Under 6 Free, www.columbiagorge.org   JN-4   Primary Trainer

Tacoma - McChord Air Museum, McChord AFB, Bldg 517, 98438-0205, Ext 125 Off I-5, E on Bridgeport Way, Main Gate to Visitors Center, Mail: POB 4205, (253) 982-2485/2419, Wed-Sat 12-4, Closed: TD, CD, ND, Free Adm, Gift Shop, www.mcchordairmuseum.org

A-10A	C-47C(TC)	F-4C	F-102A
B-18A	C-82A	F-15A	F-106A
B-23A	C-124C	F-86D	SA-10A(PBY)
B-25 Nose	C-141B	CF-101F	T-33A Last Built

Glen E Spieth Museum Antiques, 5928 Steilacoom Blvd, 98499, (253) 584-3930, Sat 11-5, By Appt, T-33A   T-33 Fuse   B-17 Parts

Mr Benhouser, AT-11 in Front Yard, 121th Ave

Tillicum - Camp Murray Air National Guard Park, Exit 122, (253) 512-8524
F-101B   M-5 Stuart   M-47 Walker Bulldog Tank

Vancouver - Pearson Air Museum, 1115 E 5th St, 98661, (360) 694-7026,Wed-Sat 10-5, Closed TD, CD, ND, Adm Adult $6, Mil/Snr $5, Child 6-12 $3, Gift Shop, Theater, Restoration Facility, www.pearsonairmuseum.org

ADOCK	Foker Dr.I	Mooney Mite M-18C	Starduster II
Aeronca C-3B	Formula 1 Racer 3ea	Nieuport Rep	Stearman 1942
AN-2	GAT-1 Link Trainer	Polan Special	Student Prince
AT-6(SNJ)	H-1(AH)	PT-17	T-28
Baby Great Lakes	J-3	PT-19B	Taylor Craft
Curtiss Pusher	JN-4D	PT-21/22	Travel Air B-4000
DH 82	L-4	Rearwin Sportster	Waco UPF-7
DC-3	Lindsey Model 2	Rutan Quickie	Wasol Racer
Fairchild 24	Meyers OTW	Ryan STA	Wright Flyer Rep
Fleet Model 2	Mini-Cab	Seahawker Biplane	WSA-1

Whidbey Island Naval Air Station, (360) 257-2211, KA-6D

Yakima - McAllister Museum of Aviation, 2008 S 16th Ave, McAllister Field, Yakima Air Terminal, (509) 457-4933, Sat 9-5, Free Adm, Tue-Sat 10-4, Contact Don Clark, www.mcallistermuseumofaviation.org, Aeronca 7AC, Starduster

WEST VIRGINIA

Charleston - Charles ANG, 25311-5000, (304) 357-5100,   P-51D

WISCONSIN

Appleton - American Legion, 3220 W College, Off I-41, 54914, (920) 733-9840

F-86L	Sherman Tank	M-60 Tank

Camp Douglas - Wisconsin National Guard Memorial Library & Museum, Camp Williams, Volks Field, 54618-5001, (800)752-6659, (608) 427-1280, Wed-Sat 9-4, Sun 12-4, Free Adm,

A-7D	F-4C	F-100C	O-2A
A-10	F-84F	F-102A (2ea)	P-51D
C-97L(KC)	F-86H	F-105B	UH-1

Fond Du Lac - Wisconsin Aviation Museum, 89 North Pioneer Rd Fond du Lac County Airport 54935, (920) 924-9998, Fax 921-3186, Only Open During EAA Show, www.fdl.net/wami,

Adventura Sea Plane	Taylor Monoplane	Woodstock Glider
Ercoupe	Pietenpol AirCamper	
Rotorway 162	Steen Skybolt	

Hardwood Range Target Range, Public Viewing Area, A-4 on Display

Target Planes:	A-6	F-4	T-33	Vigilante
Remnants:	C-135(KC)	USCG Cutter		

Janesville - Black Hawk Airways, Hwy 51 S, 53542, (608) 756-1000, Beech D18S(C-45)

Black Hawk Technical School, Aviation Center, P.O. Box 5009
53547, (608) 757-7743, HH-3 T-33

Kenosha - Gateway Technical Aviation Center, 4940 88th Ave, 53144, (262) 656-6976, F-84F

Madison - Truax Field Museum, Dane County Regional Airport, 4000 Int'l Lane, In the New Pax Terminal, 53704, (608) 246-3380,

Corben Super Ace	Cobra	F-16	H-1(UH)

Wisconsin Veterans Museum, 30 W. Mifflin St, Capitol Square,
53703-2558, (608) 264-6086, Sopwith Pup Rep P-51

Milwaukee - Milwaukee Aera Tech, 422 E College Ave, 53200, (414) 571-4799,

L-19	H-3 (HH)	T-34

Milwaukee ANG, De Havilland Heron T-33A

Mitchell Gallery of Flight, 5300 S Howell Ave, Main Terminal Gen Mitchell Int'l Airport, 53207-6156, (414) 747-4503, Fax 747-4525, Daily 24 Hours, Free Adm www.mitchellgallery.org/, B-25J-25-NC Curtiss Pusher

Oshkosh - (See Next Page)

Superior - Richard I Bong WWII Heritage Center, 305 Harborview Parkway,54880 (715) 392-7151, Mid May-Mid Oct Mon-Sat 9-5, Mid Oct-Mid May Tue-Sat 9-5, Adm Adult $9, Snrs 65 & Child 13-18 $8, Child 6-12 $7, under 6 Free, Gift Shop, www.bongheritagecenter.org, P-38L-5

Waukesha - CAF/Wisconsin Wing, N9 W24151 Blu M, 53186, Mail: PO Box 1998, 53110-1998, (262) 547-1775, www.cafwi.org, PV-2D

WISCONSIN

Oshkosh - EAA Air Adventure Museum, Wittman Airfield, 3000 Poberezny Rd, US 41 Exit 44
POB 3086, 54903-3086, (920) 426-4818, Mon-Sat 8:30-5, Sun 11-5,
Closed TD, CD, ND, Adm Adult $8.75, Snrs 62 $7.75, Child 6-17 $6.75, Under 6 Free, Family $22,
Group Rates, Gift Shop, Library, www.airventuremuseum.org

A-4B(A4D-2)	E-2	J-1
A-1E/AD-5	EAA Super Acro Sport	J-2
A-1E/AD-3	EAA A-1	J-3
Acroduster SA-700 H.G.G.	EAA P-8	J2F-6
Aero Sea Hawk	Eipper MX-1 Quicksilver	JC-1
Aeronca C-2N	Ercoupe 415-C	JC24-B
Aeronca LC	F-80C(GF)	JN-2D-1
Aeronca C-3	F-84C	JN4-D (2ea)
Aeronca K	F-84F(GF)	JP-001
Anderson Greenwood 14	F-86 Mk V	Kaminskas RK3
B-17G	F-86 Mk V/VI	Karp Pusher 107
B-25J	F-86H	Kiceniuk Icarus V
Baby Ace D Lambert	F-89J	Knight Twister
Baker 001 Special	F-100A	Kotula-Lundy Graflite
Barlow Acapella	F4U-4	L-5E-1VW
Barrage Kite	Fairchild 24W-46	LC-DW 500
Bates Tractor	Fairchild 24 C8	Learfan LF-2100
Bede XBD-2	Fairchild 24 C8A	Lincoln PT-K
Bede BD-5 Micro	Falck Racer	Lincoln Biplane
Bede BD-4 Stricker	FC-2W2	Loving Racer
Bee Honey Bee	Fi 156C-2	Luscombe Phantom 1
Bensen B-11 Gyrocopter	Fike Model C	M-1 Special
Boeing E75N1	Fokker DR-1	Mace Model III
Brock Kem 8M Gyroplane	Fokker DR-1	Marinac Flying Mercury
Brown-Bushby-Robinson	Folkerts Gullwing	MC-12
Brown Star Lite	Ford 4-AT-E	McHolland Acro-Sport
Brown B-1 Racer	Ford Flivver 268	Meyer Little Toot
Brugioni Mario Cuby	Funk B	MiG-15
Bu 133	GA-22	MiG-21
Bu 133L	GA-400-R-2J	Midgnet Pou du Ciel
Bugatti 100	Glastar 3	Miles M.2.W.
Burgess Twister Imperial	Globe OQ-2A	Mitchell Wing A-10
Cessna 150H	Globe KD2G-2	MJ-5
CG-2 186V	Great Lakes 2-T-1AE	Mong Sport
Chanute Hang Glider	Grouod Trainer	Monnett Moni Van WYK
Chester Racer	Gunderson Trainer	Monnett Sonerai II
Christen Eagle I 2ea	H-1S(AH)	Monnett Monex
Christen Eagle II	H-21B	Monnett Moni
Christen Eagle IF	H-10	Monocoupe 110 Special
Collins Aerofoil Boat	HA-1112-M1L	Monocoupe 110
Corbin D Baby Ace	Hamilton Glasair	Monocoupe 90A
Corbin C-1	Hardly Abelson	Monocoupe 90AW
Co-Z	Harlow PJC-2	Monocoupe 113
CR-4	Haufe Dale Hawk 2	MS 181
Curtiss-Wright B-2	Hawker Hunter Mk 51	N2S-2
Curtiss/Abbott	Heath Parasol	Neibauer Lancair 200
Curtiss/Thompson	Heath LNA-40 Super	Neiuport 24
Cvjetkovic CA-61	Heath Feather	Nitz Executive
DH 98B Mk.35	Heath Super Parasol	Oldfield Special BGL
DH DHC-1B2	Hegy R.C.H.I.	OQ-2A
DH 100 Mk.35	Henderschott Monoplane	OQ-19D
DH 82A	Henderson Highwing	OTW-145
DH 89A MK.IV	Hill Hummer	P-5
DC-3	HM-360	P-51(XP)
Double Eagle V	HP-10	P-64
Driggers A 891H	HP-18-LK-G Sailplane	P-6E
DSA-1	Hugo VPS HU-GO Craft	**(Continued on Next Page)**

(From Previous Page)

P-9
P-10
P-38L
P-51D
P-51D(XP)
PA-22-150
PA-28-140
PA-39
Pedal Plane
Pereira Osprey II
PG-1
Pientenpol B4A Pientenpol
Pientenpol P-9
Piper PT
Pitts P-6
Pitts 1
Pitts Racer
Pitts S-1
Pitts S-1 Special
Pitts S-1S Special 2ea
Pitts S-2
Pitts SC-1
Player Sportplane
Pober Super Ace
Pober Jr Ace
PQ-14B
PT-3
PT-19B/M-62A
Quickie Herron
Questair 200 Venture
Rand KR-1
Rasor 21

Riderf A-1
RLU-1 (2ea)
Rotorway Scorpion I
Rutan 72 Grizzly
Rutan Solitaire
Rutan Vari-eze
Rutan 50-160 Variviggen
RV-3 VanGrusven
RV-4 VanGrunsven
Ryan NX-211
Ryan SCW-145y
Schemp-Hirth Nimbus II
Scorpion II 754RW
Shafor Ganagobie
SM-8A
Smith Miniplane
Smyth Sidewinder
Sorrell DR-1
Spad VII Swanson
Spartan 7W Executive
Spinks Akromaster
Spitfire Mk.IXE
Starduster SA-300
Stinson SR-9C
Stits SA-2A
Stits SA-3A
Stits SA-8
Stits DS-1
Stits SA-11A
Stolp SA300
Stolp V Star
Stolp SA500L

Swallow Model 1924
Swenson S1
T-18
T-33 Mk 3
T-33A
T-40
Taylor Aerocar
Taylorcraft BC
Tessier Biplane
Travel Air E-4000
Travel Air 2000
UFM Solar Riser
UHM Easy Riser]
V-260/USD
Vector 27
Waco CTO
Waco RNF
Waco YKS-7
Wag-Aero Cuby
Warwick W-4
WD-A
WE-1
Welsh Rabbit Model A
Whitaker Centerwing
Wings Avid Flyer
Wisman Pusher
Wittman Midwing
Wittman DFA
Wittman Tailwind WO
Wittman W
Wittman WV
Wright Flyer

Basler's Flight Service, Whittman Field, 54901, Restores DC-3's

WYOMING

Afton - Cal Air Museum, 1042 S Washington, 83110, (307) 886-9881, Callair Airplanes (3ea)

Cheyenne - Francis E Warren ICBM & Heritage Museum, Warren AFB, 7405 Marne Loop, Bldg 210, 82005-5000,(307) 773-2980, Mon-Fri 8-4, Free Adm, Gift Shop, www.warrenmuseum.com, H-1F(UH)

WY ANG Cheyenne, BOX 2268, Mncpl Airport, 82003-2268, (307) 772-6201, CMS: MD Duncan,
F-84F   F-86L   F-86E   T-33A

CANADA
ALBERTA
Calgary - Aero Space Museum of Calgary, 4629 McCall Way NE, T2E 8A5, (403) 250-3752,
Fax 250-8399, Daily10-5, Closed ND, CD, Adm Adult $7, Snrs 60 & Child 6-11 $4.50,
Under 6 Free, Family $18, Gift Shop, Restoration Facility, Curator Anthony Worman, www.asmac.ab.ca/
(C) = Courtyard; (M) = Museum gallery; (O) = Out On Loan, (R) = Restoration Project; (S)=Storage

Avro Lancaster Mk.X (C)	DC-3 (C)	Link Trainer (M)
Avro Anson Mk V (C)	DH 100	Mitchell U-2 (M)
Bagjo BG12 Glider (M)	DH 82 (M)	Quickie II (M)
Barkley Grow T8P-1(O)	DH 98 (R)	S-51 (C)
Barkley Grow T8P-1(S)	DHC-6 (C)	S-55 (C)
Bede BD-5 (S)	F-101B (C)	Sopwith Triplane (M)
Beech D-18S Mk.III (M)	F-86 (M)	T-50 (R)
Bell 47G (M)	Harvard Mk IV (M)	Taylorcraft Auster Mk.VII (R)
Cessna 188 (C)	Hawker Hurricane XIIb (R)	WACO EQC-6 (M)

Edmonton - (See Next Page)

Innisfail - Royal Canadian Legion Branch # 104, 5108 - 49 St, T4G 1R9, (403) 227-3622, F-104F

Nanton - Nanton Lancaster Society, POB 1051, T0L 1R0, (403) 646-2270, Fax 646-2214,
May-Oct Daily 9-5, Nov-Apr Sat-Sun 10-4, Free Adm, Gift Shop, Restoration Facility
www.lancastermuseum.ca,

Avro 683 Lancaster	CF-100	Link Trainer
Avro Anson MkII (P)	CT-114	PT-18
Beech D18	DH 82 (On Loan)	PT-26
Bristol Bolingbroke /Blenheim (P)	Fleet Fawn Mk II	T-20 Crane
Bristol Blenheim Cockpit	Fleet 7C Mk.II	T-33
BT-14 Yale	Harvard Mk.II	

St Paul - UFO Landing Pad, Hwy 28, NW of City, Mail: Box 887, T0A 3A0, (888) 733-8367
(780) 645-6800, June 22-Aug 31 Mon-Fri 9-6, Sat-Sun 9-5, RoY Mon-Fri 9-5, Artifacts

Wetaskiwin - Reynolds Museum, East of Airport, 4118 57st, T9A 2B6,
(403) 361-1351, Mail: POB 6360, T9A 2G1, Sept-May9 Tue-Sun 10-5, May-Sept Daily 10-5,
Adm Adult $9, Snrs 65 $7, Child 7-17 $5, Under 7 Free, Gift Shop, Library (2,500 Books)
www.cahf.ca/   Biplane Rides Available $116.63 (780) 352-9689

Aeronca O-58	DC-3	Link Trainer
Aeronca Chief	DGA-15P	Meade Glider
Aeronca C-3	DH 60M	Meyers MAC 145
AT-6 Harvard Mk.4	DH 60	Miles M11A
Auster AOP-6	DH 82C	N-75
Avro Avian CF-CDV	DH 100	Pietenpohl Air Camper
Avro Anson MK II	DH 60GM	PT-26
B-25	DH 60X	PT-19
BC-12	DHC. 1	RC-3
Beech D17S	Fairchild 24-C8E	Reynolds Star
Beech 18 Expeditor	Fairchild 71	Reynolds Sport
Bellanca Skyrocket	Fleet 16	Stinson HW75
Boeing Stearman	Fleet Fawn II	T-50
Bristol Bolingbroke MK.IV	Focke Wulf Weihi	T-33
BT-14	Funk B.85C	T8P-1
C-64	H-34	TBM
C-1(EC)	Hawker Hurricane MK.XIII	Waco 10 GXE
C-37	J-5A	Waco YKS-7
C-64 Mk.4	J-2	Waco ZQC-6
CF-101	Jacobs Jaycopter	Waco YPT-14
CF-104	JN-4	Waco UPF-7
CT-134	L-5	
Curtiss Robin	Lincoln Sport	

ALBERTA

Edmonton - Alberta Aviation Museum Assoc, 1140 Kingsway Ave, T5G 0X4, Bldg 11, (780) 451-1175,
Fax: 451-1607, Mon-Fri 10-6, Sat 10-4, Sun 10-4, Adm Adult $7, Snrs 60 $5, Child 13-18 $4
Child 7-12 $3, Under 7 Free, Gift Shop, Manager: Pete Bushko, www.albertaaviationmuseum.com

Avro Avian Replica	CL-13	Loockheed Vega GR.V
B-25J	Cranwell CLA4 (R)	McHardy Lysander 2/3 Scale
Barkley-Grow T8P	CT-33	Noorduyn Norseman (R)
Beech D18S	DH.100	Piccard Hot Air Balloon
Bell 47G	DH.60	Quicksilver 1
Boeing 737-200	DH.82	Sindgler Hurricane 5/8 Scale
C-47/CC-129	DH.89	Stinson SR-9FM
CF-101B	DH98 Mk B35	Tocan Ultrlight
CF-100 (2ea)	Fairchild 71C	Vickers Viking Mk.IV 7/8 Scale
CIM-10B	Fokker Universal	Waco UIC

BRITISH COLUMBIA

Lazo - Comox Air Force Museum, Canadian Forces Base, 19 Wing, V0R 2K0
POB 1000 Stn Forces, V0R 2K0, (250) 339-8162, Daily10-4, Closed CD, ND, Adm Donation
Gift Shop, Library, www.comoxairforcemuseum.ca

C-47	CF-100	H-21	S2F(SC)(CP-121)
CT-114	CF-101B	MiG-21	Spitfire (Project)
DH 100	CF-104	P-107(CP)	T-33

Sidney - British Columbia Aviation Museum, 1910 Norseman Rd, V8L 5V5, (250) 655-3300,
Fax 655-1611, May-Sept Daily 10-4, Oct-Apr Daily 11-3, Adm Adult $7, Snrs & Child $3,
Under 12 Free, Gift Shop, Library, www.bcam.net

A-26	Fleet Model 2	RC-3
Auster AOP Mk VI(Project)	Harvard (Project)	Rutan Quickie
Avro Anson Mk II	Gibson Twin Plane	S-55(HO4S-2)
Bell 47D-1	Lincoln Sport (Project)	SE.5A
Bristol Bolingbroke Mk IV	Luscombe 8A Silvaire	Spitfire Rep
Chanute Glider	Nieuport 17 7/8	T-33 (Project)
DH82C	Nooruyn Norseman	Ultralight Skyseeker C-IFAI
DHC-122	Pac Aero Tradewind	Vickers Viscount
Eastman E-2	Pietenpol	

Langley - Canadian Museum of Flight & Transportation, Hangar #3 - 5333, 216th St,
Langley Airport, V2Y 2N3, (604) 532-0056, Fax 532-0056, Daily 10-4, Closed CD, Boxing D, ND,
Adm Adult $5, Snrs & Child $4, Under 6 Free, Family $12, Gift Shop, Cafe, www.canadianflight.org,

Beechcraft 3NMT	DH 82C	SE-5A Replica
Bowlus BB-1	Fleet 80	Sopwith Camel Replica (Storage)
C-45-3NM	Fleet Finch MkII Rep	Struchen Helicopter (Storage)
Canadian Quickie	Flight Simulator	T-33AN
CF-104D	Handley-Page 52	Taylor Monoplane (Storage)
CF-100 Mk.38	Harvard Mk IIB	Waco INF
CT-114	KD2R Radio Plane	Waco AQC-6
DC-3(CF-PWD)	Mignet Pou du Ciel	Westland Lysander MkIII
DH 100 Mk3	S-55D(H-19)	

MANITOBA

Brandon - Commonwealth Air Training Plan Museum, Inc, Brandon Mncpl Airport, R7A 6N3,
BOX 3, Group 520, RR5, (204) 727-2444, Fax 725-2334, N of Trans Canada Hgwy on #10,
Oct-Apr Mon-Fri 9-4:30, May-Sept, Daily 10-4, Adm Adult $5, Child $3, Under 6 Free
Exec Dir Stephen Hayter, Gift Shop, www.airmuseum.ca, E-mail: hayter@attcanada.net

Anson	CF-100	DC-3 (CC-129)	J-3
AT-6 Harvard	CF-101B	DH 82	P-121(CP)
B-25	CF-104	F-86 Mk VI	Stinson
Bristol Bolingbroke	Cornell	Fleet Fort Project	T-50
C-45 (CT-128)	CT-134A	H-136(CH)	Westland Mk.III
Casara Prayer	CT-33	Hurricane	X-44(CX)

MANITOBA

Portage La Prarie - Southport, Portage La Prarie Manitoba Airport (CFB), Cresent Rd & Royal Rd, C-45,   CT-114   CT-134A,   T-33

Fort La Reine Museum, Hwy 26 & Hwy 1A, 204-857-3259, May-Sept Mon-Sat 9-8, Sun 12-8, Adm Adult $7, Snrs & Child 13-18 $5, Child 5-12 $2, Under 5 Free, CT-134A
www.fortlareinemuseum.ca

Winnipeg - Western Canada Aviation Museum, Inc, Hangar T2, 958 Ferry Rd, R3H-0Y8, (204) 786-5503, Fax 775-4761, Mon-Fri 9:30-4:30, Sat 10-5, Sun and Holidays 12-5, Closed Boxing Day, Good Fri, CD, ND, Adm Adult $7.50, Snrs & Student $5, Child 3-12 $3, Under 3 Free,Gift Shop, Library, Restoration Facility, Facility Rental,
www.wcam.mb.ca/   e-mail: info@wcam.mb.ca

AT-6 Harvard	CP-107	H-136(CH)
Avro Anson Mk.I	CP-121	HA-1112
Avro Anson Mk.V	CT-134	Hiller Helicopter
Avro Anson Mk.II	CX-144	Ju 52/1M
Beech D18S	DC-3	Junkers F-13
Beechcraft 23 Musketeer	DGA-15	Link Trainers
Bellanca 14-19	DH 82C	Lockheed 10A
Bellanca 31-55	DH 100	NA-64
Bellanca 66-75	DHC.3	Norseman Mk IV
Bensen B-7	F-101B Cockpits	Saunders ST-28
Bristol Freighter	F-11A	Saunders ST-27
Bristol Bollingbroke	F-86 Mk.3	Schweizer 2-22
BT-13	Fairchild 24W46	Stinson SR-8
BT-14	Fairchild 71C	T-50
C-37	Fairchild Super 71	T-33A 2 ea
C-45	FC-2	U-6
CF-100	Fokker Super Universal	Vickers Viscount
CF-101B	Fokker F11	Vickers Vedette V
CF-104	Froebe Hellicopter	Waco YKS-6
CF-5	Froebe Ornithopter	
CL-84	Gruneau 2 Glider	

Air Force Heritage Museum, 500 Wing, Memorial Park, Sharpe Blvd, Off Ness, (204) 833-2500 ext 5993, Weekly 9-4, Free Adm

B-25	CF-101	Harvard(AT-6)
Beech 23 Musketeer	CF-100	H-136(CH)Kiowa
C-4/6 Canadair	CF-101	S2F(CP-121)
C-47(DC-3)	CF-104	T-33
CF-5	F-86	

NEW BRUNSWICK

Boiestown' - Central New Brunswick Woodmen's Museum, 6342 Route 8, E6A 1Z5 (506) 369-7214, Fax 369-9081, May-Oct Daily 9:30-5, Adm Adult $5, Snrs $4, Child $2.50, Under 6 Free Family $12, Gift Shop, www.woodsmenmuseum.com, TBM-3E

St. John - New Brunswick Museum, 277 Douglas Ave, Market Square, E2K 1E5, (506) 643-2300, Mon-Fri 9-9, Sat 10-6, Sun 12-5, Adm Adult $6, Snr $4.75, Child 4-18 $3.25, 3 & Under Free, Family $13, Wed 6-9 Free, TBM

NEWFOUNDLAND

Gander - North Atlantic Aviation Museum, 135 Trans Canada Hwy, Mail POB 234, A1V 1W6, (709) 256-2923, Fax 256-4477, Mid June-Aug Daily 9-6, Sept-Mid June Daily 9-4, Adm Adult $4, Senior 65 & Child 6-15 $3, Under 6 Free, Gift Shop, www.naam.ca

Beech D18S	DC-3 Cockpit	Link Trainer	PBY-5A
CF-101B	DH 82	Lockheed Hudson	Quickie 1

Goose Bay - Happy Valley, Labrador Heritage Society Museum, (709) 896-5445, F-101 XL361

NORTHWEST TERRITORIES

Hay River - Buffalo Airways, Box 4998, NWT, X0E 0R0, (403) 874-3333,
C-47(3ea) (Flights To: Yellowknife & Ft Simpson Available)

Prince of Whales - Prince of Whales Nothern Heritage Center, Box 1320
X1A 2L9, (867) 873-7551, Mon-Fri 10:30-5, Sat-Sun 12-5, DH 83C

NOVA SCOTIA

Baddeck - Alexander Grahm Bell National Historic Park, PO BOX 159,
B0E 1B0, HD-4 Hydrofoil Remains, Silver Dart 1909

Clementsport - HMCS/CFB Cornwallis Military Museum, Bldg 41-3 Cornwallis Park,
Mail: POB 31, B0S 1E0, (902) 638-8602, CF-101, T-33

Greenwood - Greenwood Military Aviation Museum, Canex Mall, Ward Rd, Mail: POB 786,
B0P 1N0, (902) 765-1494, Fax 765-1261, June-Aug Daily 9-5, Sept-May Tue-Sat 10-4,
Free Adm, Gift Shop, Library, Cafe, Restoration Facility, www.gmam.ca

Avro Lancaster Mk X	C-47 (P)	P2V-7
Avro Anson Mk II (P)	CP-107 Argus	
Bollingbrooke (P)	CT-33 (2ea)	

Halifax - Atlantic Canada Aviation Museum Society, 1747 Summer St, B3H 3H6
Exit 6 from Hwy 102, Mail: POB 44006, 1658 Bedford Hwy, Bedford, NS, B4A 3X5
Mid-May to Mid-Sept 9-5, (902) 873-3773, Gift Shop, Picnic Area, Wheelchair Acces
http:/acam.ednet.ns.ca,(R=Being Restored), (P=Project) (S=Storage)

Aeronca C-3 (S)	CT-33 Cockpit	Link Trainer
Bell 47-J-2	CT-33	Lockheed 1329-8
Bell 206B	Erco 415C Ercoupe	Lockheed Hudson Mk.6 (S)
CL-13	F-86 Mk.5	PBY-5A (R)
CF-5	Fi-103(V1)FZG-76 (R)	Pitts Special S1-C
CF-100	Hang Glider Eletroflyer	Scamp 1 Homebuilt
CF-101B	Harvard Mk.II	Silver Dart Rep
CF-104	L-19	TBM
CP-107 Simulator	L-Spatz-55	
CP-121	Lincoln Sports	

Halifax Aviation Museum - CF-5, CF-100 Mk 5, F-86, TBM 2ea

Shearwater - Shearwater Aviation Museum, Canadian Forces Base Shearwater, 12 Wing,
Mail: POB 5000 Stn Main, B0J 3A0, (902) 460-1083 & 1011 ext 2139
April-May &Sept-Nov Tue-Fri 10-5, Sat 12-4, June-Aug Tue-Fri 10-5, Sat-Sun 12-4, Closed Dec-March,
Free Adm, Gift Shop, Library & Restoration Facility 460-1011 ext 2165,
www.shearwateraviationmuseum.ns.ca,

AT-6 Mk.II	F-116B (F5B)	Harvard 277	TBM-3
CP-121	F2H-3	HO4S-3	
CT-114	Fairey Swordfish	S2F-3	
F-101	Firefly Mk.I	T-133	

ONTARIO

Barrie - RCAF Assoc, 441 Wing, Hwy 90, East of City, T-33A

Borden - CFB Borden Military Museum, L0M 1C0, Dieppe Rd & Waterloo Rd,
(705) 424-1200, Tue-Fri 9-12 & 1:15-3, Sat-Sun 1:30-4, Closed Day After Holiday Weekend.
AFA = Air Force Annex, Hangar 11, Hangar Rd, Sat & Sun 1-4, Closed Day After Holiday
AP = Air Park

Avro 504	AFA	CS2F	AP	JN-1		Panzer Tank
CF-5	AP	CT-114	AFA	L-13(CL)		Renault Tank
CF-101	AP	DH 82	AFA	T-33	AFA	Sherman Tank
CF-100	AP	F-18				Stuart M5AI Tank
CF-104	AP	F-86	AP			

ONTARIO

Bradford - Guild of Automotive Restores Inc, 44 Bridge St, (705) 775-0499, A-6 Project

Brampton - The Great War Flying Museum, 13691 McLaughlin Rd, Brampton Airport,
(905) 838-4936, May-Oct Sat-Sun 11-5, or By Appt, Adm Adult $5, All Aircraft Flyable
www.greatwarflyingmuseum.com,

Fokker D.VII Rep	Nieuport	SE-5A 7/8	Sopwith 1 ½ Strutter
Fokker DR.I (2ea)	SE-5A	Sopwith Camel (Project)	

Campbellford - Memorial Military Museum, 230 Albert St, K0L 1L0, (705) 653-4848,653-1398

Beech 18 Parts	CF-100	CT-134	PBY Parts
CF-5	CT-33	F-105 Replica	T-50 Project

Collingwood - Collingwood Classic Aircraft Foundation, Collingwood Mncpl Airport,
Mail: Box 143, L9Y 3Z4, (705) 445-7545, Thur 9-4, Mid May-Mid Sept Sat 9-4
Adm Free, www.classicaircraft.ca/homepage.htm, Rides Available

Aeronca Champ 7AC (Rides)	Fleet Canuck (Rides)	Stinson 105
DH 82A (Rides)	Smith Miniplane	

Cornwall - RCAFA 424 Wing, Water St, CT-33 2ea

Dunnville - No 6 RCAF Dunnville Assoc, Dunnville Airport, Hangar 1, Regional Rd 11, (905) 701-RCAF
DH-82,   Harvard

Ear Falls - Ear Falls Museum, Waterfront off Hwy 105, Beech 18, Mike

Goderich - Sky Harbour Gallery, 110 N St, N7A 2T8, Goderich Airport, (519) 524-2686,
Fax 524-1922, Daily, www.huroncountymuseum.on.ca/skyh.htm, Artifacts

Hamilton - Canadian Warplane Heritage, Hamilton Civic (Mt Hope)Airport,
9280 Airport Rd, L0R 1W0, (800) 386-5888, (905) 679-4183, Fax 679-4186, (800) 365-5888
Daily 9-5, Closed CD, ND, Adm Adult $10, Snrs & Student 13-17 $9, Child 6-12 $6,
Gift Shop, Library, Theater, Facility Rental, www.warplane.com, e-mail: museum@warplane.com

AN-2	CF-5	Link Trainer
AT-6G Harvard 3 ea	F-86	N.A. 64 Yale
Auster	CF-100 Mk.5	PT-26B Cornell
Avro Lancaster BX683	CF-104D	PT-27 Stearman
Avro 652 Anson V(2ea)	Fairchild F-24R	S-51
B-25J	Fairey Firefly Mk.5	Sopwith Pup Replica
Bollingbroke Nose	Fleet Finch 16B	Spitfire Mk XVI
UC-45D	Fleet 21K	T-28
CF-104D	Fleet Fort 60K	T-33A
DH 100	Fleet 7C Fawn II	Westlander Lysander 3
DH 82C	Hawker Hurricane	Widgeon
DHC. 1	Hawker Hunter Mk.IIB	
DC-3	Hurricane Replica	

Hamilton Airforce Assoc, CT-33

Hamilton Military Museum, York Blvd (Dundurn Park), L8R 3H1, (905) 546-4974
June 15-Labor Day Daily 11-5, Labour Day-June 14 Tue-Sun & Holiday Mondays 1-5
Closed CD, ND, Military Artifacts

RCAF Assoc 447 Wing, Unit 350, Mount Hope Airport, 9300 Airport Rd, L0R 1W0, CF-100

Kapuskasing - The Kap Air Collection 17 Lang Ave, P5N 1E5, Airport (705) 331-2611

Kingston - CFB Kingston, Hwy 2 East, CF-5   CH-136

London - Royal Canadian Regiment Museum, Carriageway Wolseley Hall, N5Y 4T7,
Oxford/Elizabeth Streets, (519) 660-5102, 5136

Oshawa - Oshawa Aeronautical, Military, & Industrial Museum, 1000 Stevenson Rd N, L1J 5P5, (416) 728-6199, Easter-Nov Tue-Sat 12-5, Sun 1-5

A-26	M 24 Tank	Sherman Tank

Robert Stuart Aeronatical Collection, 1000 Stevenson Rd N, Oshawa Airport, L1G 5P5
End of Stephenson Rd North, (905) 436-6325, Sat-Sun 11:30-3:30, Adm Adult $5, Child 6-11 $3, Gift Shop, www.aeronautical-museum.ca   F-86 Mk.5

Ottawa - Canadian Aviation Museum, 11 Aviation Parkway, K1K 4R3, (800) 463-2038, (613) 993-2010, Mail: POB 9724, K1G 5A3, Station T,Wed-Sun 10-5, After Laboour Day-April 30 Daily 9-5, Closed CD, Adm $6 Adult, Senior & Student $5, Child 4-15 $3, Under 4 Free, Family $14, Group Rates, Gift Shop, Library, Facility Rental, Curator Renald Fortier
www.aviation.technomuses.ca

	(R) = Restoration	(S) = Storage
AEA Silver Dart	CP-107 (S)	HUP-3
AEG G.IV	CP-121	JN-4
Aeronca C-2 (S)	CT-114	Junkers W-34f/fi
Airspeed Consul (Loan)	CT-133	Junkers J.1 (S)
APCO Astra 29 (S)	Curtiss Kittyhawk I	Lockheed Jetstar (S)
AusterAOP 6 (S)	Curtiss Seagull	Lockheed 10A
AT-6 Harvard Mk.II	Czerwinski Harbinger (S)	Lockheed 12A (S)
AT-6 Harvard Mk.II (Loan)	DC-3	Maurice Farman S.11
AT-6 Harvard Mk.IV	DC-9-32 (S)	McDowall Monoplane
AV-8A Harrier (Loan)	DH Menasco Moth	Me 163B-1a
Avro 504K	DH 60 (S)	MiG-15bis
Avro 504K (Loan)	DH 80A	MiM-10B
Avro Anson V	DH 82C (S)	Mitchell B-10 Wing (S)
Avro Avian IVM (R)	DH-82C-2	Moyes Stingray (S)
Avro C.102 Nose	DH 83C	Nieuport 12
Avro Lancaster Mk X Nose	DH 98	Nieuport 17 (L)
Avro Lancaster Mk.X	DH 100 F.1 (S)	Noorduyn Norseman VI
B-24L GR.VIII (S)	DH 100 F.3	P-51D Mk.IV (S)
B-25L Mk 3PT (S)	DHC. 7	Pitcairn-Cierva PCA-2 (S)
Bellance CH-300	DHC. 6	Pitts S-2A
Bensen B.8MG	DHC. 1B2	Quickie
Bensen B.8	DHC. 2	R-4B (S)
Bf 109-4	DHC. 3	RAF B.E.2c
Bleriot XI (S)	E-2	Sheldrake Merrel (S)
Boeing 247D	Easy Riser (S)	Sopwith Camel 2F.1
Bombardier Challenger 600 (S)	F2H-3	Sopwith Pup (L)
Borel Morane (S)	Fairchild FC-2W-2	Sopwith Snipe 7F.1
Bowers Fly Baby (S)	Fairchild 82A (S)	Sopwith Triplane (S)
Bristol Bolingbroke IVT (S)	Fairey Battle IT (S)	SPAD SVII
Bristol Beaufighter TFX (S)	Fairey Firefly FR.1 (S)	Spectrum Beaver RX550 (S)
Bristol F.2B	Fairey Swordfish	Spitfire Mk.II (L)
Buzzman Buccaneer SX (S)	Fantasy 7 (S)	Spitfire LF Mk.IX
C-119 Nose (S)	Flet 2/7 (S)	Spitfire Mk.IX-LF
C-54GM North Star (S)	Fleet 16B	Stearman 4EM
CF-86	Fleet 50K Remains (S)	Stinson SR
CF-100 Mk.5D (2ea)	Fleet 80 (S)	Stits SA-3A (S)
CF-101B	Fokker D.VII (S)	T-33AN
CF-104A	Found FBA-2C (S)	T-50 Cockpit
CF-105 Mk 2 Nose	G-21A Goose (S)	Taylorcraft BC-65 (S)
CF-116A	H-5 (L)	Travel Air 2000 (R)
CF-135	Ha-112-M1L (S)	Vickers Vedette Nose (S)
CF-188B	Hawker Hind	Vickers Vedette Hull (S)
CH-113	Hawker Hurricane XII	Vickers Viscount (S)
CH-135	Hawker Sea Fury F.B.11	Waco 10
CH-300 (S)	He 162A-1 (S)	Westland Lysander III
CL-84-A	HO4S-3	Wills Wing XC

ONTARIO

Ottawa - Canadian War Museum, Museum, 330 Sussex Dr, (613) 922-2774, Daily 1-5pm, Closed Monday Mid-Sept-Apr, Closes 9pm Tuesdays in summer, H-136(CH), Nieuport 17, Spitfire Mk VII

Petawawa - CFB Pettawawa Military Museum, (613) 687-5511 ext 6238, C-47, L-19A

Sault Ste Marie - Canadian Bushplane Heritage Centre, 50 Pim St, Station Mall Postal Outlet, P6A 3G4, Mail: POB 23050, P6A 6W6, (705) 945-6242, Fax 942-8947, Toll-Free (877) 287-4752 Mid May-Mid Oct Daily 9-6, Oct-May Daily 10-4, Adm Adult $10.50, Snrs $9.50, Student $5 Child $2, Gift Shop, Library, Theater, www.bushplane.com, email: bushplane@soonet.ca,

Aeronca 11AC	DHC 2-Mk.I	Buhl (Parts)
Beech D18S (3 ea)	DHC 2-Mk.III	RC-3 Seabee
Bell 47D-1	DHC 3	Silver Dart 1909 Rep
Buhl CA-6 Airsedan	F-11 Husky	ST-27
C-64 (CY-AYO)	Frasca IFR Simulator	Stinson SR-9 Reliant
CL-215	Link Trainer	Taylor Model 20
CS2F(CF-21) Tracker	KR-34	U-6A
DH 83C Fox Moth	Noorduyn Norseman Mk.I	U-6A Turbo
DH 89A	Noorduyn Norseman Mk.IV	

Tillsonburg - Canadian Harvard Aircraft Assoc, Tillsonburg Airport, Mail: POB 774 Woodstock, N4S 8A2, (519) 842-9922, By Appt, email: 1sunday@hangerline.com

BT-14 Yale Project	Private Flying Club with:
DH-82 Tigermoth	Harvard MKA
Harvard (4 EA) HWX, MTX, RWN, WPK	Harvard NDB

Toronto - Ontario Science Centre, 770 Don Mills Rd, Sopwith Pup Rep

Toronto Aerospace Museum, Parc Downsview Park, 65 Carl Hall Rd, M3K 2E1, (416) 638-6078, Fax 638-5509, Wed 10-8, Thur-Sat 10-4, Sun 12-4, (416) 638-6078, Fax: 638-5509, Adult $8, Snrs 60 $6, Student $5, Under 6 Free, Family $20, Gift Shop, Facility Rental www.torontoaerospacemuseum.com

CF-5	CT-114	Lancaster Project
CF-105Rep	CT-134	Ultimate 100
CS2F	DH-82 Project	Zenair Zenith

Trenton - RCAF Memorial Museum, Quinte West, 8 Wing, RCAF Rd, K0K 1B0, Mail: POB 1000, Stn Forces, Astra, K0K3W0, Exit 526 on Hwy 401, (613) 965-2208, Fax: 965-7352, May 1-Oct 1 Daily 10-5, Oct 1-May 1 Wed-Sun 10-5, Free Adm, Gift Shop www.rcafmuseum.on.ca

Argus 732	CF-5B	CT-114	Handley-Page Halifax
Auster AOP Mk6	CF-100 MkIV	CT-134	Hawker Hunter Mk9
C-47	CF-101B 2ea	CT-133	Lancaster
Canadair Mk.2	CL-41	DHC 1B (CT-120)	MiG-21 MF
CF-104D	CT-33 MkIII	F-86D MkVI	OH-58

Windsor - Canadian Aviation Historical Society Windsor, Windsor Airport Airport Rd, N8V 1A2, (519) 737-9461,   DHC-1   Fleet Fawn   Mosquito Project   Stearman

PRINCE EDWARD ISLAND

Summerside - Heritage Aircraft Society, 173 Victoria Rd, C1N 2G8, CP-107, CF-101, CS2F

QUEBEC
Bagotville Alouette - CFB, CF-5 , CF-86, CF-100 , CF-101

Gatineau - Vintage Wings of Canada, 1699 Arthur Fecteau St, Gatineau Airport, J8R 2Z9
(819) 669-9603, Jun-Sept 1st Sat 10-2 Monthly, By Appt Only Groups of 15+, www.vintagewings.ca

Beech D17S	F4U-4B	Huricane Mk.XII
DH-82C	Fairey Swordfish Mk II	P-51 Mk.IV
DH-83C	Harvard Mk 4	Spitfire Mk.XVIe
DHC-2 Mk I	Hurricane Mk.IV	Waco ATO

Knowlton - Brome County Historical Society, POB 690, J0E 1V0
Near Brome, 243-6782, Curator: Marion L Phelps, Fokker D.VII

La Baie - Air Defence Museum, Hwy 170,Station Bureau-Chief Alouette, Mail: POB 567, Alouette,
G0V 1A0, (418) 677-7159, Fax 677-4104, June-Sept Daily 9-5m , Off-Season by Appt,
Adm Adult $5, Child & Snrs $4, Under 5 Free, Gift Shop, www.bagotville.net

CF-5	CF-86	CF-101	H-21
CF-18	CF-100	CT-133	MiG-23L

SASKATCH EWAN (SK)
Moose Jaw - Western Development Museum, 50 Diefenbaker Dr, S6J 1L9, (306) 693-5989,
Fax 691-0511, Mail: POB 185, S6H 4NB, Daily 9-5, Closed CD, ND, Adm Adult $7.25,
Snrs 65 $6.25, Student $5.25, Child 6-12 $2, Under 6 Free, Family $16, Gift Shop, www.wdm.ca

Aeronca K	CT-114	H-10	Spitfire Parts
Avro Anson	DH 53	Harvard Mk IV	Stingray Hang Glider
Benson B-8	DH 60M	J-3	Stinson 105
C-64 CF-SAM	DH 82C	Jodel D-9	T-33A
Cessna 195	Eagle Ultralight	Mead C-III	T-50
CT-14	Funk B85C	PT-19	Zogling Glider

YUKON TERRITORY
Whitehorse - Yukon Transportation Museum, Mile 917 Alaska Hwy, Y1A 5L6, (403) 668-4792
Fax: 633-5547, May 22-Sept 5 Daily 10-7, Adm Adult $3, 60+ $2.50, Child 12+ $2.50,
6-12 $2, Family $7, Ryan NYP, DC-3

CITY DISPLAYED AIRCRAFT

Airport=(AP) / American Legion=(AL) / American Veterans=(AV) / Verterans of Foreign Wars=(VFW)

ALABAMA

City	Aircraft
Atmore	T-33A
Andalusia -Town of Sanford	H-1(UH)
Daleville - City of Daleville 740 South Daleville Ave	H-1(UH)
Dothan - City of Dothan	H-1(UH)
Dothan -DAV Chapter #87	H-1(AH)
Double Springs - AL Post #184, 110 Legion Drive	Nike
Elba - City of Elba 200 Buford Street	H-1(UH)
Enterprise - City of Enterprise 501 South Main Street	H-1(UH)
Eufaula -VFW Post #5850 US Highway 431 North	H-1(UH)
Florala	T-33A
Florence - AL Post #11, 318 South Court St.	H-1(AH), M3, MGR1B
Florence - Florence State College	Missile
Evergreen - Middleton Airport, 334-578-1274, 35747	FJ-3, T-28C
Huntsville - Veterans Memorial Museum, 2060A Airport Road	H-1(AH)
Jacksonville - AL Post #57 1501 Pelham Rd	H-1(UH)
Mobile - VVA Chapter #701	H-1(UH)
Mobile	T-33A, F-105
Monroeville	T-33A
Monroeville - AL Post #61	H-1(UH)
Montgomery	F-84F, F-86L 3ea
Ozark	RF-84F
Ozark - City of Ozark, 417 North Union Street	H-1(UH)
Selma	T-33A 2ea
Troy - City of Troy, 301 Railroad Ave.	H-1(AH)
Tuscaloosa - 40/8 Voiture Nationale #1060, 20 Frederick Dr	H-1(UH)
Tuscaloose - Airport	T-33A
Tuscaloose - Veterans Memorial Park (I-20/59)	A-7, UH-1, M60

ARIZONA

City	Aircraft
Apache Junction 1018 S Meridan	T-33A
Apache Jct - AL Post 27, 1880 Apache Trail, (480) 982-0220,	T-33A
Chandler	F-86D
Douglas	RF-101C
Duncan (5 Mi S of Town)	F-100
Gila Bend (AP)	RF-101C 2ea
Glendale	F-100D
Globe (VFW 1704)	F-86D
Quartzsite Plymouth & Quail Trail Rd	F-4C (2ea)
Marana - VFW Post #5990, 15850 West El Tiro Road	H-1(AH)
Peoria (AL) US60	F-84F
Phoenix - Phoenix ANG, Sky Harbor Int'l Airport, 97218-2797	F-104C
Three Points - VFW Post #10254, 10211 South Sasabe Hwy	H-1(AH)
Tucson - AL Post 109, 15921 S Houghton Rd, 84747	F-4E

ARKANSAS

City	Aircraft
Bull Shoals - VFW Post #1341,1206 Central Blvd.	H-1(AH)
Dardanelle - VFW Post #3141, 118 North Front St.	Missile (2ea)
Fort Smith - Vietnam Veterans Assoc. #467	H-1(AH)
Gravette	T-33A
Harrison	F-84F
Helena	T-33A
Holiday Island - VFW Post #77	H-1(UH)
Pocahontas - Mncpl Airport, US Hwy 67A-7	MGM-13B, Sikorsky Heliocopter
Rogers - Municipal Airport, Carter Field	F-101B
Rogers - City of Rogers, 300 W. Poplar	H-1(UH)
Trumann - City of Trumann, 225 Highway 463	MGR1B
Wynne - Cross Cnty Vet Memorial, 1205 East L'Anguille Ave	H-1(AH)

CALIFORNIA

Apple Valley Cnty Airport, 21600 Corwin Rd	F-86H
Bakersfield	T-38 (2ea)
Banning	XGAM-67
Burbank	F-104D
Lancaster - Antelope Valley College,	D-558-II Skyrocket
Lancaster - Fox Airport, 4555 West Ave G, 93536,	Apollo Boilerplate
Long Beach - Viet Nam Vet Memorial, Houghton Park,	
Atlantic & Hardong St, 90805,	UH-1
Los Gatos	T-33A
Madera	T-33A
Mojave Airport, 434 Flightline, 93501	Convair 880, F-4
Nevada Cnty	F-104A
Palmdale	F-4D
Porterville	A-4
Redands	F-104D
San Francisco Int'l Airport, North Terminal	Arrow Sport
Santa Barbara Vietnam Veterans Assoc. #218	H-1(UH)
Stockton American Legion Post #632,	
1600 Northrop Street Bldg 372	H-1(AH)
Susanville City of Susanville 66 North Lassen Street	H-1(AH), H-1(UH), RF-4C
Torrance (AP)	T-33A
Tulare American Veterans Post 56, Tulare Mcpl Airport	B-17G, BT-13, F-4C
West Covina - Palmview Park, Lark Ellen & Puente Ave	F-86D
Victorville - Souothern California Logistics Airport,	
(Old George AFB), 92394-5000,	F-4C, F-86H, F-100D, F-105D,
	F-104C, F-105G

COLORADO

Burlington - VFW Post 6491, 884 R Rose Ave (Hwy 24 E),	AH-1F
Canon City	F-4
Denver - Int'l Airport, (303) 270-1500, Main Concourse	JN-4D, Alexander Eaglerock
Denver - United Air Lines	Link Trainer
Flagler -	T-33A, TGM-13, Mace
Fruita - City of Fruita	H-1(UH)
Kremmling - Town of Kremmling	H-1(AH)
Monte Vista	XQ4
Walsenburg - Colorado State Veterans Nursing Home,	
23500 US Highway 160	H-1(AH)

CONNECTICUT

East Hampton - VFW Post #5095, 20 North Maple Street	H-1(AH)
Prospect - VFW Post #8075, 218 Cheshire Road	H-1(AH)
Stratford - Sikorsky Memorial Airport	FG-1D
Waterbury - City of Waterbury, 236 Grand Street	H-1(AH)

DELAWARE

Dover - AL Post # 2	T-33A
New Castle - ANG, Greater Wilmington Airport, 19720,	F-86H
New Castle - VVA - Delaware State Council, 12 Boston Place	H-1(UH)

FLORIDA

Arcadia - Municipal Airport, West Hanger	Fr 24, T-33A
Callaway	F-15C
Daytona Beach - Miniature Golf, South Atlantic Ave,	Beechcraft 18
Deltona - City of Deltona, 2345 Providence Blvd	H-1(AH)
DeFuniak	T-33A
Ft. Lauderdale - Holiday Park	F-86H
Ft.Walton Beach	CQM-10A
Hernando - VFW Post #4252	H-1(UH)
Homestead	F-4

FLORIDA

Inverness - Veterans Educational Team 4 Students, 1300 North Hwy 41	H-1(UH)
Lake City - (I-75N Exit 81)	A-7E
Merritt Island - Veterans Memorial Center, 400 S. Sykes Creek Parkway	H-1(AH), H-1(UH)
Milton	T-28
New Smyrna Beach - VFW Post #4250, 816 East 19th Ave	H-1(AH)
Oelwein	T-33A
Orlando - Int'l Airport, 1 Airport Blvd,Memorial Park	B-52D
Orlando/Sanford Airport, Marquette Ave & Red Cleveland Blvd, N28 45.902, W81 14.254	RA-5C
Orlando - The National Vietnam War Museum, 3400 North Tanner Rd	H-1(UH)
Panacea	CGM-13B
Pensacola - Regional Airport,	F11F-1 Blue Angels
Pensacola - Visitors Center, 3 Miles West of City,	F9-5 "Blue Angels #1"
St Augustine - St John's Cnty Airport, US Hwy 1 N Ernie Moser's Aero Sport	
St Cloud - Hwy192 & Pennsylvania Ave	AH-1
Tallahassee - VVA Chapter #96, 241 Lake Ella Dr	Helicopter
Wauchula (AM 2)	F-84F
West Orlando - -Airport	Byrid, Fr Kr 21, Taylorcraft A
Wildwood - AM 18	CGM-13B

GEORGIA

Alma - City of Alma, 1751 Old Dixie School Rd	Helicopter
Alpharetta - AL Post #201	H-1(UH)
Athens VFW	F-84F
Bainbridge - City of Bainbridge	H-1(UH)
Buford - AL Post #127, 1367 Sawnee Ave	Helicopter
Cairo - VFW Post #8433, 2513 U.S. Hwy 84 West	H-1(UH)
Chickamauga - City of Chickamauga	H-1(UH)
Cochran	Missile
Conyers - AL Post #77, 674 American Legion Rd	H-1(UH)
Cordele - Exit 32, I-75 Hwy 300	Titan I
Cordele - Georgia Veterans Memorial State Park 2459-A Highway 280 West	H-1(UH)
Donalsonville - AL Post #157	H-1(AH)
Douglas	T-33A
Griffin	T-33A
Griffin, Gryder Networks LLC, 147 Sky Harbor Way	DC-3A
Griffin-Spaulding Airport, Lance Toland LTD	DC-3C
Low Pass Inc, 127 Airport Rd, 30224,	F9F-5
Lexington - AL Post #123	H-1(UH)
Hawkinsville	MGM-1
Tallapoosa - Haralson Cnty Veterans Assoc, 71 Riverside Dr	H-1(UH)
Thomaston - Custom Air Service, Clayton Cnty Airport,	C-54B (ATL98) CVA
Thomasville	T-33A
Valdosta	F-86L
Warner Robins	CGM-13B
Waynesboro	T-33A
Willacoochee	T-33A
Williamson - City of Williamson	H-1(UH)

IDAHO

Burley	H-1(UH), T-33A
Idaho Falls Airport, 83402	F-86
Lewiston	T-33A
Malad	T-33A
Mountain Home (Carl Miller Par	F-111
Nampa	F-89B
Pocatello (AP)	F-101B

IDAHO

Sheldon (AP)	T-33A
St Maries	F-100
Twin Falls	T-33A

LLINOIS

Aurora Airport	F-105D
Aurora - City of Aurora, 44 East Downer Place	H-1(UH)
Brookfield Elhert Park, (Rte 34, Elm St)	F-86L
Canton - City of Canton, 250 South Ave	H-1(UH)
Centralia	T-33A
Chicago - Butch O'Hare Memorial Airport, Terminal 2	F4F-3
Chicago - Midway Airport, 5700 South Cicero, 60638	SBD
Chicago - Kirkland Airport,	Baby Ace Fleet
Colinsville - AL Post 365,	
1022 Vandalia St (Hwy 159), 62234,	H-1G(AH), M6A2 Cannon
Dixon - VFW Post #540, 1560 Franklin Grove Rd	H-1(UH)
Edwardsville (RC Stille Twnp Park)	LTV A-7E
Edgewood - Keeler-Adams AL Post, Hwy 57, (618) 238-4193,	5" Naval Gun
Granite City	F-84F, DC-3
Herrin - VFW Post #1567, 309 North 16th St	H-1(AH)
Highland - VFW Post #5694, 12173 Buckeye Rd	H-1(AH)
Highland	T-33A
Island Lake - Village of Island Lake, 3720 Greenleaf Ave	H-1(AH)
Kankakee - AL Post #1019, 739 South Sandbar Rd	Helicopter
Lansing Veterans Memorial,	UH-1
Lindenhurst (VFW)	A-7
Milford - Route 1	JB-2 Buzz Bomb
Oglesby - City of Oglesby, 128 West Walnut	H-1(UH)
Orland Hills - Village of Orland Hills, 16033 South 94th Ave	MGM-52
Pekin	F-84F
Pekin - VFW Post #1232, 15665 VFW Rd	H-1(UH)
Pinckneyville	T-33A
Quincy	T-33A
Quincy - Illinois Veterans Home, 1707 N 12th St	H-1(UH)
Rockford - Greater Rockford Airport,	
Midway Village & Museum, 60 Airport Dr, 61109,	T-28
Springfiled Airport Terminal	Pietenpohl Air Camper
St Charles Airport	DC-3
Versailles	T-33A
Washburn - AL Post #661, 104 E Parkside Dr	H-1(UH)
Washington - Washington Park District 815 Lincoln St	H-1(AH)
Wenona	F-84F

INDIANA

Churubusco	F-86H
Columbus Mncpl Airport, Rhoades Aviation, 47203	DC-3
Columbus - VFW Post 7964, 120 E Main Cross St,	
46124,	F-80, M1 Tank
Covington - VFW Post 2395, Liberty St & 12th,	T-33A
Elkhart - AM Post 233, 500 Memorial Dr, 46124,	T-38
Fairmount - AL Post 313, 522 E 8th St, 46928,	F-4C, UH-1A, M60 A1 Tank
Fishers - AL Post #666, 666 Wakeley dr	H-1(AH)
Ft Wayne Memorial Coliseum, 4000 Parnell Ave	F-84F
Green Castle Court House Downtown	Fi 103 Buzz Bomb
Hoagland	F-84F
Huntington	T-33A
Indianapolis	F-86E
Ligonier - Zollinger Field, 12264 Co Rd, 148& US 33, 46767	C-45G
Mentone Airport	BT-13, T-50
Mitchell - Spring Mill State Park, (812) 849-4129,	Grissom Gemini Capsule
Monroeville	F-84F

INDIANA

Montpelier	F-84F
Munster - Veterans Memorial Park , 1005 Ridge Rd	H-1(UH)
Orland - AL Post #423, 6215 N SR327 P.O. Box 448	H-1(UH)
Richmond Rte 227 S	A-6
Sellersburg - Clark Cnty Airport, 7001 Airport Rd, 47172, N38-21.93; W 085-44.29	F-86
South Bend Airport, Military Honor Park, P-80(T-33)	UH-1, M-60 Tank, M-42 Tank
South Whitley	F-84F
Sullivan - VFW Post #2459, 201 West Illinois St	H-1(UH)

IOWA

Burlington	T-33A
Carroll - Arthur N Neu Airport	A-7D
Cedar Rapids (Vet Memorial)	F-84F, T-33A
Correctionville	A-7D, F-84F
Columbus Junction - Louisa Cnty Area Vietnam Veterans	H-1(UH)
Fairfield	F-84F
Harlan	RF-84F
Ida Grove - AL Post #61, Cobb Memorial Park, Hwy 59/175, 42.351N, 95.475W ,	AH-1
Iowa City	F-86L
Manchester - VFW Post #6637 909 New St	H-1(AH)
Onawa - City of Onawa, 914 Diamond St	H-1(UH)
Parkersburg - AL Post #285,	H-1(AH)
Sheldon Airport	A-7D, T-33A
Sigourney	T-33A
Waterloo - AL Post #730, 2260 Ashland Ave	H-1(AH)
Waterloo - Hawkeye Community College, 1501 E Orange Rd	H-1(AH)

KANSAS

Atwood - AL Post #46, 112 S. 3rd St	H-1(AH)
Dodge City	B-26C
Emporia Airport Veterans Park, 522 Mechanic St	F-4E, UH-1, M-60 Tank
Independence	T-33A
Lynn	F-84F
Overbrook - AL Post #239, 16119 S Shawnee Heights Rd	H-1(UH)
Pratt, B-29 All Vets Memorial	H-1(AH), F-4
Tonganoxie - VFW Post #9271	H-1(UH)

KENTUCKY

Flatwoods - Greenup Cnty War Memorial,	H-1(UH)
Fulton	T-33A
Louisville - Clark Cnty Airport,	FJ-1, P-51, P-51D
Middlesboro Airport, 1420 Dorchester	F-86, M-60 Tank
Prestonburg - Kentucky Wing Civil Air Patrol, 1135 South Lake Dr	H-1(AH)
Sturgis	F-86D

LOUISIANA

Alexandria	F-80
Ball - Town of Ball	H-1(UH)
Houma	T-33A
Lafayette - LA Museum of Military History, 306 East Willow	H-1(UH)
Many - DAV Chapter #21, 29336 Highway 191	H-1(AH)
Many - VFW, 318-256-2143, State Rd 6 Off of US 6.	M4 Sherman Tank
Mansfield	T-33A
Ruston - VFW Post #3615, 200 Memorial Dr	H-1(UH)
Springhill	T-33A
Ville Platte - Vietnam Veterans Assoc. #632, 12407 Veterans Memorial Highway	H-1(UH)

MAINE

Blaine	AGM-28B
Marshill (AL 118)	Jet
Millinocket - AL Post #80, 970 Central St	H-1(UH)
Waterville	F-89J

MARYLAND

Cambridge Airport	UC-78CE
Cumberland	T-33A
Ellicott City (VFW)	F-86H
Handcock	Nike-Ajax
Pocomoke City	T-33A
Rockville	T-33A

MASSACHUSETTS

Beverly - VFW Post #545, 20 Whittier	H-1(UH)
Freetown - VFW Post #6643,	H-1(AH)
Worcester - VVA Chapter #5542 Brackett Court,	H-1(AH)

MICHIGAN

Adrian - VFW Post #1584, 726 North Main St	H-1(UH)
Ann Arbor - VFW Post #423, 3230 South Wagner Rd	H-1(UH)
Bay City - City of Bay City, 301 Washington Ave	H-1(UH)
Blissfield - AL Hall, High St & US 223	F-105D
Breckenridge	T-33A
Calumet - Calumet AFS, 49913	T-33A
Charlotte - AL Post #42, 1000 Lawrence Ave	H-1(AH)
Cheboygan - VVA Chapter #274, 7747 North Black River Rd	H-1(UH)
Decatur - VFW Post #6248, 560 North Phelps St	H-1(AH)
Escanaba	F-84F
Fraser - VFW Post #6691, 17075 Anita	H-1(UH)
Grand Haven	F-100A
Grayling	T-33A
Hart	T-33A
Hermansville - VVA Chapter #571,	H-1(UH)
Iron Mountain	T-33A
Lapeer - VFW Post #4139, 128 Daley Rd	H-1(UH)
Ludington - Mason Cnty Airport, E Ave, 49431	T-38
Marcellus - VFW Post #4054, M-40 South	H-1(UH)
Monroe Cnty Vietnam Veterans Chapter #142 Memorial Norman Heck Park	AH-1, F-86D, UH-1M
Mt Clemens - AL Post 4, 401 Groesbeck, F-101	
Muskegon - Hidden Cove Park, Norton Shores, Mona Lake	UH-1
Onondaga - VFW Post #6986, 5373 Gale Rd	H-1(AH)
Plainwell - Plainwell Municipal Airport, 630 10th St, 49080	T-38
Pontiac - VVA Chapter #133, 581 W Kennett Rd	H-1(UH)
River Rouge - City of River Rouge, 10600 W Jefferson Ave	H-1(UH)
Rosebush	T-33A
Sebewaing	T-33A

MINNESOTA

Albert Lea	T-33A
Alexanderia	T-33A
Arlington - AL Post #250, 807 West Chandler	H-1(AH)
Belle Plaine - City of Belle Plaine, 420 East Main St	H-1(UH)
Blaine Airport	L-39, Ryan Navion, C-123 (2ea)
Brainerd - Crow Wing Cnty Regional Airport	F9F-6
Buffalo	T-33A
Chisholm - AL Post #247,	H-1(UH)
Duluth - Duluth Int'l Airport, 6 Mi NW of City	F-4, T-38
Fosston - City of Fosston, 220 East 1st St	H-1(AH)
Hector	T-33A

MINNESOTA
Hill City - City of Hill City,	H-1(AH)
Minnesota Lake	T-33A
Proctor	F-101F
Shakopee - Vet Memorial Park, 129 Holmes St South	H-1(AH)
Winoma - Max Conrad Airfield, Winoma Mncpl Airport	F9F-5, O-1, T-33

MISSISSIPPI
Columbia	T-33A
Greneda - HS (Hwy 51S)	A-4L
Magee - VFW Post #9122, 453 Bill Blair Rd.	H-1(UH)
Purvis - Cnty of Lamar	H-1(UH)
Raymond - Hinds Community College	H-58(OH)
Walnut - Town of Walnut	H-1(UH)

MISSOURI
Bloomfield - The Stars and Stripes Museum, 17377 Stars and Stripes Way	H-1(UH)
Caruthersville	T-33A
Chillicothe - Chillicothe Municipal Airport, 64601	F-105
Ellington - VFW Post #6043	H-1(AH)
LaPlata	F-86H
Lee's Summit - VVA Chapter #243	H-1(UH)
Monett	F-4
Mountain View	T-33A
Neosho - City of Neosho, 221 N. College	H-1(UH)
O'Fallon - VFW Post #5077, 501 St. Marys Place	H-1(AH)
Springfield - AL Post #639, 2660 S. Scenic	H-1(AH), H-1(UH)
Richmond	T-33A
St. Charles	T-33A
St Louis Lambert Int'l Airport	T-33A
St Louis Lambert Int'l Airport, Terminal Entrance C Concourse	Monocoupe
St. Louis - VFW Post #3944, 10815 Midland Ave	H-1(AH)
Sikeston - Sikeston Veterans Park, One Industrial Dr, 63801	F-4J, M-60 Tank
Warsaw - AL Post #217,	H-1(AH)

MONTANA
Butte	F-86L
Dutton - AL Post 64, 201 Main East, 59433	F-104
Glasgow	T-33A
Great Falls Lion's Park, 10th Ave	F-102A, T-33A
Missoula - Rocky Mountain Museum	H-1(UH)

NEBRASKA
Beatrice - City of Beatrice, 205 N. 4th St	MGR1B, T-33A
Creighton	F-84F
David City	RF-84F
Franklin	T-33A
Fairbury - Engels J T Airport, 68352	F-100, T-33A
Gordon - AL Post #34, 404 S. Elm St	H-1(AH)
Kimball - Gotte Park, S of US 30 & E of SR 71/Chestnut St	Titan 1 First Stage
Mc Cook	F-86H
Neligh	RF-84F
Omaha - AL Post #374, 4618 S 139th St	H-1(UH)
S Sioux City	A-7D
Valley	RF-84F
Wakefield - AL Post #81, 405 Main St	H-1(AH)
York	RF-84F

New Jersey
Clark - AL Post #328, 78 Westfield Ave	H-1(AH)
Hamilton - Town of Hamilton, 2090 Greenwood Ave	H-1(AH)

New Jersey

Jackson - Amusement Park	F-104D
Milltown - AL Post #25	H-1(AH)
Monroe Township, Stone Museum,	
608 Spotswood-Englishtown Rd.	H-1(AH)
South Plainfield - 2480 Plainfield Ave	H-1(AH)

NEW HAMPSHIRE

Nashua - FAA Air Traffic Control Center	A-4
Reno-Stead Airport, 4895 Texas Ave, 89506-1237,	MiG-15, MiG-17, MiG-19

NEVADA

Amargosa Valley - VFW Post #6826	H-1(UH)
Indian Springs - City Park, West 1 Block Off I-95	F-84F
Jean - Casino, South Side of the Highway	WWI Replica
Reno Lions Park	Jet
Winemucca - Cnty of Humboldt, 50 W Fifth St	F-86D, H-1B(UH), M-3 Tank

NEW MEXICO

Alamogordo	F-80F, XQ-4
Albuquerque Int'l Airport, 4 Mi SE of City	Ingram/Foster Biplane
Albuquerque - Eileen St & Aberdeen Ave	HH-34(S-58), PBY-5(OA-10), SC-47
Angel Fire - Vietnam Veterans National Memorial	H-1(UH)
Artesia (Hwy 285)	F-84F
Carlsbad - Cavern City Mncpl Airport, 1505 Terminal Dr	AT-11
Carlsbad - VFW Post #3277 205 South Walnut St	Nike
Clovis - City Display, 7th & West Hwy 60 & Hwy 84	F-111F
Gallup - Gallup Municipal Airport, Old Hwy 66	T-38
Las Cruces Int'l Airport, 8960 Zia Blvd	C-46, F-100F
Manchester	F-86H-10-NH
Melrose	F-100A
Portales - 81 Airport Rd	F-111F
Roswell Airport, Enmur	F-105, Tank
Santa Fe - Santa Fe Municipal Airport, SW of City Off I-25	F-111
Truth	T-33A

NEW YORK

Adams - AL Post #586, 10 South Main St	H-1(AH)
Arcade - VFW Post #374, 550 West Main St	H-1(UH)
Baldwinsville	F-102A-80
Bath - VFW Post #1470,	H-1(AH)
Binghamton Regional Airport, 13901	Link Trainer
Buffalo Intl Airport	Bell 47, F-4J, F-101F
Campbell - AL Post #1279,	H-1(AH)
Central Square	F-86H
Cheecktowaga - Cal Span Cheecktowaga Airport	A-26 X-22
Cuba - VFW Post #2721, RD 2 5425 Rt. 305N	H-1(UH)
Dix Hills - Military & Vehicles & Collections Association,	228 Dix Hills Rd H-1(UH)
East Aurora - AL Post #362, Legion Dr - Box 122	H-1(UH), Nike
Eden - AL Post #880, 2912 Legion Dr	H-1(AH)
Fairport - VFW Post #8495, 300 Macedon Center Rd	H-1(UH)
Franklinville - VFW Post #9487,	H-1(AH)
Gowanda - AL Post #409, 100 Legion Dr	H-1(UH)
Hamburg - VFW Post #1419, 2985 Lakeview Rd	H-1(AH)
Horseheads - Corning Regional Airport, 6 Mi NW of City	Stuka Ju-87-B 7/8 Scale
Lowville - MCL Detachment #754	H-1(AH)
Manchester	F-86H
Massena - AMVETS Post #4, 12 Andrews St	H-1(AH)
Massena - AL Post #79, 40 East Orvis St	H-1(UH)
Monroe	F-86L
Moria - AL Post 939, Hwy 11 East of Town	T-38
New Hartford - AL Post #1376, 8616 Clinton St	H-1(AH)
North Tonwanda - Town of Wheatfield, 2800 Church Rd	H-1(UH)

NEW YORK

Oriskany - Village of Oriskany, 13424	A-4E
Parish - AL Post #601	H-1(AH)
Patterson - AL Post #1542, 113 Maple Ave	H-1(AH)
Sackets Harbor - AL Post #1757	H-1(AH)
Stittville - VFW Post #8259, 8999 Olin Rd	H-1(AH)
Tonawanda	F-9
Waterloo - VFW Post #6433, 29 West Elisha St	H-1(UH)
Westhampton Beach - Francis Gabreski Airport,	F-102A
White Plains - Westchester Cnty Airport (HPN)	T-33A

NORTH CAROLINA

Conover - VFW Post #5305, 2163 Highway 10E	H-1(UH)
Fayetteville	F-94C
Goldsboro	F-86H
Kings Mountain	F-105
Marshville - AL Post #440, 7321 Highway 218 East	H-1(AH)
Newbern - Clarendon Blvd, Hwy 17 South, City Park,	F-11A
Salisbury - VFW Post #3006, 1200 Brenner Ave	H-1(UH)
Statesville - AL Post #65, 2446 Salisbury Hwy 70 East	H-1(AH)
Waynesville - VFW Post #5202, 216 Miller St	H-1(UH)
Wilmington (Carolina Beech Rd)	T-33A

NORTH DAKOTA

Dickenson	T-33A
Fessenden	F-105
Grand Forks	F-86L
Hatton	F-80
Hettinger	F-86H
Hillsboro	T-33A
Jamestown (AP)	F-86H
Lidgerwood - City of Lidgerwood	H-1(AH)
McVille - Dam CP	H-1H(UH)
Mayville Island	F-84F
New Rockford - AL Post #30, 824 Central Ave	H-1(UH)
Vela	F-80
Walhalla	F-86H
Wahpeton	A-7D

OHIO

Arcanum - VFW Post #4161, 311 South Albright St Box 145	H-1(UH)
Batavia - VVA Chapter #649	H-1(UH)
Brooklyn 7521 Memphis Ave	T-33A
Columbus - Defense Construction Supply Center	H-1(UH)
Ellsworth - VFW Post #9571	H-1(AH)
Harrod - Village of Harrod	H-1(UH)
Heath - Newark Airport	F-4C
Holmesville - AL Post #551, 9150 ST RT 83	H-1(UH)
Jefferson - VFW Post #3334, 341 South Elm St.	H-1(AH)
Marietta	T-33A
Medina - VFW Post #5137	H-1(UH)
Newark - Vietnam Veterans Assoc. #55	H-1(UH)
Pickerington - AL Post #283 H-1(AH)	
Sidney - AMVETS Post #1986, 1319 North Fourth Ave	H-1(AH)
Sidney - VFW Post #4239, 2841 Wapak Rd	H-1(AH)
Vandalia - VFW Post #9582, 4170 Old Springfield Rd	H-1(UH)
Wadsworth	T-33A
Washingtonville - VFW Post #5532	H-1(UH)
Wilmington - Airborne Airpark	F-101B
Zanesville - VVA Chapter #42, 334 Shinnick St	H-1(AH)

OKLAHOMA

	Helicopter
Bristow - VFW Post #3656, 35530 W 261st St S	
Comanche	T-33A
Cushing - City of Cushing	H-1(UH)
El Reno (VFW 382)	A-26
Elk City	T-33A
Glencoe - VFW Post #1843 H-1(UH)	
Hattiesburg	RF-84F, RF-101C
Hazlehurst	F-86L
Jackson	F-105
Midwest	GAM-63
Oklahoma City	B-52F 2ea, AGM-28
Oklahoma City State Fair Grounds	B-47, Gulfstream SC
Roland - AL Post #339, RR 1 Box 711	H-1(UH)
Tulsa - Richard Lioyd Jones Jr Airport, Main Lobby	JN-4D

OREGON

Canby - Vietnam Veterans Assoc #392, 1000 NE 10th Ave	H-1(UH)
McMinnville Evergreen Airport	F-14
Medford - Rogue Valley Int'l Airport, 3650 Biddle Rd	F-16, KC-97
Nyssa	F-86L
Vale	F-86L
Woodburn	T-33A

PENNSYLVANIA

Beaver Falls	F-86H
Beaverdale - AL Post #460	H-1(AH)
Butler - Cnty of Butler, 475 Airport Rd	H-1(AH)
Carrolltown - AL Post #506	H-1(AH)
Chambersburg - Guilford Township, 115 Spring Valley Rd	H-1(AH)
Cory	F-94C
Doylestown - VVA Chapter #210	H-1(UH)
Du Bois - VFW Post #813, 114 Fuller Ave	H-1(AH)
East Berlin - VFW	F-14
Glenside - VVA Chapter #590, 2601 Church Rd	H-1(UH)
Greensburg - City of Greensburg, 416 South Main St	H-1(UH)
Imperial	F-86L
Jersey Shore - AL Post #36	H-1(UH)
Latrobe - AL Post #515, 1811 Ligonier St	Missile
Midland - VFW Post #8168, 700 Midland Ave	H-1(AH)
Mildred	MACE
Milford - AL Post #139	H-1(UH)
N Huntington	T-33A
New Kensington	T-33A
New Berlin - AL Post #957	H-1(UH)
New Galilee - VFW Post #8106, 100 Monroe St.	H-1(AH)
New Kensington - VFW Post #92, 1601 Wildlife Lodge Rd	H-1(UH)
Philipsburg - Mid-State Regional Airport, 457 Airport Rd	H-1(AH)
Pleasant Hills - AL Post #712, 650 Old Clairton Rd	H-1(AH)
Pottsville - AMVETS Post #227, 2333 Mahantongo St	H-1(UH)
Stoystown - AL Post #257	H-1(UH)
Towanda - VFW Post #1568, RR 1 Box 182	H-1(UH)
Waterford	F-94
West Brownsville - AL Post #940, 800 Middle St	H-1(UH)
White Haven - VFW Post #6615, 519 Ash Lane	H-1(UH)

SOUTH CAROLINA

Anderson - Anderson Cnty Airport, 100 S Main St, 29624	F-105B
Barnwell - VVA Chapter #828, 1520 Reedy Branch Rd	H-1(UH)
Chesnee - AL Post #48	H-1(AH)
Gaffney - AL Post #109	H-1(UH)
Greenville	F-86H
Greer - City of Greer, 226 Oakland Ave	H-1(AH)

SOUTH CAROLINA
Hartsville	T-33A
Huron	T-33A
Lake Norden	T-33A

SOUTH DAKOTA
Great Plains - Great Plains Airport, 57064	A-7D
Huron - Huron Regional Airport, 57350	A-7D

TENNESSEE
Athens, VFW 5146, 706 Congress Pkwy	F-4
Chattanooga - VVA Chapter #203	H-1(UH)
Collegedale - City of Collegedale	H-1(AH)
Crossville	T-33A
Crump - City of Crump	H-1(AH)
Dayton	T-33A
Dickson - VFW Post #4641, 215 Marshall Stuart Dr	H-1(UH)
Johnson City	T-33A
Knoxville	F-86D
Louisville - VFW Post #5154, 2561 Hobbs Rd	H-1(AH)
Nashville	F-86L
Pulaski	T-33A
Sweetwater - VFW Post #5156, 104 Nichols Rd	H-1(AH)

TEXAS
Bastrop, AL #533, 3003 Loop 150 East	F-4
Bastrop - VFW Post 2527, Rockne Hwy, 78602	F-4
Beeville - Courthouse, 105 W Corpus Christi	A-4
Big Springs - Vietnam Memorial, 7th & Sword St	F-4E, H-1(AH), H-1H(UH)
Conroe - VVA Chapter #734	H-1(UH)
Del Rio Commerce	T-33A
Denison	F-86L
Eagle Pass	T-33A
Eagle Pass - VFW Post #8562, 1238 Winding Ridge Dr	H-1(UH)
Ellington (VFW)	F-84G
Fulshear - Covey Trails Airport	Beech 18R
Hallettsville - Vietnam Veterans Assoc. #854	H-1(AH)
Hawkins - Greater Hawkins Veterans Memorial Assoc	H-1(AH)
Houston Smiley High School	F-80
Houston - West Houston Airport, Groeschke Rd	H-1H(UH)
Hubbard - City of Hubbard, 118 N. Magnolia	H-1(AH)
Killeen - City of Killeen	H-1(AH)
Kingsville NAS	A-4D
Manchaca - VFW Post 3377, 12921 Lowden Ln, 78652	F-4
McAllen - McAllen Miller Int'l Airport, Ceiling of Main Lobby	White Monoplane Rep.
Midland - Permian Basin Vietnam Veterans Memorial	H-1(UH)
Muenster	F-84F
Pampa - Freedom Museum of USA, 600 North Hobart St	H-1(UH)
Plainview - Hale Cnty Airport	T-33A
Port Neches - VFW Post #4820, 633 Grisby Ave	H-1(UH)
San Angelo -Vietnam Veterans Memorial	UH-1H
San Antonio - City Park Between San Antonio & Coast Off I37	A-4
Seadrift - VFW Post #4403	H-1(AH)
Sherman	F-86L
Sweetwater - City Park, 200 East 4th St	T-33A , H-1(UH)
Texarkana	T-33A
Tulia - VFW Post 1798, 300 SE 2nd St, 79088,	F-86

UTAH

Heber Airport, Russ McDonald Field, 84032, Strikemaster,   Jet Provose
Murray   T-33A
Salt Lake City Airport Municipal Airport #2   DH 100
Tooele - City of Tooele, 90 North Main St   Nike
Vernal - VFW Post #5560, 241 North - 850 West   H-1(AH)

VIRGINIA

Hampton   CIM-10A, F-84F,   F-86L,
Hampton   F-89JC, F-100C, F-104C
Bristol - City of Bristol, City Hall 497 Cumberland St   H-1(AH)
Danville - American Armoured Foundation,
    3401 U.S. Highway 29   H-1(AH), M3 Missile Hawk
South Hill - VFW Post #7166   H-1(UH)

VERMONT

Hyde Park, VFW Post #7779   H-6A(OH)

WASHINGTON

Brewster City Park   T-33A, YIM-99B
Bridgeport   F-86L, XGAM-67
Oak Harbor (City Beach Park)   EA-6B
Othello   T-33A
Spokane   T-33A
Reedsville   T-33A
River Falls   AGM-28A
Seattle - King Cnty Municipal Airport   Boeing 707, P-51D
Sherwood   T-33A
Stoughton   T-33A
Weirton City Park Rte 2 Exit 2   A-7D, AH-1F

WEST VIRGINIA

Clarksburg - Benedum Airport   AT-6
Milton   F-86L
Vienna   F-84H
Weirton, Brooke Cnty Memorail Park, US Route 2 & 22   AH-1, M-60

WISCONSIN

Almond - AL Post #339, 1401 Division St. H-1(AH)
Amery - Amery Municipal Airport   L-29 Czech Delfin (3ea)
Argyle   F-86H
Bangor - Village of Bangor, 100 North 17th Ave   H-1(AH)
Beloit - Beloit Airport, 4046 E Cnty Tk P, 53512   T-28
Black River Falls - Jackson Cnty Veterans Park, Hwy 54   H-1(AH)
Boscobel - Airport, 5178 Hwy 133 E, 53805   AT-6, T-28
Brillion   T-33A
Chippewa Falls - State of Wisconsin   H-1(AH)
Eagle River - AL Post #114, 117 W Pine St   H-1(AH) (2ea)
Elderon - VFW Post #8068   H-1(AH)
Endeavor - VVA Chapter #659, W 6901 Highway P   H-1(UH)
Fall River   T-33A
Fond du Lac - AL Post #75, 500 Fond du Lac Ave   H-1(AH)
Footville - AL Post #237, 406 Old Highway 11   H-1(AH)
Hurley - VVA Chapter #529   H-1(AH)
Janesville   F9F
Janesville - VFW Post #1621, 1015 Center Ave   H-1(AH)
Kendall - AL Post #309, 414 Medburry   H-1(AH)
Lake Geneva - AL Post #24, 935 Henry St P.O. Box 24   H-1(AH)
Lowell - VFW Post #9392   H-1(AH)
Lyndon Station - VFW Post #5970, 811 East Flint St   H-1(AH)
Madison   T-33A
Madison - Wisconsin Veterans Museum, 30 West Miffin St   H-1(UH)
Marshfield - AL Post #54, 2100 Maple Ave PO Box 54   H-1(AH)

WISCONSIN

Milwaukee's General Mitchell Int'l Airport	B-25J(TB)
Monroe - Gen Twining Park, Park Dr, 53566	F-86D
Mosinee - VFW Post #8280, 3323 Highway 153 East	H-1(AH)
New Richmond (AL 80)	P-80
New Lisbon - AL Post #110, 110 Welch Prairie Rd	H-1(AH)
North Lake - Town of Merton, W314 N7624 Hwy 83	H-1(AH)
Oak Harbor, Hwy 20 & Ault Field Rd	A-6, EA-6B
Pound - Village of Pound	H-1(AH)
Prairie du Sac - VFW Post #7694	H-1(AH)
Prentice	T-33A
River Falls - Vietnam Veterans Assoc. #331	H-1(UH)
Sparta - AL Post #100, 9929 State Hwy 21	H-1(AH)
Stoughton - VFW, W Veterans Rd, 53589,	T-33
Waterford - VFW Post #11038, 29224 Evergreen Dr	H-1(AH)
Waupaca - VFW Post #1037, N2490 W. Columbia Lake Dr	H-1(UH)
Wild Rose - AL Post #370	H-1(AH)

WYOMING

Buffalo	AGM-28A
Casper - VFW Post #9439, 1444 East Sunlight Dr	H-1(UH)
Fairmont - Marion Cnty Vietnam Veterans Memorial, Route 3	H-1(UH)
New Richmond	T-33A
Rock Springs (I-80)	F-101
Weirton - Brooke-Hancock Cnty Veterans Memorial	H-1(AH)

CANADA

ALBERTA

Airdrie - Arcot Aviation, Airdrie Airport, RR #2, T4B 2A4	Harvard Mk IV
Claresholm	SNJ
Cold Lake	CF-5, CF-101, CF-104, CT-33
Grand Center - City Diplayed	CF-5, CF-104
Harbor Grace - City Displayed	DC-3
Leduc	CT-33
Lethbridge	CT-33
Stephanville - Harmon Field	F-102
St Albert	CT-33
Vulcan	Starship Enterprise

BRITISH COLUMBIA

Abbotsford - Abbotsford Int'l Airport	CF-101
Kamloops - Kamloops Airport	CF-5
Port Alberum - Sproat Lake, Vancouver Island West of City	Martin Mars Flying Boat 2ea.
Sidney - Army, Navy and Air Force Assoc, 4th St	F-86 Mk. 6
St James	Junkers W34

MANITOBA

Brandon - Comfort Inn, Route 10 & Trans Canada	Bollingbroke
Brandon Airport, Route 10	T-33
Gimili - 1st Ave Off Center St	T-33
Moncton	CF-5
Moose Jaw	SNJ
Winnipeg - Ness Ave & Conway	F-5
Winnipeg - Woodland Park, Portage Ave & Woodhaven	T-33

ONTARIO

Belleville - Zwicks Centennial Park, Hwy 2 at Bridge, In Town	F-86 RCAF
Brockville - Brockville Marina, Blockhouse Island, Hwy 2 West	F-86, CT-134
Dunnville Library, Chestnut Ave, Off Hwy 3	Harvard
Dundas	CT-33
Fort Erie - Niagara Parks, Garrison Rd & Central Ave	T-33
Grand Bend - Pinery Antique Flea Market	T-33

ONTARIO

Ignace - City Display	Beechcraft D18 on Floats
Kingston Airport, RCAFA 416 Wing, Regional Rd 1	AT-6 Harvard, CT-134
Kingston Royal Military College, Point Frederick,Hwy 2	F-86, CF-100
Kitchener Waterloo Regional Airport, Fountain St	Diamond Katana
London Airport, Crumlin Rd	Diamond Katana, CT-133
Malton	CF-100
Moonbeam	Flying Saucer
North Bay Lee Park, Memorial Dr	Bomarc, CF-101
Ottawa Int'l Airport, Breadner Blvd & Royal Route	CF-101
Peterborough - Riverview Park, Water St, North of Town	F-86 Mk.6
Picton - Along Union St, East of City	T-33, CT-134
Red Lake - Howie Bay Waterfront, Howie St	Norseman
Sarnia - Germaine Park, East St	F-86
Smith Falls - Victoria Park, Lombard South	AT-6 Harvard IV
Toroonto Wildwood Park, Derry Rd	CF-100
Trenton - Holiday Inn, Sidney St & Hwy 401	CF-5
Trenton Town Arena, South of Dundas St	F-86
Wellington - Hwy 33 East of Town, On Garage Roof	F4U (1/3 Scale)
Windsor	Flying Saucer

QUEBEC

St Esprit	RB-57
St Hubert CFB	CF-100
St Jean-sur-Richelieu - Airport, CFB	CF-100, CF-104
St Jean-sur-Richelieu College Military Royal	CF-100

NEW BRUNSWICK

Chatham - Canadian Forces Base	CF-101
Cornwallis	CF-101
Cornwallis - Edmunston Airport,	Lancaster 10AB
Hillsborough - Preservation Park, Main Rd S of Town	CF-101
Moneton - Centenial Park	CF-100 Mk 5
Moose Bay - Labrador	CT-33

NEW FOUNDLAND

Botwood - In Town,	PBY-5A
Goose Bay - Town Hall, Hamilton River Rd	T-33
Goose Bay - 5 Wing Goose Bay Hq, Forbes Rd, Bldg 512	CF-100
Harbour Grace	DC-3

NORTHWEST TERRITORIES

Yellowknife - Yellowknife Airport, Briston 170 Freighter Mk 31M

NOVA SCOTIA

Bedford	CF-101

ONTARIO

Windsor - Jackson Park, Tecumseh Rd East, Lancaster

SASKATCH EWAN

Regina	C-45
Saskatoon	CT-33

RESTAURANTS

The following are restaurants with one or more aircraft in or around them or have been converted into a restaurant.

ARKANSAS

Hot Springs - Granny's Kitchen, 332 Central Ave, 71901, (501) 624-6183
Daily 6:30-8pm, Closed January, Home Cooking At Moderate Prices, Daily Breakfast Special, Daily Lunch Special Full Lunch and Dinner Menu With 12 Vegetables, Specialty - Blackberry Cobbler. Hanging From Ceiling Are:

A6M Zero	Ju 87 Stuka	P-38	PT-19	RC-3
DHC. 1	Nieuport 28	Pitts S-1	Super Chipmunk	
Flybaby Biplane J-3	Nieuport 17	PT-19	UC-78	

CALIFORNIA

Calabasas - Sagebrush Cantina, 3527 Calabasas Rd, 91302, (818) 222-6062
Mon-Thur 11am-10pm, Fri-Sat 11am-11pm, Sun 9am-2pm,Bar: Fri-Sat 9am-1:30am, Sun-Thur 9am-Midnight, Appetizers Avg $6, Soups and Salads$4-9, BBQ Ribs $15, Mexican Specialties $8-11, Charcaol Broiler $9-17, Bede BD-5J N007JB Ontop Restaurant

Camarillo - Camarillow Airport Cafe, Breakfast, Sandwichs

Hawthorne - Pizza Hut, 5107 El Segundo Blvd, 90250-4139, (424) 676-1100
1 Mile from Northrop Plant, Space & Aviation Artifacts

Inglewood - Proud Bird Restaurant, 11022 Aviation Blvd, (818) 670-3093
Leave 405 Freeway on Century Off Ramp, West To Aviation
Blvd, South To 11022 (Just East of LAX South Runway).
Thur-Sun 11-10, Fri-Sat 11-11,

A-4	Lockheed Vega	P-47	Spad XIII
F4U	Me-109	P-51D	Spitfire V
F6F	MiG-15	P-80	TBM
F-86	P-38	SBD Rep	X-1
Fokker D.VI	P-40	Skyhawk II	

Sacramento - Aces Restaurant, Holiday Inn, 5321 Date Ave, 95841-2597
(800) 388-9284, www.basshotels.com/h/d/hi/hr/sacne
Breakfast/Lunch/Dinner, Steaks, Seafood, P-51 Replica Above Roof

Santa Ana - Nieuport 17 Restaurant, 1615 E 17th , (714) 547-9511

San Diego - 94th Aero Sqd, 8885 Balboa Ave, 92123, (619) 560-6771

San Jose - 94th Aero Sqd, 1160 Coleman Ave, 95110, (408) 287-6150, Airplane there

Santa Monica - DC-3 Restaurant, 2800 Donald Douglas Loop North, 90405
(310) 399-2323, Mon & Sun Lunch, Tue-Sat Lunch & Dinner
Specialty - Steaks, Douglas - Sunbeam - Harley Davidson Motorcycle Display

Torrance - Doolittle's Raiders, 2780 Skypark, 90505, 428-539-6203, Manager: Keith Sulesky

Tulare - Aero Dogs, 240 North L St, (559) 685-1230, Mon-Sat 10:30-8:00pm
Seats 18, email: schoenau@comcast.net, Convair 240 (T-29)

Tustin - Nieuport 17 Restaurant, 13051 Newport Ave, 92780 (714) 731-5130

Van Nuys - 94th Aero Sqd, 16320 Raysner Ave, 91406, (818) 994-7437

COLORADO

CO Springs - Solo's Restaurnat, 1665 N Newport Rd (Off Fountain Blvd, One block East of Powers), CO Springs Mncpl Airport, (719) 570-7656, Sun-Thur 11-9 Fri-Sat 11-10, Eat inside a KC-97, Burgers to Steaks
Eat inside a KC-97, Model 8' B-17

Denver - Perfect Landing, Centennial Airport, Above Denver Jet Center, Hawker Sea Fury

CONNECTICUT

Bridgeport - Captains Cove, 1 Bostwick Ave, Restaurant (203) 335-7104, Gostave Whitehead Model 21, 1901 Glider, (203) 335-1433,

DELAWARE

New Castle - Air Transport Command Greater Wilmington Airport, 143 N du Pont Hwy(US Hwy 13), 19720, (302) 328-3527, C-47 Project

FLORIDA

Clearwater - 94th Aero Sqd, 94 Fairchild Dr, 33520, (727) 536-0409

Ft Lauderdale - Aviator's Tavern & Grille, Ft Lauderdale Int'l Airport, Under the Control Tower on the SW Side of the Airport, 1050 Lee Wagner Blvd, 33315, (954) 359-0044

95th Bomb Grp, 2500 NW 62nd St, 33309, (954) 491-4570

Lakeland - Tony's Airside Restaurant, Lakeland Linder Regional Airport,

Miami - 94th Aero Sqd, 1395 NW 57th Ave, 33126, (305) 261-4220

Mayday's, 7501 Pembroke Rd, S Side of North Perry Airport, 33024, (305) 989-2210, Manager: Mark Siple,

Spirit Restaurant, 7250 NW 11th St., 33126, (305) 262-9500
Pres Denise Noe, Lunch Specials Daily $4-7, Mon-Fri
Dinner 5pm Mon-Sat $7-11, Happy Hour Mon-Fri & D.J.
Fri/Sat, Steaks - Seafood - Pasta's - Salads - Mexican -
Cuban, Artifacts & 5' Models of Eastern & Pan Am Airlines
DC-3, DC-10, 727, 747, 757,

Orlando - 4th Fighter Grp, 4200 E Colonial Dr, 32803, (305) 898-4251
Off-The-Wall, Night Club, 4893 S Orange Blossum Tr,
(305) 851-3962,   Fokker D.VII   Fokker DR.I   SE-5A

Sarasota - 306th Bomb Grp, 8301 N Taniani Trail, 33580, (941) 355-8591

West Palm Beach - 391st Bomb Grp, 3989 Southern Blvd, 33406, (561) 683-3919
Daily, C-47, F4U, P-47, Tank

GEORGIA

Atlanta - 57th Fighter Grp, 3829 Clairmont Rd, 30341, (404) 457-7757

Air Superiorty Group, DeKalb-Peachtree Airport, POB 566726, 31156,
AT-6,   C-47,   P-51,   Rides in a N2S-3

IOWA

Cedar Rapids - Flyin Weenie, Downtown, PA-22 On Roof

ILLINOIS
Decatur - Decatur Airport Restaurant, R/C Aircraft Hanging From Ceiling,

Moline - Bud's Skyline Inn, 2621 Airport Rd, Rt 6 & 150, 61265,
(309) 764-9128, Lunch Mon-Sat 11am, Dinner: Ribs, Catfish, Steaks,
Email: skyline@qconline.com, Artifacts, Models

Wheeling - 94th Aero Sqdn, 1070 S Milwaukee Ave, 60090, (847) 459-3700
P-38 Replica   P-47 Replica   P-51 Replica

INDIANA
Muncie - Vince's Gallery, 5201 N Walnut, Muncie Airport, 47303,
(765) 284-6364, Mon-Thur 11-10, Fri 11-11, Sat 7-11,
Sun 7-9, Dinners Average: 10.00-12.00, Artifacts

Valparaiso - Strongbow Turkey Inn, 2405 Hwy 30 E, (219) 462-5121, 11-10pm

MARYLAND
College Park - 94th Aero Sqd, 5240 Calvert Rd, 20740, (301) 699-9400

MICHIGAN
Flint - Mister Gibby's Food & Spirits, Mister Gibby's Inn,
Best Western, G 3129 Miller Rd, At I-75 & US 23, 48507,
(810) 235-8561, (800)528-1234, 1/3 Scale Wings of DR.1 in
Cocktail Lounge, Bi-Plane Wings Outside Wall of Building.
Steaks, Seafood and Salad Bar.

MINNESOTA
Alexandria - Doolittle Restaurant, 4409 Hwy 29 South, 56308, (320) 759-0885,
Steaks, Ribs, Pasta, Seafood, Sandwiches, www.doolittlesaircafe.com,
R/C Aircraft, Artifacts, T-33

Coon Rapids - Doolittle Restaurants, 3420 129nd Ave NW, 55448,(612) 576-0575
Steaks, Ribs, Pasta, Seafood, Sandwiches, www.doolittlesaircafe.com,
R/C Aircraft, Artifacts,

Eagan - Doolittle Restaurants, 2140 Cliff Rd, 55122, (651) 452-6627
Steaks, Ribs, Pasta, Seafood, Sandwiches, www.doolittlesaircafe.com,
R/C Aircraft, Artifacts,

Golden Valley - Doolittle Restaurants, 550 Winnetka Ave North, 55427, (612) 542-1931
Steaks, Ribs, Pasta, Seafood, Sandwiches, www.doolittlesaircafe.com,
R/C Aircraft, Artifacts,

Plymouth - Doolittle Restaurants, 15555 34th Ave North, 55447, (612) 577-1522, Steaks, Ribs,
Pasta, Seafood, Sandwiches, www.doolittlesaircafe.com, R/C Aircraft, Artifacts,

MISSOURI
Berkeley - 94th Aero Sqd, 5933 McDonnell Blvd, 63134, (314) 731-3300

NEW JERSEY
Caldwell - 94th Bomb Grp, 195 Passaic Ave, 07006, (973) 882-5660

NEW YORK
Buffalo - Inn of the Port, Buffalo Greater Int'l Airport, (716) 632-5050, P-40 Replica

Cheektowaga - Flying Tigers, 100 Amherst Villa Rd, 14225-1432, (716) 631-3465, Seats 200, Smoking & Handicapped Sections,P-40: Tail Rudders - Parts of Wing - Propellers
Assistant General Manager: Matthew Rickrode, Appetizers: $2.95-$6.95, Entrees: $10.95-$15.95
Soups & Salads: $2.95, Desserts: $ 1.95-$ 3.95

E Farmingdale - 56th Fighter Grp, Republic Airport Gate 1, Route 110, 11735, (631) 694-8280, P-47 Replica

NORTH DAKOTA
Grand Forks - John Barley'Corn, 123 Columbia Mall, (701) 775-0501, Lunches $5.50 to Dinners $14.00, Hamburger to Lobster EAA Biplane, Hanging From Ceiling In Lounge, 11:30 am -1 am

Fargo - Doolittle Restaurants, 2112 25 th St South, 58103, (701) 478-2200
Steaks, Ribs, Pasta, Seafood, Sandwiches, www.doolittlesaircafe.com,
R/C Aircraft, Artifacts,

OHIO
Cleveland - 100th Bomb Grp, 20920 Brookpark Rd, 44135-3125, (216) 267-1010,   P-51

Columbus - 94th Aero Sqd, Port Columbus Int'l Airport, 5030 Sawyer Rd, 43219, (419) 237-9093

North Canton - 356th Fighter Grp Restaurant & Banquet Center, Akron-Canton Airport
4919 Mt Pleasant St NW, 44720, (330) 494-3500, Lounge Seats 170, Banquet Seats 60,
Non-Smoking & Handicapped Sections, Daily : Lunches $4.95-7.95; Dinners $10.95-22.95

OREGON
Milwaukie - Bomber Restaurant, 13515 SE. McLoughlin Blvd, Hwy 99E, 97222, (503) 654-6491,
B-17G (485790) Breakfast Mon-Sat 6am-1:45, 12:45 Sun, $2.25-6.95 Lunch 11am-5, $3.25-6.50,
25 Selections Dinner 11am-8:30, Till 9 Thr-Sat, $4.95-8.95 12 Selections Daily Specials: Ribs,
Seafood, Italian, Steak & Prime Rib, www.thebomber.com

PENNSYLVANIA
Reading - Dutch Colony Motor Inn, Antique Airplane Restaurant and Rudder Bar, 4635 Perkiomen Ave,
19606, (610) 779-2345 Co-Owner: R.H. Breithaupt, Suspended In Dinning Room 1927 Monocoupe,
Left Wing From A Piper Cub From WWII, 1917 Curtiss OX-5 Engine, 1930 Zekely Engine, & Artifacts

Philadelphia 94th Aero Sqd, N Philadelphia Airport, 2750 Red Lion Rd, 19154, (215) 671-9400

TENNESEE
Nashville - 101st Airborn, 1362-A Murfreesboro Rd, 37217-2619, Sat, American, $20-40, (615) 361-4212
TC-47B,   WWII Tank   Artifacts

Sam's Place, 7648 Hwy 70 South, (615) 662,7474,Large Models Hanging from Ceiling

TEXAS
Pittsburg - Warrick's Restaurant, 142 Marshall St, 75686, (903) 856-7881 Tue-Thur 11-9, Fri-Sat 11-10,
1902 Ezekiel Airship Replica Appetizers, Side Orders, Desserts, Sandwiches, Salads & Soups,
Seafood $6-9, Specialty Dishes $7-14, Steaks & Chicken $6-13, Child Menus $3-4

WISCONSIN
Dodgeville - Don Q's INN, Highway 23 N, PO BOX 53533, (608) 935-2321, KC-97 in front of the motel.

USS NAVAL SHIP MUSEUMS
ALABAMA
Mobile - Battleship Memorial Park, POB 65, 2703 Battleship Prky, 36601, (251) 433-2703, Daily 8-Sunset, Adm Adult $5, Child 6-12 $2.50, Gift Shop, Located On Battleship Parkway Between Exit #27 & #30, www.ussalabama.com   USS Alabama,   USS Drum,

CALIFORNIA
Long Beach - The Queen Mary , Pier J, 1126 Queens Hwy, (562) 435-3511, Mon-Fri 10-6, Sat-Sun 9:30-6, Adm Adult $22.95, Snrs $19.95, Child 5-11 $11.95, Overnight Stay on Queen Mary for one person $64 - $94. www.queenmary.com RMS Queen Mary,   Russian Foxtrot Submarine

Oakland - USS Potomac, 540 Water St, 94607, Mail: POB 2064, 94604, (866) 468-3399 Mon-Tue 9-1, Wed-Fri 9-5, USS Potomac

Naval Ship Visitation Tours, Terminal Island Naval Complex, Pier T (800)262-7838, USS Mobile, Tours change Monthly, Call for current ship.

USS Roncador, 7950 Deering Ave, Canoga Park, 91304

Richmond - Richmond Museum of History, POB 1267, 94802, (501) 237-2933, www.redoakvictory.org, SS Red Oak Victory Ship

San Diego - USS Midway Museum, 910 N Harbor Dr, 92101, (619) 544-9600, Daily 10-5, Adm Adult $15, Snrs 62 /Mil/ $10, Child 6-17 $8, Under 6 Free, Cafe, Gift Shop, www.midway.org **(Photo On Front Cover)**

San Francisco - National Maritime Museum , Fisherman's Wharf Pier 32-47 Changes Seasonally, POB 470310, 94147, 415-775-1943, www.maritime.org/pamphome.htm, Contact: Dave Lerma, USS Roncador (Submarine SS-301), USS Pamanito (Submarine SS-383)

National Liberty Ship Memorial, Ft Mason Center, Bldg A, 94123, (415) 441-3101 www.ssjeremiahobrien.org/   SS Jeremiah O'Brian (Liberty Ship)

San Pedro - US Merchant Marine Veterans of WW2, POB 629, 90733, (424) 519-9545, www.lanevictoryship.com, SS Lane Victory Ship

CONNECTICUT
Groton - Submarine Force Museum, X-1

New London - Nautilus Memorial & Submarine Force Library & Museum, New London Submarine Base, Mail: Box 571, 06349-5000, (800)343-0079, (860) 449-3174, 449-3558, Mid-April to Mid Oct Daily 9-5, Tue 1-5, Nov 1-May 14 Daily 9-4, Closed TueClosed: TD, CD, May 1st Week, Oct 1st Week, Free Adm, www.ussnautilus.org, USS Nautilus SSN 571
Bushnells Turtle   SS X-1   Mato-8 (Japanese Midget Sub)
Maiale (Italian Midget Sub)   Seahund (German Midget Sub)

DISTRICT OF COLUMBIA
The Navy Museum, 805 Kidder Breese St, 20374-5071, (202) 433-4882, Mon-Fri 9-4, Sat-Sun 10-5, Closed: TD, CD, ND, Adm Free, Tours Dahlgren Ave, 8th & Main St, Dir: Oscar P.Fitzgerald, Gift Shop, www.history.navy.mil
FG-1D	MXY7 Trainer	Posedon Missile	USS Barry
Maiale SSB	Turtle	USS Roncador Tower	
LCVP Higgins	Balao Fairwater		

FLORIDA
Tampa - American Victory Mariners Memorial & Museum Ship, 705 Channelside Dr, 33602, (813) 228-8766, www.americanvictory.org, SS American Victory

HAWAII

Honolulu

USS Arizona Memorial BB-39, Shoreline Dr. Pearl Harbor Navy Base off I-99
(808) 422-0561, 422-2771, 1 Arizona Memorial Place, 96818-3145,
Daily 7:30-5, Closed TD, CD, ND, Free Adm, Theater,
USS Arizona, www.nps.gov/usar/

USS Utah Memorial, www.ussutah.org,

Uss Missouri Memorial Assoc, POB 6339, 96818, (808) 973-2494, Daily 9-5, Adult $16,
Child 4-12 $8, www.ussmissouri.com   USS Missouri BB-63

USS Bowfin Submarine Museum & Park, 11 Arizona Memorial Dr.,
Pearl Harbor, 96818, (808) 423-1341, Next to USS Arizona Visitor
Center, Daily 8-5, Adm Charge, Gift Shop, www.bowfin.org
USS Bowfin SS-287, Missile & Rockets

INDIANA

Evansville - USS LST 325 Ship Memorial, Inc, 8740 LST Dr, 47713, (812) 435-8678
LST325 Hook Term, www.lstmemorial.org

LOUISIANA

Baton Rouge - Louisiana Naval War Memorial, 305 S River Rd, 70802, (225) 342-1942
Daily 9-5, Closed CD, Adm Adult $4, Sr $3, 6-12 $2.50,
USS KIDD (Camping aboard available groups of 20)www.usskidd.com/index.html

MARYLAND

Baltimore - Baltimore Maritime Museum, Pier 4 Pratt St, Inn Harbor, 21202,
(410) -396-5528, Mail: 802 S Carolina St, 21231, www.usstorsk.org
USS Torsk,   Lightship "Chesapeak",   USCG "Taney"

Liberty Ship Project, Highland Station, Pier One, 2000 block of South Clinton St,
Mail: Project Liberty Ship, POB 25846 Station, 21224-0546, (410) 558-0646
www.liberty-ship.com, email: john.w.brown@usa.net, SS John Brown

USS Constellation, DockPier One, 301 E Pratt, 21202, (410) 539-1797,
www.constellation.org,   USS Constellation

MASSACHUSETTS

Charlestown - USS Constitution Museum, 02129, (508) 242-5601, Mail: Box 1812, Boston, MA 02129
Oct 16-April 30 Daily 10-5, May 1-Oct 15 Daily 9-5, Adm Free, Gift Shop, Cafe, Over Night Stays
www.ussconstitution.navy.mil, USS Constition (Old Iron Sides), USS Cassin Young

Fall River - Fall River - Battleship Cove, 5 Water St, 02721, (508) 678-1100, I-95 Exit 5 to Braga Bridge,
Mail: POB 111, 02722-0111, Daily 9-5:00, Closed TD, CD, ND, Adm Adult $14, Snrs & Vet $12,
Child 6-18 $8, Under 6 Free, www.battleshipcove.org

USS Fall River	PT-617 Patrol Boat	Japanese Suicide Sub
USS Lionfish	PT-796 Patrol Boat	LCM
USS Joseph P Kenndey Jr	AH-1S	T-28
USS Massachusetts	Gyrodyne	UH-1M

Quincy - US Naval & Shipbuilding Museum, 739 Washington St, Next to Fore River Bridge Rte 3A
(617) 479-7900, Voice 7686, Fax 479-8792, Free Adm, April-Sept Daily 10-4,
Oct-March Sat-Sun 10-4, Closed Holidays, Adm Adult $6, Snr & Child 4-12 $4, Under 4 Free
Active Mil with ID Free, Archives James E Fahey, www.uss-salem.org, USS Salem CA 139

MICHIGAN

Douglas - Keewatin Maritime Museum, Blue Star Hwy & Union St, South of Saugatuck-Douglas Bridge
MD-LD Daily 10:30-4:30, Adm Adult $8.50, Child 6-12 $4.50, Winter (517) 589-8635
(269) 857-2464, Gift Shop, www.keewatinmaritimemuseum.com, SS Keewatin Passenger Steamer

Muskegon - USS Silversides SS-236, S Channel Wall, Pere Marquette Park, 134 Bluffton St,
(231) 755-1230, Fax 755-5883, June-Aug. Daily, 10-5:30, Sept Sat-Sun 10-5:30,
Weekdays 1-5:30, Oct Sat-Sun Only, Adm Adults $5.00, Over 62 $3.50, Child 12-18 $4,
5-11 $3, Under 12 $3.00, Free Overnight Package $15 Per Person Up To 52 People,
www.silversides.org, USS Silversides SS-236,   USCGC, LST 393

NEBRASKA

Omaha - Freedom Park, 2497 Freedom Park Rd, 68110, (402) 345-1959, From I-29 Go W
on I-480 Then N on Freedom Park Rd, Apr 15-Oct 31, Daily, 10-5, Adm Adult $4,
Snr $3, Child $2.50, Goup Rates, www.freedomparknavy.org,
A-4D   H-1(UH) USS Hazard AM-240 Mine Sweeper,   USS Marlin SST-2 (Submarine)
A-7   SH-3   USS Towers DDG-9 Captains Gig,   USS LSM-45 Landing Ship

New Hampshire

Portsmouth - Portsmouth Maritime Museum, 600 Market St, 03801, (603) 436-3680, USS Albacore Sub

NEW JERSEY

Camden - The Battleship New Jersey BB-62, Home Port Alliance, 2500 Broadway,
08104, (856) 966-1652, www.battleshipnewjersey.org, www.bb62museum.org/

Hackensack - US Naval Museum/Submarine USS Ling, 150 River St, 07601,
Mail: POB 375, 07682, (201) 342-3268, Daily 10:15-4, Closed Mon & Thur in
Dec-Jan, Adm Charge, www.njnm.com/NJNM.htm,
USS Ling (SS-297)(Submarine), German Seehund, Japanese Kaiten

Sea Girt - New Jersey National Guard Militia Museum, Intelligent Whale

NEW YORK

Albany - USS Slater (DE-766), POB 1926, 12201, (518) 431-1943, www.ussslater.org

Buffalo - Buffalo & Erie County Naval & Servicemen's Park, 1 Naval Park Cove, 14202,
(716) 847-1773, April 1-Oct 31 10-5, Nov Sat-Sun Only, Adm Adult $6.00,
6-12 $3.50, 5 & Under or Senior Citizen Free, Gift Shop,
www.buffalonavalpark.org,   PTF-17 Boat
USS Croaker SSK-246,   USS Little Rock (CLG-4),   USS Sullivans

New York City - Intrepid Sea-Air-Space Museum, **(Closed Until 2008)**,1 Intrepid Plaza, Pier 86,
46th &12th, 10036, (212) 245-0072, 2533, MD-LD 10-5, RoY Wed-Sun 10-5, Closed TD, CD, ND,
Adm Adult $4.75, Snr $4, Child 7-13 $2.50, Under 6 Free
www.intrepid-museum.com, USS Intrepid,   USS Growler,   USS Edson

NORTH CAROLINA

Kinston - CSS Neuse & Governor Caswell Memorial, 2612 W Vernon Ave (US Bus 70)
Mail: POB 3043, 28502, (252) 522-2091, Apr-Oct Mon-Sat 9-5, Sun 1-5
Nov-Mar Tus-Sat 10-4, Sun 1-4, Free Adm,
Hull of Iron Clad Gunboat CSS Neuse 1862
www.ah.dcr.state.nc.us/sections/Hs/neuse/neuse.htm

Wilmington - USS North Carolina Battleship Memorial, POB 480, 28402-0480
(910) 251-5797, Fax 251-5807, May 16-Sept Daily 8-8, RoY 8-5, Adm Adult $12, Snr 65 & Mil $10
Child $6, Child Under 6 Free. www.battleshipnc.com   USS North Carolina,   OS2U

OHIO

Cleveland - Submarine USS COD, 1089 N. Marginal Dr, Lakefront Between E & 9th St, 44114, (216) 566-8770, May-LD Daily 10-5, Adm Charged, www.usscod.org, USS Cod

Newcomerstown - National Naval Museum, 132 W Canal St, I-77 Exit 65, 43832, (740) 498-4446, www.ussradford446.org, R/C Helicopter, USS Radford & USS Helena Artifacts

OKLAHOMA

Muskogee - Muskegee - War Memorial Park, POB 253, 74401, (918) 682-6294, Mar 15-Oct 15 Mon-Sat 9-5, Sun 1-5, Closed RoY, Adm Charged, www.batfish.org, USS Batfish (Submarine)

OREGON

Astoria - Ft Stevens Historical Military Museum & Trails, Ft. Stevens State Park, Off US101, 10 Miles West of Astoria, (800) 551-6949, (503) 861-1671, Adm $3, www.oregonstateparks.org/park_179.php; 5 Inch 38 Caliber Navy Gun Sites WWII.

Deloria Beech Rd., WWII Japanese I-25 Submarine Siting Plaque

Portland - OMSI Oregon Museum of Science & Industry, Washington Park, 1945 SE Water Ave, 97208, (503) 797-4600, Daily 9-5, Adm Adult $2, Child $1, Store 9585 Sw Washington Sq Rd, 97208, (503) 684-5202, www.omsi.edu, email: Garron.Gest@omsi.edu, USS Blueback Sub

Pennsylvania

Philadelphia - Independence Seaport Museum, 131 N Dlwr Avenue & Chstnt, 19104 (215) 923-9129, Mail: POB 928, www.phillyseaport.org   USS Becuna   USS Olympia

Pittsburgh - Carnegie Science Center, One Allengeny Ave, 15212-5850, (412) 237-3400, March 1-Jun 14 & Sept 2-Dec 8: Sun-Fri 9-4:30, Sat 10-5:30, June 14-Sept 2 10-5:30, Dec 8-March 1: Sat-Sun 10-4:30, Closed Weekdays, Dec 26-31 10-5, Martin Luther King Birthday & President's Day 10-4:30, Adm Adult $4, Child 3-18 & Snr $2, www.carnegiesciencecenter.org, 45 Min Tours Every 15 Min, USS Requin SS-481 Submarine

RHODE ISLAND

Providence - USS Saratoga Museum, Not Open - Still Building, Coddington Cove, Naval Station Newport, Next to Quonset Air Museum, POB 28581, 02908, (401) 831-8696, www.saratogamuseum.org, email: SaveSara@aol.com, Aircraft Carrier CV-60, Restoration at Quonset: AV-8B, F-4B, VH-3

Russian Submarine Museum (Part of US Saratoga Museum), Collier Point Park, Off I-95 next to Manchester Station Generating Station, POB 28581, 02908, (401) 831-8696, Daily 10-6, Adm Adult Adult $8, Mil/Snr 65 $6 Child 6-17 $5, www.juliett484.org/juliett/index.html, Juliett 484 (K-77) Russian Submarine

SOUTH CAROLINA

Mt Pleasant - Patriots Point Museum, 40 Patriots Point Rd, 29464-4377, Mail: POB 986, 29464, (800) 248-3508, (843) 884-2727, Apr-Sept Daily 9-6, Oct 1-Mar 31 9-5, Closed CD, Adm Charged, www.state.sc.us/patpt, USS Clamagore SS-343, USCG Ingham, USS Laffey, USS Yorktown, MARK I Patrol Boat, UH-1 (2ea)

TEXAS

Corpus Christi - USS Lexington Museum, 2914 Shoreline Dr, Mail: POB 23076, 78403-3076, (361) 888-4873, Daily 9-5, Adm Adult $7, Child 4-17 $3.75, Seniors & Military W /ID $5, Closed CD, Gift Shop, Food Court, On-Going Restoration Projects, Asst Curator: Margaret W ead, www.usslexington.com
USS Lexington,   USS PINTA,   USS MARIA

Galveston - Seawolf Park, Pelican Island, Mail: POB 1575, 77550, (409) 744-5738, Daily 9-5, Adm Charged, www.cavalla.org, USS Cavalla (Submarine), USS Stewart (Destroyer), F-86

Houston - USS Houston Museum, (800)231-7799, 8:30-5,

La Porte - USS TEXAS BB-35 Battleship SMS, 3527 Battleground Rd, 77571, (281) 479-4414, Closed Mon-Tue, www.usstexasbb35.com

Orange - Southeast Texas W ar Memorial, 2606 Eddleman Rd, 77632, (409) 883-8346, Tue/Fri 9-2, Sat 9-4, Sun 1-4, Adm Donation, www.ussorleck.org, USS Orleck

VIRGINIA

Newport News - USS Savannah

Norfolk - Battleship W isconsin Foundation, National Maritime Center, 224 E Main, 23510, Mail: One W aterside Dr, Suite 248, (757) 322-2987, Memorial Day-Labor Day, Daily 9-6, RoY Tue-Sat 10-5, Sun 12-5, Closed TD, CE, CD, www.hrnm.navy.mil, USS W isconsin (BB-64)

WASHINGTON

Bremerton - Puget Sound Naval Shipyard, 130 W ashington Ave, 98337, (360) 479-7447, Tue-Sat 10-5, Sun & Holidays 1-5, One Block from Port Orchard Ferry or Hwy 304 These Ships Change and May Be Gone, Check Ahead. www.psns.navy.mil
USS Camden   (AOE-2)   Others Included:
USS Nimitz   (CVN-68)   Destroyers
USS Sacramento (AOE-1)   Battleships

Bremeerton Historic Ship Assn, 300 W ashington Beach Ave, 98337, (360) 792-2457 North of Ferry at W aterfront, Mon/Thr/Fri 11-4, Sat-Sun 10-4,
USS Turner Joy (DD-951) Destroyer,

Keyport - Naval Undersea Museum, End of Route 308, POB 408, 98345-5000, (360) 396-4148, Daily 10-4 Summer, Closed Tue Oct-May, Free Adm
Kaiten Japanese Suicide Mini-Sub   USS Etlah Netlayer
Trieste II Deep Submerge Vehicle   USS Safeguard Salvage Vessel

WISCONSIN

Manitowoc - W isconsin Maritime Museum, 75 Maritime Dr, 54220-6823, (920) 684-0218, Daily 9-5, Nov-March Daily 9-5, Sun 11-5, Closed NYD, ED, TD, CD
Adm Museum & Sub Adult $7, Child 6-12 $5, Family $20, Child 5 & Under Free, Museum only Adult $5, Child 6-12 $4, 5 & Under Fee, USS Cobia Submarine www.wimaritimemuseum.org/

Canada
Alberta

Calgary - Naval Museum of Alberta - 1820-24th St SW , T2T 0G6, (403) 242-0002, Tue-Fri 1-5, Sat-Sun 10-6, Closed: CD, ND, www.navalmuseum.ab.ca/aircraft.html
F2H-3, Hawker FB.11 Sea Fury, Supermarine Seafire Mk XV, T-33

Nova Scotia

Halifax - Maritime Museum of the Atlantic, www.hmcssackville-cnmt.ns.ca, HMCS Sackville,

ONTARIO

Hamilton - HMCS Haida Tribal Class Destroyer W W II # G63

ARMORED VEHICLE & ARTILARY MUSEUMS

California

Chiriaco Summit - General Patton Museum, 62510 Chiriaco Rd, 92203, (760) 227-3483,
Daily 9:30-4:30, Closed TD, CD, Adm Adult $4, Snrs $3.50, Child Under 12 Free

M4	M5A1	M47 (3ea)
M5	M26	M-60 (7ea)

CONNECTICUT

Danbury - Military Museum of Southern New England, 125 Park Ave, 06810, (203) 790-9277
April 1-Nov 30 Tue-Sat 10-5, Sun 12-5, Dec 1-March 31 Fri-Sat 10-5, Sun 1-5, Adm Adult $6,
Military & Snrs 62+ $4, Child Under 5 Free, www.usmilitarymuseum.org

Anti-Tank Guns	M-47	M3A1	Schutz 12-3
Fv603	M-48	M5	SPZ Observation
M-1	M-60	M40A1	SPZ 42-1
M-2	M-108	M578	
M-20	M-551	MBT-70	
M-39	M-656	PBV 302	

FLORIDA

Clearwater - Ft Desoto Museum, Tampa Bay, 12 Inch Motar

HAWAII

Honolulu - US Army Museum, Historic Battery Randolf, Kalia Rd Ft. DeRussy
(808) 438-2821, Mail: DPTMSEC, USAG-HI, Schofield Barracks, 96857, Tue-Sat 10-4,
Closed Mon, CD, Nd, Free Adm, Gift Shop 955-9552, AH-1, Japanese Tank, 14" Gun

ILLINOIS

Salem - Route 37 North of Salem,   WWI Howitzer

Wheaton - Cantigny 1st Divison Museum, 1S151 Winfield Rd, 60187, (630) 668-5161
10-5 Tue-Sun Memorial-Labor Day, 10-4 Tue-Sun Remaining Year, Free Adm

Howitzer 75mm	M41A3	M60	M1902
M4A3E8	M46	M113A2	M1917
M5	M47	M551	T26E4
M24	M48	M1896	

INDIANA

Auburn - WWII Victory Museum, 5634 County Rd 11A, 46706, (260) 927-9144, Mail POB 1, 46706
Daily 9-5, Closed TD, CD, ND, Adm Adult $10, Snrs 55 $8, Child 7-12 $6, Under 7 Free, Gift Shop,
Facility Rental, www.wwiivictory.org, Stinson 10A, 150 WWII Vehicles from Around the World

Brooksburg - City Hall, Main St, Cannon 120 mm

Cromwell - North of Rail Road Track,   Patton Tank

Huntington - Huntington Memorial Park, W Park & Bartlett St, T-33A,   M4A1 Tank

Jeffersonville - US Army Reserve, 11th Pennsylvania Ave, 47130-2702, N38' 17.109, W 085" 44.275
M48 Tank

Michigan City - Great Lakes Museum of Military History, 1710 E Hwy 20, Evergreen Plaza 46360
(219) 872-2702, May 20-Labor Day Tue-Fri 10-5, Sat 10-4, Sun 10-2: Labor Day-May 20 Tue-Sat 12-4:
Closed ES, TD, CD, Military Vehicles

Scottsburg - Indiana National Guard Center, Sherman Tank

Sunman - Aerican Legion, St Leon Exit, M4A3(75)VVSS Sherman Tank,

Van Buren - VFW, 7595 E 450N PO Box 441, Army Tank

INDIANA
Warsaw - City Court House, 301 N Buffalo St, M-4 Tank

MARYLAND
Aberdeen - VFW Post 10028, 821 Old Philadelphia Rd, POB T, 21001, Tank

Crisfield - VFW Post 8274, Somerset County memorial Post, Rocket

Federalsburg - VFW Post 5246, 203 Vernon Ave, 21632, (410) 754-5020, Tank

Grasonville - VFW Post 7464, Grasonville Memorial, Tank

Jarrettsville - VFW Post 8672, Manor Memorial, 3713 Federal Hill Rd, 21084-9998, Tank

Port Deposit - VFW Post 8185, Jerry Skrivanes Post, Tank

Powellville - VFW Post 2996, East Side Memorial Post, POB 51, 21850, (410) 835-8785, M-64 Tank

MONTANA
Helena - Montana Military Museum Ft Harrison Complex, 324-3550, (406) 841-3550, Thur 9-4, Free Adm, Tank

New Hampshire
Wolfeboro - E Stanley Wright Museum, 77 Center St, Mail POB 1212, 039894, (603) 569-1212, WW II Artifacts, www.wrightmuseum.org

NORTH CAROLINA
Camp Mackall - 4 Acres of WW II Jeeps, 10 Miles West of Fort Bragg
Near Addor, NC Just Off US 1, Between Southern Pines and Hoffman
Places where to purchase Military Aircraft, Vehicles:

Camp Lejeune - Camp Lejeune,Visitors Center (Bldg 812) at Main Gate on Holcomb Blvd, Off NC 24, (910) 451-2197, www.lejeune.usmc.mil or www.ci.jacksonville.nc.us
M-48 & M-60 Tank Infront of Bldg 407, At Courthose Bay: LVTPX12,
LVTP-4, LVTP-5A1, BMP-76PB (From Desert Storm)

Greenville - VFW Post 7032, 1108 Mumford Rd, PO Box 8387, 27835, Tank

Hollyridge Beach - Topsail Island Museum, The Assembly Bldg, 720 Channel Blvd,
Mail: POB 2645, 28445-9821, Mid April-Oct Mon, Tue, Fri-Sat, 2-4,
Nov-March Appt Only, (910) 328-8663, Gift Shop,
www.topsailmissilesmuseums.org, Talos Rocket from Operation Bumblebee 1959

OHIO
Hubbard - World War II Vehicle Museum, 5959 W Liberty St (Rt 304), 44425,
(330) 534-8125, Fax 534-3695, Mon-Fri 9-12 & 1-5, Adm Adult $5,
Child 10 & Under $3, Tanks: M4A1E8, M4A3, M7B1, M19, LVT(A)4
Half Track 3ea, 8 Inch Howitzer, DUKW, 6 Towed Guns 37mm to 175mm

PENSYLVANNIA
Dry Run - American Legion Post 232, James W McCartney memorial, 17319 Path Valley Rd
M-60 Tank SN 28-2-103

Virginia
Danville - American Armoured Foundation Tank Museum, 3401 US Hwy 29, 24540,
(434) 836-5323, Fax: 836-532, Mon-Sat 10-5, Closed TD, CD, Adm Adult $10,
Snr & Child Under 12 $8, Gift Shop, Tanks: M5A1, M42A1, M551A1, T54-55
M110A1, M-20, Daimler Dingo

Virginia
Petersburg - Fort Lee, Army Quartermaster Museum, 1201 22nd St, 23801-1601
(804) 734-4203, Tue-Fri 10-5, Sat-Sun 11-5, Closed TD, CD, ND, Free Adm
http://www.qmmuseum.lee.army.mil/index.html, Artifacts

Fort Lee, US Army Women's Museum, 2100 Adams Ace, Bldg P-5219, 23801-2100
Tue-Fri 10-5, Sat-Sun 11-4:30, Closed TD, CD, ND, Free Adm, Gift Shop 734-4636

Port Townsend - Coast Artillery Museum, 200 Battery Way, 98368, (360) 385-0373
Daily 12-4, Artifacts from Fort Casey, Fort Flager & Fort Worden

WISCONSIN
Racine - American Legion K Rd, Exit 329 Off I-94, Tank, Cannon

CANADA
Manitoba
Shilo - The Central Museumof the Royal Regiment of Canadian Artillery, Bldg N-118, Patricia Rd
CFB Shilo, Mail Box 5000 Station Main, R0K 2A0, (204) 765-3000 Ext 3534,
Victoria Day - Thanksgiving Day, Sat-Sun 1-5,Rest of Year Mon-Fri 9-5, Adm Adult $5
Snrs & Child 6-18 $3, Gift Shop, www.artillery.net, E-mail: rcamuseum@artillery.net,
Cannons, Rocket, 22 Guns & Vehicles

LANDMARKS
CALIFORNIA
Point Loma - Cabrillo National Monument, 1800 National Monument Dr, San Diego,
92106, (619) 557-5450, Daily 9-5:15, Adm Charged, Two 16" Gun Mounts
& Station used for WWII Costal Defenses.

San Francisco - Battery Davis Fort Funston, Pacific Side of City, 16" Gun Bunker.
Fort Point National Historical Site, 3" Gun Observation Posts,
South End Under the Golden Gate Bridge,

San Miguel Island - Green Mountain, Channel Island National Park, B-24 Crash Remains
Story on VHS "Wreckfinding, Lost But Not Forgotten".

Ventura - Battery 2 & Camp Seaside, Emma Wood State Beach, Panama Gun Mounts,
West 100 Yards from the Ventura River Mouth.

DELAWARE
Lewes - Cape Henlopen State Park, 42 Cape Henlopen Dr, 19958, (302) 645-8983
This is where you'll find a 12 Inch Gun & Tower 4A, a WWII observation tower that was
used to spot enemy submarines & vessels. These towers helped direct eight 16 inch guns
buried in sand along the coast. The guns had a range of 24 miles but were never called upon.
At the end of the war a German sub surrendered in the area, which claimed the sinking of
400 vessels along the east coast.

FLORIDA
Miami - Dade Metro Zoo. Here you will find still standing a tall blimp
support that was part of the NAS Hangar in Richmond during WWII.

New Smyrna - Target Rock, Rings of Port, WWII Gunnery & Bombing Target, Beach 13
Miles S of H-1A Hwy, Along Canaveral National Seashore, Remains of
an F6F Target, See Ranger Station on Directions.

HAWAII

Honolulu - Historic Battery Randolf, US Army Museum,, Kalia Rd Ft. DeRussy, (808) 438-2821,
Mail: POB 8064, 96830-0064, Tue-Sun 10-4:30, Closed Mon, CD, Nd, Free Adm,
Gift Shop 955-9552, AH-1, Japanese Tank, 14" Gun

MICHIGAN

Porcupine Mountain Wilderness State Park, On April 19, 1944 a B-17
crashed inside the wilderness where you can still find remains of
small parts along with the marks. To see this stop at the park
visitor center near junction of M-107 and South Boundary Rd.

NEBRASKA

Mc Cook - Mc Cook Air Base Historical Box 29 or Box B-337, 69001-0029
(308) -345-3200, under restoration of the facility. Training base
for B-24 & B-29 Bomb Groups. Remains are the buildings, hangars,
water tower, runways and aprons.

NEW JERSEY

Sandy Hook - The Gunnery, Sandy Hook State Park, Long Branch area,
Formerly Ft Hancock, 6" Shore Battery & Bunker System,
Tour Bunkers Used To Protect NY Harbor, Slide Show Twice,
Twice per Season Only, All Evening Tour

OREGON

Brookings - Siskiyou National Forest, From Hwy 101 - S Bank Chetco River Rd 6mi
Right on Forest Rd 1205 - At 12.7 mi - Take Wheeler Creek Research
Natural Area (#260) - This is a incendiary bomb site of a Japanese
aircraft launched off of a submarine near Gold Beach.

OREGON

Hillsboro - Bruce Campbell, 15270 SW Holly Hill Rd, 97123-9074, (503) 628-2936
www.leppo.com/~hypatiainc/BC727200.html,   Home Built Out of a Boeing 727

Tillamook - Municipal Airport, Blimp Hangar, Used for patrol along the west
coast during WWII.

WASHINGTON

Coupeville - Fort Casey State Park, 1280 S Fort Casey Rd, 98239, (360) 678-4519
Apr 1-Oct 31 Daily 6:30-Dusk, Oct 16-Mar 31 Daily 8-Dusk, Free Adm,
Manager: John Harris, 2 each 3" WWII Guns, 2 each 6" WWII Guns

Ft Columbia - Ft Columbia, 6 Inch Guns

Biplane & Warbird Rides
ARIZONA

Scottsdale - Sun Air Aviation, Inc, 15115 Airport Dr, Scottsdale Airpark, 85260,
(480) 991-0611, (800) 382-5030, Rides In The Following Aircraft:
Pitts Special   T-34   Waco   Helicopter & Balloon

CALIFORNIA

Chino - Planes of Fame, 7000 Merrill Ave, Chino Airport, 91710, (909) 597-3722
www.planesoffame.org, Rides in: SNJ (T-6) $1,000; P-51 $2,500; B-25 $5,000

Fullerton - Air Combat USA, 230 N Dale Pl, Mail: POB 2726, 92633-2524,
(800) 522-7590 Fly Laser Dog Fights in the SIAI Marchetti SF260. $695 Phase I/II,
$1295 Full Day Training & 2 Flight Missions & G-1 Jacket.

CALIFORNIA
Mesa - CAF - Arizona Wing & Museum, 2017 N Greenfield Rd, 85219, (480) 924-1940
May 15-Oct 14 Wed-Thur 9-3, Oct 15-May 14 Mon-Fri 10-4, Adm $7 Donation,
Gift Shop, Library, Restoration facility, www.arizonawingcaf.com
B-17G $425   C-45 $250   SNJ $250

COLORADO
Aurora - Airpower West, 2850 Kerr Gulch Rd, Mail: 3641 S Yampa St, 80013,
(303) 674-7864, Fax 670-6529, Airshow Coordinator: Mike Baldwin, apwrwest@rmi.net
Scheduled Airshows Flying: A-1, A-37, AT-6's, Beechcraft D17S & 18S, N2S, OV-1

Ft Lupton - CAF - Mile High Wing, Front Range Airport, 7607 County Rd 39, 80034-0528,
Mail: POB 471596, Aurora, CO, 80047-1596, (303) 851-1499, Info (303) 841-3004,
3rd Sat Monthly 10am, www.milehighcaf.org, C-60A (Rides Available)

FLORIDA
Kissimmee - Stallion 51 Corp, 3951 Merlin Dr, 34741, (407) 846-4400,
Fax 846-0414, Ride/Fly an AT-6 or TF-51 (Dual Cockpit) Mustang $2,850 Per Hour
www.stallion51.com

Warbird Adventures, 233 N Hoagland, Ramp 66, Grand Strand Airport, Adjacent to Flying Tigers Warbird
Restoration Museum, (800) 386-1593, (407) 870-7366, www.warbirdadventures.com,
E-mail: programs@warbirdmuseum.com, AT-6/SNJ Rides 15 Min $160, 60 Min $490

St Augustine - North American Top Gun, 270 Estrella Ave, 32095, (800) 257-1636, (904) 823-3505
AT-6 Rides $195-595, www.natg.com, AT-6G, AT-6D/G, SNJ-4, SNJ-5, SNJ-6

GEORGIA
Atlanta - Sky Warriors, Inc, 3996 Aviation Circle, Hangar B-3, Fulton County
Airport, Brown Field, 30336, (404) 699-7000, Fax 699-7200,
T-34A Aerial Laser Combat (75 Minute Flights)

Air Superiority Group, DeKalb-Peachtree Airport, POB 566726, 31156, Rides in a N2S-3

IDAHO
Driggs - Teton Aviation Center. 675 Airport Rd, Off Hwy 33, Mail: POB 869, 83422
(800) 472-6382, (208) 354-3100, Fax 354-3200, Daily 8-5, Closed TD, CD, Free Adm
www.tetonaviation.com, Glider Rides Available & Aviat Husky A-1 Rides

INDIANA
Valparaiso - Indiana Aviation Museum, Porter County Municipal, 4601 Murvihill Rd,
46383, (219) 548-3123, Sat 10-4, Sun 1-4, Adm Adult $3, Child Under 13 Free.
Curator: Jim Read, www.in-am.org, Rides Available in the following:
AT-6G   P-51D   T-28B
F4U-5N   PT-17   T-34B

KANSAS
Wichita - CAF Jayhawk Wing, 2560 S Kessler St, Westport Airport, 67217, (316) 943-5510,
(Rides Available for $75), www.cafjayhawks.org
PT-23 (Rides)   UC-78 (Rides)

KENTUCKY
Louisville, Bowman Field, (502) 368-6524, AT-6

MISSOURI
Maryland Heights - Historic Aircraft Restoration Museum, Dauster Flying Field,
Creve Coeur Airport, 3127 Creve Coeur Mill Rd, 63146, (314) 434-3368, Fax 878-6453
Sat-Sun 10-4,Rides: SNJ $75, Stearman $50, www.historicaircraftrestorationmuseum.org

NORTH CAROLINA

Durham - Carolina Barnstormers, Durham Skypark Airport, 4340 Ger St, 27704, (919) 680-6642,
Rides: Waco YPF-7, Two People for 25 Min. $90, 1 Hr $175; PT-17 One Person 25 Min. $75, 1 Hr $150

NEW YORK

Ghent - Parker-O' Malley Air Museum, 435 Old Rte 20, SW Side of Columbia County Airport,
POB 216, 12075, (518) 392-7200, www.parkeromalley.org   PT-17 (Rides $75)

Rhinebeck - Old Rhinebeck Aerodrome, 44 Stone Church Rd, Mail: BOX 229, 12572
(845) 752-3200, Fax: 758-6481, May 15-Oct31, Daily 10-5, www.oldrhinebeck.org/
1929 New Standard Biplane Rides 15 Min $40 Per Person

OHIO

Norwalk - Firelands Museum of Military History, 4755 SR601, (419) 668-8161, Mail: c/o Richard Rench,
202 Citizens Bank Bldg, 448547, www.huey.org   UH-1H (Rides Available)

Miamisburg - Wright B Flyer Museum, 10550 Springboro Pike, Off Rte 741, Wright Brothers Airport
(Dayton General Airport), 45342, (937) 885-2327, Tue,Thur,Sat 9-2:30,
Closed Holidays, www.wright-b-flyer.org, Wright B Flyer Flyable Rides for $150

TEXAS

Houston - CAF - West Houston Squadron, West Houston Airport, Hangar B-5, 18000 Groeschke Rd
77084, Hangar: (281) 578-1711, 3rd Sunday each Month, (Rides) Rides Available
AT-6D $250   BT-13A (Late 2007)   C-60A (Mid 2007)   S-108 (Late 2007)

Lancaster - CAF - Dallas / Ft. Worth Wing Museum, Lancaster Airport, Belt Line Rd, 75146
(972) 227-9119, 6 Mi East of I-35E in SE Dallas County, Sat 9-4,www.dfwwing.com,
BT-15 (Rides Available)   L-5 (Rides Available)   R4D-S (Rides Available)

VIRGINIA

Bealeton - Flying Circus Aerodrome, 15S. Route 17, BOX 99, 22712, (540) 439-8661,
Daily 11-Sunset, J-3 $35   Stearman $60   Fleet $120

WASHINGTON

Vashon - Olde Thyme Aviation Inc, 21704 141st. Avenue SW, 98070, Rides starting at
$107 for 2 people, 2 Travel Airs, 2 Waco UPF-7s, 2 Stearman Kaydets (1944 N2S-4 Navy
& 1944 PT-17 Army), and 2 Cabin Waco Biplanes (1936 YKS-6 & 1937 YKS-7),
http://www.oldethymeaviation.com/index.html, email: Waco@oldethymeaviation.com,

WISCONSIN

Oshkosh - EAA Air Adventure Museum, 3000 Poberezny Rd, POB 3065, 54903-3065, US 41 Exit 44,
(920) 426-4818, Mon-Sat 8:30-5, Sun 11-5, Closed TD, CD, ND,
Ford Tri-Motor Adult $30, Child $20   Travel Air E-4000 Biplane $50
Waco YKS-7 Biplane $40, 2 for $70, 3 for $90   Bell 47 $30 , 2 for $50
Spirit of St Louis Replica $100   New Standard D-25 Biplane $50

Canada
Alberta

Wetaskiwin - Reynolds Museum, East of Airport, 4118 57st, T9A 2B6,
(403) 361-1351, Mail: POB 6360, T9A 2G1, Sept-May9 Tue-Sun 10-5, May-Sept Daily 10-5,
www.cahf.ca/   Biplane Rides Available $116.63 (780) 352-9689

Ontario

Collingwood - Collingwood Classic Aircraft Foundation,
Collingwood Mncpl Airport, Mail: Box 143, L9Y 3Z4, (705) 445-7545, Thur 9-4, Adm Free,
www.classicaircraft.ca/homepage.htm, Smith Miniplane, Stinson 105
Rides in: Aeronca Champ 7AC, DH 82A, Fleet Canuck

DC-3 Rides

CALIFORNIA
San Clemente - Air Cruise America, 1 Via Pasa, 92673-2750, (949) 661-8410, DC-3 (Rides Available)

GEORGIA
Griffin - Alexander Aeroplane Co, Spalding County Airport, 118 Huff Daland Cir, 30223, (770) 228-3901, (800)831-2949, DC-3 (2 Hour Flights), T-33

ILLINOIS
Prairie Aviation Museum, Bloomington-Normal Airport, 2929 E Empire St, 61704, Mail POB 856, 61702, (309) 663-7632, Fax 663-8411, Tue-Sat 11-4, Sun 12-4,DC-3 Rides $80, www.prairieaviationmuseum.org

KENTUCKY
Louisville - Bowman Field, 5 Mi SE of City, (502) 368-6524, AT-6, DC-3/C-47 Flights

OKLAHOMA
Ames - Bygone Aviation, POB 22, 73718, (580) 753-4445, DC-3 Rides Available

CANADA
YUKON TERRITORY
Whitehorse - Whitehorse Airport, (403) 667-8440, DC-3(3ea) Flights To:
Dawson City, Fairbanks, Juneau, Old Crow

Glider Rides
NEW YORK
Elmira - National Soaring Museum, 51 Soaring Hill Dr, 14903-9204, (607) 734-3128, Fax 732-6745, Daily 10-5, Adm Adult $6.50, Snrs 60 $5.50, Child 5-17 $4, Under 5 Free Gift Shop, Sailplane Rides, www.soaringmuseum.org

TEXAS
Marfa - Marfa Gliders, Texas Hwy 17, Mail POB 516, 79843, (800) 667-9464, Daily 11-4, Free Adm, Glider Rides, Contact Burt Compton, www.flygliders.com **(See Classified Ad Section)**

Blanik L-23 (2ea)	Schempp-Hirth Cirrus (2ea)
Schweizer 1-36	Scheicher ASK-13

Credits
Carry Patrick from Waukegan, IL

Has provided me with endless letters each month with lots of useful information on museums & aircraft. He saved me Months of work.

I would like to thank all museums who have sent me information on their facility and for the following people who have provided me with information for this edition.

Baleria	Dave	Rapid City,	SD
Bauer	Richard	Battle Creek,	MI
Baumann	Richard	Los Angeles,	CA
Besecker	Roger	Bethlehem,	PA
Bonoit	Christen P	Ridgefield,	CT
Browning	Scott	Cincinnati,	OH
Ford	Larry	Goshen,	IN
Gaskins	Robert	Drapers,	UT
Gelford	Mark	Los Angles,	CA
Grose	Jim	Lake Hughes,	CA
Holm II	Robert D	Long Island,	NY
Houser	Allen E	Jeffersonville,	IN
Howe	William	Casa,	AZ
Idol	Paul E	Wichita,	KS
Johnston	Bill	Lacombe,	Alberta, Canada
Kloek	Ludo	Hoevenen	Belgium
Malin	Robert	Commerce Twp,	MI
Mihavics	George	Auburn,	IN
Nelson	Gerald D	Big Lake,	MN
Olson	Larry	Silver Springs,	MD
Porter	Liz	Woodstock,	GA
R&D	Diane	Wyoming,	MI
Richard	Baumann	Los Angles,	CA
Roe	Bruce	Aurora,	IL
Roesky Jr	Emil	Coffeyville,	KS
Smalley	Erville G	Colorado Springs,	CO
Stocker	Bill	London,	Ontario, Canda
Summer	Howard L	Mesa,	AZ
Symer	Richard P	Griffith,	IN
Walter	John C	Columbus,	OH
Wilburn	Nate	Great Falls,	MT
Williams	John	Fall River	

Last I want to thank my wife Sylverta M Blaugher
for her help and support in my long hours and months putting
this edition together.

Glider Rides
by appointment at

Marfa Airport on Texas Highway 17
www.flygliders.com

Call for flying schedule: 800-667-9464

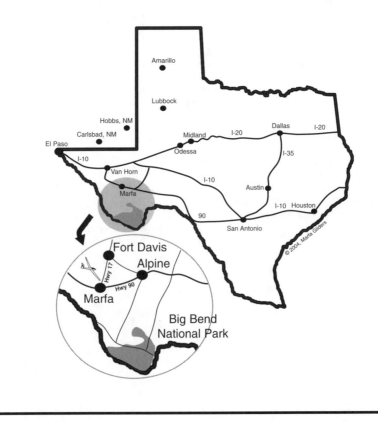

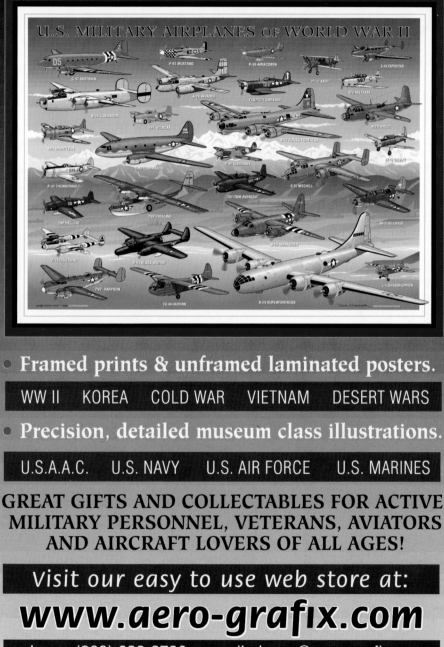
132A

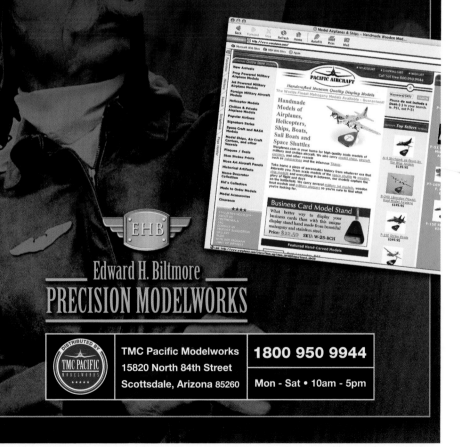

Wings of Freedom, Willow Grove NAS, PA; P-80C Photo by Author

The Bomber Restaurant, Milwaukie, OR; B-17 Photo by Terry Scott

(Model)	State	City Abv.	Museum Abv.	Manufacture	Aircraft Name/ SN, N#, Tail#, Side#, Sq#, Nick Name
A-1	CO	Pueblo	PWAM	Martin-Marietta	Pershing 15
A-1	FL	Pensacola	NMoNA	Curtiss	Triad N6077V
A-1 EAA	WI	Oshkosh	EAAAAM	Curtiss	Triad

A-1 Douglas Skyraider

(Model)	State	City Abv.	Museum Abv.	SN / Tail / Side #
A-1(BTD-1)	NY	Horseheads	NWM	04959
A-1(AD)	CA	San Diego	SDACM	127922
A-1A(AD-1)	VA	VBeac	ONAS	9102, 500, VA-176
A-1A(AD-1H)	CA	El Cajon	WW	
A-1C(AD-3)	WI	Oshkosh	EAAAAM	122811
A-1D	CO	Denver	69thB	Tail: TT822
A-1D(AD-4N)	AZ	Grand Canyon	VGCM	
A-1D(AD-4N)	CT	Winds	NEAM	
A-1D(AD-4N)	ID	Rexburg	LFM	
A-1D(AD-4N)	WA	Bellingham	FHC	126924, N2692
A-1D(AD-4N)	VA	Suffolk	FF	123827, VA-195
A-1D(AD-4NA)	MI	Kalamazoo	KAHM	127888, N92334
A-1D(AD-4W)	NV	Fallon	NASF	132261, VA-145, 500, NK
A-1D(AD-4W)	OR	Tillamook	TAM	

(Model)	City Abv.	State	Museum Abv.	SN / Tail / Nick Name
A-1E(AD-5)	Lemoore	CA	LNAS	
A-1E(AD-5)	McClellan	CA	McCelAFB	132463, 552, 2 Seater
A-1E(AD-5)	FtWal	FL	HF	52-598, 2 Seater
A-1E(AD-5W)	Geneseo	NY	1941AG	
A-1E(AD-5)	Dayton	OH	NMUSAF	52-13264, 9, Twin Seater
A-1E(AD-5)	MtPleasant	SC	PPM	Twin Seater
A-1E(AD-5)	RioHo	TX	TAM	BU132443, Twin Seater
A-1E(AD-5)	Tyler	TX	HAMM	
A-1E(AD-5)	Ogden	UT	HAM	52-0247
A-1E(AD-5)	Oshkosh	WI	EAAAAM	132789, Twin Seater
A-1F(AD-5Q)	Tucson	AZ	PAM	135018, VR703, 2 Seater
A-1H(AD-6)	Pensacola	FL	NMoNA	135300, NL405, VA-25
A-1H(AD-7)	Suitland	MD	PEGF	
A-1H(AD-6)	Dayton	OH	NMUSAF	51-630

(Model)	State	City Abv.	Museum Abv.	Manufacture	Name
A-2	CA	China Lake	USNMAT	Lockheed	Polaris
A-2	VA	Hampton	APM	Lockheed	Polaris

A-3A(A3D-1) Douglas Skywarrior

(Model)	State	City Abv.	Museum Abv.	SN
A-3A(A3D-1)	FL	Pensacola	NMoNA	135418, 70
A-3B(A3D-2)	CA	San Diego	SDACM	142551
A-3B(A3D-2)	MD	Ft Meade	NVP	
A-3B(A3D-2)	CT	Winds	NEAM	142246
A-3B(A3D-2)	NY	NYC	ISASM	
A-3D(A3D-1)	AZ	Tucson	PAM	130361

(Model)	City Abv.	State	Museum Abv.	SN / Nick Name
A-3D(A3D-4)	Rosamond	CA	EAFB	135434
A-3D(A3D-4)	NYC	NY	ISASM	"Whale"
A-3D(KA-3B)	Oakla	CA	OWAM	
A-3D(KA-3B)	C Christi	TX	USS Lexi	

A-4

McDonnell-Douglas Skyhawk

Type	State	City	Code	Serial/Notes
A-4J(TA)	AL	Birmingham	SMoF	
A-4	AZ	Yuma	YUSMAB	SC01
A-4	CA	Alame	ANAS	
A-4	CA	El Centro	ECNAF	159798
A-4	CA	Inglewood	PBR	
A-4	CA	Lemoore	LNAS	
A-4	CA	Twentynine	TPMC	5133
A-4	FL	Kissi	FTWAM	
A-4	FL	Orlan	ONTC	
A-4	HI	Oahu	BPNAS	152061
A-4	HI	Oahu	BPNAS	153689
A-4	IL	Great Lakes	GLNTC	
A-4	LA	Reser	AMHFM	
A-4	NB	Omaha	FP	
A-4	NC	CPoin	CPMB	
A-4	NC	Havelock	HI	
A-4	NH	Nashu	FAAATCC	
A-4	NJ	Millville	MAAFM	
A-4	NV	Fallon	NASF	142100, VFC-13, 01
A-4	NV	Fallon	NASF	
A-4	NY	Brooklyn	FAAATCC	
A-4	SC	Mt Pleasant	PPM 1	49623, VA 163 USS Oriskany
A-4	TX	Beevi	CrtHouse	
A-4	TX	San A	CityPark	
A-4	VA	Norfolk	NMM	
A-4(Tail Only)	TN	Memph	LS	
A-4A	CA	Alameda	USSHM	139929
A-4A	CA	Paso Robles	EWM	137826
A-4A	CT	Winds	NEAM	2219 , 36
A-4A	IL	Rantoul	OCAM	139947, Blue Angle #6 "Lucy"
A-4A Cockpit	KS	Liberal	MAAM	
A-4A	KS	Topeka	CAM	142168
A-4A	MD	Annap	USNAM	
A-4A	NY	NYC	ISASM	2833, AF, 300
A-4A	TX	Kings	CityPark	
A-4A	TX	Paris	FTAM	
A-4B(TA)	AZ	Tucson	PAM	14928 (A4D-2)
A-4B	CA	Chino	PoF	
A-4B	CA	Chino	YAM	
A-4B	CA	San Diego	SDAM	P302, VA-212
A-4B	DC	Washi	NA&SM	
A-4B	IN	Crawfordsville	RAM	142834
A-4B(A4D-2)	MI	Kalamazoo	KAHM	057182, 145011
A-4B	MI	Mt Clemens	SMAM	142761, Side # 01
A-4B	NY	NYC	ISASM	
A-4B	OR	Tillamook	TAM	
A-4B	TN	Crossville	CCHS	148572, "Blue Angles"
A-4B	TX	C Christi	USS Lexi	
A-4B	TX	C Christi	USS Lexi	
A-4B	WI	Oshkosh	EAAAAM	685
A-4C	AR	Fayet	AAM	147733
A-4C	AZ	Tucson	PAM	148571, N401FS
A-4C	CA	Chino	YAM	
A-4C	CA	El Cajon	SDAMGF	201, NM
A-4C	CA	Miramar	FLAM	DT, VMA-242, "Advisary"
A-4C(TA)	CA	Miramar	FLAM	
A-4C	CA	Palmdale	PPHP	145067
A-4C	CA	San Diegoe	SDAM	
A-4C	FL	Clear	FMAM	
A-4C	FL	Jacksonville	NASJ	147788, AK 301, VA-106
A-4C	NJ	Lumberton	AVM	145072
A-4C	NJ	Lexington	NASWAM	
A-4C	NY	NYC	ISASM	
A-4C	RI	NKing	QAM	147790 "Mighty Midget"
A-4C	VA	Richmond	VAM	
A-4D	IN	Goshen	AM	
A-4D	NB	Omaha	FP	149618, "USS Enterprise"
A-4D-1	NC	Charlotte	CAM	14-226
A-4D-2	CO	Pueblo	PWAM	147702
A-4E	CA	Chino	YAM	
A-4E(A4D)	FL	Pensacola	NMoNA	149656, VA-164, "AH", #303
A-4E(A4D)	FL	Pensacola	NMoNA	"Blue Angels", 150076 154180 1

Model	State	City	Location	BuNo / Notes
A-4E	HI	Kalaeloa	NASBP	
A-4E	HI	Kalaeloa	NASBP	
A-4E	HI	Kalaeloa	NASBP	
A-4E	VA	Triangle	NMMC	
A-4F(NT)	CA	China Lake	USNMAT	
A-4F	NY	Scotia	ESAM	155009
A-4F	CA	San Diego	SDACM	154977
A-4F	RI	NKing	QAM	155027
A-4F	VA	VBeac	ONAS	155176, VF-43
A-4F	WA	Seattle	MoF	"Blue Angels", 154180 4
A-4F(A4D)	FL	Pensacola	NMoNA	"Blue Angels", 154217 4
A-4F(A4D)	FL	Pensacola	NMoNA	"Blue Angels", 155033 3
A-4F(A4D)	FL	Pensacola	NMoNA	"Blue Angels", 154983 2
A-4L	AL	Mobile	BMP	147787
A-4J(TA)	CA	Palm Springs	PSAM	153678
A-4J(TA)	IL	Sugar Grove	ACM	153671, VT-7, CTW-1, 716
A-4J(TA)	IN	Elkhart	NIAM	158716, 771, A, VT-7(CTW-1)
A-4J(TA)	KS	Topeka	CAM	
A-4J(TA)	MD	Lexington	USNTPS	158106, Side # 8, TPS Tail
A-4J(TA)	TX	Beevi	CFAFB	
A-4J(TA)	TX	Corpus Christi	NASCC	
A-4J(TA)	TX	FWort	NASFWJRB	
A-4J(TA)	TX	Tyler	HAMM	
A-4L	KS	Liberal	MAAM	
A-4L	KY	Lexington	AMoK	147708
A-4L	MS	Greneda	HS	160255, NMF-213
A-4L	SC	Beauf	MAS	147772, EX 01, MALS-31
A-4M	CA	Miramar	FLAM	
A-4M	CA	Oakla	OWAM	SI 59
A-4M	IL	Bloomington	PAM	160036
A-4M	ME	Lexin	PNAT&EM	
A-4M	NC	Havelock	HTC	
A-4M	PA	Willow Grove	NVHAA	158182, WA 00
A-4M	RI	NKing	QAM	158148
A-4M	TX	FWort	NASFWJRB	

A-5 NA-Rockwell Vigilante

Model	State	City	Location	BuNo / Notes
A-5	FL	KeyWe	NASKW	
A-5	FL	Orlan	MGNTC	
A-5C	FL	Sanford	Airport	
A-5(A3J)	MD	Lexington	PRNAM	156643, Side# 643, NATC Tail
A-5A(A3J)	MD	Lexington	SWD	146697
A-5	TN	Millington	NASM	

A-6 Grumman Intruder

Model	State	City	Location	BuNo / Notes
A-6	CA	San Diego	SDAM	
A-6	GA	Marietta	NASA	
A-6	MI	Lapee	YAFDLA	
A-6	NV	Fallon	NASF	
A-6	NY	NYC	ISASM	155627
A-6	PA	Smethport	AAAM	147867
A-6	VA	Norfolk	NASN	
A-6	WA	Oak Harbor	City Park	
A-6 Simulator	CA	Oakla	OWAM	
A-6A	AL	Starke	CBM	155661,
A-6A	MD	Lexington	PRNAM	VA-35, 507, 07, USS America / 156997, 500, NAWC/AD
A-6A	MI	Belleville	YAM	156981, "Flight of the Intruder" Movie
A-6A	NY	NYC	ISASM	162185
A-6B Cockpit	CA	Chino	YAM	
A-6B	SC	Mt Pleasant	PPM	152599
A-6B(EA)	WI	Oak Harbor	CP	
A-6D(KA-6D)	AL	Mobile	BPM	151826
A-6D(KA-6D)	CA	Oakla	OWAM	
A-6E	AZ	Tucson	PAM	155713, NJ 562, VA-128
A-6E	CA	Chino	YAM	
A-6E	CA	Paso Robles	EWM	154717

Vought Corsair II / A-6 Intruder listing

Column 1

Type	Code	City	State	Serial / Notes
A-6E	USNMAT	China Lake	CA	NAWC
A-6E	FLAM	Miramar	CA	154162, #500, VA-36, AJ, USS Theodore Roosevelt
A-6E	PSAM	Palm Springs	CA	
A-6E	PCAM	SRosa	CA	
A-6E	SDAMGF	El Cajon	CA	
A-6E	SDACM	San Diego	CA	
A-6E	CAF-RMW	Grand Junction	CO	VMA-533, #7
A-6E	NMoNA	Pensacola	FL	155610

A-7 — Vought Corsair II

Type	Code	City	State	Serial / Notes
A-7	CBM	Starke	AL	157503, 301, NE 01, Lt PS Clark
A-7	I-20/59	Tuscalloose	AL	400
A-7	PMA	Pocahontas	AR	153150, 300,
A-7	ANAS	Alame	CA	Tail NL, VA-22, USS Nmitz
A-7	YAM	Chino	CA	400
A-7	SDAM	San Diego	CA	
A-7	SDACM	San Diego	CA	
A-7(LTV)	FTWRM	Kissimmee	FL	
A-7	ONTC	Orlan	FL	
A-7	VACM	Titus	FL	
A-7	ING	Des Moines	IA	75403
A-7	IAM	Greenfield	IA	
A-7	Belle Chasse NAS	New Orleans	LA	
A-7	PNA&EM	Lexin	MD	
A-7	FP	Omaha	NB	
A-7E2	CAM	Charlotte	NC	159971, VA-72
A-7	CPMB	CPoin	NC	
A-7	DTAM	Minot	ND	
A-7	NASF	Fallon	NV	154420, 00
A-7	NASF	Fallon	NV	
A-7	AHS	Alliance	OH	153142, VA-86
A-7	EAM	Tillamook	OR	153142, VA-86
A-7A	VACM	Tittusville	FL	
A-7A	PAM	Bloomington	IL	152681, NJ412
A-7B Cockpit	YAM	Chino	CA	

Column 2

Type	Code	City	State	Serial / Notes
A-6E	VACM	Tittusville	FL	164384
A-6E	GMP	Calverton	NY	155629
A-6E	QAM	NKing	RI	
A-6E	USS Lexi	C Christi	TX	151579, AC501, VA-75
A-6E	ONAS	VBeac	VA	151579, AC501, VA-75
A-6E	NASMUVC	Chantilly	VA	158794
A-6E	MoF	Seattle	WA	
A-6E(EA)	City Beach	Tacoma	WA	152907, VA-128, NJ, Side # 800
A-6F	CoAM	Garde	NY	162184
A-7	SDAMGF	El Cajon	CA	154449
A-7B	PPHP	Palmdale	CA	154550
A-7B	AVM	Lumberton	NJ	144345, VA-82
A-7B	HRA	Hickory	NC	154431
A-7B	USS Lexi	C Christi	TX	154431
A-7C	TAM	Slaton	TX	
A-7C	OMM	Fayettville	AR	
A-7C	USNMAT	China Lake	CA	
A-7C	EWM	Paso Robles	CA	156739
A-7C(TA)	MMM	Russell	IL	156751, VAQ33, #120
A-7D	NAM	Albuq	NM	
A-7D	DMAFB	Tucson	AZ	
A-7D	PAM	Tucson	AZ	70-973, "Big D"
A-7D	TANG	Tucson	AZ	
A-7D	MAFM	Riverside	CA	69-6188
A-7D	McCelAFB	McClellan	CA	70-998
A-7D	WOTR	Denver	CO	
A-7D	SWYC	Altoona	IA	71334, Tail IA AF
A-7D	Airport	Carroll	IA	
A-7D	CityPark	Corre	IA	
A-7D	CD	Johnston	IA	
A-7D	MAAM	SBluf	IA	
A-7D	CityPark	Sheld	IA	
A-7D	SCANG	Sioux	IA	
A-7D	OCAM	Rantoul	IL	75403, Tail IA, AF,
A-7D	GLMAM	Middle River	MD	69-6190

Model	State	City	Location	Serial/Notes
A-7D	MI	Mt Clemens	SMAM	72-0261
A-7D	MT	Helena	FFTC	
A-7D	NC	Fayet	PAFB	
A-7D	ND	Wahpe	CityPark	
A-7D	NE	S.Sio	CityPark	
A-7D	NE	SSiou	MA	
A-7D	NM	Albuquerque	KAFB	72045
A-7D	NY	Horseheaed	WoE	69-6200
A-7D	OH	Cincinnati	123ACS	76360
A-7D	OH	Dayton	NMUSAF	70-0970
A-7D	OH	Lockb	RANGB	73-999
A-7D	OH	Lockb	RANGB	73-1006
A-7D	OH	Springfield	178FW	72-00178
A-7D	OH	Wilmington	AA	57-00308
A-7D	OK	Oklahoma	45IDM	72-0240
A-7D	RI	NKing	QAM	75-0408
A-7D	SC	McEnt	MEANGB	
A-7D	SD	Huron	Airport	
A-7D	SD	McEnt	MEANGB	
A-7D	SD	Pierr	SDNGM	
A-7D	SD	Sioux	SDANGSF	
A-7D	SD	Tea	Airport	
A-7D	TX	Burnet	CAFHLS	
A-7D	VA	Richm	SMAM	72-0
A-7D	VA	Sands	VAM	"Death Dealer"
A-7D	WA	Weirton	CP	
A-7D	WI	CDoug	WNGML&M	
A-7D(YA)	CA	Rosamond	EAFB	67-14583
A-9A(YA)	CA	Riverside	MFAM	Northrop
A-10 Wing	WI	Oshkosh	EAAAAM	Mitchell

Fairchild

Thunderbolt II

Model	State	City	Location	Serial/Notes
A-10	CA	Chino	YAM	
A-10 Cockpit	KY	Ft Campbell	DFPMM	
A-10	LA	Alexandria	EAB	23-3667, EL 23TFW
A-10	LA	New Orleans	Belle Chasse NAS	

Model	State	City	Location	Serial/Notes
A-7D-3-CV	MI	Belleville	YAF	69-6193
A-7E	Al	Birmingham	SMoF	
A-7E	AZ	Tucson	PAM	160713
A-7E	CA	Lemoore	LNAS	
A-7E	CA	Oakla	OW AM	NJ250
A-7E	FL	Colum	CityPark	158003
A-7E	FL	Jacksonville	NASJ	160715, 301, VA-46
A-7E	FL	LakeCity	CityPark	Thunderbird colors
A-7E	FL	Pensacola	NMoNA	160714
A-7E	GA	Marietta	NASA	158842
A-7E	IL	Sugar Grove	ACM	158842
A-7E	IL	Edwardsville	CityPark	159303, #401
A-7E	IL	Linco	HIFM	
A-7E	KS	Liberal	MAAM	20
A-7E	LA	Alexandria	EAB	69-234, EL 23TFW
A-7E	LA	Baton Rouge	LNW M	160724
A-7E	LA	Reser	AMHFM	
A-7E	NM	St Teresa	WEAM	
A-7E	NV	Fallon	NAS	
A-7E	SC	Mt Pleasant	PPM	Side 301
A-7E	TN	Memph	MBMA	160869, 401, VA-27
A-7E	VA	Hampton	APM	157500, AC-300, VA-37
A-7E Cockpit	OR	Tillamook	TAM	
A-7F(YA)	OR	Tillamook	TAM	71-344
A-7F(YA)	CA	Rosamond	EAFB	70-1039
A-7K	UT	Ogden	HAFBM	
	IA	SBluf	MAAM	

Model	State	City	Location	Serial/Notes
Wing				71-1368

Model	State	City	Location	Serial/Notes
A-10	CT	Windsor	ANG	
A-10 Cockpit	TX	Big Springs	H25	
A-10	WI	CDoug	WNGML&M	
A-10A	AZ	Tucson	DMAFB	
A-10A	AZ	Tucson	PAM	75-298

Designation	State	City	Location	Serial/Notes
A-10A	CA	McClellan	McCelAFB	76-540
A-10A	CT	Winds	NEAM	173
A-10A	FL	Shalimar	USAFAM	77-205, NO
A-10A	IN	Peru	GAFB	77-228
A-10A	NC	Fayet	PAFB	
A-10A	NY	Garde	CoAM	760535
A-10A	NY	Horseheads	NWM	
A-10A	NY	Scotia	ESAM	75-263
A-10A	OH	Dayton	NMUSAF	78-0681, TW F-23
A-10A	TX	San Antonio	LSAD	76-547
A-10A	UT	Ogden	HAFBM	
A-10A	WA	Tacoma	MAFB	270
A-10A(OA)	NC	Fayet	PAFB	
A-10B(YA)	CA	Rosamond	EAFB	73-1664

Lockheed — Blackbird (See also SR-71)

Designation	State	City	Location	Serial
A-12	AL	Birmingham	SMoF	60-6937
A-12	AL	Huntsville	HSRM	60-6930
A-12	AL	Mobile	BMP	60-6938
A-12	CA	Los Angeles	CMoS	60-6927
A-12	CA	Palmd	PAFB	60-6924
A-12	CA	San Diego	SDAM	60-6933
A-12	NY	New York City	ISASM	60-6925
A-12(M-21)	WA	Seattle	MoF	60-6940

Designation	State	City	Location	Serial
A-17A	OH	Dayton	NMUSAF	Northrop

Nomad 36-0207

Douglas — Havoc

Designation	State	City	Location	Serial
A-20	AZ	Tucson	PAM	43-21627
A-20	VA	Suffolk	FF	
A-20G	OH	Dayton	NMUSAF	43-22200
A-20G	TX	Galveston	LSFM	43-21709, N3WF
A-20H	PA	Beave	AHM	44-0020

A-24 (* See SBD*)

Douglas — Invader

Designation	State	City	Location	Serial/Notes
A-26(JD-1)	CA	Palm Sprg	PSAM	43-5721, N94257, Target Tug, Tail BP
A-26(JD-1)	FL	Pensacola	NMoNA	44-6928, 77141, UH2, Target Tug, VH-5
A-26	AL	Birmingham	SMoF	
A-26	AL	Troy	TMA	
A-26	AR	PineB	CAF-RW	N2268N
A-26	AZ	PBluf	RWCAF	
A-26	BC-C	Sidne	BCAM	
A-26	CA	Marys	BAFB	
A-26A	CA	SRosa	PCAM	
A-26	LA	New Orleans	JBMM	44-35937
A-26	MA	Stow	BCF	
A-26	MS	Jacks	ThompANG	
A-26	NM	St Teresa	WEAM	
A-26	NY	Cheec	CSCA	
A-26	OK	ElRen	VFW	"Sonny"
A-26	ON-C	Bradford	GoAR	
A-26	ON-C	Oshaw	MT	
A-26	ON-C	Oshaw	OAM&IM	
A-26	OR	Tillamook	TAM	44-35439, N3222T
A-26	TX	SMarc	CTWCAF	
A-26	TX	Waco	WRA	N240P
A-26A	SC	Flore	FA&MM	
A-26B	CA	Rosamond	EAFB	44-34165
A-26B(VB)	MD	Suitland	PEGF	
A-26B	MS	Jacks	JANG	
A-26B(VA)	NE	Ashland	SACM	44-34665
A-26B	NM	Las Cruces	SA	
A-26B	NY	Horseheads	NWM	41-39516, N237Y, VA ANG

Type	State	Location	Collection	Serial / Notes
A-26B	OH	Carroll	HAS	44-34104, N99420
A-26B	OK	Fredi	AAM	
A-26B	VA	Suffolk	FF	Project
A-26B	UT	Ogden	HAFBM	44-35617
A-26C	AR	Mesa	CAFAWM	28880, NL202R
A-26C	AZ	Tucson	PAM	43-22494
A-26C(K)	AZ	Tucson	PAM	44-35372, N8028E, "Grim Reaper"
A-26C	CA	Atwater	CAM	43-5648
A-26C	CA	Riverside	MFAM	44-35224, "Midnight Endeavors", BC-224
A-26C	CO	Pueblo	PWAM	44-35892
A-26C	CT	Winds	NEAM	
A-26C	FL	Miami	WOM	N3941
A-26C(TB)	GA	Pooler	MoF	44-35732, BC-732
A-26C(RB)	AZ	Grand Canyon	PoFGCVA	
A-26C(RB)	HI	Oahu	HAFB	44-35596/BC-596
A-35A	VA	Suffolk	FF	North American
A-36A	OH	Dayton	NMUSAF	North American
A-36	MA	Stow	BCF	
Apache				
Apache				
A-37		Cessna		Dragonfly
A-37	CA	Chino	PoF	
A-37	CO	Denver	69thB	
A-37	FL	Clear	FMAM	
A-37	TX	San Antonio	LSAD	
A-37A	GA	Pooler	MoF	67-14525
A.E.G.GIV	ON-C	Ottaw	CAM	Allquemeine/Elektrizitat/Gesellschaft
A.W.650-101	MI	Belleville	YAF	Armstrong-Whitworth
A6M		Mitsubishi		Zero
A6M	FL	Pensacola	NMoNA	
A6M-2B	HI	Honolulu	PAM	5450
A6M2	ND	Fargo	FAM	
A6M2	OH	Dayton	NMUSAF	11593
A6M2	TX	Breck	CAF-DP	5356, N58245
A6M2	TX	Midland	AAHM	15799
A-26B	KS	Dodge	CityPark	43-5884 (43-5986)
A-26C(GA)	MI	Mt Clemens	SMAM	
A-26C	ND	Grand Forks	GFAFB	
A-26C	NC	Charlotte	CAM	44-35752
A-26C	OH	Dayton	NMUSAF	44-35733, "Dream Girl"
A-26C(K)	OH	Dayton	NMUSAF	42-54582
A-26C	OR	Hillsboro	CAAM	44-35444, N269J
A-26C	OR	Hillsboro	CAAM	44-35708, N26FK
A-26C	OR	Mc Minnville	EAV	44-35439, N74833
A-26C	TX	Abilene	DLAP	44-35913
A-26C	TX	San Antonio	LSAD	44-35918
A-26C	UT	Ogden	HAM	44-35617
A-26C	WA	Seattle	MoF	
A-26C	CA	Farfield	DA&SM	
Apache				42-83665
Apache				
A-37A(GY)	TX	Whichita Falls	SAFB	
A-37A(YA)	OH	Dayton	NMUSAF	62-5951
A-37B(NA)	CA	Rosamond	EAFB	
A-37B	FL	Mary Esther	HF	70-1293
A-37B	NY	Horseheads	NWM	71-0826
A.E.G.GIV				574/18
A.W.650-101		Argosy		6651, N896U, "City of Leamington Spa"
A6M2	WA	Olympia	OFM	9403
A6M3-22	CA	Camarillo	CAF-SCW	3869, X-133, N712Z
A6M3	ID		T&S	3318 Model 32
A6M3	ID		T&S	3685 Model 22
A6M3	OR	Mc Minnville	TNSAM	3318
A6M5	CA	Chino	PoFAM	5357, N46770
A6M5	CA	Chino	PoFAM	4400

Name	Builder	Model	State	City	Museum	Registration
A6M5			DC	Washington	NA&SM	4340
A6M5			FL	Miami	WOM	4043
A6M7			CA	San Diego	SDAM	23186
Air Command Autogyro	Air Command	Autogyro	PA	W Chester	AHM	
Abernathy Streaker	Abernathy	Streaker	FL	Polk	FoF	
Abrams Explorer	Abrams	Explorer	MD	Suitland	PEGF	
Acro Sport P-8 EAA	Acro	Sport	WI	Oshkosh	EAAAAM	N9PH
Acro Sport P-8 EAA	Acro	Sport	WI	Oshkosh	EAAAAM	N1AC
Acro Sport S1	Acro	Sport	WI	Oshkosh	EAAAAM	N15HS
Acro Sport Super	Acro	Super Sport	WI	Oshkosh	EAAAAM	N76BM
ADOCK		Bi-plane	WA	Vancouver	PAM	
Addventura	Arnet Peryra	Ultralight	AR	Little Rock	AEC	
Adventure Sea Plane	Adventure	Sea Plane	WI	Oshkosh	WAM	
AEC Ace	Aircraft Eng Co	Ace 1	NY	Garde	CoAM	1
Aero Vodochody L-39C	Aero	Albatros	AL	Birmingham	SMoF	931332, N4679B
Aero Commander 680 (See also L-26, U-4B)						
Aero Commander A-9	Quail Agricultural		AR	Eureka Springs	ACM	
Aero Commander	Rockwell		TX	Laredo	Airport	N25130
Aero Commander	Rockwell		VA	Chantilly	NASMUVC	12, N23JF
Aero Commander 500U			IL	Springfield	ACM	
Aero Commander 520			KS	Liberal	MAAM	
Aero Commander 520			OK	Fredi	AAM	
Aero Commander 680			AL	Birmingham	SMoF	
Aero Commander 680			LA	Patte	WWMAM	
Aero Commander 690B			KS	Liberal	MAAM	
Aero Commander 690B			OK	Fredi	AAM	
Aero Sport	Aero	Sport	FL	St. A	EM	
Aero Sport Champ	Aero	Sport Champ	FL	Lakel	SFAF	
Aero Sport-3	Aero	Sport	WA	Seattle	MoF	
Aero Star	Aero	Starr	IL	Springfield	ACM	
Aerocar	Taylor	Aerocar	MN	Blaine	GWFM	
Aerocar	Taylor	Aerocar	WA	Seattle	MoF	1, N100D
Aerocar Model	Taylor	Aerocar	ID	Athol	NAM	
Aerojet V-260	Aerojet-General	Aerojet	WI	Oshkosh	EAAAAM	V-260
Aerolift X.2	Aerolift	Helicopter	CA	Ramona	CR	
Aeromarine 39B	Aeromarine		NY	Rhine	ORA	Navy Two Seater Biplane
Aeromarine AKL-26ANY	Aeromarine-Klemm	AKL-26A	NY	Rhine	ORA	
Aeronaut	Armstrong	Aeronaut	KS	Liberal	MAAM	
Aeronca Champ	Aeronca	7AC	GA	Pooler	MoF	

Aeronca

Model	State	Location	Museum	Registration / Notes
Aeronca 7AC	IA	Ottumwa	MAAM	
Aeronca 7AC	KS	Liberal	MAAM	
Aeronca 7AC	NY	Bayport	BA	
Aeronca 7AC	NY	River	TFAC	7AC-6740, N3144E
Aeronca 7AC	OH	Madis	CFR	
Aeronca 7AC	OH	Wapak	NAA&SM	
Aeronca 7AC	OK	Fredi	AAM	
Aeronca 7AC	ON-C	Collingwood	CCAF	
Aeronca 7AC	WA	Port Townsend	PTAM	6597, N3011E
Aeronca 7AC	WA	Port Townsend	PTAM	732, N82106
Aeronca 7DC	NC	Hende	WNCAM	N4537E

Aeronca Chief

Model	State	Location	Museum	Registration / Notes
Aeronca 11AC	AL	Birmingham	SMoF	
Aeronca 11AC	AR	Pine Bluff	REAA	
Aeronca 11AC	IA	Ottumwa	AM	
Aeronca 11AC	IN	Mario	MMA	11AC-956, N9318E
Aeronca 11AC	IN	Mario	MMA	C-FNGV
Aeronca 11AC	NY	Bayport	BA	
Aeronca 11AC	ON-C	Sault Ste Marie	CBHC	CF-NGV
Aeronca 11AC	TX	Ft Worth	VFM	

Aeronca Super Chief

Model	State	Location	Museum	Registration / Notes
Aeronca 65C	HI	Ford Island	PAM	Airborne During 12/07/41 Attack
Aeronca 65C	KS	Liberal	MAAM	Aeronca 65C
Aeronca 65C	MD	College Park	CPAM	
Aeronca 65C	MI	Kalamazoo	KAHM	12231
Aeronca 65C	OK	Fredi	AAM	Aeronca 65C
Aeronca 65CA	IA	Ottumwa	AM	N29427
Aeronca 65LA	IA	Ottumwa	AM	L-750, N24276
Aeronca 65LB	IL	Cul	OCAM	L-14881, N3449
Aeronca 65TC	HI	Honolulu	PAM	

Aeronca Robin

Model	State	Location	Museum	Registration / Notes
Aeronca C-2	IA	Ottumwa	APM	301-44
Aeronca C-2	ON-C	Ottaw	CAM	CF-AOR, N525
Aeronca C-2	WA	Port Townsend	PTAM	
Aeronca C-2	WA	Seattle	MoF	301-23, N30RC
Aeronca C-2	VA	Chantilly	NASMUVC	
Aeronca C-2N	VA	Sands	VAM	151, N11417
Aeronca C-2N	WI	Oshkosh	EAAAAM	NC13089

Aeronca Duplex

Model	State	Location	Museum	Registration / Notes
Aeronca C-3	CA	Hayward	VAM	
Aeronca C-3	CA	San Diego	SDAM	N13094
Aeronca C-3	FL	Kissi	FTWAM	
Aeronca C-3	FL	Lakel	SFAF	N17449
Aeronca C-3	IA	Ottumwa	APM	A-405, NC14098
Aeronca C-3	MN	Blaine	GWFM	
Aeronca C-3	NC	Hende	WNCAM	NC11923
Aeronca C-3	NY	Bayport	BA	
Aeronca C-3	NY	Mayville	DA	
Aeronca C-3	NY	Rhine	ORA	
Aeronca C-3	OR	Hood	WAAAM	Year 1931
Aeronca C-3	OR	Hood	WAAAM	Year 1931 Project
Aeronca C-3	OR	Hood	WAAAM	Year 1932
Aeronca C-3	PA	Bethel	GAAM	
Aeronca C-3	PA	Readi	MAAM	
Aeronca C-3	PA	Tough	CFCM	
Aeronca C-3	VA	Sands	VAM	426, NC14640
Aeronca C-3	WI	Oshkosh	EAAAAM	NC16291
Aeronca C-3 (Fuse)	NS	Halifax	Halifax	ACAM
Aeronca C-3B	WA	Port Townsend	PTAM	A673, NC16529
Aeronca C-3B	WA	Vancouver	PAM	Flying Bathtub

Aeronca Scout

Model	State	Location	Museum	Registration / Notes
Aeronca K	AL	Birmingham	SMoF	

Aircraft	State	City	Museum	2nd State	2nd City	2nd Museum	Mfr / Model	Name	Registration / Notes
Aeronca K	IA	Ottumwa	APM	SK-C	MJaw	WDM	Aeronca K		K-147, NC18872, Model 8135; CF-BIN
Aeronca K	KS	Liberal	MAAAM	WI	Oshkosh	EAAAAM	Aeronca K		NC19732
Aeronca K	KY	Lexington	AMoK	IA	Ottumwa	APM	Aeronca LC		K165, NC18896; 90 Hp Warner Junior
Aeronca K	OK	Fredi	AAM	OR	Hood	WAA&AM	Aeronca K		
Aeronca K	OR	Hood	WAAAM	WI	Oshkosh	EAAAAM	Aeronca LC		NC17484, 90 Hp Warner Junior
Aeronca K	PA	Readi	MAAM						
Aerospatial SA 341	CA	Ramona	CR				Aerospatial	Gazelle	
Aerospatial Tampico	FL	Dayton	ERAU				Aerospatial	Tampico	54716941, Q547169410
Aerosport Quail	AZ	Tucson	PAM				Aerosport	Quail	
Aerosport Scamp	FL	Lakeland	SNFAM				Aerosport	Scamp	
Aetna-Timm #4	IA	Greenfield	IAM						
AEW.2	TX	Midland	AAHM				Avro-Shackleton	Gannet	AS.1-4 1949 Anti-Sub
AEW.3	CT	Winds	NEAM				Fairey-Gannet	Gannet	
AF-2S(G-82)	WA	Seattle	MoF				Grumman	Guardian	
AF-2S(G-82)	AZ	Mesa	CAFAWM				Grumman	Guardian	126731
AF-2S(G-82)	AZ	Tucson	PAM				Grumman	Guardian	129233, N9995Z
AF-2S(G-82)	FL	Pensacola	NMoNA				Grumman	Guardian	123100, SK30, VS-25
AG Tiger	FL	Dayton	ERAU				American-General	Tiger	
Agena Space Vehicle	OH	Dayton	NMUSAF				Agena	Space Vehicle	
Aichi D3A Val	TX	Frede	NMofPW				Aichi	Val	
Aichi D3A2 Val	CA	Chino	PoFAM				Aichi	Val	
Alien Blimp	OR	Tillamook	TAM				Blimp		
AJ-2	FL	Pensacola	NMoNA				North American	Savage	130418
Akerman Tailless	WI		GHG-UoW				Akerman	Tailless	
Albatros D.Va	WA	Seattle	MoF				Albatros	Scout	NX36DV
Albatros D.Va Rep	CA	San Diego	SDAM				Albatros	Scout	
Albatros D.Va	DC	Washi	NA&SM				Albatros	Scout	
Albatros D.Va	NY	Rhine	ORA				Albatros	Scout	AA, 106, N3767A
Albatros D.Va Rep	OH	Dayton	NMUSAF				Albatros	Scout	
Albatros D.VII	AL	Gunte	LGARFM				Albatros	Scout	
Alexander Primary Glider	CA	Santa Martin	WoHAM				Alexander	Glider	Year 1930, NC205Y
Alexander Eagle Rock A-14	CO	Denve	DIA						NC205Y
Alexander Eagle Rock	CO	Denve	DIA						469, N4648, Combo Wing
Alliance Argo	MN	Blaine	GWFM				Alliance	Argo	
Allison Sport	PA	Bethel	GAAM				Allison	Sport	
AM-1	FL	Pensacola	NMoNA				Martin	Mauler	122397

AM-1 OR Tillamook TAM Martin Mauler N7163M 22275
American Aerolights IL Rantoul OCAM American Aerolights
American Aerolights VA Chantilly PEGF American Aerolights
American Aerolights PA Readi MAAM American Aerolights430R, "Double Eagle"
American BAT TX Frede NMofPW American Bat

American Eaglet
American Eaglet A-101 AZ Tucson PAM 538
American Eaglet A-101 OR Hood WAAAM
American Eaglet VA Richmond VAM
American Eaglet AR Fayetteville AAM
American Eaglet CA Santa Martin WoHAM
American Eaglet FL Lakel SFAF N5AQ
American Eaglet KS Wichita KAM 8-129
American Eaglet NY Rhine ORA
American Eaglet OK Oklahoma OSM
American Eaglet A 1 CA Chino YAM
American Eaglet A 1 CA San Diego SDAM N4289
American Eaglet B-31 IA Ottumwa APM 1111, N17007

Antonov Colt
AN-2 CA Chino PoFAM
AN-2 CA Riverside MAFM ANATDSR-IR-16550, N22AN
AN-2 FL Titusville VACM
AN-2 MO Maryland Hts HARM
AN-2 NC Charl CHAC
AN-2 NY Geneseo 1941AG
AN-2 NC CPoin CPMB
AN-2 ON-C Hamilton CWHM Colt
AN-2 WA Seattle MoF 1G17527, N615L
AN-2 WA Vancouver PAM

Anderson Greenwood 14 WI Oshkosh EAAAAM Anderson-Greenwood N314AG
Anderson Z IA Ottumwa APM Anderson 2A, N12041
Antoinette ME Owls Head OHTM Antoinette
Anglin Spacewalker II FL Lakel SFAF Anglin Spacewalker II N168CM
Anzani Longester Rep OR Eugen OAM Anzani Longester
APCO Astra 29 ON-C Ottawa CAM Astra 29

Apollo North American Command Module
Apollo AR Little Rock AEC
Apollo AZ Flags MC
Apollo CA Chino PoFAM
Apollo CA San Diego SDAM
Apollo FL Shalimar USAFAM
Apollo GA Atlan FSC
Apollo NY NYC ISASM
Apollo OH Dayton NMUSAF
Apollo OK Oklahoma OSM
Apollo WA Seattle MoF
Apollo WA Vanco PAM
Apollo 8 IL Chica MoS&I First Moon Orbit
Apollo 12 VA Hampton VA&SC Last Apollo
Apollo 13 KS Hutch KC&SC

Apollo 14 BP1102A CA Alameda USSHM Training

Left listing

Designation	State/Prov	City	Museum	Serial / Notes
Apollo 14 MQF004	CA	Alameda	USSHM	
Apollo Skylab III	OH	Cleve	NASALRC	
Applebay Zuni II	MD	Suitland	PEGF	
Arado Ar.196A	FL	Pensacola	NMoNA	
Arado Ar.196A	MD	Suitland	PEGF	
Arado Ar.234B-2	VA	Chantilly	NASMUVC	
Argo D-4	VA	Hampton	APM	
Arilington Sisu 1A	VA	Chantilly	NASMUVC	
Arrow Sport				
Arrow Sport	CA	San F	SFIA	
Arrow Sport	VA	Chantilly	PEGF	
Arrow Sport	MN	Blaine	GWFM	
AS.65	ON-C	Ottaw	CAM	
ASG-21	CA	San Diego	SDAM	
ASV-3	OH	Dayton	NMUSAF	
AT-6 / North American / Harvard				
AT-6	AB-C	Claresholm	CFB	
AT-6	AB-C	Edmonton	AAM	
AT-6	BC-C	Sidney	BCAM	Restoration Project
AT-6	AR	Pine Bluff	REAA	
AT-6	MB-C	Brand	CATPM	2557
AT-6	MB-C	Winni	WCAM	20301
AT-6	MB-C	Winni	WCAM	
AT-6	MB-C	Winni	WCAM	
AT-6	ON-C	Dunnville	CL	2766
AT-6	ON-C	Kingtons	CFBK	AJ-693
AT-6	ON-C	Smith Falls	WCAM	Xx443
AT-6	ON-C	Tillsonburg	CHAA	HWX
AT-6	ON-C	Tillsonburg	CHAA	MTX
AT-6	ON-C	Tillsonburg	CHAA	RWN
AT-6	ON-C	Tillsonburg	CHAA	WPK
AT-6	ON-C	Tillsonburg	CHAA	MKA
AT-6	ON-C	Tillsonburg	CHAA	NDB
AT-6 (SNJ)	CA	Oakland	CAF-GGW	51697
AT-6G (SNJ)	CA	Palm Sprg	PSAM	49-3402, N85JR

Right listing

Designation	Location	Museum	Serial / Notes
North American	Mobile Quarantine Facility		
North American	Skylab III		
Applebay Zuni			
Ar.196A			
Ar.196A			
Arado	Blitz(Lightning)		
Javelin Launcher	4 Stage Launch Vehicle		
Arlington Sisu			
Arrow Sport			
Arrow Sport	ND Minot	DTAM	
Arrow Sport	OR Hood	WAAAM	
Arrow Sport F	CA Oakla	OWAM	
Arrow Sport F	IA Ottumwa	APM	18, N18000
Airspeed	Consul		
Sails HG	Hang Glider 1976		
Lifting Body			
AT-6 Mk IV	KS Topek	CAM	N-294CH, 29, CCF-4-85
AT-6C Mk.II	AB-C Wetas	RM	
AT-6C	NY Geneseo	1941AG	
AT-6 Mk.II	NS-C Shear	CFBS	
AT-6 Mk.II	ON-C Ottaw	CAM	66-2265
AT-6F Mk.II	ON-C Ottaw	CAM	20387
AT-6F Mk.II	ON-C Ottaw	CAM	81-4107
AT-6F Mk.II	NS-C Halifax	ACAM	
AT-6F Mk.IV	ON-C Ottaw	CAM	
AT-6F Mk.IV	AB-C Calga	NAM	
AT-6F Mk.IV	AB-C Nanton	NLS	29419
AT-6F Mk.IV	BC-C Langley	CMoF	07-144, RCAF 3275, YRI
AT-6F Mk.IV	MN S St Paul	CAF-SMW	N13595
AT-6F Mk.IV	NY Ghent	POMAM	
AT-6F Mk.IV	ON-C Hamilton	CWH	20431, CF-UZW
AT-6F Mk.IV	ON-C Hamilton	CWH	3372
AT-6F Mk.IV	ON-C Hamilton	CWH	20213, RAF, CF-UUU
AT-6F Mk.IV	ON-C Ottawa	VVoC	
AT-6F Mk.IV	TX Galve	LSFM	20247 NX 1811B
AT-6G	ON-C Hamilton	CWH	

North American Texan

AT-6	State	City	Org	Notes
AT-6	AZ	Glndale	LAM	
AT-6	AZ	PBluf	RWCAF	
AT-6	AZ	Tempe	AHSM	
AT-6	CA	Atwater	CAM	Side # TA-684
AT-6	CA	Shafter	MFAM	"Miss T-N-T""
AT-6	CA	Shafter	MFAM	"Warlock"
AT-6	CO	Denve	JWDAS	
AT-6	CO	Lafayette	SoFC	
AT-6	CT	Winds	NEAM	
AT-6	FL	Kissimmee	AA	055
AT-6	FL	Kissimmee	AA	
AT-6	FL	Kissimmee	AA	
AT-6	FL	Titusville	VACM	
AT-6	GA	Atlanta	ASG	
AT-6	GA	Douglas	LF	
AT-6	GA	Marietta	NASA	
AT-6	IL	Aurora	RH	
AT-6	IL	Cahok	PCUSL	
AT-6	IN	Ft. W	FWAS	
AT-6	KS	New Century	CAF-HoAW	49-3349
AT-6	KY	Louis	BF	
AT-6	MA	Stow	BCF	
AT-6	MD	Hager	HRegAirP	
AT-6	MN	Minne	JJ	
AT-6	MO	SLoui	SLAM	
AT-6	ND	Fargo	FAM	
AT-6	ND	Fargo	WEAM	
AT-6	NM	St Teresa	WEAM	
AT-6	OR	Tillamook	TAM	
AT-6	TX	Amarillo	CAFDS	
AT-6	TX	Breck	BAM	
AT-6	TX	C Christi	USS Lexi	
AT-6	TX	Addison	CFM	
AT-6	TX	Addison	CFM	
AT-6	TX	D Rio	LAFB	
AT-6	TX	FtWorth	VFM	
AT-6	TX	Galve	LSFM	77-4601, N78RN
AT-6	TX	Houston	CAF-GCW	N4447
AT-6	TX	Houston	CAF-GCW	N15797
AT-6	TX	Houston	CAF-GCW	N11171
AT-6	TX	Houston	CAF-GCW	N15799
AT-6	TX	Houston	CAF-GCW	N9097
AT-6	TX	Houston	CAF-GCW	N3725G
AT-6	TX	Paris	CAF-WHS	"Ace In The Hole", N97902
AT-6	TX	S Antonio	FTAM	
AT-6	TX	SMarc	TAM	
AT-6	UT	Ogden	CAF-WF	N2047
AT-6A	UT	Ogden	HAFBM	039
AT-6	WA	Olympia	OFM	Side # 6N6
AT-6	WA	Tillamook	TNAM	
AT-6	WA	Vanco	PAM	"Scrap Iron IV", 486
AT-6	WI	Bosco	BA	
AT-6	WV	Bride	BA	
AT-6 (BC-1A)	MN	Minne	MAGM	40-2122, 798
AT-6 (P-64)	TX	Galve	LSFM	
AT-6 (SNJ)	AR	Fayetteville	OMM	
AT-6 (SNJ)	AR	Pine Bluff	REAA	
AT-6 (SNJ)	ID	Driggs	TAC	Side # 69
AT-6 (SNJ)	MO	Maryland Hts	HARM	
AT-6 (SNJ)	PA	Tough	CFCM	
AT-6 (SNJ)	TX	C Christi	USS Lexi	
AT-6 (SNJ)	WA	Seattle	MoF	
AT-6 (SNJ-2)	VA	Suffolk	FF	
AT-6 (SNJ-3)	FL	Kissi	FTW AM	
AT-6 (SNJ-3)	ID	Rexburg	LFM	
AT-6 (SNJ-4)	CA	Riversideside	MFAM	51360, N6411
AT-6 (SNJ-4)	FL	Kissi	FTW AM	
AT-6 (SNJ-4)	FL	St Augustine	NATG	N55A
AT-6 (SNJ-4)	IN	Elkhart	NIAM	
AT-6 (SNJ-4)	NM	Hobbs	CAF-RB	N7024C
AT-6 (SNJ-4)	OH	Elyri	CAF-CW	N224X
AT-6 (SNJ-4)	OR	Mc Minnville	EAM	88-13466, N33CC
AT-6 (SNJ-4)	TX	Burnet	CAFHLS	88-13517

Type	State	City	Org	Notes
AT-6 (SNJ-4)	WA	Bellingham	HFM	
AT-6 (SNJ-4)	VA	Suffolk	FF	
AT-6 (SNJ-5)	AZ	Mesa	CAFAWM	N3246G
AT-6 (SNJ-5)	CA	Oklan	CAF-GGS	N3195G
AT-6 (SNJ-4)	CA	Camarillo	CAF-SCW	10198, N64110
AT-6 (SNJ-5)	CA	Camarillo	CAF-SCW	84865, N89014, 290, Tail SB
AT-6 (SNJ-5)	CA	Chino	PoFAM	39
AT-6 (SNJ-5)	CA	Chino	YAM	
AT-6 (SNJ-5)	CA	Miramar	FLAM	WD, VMT-2
AT-6 (SNJ-5)	CA	S. Mon	MoF	90952, N3204G, "Big Thunder"
AT-6 (SNJ-5)	FL	St Augustine	NATG	N1617F
AT-6 (SNJ-5)	MI	Kalamazoo	KAHM	49-3509, 112493
AT-6(SNJ-5)	NC	Hendersonville	WNCAM	
AT-6 (SNJ-5)	NY	Shirley	WOLI	
AT-6 (SNJ-5C)	NC	Charlotte	CAM	90906
AT-6 (SNJ-5)	TX	C Christi	USS Lexi	
AT-6 (SNJ-5)	TX	Midland	AAHM	101X
AT-6 (SNJ-5)	VA	Quantico	NMMC	84962
AT-6 (SNJ-5B)	HI	Kalaeloa	NAMBB	90599
AT-6 (SNJ-5B)	IN	Indianapolis	AMHF	43963
AT-6 (SNJ-5B)	MD	Ft Meade	QM	
AT-6 (SNJ-7)	CA	San Diego	SDACM	
AT-6A(SNJ-4A)	MD	Suitland	PEGF	
AT-6A	CO	Auror	BANGB	
AT-6A	MN	Eden Prairie	WotN	N77TX, #42
AT-6B	AZ	Tucson	PAM	41-17246
AT-6B-NT	IL	Rantoul	OCAM	41-17372
AT-6B(SNJ-4B)	PA	Readi	MAAM	88-12281, N24554
AT-6C	FL	Miami	WOM	
AT-6C(SNJ-5C)	FL	Pensacola	NMoNA	51849
AT-6C(SNJ-5C)	NC	Charl	CHAC	
AT-6C(SNJ-5C)	NC	CPoin	CPMB	
AT-6D	AK	Ancho	KANGB	
AT-6D/G	FL	St Augustine	NATG	N1364N
AT-6D	FL	Polk	FoF	
AT-6D	IN	Bippu	PAC	
AT-6D-NT	MI	Belleville	YAF	42-85377, N555Q
AT-6D-NT	MI	Belleville	YAF	42-84678, N7095C, 26, "Turtle Bay"
AT-6D-NT	MI	Belleville	YAF	44-81346, N6637C
AT-6D	MI	Detro	WR	
AT-6D	NY	eads	NWM	41-16667
AT-6D	NY	longl	TC	
AT-6D	OH	Batavia	TSWM	"Tweety"
AT-6D)	OH	Dayton	NMUSAF	42-84216
AT-6D(SNJ-5)	TN	Sevierville	TMoA	49-2977, N29963 Flyable
AT-6D	TX	San Antonio	LSAD	
AT-6D	TX	San A	RAFB	
AT-6D	WA	Bellingham	HFM	
AT-6D	WI	Oshkosh	EAAAAM	42-44629
AT-6F	ID	Zellw	BWA	
AT-6F	OK	Fredi	AAM	
AT-6F	TX	San Antonio	TAM	SN112501, N9806C
AT-6F(T-6)	TX	Abilene	DLAP	44-81819
AT-6F	WA	Bellingham	HFM	
AT-6G	AL	Birmingham	SMoF	
AT-6G	AR	Fayet	AAM	N6FD
AT-6G	AZ	Grand Canyon	PoFGCVA	
AT-6G	CA	McClellan	McCelAFB	51-5124
AT-6G (SNJ-5)	FL	Kissi	FTWAM	
AT-6G(SNJ-6)	FL	Miami	WOM	
AT-6G	FL	St Augustine	NATG	N49NA
AT-6G (SNJ-6)	FL	St Augustine	NATG	N1044C
AT-6G	GA	Pooler	MoF	
AT-6G	IL	Waukegan	WHM	197092, N584M
AT-6G	IN	Hunti	WoF	53- 4568, N153NA, 13, TA-568, "Lackland"
AT-6G	IN	Valparaiso	IAM	51-14726
AT-6G	NC	Asheboro	PFAC	
AT-6G	NJ	Trent	MGAFB	
AT-6G(SNJ-5)	MI	Kalamazoo	KAHM	91005, N333SU, 1
AT-6G(T-6)	AL	Birmi	Southe	TA-963
AT-6G(T-6)	GA	Pooler	MoF	49-3217, TA 217
AT-6G(T-6)	LA	Reser	AMHFM	
AT-6G(T-6)	MI	Ypsilanti	YAF	

Type	State	Location	Collection	Serial / Notes
AT-6G(T-6)	OH	Dayton	NMUSAF	49-3368
AT-6G(T-6)	OH	Dayton	NMUSAF	50-1279
AT-6G(T-6)	TX	Gilmer	PotP	
AT-6G(T-6)	TX	Slaton	TAM	
AT-6G	TX	Dallas	FoF	
AT-6H	WA	Olympia	MAHSM	Side # 25, Tail ZE
AT-9	OH	Dayton	NMUSAF	Curtiss-Wright — Fledgling Jeep — 41-12150
AT-9A	AZ	Tucson	PAM	Curtiss-Wright — Fledgling Jeep — 42-56882
AT-10	OH	Dayton	NMUSAF	Beech — 42-35143
AT-10	OH	Dayton	NMUSAF	Beech — 42-35180
AT-11(Beech D18S)	**Beech**			**Kansan**
AT-11(Beech D18S)	AZ	Tucson	PAM	41-9577, N6953C
AT-11(Beech D18S)	CA	Farfield	DA&SM	
AT-11(Beech D18S)	CA	Paso Robles	EWM	
AT-11(Beech D18S)	CA	McClellan	McCelAFB	
AT-11(Beech D18S)	CA	Santa Martin	WoHAM	
AT-11(Beech D18S)	CO	Denve	JWDAS	
AT-11(Beech D18S)	FL	Clear	FMAM	9639, 619
AT-11(Beech D18S)	FL	Lakeland	SNF	
AT-11(Beech D18S)	FL	Polk	FoF	
AT-11(Beech D18S)	GA	Pooler	MoF	41-27391
AT-11(Beech D18S)	IL	Springfield	ACM	
AT-11-BH(Beech D18S)	IN	Auburn	HW	On Loan
AT-11-BH(Beech D18S)	LA	New Orleans	JBMM	44951
AT-11(Beech D18S)	MI	Belleville	GRapi	YAF 43-10404, N7340C
AT-11(Beech D18S)	MI	Dayton	CAF-WMW	N320A
AT-11(Beech D18S)	OH	Dayton	NMUSAF	41-27561
AT-11(Beech D18S)	TX	Big Springs	H25	
AT-11(Beech D18S)	TX	Galve	LSFM	42-37240, N81Y
AT-11(Beech D18S)	WI	Janes	YAFS	
AT-12A/2PA	CA	Chino	PoFAM	Sikorsky — Guardian
AT-19				**Stinson** / **Gullwing**
AT-19	AK	Ancho	AAHM	
AT-19-VW(V-77)	MI	Belleville	YAM	43-44165, N15JH
AT-19(V-77)	IN	Auburn	HW	
AT-19	NC	Morga	CWCAF	
AT-19	NC	S.Pin	CAF-CW	1335, V77-333, N60634
AT-19	NM	St Teresa	WEAM	
AT-19	NV	Las Vegas	CAFNW	
AT-19	OK	Fredi	AAM	
AT-19	PA	Beave	AHM	
AT-19	TX	Slaton	TAM	477
AT-19	UT	SLake	CAF-UW	N67227
AT-19(V-77)	AK	Fairbanks	PAM	"Peter Pan", NC60924
AT-19(V-77)	TX	Lancaster	CAF-DFW	
AT-19(V-77)	TX	Ft Worth	VFM	
Atlas Mercury	NY	Coron	NYHoS	Atlas — Mercury
Auster				
Auster AOP Mk VI	AB-C	Wetas	RM	16662,
Auster AOP Mk VI	BC-C	Sidney	BCAM	
Auster AOP	NY	Bayport	BA	
Auster AOP Mk VI	ON-C	Ottawa	CAM	VF582

Auster AOP Mk VI	ON-C	Trenton	RCAFMM	VF-582, C-FLWK
Auster AOP.9 Mk.IX	FL	Lakel	SFAF	N408XN
Auster MK.V1-J	PA	Readi	MAAM	
AV-8	**McDonnell**		**Harrier**	
AV-8	AZ	Yuma	YUSMAB	
AV-8(YAV)	IL	Cahokia	GSLA&SM	
AV-8	NC	Havel	CPMCAS	
AV-8	TX	Big Springs	H25	
AV-8A	CA	El Cajon	SDAMGF	
AV-8A	CA	China Lake	USNMAT	
AV-8A	ONT-C	Ottawa	CAM	
Avian Falcon II	AZ	Tucson	PAM	12, N4369Z, N3AV
Aviat A-1	ID	Driggs	TAC	Huskey
Aviat Christen Eagle	TX	Dallas	FoF	Christen Eagle
Aviatik D.II	WA	Seattle	MoF	Berg Scout 101,40
Avid Flyer	KS	Agusta	AAM	Avid Flyer
Avid Flyer	MI	Kalamazoo	KAHM	Avid Flyer
Avid Flyer	OK	Fredi	AAM	Avid Flyer
Avid Flyer	WI	Oshkosh	EAAAAM	Avid Flyer N4636J
Avitor Hermes, Jr.	CA	San Carlos	HNCAVM	Hermes Jr.
Avro 504 (3 ea)	ON-C	Ottaw	CAM	Gosport D-8971
Avro 652	**Anson**			
Avro 652	MB-C	Brandon	CATPM	
Avro 652	SK-C	MJaw	WDM	R9725
Avro 652 Mk.I	MB-C	Winni	WCAM	
Avro 652 Mk.II	AB-C	Calga	AMoC	
Avro 652 Mk.II	AB-C	Nonton	NLS	
Avro 652 Mk.II	AB-C	Wetas	RM	
Avro 683	**Lancaster**			
Avro 683 Mk.X	AB-C	Calga	AMoC	FM136, BX
Avro 683 Mk.X	AB-C	Nanto	NLS	FM159
Avro 683 Mk.X	NB-C	Edmunston	EA	KB882
Avro 683 Mk.X	NS-C	Greenwood	GMAM	KB829

Auster	ON-C	Hamilton	CWH	16652	
Auster Mk.VI	ON-C	Ottaw	CAM	16652	
AV-8B	AL	Huntsville	AC		
AV-8B	MD	Lexington	PRNAM	161396, Side # 623, SD Tail	
AV-8B-1	NC	Charlotte	CAM	161397	
AV-8B	VA	Triangle	NMMC		
AV-8C	AZ	Tucson	PAM	159241	
AV-8C	CA	Oakla	OWAM		
AV-8C	FL	Pensacola	NMoNA	158975, WF	
AV-8C	NY	NYC	ISASM		
Avro 504J/K	FL	Polk	FoF	Gosport	
Avro 504K	MB-C	Winni	WCAM	Gosport	
Avro 504K	NY	Rhine	ORA	Gosport	
Avro 504K Rep	OH	Dayton	NMUSAF	Gosport	G-CYEI
Avro 504K Replica	MB-C	Winni	WCAM	Gosport	
Avro 581	AB-C	Wetas	RM	Avian	
Avro 581	MN	Blaine	GWFM	Avian	
Avro 595	CA	Santa Martin	WoHAM	Avian	
Avro 616 Mk.IV M	ON-C	Ottaw	CAM	Avian	
Avro 652 (See also: AT-20; C.18; C.19; T-20; T-21; T-22)					
Avro 652 Mk.II	MB-C	Winni	WCAM		
Avro 652 Mk.II	NS-C	Greenwood	GMAM	7135	
Avro 652 Mk.V	MB-C	Winni	WCAM		
Avro 652 Mk.V	AB-C	Edmonton	AAM		
Avro 652 Mk.V	ON-C	Ottawa	CAM	12518	
Avro 652 Mk.VI	ON-C	Hamilton	CWH		
Avro 683 Mk.X	ON-C	Hamilton	CWH	BX	
Avro 683 Mk.X	ON-C	Ottaw	CAM	BX	
Avro 683 Mk.X Nose	ON-C	Ottaw	CAM	KB848	
Avro 683 Mk.X	ON-C	Trenton	JP		
Avro 683 Mk.X	ON-C	Windsor		FM212	

Type	State	City	Org	Registration / Name
Avro C.102 Jetliner Nose	ON-C	Ottawa	CAM	Avro Jetliner CF-EJD,
B 1	CA	Chino	YAM	Mahoney 141, NC6956
B-1	WA	Seattle	SHSM	Boeing Flying Boat, I-13, M-92, Model 6, "U.S. Mail"
B-1A	NE	Ashland	SACM	Rockwell Lancer 76-174
B-1B	OH	Dayton	NMUSAF	Rockwell Lancer 84-0051
B-1A	CO	Denver	WOTR	Boeing Stealth
B-1B	SD	Ellsworth	SDA&SM	Boeing Stealth
B-1B	UT	Ogden	HAM	Boeing Stealth 83-0070
B-2	PA	WChes	AHM	Brantly Model 305
B-2	OH	Dayton	NMUSAF	Ryan Spirit TA-100
B-5	CA	San Diego	SDAM	Ryan Brougham NC9236
B-10	AK	Fairbanks	PAM	Mitchell Wing
B-10	AZ	Tucson	PAM	Mitchell Wing 285, N4232A
B-10	NM	Moriarty	SSM	Mitchell Wing
B-10	OH	Dayton	NMUSAF	Martin Bomber

Boeing — Flying Fortress — B-17

Type	State	City	Org	Registration / Name
Ball Turret	FL	Lakeland	SNF	
B-17	FL	Polk City	FoF	44-83525, "Suzy Q", Storage
B-17	WA	Arlington	GPAM	
B-17D	MD	Suitland	PEGF	40-3097, "Swoose"
B-17E	OH	Cincinnati	BR	41-9032, 2504, "My Gal Sal"
B-17E	IL	Marengo	MK	41-2595, 2406, "Desert Rat"
B-17F	NE	Offutt	OAPB	42-30230, "Homesick Angel", Sq/Yel L
B-17F	OH	Dayton	NMUSAF	41-24485, 3170, "Memphis Belle"
B-17F	WA	Seattle	MoF	42-29782, N17W, 4896, "Boeing Bee"
B-17G	AZ	Mesa	CAFAWM	44-83514, N9233, "Sentimental Journey"
B-17G	AZ	Tusco	390thMM	44-85828, N9323R, JDIH, "I'll Be Around"
B-17G(PB-1G)	CA	Atwater	CAM	43-38635, N3702G, "Virgin's Delight",
B-17G-105VE	CA	Palm Sprg	PoF	44-85778, N3509G, 8687, "Miss Angela"
B-17G	CA	Riverside	MFAM	44-6393, "Starduster II"
B-17G	CA	Tular	VMVETS56	44-85738, K,8647, "Reston's Pride"
B-17G	VA	Chantilly	NASMUVC	44-83814, NASM/Storage
B-17G	DE	Dover	DAFB	44-83624, 381BG, "Sleepy Time Gal"
B-17G	GA	Douglas	FTWAM	44-85734, N5111N, 8643, "Liberty Belle"
B-17G	GA	Douglas	FTWAM	
B-17G	FL	Polk	FoF	44-83542, N9324Z, "Picadilly Princess"
B-17G	FL	Shalimar	USAFAM	44-83863, 32504, "Gremlins Hideout"
B-17G	IN	Peru	GAFB	44-83690, XK-D, 305BG "Miss Liberty Bell"
B-17G	LA	Barksdale	BAFB	44-83884, 32525 / 333284, "Yankee Doodle"
B-17G-110-VE	MA	Stow	BCF	44-83575, N93012, OR-R,
B-17G	MI	Belleville	YAF	44-85829, N3193G, "Yankee Lady"
B-17G-35-BO	NE	Ashland	SACM	44-83559, EP-B, 32200 / 23474, "King Bee"
B-17G	NY	Horsehead	NWM	44-83563, "Fuddy Duddy"
B-17G	OH	Dayton	NMUSAF	42-32076, 7190, 91, "Shoo Shoo Baby"
B-17G	OR	Milwa	BG	44-85790, "Lacey Lady"
B-17G	OR	Mc Minnville	EAM	44-83785, N207EV, K32426, "Shady Lady"
B-17G	TX	Abilene	DLAP	44-85599, 8508, 238133
B-17G	TX	FW ort	VFM	44-8543, N3701G, 7943, "Chuckie",
B-17G	TX	Galve	LSFM	44-85718, N900RW, "Thunder Bird"
B-17G	TX	Houston	CAF-GCW	44-83872, N7227C, "Texas Raiders"
B-17G-90-DL	TX	San Antonio	LSAD	44-83512, HT, "Heavens Above"
B-17G-VE	UT	Ogden	HAFBM	44-83663, 32304, "Short Bier"
B-17 Parts	WI	Oshkosh	EAAAAM	44-85740, N5017N, "Aluminum Overcast"
B-17G (Parts)	CO	Denve	JWDAS	44-83722, 32363
B-17G (Parts)	CA	Wells	Ocotillo	44-85813
B-17G (Parts)	FL	Kissi	FTWAM	

Douglas — Bolo — B-18

Type	State	City	Org	Registration / Name
B-18A	CA	Atwater	CAM	37-029, Tail # BI
B-18A	CO	Denver	WOTR	39-025
B-18A	OH	Dayton	NMUSAF	37-0469
B-18A	WA	Tacoma	MAFB	38-593, N66267

Douglas — Dragon — B-23

Type	State	City	Org	Registration / Name
B-23	CA	Atwater	CAM	39-045, Tail # 112MD
B-23	FL	Polk City	FoF	39-057
B-23	OH	Dayton	NMUSAF	39-0037
B-23	TX	Midland	AAHM	39-038, 62G
B-23	WA	Tacoma	MAFB	39-036, 1089R
B-23(UC-67)	AZ	Tucson	PAM	39-051, N534J

B-24 Consolidated Liberator (One Tail version See PB4Y)

Model	State	Location	Registration / Name
B-24M-5-CO	CA	Atwater CAM	44-41916, "Shady Lady"
B-24(LB-30)		TX, Midland, CAF-B29/24, AM927, N24927, "Diamond Lil"	
B-24J Nose	MD	Ft Meade QM	44-40332
B-24L Fuse	MD	Ft Meade QM	44-50022
B-24M Replica	TX	San Antonio LSAD	
B-24 Nose	GA	Pooler M8thAFHM	42-40557, "Fightin Sam"
B-24 Nose	VA	Hampton VA&SC	42-40461
B-24 Nose Turret	MI	Lansi MHM	44-49112
B-24D-160-CO	OH	Dayton NMUSAF	42-72843, "Strawberry Bitch"
B-24D	UT	Ogden HAFB	41-23908, N58246, Project
B-24J-90-CF	AZ	Tucson, PAM	44-44175, N7866, "Bungay Buckaroo"
B-24J-95-CF	FL	Polk City FoF	44-44272, N94459, "Joe"
B-24J-25-FO	LA	Barksdale AFB, BAFB,	44-48781, "Laden Maiden"
B-24J	MA	Stow BCF	44-44052, N224J, JHK191, "Witchcraft"
B-24L-20-FO	ON-C	Ottaw CAM	44-50154, 11130

B-25 North American Mitchell

Model	State	Location	Registration / Name
B-25 Nose	WA	Tacoma MAFB	
B-25	AB-C	Westaskiwin RM	44-86726
B-25(PBJ)	CA	Miramar FLAM	
B-25	CA	San Diego MCAS	44-86727
B-25	FL	Pensacola NMoNA	44-29035
B-25	FL	Polk City FoF	43-28059, "Apache Princess"
B-25	HI	Honolulu PAM	
B-25	OH	Batavia TSM	45-8898, "Axis Nightmare"
B-25	MB-C	Brandon CATPM	44-86724
B-25 Sim	MN	Duluth CAF-LSS	
B-25	NB	Bellevue SASM	43-30772
B-25	ND	Fargo FAM	44-30010, N9641C
B-25	ND	Grand Forks	GFAFB 44-28834
B-25	OH	N Canton MAM	44-30324
B-25	ON-C	Ottaw CAM	44-86699
B-25	OR	Pendleton PAM	44-30243
B-25	TX	Addison CFM	
B-25	TX	Ft Worth VFM	
B-25	TX	Galve LSFM	
B-25	WA	Arlington FHCM	44-30254, N41123
B-25A	CA	Atwater CAM	44-86891, "Lazy Daisy Mae"
B-25C	AL	Birmingham SMoF	41-12634
B-25C	OH	Dayton NMUSAF	43-3374
B-25D	MI	Bellevue YAM	43-3634, "Yankee Warrior"
B-25D-NC	SC	Mt Pleasant PPM	41-29784, "Fertile Myrtle"
B-25H	IL	Aurora WWS	43-4106, "Barbie III"
B-25H	AL	Mobile BMP	44-31004, NC44310004
B-25H	CT	Windsor Locks NEAM	43-4999, "Dog Daize"
B-25J	TX	San Antonio LSAD	44-29835J, 35103
B-25J	AL	Montg MAFB	44-30649
B-25J	AB-C	Edmonton AAM	
B-25J	AZ	Mesa CAFAWM	43-35972, N125AZ, "Maid in the Shade"
B-25J(PBJ-1J)		CA, Camarillo, CAF-SCW,	44-30988, N5865V, "Semper Fi"
B-25J	CA	Chino PoFAM	44-30423, N3675G, "Photo Fanny"
B-25J	CA	Chino YAM	44-86791, N6116X
B-25J	CA	Rialto KA	44-29199, N9117Z, "In The Mood"
B-25J	CA	Riverside MFAM	44-31032, "Problem Child"
B-25J	CA	San Marcos	CAF-YRS, 43-27868, "Yellow Rose"
B-25J	FL	Shalimar USAFAM	44-30854, "Doolittle Raider"
B-25J	GA	Pooler MoF	44-86872, N2888G, "little King"
B-25J-25-NA	IL	Rantoul OCAM,	44-30635, "Whiskey Pete"
B-25J	IN	Peru GAFB	44-86843, "Passionate Paulette"
B-25J	KS	Liberal, MAAM,	44-30535, N9462Z, "Iron Laiden Maiden"
B-25J	MA	Stow, BC,	44-28932, N3478G, "Tondelayo"
B-25J	MN	S St Paul, CAF-SMW,	44-29869, N27493, "Miss Mitchell"
B-25J	MI	Kalamazoo AZ	
B-25J	MO	SChar CAF-MW	44-31385, N3481G, "Show Me"
B-25J	ON-C	Hamilton CWH	45-8883, C-GCWM, "Grumpy"
B-25J-10-NA		PA, Reading, MAAM,	44-29939, N9456Z, "Briefing Time"
B-25J	TX	Frede NMofPW	44-86880
B-25J	TX	Midland AAHM	44-86758, 25YR, "Devil Dog"
B-25J	UT	Ogden HAFBM	44-86772
B-25J	VA	Chantilly NASMUVC,	44-29887, "Carol Jean", Storage

B-25J	VA	Suffolk	FF	44-30129
B-25J-25-NC	WI	Milwaukee	GMF	44-30444
B-25J	WI	Oshkosh	EAAM	43-4432
B-25M	MT	Great Falls	MAFB	44-50493, 44-30493
B-25N	CA	Palm Sprg	PSAM	44-86747, N8163H, "Mitch the Witch II"
B-25N	FL	Mary Esther	HAP	43-28222
B-25N	NY	Farmingdale	AAM	40-2168, "Miss Hap"
B-26	**Martin**		**Marauder**	
B-26	AZ	Tucson	PAM	40-1501
B-26	FL	Polk	FoF	40-1464 N 4297J
B-26	OH	North Canton	MAM	40-1459
B-26	UT	Ogden	HAM	40-1370
B-26B	DC	Washi	NA&SM	41-31773, "Flak Bait"
B-26G-MO	OH	Dayton	NMUSAF	43-34581, "Shootin In"
B-26K	**Douglas**		**Counter Invader**	
B-26K	FL	Mary Esther	HAP	44-35483 (64-17666)
B-26K	OH	Dayton	NMUSAF	41-39596, 64-17676
B-26K	AZ	Tucson	PAM	41-39378 (64-17653)
B-26K	SD	Ellsworth	A&SM	44-35896 (64-17640)
B-29	**Boeing**		**Super Fortress**	
B-29	CA	Farfield	DA&SM	42-65281, R, "Miss America 62"
B-29	FL	Polk City	WAM	44-70049, Nose at Borrego Springs, CA
B-29	FL	Polk City	WAM	44-84084, at Borrego Springs, CA
B-29 Nose	FL	Lakeland	SNF	Nose
B-29	GA	Cordele	GVMSP	42-93967
B-29	GA	Marie	DAFB	44-70113, "Sweet Loise"
B-29	KS	Wichita	KAM	44-69972, "Doc"
B-29	LA	Barksdale	BAFB	44-87627
B-29	VA	Chantilly	NASMUVC	44-86292, "Enola Gay"
B-29	MO	White	WAFB	44-61671, "The Geat Artist"
B-29	NM	Albuq	NAM	45-21748, "Duke of Albuquerque"
B-29	NY	Farmingale	AAM	
B-29	OH	Dayton	NMUSAF	44-27297, "Bockscar"
B-29 Cockpit	OH	Dayton	NMUSAF	44-62139, "Command Decision"
B-29	OK	Tinke	TAFB	44-27343, "Tinker Heritage"
B-29	SD	Rapid City	SDA&SM	44-87779, "Legal Eagle II"
B-29-55-MO	UT	Ogden	HAFBM	44-86408, "Haggerty's Hag"
B-29	WA	Seattle	MoF	44-69729, "T-Squre 54"
B-29(TB)	AZ	Tucson	PAM	44-70016, "Sentimental Journey"
B-29-60-BA(TB)	NE	Ashland	SACM	44-84076, "Man O" War"
B-29A(B-50)	CA	Atwater	CAM	44-61535, "Raz'n Hell"
B-29A	CA	Riverside	MFAM	44-61669, E, "Flag Ship 500"
B-29A	CO	Pueblo	PWAM	44-62022, "Peachy"
B-29A	CT	Winds	NEAM	44-61975, "Jack'S Hack"
B-29A	TX	Midland	AAHM	44-62070, N5298, "FiFi"
B-29A	TX	San Antonio	LSAD	44-62220
B-29B-55	GA	Pooler	MoA	44-87627

B-36J-111-10	AZ	Tucson	PAM	Convair	Peacemaker	52-2827A
B-36J-65-CF	NE	Ashland	SACM	Convair	Peacemaker	52-2217A
B-36J	OH	Dayton	NMUSAF	Convair	Peacemaker	52- 22220
B-36H(RB)	CA	Atwater	CAM	Convair	Peacemaker	51-13730, Circle W
B-37(RB)	AB-C	Edmonton	AAM	Lockheed	Ventura	5324
B-37(RB)	AB-C	Edmonton	VMFA	Lockheed	Ventura	2195, CF-FAV, CAF447
B-37(RB)	CO	Pueblo	PWAM	Lockheed	Ventura	342-17
B-37(RB)	QU-C	St Esprit	Airport	Lockheed	Ventura	CF-SEQ

Designation	State	City	Museum	Manufacturer	Type	Serial / Notes
B-37(RB)(PV-1)	VA	Quantico	NMMC	Lockheed Ventura		
B-377SG	AZ	Tucson	PAM	Aero Spacelines	Super Guppy 201	52-2693, N940NS
B-42A(XB)	MD	Suitland	PEGF	Douglas	Mixmaster	
B-43(XB)	MD	Suitland	PEGF	Douglas	Jetmaster	
B-45A	AZ	Tucson	PAM	North American	Tornado	47-63
B-45A	CA	Atwater	CAM	North American	Tornado	47-008, Tail B
B-45C	OH	Dayton	NMUSAF	North American	Tornado	48-0010
B-45C(RB)	NE	Ashland	SACM	North American	Tornado	48-0017

B-47 Boeing Stratojet

Designation	State	City	Museum	Serial / Notes
B-47A Nose	AZ	Tucson	PAM	49-1901
B-47B Parts	CA	Rosamond	EAFB	51-2075
B-47B	MO	Knob	WAFB	51-2120
B-47B(WB)	GA	Pooler	M8thAFM	50-062
B-47D	IN	Peru	GAFB	51-2315
B-47E	AR	Littl	LRAFB	52-595, 384th BW
B-47E	CA	Atwater	CAM	52-0166, 0166, "Spirit"
B-47E	CA	Riverside	MFAM	53-2275, "Betty Boop", In movie "Strategic Air Command"
B-47E	CO	Pueblo	PWAM	53-2104
B-47E	LA	Barksdale	BAFB	53-2276
B-47E	NY	Platt	PAFB	53-2385
B-47E	KS	Wichita	MAFB	53-4213
B-47E	OH	Dayton	NMUSAF	53-2280
B-47E-55-BW	UT	Ogden	HAFB	51-2360
B-47E(WB)	WA	Seattle	MoF	51-7066
B-47E(EB)	AZ	Tucson	PAM	53-2135, 44481
B-47E(XB)	IL	Rantoul	OCAM	46-0066
B-47E(EB)	OK	Tinke	TAFB	53-4257
B-47E(EB)	TX	Abilene	DLAP	52-4120
B-47E(WB)	OK	Oklahoma	SFG	51-2387
B-47E-35-DT	NE	Ashland	SACM	52-1412
B-47H(RB)	OH	Dayton	NMUSAF	53-4299
B-47N(RB)	FL	Shalimar	USAFAM	53-4296

B-50 Boeing Superfortress

Designation	State	City	Museum	Serial / Notes
B-50(WB)	CA	Atwater	CAM	49-351
B-50A Fuse	CA	Chino	PoFAM	46-0010
B-50D(WB)	OH	Dayton	NMUSAF	49-0310
B-50J(KB)	AZ	Tucson	PAM	49-372
B-50J(KB)	FL	Tampa	MAFB	49-389, 48-114A, 0-80114

B-52 Boeing Stratofortress

Designation	State	City	Museum	Serial / Notes
B-52 Trainer	CA	Riversideside	MAM	Gunner Trainer
B-52 Nose	CA	Chino	YAM	
B-52 Nose	CA	El Cajon	SDAMGF	
B-52 Nose	CA	Big Springs	H25	
B-52 Nose	AZ	Tucson	PAM	52-003
B-52A(NB)	NM	Albuq	NAM	52-0013
B-52B	CO	Denver	WOTR	52-005
B-52B(GB)	NE	Ashland	SACM	52-8711
B-52B(RB)-15-BO	IL	Rantoul	OCAM	
B-52C Cockpit				
B-52D	AL	Mobile	BMP	55-0071, "Calamity Jane"
B-52D	AL	Montgomery	MAFB	55-0057
B-52D	AZ	Tucson	DMAFB	56-0659
B-52D	AZ	Tucson	PAM	55-0067
B-52D	CA	Atwater	CAM	56-0612
B-52D	CA	Fairfield	DA&SM	56-0696
B-52D	CA	Rosamond	EAFB	56-0585
B-52D	CO	CSpri	USAFA	55-0083, "Diamond Lil"
B-52D	FL	Orlan	OIAMP	56-0687
B-52D	KS	Wichita	KAM	55-0094

B-52

Model	State	City	Museum	Serial / Notes
B-52D	GA	Pooler	MoF	55-0085
B-52D	LA	Barksdale	BAFB	56-0629
B-52D-25-BW	MI	Belleville	YAF	55-0677, N464024, "Clyde"
B-52D	MI	Gwinn	KISHAM	55-0062
B-52D	NE	Offut	OAFB	57-6468
B-52D	OH	Dayton	NMUSAF	56-0665
B-52D	OK	Tinker	TAFB	56-0695
B-52D	SD	Rapid City	SDA&SM	56-0657
B-52D	TX	Abilene	DLAP	56-0685
B-52D	TX	San Antonio	LSAD	55-0068
B-52D	TX	Wichita Falls	SAFB	56-0589
B-52D	WA	Spokane	AF&AM	56-0676
B-52D	CA	Riverside	MFAM	56-0679
B-52D(GB)	MO	White	WAFB	56-0683, "Necessary Evil"
B-52D-40BW	CA	Palmdale	PP42	57-0038
B-52F	AZ	Tucson	PAM	58-0183
B-52G	FL	Shalimar	USAFAM	58-0195
B-52G	LA	Barksdale	BAFB	57-6509
B-52G	ND	Grand Forks	GFAFB	59-2577
B-52G	NY	Rome	MVBM	58-0225
B-52G	UT	Ogden	HAFBM	58-0191
B-52G	VA	Hampton	LAFB	59-2601
B-52G	WA	Everett	MoF	56-2584
B-52G-105-BW	NY	Rome	GAFBM	58-0225, "Mohawk Valley"

B-57 — Martin Canberra

Model	State	City	Museum	Serial / Notes
B-57	FL	Melbourne	FITA	
B-57	KS	Topek	FF	
B-57	KS	Wichita	MoKNG	
B-57A(RB)	UT	Ogden	HAFBM	52-1492
B-57A(RB)	CT	Winds	NEAM	52-1488
B-57A(RB)	GA	Pooler	MoF	52-1475A
B-57A(RB)	MD	Middle River	GLMAM	52-1446
B-57A(RB)	MD	Middle River	GLMAM	52-1447
B-57A(RB)-MA	MI	Belleville	YAF	52-1426
B-57A(RB)	MI	Mt Clemens	SMAM	52-1485
B-57A(RB)	NY	Horseheads	NWM	52-1459
B-57B	SC	Flore	FA&MM	
B-57B	CA	Rosamond	EAFB	52-1576
B-57B	FL	Shalimar	USAFAM	52-1516
B-57B(EB)	CA	Riverside	MFAM	52-1519
B-57B(EB)	VA	Chantilly	NASMUVC	
B-57B	MI	Kalamazoo	KAHM	52-1584
B-57B(EB)	MT	Great Falls	MAFB	52-1505
B-57B(EB)	OH	Dayton	NMUSAF	52-1499
B-57B(EB)	SD	Rapid City	SDA&SM	
B-57B(EB)	TX	D Rio	LAFB	
B-57B(EB)	VT	Nurii	BANG	
B-57C(EB)	AR	Littl	LRAFB	53-521
B-57D(RB)	TX	Abilene	DLAP	52-1504
B-57D(RB)	AZ	Tucson	PAM	53-3982
B-57D(RB)	OH	Dayton	NMUSAF	53-3982
B-57E(EB)	AZ	Tucson	PAM	55-4274
B-57E(EB)	CA	Atwater	CAM	54-00253
B-57E(EB)	CO	CSpri	EJPSCM	55-4279
B-57E(EB)	CO	Denver	WOTR	
B-57E(EB)	NE	Ashland	SACM	55-4244, MA
B-57F(WB)	AZ	Tucson	PAM	63-13501, N925NA
B-57F(WB)	GA	Pooler	MoF	63-13293A

B-58 — Convair Hustler

Model	State	City	Museum	Serial / Notes
B-58A	AZ	Tucson	PAM	61-2080
B-58A	IL	Rantoul	OCAM	55-0666, "Greased Lightning"
B-58A Escape Capsule, MD, Suitland, PEGF				
B-58A	OH	Dayton	NMUSAF	59-2458
B-58A(N)	CA	Rosamond	EAFB	55-665, "Snoopy"
B-58A(TB)	IN	Peru	GAFB	55-663
B-58A(Rocket Sled Fuse), LA, Louisiana, 8thAFM,				
B-58A(TB)	TX	Galve	LSFM	55-668
B-58A-CF	NE	Ashland	SACM	61-2059

Type	State	City	Museum	Name	Serial/Notes
B-66 (Douglas Destroyer)					
B-66(RB)	TX	Abilene	DLAP		53-0466
B-66(RF)	TX	Austi	BAFMlark		
B-66(WB)	SC	Flore	FA&MM		
B-66A(RB)	SC	Sumte	SAFB		
B-66B(RB)	OH	Dayton	NMUSAF		53-0475
B-66D	IL	Rantoul	OCAM		53-0412, BB
B-66D(WB)	AZ	Tucson	PAM		55-395
B-66D(WB)	GA	Pooler	MoF		55-392, RB
B-66D(WB)	TX	San Antonio	LSAD		55-390
B-69A(RB)	GA	Pooler	MoF	North American [Neptune]	54-4037
B-70(XB)	OH	Dayton	NMUSAF	North American Valkyrie	62-001
B.2 Mk.II	LA	Barksdale AFB	BAFB	Avro Vulcan	Model 698
B.2 Mk.II	NB	Belle	SAC	Avro Vulcan	Model 698
B.2 Mk.II	NE	Ashland	SACM	Avro Vulcan	XM573
B.2 Mk.II	CA	Atwater	CAM	Avro Vulcan	
B.E.2c	ON-C	Ottaw	CAM	Royal Aircraft B.E.2c	4112
B290	WI	Oshkosh	EAAAAM	Bauman Brigadier	N90616
B6N2	MD	Suitland	PEGF	Nakajima Jill (Tenzan)	Jill
B7A1	MD	Suitland	PEGF	Aichi Grace (Ryusei)	
BAC-167	WA	Olympia	OFM	Bachem Strikemaster	
Ba 349	CA	Chino	PoFAM	Bachem Natter	
Ba 349	MD	Suitland	PEGF	Bachem Natter	
Backstrom EPB-1C	WI	Oshkosh	EAAAAM	Cleave Plank	N19C
BAE Mk 53	GA	Pooler	MoF	British Lightning	
BAE	WA	Olympia	OFM	British Lightning	
Baby Great Lakes	AZ	Grand Canyon	PoFGCVA	Baby Great Lakes Bi	
Baby Great Lakes	KS	Liberal	MAAM	Baby Great Lakes Bi	6907M-187, N44ET
Baby Great Lakes	OR	Mc Minnville	EAM	Baby Great Lakes Bi	7318B471, N15RF
Baby Great Lakes	TX	Galveston	LSFM	Baby Great Lakes Bi	
Baby Great Lakes	WA	Vancouver	PAM	Baby Great Lakes Bi	
Backstrom Plank	IA	Ottumwa	APM	Backstrom Plank	1, N20WB
Bagjo BG12	AB-C	Calga	AMoC	Bagjo Glider	
Baker 001 Special	WI	Oshkosh	EAAAAM	Baker Special	N3203
Baking Duce II	AK	Fairbanks	PAM	Baking Duce II	N75FD
Baldwin Red Devil	VA	Chantilly	NASMUVC	Baldwin Red Devil	
Ballistic Silo	IL	Rantoul	OCAM	Ballistic Silo	
Balloon Basket	CT	Winds	NEAM	Blanchard Balloon Basket	
Balloon Capsule	SD	Mitch	S&TIB&AM	Balloon Capsule "Zanussi"	
Balloon D	TX	FWort	VFM		
Balloon Gondola	SD	Mitch	S&TIB&AM	Balloon Gondola "Super Chicken"	

Balloon Helium IA India USNBM
Balloon Hot Air IA India USNBM
Balloon Hot Air SD Mitch S&TIB&AM
Balloon Hot Air SD Mitch S&TIB&AM
Balloon Hot Air SD Mitch S&TIB&AM
Balloon Hot Air SD Mitch S&TIB&AM
Balloon Hot Air SD Mitch S&TIB&AM
Balloon Hot Air SD Mitch S&TIB&AM
Balloon Montgolfiere CA San Diego SDAM
Balloon WWI Gas SD Mitch S&TIB&AM
Balloon Works Firefly 7, AZ Tucson PAM
Barlow Acapella, WI, Oshkosh EAAAAM Barlow
Baracuda MI Oscoda YAF
Barrage Kite WI Oshkosh EAAAAM
Bates Tractor WI Oshkosh EAAAAM
BB-1 VA Chantilly NASMUVC
BC-12D AZ Tucson PAM

Bede BD-4 Micro Jet

Bede BD-4 AL Birmingham SMoF
Bede BD-4 AZ Tucson PAM
Bede BD-4 FL Lakel SFAF N8826
Bede BD-4 IA Ottumwa APM
Bede BD-4 KS Wichita KAM
Bede BD-4 WI Oshkosh EAAAAM N200SS
Bede BD-5 AB-C Calga AMoC
Bede BD-5 AZ Tucson PAM
Bede BD-5 CA Santa Rosa PCAM
Bede BD-5 KS Augusta AAM
Bede BD-5 OK Oklahoma OSM

Bee Honey Bee CA El Cajon SDAMGF

Beech B17S (See also UC-43) Beech

Beech Staggerwing

Beech A17R TN Tullahoma SMF 1, NC499N
B17S TN Tullahoma SMF 21, NC14409

Balloon Helium
Balloon Hot Air
Balloon Hot Air "Hilda"
Balloon Hot Air "Chic I Boom"
Balloon Hot Air "Chesty"
Balloon Hot Air "Matrioshk"
Balloon Hot Air "Uncle Sam"
Balloon Hot Air "Aero Star"
Montgolfiere Balloon
Balloon Gas
Balloon Works Firefly 7 N4065D
Acapella N455CB
Baracuda Homebuilt N29M
Barrage Kite
Bates Tractor
Nelson Dragonfly
Taylorcraft T-Craft N43584

Bede BD-5 WI Oshkosh EAAAAM N500BD
Bede BD-5B AL Birmingham SMoF
Bede BD-5B CA Oakla OWAM
Bede BD-5B FL Lakel SFAF N51GB
Bede BD-5B VA Chantilly NASMUVC
Bede BD-5B OR Mc Minnville EAV 2392, N110CJ
Bede BD-5B PA Readi MAAM N5BE
Bede BD-5 AZ Tucson PAM N505MR
Bede BD-5J CA Calab SC
Bede BD-5V AZ Grand PoFGCVA N64DS
Bede XBD-2 WI Oshkosh EAAAAM N327BD

Bee Honey Bee WI Oshkosh EAAAAM N90859

Traveler

C17L DC Washi NA&SM
C17S TN Tullahoma SMF 100, N962W
D17A OR Mc Minnville EAM

Model	State	City	Code	Serial/Registration
D17S	CA	Modesto	HAM	
D17S	CA	Santa Monica	MoF	
D17S	CA	Santa Paula	SPAA	
D17S	ID	Rexburg	LFM	3098, N217SD
D17S	ID	Zellw	BWA	
D17S	KS	Liberal	MAAM	
D17S	KS	Wichita	KAM	
D17S	LA	Patte	WWMAM	
D17S	NC	Fargo	FAM	
D17S	OC-C	Ottawa	VWoF	
D17S	TN	Tullahoma	SMF	6914, N35JM
D17S	TN	Tullahoma	SMF	395, NC20753
D17S	TN	Tullahoma	SMF	231, NC19467
E17S	TN	Tullahoma	SMF	BA-453, N712JS
E18S	TN	Tullahoma	SMF	333, NC20798
F17D	TN	Tullahoma	SMF	B-7, NC80308
G17S	TN	Tullahoma	SMF	178, CF-BKO
S18D	TN	Tullahoma	SMF	

Beech D18S See Also (C-45)(AT-11)

Beech D18 **Beech** **Twin Beech**

Model	State	City	Code	Serial/Registration
Beech D18H-4D	TX	Galve	LSFM	
Beech D18R	TX	Fulsh	CTA	670, N954
Beech D18S	AB-C	Edmonton	AAM	
Beech D18S	AB-C	Nanton	NLSAM	2366, CA-245
Beech D18S	AB-C	Wetas	RM	CF-MPI
Beech D18S	AZ	Tucson	PAM	
Beech D18S	CO	Denver	WOTR	N55681
Beech D18S	IN	Ft.W	BAI	
Beech D18S	LA	Barksdale AFB	BAFB	
Beech D18S	MB-C	Winni	WCAM	
Beech D18S	VA	Chantilly	NASMUVC	
Beech D18S	NF-C	Gander	NAAM	CA-110
Beech D18S	OK	Fredi	AAM	
Beech D18S	ON-C	Campbellford	MMM	
Beech D18S	ON-C	Ear FAlls	EFM	
Beech D18S	ON-C	Ignace	City	
Beech D18S	ON-C	Sault Ste Marie	CBHC	CF-MGY
Beech D18S	TN	Gatlinburg	PHLTG	
Beech D18S	OR	Hood	WAAAM	
Beech D18S	TX	Ft Worth	VFM	
Beech D18S	TX	Gilmer	PotP	
Beech D18S	TX	Houston	1940AT	
Beech D18S	WA	Seattle	MoF	
Beech D18S	WI	Janesville	BHA	
Beech D18S(AT-7)	AZ	Tucson	PAM	42-2438, N8073H, Navigation Trainer

Beech 23 (See C-45)

Model	State	City	Code	Serial/Registration
Beech 73	KS	Wichita	KAM	
Beech Starship	KS	Wichita	KAM	
Beech Starship 2000A	TN	Tullahoma	SFM	
Beech 3NM	AR	Fayetteville	OMM	
Beech 3NMT	BC-C	Langley	CMoF&T	
Beech		Mentor	Jet	
Beech		Starship		
Beech		Starship		NC-49, XA-TQF
Beechcraft		Expeditor		
Beechcraft		Expeditor		

Beechcraft 35 Bonanza

Model	State	City	Code	Serial/Registration
Beechcraft 35	CA	Modesto	HAM	
Beechcraft 35	KS	Liberal	MAAM	
Beechcraft 35	KS	Wichita	KAM	
Beechcraft 35	VA	Chantilly	NASMUVH	"Waikiki Beach"
Beechcraft 35	OK	Fredi	AAM	
Beechcraft 35	OR	Mc Minnville	EAV	D-1111, N3870N
Beechcraft 35	TN	Tullahoma	SMF	D-9, NC80409

Type	State	City	Code	Registration / Notes	Name
Beechcraft 35	TN	Tullahoma	SMF	D-18, nc80418	
Beechcraft 35	TX	Laredo	AAM		
Beechcraft 35(N)	AZ	Tucson	PAM	N9493Y	Bonanza
Beechcraft A36	TN	Tullahoma	SFM	E-2503, N9675R	Bonanza
Beechcraft Super V	TN	Tullahoma	SFM	SV-109D-549, N3124V	Bonanza

Beechcraft 50 Seminole (Twin Bonanza)

Type	State	City	Code	Registration / Notes	
Beechcraft D50	TN	Tullahoma	SFM		
Beechcraft 50(L-23)	IN	Mento	LB		
Beechcraft 50(L-23)	OK	Fredi	AAM		
Beechcraft 50(L-23D)(U-8D)	AZ	Tucson	PAM	56-3701	
Beechcraft 50(RU-8D)	KS	Topek	CAM	"Lonely Ringer"	
Beechcraft 50(RU-8D)	MD	Ft Mead	NVP	58-3051	
Beechcraft 50(RU-8D)	VA	FtEus	USATM		
Beechcraft 50(U-8A)	AL	Ozark	USAAM		
Beechcraft 50(U-8A)	AL	Ozark	USAAM	52-1700	
Beechcraft 50(U-8D-5J)	SD	Rapid City	SDA&SM		
Beechcraft 50(U-8F)	GA	Hampton	AAHF		
Beechcraft 55(T-42)	AL	Ozark	USAAM		Baron
Beechcraft 55(T-42)	IN	Valparaiso	IAM		Baron
Beechcraft 55(T-42A)	GA	Hampton	AAHF	65-12685	Baron
Beechcraft 58P	MT	Misso	AFDSC		Baron
Beechcraft 95-55	TN	Tullahom	SFM	TC-1, N9695R	Baron
Beechcraft 99	MT	Misso	AFDSC		Airliner
Bell 204	CO	Denve	JWDAS		Model 204
Bell 206	FL	Starke	ACAM		Long Ranger
Bell 206B	NS	Halifax	ACAM		Long Ranger
Bell 206L	MD	Suitland	PEFG	3980, CF-DOI	Long Ranger
Bell 214	CA	Miramar	FLAM		Huey Super
Bell 222A	TN	Pigeon Forge	HH	N414WW, "Airwolf"	Huey Super
Bell 260	MD	Suitland	PEGF		Jet Ranger
Bell 260	PA	WChester	AHM		Jet Ranger
Bell 260	OR	Tillamook	TNAM		Jet Ranger
Bell 47	AB-C	Edmonton	AAM		Ranger
Bell 47	VA	Chantilly	NASMUVH		Ranger
Bell 47	WA	Seattle	PSC		Ranger
Bell 47A	TX	Addison	CFM		Ranger
Bell 47B	PA	WChes	AHM	NC5H	Ranger
Bell 47B-3	NY	Niagara Falls	NIA		Ranger

Bell 47 (H-13) Sioux

Type	State	City	Code	Registration / Notes
Bell 47D (H-13)	AB-C	Calga	AMoC	
Bell 47D (H-13)	AL	Birmingham	SMG	
Bell 47D (H-13)	ON-C	Sault Ste Marie	CBHC	665-8, CF-ODM

Aircraft	State/Prov	City	Museum	Name	Registration
Bell 47D-1(H-13)	BC-C	Sidne	BCAM		CD-FZX
Bell 47D-1(H-13)	CA	Chino	YAM		51-4175, N55230
Bell 47D-1(H-13)	CT	Winds	NEAM		LV AEF
Bell 47D-1(H-13)	PA	WChes	AHM		
Bell 47D-1(H-13)	PA	Willow Grove	NVHAA		
Bell 47D-5(H-13)	NY	Niagara Falls	NAM		
Bell 47G (HTL-6)	ON-C	Ottaw	CAM		1387
Bell 47G-5(HTL-5)	CA	LAnge	CMoS&I		
Bell 47G	CO	Pueblo	PWAM		N62178, "Spike"
Bell 47G3-B1	TN	Pigeon Forge	HH		
Bell 47G	TX	Laredo	Airport		
Bell 47J-2(H-13)	NS	Halifax	ACAM		1827, CF-PQZ
Bell 47H-1	NY	Niagra Falls	NAM	Ranger	
Bell 47H-1	PA	WChester	AHM	Ranger	
Bell 47J	PA	WChes	AHM	Ranger	
Bell ATV VTOL	MD	Suitland	PEGF	VTOL	
Bell Boeing Tiltrotor RPV	PA	WChester	AHM	RPV	
Bell Model 30	MD	Suitland	PEGF	Model 30	
Bell Model 30	PA	WChes	AHM	Model 30	NX41867
Bell Rocket Belt	MD	Suitland	PEGF	Rocket Belt	
Bell Rocket Belt	VA	FtEus	USATM	Rocket Belt	
Bellanca	NV	Carso	YF		
Bellanca 14-9	FL	Lakeland	SNF		
Bellanca 14-9L	NC	Charlotte	CAM	Crusair	1037, N1KQ
Bellanca 14-13-2	AZ	Tucson	PAM	Crusair	1551, XB-FOU
Bellanca 14-13-2	AZ	Tucson	PAM	Crusair	1073, N46LW
Bellanca 14-13-3	KS	Liberal	MAAM	Crusair	
Bellanca 14-13-3	VA	Chantilly	NASMUVC	Crusair	
Bellanca 14-13-3	OK	Fredi	AAM	Crusair	
Bellanca 14-19C (260)	OK	Fredi	AAM	Cruisemaster	
Bellanca 190	KS	Liberal	MAAM	Cruisemaster	
Bellanca CH-400(1-87)	VA	Sands	VAM	Skyrocket	187, NX237, "Columbia"
Bellanca 66-75 BTW	MB-C	Winni	WCAM	Aircruiser	
Bellanca 66-75 BTW	OR	Tillamook	TAM	Aircrusier	
Bellanca C.F.	VA	Chantilly	NASMUVH		
Bellanca CH.300	AK	Ancho	AAHM		
Bellanca Pacemaker CH-300	ON-C	Ottaw	CAM	Pacemaker	CF-ATN
Bellanca Replica	ME	Owls Head	OHTM		
Bennett Matiah M-9	VA	Chantilly	NASMUVC	Matiah M-9	
Bennett Model 162	VA	Chantilly	NASMUVC	Model 162	
Bennett Phonix 6	VA	Chantilly	NASMUVC	Phonex 6	
Bennett Phonix 6B	VA	Chantilly	NASMUVC	Phonex 6B	

Listing	Variant	State	City	Museum	Registration
Bennett Phonix Viper	Phonix Viper	VA	Chantilly	NASMUVC	
Bennett Streak 130	Streak 130	VA	Chantilly	NASMUVC	
Bennett (See also Rogallo)					
Benoist Air Boat 1914	Air Boat	FL	Largo	HPPCHM	
Benoist-Korn	Benoist-Korn	VA	Chantilly	NASMUVC	
Bensen B- 6	Gyro-Glider	VA	Chantilly	NASMUVH	
Bensen B- 6	Gyro-Glider	NE	Minde	HWPV	
Bensen B- 7	Gyro-Glider	NE	Minde	HWPV	
Bensen B- 7M	Gyro-Copter	MB-C	Winni	WCAM	

Bensen B- 8M Gyro-Copter

Listing	Variant	State	City	Museum	Registration
Bensen B- 8M	Bensen B- 8MG	AL	Birmingham	SMoF	
Bensen B- 8M	Bensen B- 8M	CA	Riverside	MAFM	
Bensen B- 8M	Bensen B- 8M	CT	Winds	NEAM	
Bensen B-8M	Bensen B- 8M	FL	Lakel	SFAF	
Bensen B- 8M	Bensen B-8M	KS	Coffeyville	CAHM	
Bensen B- 8M	Bensen B- 8M	VA	Chantilly	NASMUVH	
Bensen B- 8M	Bensen B-11	NC	Ralei	NCMoH	
Bensen B- 8M(X-25A)	Bensen B-11	OH	Dayton	NMUSAF	68-10770
Bensen B- 8M		ON-C	Ottawa	CAM	GGSXV
		ON-C	Ottawa	CAM	C-GPJE
		OR	Eugen	OAM	
		OR	Tillamook	TNAM	
		PA	Reading	MAAM	
		PA	Wchester	AHM	
		SK-C	Moose Jaw	WDM	
		WA	Seattle	MoF	1, N8533E
		CA	Chino	PoFAM	
		WI	Oshkosh	EAAAAM	N63U

Listing	Variant	State	City	Museum	Registration
Bergfalke 11 Glider	Glider	PA	Tough	CFCM	
Berliner Helicopter	Helicopter	MD	College Park	CPAM	
Berliner Helicopter	Helicopter	MD	Suitland	PEGF	
Bertelson Aeromobile Hover	Bertelson / Aeromobile Hover	MD	Suitland	Suitland	

Bf- 109 Messerschmitt Gustav

Listing	Variant	State	City	Museum	Registration
Bf -109	Bf -109F	GA	Savan	MEHM	
Bf -109	Bf -109F-4	MD	Suitland	PEGF	
Bf -109	Bf -109F-4	OR	Tillamook	TAM	
Bf -109 (1/2 Scale)	Bf -109G	LA	Patte	WWMAM	
Bf -109E-7	Bf -109G-10/U4	VA	Suffolk	FF "Black 9"	
Bf -109F	Bf -109G-10	CO	Lafayette	SoFC	10256, N109WR
Bf -109F	Bf -109G-14(Mock Up)	CO	Lafayette	SoFC	10144, N441WR
	Bf -109G	CO	Lafayette	SoFC	10145, N541WR
		ON-C	Ottaw	CAM	471-39
		TX	Slaton	TAM	
		DC	Washi	NA&SM	
		AZ	Grand	PoFGCVA	13
		OR	Mc Minnville	EAM	610937, N109EV
		CA	San Diego	SDAM	
		VA	Suffolk	FF	

Listing	Variant	State	City	Museum	Registration
BFC-2(F11C)	Goshawk	FL	Pensacola	NMoNA	9332 2-B-13

Aircraft	Name / Type	State	City	Museum	Reg. No. / Notes
BG-12B	Sailplane / Brieglab	ND	Fargo	BUSAHM	
BG-12BD	Sailplane / Brieglab	NY	Elmir	NSM	
BG-12BD	Sailplane / Brieglab	PA	Reading	MAAM	162, N12RK
Biplane	Biplane	IN	India	CMol	
Biplane	Biplane	KS	Topek	KSHS	"Lil Chil"
Biplane	Biplane	TX	C Christi	USS Lexi	
Bird CK	CK / Bird	PA	Bethel	GAAM	
Birdwing Imperial	Imperial / Birdwing	NY	River	RE	
Blanik	Glider / Blanik	ID	Driggs	TAC	1930
Blanik L-13	Glider / Blanik	NM	Hobbs	NSF	
Blaty	Orion Hang Glider / Blaty	CA	Chino	PoFAM	
Bleriot X		NY	Rhine	ORA	
Bleriot XI Replica		AZ	Mesa	CAFAWM	
Bleriot XI		CA	San Diego	SDAM	
Bleriot XI		CT	Winds	NEAM	
Bleriot XI		DC	Washi	NA&SM	"Domenjoz"
Bleriot XI		FL	Pensacola	NMoNA	
Bleriot XI		IA	Des M	ISHD	
Bleriot XI		MA	Stow	BCF	
Bleriot XI		MD	College Park	CPAM	
Bleriot X		ME	Owls Head	OHTM	1, "Boneshaker"
Bleriot XI Replica		MI	Dearb	HFM	153
Bleriot XI		NY	Garde	CoAM	Original 1909
Bleriot XI		NY	River	RE	
Bleriot XI		OH	Dayton	NMUSAF	
Bleriot XI		ON-C	Ottaw	CAM	
Bleriot XI		TX	Kingsbury	VAHF	
Bleriot XI		TX	San Antonio	TAM	
Blimp (2ea)		OR	Tillamook	TAM	
Block IV Satellite	Block	OH	Dayton	NMUSAF	IV Satellite
BobCat		GA	Woodstock	NGWS	BobCat Kit
Boeing 100	Boeing	WA	Seattle	MoF	Boeing 247D — 1143, N872H
Boeing Airliner					
247D(C-73)		DC	Washi	NA&SM	1930 - 10 Passenger
247D(C-73)		ON-C	Ottaw	CAM	1930 - 10 Passenger
247D(C-73)		WA	Everett	MoF	1729, NC13347, "Cpt George Juneau"
307		VA	Chantilly	NASMUVC	
367-80		VA	Chantilly	NASMUVC	
367-80		WA	Seattle	MoF	
377(C-97)	Mini Guppy	OR	Tillamook	TAM	NC285
40B-2		MI	Dearb	HFM	
40B-2 (727-100)		IL	Chica	MoS&I	7017, "United Airlines"
707 Cockpit		NY	NYC	ISASM	
707-131B		AZ	Tucson	PAM	99-18390, N751TW
707-320		CA	Simi VAlley	RL	Air Force One, 27000, VC-137C
720 Cockpit		NV	Las Vegas	LBAHSM	"Kay O"II"
727		IL	Chicago	MoS&I	
727-22		WA	Seattle	MoF	18293, N7001U
727-25C		MI	Kalamazoo	KAHM	19301, N119FE

Aircraft	State	City	Museum	Registration / Notes
727	OR	Hillsboro	BC	
727-100	KS	Wichita	KAM	
727-100	WA	Everett	MoF	N7001U, 1st Built
727-130	WA	Seattle	MoF	19437, 515
737-200	AB-C	Edmonton	AAM	
737-200	KS	Wichita	KAM	
727-200	WA	Seattle	MoF	
737-200 Nose	TX	Dallas	FoF	
747-100 Cockpit	CA	San Carlos	HNCAVM	
747-121	WA	Seattle	MoF	20235
747 Fuse	DC	Washington	NASM	N747001

Aircraft	Type	State	City	Museum	Registration / Notes
Boeing 80A-1	Tri-Motor	WA	Seattle	MoF	1082, NC224M
Boeing B&W Replica	B&W	WA	Seattle	MoF	N1916
Boeing B-100	B-100	FL	Polk	FoF	
Boeing Bird of Prey	Bird of Prey	OH	Dayton	NMUSAF	
Boeing Condor	Condor	CA	San Carlos	HNCAVM	
Boeing E75N1		WI	Oshkosh	EAAAAM	
Boeing Inertial Upper Stage	Boeing	WA	Seattle	MoF	Upper Stage
Boeing Lunar Rover	Lunar Rover	WA	Seattle	MoF	
Boeing MIM-10B	Super Bomarc	ON-C	Ottaw	CAM	60446
Boeing 2707-300(SST)	SST	CA	San Carlos	HNCAVM	
Boeing 2707-300(SST)	SST	FL	CapeC		
Bolkow Bo 208A-1 Jr		IA	Ottumwa	APM	525, N208JR
Bombardier Challenger	Challenger	ON-C	Ottawa	CAM	600
Boost Glide Reentry Vehicle		OH	Dayton	NMUSAF	Reentry Vehicle
Borel Morane	Morane	ON-C	Ottawa	CAM	

Bowers Fly Baby

Aircraft	State	City	Museum	Registration / Notes
Bowers Flybaby 1-A	FL	Lakel	SFAF	
Bowers Flybaby 1-A	AZ	Tucson	PAM	N49992
Bowers Flybaby 1-A	CA	Santa Martin	WoHAM	
Bowers Flybaby 1-A	CA	Santa Maria	SMMoF	
Bowers Flybaby 1-A	CA	San Diego	SDAM	
Bowers Flybaby 1-A	ND	W Farg	Bonanzav	
Bowers Flybaby 1-A	OH	Madis	CFR	
Bowers Flybaby 1-A	ON-C	Ottawa	CAM	
Bowers Flybaby 1-A	WA	Seattle	MoF	68-15, N4339

Aircraft	Type	State	City	Museum	Registration / Notes
Bowlus Albatross	Falcon	CA	Santa Martin	WoHAM	N6219Y, 25
Bowlus Albatross	Falcon	NY	Elmir	NSM	
Bowlus Albatross	Falcon	VA	Hampton	APM	
Bowlus Albatross D.V	Falcon	VA	Suffolk	FF	
Bowlus Albatross I-S-2100	Senior	VA	Chantilly	NASMUVC	
Bowlus Albatross SP-1	Falcon	CA	San Diego	SDAM	
Bowlus BB-1	Bumblebee	BC-C	Langley	CMoF	
Bowlus Baby Ace	Baby Ace	CA	Santa Martin	WoHAM	506, N34922, CF-MB/CF-VFA

Model	State/Prov	City	Museum	Name/Type	Registration / Notes
Bowlus Baby Ace	NM	Kirkl	KA	Baby Ace	
Bowlus Baby Ace	NY	Elmir	NSM	Baby Ace	
Bowlus Baby Ace	NY	Elmir	NSM	Baby Ace	
Bowlus Baby Albatross	VA	Chantilly	NASMUVC	Falcon	
Bowlus Baby Albatross	WA	Everett	MoF		N25605
Bowlus Nelson Motor Glider	NY	Mayville	DA	Motor Glider	
Bowlus Super Albatross	CA	M.Maria	WoHAM	Super Albatross	
Brantly 305	CA	Ramona	CR	305	
Breese Penquin	NY	Garde	CoAM	Penquin	33622
Breese Penquin	NY	Mayville	DA	Penquin	
Breguet G-3	NY	Rhine	ORA	Breguet	1911, 3 Seater Biplane
Brewster B-1	IA	Ottumwa	APM	Brewster	1, NC-20699
Brewster Fleet 7	PA	Reading	MAAM	Fleet 7	
Bristol Beaufighter	ON-C	Ottaw	CAM		RD 867
Bristol Beaufighter Mk.Ic	OH	Dayton	NMUSAF		A19-43
Bristol Beaufighter	TX	Kingsbury	VAHF	Bristol Beaufighter Mk.I	Project
Bristol Beufort Mk.I	TX	Hawki	RRSA		
Bristol Blenheim Mk.IV	AB-C	Nanton	NLSAM	Bolingbroke	9989 (L-WV)
Bristol Bolingbroke Mk IV	AB-C	Wetas	RM		
Bristol Bolingbroke Mk IV	BC-C	Sidne	BCAM		
Bristol Bolingbroke	MB-C	Brand	CI		
Bristol Bolingbroke	MB-C	Brand	CATPM		9944
Bristol Bolingbroke	MB-C	Winni	WCAM		9892
Bristol Bolingbroke Mk.IVT	ON-C	Ottaw	CAM		903
Bristol Bolingbroke Mk.IVW	ON-C	Hamilton	CWH		
Bristol Bolingbroke	NS-C	Greenwood	GMAM		
Bristol F.2B	AL	Gunte	LGARFM	Brisfit	
Bristol F.2B Rep	AZ	Grand	PoFGCVA	Brisfit	PWZ
Bristol F.2B Rep	CA	Chino	PoF	Brisfit	PWZ
Bristol 170 Freighter Mk.31	NT-C	Yellowknife	YA	Freighter	13137, CF-TFX
Bristol Type 170 Mk.31	MB-C	Winni	WCAM	Freighter/Wayfarer	
Brock Keb 8BM Gyroplane		WI	Oshkosh	Brock	Gyro-Plane, N2303
Broussard MH.1512	CA	SRosa	PCAM	MH.1512	
Brown B-1	IL	Chica	MoS&I	B-1 Racer	NR 83Y
Brown B-1	WI	Oshkosh	EAAAAM	B-1 Racer	Suzie Jane 19
Brown-Bushby-Robinson	WI	Oshkosh	EAAAAM	Star Lite	
Brown Star Lite	WI	Oshkosh	EAAAAM	Star Lite	N81197
Brugioni Mario	WI	Oshkosh	EAAAAM	Cuby	

Brunner-Winkle Bird

Type	State	City	Museum	Reg / Notes
Brunner-Winkle Bird	NY	Bayport	BA	
Brunner-Winkle Bird	NY	Garde	CoAM	NC78K
Brunner-Winkle Bird	PA	Bethel	GAAM	NC726N
Brunner-Winkle Bird A-1	PA	Reading	MAAM	
Brunner-Winkle Bird BK	VA	Sands	VAM	20250-96, N831W
Brunner-Winkle Bird BK	CA	Chino	YAM	
Brunner-Winkle Bird BK	CA	San Diego	SDAM	
Brunner-Winkle Bird BK	NY	Rhine	ORA	
Brunner-Winkle Bird BK	NY	River	TFAC	N731Y
BT-9B	OH	Dayton	NMUSAF	

BT-13 Vultee Valiant

Type	State	City	Museum	Reg / Notes
BT-13	AZ	Pine Bluff	REAA	
BT-13	CA	Atwater	CAM	42-16978, Side # E-205
BT-13	CA	Shafter	MFAM	
BT-13	CA	Farfield	DA&SM	
BT-13	CT	Winds	NEAM	
BT-13	DE	Dover	DAFB	K-11
BT-13	IL	Danville	TSM	
BT-13	IN	Mento	LB	
BT-13	KS	New Century	CAF-HoAW	41-21216, N56665, "Good Vibrations"
BT-13	KS	New Century	CAF-HoAW	
BT-13	KS	Topek	CAM	N2808
BT-13	MN	Minne	JJ	
BT-13	MS	Petal	MWHMM	
BT-13	NM	St Teresa	WEAM	
BT-13	NV	Carso	YF	
BT-13	NY	Geneseo	1941AG	
BT-13	TX	Brown	RGVW-CAF	
BT-13	TX	Brown	RGVW-CAF	
BT-13	OH	Carroll	HAS	
BT-13	TX	Houston	CAF-GCW	N67208
BT-13	MI	Kalamazoo	KAHM	11676, (SNV-1)
BT-13	MI	Ypsilanti	YAF	(SNV-1VU)
BT-13	TX	Addison	CFM	13 (SNV-2)
BT-13	VA	Manassass	CAF-NCS	42-42353
BT-13A	AZ	Tucson	PAM	41-1414, Side BI-211
BT-13A	CA	Riverside	MFAM	41-1306, 21487
BT-13A	CA	Riverside	MFAM	P-101
BT-13A	CO	Ft Lupton	VA	42-90018
BT-13A	GA	Pooler	MoF	"Vibrator"
BT-13A	IN	Indianapolis	AMHF	
BT-13A	KS	Liberal	MAAM	
BT-13A	KS	New Century	CAF-HoAW	N57486
BT-13A	MB-C	Winni	WCAM	
BT-13A	MN	S St Paul	CAF-SMW	N52411
BT-13A	NC	Asheboro	PFAC	
BT-13A	OK	Fredi	AAM	
BT-13A	SD	Rapid City	SDA&SM	41-22204
BT-13A	TX	San Angelo	GAFB	42-04130
BT-13A	TX	Houston	CAF-GCW	N56336
BT-13A	TX	Houston	CAF-WHS	N27003
BT-13A	PA	Readi	MAAM	41-22441, N60277, (SNV-1)
BT-13B	AL	Birmingham	SMoF	
BT-13B	CA	Chino	YAM	79-326, N4425V
BT-13B	OH	Dayton	NMUSAF	42-90629
BT-13B	UT	Ogden	HAM	42-90406

BT-14 (NA-64) North American Yale

Type	State	City	Museum	Reg / Notes
BT-14 (NA-64)	AB-C	Nanton	NLSAM	64-2157
BT-14 (NA-64)	AB-C	Wetas	RM	
BT-14 (NA-64)	AZ	Tucson	PAM	3397, N4735G
BT-14 (NA-64)	MB-C	Winni	WCAM	
BT-14 (NA-64)	OH	Dayton	NMUSAF	38-224
BT-14 (NA-64)	ON-C	Dunnville	RCAFDA	
BT-14 (NA-64)	ON-C	Hamilton	CWH	CF-CWZ, 3350

Type	State	Location	Museum	Serial		Type / Mfr	State	Location	Museum	Serial
BT-14 (NA-64)	ON-C	Tillsonburg	CHAA	3399		BT-14 (NA-64)	TX	Slaton	TAM	
BT-15	CA	Grand Canyon	PoFGCVA			Vultee Valiant	VA	Sands	VAM	251N133BU
BT-15	TX	Lancaster	CAF-DFW			Vultee Valiant	OK	Oklahoma	OSM	
Bu.131	TX	Gilmer	PotP			Bucker Bucker	VA	Suffolk	FF	

Bu.133 Bucker Jungmeister

Type	State	Location	Museum	Serial		Type / Mfr				Serial
Bu.133	FL	Polk	FoF			Bu.133-C	WI	Oshkosh	EAAAAM	N515
Bu.133	ID	Athol	NAM			Bu.133	WI	Oshkosh	EAAAAM	N258H
Bu.133	MD	Suitland	PEGF			Bu.133				
Bu.133	OK	Oklahoma	A&SM			Bu.133				
Bu.133	OK	Oklahoma	OSM			Bu.133L				
Bu.181	MD	Suitland	PEGF			Bucker Bestmann				
Bugatti 100	WI	Oshkosh	EAAAAM			Bugatti 100				
Buhl CA-6 Air Sedan	ON-C	Sault Ste Marie	CBHC			Buhl Air Sedan				CF-OAR
Buhl Pup	OR	Hood	W AAAM			Buhl Airsedan				
Buhl Sport	MN	Blaine	GWFM			Buhl Airsedan				
Buhl Sport	ON-C	Sault Ste Marie	CBHC			Airsedan				CF-OAT
Buhl Sport	ON-C	Sault Ste Marie	CBHC			Airsedan				CF-OAR Wreckage
Bunce-Curtiss Pusher	CT	Winds	NEAM			Bunce-Curtiss Pusher				
Bunker 154	OK	Oklahoma	OSM			Bunker Model 154				
Burgess-Curtis SC	MD	Suitland	PEGF			Burgess-Curtiss SC				
Burgess-Dunne Rep	ON-C	Trenton	RCAFMM			Burgess-Dunne				
Burgess Twister	WI	Oshkosh	EAAAAM			Burgess-Knight Twister Imperial				
Burgess-Wright B	ME	Owls Head	OHTM			Burgess-Wright Flyer				
Burgess-Wright B	UT	Ogden	HAM			Burgess-Wright Flyer				69115
Bushby Mustang II	AL	Birmi	SMoF			Bushby Mustang II				Mustang Mk.2
Bushby Mustang II(MM-2)	AZ	Tucson				PAM Bushby				Man Sn 581, N53RM
Bushby Mustang II	KS	Liberal	MAAM			Bushby Mustang II				
Bushmaster 2000	MN	Blaine	GWM			Bushmaster 2000				
Buzzman Buccaneer SX	ON-C	Ottawa	CAM			Buzzman Bucaneer SX				C-IDWT
BV 155B	MD	Suitland	PEGF			Blohm & Voss Model 155B				
C-1	CA	San Diego	SDACM			Grumman Trader				146036
C-1	FL	Kissi	FTWAM			Grumman Trader				
C-1										

Desig	State	Location	Org	Mfr	Name	Serial / Notes
C- 1	IN	Peru	GAM	Grumman	Trader	136754, 754, "Bicentenial"
C- 1A	FL	Pensacola	NMoNA	Grumman	Trader	146034, # 62
C- 1A	PA	Willow Grove	NVHAA	Grumman	Trader	
C- 1A	CA	Palm Sprgs	PoFAM	Grumman	Cod	136792
C- 1A	RI	NKing	QAM	Grumman	Cod	
C- 1A	SC	Flore	FA&MM	Grumman	Cod	146052, N81193
C- 1A	TX	Galve	LSFM	Grumman	Cod	Tail RW, Nose 30, Side VRC 30
C- 2	CA	San Diego	NINAS	Spartan		
C- 2	OK	Tulsa	TA&SC	Spartan		
C- 2	VA	Chantilly	NASMUVH	Spartan		
C- 2-60	OR	Hood	WAAAM	Spartan		
C- 3	OK	Tulsa	TA&SC	Spartan	Spartan	
C- 5A	NS-C	Halifax	ACAM	Lockheed	Galaxy	116748
C- 5A Simulator	NM	St Teresa	WEAM	Lockheed	Galaxy	
C- 6A(VC)	IA	Sioux City	MAAM	Beechcraft	King Air	
C- 6A(VC)	NM	Las Cruces	WSMP	Beechcraft	King Air	66-7943
C- 6A(VC)	OH	Dayton	NMUSAF	Beechcraft	King Air	
C- 6A(VC)	VA	Chantilly	NASMUVH	Beechcraft	King Air	
C- 6A(VC) 65-90	VA	Chantilly	NASMUVH	Beechcraft	King Air	

C- 7 de Havilland Caribou

Desig	State	Location	Org	Serial / Notes
C- 7(YAC-1)	NC	Fayet	FBADM	57-3083
C- 7A(CV-7)	VA	FtEus	USATM	57-3079, (Golden Knights)
C- 7A	CT	Winds	NEAM	62-4188
C- 7A	DE	Dover	DAFB	
C- 7A(CV2B)	GA	Hampton	AAHF	
C- 7A	GA	Pooler	MoF	63-9756, 756, "Dixie Pub"
C- 7A	OH	Dayton	NMUSAF	62-4193
C- 7A	TX	Abilene	DLAP	58-82
C- 7A	TX	Amarillo	EFA&SM	63-9719
C- 7A	UT	Ogden	HAFBM	
C- 7B	CA	Rosamond	EAFB	63-9765

Desig	State	Location	Org	Mfr	Name	Serial / Notes
C- 9	DE	Dover	AMCM			
C- 12B(UC)	TX	Corpus Christi	NASCC	Beechcraft	Huron	161185
C- 14(YC)	AZ	Tucson	PAM	Boeing		72-1873
C- 15(YC)	AZ	Tucson	PAM	McDonnell		72-1875
C- 21B(CH)	AK	Palme	MOAT&I			
C- 35(AC)	VA	Chantilly	NASMUVC	Lockheed	Autogiro	
C- 35B (XC)	VA	Chantilly	NASMUVC	Lockheed	Electra	
C- 36(UC)	AZ	Tucson	PAM	Lockheed	Lockheed 10	43-56638, N4963C
C- 37	AB-C	Wetas	RM	Airmaster		

Model	Type	Museum	City	State	Registration / Notes
C-37	Airmaster	W CAM	Winni	MB-C	
C-39A	Douglas	NMUSAF	Dayton	OH	
C-40A/L-12	Lockheed Electra Jr	YAM	Chino	CA	38-515
C-41	Douglas	OSA	SLean	CA	2053, NC41HQ, "General Hap Arnold"
C-43(UC)	Beech Traveler	YAM	Chino	CA	4890, N51746
C-43(UC)	Beech Traveler	NMUSAF	Dayton	OH	44-76068
C-43(UC)	Beech Traveler	1941HG	Geneseo	NY	

C-45 Beech Twin Beech

Model	State	City	Museum	Registration
C-45	WA	Seattle	MoF	51-11696, N115ME
C-45	AZ	Mesa	CAFAWM	N145AZ
C-45	AZ	PBluf	RWCAF	
C-45	CA	Farfield	DA&SM	
C-45	GA	Atlan	CAF-DW	N70GA
C-45	IL	Linco	HIFM	
C-45	KS	Liberal	MAAM	
C-45	LA	Reser	AMHFM	
C-45B	MI	Mt Clemens	SMAM	42-37511
C-45	MN	Minne	MAGM	51-338
C-45	MN	Winoma	WTI	N3785
C-45	MO	Missoula	MMF	
C-45	MS	Canto	CAF-MW	N4207
C-45	NM	Hobbs	CAF-NMW	N79AG
C-45	NC	Asheboro	PFAC	90536
C-45	NY	Brooklyn	PFAC	
C-45	NY	Manhattan	CUSA	67103, N200KU
C-45 Cockpit	OH	N Canton	MAM	N40074
C-45(SNB-5)	OK	Enid	CAF-CSW	
C-45	SD	Rapid City	SDA&SM	
C-45	TX	Ladero	Airport	
C-45 (2 EA)	CO	Denve	JW DAS	

Model	State	City	Museum	Registration / Notes
C-45 (UC)	AK	Fairbanks	PAM	N9199Z
C-45A	CA	Atwater	CAM	51-1897
C-45F(UC)	AK	Ancho	AAHM	
C-45F(UC) Cockpit	MD	Ft Meade	QM	
C-45G	DE	Dover	DAFB	
C-45G	IN	Ligonier	ZF	AF95, British
C-45H	AK	Ancho	AAHM	
C-45H	FL	Titusville	VACM	
C-45H	IL	Belle	SAFB	
C-45H	ND	Fargo	BUSAHM	
C-45H	OH	Dayton	NMUSAF	52-10893
C-45H	TN	Tullahoma	SFM	5AF-824, N7916A
C-45H	TN	Tullahoma	SFM	8142, N20003
C-45H Simulator	UT	Ogden	HAFBM	52-10862
C-45J	IL	Belle	SAFB	
C-45J	TX	Midland	AAHM	70GA
C-45J	TX	San Antonio	LSAD	29639, #637
C-45J(UC)	GA	Woodstock	NGWS	
C-45J(RC)	CA	McClellan	McCelAFB	51-291
C-45J(UC)	ON-C	Hamilton	CWH	
C-45J(UC)	TX	D Rio	LAFB	
C-45J(UC)(SNB-2)	CA	Rosamond	EAFB	67161

CT-134(C-45) Beech Musketeer

Model	State	City	Museum	Registration
C-45(CT-134)	CA	Santa Martin	WoHAM	Model 23
C-45(CT-134)	AB-C	Wetaskawin	CFB	134232
C-45(CT-134)	MB-C	Brandon	CATPM	
C-45(CT-134)	MB-C	Portage	S	134201
C-45(CT-134)	MB-C	Portage	S	134238
C-45(CT-134)	MB-C	Winni	WRCFB	134228
C-45(CT-134)	ON-C	Campbellford	CFB	134219
C-45(CT-134)	ON-C	Picton	CFB	134211
C-45(CT-134)	ON-C	Toronto	TAM	

Designation	State/Prov	Location	Museum	Serial / Registration
C-45(CT-134)	ON-C	Trenton	RCAFMM	
C-45(CT-134A)	ON-C	Brockville	Park	
C-45(CT-134A)	ON-C	Campbellford	MMM	23

C-45 Beech Expeditor

Designation	State/Prov	Location	Museum	Serial / Registration
C-45 Fuse	AL	Birmingham	SMF	
C-45 (JRB Mk.III)	AB-C	Calga	AMoC	
C-45 (D-18 / CT-128)	MB-C	Brandon	CATPM	
C-45 (JRB Mk.III)	MB-C	Portage	S	1560
C-45 (JRB Mk.III)	MB-C	Winni	WCAM	1528
C-45 (JRB Mk.III)	VT	Burli	BANG	

C-45 Beech Kansan

Designation	State/Prov	Location	Museum	Serial / Registration
C-45 (SNB) Trainer	AR	Walnut Ridge	WRAFSM	
C-45 (SNB)	CA	Chino	PoFAM	BG-33
C-45 (SNB)	KS	Topek	CAM	

C-46 Curtiss Commando

Designation	State/Prov	Location	Museum	Serial / Registration
C-46	CA	Chino	YAM	43-47218
C-46	NM	Las Cruces	LCIA	
C-46	NM	Las Cruces	SA	
C-46	TX	Midland	AAHM	78774
C-46(EC)(R5C)	FL	Pensacola	NMoNA	N611Z, 39611, MARS-37
C-46(EC)(R5D-2Z)	CA	Miramar	FLAM	
C-46A	GA	Pooler	MoF	42-101198, N68851

C-47 Douglas Sky Train (See C-53, DC-3 & R4D)

Designation	State/Prov	Location	Museum	Serial / Registration
C-47	AA	Starke	CBM	12436, nose Z7
C-47	AB-C	Edmonton	AAM	
C-47	AR	St Louis	OAM	4463
C-47	AZ	Tucson	PAM	41-7723, 4201
C-47	CA	Chino	YAM	
C-47	CA	Fairfield	TAM	42-92990
C-47	CA	Palm Springs	PSAM	0106, N60154, #44
C-47(R4D-6R)	DE	New Castle	ATC	"Kilroy Was Here"
C-47(AC)	FL	Clear	FMAM	
C-47	FL	Kissimmee	FTWRM	

Designation	State/Prov	Location	Museum	Serial / Registration
C-45(CT-134A)	ON-C	Prairie LP	PA	11400
C-45(CT-134A)	ON-C	Prairie LP	FLPRM	
C-45(CT-134A)	SK-C	Moose Jaw	WDM	230
C-45F(JRB-4)	CA	Riverside	MFAM	44588, 52-10588A
C-45H	AL	Ozark	USAAM	51-11638
C-45H	GA	Pooler	MoF	51-11653, N141ZA
C-45J(UC)	AL	Ozark	USAAM	43-9767
C-45J(UC)(SNB-2C)	AZ	Tucson	PAM	43-50222, N1082
C-45J(YC)(SNB-5)	AZ	Tucson	PAM	39123, N75018,
C-45 (SNB-5)	AZ	Tucson	PAM	N40090, 39213
C-45H(SNB)	NY	Geneseo	1941HAGM	52-01539
C-45J(RC)(SNB-5P)	FL	Pensacola	NMoNA	9771, 4P, NATTU
C-46D	AZ	Tucson	PAM	44-77635
C-46D	AZ	Tucson	PAM	44-78019, N32229
C-46D	CA	Atwater	CAM	44-77575
C-46D	FL	FtWal	HF	44-424
C-46D	OH	Dayton	NMUSAF	44-78018
C-46F	CA	Camarillo	CAF-SCW	44-78663, N53594, "China Doll"
46F(NC)	NC	Fayet	FBADM	44-78573
C-47	FL	Polk	FoF	
C-47	FL	Stark	CB-FANTC	
C-47	FL	Titus	VACM	2100591, S U 5, "Tico Belle"
C-47	FL	WPalm	391BG	
C-47	GA	Atlanta	ASG	
C-47	GA	Douglas	LF	
C-47	HI	Kalaeloa	NAMBB	42-100486
C-47(R4D-6R)	IL	Chica	CAF-GLW	99854, N227GB, "Black Sparrow"
C-47(AC)	KS	Topeka	AFM	43-16369, N2805J, "Spooky"
C-47	KY	FKnox	FC	
C-47	LA	New Orleans	DDM	42-93096

Type	Loc	City	Collection	Serial / Registration / Notes
C-47	MB-C	Winnipeg	WRCAFB	
C-47	MI	Kalamazoo	KAHM	42-93168
C-47	NC	Charlotte	CAM	
C-47	NC	Charlotte	CAM	43-49926, 12907
C-47	ND	Minot	DTAM	
C-47 Cockit	ND	Minot	DTAM	
C-47(SC)	NM	Albuquerque	KAFB	035732
C-47	NY	Brooklyn	Bonanzav	
C-47	NY	Geneseo	1941HAGM	
C-47(R4D-5)	NY	Horsehead	WoE	43-13860, N293WM
C-47	OH	N Canton	MAM	45-0928, N54599, "Raptured Duck"
C-47	ON-C	Ottaw	CAM	
C-47	ON-C	Petawawa	CFBPMM	
C-47	ON-C	Trenton	RCAFMM	
C-47	OR	Mc Minnville	EAM	
C-47	OR	Tillamook	TAM	43-15512, N62376
C-47B	TX	Burnet	HLSCAF	43-49942
C-47	TX	FWort	PMoT	
C-47	TX	Houston	1940ATM	
C-47	TX	Lubbock	SWM	
C-47(EC)	TX	San Antonio	VMP	43-48415 as 43-49201
C-47	VA	Peter	FL	
C-47 (R4D)	CO	Pueblo	PWAM	17217
C-47 Simulator	NY	Garde	CoAM	
C-47A Damaged	MS	Petal	SFC	42-92864, N37906
C-47(VC)	CA	Riverside	MFAM	43-15579, "Golden Bear"
C-47(VC)	ND	WFarg	Bonanzav	
C-47A	AK	Ancho	KANGB	
C-47A	AK	Palme	MOAT&I	
C-47A	CA	Atwater	CAM	43-15977, Tail N, Side L7
C-47A	DE	Dover	DAFB	292841, Q9, R, "Turf & Sport Special"
C-47A	LA	Barksdale AFB	BAFB	"Hi Honey"
C-47A-90-DL	MT	Missoula	MMF	43-15731, 20197, N24320
C-47A	NY	Scotia	ESAM	43-12061
C-47A	NC	Fayetteville	A&SOM	43-15623
C-49	IL	Chica	CAF-GLW	N17332
C-47A	SD	Rapid City	SDA&SM	4226GB
C-47A	TX	Abilene	DLAP	41-8808
C-47A	TX	Addison	CFM	
C-47A RAF		NWTC HayRi	BA	12327, C- GWZS
C-47A RAF		NWTC HayRi	BA	13155, C- FLFR
C-47A RAF		NWTC HayRi	BA	13333, C- GPNR
C-47A(AC)	FL	FtWal	HF	42-510, AH
C-47A(AC)	FL	Shalimar	USAFAM	43-10, O
C-47A(VC)	MO	SLoui	NMoT	43-15635
C-47A(VC)	ND	WFarg	Bonanzav	42-93300
C-47A-30-DK	NE	Ashland	SACM	43-48098
C-47B	AL	Montg	GAFB	
C-47B	LA	ASI	HTA	N4994N, "Flying Dove"
C-47B	LA	ASI	HTA	42-24337, N64767
C-47B	LA	ASI	HTA	49957, N64766, "Nancy B"
C-47B	MN	Minne	MAGM	44-7462
C-47B	NC	Fayet	FBADM	43-48932
C-47B	NC	Fayet	PAFB	
C-47B(TC)	WA	Tacoma	MAFB	44-76502
C-47D	AZ	Tucson	PAM	41-7723
C-47D	IL	Rantoul	OCAM	43-49336
C-47D	IN	Peru	GAFB	43-49270
C-47D	KS	Topek	CAM	45-1074, "Kilroy", J8
C-47D	MI	Belleville	YAF	44-76716, N33048, "Yankee Doodle Dandy"
C-47D	MI	Ypsilanti	YAF	43-49507
C-47D	OH	Dayton	NMUSAF	44-76671
C-47D	TX	San Antonio	LSAD	
C-47D	WA	Spokane	AF&AM	
C-47D(VC)	AL	Mobile	BMP	40-76326
C-47D(VC)	SC	Charl	CAFB	
C-47H	UT Ogden		HAFBM	43-49281
C-47H	AL	Ozark	USAAM	41-12436
C-47H(R4D-5)	FL	Pensacola	NMoNA	12418, 18
C-47J(R4D-6)	GA	Pooler	MoF,	43-48442, 15090 EL, "Saylor's Trailer"

C-54 Douglas Skymaster

Model	Type	State	City	Organization	Serial / Notes
C-50	Douglas Skytrooper	CT	Winds	NEAM	
C-53	Douglas Skytrooper	CA	Rosamond	EAFB	
C-53D	Douglas Skytrooper	CA	Riverside	IES	
C-53D	Douglas Skytrooper	CA	McClellan	McCelAFB	42-68835
C-53D Parts	Douglas Skytrooper	MS	Petal	SFC	42-68804, Southern Flyer Co.
C-53D	Douglas Skytrooper	MS	Petal	MWHMM	42-68745, N4003

Model	State	City	Organization	Serial / Notes
C-54(DC-4)	AK		CAS	"Fat Annie"
C-54	CA	Riverside	WFAM	42-72636
C-54	NJ	Farmi	BAHF	"Spirit of Freedom"
C-54	NY	Brooklyn	BAHF	42-72592
C-54	SD	Rapid City	SDA&SM	
C-54	TX	Brown	RGVW-CAF	N89F
C-54	WA	Seattle	MoF	
C-54B(ATL98)	LA	Houma	CAS	N44914, 56498, "Air Transport Command"
C-54B(R5D-2)	MA	Nando AW	NMUSAF	42-107451, "Sacred Cow"
C-54C(VC)	OH	Dayton		
C-54D(DC-4)	AZ	Tucson	PAM	42-72488
C-54D	CA	Riverside	MAFB	42-72636, 56514, N67062
C-54D	CA	McClellan	McCelAFB	42-72449
C-54D-1-DL	LA	Houma	ASI	50871, N67024
C-54E	NE	Ashland	SACM	42-72724
C-54G	CA	Atwater	CAM	1373
C-54G-1-DO	GA	Pooler	MoF	45-579, A
C-54M	UT	Ogden	HAM	45-0502
C-54Q	DE	Dover	DAFB	
	CA	Farfield	DA&SM	

C-56 (L.18) Lockheed Lodestar

Model	State	City	Organization	Serial / Notes
C-56 (L.18)	CA	Atwater	CAM	
C-56 (L.18)	CA	Farfield	DA&SM	
C-60 (L.18)	CA	Chino	PoFAM	
C-60 (L.18)	CA	SAnto	CAF-AW	N6371C
C-60 (L.18)	TX	Houston	1940AT	
C-60 (L.18)	VA	Chesa	CAF-ODS	N30N
C-60A(L.18)	CO	Westminster	CAF	43-16438, (PV1)(R50)
C-60A(L.18)	GA	Pooler	MoF	42-55918, N18198
C-60A(L.18)	OH	Dayton	NMUSAF	43-16445, Military Version
C-60C(L.18C)	VA	Chesapeake	CAFODW	
	CA	Atwater	CAM	

UC-61 Fairchild Argus

Model	State	City	Organization	Serial / Notes
C-61(UC)(FC-24)	AK	Ancho	AAHM	
C-61(UC)(FC-24)	KS	Liberal	MAAM	
C-61(UC)(FC-24)	PA	Reading	MAAM	NC19133
C-61(UC)(FC-24)	VA	Sands	VAM	2983, Model G, N19123
C-61(UC)(FC-24)	WA	Seattle	MoF	
C-61(UC)(FC-24)	AB-C	Edmonton	AAM	
C-61B(UC)(FC-24J)	AK	Fairbanks	PAM	NC20617, "Pollack Flying Service"
C-61C(UC)(FC-24)	PA	Hagerstown	HAM	
C-61F(UC)(FC-24R)	ON-C	Hamilton	CWH	C-FGZL, 4809
C-61G(UC)(FC-24H)	OK	Fredi	AAM	
C-61G(UC)(FC-24W)	AL	Birmi	Southe	
C-61G(UC)(FC-24W)	OK	Fredi	AAM	
C-61G(UC)(FC-24W-46) MB-C		Winni	WCAM	N81318
C-61G(UC)(FC-24W-46) WI		Oshkosh	EAAAAM	
C-61G(UC)(FC-2W) Frame AK		Ancho	AAHM	
C-61J(UC)(FC-24 C8) WI		Oshkosh	EAAAAM	N13191
C-61J(UC)(FC-24C-8A) WI		Oshkosh	EAAAAM	N957V
C-61K(UC)	KS	Topek	CAM	N-18395

C-64 Noorduyn Norseman

Model	State	City	Museum	Notes
C-64	AB-C	Edmonton	AAM	
C-64	ON-C	Red Lake	HB	
C-64A Mk.I	ON-C	Sault Se Marie	CBHC	CF-AYO
C-64	AK	Ancho	AAHM	N725M
C-64	BC-C	Sidne	BCAM	"Thunder Chicken"
C-64A Mk.IV	ON-C	Sault Ste Marie	CBHC	17, CF-BFT
C-64	SK-C	MJaw	WDM	CF-SAM
C-64(UC)	CO	Denve	JWDAS	
C-64(YC)	MD	Suitland	PEGF	
C-64(YC) Mk.IV	MD	Suitland	PEGF	
C-64A Mk.IV	AB-C	Wetas	RM	
C-64A Mk.IV	MB-C	Winnipeg	WCAM	
C-64A Mk.VI	AK	Fairbanks	PAM N55555, "Alaska Airways"	
C-64A Mk.VI	ON-C	Ottaw	CAM	QT787
C-64A(UC)	OH	Dayton	NMUSAF	44-70296

UC-78 Cessna Bobcat (See Also AT-17)

Model	State	City	Museum	Notes
C-78(UC)	AZ	Tucson	PAM	42-39162, N66794,
C-78(UC)	CA	Atwater	CAM	
C-78(UC)	CA	Farfield	DA&SM	
C-78(UC)	CO	Denve	JWDAS	3806 806
C-78(UC)	MD	Cambr	CA	
C-78(UC)	NY	River	RE	
C-78(UC)	PA	Reading	MAAM	N 41793
C-78(UC)	TX	SMarc	CTWCAF	
C-78B(UC)	AZ	Tucson	PAM	42-71830
C-78B(UC)	GA	Pooler	MoF	42-71714
C-78B(UC)	OH	Dayton	NMUSAF	42-71626

Model	State	City	Museum	Notes
C-82	PA	Hagerstown	HAM	Fairchild Packet
C-82	WA	Tacoma	MAFB	Fairchild Packet
C-82A	AZ	Tucson	PAM	Fairchild Packet
C-82A	OH	Dayton	NMUSAF	Fairchild Packet
	Packet			48-57574
	Packet			44-23006, N6997C
	Packet			48-581

KC-97 Boeing Stratocruiser

Model	State	City	Museum	Notes
C-97(KC)	CO	Colorado Sprs	SR	3-0283
C-97(KC)	WI	Dodge	Restaura	
C-97G	AZ	Tucson	PAM	52-2626, HB-ILY
C-97G	CA	Lanca	MoFM	
C-97G	IL	Rantoul	OCAM	52-0898
C-97G(KC)	AZ	Tucson	PAM	53-151
C-97G(KC)	MO	White	WAFB	0-30327
C-97G(KC)(Cockpit)	NC	Charlotte	CAM	53-0335
C-97G(KC)	NJ	Farmi	BAHF	52-2718, N117GA, "Deliverance"
C-97G(KC) Cockpit,	NV	Las Vegas	LBAHSM	53-0317, N971HP, #377
C-97G(KC)	OR	Medford	RVIA	2-0895
C-97G(KC)-BN	NE	Ashland	SACM	53-0198
C-97K(KC)	SC	Flore	FA&MM	
C-97L(KC)	CA	Atwater	CAM	0-0354,
C-97L(KC)	CA	Marys	BAFB	53-0363
C-97L(KC)	CA	Riverside	MFAM	53-298
C-97L(KC)	GA	Pooler	MoF	52-2297
C-97L(KC)	IN	Peru	GAFB	0240
C-97L(KC)	LA	Barksdale AFB	BAFB	
C-97L(KC)	MD	Suitland	PEGF	
C-97L(KC)	MT	Great Falls	MAFB	53-360,
C-97L(KC)	NH	Ports	PAFB	
C-97L(KC)	OH	Dayton	NMUSAF	52-2630
C-97L(KC)	TX	Abilene	DLAP	53-282
C-97L(KC)	TX	FWort	NASFW JRB	
C-97L(KC)	TX	FWort	SAM	
C-97L(KC)	WI	CDoug	WNGML&M	905

C-103A
C-117D *See R4D*

AZ Tucson DMAFB

VC-118 Douglas Liftmaster

Model	State	Location	Facility	Serial/Notes
C-118(VC)	OH	Dayton	NMUSAF	46-505
C-118(YO)	CA	Farfield	DA&SM	
C-118A	NJ	Trent	MGAFB	
C-118A	TX	San Antonio	LSAD	51-17640
C-118A(VC)(DC-6)	AZ	Tucson	PAM	53-3240, 33240, "Air Force One"
C-118B	OK	Altus	AAFB	
C-118B(R6D-1)	FL	Pensacola	NMoNA	128424, 424

C-119 Fairchild Flying Boxcar

Model	State	Location	Facility	Serial/Notes
C-119	CO	Pueblo	PWAM	131688
C-119	GA	FtBen	IM	
C-119	KY	FKnox	FC	
C-119	NV	Battl	BMAM	N5216R, 137
C-119F	PA	Readi	MAAM	N175ML, VMR-52
C-119	TX	FWort	PMoT	0-12675
C-119	WI	Milwa	MANG	
C-119(R4Q-2)	CA	Miramar	FLAM	708, VMR-352
C-119B	CA	Rosamond	EAFB	48-352
C-119B	GA	Pooler	MoF	51-2566
C-119C	AZ	Tucson	PAM	49-0157
C-119C	AZ	Tucson	PAM	49-132, N13743
C-119C	CA	Atwater	CAM	49-199, N13744
C-119F	NY	Geneseo	1941AG	10678
C-119F Nose	ON-C	Ottawa	CAM	134
C-119G	CA	Farfield	DA&SM	
C-119G	CA	Riverside	MFAM	RCAF 22122, 452 TCW
C-119G	CA	McClellan	McCelAFB	52-114
C-119G	DE	Dover	DAFB	
C-119G	FL	FtWal	HF	33144
C-119G	IN	Peru	GAFB	52-5850, "Hash-2-Zero"
C-119G	UT	Ogden	HAFBM	52-2107
C-119J	AR	Littl	LRAFB	53-8084, 314th TAW
C-119J	OH	Dayton	NMUSAF	51-8037
C-119L	NC	Fayet	FBADM	53-8087A

Model	State	Location	Facility
C-120(EC)	TX	Addison	CFM

C-121 Lockheed Constellation (Warningstar)

Model	State	Location	Facility	Serial/Notes
C-121 (L-0749)	MT	Helena	CoT	52-3417
C-121A(L-0749)	AZ	Tucson	PAM	48-614, USAF
C-121A(VC)(L-0749)	AL	Ozark	USAAM	USAF
C-121A(VC)(L-0749)	AZ	Grand	PoFGCVA	48-613, N422NA, "Bataan"
C-121C(L-0749)	DE	Dover	DAFBHC	
C-121C(L-0749)	SC	Charl	CAFB	54-180, USAF
C-121C(L-1049)	TX	San Antonio	LSAD	54-155
C-121C(L-1049G)	WA	Seattle	MoF	
C-121C(L-1049)	VA	Chantilly	NASMUVC	54-177
C-121D(EC)(L-1049)	CO	Colorado Sprs	PA&SM	52-3425
C-121D(EC)(L-1049)	OH	Dayton	NMUSAF	53-555, USAF

Super

Model	State	Location	Facility	Serial/Notes
C-121E(VC)(L-0749)	OH	Dayton	NMUSAF	53-7885, "Columbine III"
C-121K(EC)(L-1049)	CA	McClellan	McCelAFB	141309, 53-552
C-121K(EC)(WF-2)	FL	Pensacola	NMoNA	143221, VT 86
C-121K(EC)(L-1049)	GA	Pooler	MoF	141297, USAF Super
C-121K(EC)(L-1049)	IL	Rantoul	CAM	141311
C-121K(EC)(L-1049)	OK	Oklahomaoma	TAFB	137890
C-121T(EC)(L-1049)	AZ	Tucson	PAM	53-554, USAF
C-121T(EC)(L-1049)	CA	Chino	YAM	53-0548
C-121T(EC)(L-1049)	KS	Topeka	CAM	52-3418
C-121T(EC)(L-1049)	MO	Kansas City	AHM	N6937C

C-131 Fairchild Provider

Model	State	City	Org	Serial / Notes
C-123B	AZ	Tucson	PAM	55-4505
C-123J	AK	Ancho	KANGB	
C-123J	AK	Palme	MOAT&I	N98
C-123K	AZ	Tucson	PAM	54-580, N3142D, 731TAS, "War Wagon"
C-123K	AZ	Tucson	PAM	54-0659, N2129J
C-123K	CA	Atwater	CAM	54-512, Tail WX
C-123K	CA	Riverside	MFAM	54-612, "The Chief"
C-123K	CA	Rosamond	EAFB	54-683
C-123K	DE	Dover	DAFB	WM
C-123K	FL	Titusville	AAF	54-674
C-123K	FL	Titusville	AAF	54-603
C-123K(UC)	FL	FtWal	HF	55-533
C-123K	MN	Aonka	Airport	N681DG
C-123K	MN	Aonka, SEAC		54603, NX-4254H, #603, "Cat House"
C-123K	MN	Minneapolis	MAGM	
C-123K	NC	Fayet	FBADM	54-609
C-123K	NC	Fayet	PAFB	
C-123K	NJ	Trent	MGAFB	
C-123K	OH	Dayton	NMUSAF	56-4362
C-123K	PA	Beave	AHM	"Thunder Pig"
C-123K	TX	Abilene	DLAP	54-604 A
C-123K	TX	D Rio	LAFB	
C-123K	TX	San Antonio	LSAD	54-668
C-123K	UT	Ogden	HAFBM	54-610
C-123K(UC)	GA	Pooler	MoF	54-633

C-124 Douglas Globemaster

Model	State	City	Org	Serial / Notes
C-124A	DE	Dover	AMCM	49-0258
C-124C	AZ	Tucson	PAM	52-01004
C-124C	CA	Farfield	DA&SM	52-01000
C-124C	GA	Pooler	MoF	51-0089
C-124C	OH	Dayton	NMUSAF	51-1066
C-124C	SC	Charl	CAFB	52-1072
C-124C	UT	Ogden	HAFBM	52-0050
C-124C	WA	Tacoma	MAFB	52-0994, MATS

Model	State	City	Org	Serial / Notes
C-125A(YC)	AZ	Tucson	PAM	
C-125B(YC)	OH	Dayton	NMUSAF	
C-126A(LC)	CA	Farfield	DA&SM	
C-126A(LC)	IN	Indianapolis	AMHF	
C-126A(LC)	OH	Dayton	NMUSAF	
C-126A(LC)	TX	Denton	H10FM	
Northrop	OH	Raider		48-0636 N 2573B
Northrop	SC	Raider		48-622 N 2566B
Cessna		Businessliner		Model 195
Cessna		Businessliner		
Cessna		Businessliner		49-1949, Model 195

C-130 Lockheed Hercules

Model	State	City	Org	Serial / Notes
C-130 Fuse Only 2ea	LA	Alexandria		EAP
C-130	AR	Littl	LRAFB	
C-130	DE	Dove	AMCM	
C-130	GA	Colum	FB	
C-130	FL	Pensacola	NMoNA	149798
C-130	MN	Minne	MAGM	70485
C-130A	AZ	Tucson	PAM	57-457
C-130A	CA	Hemet	HAAB	
C-130A	VA	Chantilly	NASMUVC	
C-130A	IL	Rantoul	OCAM	55-0037, MA ANG
C-130A	MD	Ft Meade	NVP	60528, 60528
C-130A	MI	Mt Clemens	SMAM	57-0514
C-130A	TX	Abilene	DLAP	55-23

C-130

Designation	City	State	Facility	Serial / Notes
C-130A	Whichita Falls	TX	SAFB	54-1626
C-130A(AC)	Shalimar	FL	USAFAM	54-1630
C-130A(AC)	Dayton	OH	NMUSAF	55-14
C-130A(JC)	Dayton	OH	NMUSAF	57-0526
C-130A(YMC)	Pooler	GA	MoF	
C-130B(NC)	Ogden	UT	HAFBM	
C-130B Cockpit	Ogden	UT	HAFBM	
C-130D	Tucson	AZ	PAM	57-493
C-130E	Fayetteville	NC	FBADM	64-0525, POPE"
C-130E	Whichita Falls	TX	SAFB	
C-130H(YMC)	Pooler	GA	MoF	74-1686

C-131 Convair Samaritan

Designation	City	State	Facility	Serial / Notes
C-131	Farfield	CA	DA&SM	Model 340
C-131	Minne	MN	MAGM	54-757,
C-131D	Rapid City	SD	SDA&SM	55-0292, Model 340
C-131D	McClellan	CA	McCelAFB	54-2822, Model 340
C-131A(HC)	Littl	AR	LRAFB	Model 340
C-131A(HC)	Burli	VT	BANG	
C-131A(T-29A)	Chino	CA	PoFAM	Model 240
C-131A(T-29A)	Suitland	MD	PEGF	"Caroline" Model 240
C-131A(VC)(T-29A)	Tusco	AZ	HA	Allison Model 580
C-131B	Chino	CA	PoFAM	Model 340
C-131D	Dover	DE	DAFB	Model 340
C-131B	Shalimar	FL	USAFAM	Model 340
C-131D(VC) "samaritan"	Camarillo	CA	CAF-SCW	54-2809, N131CW,
C-131D	Riverside	CA	MFAM	54-2808
C-131D	Mt Clemens	MI	SMAM	52-0293, Model 340
C-131D	Dayton	OH	NMUSAF	55- 301 Model 340
C-131E	Ogden	UT	HAFBM	55-0300
C-131F(R4Y-1)	Lockb	OH	RANGB	55- 4751
C-131F(R4Y-1)	Tucson	AZ	PAM	141017
C-131F(R4Y-1)	Tucson	AZ	PAM	141025
C-131F(R4Y-2)	Chino	CA	YAM	
	Pensacola	FL	NMoNA	141015 615 Model 340

C-133

Designation	City	State	Facility	Serial / Notes
C-133A	Rantoul	IL	OCAM	Douglas Cargomaster, 56-2009
C-133A	Dayton	OH	NMUSAF	Douglas Cargomaster, 56-2008
C-133B	Tucson	AZ	PAM	Douglas Cargomaster, 59-0527
C-133B	Dover	DE	AMCMM	Douglas Cargomaster, 59-0536

C-135 Boeing Startotanker

Designation	City	State	Facility	Serial / Notes
C-135C(EC)-BN	Ashland	NE	SACM	63-8049
C-135 (EC)	Dayton	OH	NMUSAF	60-0374
C-135 (EC)	Rapid City	SD	SDA&SM	61-0262
C-135(EC)	Whichita Falls	TX	SAFB	Looking Glass
C-135J(EC)	Tucson	AZ	PAM	63-8057
C-135L(EC)	Peru	IN	GAFB	61-269, "Excalliber"
C-135(KC)	Belle	IL	SAFB	
C-135(KC)	Barksdale AFB	LA	BAFB	
C-135(KC)	Offut	NE	OAFB	10287
C-135(KC)	Oklahoma	OK	TAFB	
C-135A(KC)	Rosamond	CA	EAFB	
C-135A(KC)	Atwater	CA	CAM	55-3139
C-135A(KC)	Riverside	CA	MFAM	55-3130, "Old Grandad"
C-135A(NKC)	Abilene	TX	DLAP	56-3639
C-135E(KC)	Dayton	OH	NMUSAF	55-3123
	Wichita	KS	KAM	

C-137

Designation	City	State	Facility	Serial / Notes
C-137B(VC)	Tucson	AZ	PAM	Boeing, Air Force One, 58-6971, "Freedom One"
C-137B(VC)	Dayton	OH	NMUSAF	Boeing, Air Force One, 62-6000

Designation	State	City	Museum	Mfr	Name	Serial / Notes
C-137B(VC)	WA	Seattle	MoF	Boeing	Air Force One	58-6970, 1958

C-140 Lockheed Jetstar

Designation	State	City	Museum	Serial / Notes
C-140	IL	Belle	SAFB	
C-140((1329-8))	NS	Bedford	ACAM	
C-140	ON-C	Ottaw	CAM	
C-140	UT	Ogden	HAFBM	
C-140	WA	Seattle	MoF	
C-140 NASA	CA	Palmdale	PPHP	N814NA
C-140(VC)	GA	Pooler	MoF	61-2488
C-140(VC)	IL	Belle	SAFB	
C-140A	CA	Farfield	DA&SM	
C-140A	CA	Rosamond	EAFB	59-5962
C-140B(VC)	AZ	Tucson	PAM	61-2489
C-140B(VC)	OH	Dayton	NMUSAF	61-2492
C-140B	UT	Ogden	HAM	62-4201

C-141 Lockheed Starlifter

Designation	State	City	Museum	Serial / Notes
C-141	IL	Belle	SAFB	
C-141	CA	Riverside	MFAM	65-0257
C-141B(NC)	CA	Rosamond	EAFB	65-0257
C-141A	DE	Dover	DAFB	
C-141B	DE	Dover	DAFB	
C-141B	GA	Pooler	MoF	66-0180A
C-141C	OH	Dayton	NMUSAF	66-0177

Designation	State	City	Museum	Mfr	Name	Serial / Notes
C-142A(XC)	OH	Dayton	NMUSAF		VSTOL	65-5924
C-144(CX)	MB-C	Winnipeg	CFB			144612
C6N1-S	MD	Suitland	PEGF	Nakajima	Myrt (Saiun)	
CA-61 Mini-Ace	WI	Oshkosh	EAAAAM	Cvjetkovic	Mini-Ace	N94283
Callair A-2	MN	Blaine	GWFM	Callair	Callair	
Callair	WY	Afton	CAM	Callair	Callair	
CAM 3	WA	Seattle	MoF	Swallow-Stearman		
Canard Quickie	PA	Phila	FI	Canard	Quickie	
Cangley Aerodome	VA	Hampton	VA&SC	Cangley	Aerodome	
Cap 231	FL	Polk	FoF	Cap	Cap	
Caproni CA 20	WA	Seattle	MoF	Caproni		1
Caquot Type R Balloon	OH	Dayton	NMUSAF	Caquot	Observation	
Caravelle VI-R	CT	Winds	NEAM	Caravelle	Sud	
CASA Saeta	NY	New Windsor	RSAM	CASA	Trainer	
Casade 180B	MD	Suitland	PEGF	Casade	Kasperwing	
Casade 180B	WA	Seattle	MoF	Casade	Kasperwing	
Cassutt B Special	NY	Garde	CoAM	Cassutt	B Special	
Caudron 276	AL	Gunte	LGARFM	Caudron	Model 276	
Caudron G.III	NY	Rhine	ORA	Caudron	France	Biplane
Caudron G.IV	VA	Chantilly	NASMUVC	Caudron	France	2 Engine Bomber WWI
Cavalier	NY	Ghent	POMAM	Star	Cavalier	
Cavalier	OK	Oklahoma	OSM	Star	Cavalier	

Type	State	City	Museum	Notes
Cavalier Model B	PA	Winoma	WTI	
Cavalier Model E	PA	Winoma	WTI	
Cayley Glider	CA	SLoui	SLDPA	
Cayley Glider	ME	Ft Worth	VFM	
CBY-3 Burnelli	CT	Tucson	PAM	
CCW-1	MD	SBluf	MAAM	
CCW-5	PA	Rantoul	OCAM	
Cessna	MN	Winoma	WTI	N6766S
Cessna	MN	Winoma	WTI	N15153
Cessna	MO	SLoui	SLDPA	
Cessna 02	TX	Ft Worth	VFM	02
Cessna 120	AZ	Tucson	PAM	Model 120, NC4191N
Cessna 120	IA	SBluf	MAAM	Model 120
Cessna 120	IL	Rantoul	OCAM	Model 120, NC2660N
Cessna 120	KS	Liberal	MAAM	Model 120
Cessna 120	NC	Henders	WNCAM	Model 120
Cessna 120	OK	Fredi	AAM	Model 120
Cessna 140	CA	Modesto	HAM	Model 140
Cessna 140	KS	Liberal	MAAM	Model 140
Cessna 140	NY	Bayport	BA	Model 140
Cessna 140A	NM	St Teresa	WEAM	Model 140A
Cessna 145	KS	Liberal	MAAM	Airmaster, NC32450
Cessna 150H	KY	Lexington	AMoK	Commuter, N6598S
Cessna 150H	WI	Oshkosh	EAAAAM	Commuter, N23107
Cessna 150K	WI	Oshkosh	EAAAAM	Commuter, N5799G
Cessna 150L	AZ	Tucson	PAM	Commuter, N18588
Cessna 150L	MD	Suitland	PEGF	Commuter
Cessna 150M	PA	Readi	MAAM	Commuter, N714GR
Cessna 165	KS	Liberal	MAAM	Airmaster
Cessna 172	AR	Pine Bluff	REAA	Skylane
Cessna 172	FL	Dayton	ERAU	Skylane
Cessna 172	NV	LasVe	MIAHM	Skylane, N9712B, "Hacienda"
Cessna 172H	CA	Inglewood	PBR	Skylane
Cessna 172Q	PA	Reading	MAAM	Skylane
Cessna 172	FL	Dayton	ERAU	Skylane
Cessna 175(T-41B)	OK	Fredi	AAM	Mescalero, 67-15140

Type	State	City	Museum	Notes
Star				Cavalier
Star				Cavalier
Cayley				Glider
Cayley				Glider
Burnelli				
Custer				Channel Wing
Custer				Channel Wing
Cessna 175(T-41B)	KS	Liberal	MAAM	Mescalero
Cessna 175(T-41B)	FL	Clear	FMAM	Mescalero
Cessna 175(T-41B)	OK	FtSil	USAFAM	Mescalero
Cessna 180	CA	Hayward	VAM	Model 180
Cessna 180	GA	Woodstock	NGWS	Model 180
Cessna 180	VA	Chantilly		Chantilly, NASMUVC, Model 180, "Spirit of Columbus"
Cessna 180	OR	Tillamook	TAM	Model 180
Cessna 180F	FL	Pensacola	NMoNA	Model 180F, N 2146Z, 18051246
Cessna 182RG	FL	Dayton	ERAU	Model 182RG
Cessna 182	AR	Pine Bluff	REAA	Model 182
Cessna 182	GA	Woodstock	NGWS	Model 182
Cessna 182P	OH	Cleveland	FCAAM	Model 182P, N20920
Cessna 185	PA	Tough	CFCM	Model 185
Cessna 195	KS	Liberal	MAAM	Businessliner
Cessna 195A	KS	Liberal	MAAM	Businessliner
Cessna 195A	ND	Minot	DTAM	Businessliner
Cessna 195A	OK	Fredi	AAM	Businessliner
Cessna 195A	PA	Bethel	GAAM	Businessliner, N195PD
Cessna 206	KS	Wichita	KAM	Model 206
Cessna 206	MI	Belle	AFDSC	Model 206
Cessna 210	CA	Chino	PoF	Model 210
Cessna 303	FL	Dayton	ERAU	Model 303
Cessna 310	AL	Birmingham	SMF	Blue Canoe
Cessna 310F(U-3)	AZ	Tucson	PAM	PAM, Blue Canoe N182Z, U-3, L-27
Cessna 310F(U-3)	KS	Wichita	KAM	Blue Canoe U-3, L-27
Cessna 310 (U-3)	MO	SLoui	SLUPC	Blue Canoe U-3, L-27
Cessna 310 (U-3)	OK	Fredi	AAM	Blue Canoe U-3, L-27
Cessna 320	MO	SLoui	SLUPC	Blue Canoe U-3, L-27
Cessna 401	PA	Beaver Falls	AHM	Skynight

Cessna C-402 NV, Las Vegas, LBAHSM, N59SA, Fuse Only, "Scenic Airlines" Model AW 167 N8782

Cessna AW CA Chino YAM Model AW 167

Type	State	City	Museum	Serial		Type	State	City	Museum	Serial
CF-CPY	YT-C	W Hors	WA							
CG-15A	NC	Charl	CHAC	Waco						
CG-2	CA	El Cajon	SDAMGF	Cessna	Primary Glider					
CG-2	WI	Oshkosh	EAAAAM	Cessna	Primary Glider 1				86, V	
CG-2A	WA	Seattle	MoF	Cessna	Primary Glider 1				50, N178V	

CG-4 Waco Hadrian

Type	State	City	Museum	Serial		Type	State	City	Museum	Serial
CG-4	NY	Garde	CoAM	15574		CG-4A	MI	Kalamazoo	KAHM	45-15965
CG-4A	AZ	Tucson	PAM	45-14647		CG-4A	MI	Oscoda	YAF	45-15073
CG-4A	CA	Atwater	CAM			CG-4A	NC	Fayetteville	A&SOM	
CG-4A	CA	Chino	YAM	45-13696		CG-4A	NJ	Farfield	YAFDCWA	
CG-4A	CT	Washi	TFC			CG-4A	NY	Elmir	NSM	
CG-4A	DE	Dover	DAFB			CG-4A	OH	Dayton	NMUSAF	527948, 42-43734
CG-4A	GA	Ft Benning	AFBNIM			CG-4A	OR	Hood	W AAAM	
CG-4A Nose	IN	Columbus	ABAM			CG-4A	OR	Hubbard	LC	
CG-4A	MI	Belleville	YAF			CG-4A	TX	Lubbock	SWM	
CG-4A	MI	Greenville	FFMM	43-40833		CG-15A	NC	Charlotte	CAM	
						CG-15A	NC	Fayetteville	FBADM	45-5276A

Type	State	City	Museum		Type
CH-135	ONT - C	Ottawa	CAM	Bell	
CH-136	ON-C	Kingston	CFBK		
CH-136	ON-C	Ottawa	CWM		
CH-136	ON-C	Trenton	RCAFMM		
CH-300	ON-C	Ottaw	CAM	Zenair	Tri-Zenith

Chanute Glider

Type	State	City	Museum		Type	State	City	Museum
Chanute Glider	BC-C	Sidne	BCAM		Chanute Glider	ME	Owls Head	OHTM
Chanute Glider	CA	Chino	PoFAM		Chanute Glider	NY	Hammond	CM
Chanute Glider	CT	Winds	NEAM		Chanute Glider	NY	Rhine	ORA
Chanute Glider	GA	Pooler	MoF		Chanute Glider	WA	Seattle	MoF
Chanute Glider	IN	LaPorte	LCHSM		Chanute Glider	WI	Oshkosh	EAAAAM

Type	State	City	Museum		Type		Serial
Chester Special	OH	Cleveland	FCAAM	Chester	Special Racer		NX-93-Y-Goon
Chester Special	WI	Oshkosh	EAAAAM	Chester	Special Racer		N12930, "Jeep"
Chief Oshkosh							

Designation index

Designation	State	Location	Museum
Chris-Tena	OR	Tillamook	
Christen Eagle			
Christen Eagle	CA	San Carlos	HNCAVM
Christen Eagle	CO	Denver	WOTR
Christen Eagle II	MI	Kalamazoo	KAM
Christen Eagle	TX	Addison	CFM
Christen Eagle1	WI	Oshkosh	EAAAAM
Circa 1920	WI	Poplar Grove	VW&W
Cirrus 2	VA	Richmond	VAM
Cirrus 3	OK	Oklahoma	OSM
CJ6A	FL	Miami	WOM
CL-28(CP-107)	ON-C	Ottaw	CAM
CL-28(CP-107)	ON-C	MtVie	MVRCAF
CL-28(CP-107)	ON-C	Trenton	RCAFMM
CL-28(CP-107)	PE-C	Summe	PEIHAS
CL-28(CP-107) Mk I	NS	Greenwood	GMAM
CL-28(CP-107)	NS	Halifax	ACAM
CL-84	MB-C	Winni	WCAM
CL-84	ON-C	Ottaw	CAM
CL-215	ON-C	Sault Ste Marie CBHC	Canadair
CL-475	AL	Ozark	USAAM
Clark Bi Wing	ME	Owls Head	OHTM
Clement-Bayard Demoiselle	IN	LaPorte	LaPorte
Clemson Plane	SC	Colum	SCSM
Cloud Cutter	OK	Oklahoma	OSM
CM-170R	TX	Brownsville	BIA
CM-170	WA	Everett	MoF
CMQ-10A	CO	Pueblo	PWAM
CNA-40	PA	Readi	MAAM
Coffman Glider	TX	Lubbock	SWM
Collins Aerofoil Boat	OK	Oklahoma	OSM
Colt	WI	Oshkosh	EAAAAM
Comet Glider	MN	Winoma	WTI
Command-Aire 5-C-3	CA	LAnge	CMoS&I
Command-Aire 5-C-3	AR	Little Rock	AEC
Command-Aire 5-C-3	OR	Hood	WAAAM

Name / Model index (Mini-Coupe group)

Name	State	Location	Museum	Model	Reg./Notes
Christen Eagle1	WI	Oshkosh	EAAAAM		
Christen Eagle II	WI	Oshkosh	EAAAAM		
Christen Eagle III	OR	Mc Minnville	EAM		
Christen Eagle 1F	WI	Oshkosh	EAAAAM		
Circa					
Cirrus				Cirrus 3	
Electra					
Canadair				Argus Mk.1	10742
Canadair				Argus Mk.1	
Canadair				Argus Mk.1	10732
Canadair				Argus Mk.1	20739
Canadair				Argus	10717, 732
Canadair				Argus	
Canadair				Dynavert	
Canadair				Dynavert	CX8402, Twin Engine 1970
Water Bomber				F-ZBBT	56-4320, N6940C
Lockheed				Rigid Rotor	
Clark				Bi Wing	
LCHSM				Clement-Bayard	Demoiselle
Clemson					
Cloud				Cutter	N157CK
Fouga				Magister	N405DM, pVM 3362
Fouga				Magister	N505DM
Boeing				Bomarc	56-4029
Health				Midwing	
Coffman				Glider	
Coffman				Monoplane	N569E
Collins				Aerofoil	
Comet				Colt	N1985AP
Command-Aire				Glider	
Command-Aire					

Aircraft	ST	City	Museum	Notes
Command-Aire	FL	Lakel	SFAF	
Commonwealth	NY	Garde	CoAM	
Commonwealth 185	PA	Readi	MAAM	
Continental R670	NY	River	TFAC	
Convair 240 (see also C-131)				
Convair 240	CA	Chino	PoF	
Convair 240	CT	Hartford	PLoA	
Convair 240 (T-29)	CA	Tulare	AD	
Convair 240	MD	Suitland	PEGF	
Corben Super Ace	OH	Dayton	NMUSAF	
Corben Super Ace	WI	Madison	MTFMDCRA	
Corben Jr. Ace	NC	Hende	WNCAM	N28LW
Corben C-1	WI	Oshkosh	EAAAAM	N9050C, "Box Full"
Corben D	WA	Port Twonsend	PTAM	1, N49A
Covertawings A	NY	Garde	CoAM	
Co-Z Corp	WI	Oshkosh	EAAAAM	
CP-40	IA	Ottumwa	APM	
CP-65	FL	Lakeland	SNFAM	
CQM-10A	FL	FtWal	CityPark	
CR-4	VA	Marti		
Cranwell CLA4	AB-C	Edmonton	AAM	
Cricket	OK	Oklahoma	OSM	
Cricket MC-10	FL	Lakeland	SNF	
Cricket NC-2	CA	Chino	PoFAM	
Crosley	KY	Lexington	AVoK	
Crosley CR-4	WI	Oshkosh	EAAAAM	
Crowley Hydro-Air	MD	Suitland	PEGF	
CT-114	AB-C	Nanton	NLS	
CT-114	BC-C	langley	CMoF&T	
CT-114	ON-C	Ottawa	CAM	
CT-114	ON-C	Toronto	TAM	
CT-114	ON-C	Trenton	RCAFMM	
CT-114	SK-C	Moose Jaw	WDM	

Make	Model	ST	City	Notes
Command-Aire	Skyranger			N345JA, "Little Rocket"
Commonwealth				N92972
Commonwealth				N93248
Continental				
Convair 340		TX	Ladero	Airport
Convair 440 (2ea)		TX	Ladero	Airport
Convair 880		NV	Las Vegas	LB, Golden Arrow, 23, N817TW,
Convair Airliner		TX	FtWorth	VFM
Convair Airliner		TX	FtWorth	VFM
Corben D		WI	Oshkosh	EAAAAM
Corben Jr. Ace		CT	Winds	NEAM
Corben Jr. Ace		TX	Bealt	FCA
Corben Jr. Ace		VA	Bealt	FCA
Convertawings		WI	Oshkosh	N63N
Co-Z Development Corp				Co-Z
Porterfield				529, NC18743
Porterfield	Collegiate			
Crosby				
Cranwell				
Cricket	MC-10			N32236
Cricket	Kid Display			
Crosley	Moonbeam			#4, NX147N
Crosley	CR-4			
Crowley	Hydro-Air			
Canadair	Tutor			
Canadair	Tutor			
Canadair	Tutor			
Canadair	Tutor			
Canadair	Tutor			114021
Canadair	Tutor			

Culver (Also See PQ-14)

Aircraft	State	Location	Museum
Culver Cadet	AL	Birmingham	SMF
Culver Cadet	CA	Santa Martin	WoHAM
Culver Cadet LCA	IA	Ottumwa	APM 443, N-41725
Culver Dart	CO	Lafayette	SoFC
Culver Dart	MN	Stewa	CCC
Culver Dart	MO	HARM	CCC
Culver Dart	TX	Dallas	FoF
Culver V Cadet	KS	Liberal	MAAM
Culver V Cadet	OK	Fredi	AAM

Aircraft	State	Location	Museum
Cumulus Glider	AL	Birmingham	SmoF
Cumulus Glider			

Curtiss

Aircraft	State	Location	Museum
Curtiss A-1 Triad	NE	Minde	HWPV
Curtiss A-1 Triad	CA	San Diego	SDAM
Curtiss Canuck	VA	Chantilly	NASMUVH
Curtiss Canuck	MI	Dearb	HFM
Curtiss Canuck	TX	Kingsbury	VAHF
Curtiss E Boat	MD	Suitland	PEGF
Curtiss E-8.75	WI	Oshkosh	EAAAAM, N24034, "Sweetheart"
Curtiss H America	NY	River	TFAC
Curtiss J6-7	NY	River	TFAC
Curtiss June Bug Rep	NY	Hammond	CM
Curtiss Junior	AR	Fayet	AAM
Curtiss Junior	OR	Hood	WAAAM
Curtiss Junior Teal	NV	Carso	YF
Curtiss Little Looper	CA	San Diego	SDAM N5599N
Curtiss MF Seagull	OH	Cleve	FCAAM
Curtiss MFSeagull	ON-C	Ottaw	CAM
Curtiss Monoplane 1912	AL	Birmi	Southe
Curtiss N-9	NE	Minde	HWPV
Curtiss N-9	NY	River	TFAC
Curtiss N2C Fledgling	NY	Rhine	ORA
Curtiss NC-4	FL	Pensacola	NMoNA A 2294 4
Curtiss Oriole	MN	Minne	MAGM
Curtiss Oriole	NY	Hammond	CM
Curtiss Pusher D	CA	Chino	PoF
Curtiss Pusher D	CA	San Carlos	HNCAVM
Curtiss Pusher D	DC	Washi	NA&SM
Curtiss Pusher D	IA	Des M	ISHD
Curtiss Pusher D	IL	Chica	MoS&I
Curtiss Pusher D	KS	Topek	KSHS
Curtiss Pusher D	ME	Owls Head	OHTM
Curtiss Pusher D	MI	Kalamazoo	AZ
Curtiss Pusher D	NY	Hammond	CM
Curtiss Pusher D	NY	NYC	ISASM
Curtiss Pusher D	NY	Rhine	ORA
Curtiss Pusher D III	ND	Fargo	BUSAHM
Curtiss Pusher D	OH	Dayton	NMUSAF
Curtiss Pusher D	OK	Oklahoma	AM
Curtiss Pusher D	OK	Oklahoma	OSM
Curtiss Pusher D	OK	Weatherford	SA&SC
Curtiss Pusher D	OR	Mc Minnville	EAM
Curtiss Pusher D	OR	Hood	WAAAM
Curtiss Pusher D	OR	Hood	WAAAM Project
Curtiss Pusher D	SC	MtPleasant	PN&MM
Curtiss Pusher D	WA	Vancouver	PAM
Curtiss Pusher D	WI	Milwa	MGoF
Curtiss Pusher D	WI	Oshkosh	EAAAAM N 37864
Curtiss Pusher D-5	AL	Birmingham	SMoF
Curtiss Robin	AK	Ancho	AAHM
Curtiss Robin	AZ	Grand Canyon	PoFGCVA
Curtiss Robin	CA	Oakland	OWAPM
Curtiss Robin	IA	Greenfield	IAM 6
Curtiss Robin	ID	Athol	NAM
Curtiss Robin	MO	Maryland Hts	HARM
Curtiss Robin	NV	Niagra Falls	NAM
Curtiss Robin	NV	Carso	YF
Curtiss Robin	NY	Bayport	BA
Curtiss Robin	NY	Hammond	CM
Curtiss Robin	OR	Hood	WAAAM

Type	State	Location	Museum	Model/Name	Notes
Curtiss Robin J-1D	VA	Sands, VAM	733, "Ole Miss", NC532N		
Curtiss Robin 4C-1A	NC	Hende	WNCAM		NC563N
Curtiss Robin B	FL	Delan	OHA		
Curtiss Robin B1	CA	San Diego	SDAM		N9265
Curtiss Robin B2	WI	Oshkosh	EAAAAM		N50H
Curtiss Robin C1	CA	Chino	YAM		538, N384K
Curtiss Robin C1	WA	Seattle	MoF		628, N979K
Curtiss Robin C2	CA	Chino	YAM		
Curtiss Robin J2	CA	Chino	YAM		
Curtiss Robin J1	NY	Niagara Falls	NAM		
Curtiss Robin 50C	NY	Garden	CoAM		
Curtiss CW-1 Junior	CA	San Diego	SDAM		
Curtiss CW-1 Junior	KS	Liberal	MAAM		NC11850
Curtiss CW-1 Junior	MD	Suitland	PEGF		
Curtiss CW-1 Junior	NY	Mayvi	DA		
Curtiss CW-1 Junior	NY	Rhine	ORA		
Curtiss CW-1 Junior	OK	Fredi	AAM		
Curtiss CW-1 Junior	WA	Port Townsend	PTAM		N11809
Curtiss CW A-14D Speedwing	VA	Sandston	VAM		2009, N12329
Curtiss CW A-22 Falcon	OR	Mc Minnville	EAM		A22-1, N500G
Curtiss CW X-100 Robin	MD	Suitland	PEGF		
Curtiss CW-15 Sedan	MO	Maryland Hts	Harm		
Curtiss CW 15-C Sedan	AZ	Tucson, PAM	Man Sn 15C-2211. NC12302		
Curtiss CW 15-D Sedan	OR	Mc Minnville	EAM		15-D-2214, N12314
Curtiss Travel Air 12-W	OR	Hood	WAAM		
Czerwinski/Shenstone	ON-C	Ottawa	CAM	Harbinger	C-FZCS
D4Y	AZ	Grand Canyon	PoFGCVA	Judy	
D-21	AZ	Tucson	PAM	Mini Blackbird	Drone, 3, Carried By Blackbird
D-21	CA	Palmd	PAFB	Mini Blackbird	Drone
D-21	CA	Rosamond	EAFB	Mini Blackbird	Drone
D-21	GA	Pooler	MoF	Mini Blackbird	Drone
D-21	OH	Dayton	NMUSAF	Mini Blackbird	Drone
D-21B	WA	Seattle	MoF	Mini Blackbird	90-0510 Drone
D-25	NY	Rhine	ORA	New Standard	
D-25	OH	Chard	CA	New Standard	
D-558-1(H-76)	FL	Pensacola	NMoNA	Skystreak	37970
D-588-1	NC	Charlotte	CAM	Skyrocket	37972
D-558-2	CA	Chino	PoFAM	Skyrocket	
D-558-2	CA	Lancaster	AVC	Skyrocket	#3 Bu 37975
D-558-2	CT	Winds	NEAM	Skyrocket	
D-588-2	DC	Washi	NA&SM	Skyrocket	
D.H. 1	OR	Mc Minnville	EAM		
D.H. 1A5	AL	Ozark	USAAM	Whirlymite	2
D.H. 2	CA	San Diego	SDAM	1915 Pusher	N32DH
D.H. 2	ID	Athol	NAM	1915 Pusher	
D.H. 4	DC	Washi	NA&SM	1915 Pusher	
D.H. 4	DC	Washi	USPM	1915 Pusher	
D.H. 4B	OH	Cleve	FCAAM	1915 Pusher	

Model	State	City	Reg.	Museum	Mfr.	Model / Type	State	City	Museum	Reg.
D.H. 4 Rep	VA	Triangle		NMMC	de Havilland	1915 Pusher				6424, N888WA, N6424
D.H. 4C	WA	Everett		MoF	de Havilland	Comet				
D.H. 4M-1	OR	Mc Minnville		EAM	de Havilland	ET-4, N3258				
D.H. 4M	WA	Seattle		MoF	de Havilland	1915 Pusher				
D.H. 5	AL	Gunte		LGARFM	de Havilland	1915 Pusher				
D.H. 53	SK-C	MJaw		WDM	de Havilland	Hummingbird				CF-OVE
D.H. 60 de Havilland Gipsy Moth										
D.H. 60	AB-C	Edmonton		AAM	de Havilland	D.H. 60	ON-C	Ottaw	CAM	G-CAUA
D.H. 60	AB-C	Wetas		RM	de Havilland	D.H. 60GM	AB-C	Wetas	RM	N 917M
D.H. 60	CA	Chino		YAM	de Havilland	D.H. 60GM	CA	San Diego	SDAM	
D.H. 60	MT	Helen	N617Y	MHSM	de Havilland	D.H. 60M	SK-C	MJaw	WDM	CF-ADI Trainer
D.H. 61	TX	Brown		RGVW-CAF	de Havilland	Super Moth				
D.H. 80A	NY	Rhine		ORA	de Havilland	Puss Moth				
D.H. 80A	ON-C	Ottaw		CAM	de Havilland	Puss Moth				CF-PEI
D.H. 82 de Havilland Tiger Moth										
D.H. 82	AB-C	Edmonton		AAM	de Havilland	D.H. 82A	TX	Galveston	LSFM	T7467, N9714
D.H. 82	AR	Fayetteville		OMM	de Havilland	D.H. 82A	WI	Oshkosh	EAAAAM	N16645, CF-IVO
D.H. 82	FL	Miami		WOM	de Havilland	D.H. 82B	VA	Suffolk	FF	
D.H. 82	NM	St Teresa		WEAM	de Havilland	D.H. 82C	WA	Port Townsend	PTAM	V4760, N2726A
D.H. 82	NF-C	Gander	CF-GPE	NAAM	de Havilland	D.H. 82C Fuse	AB-C	Calga	AMoC	
D.H. 82	NY	Bayport		BA	de Havilland	D.H. 82C	AB-C	Nanton	NLSAM	
D.H. 82	OH	Dayton	N-39DH	NMUSAF	de Havilland	D.H. 82C	AB-C	Wetas	RM	
D.H. 82	ON-C	Dunnville		RCAFDA	de Havilland	D.H. 82C	BC-C	Langley	CMoF	C1178, RCAF5875, C-GFT
D.H. 82	ON-C	Tillsonburg	5030	CHAA	de Havilland	D.H. 82C	IA	Greenfield	IAM	Canadian
D.H. 82	TX	Addison	R5130	CFM	de Havilland	D.H. 82C	MB-C	Brand	CATPM	
D.H. 82	TX	Dallas		FoF	de Havilland	D.H. 82C	MB-C	Winni	WCAM	
D.H. 82	TX	Gilmer		PotP	de Havilland	D.H. 82C	ME	Owls Head	OHTM	
D.H. 82	WA	Vanco		PAM	de Havilland	D.H. 82C	ON-C	Hamilton	CWH	C-GCWT, 8922
D.H. 82A	IA	Greenfield	Australian	IAM	de Havilland	D.H. 82C	ON-C	Ottaw	CAM	4861
D.H. 82A	ON-C	Collingwood	86508, C-GSTP	CCAF	de Havilland	D.H. 82C	ON-C	Ottaw	VWoC	
D.H. 82A	PA	Toughkenamon	N4808	CFCM	de Havilland	D.H. 82C	SK-C	MJaw	WDM	C-GYCU
D.H. 83C	NT-C	Yellowknife		PWNHC	de Havilland	Fox Moth				
D.H. 83C	ON-C	Ottawa		CAM	de Havilland	Fox Moth				CF-DJB

D.H. 83C ON-C S Ste Marie CBHC de Havilland Fox Moth CF-BNO Replica
D.H. 88 Rep CA Santa Martin WoHAM de Havilland Comet

D.H. 89 de Havilland Dragon Rapide
D.H. 89 AB-C Edmonton AAM
D.H. 89 CA Hayward VAM
D.H. 89 MO Maryland Hts HARM
D.H. 89 ON-C S Ste Marie CBHC 697, C-FAYE
D.H. 89A Mk.IV WI Oshkosh EAAAAM N683DH
D.H. 89B OH Dayton NMUSAF NR695

D.H. 94 TX Brown CAF-RVGW de Havilland Minor Moth N940H
D.H. 94 TX Brown CAFRGVW de Havilland Moth Minor

D.H. 98 de Havilland Mosquito
D.H. 98 AB-C Calga AMoC
D.H. 98 Mk B35 AB-C Edmonton AAM CF-HMQ, VP-189
D.H. 98 FL Polk FoF
D.H. 98 OH Dayton NMUSAF RS709
D.H. 98 ON-C Ottaw CAM KB336
D.H. 98 ON-C Windsor CAHS
D.H. 98 Mk.35 VA Chantilly NASMUVC
D.H. 98 VA Suffolk FF
D.H. 98 Mk.35 WI Oshkosh EAAAAM

D.H. Menasco Moth ON-C Ottawa CAM de Havilland Moth 4861

D.H. U-6 de Havilland Beaver
D.H. U-6 CA SanLu CSLO
D.H. U-6 MB-C Winni WCAM
D.H. U-6A CA Atwater CAM
D.H. U-6A CA Rosamond EAFB 53-2781
D.H. U-6A CO Denve JWDAS
D.H. U-6A CT Winds NEAM 57-2570
D.H. U-6A MO SLoui SLDPA
D.H. U-6A OH Dayton NMUSAF 51-16501
D.H. U-6A ON-C Ottaw CAM CF-FHB
D.H. U-6A ON-C Ottaw CAM
D.H. U-6A ON-C Sault Ste Marie CBHC CF-PSM
D.H. U-6A(L-10) VA FtEus USATM 58-1997
D.H U-6A GA Pooler MoF 26087
D.H U-6A OH Dayton NMUSAF 51-16501
D.H. U-6A(L-20A) AZ Tucson PAM, 55-4595, N43906
D.H. U-6A(YU) AL Ozark USAAM 51-6263
D.H. U-6A6D(L-20A) GA Pooler MoF, 52-6087, N30AR
D.H U-6A(L-20A) OK Oklahoma 45IDM 56-0367
D.H U-6A(L-20A) CA Atwater CAM
D.H U-6A(L-20A) FL Clear FMAM
D.H U-6A(L-20A) PA Readi MAAM, 52- 6112, N4957

D.H.100 de Havilland Vampire
D.H.100 AB-C Calga AMoC
D.H.100 AB-C Edmonton AAM
D.H.100 AB-C Lazo CAFM
D.H.100 Mk 3 BC-C, Langley, CMoF, EEP42376, N6860D, RCAF17058
D.H.100 FL Kissi FTWAM
D.H.100 MB-C Winni WCAM
D.H.100 ON-C Hamilton CWH
D.H.100 OR Mc Minnville EAM, 1B-1686, N174LA
D.H.100 WA Seattle MoF, FLDH1367, N25776
D.H.100 Mk 35 WI Oshkosh EAAAAM N11926
D.H.100 Mk III AZ Grand PoFGCVA 17018

de Havilland aircraft index

Index by designation

Designation	St	City	Collection	Serial
D.H.100 Mk VI	CA	Chino	PoFAM	18
D.H.100 Mk. VI F.1	ON-C	Ottaw	CAM	TG372
D.H. 104	PA	Reading	MAAM	
D.H. 104	TX	Slaton	TAM	

D.H.C. 1 de Havilland Chipmunk

Designation	St	City	Collection	Serial
D.H.C. 1	AB-C	Wetas	RM	
D.H.C. 1	AZ	Tucson	PAM	N48273
D.H.C. 1	BC-C	Sidney	BCAM	
D.H.C. 1	KS	Ashla	HKAM	
D.H.C. 1	ON-C	Hamilton	CWH	B-2-S5, 035
D.H.C. 1	ON-C	Windsor	CAHS	
D.H.C. 2	ON-C	Ottawa	CAM	
D.H.C. 2 Mk.I	ON-C	Sault Ste Marie	CBHC	
D.H.C. 2 Mk.II	ON-C	Sault Ste Marie	CBHC	
D.H.C. 2 Mk.II	ON-C	Sault Ste Marie	CBHC	
D.H.C. 3	MB-C	Winni	WCAM	
D.H.C. 3	ON-C	Ottaw	CAM	
D.H.C. 3	ON-C	Sault Ste Marie	CBHC	
D.H.C. 3(U-1)NU-1B	FL	Pensacola	NMoNA	
D.H.C. 3(U-1A)	AL	Ozark	USAAM	
D.H.C. 3(U-1A)	VA	FtEus	USATM	
D.H.C. 5	ON-C	MtVie	MVRCAF	
D.H.C. 6	MT	Misso	AFDSC	
D.H.C. 6	OH	N Canton	MAM	
D.H.C. 6	ON-C	Ottaw	CAM	
D.H.C. 6-300	CA	Carls	CAJM	
D.H.C. 7	ON-C	Ottawa	CAM	
D-1K	OR	Hood	WAAM	
DA-1W	FL	Miami	WOM	
DA-1W	IN	Richmond	WCHM	
DA-1W	NY	Rhine	ORA	
DA-2	AL	Birmingham	SMF	
Daedalus 88	MD	Suitland	PEGF	
Daphne 1	TX	Ft Worth	VFM	

Index by name / manufacturer

Designation	Mfr	Name	St	City	Collection	Registration
D.H.100 Mk. VI F.3			ON-C	Ottaw	CAM	17074, AAP
	de Havilland	Dove				
	de Havilland	Dove				
D.H.C. 1	de Havilland		PA	Tough	CFCM	
D.H.C. 1	de Havilland		VA	Suffolk	FF	
D.H.C. 1A	de Havilland		VA	Chantilly	NASMUVC	
D.H.C. 1B2	de Havilland		ON-C	Ottaw	CAM	18070, CF-CIA
D.H.C. 1B-2	de Havilland		ON-C	Trenton	RCAFMM	
D.H.C. 1B2	de Havilland		WI	Oshkosh	EAAAAM	N 1114V
	de Havilland	Beaver				CF-FHB
	de Havilland	Beaver				2, CF-OBS
	de Havilland	Beaver				1650TB28, C-FOEK
	de Havilland	Beaver				1525TB1, C-FPSM
	de Havilland	Otter				9408
	de Havilland	Otter				369, C-FODU
	de Havilland	Otter				3824, 144672, F 699
	de Havilland	Otter				57-6135
	de Havilland	Otter				55-3270
	de Havilland	Otter				
	de Havilland	Buffalo				
	de Havilland	Twin Otter				
	de Havilland	Twin Otter				
	de Havilland	Twin Otter				CF-DHCX
	de Havilland	Twin Otter				
	de Havilland	Dash 7				C-GNBX
	Davis					
	Davis					
	Davis					
	Davis					
	Davis					
	Daedalus					
	Daphne					

Model	State	City	Museum	Registration / Notes
Dart	OH	Dayton	NMUSAF	Aerial Target
D.A.S.H.	SC	MtPleasant	PPM	Drone Anti Sub Helio
DC-2	WA	Seattle	MoF	Dakota — 1368, N1934D

DC-3 Douglas Dakota (See C-47)

Model	State	City	Museum	Registration / Notes
DC-3	AB-C	Calga	AMoC	
DC-3	AB-C	Harbor Grace	City	
DC-3	AL	Troy	TMA	
DC-3	BC-C	Langley	CMoF, CF-PWH, "Spirit of Skeena"	
DC-3	CA	Ames	BA	
DC-3	CA	Chino	YAM	
DC-3(R-4B)	CA	SClem	ACA	11693, N7500A
DC-3	CO	Denver	WOTR	
DC-3	CT	Winds	NEAM	"Taino Air"
DC-3	DC	Washi	NA&SM	
DC-3	GA	Atlanta	DATHM	NC28341, Ship 41
DC-3	GA	Dougl	BA	42-92606, N99FS
DC-3A	GA	Griff	AAC	2239, N28AA
DC-3	IL	Bloomington	PAM	4894, N763A, "Ozark Airlines"
DC-3	IL	Grant	CityPark	
DC-3	IL	St. C	SCA	
DC-3	KY	Louis	BF	
DC-3(CC-129)	MB-C	Brandon	CATPM	12949
DC-3	MB-C	Winni	WCAM	
DC-3	MD	Hager	HRegAirP	
DC-3	MN	Minneapolis	MAG	
DC-3	MI	Dearb	HFM	Northwest Airlines
DC-3	MO	Kansas City	AHM	SN3294, NC1945
DC-3-362	MS	Petal	MWHMM	
DC-3A-S4C4G	MT	Misso	AFDSC	
DC-3C	NC	Charlotte, CAM, 53-R1830, N44V, 4900, "Piedmont Airlines"	FAM	0-93800
DC-3C Parts	ND	Fargo		
DC-3	NF-C	Harbour Grace	Grace	6179
DC-3	NM	St Teresa	WEAM	
DC-3	NS-C	Greenwood	GMAM	655B
DC-3 Cockpit	NV	Las Vegas	LBAHSM	3252, N19968, "Trans-Texas Airways"
DC-3	OK	Fredi	AAM	
DC-3	ON-C	Hamilton	CWH	C-GDAK, KN456, Z
DC-3	ON-C	Ottaw	CAM	
DC-3	OR	Mc Minnville	EAM	1910, N16070, "United Airlines"
DC-3	TX	Brown	RGVW-CAF	
DC-3	TX	FWort	AACRS	
DC-3	TX	Galveston	LSFM	2213, N25673
DC-3 (3ea)	TX	Ladero	Airport	
DC-3	WA	Seattle	MoF	2245, N138D, NC91008, "Alaska Airlines"
DC-3	WA	Vancouver	PAM	
DC-3	WI	Oshkosh	BFBO	
DC-3	WI	Oshkosh	EAAAAM	
DC-3	YK-C	White Horse	YTM	N7772
DC-3	YK-C	White Horse	WA	20833 C- GZOF, CF-CPY
DC-3 Cockpit	CA	Chino	PoFAM	
DC-3 Cockpit	MD	Suitland	PEGF	
DC-3 Cockpit	NF-C	Gander	NAAM	
DC-3 Fuseelage	FL	Polk	FoF	
DC-3 Parts	CO	Denve	JWDAS	
DC-3A-S4C4G	GA	Atlanta	GSA	2054, N143D, Gryder Networks LLC
DC-3C	IN	Columbus	RA	19366, N141JR, 41, CFFCUC
DC-3C Parts	IN,	Columbus,	RA,	20550, N139JR, 40, "Miss Daisy"
DC-3C	IN	Columbus	RA	26815, N140JR, 40
DC-3C(C-47A)	IN	Columbus	RA	32845, N142JR, 42-100903

Model	State	City	Museum	Manufacturer	Registration / Notes
DC-4M	ON-C	Ottaw	CAM	Canadair	North Star, 17515
DC-6(C-118)	CA	SRosa	PCAM	Cessna	
DC-6	NE	Minde	HWPV	Cessna	1929
DC-6B	MI	Belleville	YAF	Douglas	44913, N4913R, "Yankee Volunteer"

Model	State	City	Museum	Manufacturer	Type/Name	Registration
DC-7	DC	Washi	NA&SM	Douglas		N 51701
DC-7B	AZ	Tucson	PAM	Douglas		
DC-8-52	CA	LAnge	CMoS&I	McDonnell-Douglas	Jet Trader	45856, N6161C
DC-8-55	MI	Oscoda	YAM	McDonnell-Douglas	Jet Trader	CF-TLL
DC-9-32	ON-C	Ottawa	CAM	Douglas		
DC-9	OR	Mc Minnvile	EAM	Douglas		
DC-9	VA	Hampton	VA&SM	Douglas		
DC-65	MI	Saginaw	YAF	Taylorcraft	Tandem	L-4874, N48102, "Yankee Hopper"
DC-65	NJ	Fairfield	YAF	Taylorcraft	Tandem	L-5041, N9666N
HZ-1	VA	FtEus	USATM	DeLackner	Aerocycle	
Decathlon	AL	Birmingham	SMF	Decathlon		
Deperdussin	CA	Chino	PoFAM	Deperdussin	Schneider Cup Racer	
Deperdussin	ME	Owls Head	OHTM	Deperdussin		
Deperdussin	NV	Carso	YF	Deperdussin		
Deperdussin	NY	Rhine	ORA	Deperdussin		
Deperdussin Model C	CA	San Diego	SDAM	Deperdussin		
der Kricket	CO	Denver	WOTR		der Kricket	
Dewoitine D.26	FL	Polk	FoF	Dewoitine		
DGA 1A	FL	Lakel	SFAF	DGA	Sportfire	N37835
DGA	CA	Santa Paula	SPAA	Howard	Nightingale	
DGA	TX	C Christi	USS Lexi	Howard		
DGA	TX	Denton	H10FM	Howard		
DGA	WA	Seattle	MoF	Howard	Nightingale	559, N52947
DGA 3	OH	Cleveland	FCAAM	Howard	Racer	"Pete"
DGA 5	CA	Chino	PoFAM	Howard	Racer	"Ike"
DGA 6	AR	Fayet	AAM	Howard	Racer	NR273Y, "Mister Mulligan"
DGA 11	AR	Fayet	AAM	Howard		NC18207
DGA 18K	AR	Fayet	AAM	Howard	Nightingale	N39668
DGA-15	MB-C	Winni	WCAM	Howard	DGA	
Diamond 1910	CA	San Carlos	HNCAVM	Diamond	Bi Plane	
Diamond Katana	ON-C	Kitchener	KWRA	Diamond	Katana	
Diamond Katana	ON-C	London	AH	Diamond	Katana	
Diamond Katana	ON-C	London	LA	Diamond	Katana	
Dickerson	NY	Rhine	ORA	Diskerson	Primary Glider	
Do 27	WA	Everett	MoF	Dornier		
Do 335	VA	Chantilly	NASMUVC	Dornier	Pfeil	
Domenjoz	ME	Owls Head	OHTM	Domenjos	Old Orchard Beach	

Aircraft	State	City	Museum	Manufacturer	Type	Reg./Notes
Dormoy Bathtub	PA	Bethel	GAAM	Dormoy	Bathtub	
Double Eagle II	CA	Chino	YAM	Anderson	Double Eagle	
Double Eagle II	VA	Chantilly	NASMUVC	Anderson	Double Eagle	
Double Eagle V	WI	Oshkosh	EAAAAM	Anderson	Double Eagle V	
DQ-14	MD	Suitland	PEGF	Radioplane		
DQ-2A/TDD-1	MD	Suitland	PEGF	Radioplane		
Driggers A 891H	WI	Oshkosh	EAAAAM	Driggers		"Sunshine Girl III"
Drone (Jet)	PA	Middl	CityPark			
DSI/NASA RPRV	VA	Chantilly	NASMUVH		Oblique Wing	
DSP Satellite	OH	Dayton	NMUSAF		Satellite	
Dumont Demoiselle	NV	Carso	YF	Dumont	Demoiselle	
Dumont Demoiselle	NY	NYC	ISASM	Dumont	Demoiselle	
Durand Mk.V	WA	Seattle	MoF	Durand		
DWC	AK	Palme	MOAT&I	Douglas	World Cruiser	5, N444JF
DWC	DC	Washi	NA&SM	Douglas	World Cruiser	"Seattle"
Dyndivic Sport	CT	Winds	NEAM	Dyndivic	Sport	"Chicago"
E-1	VA	Sands	VAM	Standard		
E-1	WI	Oshkosh	EAAAAM	Standard		
E-1B	SC	MtPleasant	PPM	Grumman	Tracer	N3783C
E-2	BC-C	Sidne	BCAM	Eastman	Sea Rover	147225 / Float Plane

E-2 Taylor Cub

Aircraft	State	City	Museum	Reg./Notes
E-2	NC	Hende	WNCAM	NC12644
E-2	NJ	Lumberton	AVM	
E-2	NY	Niagra Falls	NAM	
E-2	ON-C	Ottaw	CAM	
E-2	OR	Hood	WAAAM	
E-2	PA	Bethel	GAAM	NC13146
E-2	VA	Sandston	VAM	33, N15045
E-2	WI	Oshkosh	EAAAAM	N15045

E-2 Grumman Hawkeye

Aircraft	State	City	Museum	Reg./Notes
E-2B	FL	Pensacola	NMoNA	150540
E-2B	ME	Lexin	PNAT&EM	
E-2C	CA	Chino	YAM	
E-2C	CA	San Diego	SDACM	AA, 600, VAW-125
E-2C	GA	Marietta	NASA	949603, NSAW
E-2C	NV	Fallon	NASF	AA, 600, VAW-125
E-2C	VA	Norfo	NNAS	

Aircraft	State	City	Museum	Manufacturer	Type
EAA Acro-Sport	FL	Lakeland	SNF	EAA	Acro-Sport
EAA Biplane	AR	Pine Bluff	REAA	EAA	Biplane
EAA Biplane	ND	Grand Forks	JBC	EAA	Biplane
EAA P-9 Pober Pixie	OK	Fredi	AAM	EAA	Pober Pixie
Eagle Eye	AR	Little Rock	AEC	Bell	UASV

Type	ST	City	Museum	Serial / Notes
Etrich Taube	ME	Owls Head	OHTM	
Eurocopter SO.1221	PA	W chester	AHM	
Excelsior Gondola	OH	Dayton	NMUSAF	
Experimental	KS	Topek	KSHS	
Explorer II	DC	Washi	NA&SM	
Extra 260	MD	Suitland	PEGF	
Extra 300L	IL	Springfield	ACM	
Ezekiel Airship Rep	TX	Pitts	Restrant	

Type	Category
Etrich Taube	Taube
Eurocopter Djinn	
Excelsior	Gondola
Explorer	Helicopter
Extra	Gondola
Extra	
Ezekiel	Airship

F- 4 McDonnell Phantom II

Type	ST	City	Museum	Serial / Notes
F- 4 Cockpit	CA	Riverside	MFAM	
F- 4 Cockpit	ME	Lexin	PNAT&EM	
F- 4 Cockpit	OH	Daton	NMUSAF	
F- 4 Cockppit	IL	Russell	MMM	
F- 4 Cockpit	CA	Riverside,	MFAM, Weapons System Trainer	
F- 4C(RF) Cockpit	NC	Charlotte	CAM	155853, VMFA-235
F- 4S (Cockpit Only)	CA	Paso Robles	EWM	155861
F- 4S Cockpit				
F- 4 Rear Fuse	WA	Seattle,	MoF, 45-3016, NE 211, VF-21, "NAVY"	
F- 4	AL	Birmi	Southe	
F- 4	AR	FSmit	EANG	
F- 4	CA	Alameda	USS Hornet	
F- 4	CA	Boron	SAM	
F- 4	CA	Fresn	FANG	
F- 4	CA	Mojav	MA	
F- 4	CO	Cannon	CA	63-07551
F- 4	FL	KeyWe	NASKW	
F- 4	GA	Pooler	M8AFHM	64-815
F- 4	HI	Kaneohe	MB	
F- 4	IL	Sprin	SMAM	SI 468
F- 4	IN	Columbus	ABAM	64844 BA
F- 4	IN	FtWay	IANG	
F- 4	KS	Pratt	City Park	37702
F- 4	MD	Andrews	APG	AF66661
F- 4	MD	Lexin	PNA&EM	
F- 4	MI	Sterling Hts	FHCMP	66-8755
F- 4	MN	Dulut	DIA	
F- 4	NC	CPoin	CPMB	
F- 4	NJ	Wrightstown	McGAFB	67-0270
F- 4	NV	Fallon	NASF	
F- 4	NV	Fallon	NASF	
F- 4	OH	N Canton	MAM	
F- 4	OR	Klamath Falls	OANG	37479
F- 4	SC	McEnt	MEANGB	
F- 4	TN	Athen	VFW 5146	
F- 4	TX	Bastr	VFW 2527	
F- 4	TX	C Christi	USS Lexi	DC 3 VMFA-122
F- 4	TX	Dalla	DNAS	
F- 4	TX	Ft Worth	VFM	
F- 4	TX	Manch	VFW 3377	
F- 4	TX	Midland	AAHM	
F- 4	WI	Milwa	MANG	
F- 4A	CO	Pueblo	PWAM	
F- 4A	CT	Winds	NEAM	
F- 4A	FL	Clear	FMAM	
F- 4A	FL	Kissimmee	FTWAM	
F- 4A	NJ	Lumberton	AVM	148273
F- 4A	RI	NKing	QAM	
F- 4A	TX	C Christi	USS Lexi	"Sageburner"
F- 4A	VA	Chantilly	NASMUVC	
F- 4A	VA	Quantico	NMMC	143388
F- 4B	CT	Winds	NEAM	
F- 4B	IL	Sugar Grove	ACM	148407
F- 4B	IL	Linco	HIFM	
F- 4B	NC	Hickory	HRA	148400
F- 4B	NY	Horseheads	NWM	152256, VF-21, NE2219

Model	State	City	Location	Serial
F- 4B	TX	San Antonio	LSAD	149421
F- 4B	VA	VBeac	ONAS	7920, VF- 84
F- 4B(RF)	CA	China Lake	USNMAT	
F- 4B(RF)	CA	Miramar	FLAM	RF, VMFP-3
F- 4B(RF)		NC	Havelock	HTC
F- 4C	AK	Ancho	EAFB	
F- 4C	AL	Huntsville	AC	
F- 4C	AL	Mobile	BMP	637487
F- 4C	AL	Montg	MAFB	
F- 4C	AZ	Tucson	PAM	64-673
F- 4C	CA	Chino	YAM	
F- 4C	CA	Farfield	DA&SM	
F- 4C	CA	Boron	VFW	66-7716
F- 4C	CA	Riverside	MFAM	63-7693
F- 4C	CA	Rosamond	EAFB	63-7407
F- 4C	CA	McClellan	McCelAFB	64-705, MI40706
F- 4C	CA	San Luis	CSLO	64-0827
F- 4C	CA	SRosa	PCAM	
F- 4C(RF)	CA	Susanville	Airport	64-01022
F- 4C	CA	Tulare	AVP56	64-0912
F- 4C	CA	Victorville	GAFB	63-7519
F- 4C	CO	CSpri	EJPSCM	64-0799
F- 4C	CO	CSpri	USAFA	
F- 4C	CO	Denver	WOTR	
F- 4C	FL	Panama City	TAFB	63-7408
F- 4C	FL	Shalimar	USAFAM	40-813, XC
F- 4C	GA	Marie	DAFB	
F- 4C	GA	Pooler	MoF	63-7465
F- 4C	HI	Oahu	HAFB	63-15796
F- 4C	HI	Oahu	HANG	40792, Blue
F- 4C	HI	Oahu	HAFBFU	64-00793
F- 4C	HI	Oahu	HAFBFU	66-07540
F- 4C	HI	Oahu	BPNAS	1522291
F- 4C	IA	Marsh	ClAVM AM	
F- 4C	IN	Fairmount	ALP313	63-7623
F- 4C	IN	Peru	GAFB	64-783
F- 4C	IN	Terre Haute	THANG	63-565
F- 4C	LA	New Orleans	JBMM	63-556
F- 4C-19-MC	MI	Belleville	YAF	63-7555
F- 4C	MI	Mt Clemens	SMAM	63-7534
F- 4C	NC	Goldsboro	SJAFB	64-770 "Jeannie"
F- 4C	ND	Castl	CA	
F- 4C	NM	Alamo	HAFB	
F- 4C	NV	LasVe	NAFB	
F- 4C	NY	Niaga	NFANG	
F- 4C	OH	Newar	NAFM	
F- 4C	OH	Daton	NMUSAF	
F- 4C	SC	Charl	CAFB	
F- 4C	SC	Citid	CC	
F- 4C	TN	Arnol	AAFS	
F- 4C	TX	Austi	AGDTAG	
F- 4C	TX	Austi	BAFB	
F- 4C	TX	Addison	CFM	
F- 4C	TX	Dalla	FoF, 64-0777, AT, AF-477 Sq, Red Star	
F- 4C	TX	San Antonio	TANG	63-7515
F- 4C	TX	Whichita Falls	SAFB	
F- 4C	WA	Seattle	MoF	
F- 4C	WA	Tacoma	MAFB	63-7584
F- 4C	WI	CDoug	WNGML&M	
F- 4C-16-MC	UT	Ogden	HAFBM	63-7424
F- 4C-21-MC	UT	Ogden	HAFBM	64-0664
F- 4C(RF)	AR	Littl	LRAFB	64-0748,
F- 4C(RF)	CA	Riverside	MFAM	63-7746
F- 4C(NF)	CA	Rosamond	EAFB	64-1004
F- 4C(RF)	FL	Shalimar	USAFAM	67-452 ET
F- 4C(RF)-14-MC	IL	Rantoul	OCAM	62-12201
F- 4C(RF)	KY	Louisville	LANGS	64-081
F- 4C(RF)	MN	Minne	MAGM	64-61
F- 4C(RF)	MN	Minne	MAGM	64-665
F- 4C(RF)	NE	Lincoln	LANGB	64-0998, Nebraska AF
F- 4C(RF)	OH	Dayton	NMUSAF	64-1047
F- 4C(RF)	OH	Lockb	RANGB	65-903
F- 4C(RF)	SC	Sumte	SAFB	
F- 4C(RF)	TX	San Angelo	GAFB	69-0367

Type	State	City	Facility	Serial / Notes
F- 4C(RF)	TX	LV	LVAM	63-7744 as 67-0467
F- 4C(RF)	TX	San A	VMP	65-0905
F- 4C(RF)	UT	Ogden	HAM	66-0469
F- 4C-32-MC(RF)	UT	Ogden	HAM	69-0372, ZZ
F- 4C(RF)	VA	Hampton	APM	134748
F- 4D-1	AZ	Tucson	PAM	
F- 4D	CA	Miramar	FLAM	
F- 4D	CA	Palmdale	PPHP	64-0952
F- 4D(XF)	CA	China Lake	USNMAT	
F- 4D	FL	Homes	HAFB	
F- 4D	KS	Liberal	MAAM	
F- 4D	KS	Topek	CAM	268
F- 4D	KS	Wichi	K&HAP	66-0271
F- 4D	KS	Wichi	MoKNG	65-0801
F- 4D	KY	Bowling Green	Airport	#550
F- 4D	MA	Stow	BCF	
F- 4D	MD	Middle River	GLMAM	64-0919
F- 4D	MN	Minne	MAGM	
F- 4D	ND	Fargo	FANG	
F- 4D	NY	Scotia	ESAM	65-626
F- 4D	OH	Dayton	NMUSAF	66-7554
F- 4D	OH	Dayton	NMUSAF	66-7626
F- 4D	OH	Enon	VFW	67-5550
F- 4D-1 Fuse	TN	Memph	LS	
F- 4D	TX	Abilene	DLAP	65-0796
F- 4D	TX	Corsicana	NC	65-0747
F- 4D	TX	FWort	NASFWJRB	
F- 4D	TX	Whichita Falls	SAFB	
F- 4D	UT	Ogden	HAM	66-8711
F- 4D	VT	Burli	BANG	
F- 4D-1	VA	VBeac	ONAS	134950, 101, VF-41
F- 4E	AZ	Tucson	PAM	66-329
F- 4E	CA	Riverside	MFAM	68-0382
F- 4E	FL	Tampa	MAFB	
F- 4E	KS	Emporia	EMA	
F- 4E	MI	Kalamazoo	KAHM	74-0658
F- 4E	MO	SLoui	MOANGSLL	
F- 4E	NC	Goldsboro	SJAFB	74-649
F- 4E	OH	Cleveland	BLA	Thunder Birds #1
F- 4E	TX	FWort	NASFWJRB	
F- 4E	TX	Whichita Falls	SAFB	
F- 4E	UT	Ogden	HAM	68-0304
F- 4E	VA	Hampton	VA&SC	67-392, JJ
F- 4E(NF)	MO	Monet	CityPark	
F- 4E(NF)	NV	Battl	BMAM	66-286, ED
F- 4E(RF)	MN	Minne	MAGM	
F- 4E(YF)	CA	Rosamond	EAFB	
F- 4E(YF)	OH	Dayton	NMUSAF	62-12200
F- 4F	MD	Annap	USNAM	
F- 4F	OR	Tillamook	TAM	
F- 4G	OH	Dayton	NMUSAF	
F- 4J	FL	Tittusville	VACM	6-7263
F- 4J	MD	Lexington	PRNAM	153071, Side # 100, SD Tail
F- 4J	MO	Sikeston	SVP	153839, "USS Enterprise
F- 4J	NY	NYC	ISASM	
F- 4J	OH	Cleveland	BLA	153812, Blue Angeles #1
F- 4J	SC	Mt Pleasant	PPM,	153077, VMFA 333, USS America, 202
F- 4J(YF)	AZ	Tucson	PAM	151497
F- 4N	AL	Birmingham	SMoF	152996
F- 4N	AZ	Mesa	CAFAWM	3016, VF21
F- 4N	AZ	Phoen	LAFB	
F- 4N	AZ	Tucson	DMAFB	
F- 4N	HI	Kalaeloa	NAMBB	152291
F- 4N	IL	Bloomington	PAM	150444, VF-161, CV-41
F- 4N	NY	NYC	ISASM	
F- 4N	SC	Beauf	MAS	152270, DW 2270, VMFA-251
F- 4N(F4H)	FL	Pensacola	NMoNA	153915, NK 101, VF-154
F- 4S	CA	San Diego	SDAM	153030
F- 4S	CA	Santa Maria	SDAM	SMMoF 55014
F- 4S	VA	Chantilly	NASMUVC	
F- 4S	HI	Kaneohe	KBMCAS	153689, VMFA-212
F- 4S	KY	Lexington	AMoK	153904, VMFA-321
F- 4S	NC	Charlotte	CAM	155872, VMFA-235
F- 4S	TX	Slaton	TAM	

F- 5 Northrop Freedom Fighter

Type	State	City	Museum	Serial
F- 5	AK	Eureka Springs	ACM	
F- 5	TX	Ft Worth	VFM	
F- 5(CF)	MB-C	Brandon	CATPM	
F- 5(CF)	NS-C	Halifax, HAM, 116748, 434 Bluenose Squadron		
F- 5(CF)	AB-C	Cold Lake	CFB	116736
F- 5(CF)	AB-C	Grand Center	City	
F- 5(CF)	BC-C	Kamloops	CFB	116740
F- 5(CF)	ON-C	Bagotville	CFB-3WB	116733
F- 5(CF)	ON-C	Borden	TAM	116769
F- 5(CF)	ON-C	Kingston	CFBK	
F- 5(CF)	ON-C	Ottawa	CAM	116763
F- 5(CF)	ON-C	Toronto	TAM	
F- 5(CF)	ON-C	Trenton	HI	
F- 5(CF)	ON-C	Trenton	RCAFMM	116721
F- 5(CF)	QB-C	LaBaie	ADM	
F- 5A	IN	Ft Wayne	Mercury	
F- 5A(YF)	OH	Dayton	NMUSAF	59-4989
F- 5A	ON-C	Hamilton	CWH	116757
F- 5A(YF)	WA	Seattle	MoF	59-4987
F- 5B	TX	San Antonio	LSAD	C8123
F- 5B-5-NO(T-38)	IL	Rantoul	OCAM	63-8441
F- 5E	AZ	Yuma	MCAS	
F- 5E	CA	Palmdale	PPHP	
F- 5E	NV	LasVe	NAFB	
F- 5E	TX	Whichita Falls	SAFB	
F- 5E	UT	Ogden	HAM	73-01640

Type	State	City	Museum	Serial
F- 5L	MD	Suitland	PEGF	
F- 5L		FelixStow	America Flying Boat	
F- 11	MB-C	Winni	WCAM	
F- 11		Fairchild	Husky	
F- 11	ON-C	Sault Ste Marie	CBHC	
F- 11		Fairchild	Husky	12, CF-EIR

F- 11 Grumman Tiger

Type	State	City	Museum	Serial
F- 11A	CO	Pueblo	PWAM	
F- 11A	NC	Newbe	CityPark	
F- 11A (F9F-9)	NY	Garde	CoAM	141832
F- 11A(F11F-1)	FL	Pensacola	NMoNA, 141828, AD201, VF-21	
F- 11B	CA	Ridecrest	USNMAT	
F- 11F	IN	Peru	GAM	

Type	State	City	Museum	Serial
F- 12A(YF)	OH	Dayton	NMUSAF	60-6935

F- 14 Grumman Tomcat

Type	State	City	Museum	Serial
F- 14	AL	Birmingham	MoF	162608
F- 14	AL	Huntsville	AC	160661
F- 14	AL	Mobile	BAM	161611
F- 14 Cockpit	CA	Chino	YAM	158985
F- 14	CA	Atwater	CAM	164601
F- 14	CA	McClellan	AM	163897
F- 14	CA	Oakland	OWAM	160666
F- 14	CA	Paso Robles	EWM	162911
F- 14	CA	Riverside	MFAM	157990, VF-1, 100
F- 14	CA	San Diego	SDACM	15878
F- 14	FL	Jacksonville	NASJ	161863
F- 14	FL	Lakeland	FAM	159619
F- 14	FL	Miami	WOM	164342
F- 14	GA	Atlanta	NASA	160909
F- 14	KY	Lexington	AMoK	161860
F- 14	NV	Fallon	NASF	159626
F- 14	NY	Farmingdale	AAM	164603
F- 14	NY	Glenvile	ESAM	160411
F- 14	NY	NYC	ISASM	157986

Type	State	City	Code	Serial & Notes
F-14	OH	Lockbourne	RANGB	160925
F-14	OR	McMinnville	EAM	164343
F-14	PA	East Berlin	VFW	162916
F-14	PA	Willow Grove	NVHAA	160386
F-14	RI	N Kingstown	QAM	162591
F-14	SC	Patriots Point	PPM	159025
F-14	TX	Midland	AAHM	16902
F-14	VA	Norfolk	NASN	159445
F-14	VA	Richmond	DSC	159853
F-14	VA	Richmond	VAM	164346
F-14	WA	Tillamook	TAM	159848
F-14A	AL	Mobile	BPM	161611
F-14A	AZ	Tucson	PAM	160684, VF-124
F-14A	CA	Alameda Pt	USSHM	162689
F-14A	CA	Chino	YAM	16100, VX-9
F-14A	CA	Chino	PoF	160686
F-14A	CA	Imperial	PM,	159620, Side # 100, Tail NJ
F-14A	CA	Palm Springs	PSAM, 160898, USS Teodore Roosevelt	
F-14A	CA	Palmdale	PPHP	164350
F-14A	CA	Simi Valley	RRL	162592, VF-41, Black Aces
F-14A	CA	El Cajon	SDAMGF	159631, VF-24
F-14A	CA	SRosa	PCAM	160889
F-14A	CO	Denver	WOTR	159829
F-14A	FL	Pensacola	NMoNA	157984, NK201, VF-21
F-14A	FL	Pensacola	NMoNA	162710
F-14A	FL	Tittusville, VAC, 161134, VF-41 Black Aces, "Tico Bell"		
F-14A	HI	Honolulu	PAM	163904
F-14A	KS	Liberal	MAAM	160903
F-14A	KS	Topeka	CAM	161615

F-15 McDonnell-Douglas Eagle

Type	State	City	Code	Serial & Notes
F-15A	WA	Tacoma	MAFB	76-048
F-15A	AZ	Tucson	PAM	74-118
F-15A	CA	Atwater	CAM	74-119
F-15A	CO	CSpri	EJPSCM	76-024
F-15A	HI	Honolulu	HAFB	76018
F-15A	IL	Rantoul	OCAM	71-0286

Type	State	City	Code	Serial & Notes
F-14A	MD	Lexington	NASPR	162595, 221, SD
F-14A	MD	Lexington	PRNAM	161623, Side # 220
F-14A	MI	Kalamazoo	KAHM	160395
F-14A	MI	Mt Clemens	SAM	161620
F-14A	NJ	Lakeland	NAVEC	160658
F-14A	NJ	Lumberton	AVM	158898
F-14A	NY	Horseheads	NWM	161605, VF-32, AC, 100
F-14A	NY	Calverton	GMP	160902
F-14A	NY	Garde	CoAM	157982
F-14A	OK	Tulsa	TA&SC	161598
F-14A	OR	Tillamook	TAM	159848
F-14A	TX	C Christi	USS Lexi	160694
F-14A	TX	FWort	NASFWJRB	158999
F-14A	TX	Ft Worth	VFM	159600
F-14A	TX	Midland	AAHM, 160403, VF-211, "Sukhoi Killer"	
F-14A	TX	Slaton	TAM	160391
F-14A	WA	Seattle	MoF	160382
F-14A	VA	VBeac	ONAS	164604, 9, VF-103
F-14B	CT	Windsor Locks	NEAM	162926, VF-143
F-14B	FL	Deland	DNAS	161426, VF-101
F-14B	FL	Key West	KWNAS	162910, VF-103
F-14B	IN	Peru	GAM	162912, VF-11
F-14B	MD	Lexington Park	PNAS	
F-14B	NJ	Rio Grande	WNAS	161422, VF-103
F-14B	OH	N Canton	MAM	162694
F-14D	IL	Bloomington	PAM	161163, VF-213
F-14D	NC	Charlotte	CAM	161166
F-14D	VA	Chantilly	NASMUVC	159610, VF-31
F-15A	FL	Panama City	TAFB	74-0095, 325 FW
F-15A	FL	Shalimar	USAFAM	75-0033, 74-124, OT
F-15A	FL	Tampa	MAFB	
F-15A	GA	Pooler	MoF	73-85, RG
F-15A	LA	NewOrleans	JBMM	73-086
F-15A	LA	NewOrleans	Belle Chasse	
F-15A	MO	SLoui	MOANGSLL	

Type	State	City	Location	Serial / Notes
F-15A	OH	Dayton	NMUSAF	72-0119
F-15A	OH	Dayton	NMUSAF	76-0027
F-15A	OH	Fairborn	WPMC	
F-15A	OH	Lockb	RANGB	77-68
F-15A	OR	Klamath Falls	OANG	
F-15A	OR	Mc Minnville	EAM	76-0014
F-15A	TX	San Antonio	LSAD	71-280
F-15A	TX	Whichita Falls	SAFB	
F-15A	UT	Ogden	HAFBM	
F-15A(YF)	VA	Hampton	Hampton	
F-15B	AZ	Phoen	LAFB	LAFB
F-15B/E	NC	Goldsboro	SJAFB	77-0161
F-15C	FL	Callaway	City Park	

F-16 General Dynamics Fighting Falcon

Type	State	City	Location	Serial / Notes
F-16	CO	CSpri	USAFA	
F-16	FL	Pinellas Park	FLP	80-0528
F-16	NM	Albuq	KAFB	
F-16	NM	Albuq	KAFB	
F-16	ND	Fargo	FANG	
F-16	NV	Fallon	NASF	
F-16	NY	NYC	ISASM	
F-16	OH	Fairborne	WPMC	
F-16	OK	Weatherford	SA&SC	
F-16	WI	Madison	MTFMDCRA	
F-16A	AL	Mobile	BMP	79-0334
F-16A	MI	Mt Clemens	SMAM	78-0059
F-16A	NC	Sumter	SAFB	
F-16A	VA	Hampton	LAFB	
F-16A	OH	Dayton	NMUSAF	81-0663
F-16A(YF)	OH	Dayton	NMUSAF	75-0750, "Thunderbirds"
F-16A	OR	Klamath Falls	OANG	81-759
F-16A	OR	Medford	RVIA	81-759
F-16A	UT	Ogden	HAFBM	Side # 399FW, Tail HL
F-16A(YF)	VA	Hampton	VA&SC	1567
F-16B	CA	Rosamond	EAFB	
F-16B	TX	Dallas	FoF	
F-16B	TX	San Antonio	LSAD	
F-16C	FL	Shalimar	USAFAM	80-573, ET
F-16N	CA	Palm Sprgs	PoFAM	163277
F-16N	CA	El Cajon	SDAMGF	
F-16N	CA	SRosa	PCAM	
F-16N	TX	FWort	NASFWJRB	

Type	State	City	Location	Serial / Notes
F-17(YF)	AL	Mobile	BMP	

F/A-18 Northrop Hornet

Type	State	City	Location	Serial / Notes
F/A-18 Mock-Up	NY	NYC	ISASM	
F/A-18	CA	Lemoore	LNAS	161366
F/A-18	CA	China Lake	USNMAT	160775
F/A-18	CA	Miramar	FLAM	SH, VMF AT-101
F/A-18	CA	Lancaster	AVC	161214
F/A-18	CA	San Diego	SDACM	161749
F/A-18A-9-MC	FL	Jacksonville,	NASJ,	162462, AC401, VFA-105
F/A-18	FL	Pensacola	NMoNA	161961
F/A-18A	GA	Marietta	NASA	161957
F/A-18	LA	New Orleans	Belle Chasse	161726
Northrop		Cobra		AC1002
F/A-18	MD	Lexington	PRNAM	161353, 120, SD
F/A-18	MI	Kalamazoo	KAHM	161984
F/A-18	NV	Fallon	NASF	161708
F/A-18	PA	Willow Grove	NVHAA	162436
F/A-18	SC	Beaufort	MCASB	163157
F/A-18	TX	FWort	NASFWJRB	161712
F/A-18A-9-MC	UT	Ogden	HAFBM	161725
F/A-18	VA	Oceana	NASO	162454
F/A-18	VA	Hampton	VA&SM	160780
F/A-18	MD	Andrews	AAFB	161982, 120, SD
F/A-18A(CF)	ON-C	Borden	CFBBMM	160778

F/A-188B(CF)	ON-C	Ottawa	CAM	188901	F/A-188B(CF)	QB-C	LaBaie		ADM
F-20	CA	LAnge	CMoS&I		Northrop	Tigershark			
F-20	CA	Rosamond	EAFB		Northrop	Tigershark			
F-20	OH	Dayton	NMUSAF		Northrop	Tigershark			87-0700
F-23(YF)	OH	Dayton	NMUSAF		Northrop	Black Widow II			87-0800
F-80 Lockheed Shooting Star									
F-80	AK	Anchr	KANGB		F-80B(P)	AZ	Tucson	PAM	45-8612
F-80	IN	Columbus	VFW		F-80B(P)	CA	McClellan	McCelAFB	45-8704
F-80	ND	Hatton	CityPark		F-80B	CA	Atwater	CAM	45-8490, Side FT-490
F-80	ND	Vela	CityPark	19100	F-80C	CA	Chino	YAM	
F-80	NM	Albuquerque	KAFB	48501	F-80C	FL	Shalimar	USAFAM	53-2610
F-80	SC	McEnt	MEANGB		F-80C(P)	GA	Pooler	MoF	45-8357 FN
F-80	TX	Beevi	CourtHse		F-80C	KS	Liberal	MAAM	
F-80	TX	Houston	SHS		F-80C	KS	Wichita	K&HAP	45-8612, "City of Wichita"
F-80	IN	South Bend	MHP		F-80C	NC	Charl	CHAC	
F-80 (P)	CA	Inglewood	PBR		F-80C	NM	Alamo	HAFB	
F-80 (P)	NC	Charl	CHAC		F-80C (P)	PA	Willow Grove	NVHAA	33824, 28
F-80 (P)	NC	CPoin	CPMB		F-80C	OH	Dayton	NMUSAF	49-696
F-80 (P)(TV-1)	WA	Seattle	MoF	47-1388, 33841	F-80C	OH	Lockb	RANGB	47-171
F-80 (XP)	DC	Washi	NA&SM		F-80C	OK	Oklahoma	maoma45thIDM	
F-80-1D	FL	Shalimar	USAFAM	49713	F-80C	TX	Austi	BAFB	
F-80A	CA	Chino	PoFAM		F-80C	WA	Seattle	MoF	3841
F-80A-1-LO	UT	Ogden	HAFBM	44-8499	F-80C(EF)	CA	Rosamond	EAFB	49-851
F-80A(P)	CA	Chino	PoFAM		F-80C(GF)	WI	Oshkosh	EAAAAM	48-868
F-80A(EF)	CA	Rosamond	EAFB		F-80F	NM	Alamo	CityPark	
F-80A(P)	FL	Pensacola	NMoNA	44-85235, 29689	F-80L	NY	NYC	ISASM	
F-80A(P)	GA	Pooler	MoF		F-80L	TX	Dalla	DNAS	
F-80B	NM	Clovi	CAFB		F-80R(XP)	TX	FWort	NASFWJRB	
						OH	Dayton	NMUSAF	44-85200
F-81(ZXF)	OH	Dayton	NMUSAF		North American		Twin Mustang		44-91000
F-81(ZXF)	OH	Dayton	NMUSAF		North American		Twin Mustang		44-91001
F-82B	OH	Dayton	NMUSAF		North American		Twin Mustang		44-65168, "Betty Jo", naca-132
F-82B	TX	Midland	AAHM		North American				44-65162
F-82E(EF)(P)	TX	San Antonio	LSAD		North American				46-262

F-84 Republic Thunderjet

Model	State	City	Location	Serial
F-84	AR	Little Rock	LRAFB	0-37543
F-84	CA	Chino	YAM	
F-84	IA	Des Moines	ING	40-26497
F-84	IA	SBluf	MAAM	
F-84	IN	Ft. W	MC	50-19514
F-84	KS	Coffeyville	CAHM	
F-84	TX	FWort	PMoT	
F-84 (XP)	MD	Suitland	PEGF	
F-84(RF)	AR	FSmit	EANG	
F-84(RF)	IA	SBluf	MAAM	
F-84A(YP) Fuse	CA	Chino	PoFAM	
F-84A	IL	Rantoul	OCAM	45-59494
F-84B	AZ	Grand	PoFGCVA	45-59566
F-84B	AZ	Tucson	PAM	45-55554
F-84B	NY	Garde	CoAM	45-59504
F-84B-35-RE	PA	Readi	MAAM	
F-84B	TX	San Antonio	Lackland	
F-84C	AZ	Tucson	PAM	47-1433
F-84C	CA	Riverside	MFAM	47-1595
F-84C	KS	Wichi	K&HAP	47-1513
F-84C	NM	Clovi	CAFB	
F-84C	OH	Sprin	OHANG	
F-84C	OH	Sprin	SMAM	
F-84C	WI	Oshkosh	EAAAAM	51-9456
F-84D	GA	Savan	SMAM	
F-84E	HI	Oahu	HAFB	
F-84E	OH	Dayton	NMUSAF	50-1143
F-84E(RF)	AR	Littl	LRAFB	
F-84E-25-RE	GA	Pooler	MoF	51-604A

F-84 Republic Thunderstreak

Model	State	City	Location	Serial
F-84F	AL	Birmingham	SMoF	
F-84F	AL	Birmingham	SMoF	
F-84F	AL	Montg	CityPark	
F-84F	AR	Harri	VWF	
F-84F	AZ	Peori	VWF	
F-84F	AZ	Tucson	AM 109	46-0294
F-84F	AZ	Phoen	LAFB	
F-84F	AZ	Tucson	PAM	52-6563
F-84F	AZ	Tucson	TANG	
F-84F	CA	Atwater	CAM	51-9433, Side FS-433
F-84F	CA	Chino	PoFAM	FU-849
F-84F	CA	Farfield	DA&SM	52-6359 FS-359
F-84F	CA	Riverside	MFAM	51-9432
F-84F	CA	Rosamond	EAFB	51-9350
F-84F	CA	McClellan	McCelAFB	54-1772
F-84F	CA	Santa Rosa	PCAM	52-6475, AF
F-84F	FL	Shalimar	USAFAM	51-495 FS-495
F-84F	FL	Titusville	VAC	
F-84F	FL	Wauch	AL P-2	
F-84F	GA	Athen	VFW 2872	
F-84F	GA	Calhoun	WAM	
F-84F	GA	Corde	ALP-38	
F-84F	GA	Corde	GVMSP	
F-84F	GA	Dobbi	DAFB	
F-84F	GA	Marie	CCYM	
F-84F	IA	Corre	CityPark	
F-84F	IA	Farfield	CityPark	
F-84F	IA	FtDod	FtDIAANG	
F-84F	IA	Grime	GANG	
F-84F	IA	Sergant Bluff	SCANG	
F-84F	ID	Mount	MHAFB	
F-84F	IL	Cahok	PCUSL	
F-84F	IL	Grani	AMVETS51	
F-84F	IL	Peori	PANG	
F-84F	IL	Perki	CityPark	
F-84F	IL	Rantoul	OCAM	51-9531
F-84F	IL	Sprin	SMAM	2844
F-84F	IL	Wenan	ALP1130	
F-84F	IN	Hagerstown	WWB	52-6993
F-84F	IN	Hoagl	CityPark	
F-84F	IN	Monro	CityPark	

Type	State	City	Location	Serial
F-84F	IN	Montp	CityPark	
F-84F	IN	Peru	GAFB	
F-84F	IN	South	CityPark	
F-84F	IN	Terre Haute	THANG	027202
F-84F	KS	Lynn	ALP237	
F-84F	KS	Wichita	KAM	
F-84F	KY	Frank	BNGC	
F-84F	LA	Alexandria	EHP	11386
F-84F	LA	Barksdale AFB	BAFB	
F-84F-25-GK	MI	Belleville	YAF	51-9361
F-84F-35-GK	MI	Belleville	YAF	51-9501, N5006
F-84F	MI	Escan	CityPark	
F-84F	MI	Lapee	YAFDLA	
F-84F	MI	Mt Clemens	SMAM	51-1664
F-84F	MT	Great Falls	MAFB	52-6969
F-84F	NE	Creig	CityPark	
F-84F	ND	Mayville	IslandCP	11662
F-84F	NJ	Wrightstown	McGAFB	27066, NJANG
F-84F	NM	Alamo	HAFB	
F-84F	NM	Artes	CityPark	
F-84F	NM	St Teresa	WEAM	
F-84F	NV	Indian Springs	City Park	948051
F-84F	NY	Garde	CoAM	948051
F-84F	NY	NYC	ISASM	
F-84F	NY	Scotia	ESAM	51-1620
F-84F	NC	Asheboro	PFAC	
F-84F	OH	Dayton	NMUSAF	52-6526
F-84F	OH	Lockb	RANGB	51-1346
F-84F	OH	Mansf	MANG	
F-84F	OH	Sprin	OHANG	51-1797
F-84F	OH	Sprin	SMAM	92348
F-84F	OH	Swant	TANG	
F-84F	PA	Pitts	PANG	
F-84F	SD	Rapid City	SDA&SM	52-8886
F-84F	TX	Abilene	DLAP	51-9364
F-84F	TX	Amarillo	EFA&SM	52-6553
F-84F	TX	D Rio	LAFB	
F-84F	TX	Houston	ALP490	
F-84F	TX	Muens	CityPark	
F-84F-26-RE	UT	Ogden	HAFBM	27080, FS-080, EL 23 TFW; 51-1640
F-84F	VA	Hampton	VA&SC	51-1786, FS-786
F-84F	VA	Richm	DGSC	
F-84F	VA	Richm	SMAM	
F-84F	VA	VBeac	VANG	
F-84F	WI	CDoug	WNGML&M	
F-84F	WI	Kenosha	GTAC	52-6370
F-84F	WI	Oshkosh	EAAAAM	47-1498
F-84F	WY	Cheye	WYANG	
F-84F	IA	Cedar	CityPark	51-9444
F-84F (2ea)	KS	Topek	CAM	0-26458
F-84F-20-RE	GA	Pooler	MoF	52-7244
F-84F-30	NC	Asheb	AMA	51-1786
F-84F-30	VA	Hampton	APM	52-6486
F-84F-35RE	MI	Kalamazoo	KAHM	52-6701A, FS-701
F-84F-45-RE	GA	Pooler	MoF	51-1714
F-84F-RE	NE	Ashland	SACM	71562
F-84G	CO	Pueblo	PWAM	
F-84G	IL	Ellington	EFM	
F-84G	NY	Niagara Falls	NAM	
F-84G-30RE	NC	Charlotte	CAM	53-3253
F-84G-25-RE	UT	Ogden	HAFBM	52-3242, FS-275
F-84H(XF)	OH	Dayton	NMUSAF	51-17059

RF-84F Thunderflash

Type	State	City	Location	Serial
RF-84F	AL	Ozark	CityPark	
RF-84F	AR	Littl	LRAFB	
RF-84F	AZ	Tucson	PAM	51-1944
RF-84F	GA	Pooler	MoF	
RF-84F	IA	Harla	CityPark	
RF-84F	IA	Sergant Bluff	SCANG	
RF-84F	MD	Middle River	GLMAM	53-7554
RF-84F	MI	Belle	VFW 4434	
RF-84F	MI	Mt Clemens	SMAM	51-1896

RF-84F / RF-84K Thunderflash

Type	State	Location	Collection	Serial / Notes
RF-84F	MI	Lapee	YAFDLA	
RF-84F	MI	Ypsilanti	YAF	
RF-84F	MS	Hatti	CityPark	
RF-84F	MS	Jacks	JANG	
RF-84F	NC	Inca	IJHS	
RF-84F	NE	David	ALP125	
RF-84F	NE	Linco	LANG	51-11259, NEBR 0-11259
RF-84F	NE	Nelig	CityPark	
RF-84F	NE	Valle	CityPark	
RF-84F	NE	York	CityPark	
RF-84F	OH	Dayton	NMUSAF	49-2430
RF-84F	TN	Nashv	NANG	
RF-84F	TX	Abilene	DLAP	51-1123
RF-84F	TX	Austi	BAFB	
RF-84K	CA	Chino	PoFAM	
RF-84K	CO	Denver	WOTR	
RF-84K-17-RE	OH	Dayton	NMUSAF, 52-7259, "Ypsi Gypsy Rose"	
RF-84K-17-RE	MI	Belleville	YAF	52-7259
RF-84K-17-RE	MI	Ypsilanti	YAF	52-7260
RF-84K	MI	Ypsilanti	YAF	52-7259
RF-84K	MI	Ypsilanti	YAF	

Type	State	Location	Collection	Mfr	Name	Serial
F-85(XF)	OH	Dayton	NMUSAF	McDonnell	Goblin	46-0523
F-85(XF)-MC	NE	Ashland	SACM	McDonnell	Goblin	46-0524

CL-13(F-86) Canadair Sabre

Type	State	Location	Collection	Serial / Notes
F-86(CL-13)	AB-C	Bagotville	CFB	19454
F-86(CL-13)	AB-C	Edmonton	AAM	
F-86(CL-13)	BC-C	Sidney	YAM	
F-86(CL-13)	CA	Chino	WRCAFB	23060
F-86(CL-13)	MB-C	Winnipeg	ACAM	23355
F-86(CL-13)	NS	Halifax	BIBM	23649
F-86(CL-13)	ON-C	Brockville	BHT	
F-86(CL-13)	ON-C	CFB Borden	RCAFMM,	23257, RCAF 428
F-86(CL-13)	ON-C	Trenton,	CWH	23651, GH
F-86(CL-13)	ON-C	Hamilton	RMC	23221
F-86(CL-13)	ON-C	Kingston		23228
F-86(CL-13)	ON-C	Borden	ZPark	23053,
F-86(CL-13)	ON-C	Belle	GP,	23164, RCAF 428
F-86(CL-13)	ON-C	Sarnia	RP&Z	23428
F-86(CL-13)	ON-C	Petersburg		23047, "City of Oshawa", 416
F-86(CL-13)	ON-C	Oshawa,		
F-86(CL-13)	ON-C	Oshwa	OAM&IM	
F-86(CL-13)	QB-C	LaBaie	OAM&IM	
F-86 (CL-13Mk III)	MB-C	Winni	WCAM	
F-86(CL-13Mk.V)	NS -C	Halifax	HAM	23355
F-86(CL-13Mk.V)	ON-C	Oshawa	OA	"Golden Hawks"
F-86 (CL-13Mk V)	WI	Oshkosh,	EAAAAM, N8687D, "The Huff"	
F-86(CL-13B Mk.VI)	NJ	Lumberton	AVM	Mk.6, 31186
F-86(CL-13B Mk.VI)	ON-C	Peterborough	RP	
F-86(CL-13B Mk.VI)	ON-C	Trenton	MP	23641,
F-86(CL-13B Mk.VI)	ON-C	Ottaw	CAM	23651
F-86(CL-13B Mk.VI)	ON-C	Ottaw	CAM	23455
F-86(CL-13B Mk.VI)	OR	Hillsboro	CAAM	1710, N186PJ
F-86(CL-13B Mk.VI)	WA	Seattle	MoF	23363, N8686F
F-86(CL-13B Mk.VI)	WI	Oshkosh	EAAAAM	N86JR
F-86F(CL-13)	QC-C	La Baie	ADM	
F-86(QF)	CA	China Lake	USNMAT	627479

F-86 North American Sabre

Type	State	Location	Collection	Serial / Notes
F-86	CA	San Diego	SDAM	
F-86	CA	Santa Maria	SMMoF	
F-86	D.C.	Washington	USS&AH	
F-86	IN	Sellersburg	Clark Airport	
F-86	KY	Middleboro	LS	31361, FU-361
F-86	MI	Frankenmuth	MOM&SM	
F-86	NC	CPoin	CPMB	

Model	State	Location	Org	Serial
F-86	NM	St Teresa	WEAM	
F-86	NV	Fallon	NASF	
F-86	NV	LasVe	NAFB	
F-86	OK	Weatherford	SA&SC	
F-86	TN	Sevierville	TMoA	
F-86	TX	FWort	PMoT	
F-86	TX	FWort	VFM	
F-86	TX	Galveston	SP	
F-86	TX	Inglewood	PBR	
F-86	TX	Tulia	VFWP1798	
F-86	UT	Draper	UNGH	91273
F-86	VA	Suffolk	FF	
F-86	WA	Seattle	MoF	
F-86	WI	Monroe	TP	
F-86A	AK	Ancho	KANGB	
F-86A	CA	Fresn	FANG	
F-86A-5-NA	CA	Port Hueneme	CIANGB	49-1046
F-86A	CT	Winds	NEAM	
F-86A	IL	Rantoul	PEGF	47-615
F-86A	VA	Chantilly	NASMUVC	
F-86A	MI	Mt Clemens	SMAM	52-4387
F-86A	MT	Great	GFANG	47-00637
F-86A	OH	Dayton	NMUSAF	49-1067
F-86A	TX	San Antonio	LSAD	59-1605
F-86A	UT	Salt	SLCANG	
F-86A(P)	WA	Seattle	MoF	
F-86C	GA	Calhoun	WAM	15896
F-86D	AZ	Chand	CityPark	
F-86D	AZ	Globe	VWF1704	
F-86D	AZ	Tucson	DMAFB	16071
F-86D	CA	McClellan	McCelAFB	51-2968
F-86D	CA	West	VWF	52-3784
F-86D	CO	Auror	BANGB	
F-86D	FL	Clear	FMAM	
F-86D	FL	Panama City	TAFB	52-10133
F-86D	FL	Shalimar	USAFAM	51-2831, FU-831
F-86D	ID	Idaho Falls	PM	53-1022
F-86D	LA	New Orleans	JBMM	23747
F-86D-60-NA	MI	Belleville	YAF	53-1060, N201504
F-86D	NV	Reno	NAHS	
F-86D	OH	Dayton	NMUSAF	50-477
F-86D	OK	Oklahoma	45IDM	52-4043
F-86D	OK	Oklahoma	45IDM	
F-86D	OK	Tinke	TANG	
F-86D	OK	Tulsa	TANG	
F-86D	TN	Knoxv	CityPark	
F-86D	TX	Austi	AGDTAG	
F-86D	TX	FWort	SAM	
F-86D	TX	Paris	FTAM	
F-86D	WA	Tacoma	MAFB	52-3669
F-86D	WI	Monroe	Park	NAtch
F-86E	CA	Chino	YAM	
F-86E	CA	PHuen	CIANGB	
F-86E	HI	Honolulu	HAFB	50-00653
F-86E	HI	Honolulu	HANG	52-04191
F-86E	IN	India	VFWP7119	
F-86E	LA	Alexandria	EAB	24931, FU-931
F-86E-15NA	NC	Goldsboro	SJAFB	51-12972, N1028
F-86E	NM	Alamo	HAFB	
F-86E	TX	Addison	CFM	51-12821, N4689H, FU-821, 23293
F-86E	WA	Spokane	AF&AM	
F-86E	WY	Cheye	WYANG	
F-86F	AL	Birmingham	SMoF	
F-86F	AZ	Phoen	LAFB	
F-86F	CA	Chino	PoFAM	
F-86F	CA	El Cajon	SDAMGF	
F-86F(QF)	CA	Paso Robles	EWM	555082, N454
F-86F	CA	Rosamond	EAFB	52-5241
F-86F	CA	McClellan	McCelAFB	51-13082
F-86F-30NA	CO	Auror	BANGB	52-4913, AF. JASDF, 609
F-86F(RF)	CO	Auror	BANGB	
F-86F	FL	Clear	FMAM	
F-86F	FL	Miami	WOM	

Model	State	City	Location	Serial / Notes
F-86F	FL	Titusville	VAC	
F-86F	GA	Pooler	MoF	53-1511
F-86F(RF)	IL	Sugar Grove	ACM	51-13990
F-86F	IL	Sprin	S.ArmyNG	50-27051 IL
F-86F	IL	Sprin	SMAM	50-10822 IL
F-86F-30	IL	Waukegan	WHF	52-4986, NX188RL, FU-584, "Mig Mad Marine"
F-86F	IN	Ft. Wayne,	FWAS,	52-5139, NX86F, "No Jokes"
F-86F	MI	Kalamazoo	KAHM	52-5143
F-86F	MI	Ypsilanti	YAF	
F-86F(RF)	OH	Dayton	NMUSAF	
F-86F	OR	Clack	CANG	
F-86F(QF)	OR	Clack	CANG	
F-86F-25	PA	Readi	MAAM	52-4492
F-86F-30-NA	UT	Ogden	HAM	51-13417 N51RS
F-86F	WA	Seattle	MoF	52-4978
F-86H	AZ	Tucson	PAM	51-13371, 371, FU-371
F-86H	CA	Apple Valley	Airport	53-1525
F-86H	CA	Victorville	GAFB	53-1515
F-86H	CA	Atwater	CAM	53-1230, Tail A
F-86H	CA	Palmdale	PPHP	N91FS
F-86H	CA	Riverside	MFAM	53-1304
F-86H-10NA	CA	Victorville	GAFB	53-1378A, AF
F-86H	CO	Denver	WOTR	
F-86H	DE	New C	NCANG	
F-86H	FL	Ft. Lauderdale HP		53-1255
F-86H	IN	Churu	CityPark	56-298, 64, 66N
F-86H	IN	Peru	GAFB	
F-86H	KS	Liberal	MAAM	
F-86H	KS	Topek	CAM	
F-86H	MA	Bedfo	HAFB	
F-86H	MD	Balti	BANG	
F-86H	MD	Ellic	VFW P7472	
F-86H	MO	LaPla	CityPark	
F-86H	NC	Goldsboro	CityPark	53-1370
F-86H	ND	Hetti	CityPark	
F-86H	ND	James	CityPark	
F-86H	ND	Walha	CityPark	
F-86H	NE	Mc Co	CityPark	
F-86H	NM	Clovi	CAFB	
F-86H	NY	Centr	ALP915	
F-86H	NY	Manch	ALP	
F-86H	NY	Syrac	SMAMB	
F-86H	OH	Cinncinnati	LABA	
F-86H	OH	Dayton	NMUSAF	53-1352
F-86H	PA	Beave	CityPark	53-1333
F-86H	SC	Flore	FA&MM	
F-86H	SC	Green	CityPark	
F-86H	SC	McEnt	MEANGB	
F-86H	SD	Rapid City	SDA&SM	53-1375
F-86H	VA	Hampton	LAFB	
F-86H	WI	Argyl	CityPark	
F-86HL-26	WI	CDoug	WNGML&M	51-3064, FU-064
F-86H	WI	Oshkosh	EAAAAM	52-1993
F-86H	WVA	Vienn	CityPark	
F-86H(QF)	CA	Chino	PoFAM	
F-86H-10-NH	NM	Manch	CityPark	
F-86H-NH	NE	Ashland	SACM	53-1375

F-86L North American Sabre Dog

Model	State	City	Location	Serial / Notes
F-86L	AL	Mobile	BMP	51-2993
F-86L	AL	Montg	MAFB	
F-86L Cockpit	AZ	Grand	PoFGCVA	49-1217
F-86L	AZ	Tucson	PAM	56-965, FU-965
F-86L	CA	Farfield	DA&SM	30704, FU-704
F-86L	CA	Fresn	FANG	
F-86L	CA	Riverside	MFAM	50-0560
F-86L	CO	CSpri	EJPSCM	53-0782
F-86L	FL	Wauchula	FMAM	53-0658
F-86L	GA	Macon	MACF	
F-86L	GA	Savan	SMAM	
F-86L	GA	Valdo	CityPark	
F-86L	HI	Oahu	HAFB	

Model	State	City	Org	Serial / Notes
F-86L	HI	Honolulu	HANG	52-02841
F-86L	IA	Iowa	CityPark	53-0750
F-86L	ID	IFall	CityPark	
F-86L	IL	Brook	Village	
F-86L-50	KS	Wichi	K&HAP	52-4256
F-86L	MI	Ypsilanti	YAF	
F-86L	MS	Hazle	VFW 2567	
F-86L	MT	Butte	CityPark	53-997
F-86L	NC	Charlotte	CAM	52-4159
F-86L	NC	Charlotte	CANG	
F-86L	ND	Grand Forks	CityPark	
F-86L-31-NA	NE	Linco	LANG	53-0831, Tail ANG 0-23760
F-86L	NJ	Lumberton	AVM	FU-110
F-86L	NV	Battl	BMAM	53-1045
F-86L	NY	Monro	Village	
F-86L	OR	Nyssa	CityPark	
F-86L	OR	Vale	CityPark	
F-86L-26	PA	Imper	VFW P7714	
F-86L	PA	Pitts	PANG	
F-86L	SC	McEnt	MEANGB	
F-86L	TN	Nashv	CityPark	
F-86L	TX	Abilene	DLAP	
F-86L	TX	Dalla	DNAS	
F-86L	TX	Dalla	FOF	
F-86L	TX	Denis	VFW P2773	
F-86L	TX	FWort	NASFW JRB	
F-86L	TX	FWort	SAM	
F-86L	TX	Sherm	ALP29	406Th Fl Wing of Manstan
F-86L	UT	Ogden	HAFBM	51-6055
F-86L	WA	Bridg	CityPark	
F-86L	WI	Apple	ALP38	51-5938
F-86L	WVA	Milto	CityPark	
F-86L (3 ea)	WY	Cheye	WYANG	
F-86L	AL	Montg	CityPark	
F-86L-26	VA	Hampton	APM	51-3064, FU-064

F-89 Northrop Scorpion

Model	State	City	Org	Serial
F-89 Fuse Only	TN	Memph	Memph	LS
F-89 Fuse Only	TN	Peru	Peru	GAM
F-89B	IA	Nampa	CityPark	49-2457
F-89D	CA	Rosamond	EAFB	52-1959
F-89D	GA	Pooler	MoF	53-2463
F-89D	VT	Burli	BANG	
F-89H	MN	Minne	MAGM	53-2677, 373
F-89H	TX	Abilene	DLAP	54-298
F-89H-5-NO	UT	Ogden	HAFBM	54-0322
F-89J	AZ	Tucson	PAM	53-2674
F-89J	CA	Atwater	CAM	52-1927
F-89J	CA	Riverside	MFAM	52-1949
F-89J	CO	CSpri	EJPSCM	52-1941
F-89J	CT	Winds	NEAM	52-2494
F-89J	FL	Shalimar	USAFAM	53-2610
F-89J	ME	Bangor	MAM	52-1856
F-89J	MT	Great Falls	GFANG	53-2547
F-89J	MT	Helena	CoT	53-2453
F-89J	ND	Fargo	FANG	53-2465
F-89J	OH	Dayton	NMUSAF	52-1911
F-89J	OR	Mc Minnville	EAM	53-2534
F-89J	SC	Flore	FA&MM	53-2646
F-89J	TX	FWort	SAM	
F-89J	VT	Nurli	BANG	52-1883
F-89J	WI	Oshkosh	EAAAAM	53-3546
F-89J (2ea)	CA	Chino	PoFAM	
F-89J-50	VA	Hampton	APM	52-2129

Model	State	City	Org		Serial
F-90(XF)	OH	Dayton	NMUSAF	Republic	46-0688
F-91(XF)	OH	Dayton	NMUSAF	Thunderceptor	46-680
F-92A(XF)	OH	Dayton	NMUSAF	Convair	46-682

F-94 Lockheed Starfire

Model	State	City	Org	Serial/Notes
F-94	PA	Water	I79&RT19	
F-94A	NY	Niagara Falls	NAM	49-2500
F-94A	OH	Dayton	NMUSAF	49-2498
F-94A(YF)	CA	Rosamond	EAFB	
F-94B	NY	Syrac	SMAMB	51-5623
F-94C	AZ	Tucson	PAM	50-1006
F-94C	CO	CSpri	EJPSCM	
F-94C	CT	Winds	NEAM	51-13575
F-94C	MN	Chish	MMoM	
F-94C	MN	Minne	MAGM	51-13563
F-94C	NC	Fayet	VFW P670	
F-94C	ND	Fargo	FANG	
F-94C	OH	Dayton	NMUSAF	50-980
F-94C	PA	Cory	VFW P264	
F-94C	VT	Burli	BANG	

CF-100 Avro Canuck

Model	State	City	Org	Serial/Notes
F-100(CF)	CA	Atwater	CAM	100779
F-100(CF)	CO	CSpri	EJPSCM	18126
F-100(CF)	AB-C	Calga	AMoC	
F-100(CF)	AB-C	Edmunton	AAM	18152
F-100(CF)	AB-C	Nanton	NLSAM	100747
F-100(CF)	NS-C	Halifax	ACAM	18241
F-100(CF) Mk IV	OH	Dayton	NMUSAF	
F-100(CF)	ON-C	Belle	BA	181106
F-100(CF)	ON-C	Campbellford		
F-100(CF)	ON-C	Hamilton	RCAF	
F-100(CF)	ON-C	Missi	DR	
F-100(CF)	ON-C	MtVie	MVRCAF	
F-100(CF)	ON-C	Toronto	WP	100741
F-100(CF)	QB-C	Bagotville	CFB-3WB	
F-100(CF)	QB-C	LaBaie	CFB-3WB	
F-100(CF)	PE-C	Summe	PEIHAS	
F-100(CF) Mk.V	MB-C	Winni	W CAM	
F-100(CF) Mk V	MB C	Winnipeg	W RACFB	
F-100(CF) Mk V	NS -C	Halifax	HAM	18747, #2 OTU
F-100(CF) Mk V	ON-C	CFB Borden	BHT	18488, "RCAF"
F-100(CF) Mk.V	ON-C	CFB Borden	BHT	100785, C
F-100(CF) Mk V	ON-C	Hamilton	CWH	
F-100(CF)	ON-C	Burlington	WP	
F-100(CF)	ON-C	Burlington	WP	
F-100(CF)	ON-C	Goose Bay	5W GB	
F-100(CF)	ON-C	Kingston	RMC	100731
F-100(CF)	ON-C	North Bay	CFBNB	
F-100(CF)	ON-C	North Bay	LP	
F-100(CF) Mk IV	ON-C	Trenton	RCAFMM	18774
F-100(CF)	Quebec-C	St Hubert		CFB, 100760, CAF 760
F-100(CF)	Quebec-C	St Jean		CFB, 104784, CAF 746
F-100(CF) Mk 38	BC-C	Langley		CMoF, 18138, RCAF18138

F-100 North American Super Sabre

Model	State	City	Org	Serial/Notes
F-100	CA	Palmdale	PPHP	54-2299
F-100	FL	Clear	FMAM	
F-100	MD	Middle River	GLMAM	56-3899
F-100	MD	Middle River	GLMAM	56-3905
F-100	NB	Fairb	A	
F-100	NM	Melrose	MBR	
F-100	SD	Ellsworht	SDA&SM	
F-100	TX	FWort	PMoT	
F-100	TX	Galve	LSFM	56-3154
F-100	TX	Midland	AAHM	
F-100	TX	Tyler	HAMM	
F-100 Cockpit	CT	Winds	NEAM	
F-100A	CA	Rosamond	EAFB	52-1688
F-100A	CA	Rosamond	EAFB	52-5760
F-100A(YF)	CA	Rosamond	EAFB	52-5755
F-100A	CO	Auror	BANGB	
F-100A	CT	Winds	NEAM	
F-100A	MI	Grand	CityPark	
F-100A	NM	Albuq	AANG	

Model	State	City	Location	Serial / Notes
F-100A	NM	Melro	Village	
F-100A	OH	Sprin	OHANG	
F-100A	TX	San Angelo	GAFB	
F-100A	TX	San Antonio	LSAD	52-5759
F-100A-5-NA	UT	Ogden	HAFBM	52-5777, FW-777
F-100A	WI	Oshkosh	EAAAAM	
F-100C	AL	Birmingham	SMF	53-1553
F-100C	AL	Montg	MAFB	
F-100C	AZ	Phoen	LAFB	
F-100C	AZ	Tucson	PAM	54-1823
F-100C	CA	Chino	YAM	
F-100C	CA	Riverside	MFAM	54-1786
F-100C	FL	Shalimar	USAFAM	54-954 SS
F-100C	GA	Kenne	AFAMA	
F-100C	GA	Pooler	MoF	54-1851 FW 851
F-100C	IA	Sioux	SCANG	
F-100C	ID	Mount	MHAFB	
F-100C-5-NA	IL	Rantoul	OCAM	54-1785
F-100C	IN	Peru	GAFB	56-3232, 712Th FW
F-100C	KS	Wichita	K&HAP	54-1993
F-100C	TX	Abilene	DLAP	54-1752
F-100C	VA	Hampton	CityPark	
F-100C	WI	CDoug	WNGML&M	
F-100D	AZ	Glend	CityPark	
F-100D	AZ	Tucson	TANG	
F-100D	CA	Victorville	GAFB	
F-100D	CA	Chino	PoFAM	
F-100D	CA	McClellan	McCelAFB	56-3288
F-100D	CO	Pueblo	PWAM	55-3503
F-100D	CT	Winds	BANGB	55-3805
F-100D	FL	Clearwater	FMAM	
F-100D	FL	Homes	HAFB	
F-100D	FL	Kissimmee	FTWM	
F-100D	GA	Marie	DAFB	
F-100D	IL	Rantoul	OCAM	54-1784
F-100D	IN	Terre Haute	THANG	
F-100D	LA	New Orleans	JBMM	63020
F-100D	MA	Otis	OANG	
F-100D	MA	Westf	MAANG	
F-100D	MD	Suitland	PEGF	
F-100D	ME	Westf	MAANG	
F-100D	MI	Mt Clemens	SMAM	56-3025
F-100D	MO	SLoui	MOANGSLL	
F-100D	NM	Alamo	HAFB	
F-100D	NM	Clovi	CAFB	
F-100D	NV	LasVe	NAFB	
F-100D	NY	Niaga	NFANG	
F-100D	NC	Charlotte	CAM	56-2992
F-100D	OH	Colum	CDCSC	
F-100D	OH	Dayton	NMUSAF	55-3754
F-100D	OH	Lockb	RANGB	55-2884 Model 224
F-100D	OH	Sprin	SMAM	
F-100D	OH	Swant	TANG	
F-100D	OK	Tulsa	TANG	
F-100D	SC	Myrtl	MBAFB	
F-100D	TX	FWort	SAM	
F-100D	TX	San Antonio	TANG	56-3000
F-100D(GF)	TX	San A	MoAMM	
F-100D(GF)	CO	Denver	WOTR	
F-100D-5	TX	Whichita Falls	SAFB	
F-100F	VA	Hampton	APM,	54-2145, "Thunderbirds"
F-100F	AK	Eureka Springs	ACM	
F-100F	AZ	Tucson	DMAFB	
F-100F-16	IN,	Ft Wayne,	Mercury,	56-3948, N2011V, FW-948, "Victor in Valor"
F-100F	MI	Mt Clemens	SMAM	56-3894
F-100F	NJ	Pomon	ANG	
F-100F	NM	Las Cruces	LCIA	
F-100F	OH	Dayton	NMUSAF	
F-100F	TX	Burnet	CAFHLS	56-3837
F-100G	AK	Eureka Springs	ACM	

F-101 McDonnell Voodoo

Type	State	City	Location	Serial
F-101	AL	Birmingham	SMoF	
F-101	CA	Palmdale	PPHP	0-80324
F-101	ID	Pocatello	Airport	57-0430
F-101	MO	SLoui	SLAM	
F-101	TX	Slaton	TAM	
F-101	WY	RockS	CityPark	58-0312
F-101 (Black)	MN	Minne	MAGM	67
F-101(CF)	AB-C	Abbotsford	CFB	101055
F-101(CF)	AB-C	Bagotville	CFB-3W B	101027
F-101(CF)	AB-C	Cold Lake	CFB	101056
F-101(CF)	AB-C	Wetaskiwin	CFB	101038
F-101(CF)	BC-C	Lazo	CFB Comox	101030
F-101(CF)	BC-C	Lazo	CFB Comox	101057
F-101(CF)	MB-C	Winnipeg	CFB	101034
F-101(CF)	ON-C	CFB Borden	BHT	101011
F-101(CF)	ON-C	Haliburton		A683
F-101(CF)	ON-C	Levis	CFB	101015
F-101(CF)	ON-C	Malton		18619
F-101(CF)	ON-C	Mt Hope		18506
F-101(CF)	ON-C	North Bay	CFBNB	101054
F-101(CF)	ON-C	Ottawa	OIA	101025
F-101(CF)	ON-C	Ottawa	OIA	101045
F-101(CF)	ON-C	Trenton	RCAFMM	101040
F-101(CF)	QB-C	LaBaie	ADM	
F-101(CF)	NB-C	Hillsborough	P, 101028, 416 LYNX Sq, 28	
F-101(CF)	NF-C	Goose Bay	CFB	101003
F-101(CF)	NS-C	Bedford	CBF	101043
F-101(CF)	NS-C	Chatham	CFBC	101053, 416 LYNX Sq
F-101(CF)	NS-C	Cornwallis	CFRSC	101006, 416 LYNX Sq 6
F-101(RF)	PEI-C	Summerside	CFB	101037
F-101(RF)	TX	Beaum	BDZMP	
F-101A	CO	Pueblo	PWAM	53-2418
F-101A	FL	Kissi	FTWAM	
F-101A	NM	Clovi	CAFB	
F-101A-25-MC Nose	UT	Ogden	Ogden	HAM 54-1503

Type	State	City	Location	Serial
F-101B	AB-C	Edmonton	AAM	101021
F-101B	AB-C	Edmonton	AAM	101032
F-101B-110-MC	AB-C	Edmonton	AAM	101060, 57-433, 101-590
F-101B	AZ	Tucson	PAM	57-282
F-101B	CA	Atwater	CAM	57-0412
F-101B	CA	Farfield	DA&SM	
F-101B	CA	Riverside	MFAM	59-0418
F-101B	CA	Rosamond	EAFB	58-288
F-101B	CA	McClellan	McCelAFB	57-427
F-101B	CO	CSpri	EJPSCM	58-274
F-101B	CO	Denver	WOTR	
F-101B	DE	Dover	DAFB	
F-101B	FL	Kissimmee	FTWM	60417
F-101B	FL	Panama City	VMP	90478
F-101B	FL	Panama City	GCCC	70438
F-101B-115-MC	FL	Titusville	VAC	59-0400
F-101B-70-MC	IL	Rantoul	OCAM	56-0273
F-101B	IN	Peru	GAFM	
F-101B	KS	Topek	CAM	
F-101B	MD	Middle River	GLMAM	58-0303
F-101B	ME	Bangor	MANG	57-0377/04; CAF 101041
F-101B	MI	Mt Clemens	ALP4	57-0430
F-101B	ND	Fargo	FANG	
F-101B	ND	Grand Forks	GFAFB	
F-101B	NC	Charlotte	CAM	56-0243
F-101B	OH	Dayton	NMUSAF	58-325
F-101B	OH	Oberl	OFAA	
F-101B	OR	Portl	ORANGP	
F-101B	SD	Rapid City	SDA&SM	
F-101B	TN	Chatt	CANG	
F-101B	TX	Abilene	DLAP	57-287
F-101B	TX	San Antonio	LSAD	56-241
F-101B-80-MC	UT	Ogden	HAFBM	57-0252
F-101B	WA	Spokane	AF&AM	
F-101B (2 ea)	MI	Gwinn	KISHAM	
F-101B(CF)	CO	CSpri	EJPSCM	101044

Type	State	City	Location	Serial
F-101B(CF)	NS	Halifax	ACAM	101043
F-101B(CF)	NS-C	Shearwater	SAM	
F-101B(CF)	NF-C	Gander	NAAM	101065
F-101B(CF)	ON-C	Ottaw	CAM	101025
F-101B(CF)	ON-C	Trenton	RCAFMM	101046
F-101B(EB)	MN	Minne	MAGM	58-350
F-101B(NF)-40-MC	MI	Belleville	YAF	56-235
F-101B(NF)	MI	Ypsilanti	YAF	
F-101B(RF)	NV	Reno	MANG	
F-101B-55	VA	Hampton	APM	56-0246
F-101C	FL	Shalimar	USAFAM	60250
F-101C	GA	Pooler	MoF	41518-5656
F-101C	TX	Whichita Falls	SAFB	
F-101C(RF)	AL	Montg	MAFB	56-231
F-101C(RF)	AR	Littl	LRAFB	
F-101C(RF)	AZ	Dougl	CityPark	
F-101C(RF)	AZ	Gila	CityPark	
F-101C(RF)	AZ	Tucson	PAM	56-214
F-101C(RF)	GA	Pooler	MoF	56-229
F-101C(RF)	KY	Frank	BNGC	
F-101C(RF)	MD	Suitland	PEGF	56-048; C/N697
F-101C(RF)	MI	Mt Clemens	SMAM	56-068
F-101C(RF)	MS	Bilox	KAFB	
F-101C(RF)	MS	Hatti	CityPark	
F-101C(RF)	MS	Jacks	JANG	
F-101C(RF)	NY	Niaga	NFANG	
F-101C(RF)	OH	Dayton	NMUSAF	56-166
F-101C(RF)	SC	Sumte	SAFB	
F-101D	TX	Austi	BAFB	
F-101F	WA	Tilli	CMANGP	50-70294
F-101F	FL	Clear	FMAM	
F-101F	GA	Pooler	MoF	58-276
F-101F	MN	Proct	CityPark	
F-101F	MT	Great Falls	MAFB	59-0419
F-101F	NY	Buffalo	B&ECNP	80338
F-101F	NY	Buffalo	City	
F-101F	NY	Niaga	NFANG	
F-101F	NY	Scotia	ESAM	59-413
F-101F	TX	Ellin	EANGB	
F-101F	TX	San Antonio	LSAD	58-290
F-101F(CF)	MB-C	Winni	WRCAF	101008
F-101F(CF)	WA	Tacoma	MAFB	57-0332
F-101F(TF)	SC	Flore	FA&MM	
F-101H(RF)	AZ	Tucson	PAM	56-11
F-101H(RF)	KY	Louis	LANG	56-001

F-102 Convair Delta Dagger

Type	State	City	Location	Serial
F-102	NY	Scotia	ESAM	61515
F-102	WA	Spokane	AF&AM	
F-102(YF)	LA	New Orleans	JBMM	62394
F-102A	AB-C	Stephanville	HF	
F-102A	AK	Ancho	EAFB	
F-102A	AK	Palme	MOAT&I	
F-102A	AZ	Phoen	LAFB	
F-102A	AZ	Tucson	PAM	
F-102A	AZ	Tucson	TANG	56-1393
F-102A	CA	Chino	PoFAM	
F-102A	CA	El Cajon	SDAMGF	
F-102A	CA	Farfield	DA&SM	
F-102A	CA	Fresn	FANG	
F-102A	CA	Riverside	MFAM	56-1114, "Keith's Kitten"
F-102A	CA	McClellan	McCelAFB	51-1140
F-102A	CO	CSpri	EJPSCM	56-1109
F-102A	CT	Winds	NEAM	56-1264
F-102A	GA	Pooler	MoF	57-907
F-102A	HI	Oahu	HAFB	54-01373
F-102A	ID	Boise	BANG	
F-102A	MN	Minne	MAGM	50-61432
F-102A	MT	Helena	CoT	0-6116
F-102A	MT	Great	LP	56-1105
F-102A	ND	Fargo	FANG	
F-102A	ND	Grand Forks	GFAFB	

Type	State	City	Location	Serial
F-102A	ND	Minot	MAFB	
F-102A	NY	Syrac	SMAMB	
F-102A	NY	W Hamp	SMAM	
F-102A	OH	Dayton	NMUSAF	56-1416
F-102A	OR	Mc Minnville	TNSAM	56-1368
F-102A	PA	Pittsburgh	PANG	56-01415
F-102A	SC	McEnt	MEANGB	
F-102A	SD	Rapid City	SDA&SM	
F-102A	SD	Sioux	SDANGSF	
F-102A	TX	Ellin	EANGB	
F-102A	TX	Whichita Falls	SAFB	
F-102A	UT	Ogden	HAFBM	75833, FC-833
F-102A	VT	Nurli	BANG	
F-102A	WA	Tacoma	McCordAFB	57-0858

F-104 Lockheed Starfighter

Type	State	City	Location	Serial
F-104	AL	Birmingham	SMF	
F-104	AR	Little Rock	CRNGA	AUG00
F-104	AZ	Presc	ERAU	
F-104	CA	Moffe	NASAAVC	
F-104	CA	Riverside	MFAM	
F-104	FL	Clearwater	SI	104632, N103RB
F-104	FL	Clearwater	SI	104850, N 104RD
F-104	FL	Kissi	FTWAM	
F-104	MT	Dutton	AM	57-1332
F-104	OK	Oklahoma	A&SM	
F-104(CF)	AB-C	Cold Lake	CFB	12702
F-104(CF)	AB-C	Cold Lake	CFB	
F-104(CF)	AB-C	Wetaskiwin	CFB	104763
F-104(CF)	AB-C	Grand Center	City	
F-104(CF)	MB-C	Winnipeg	WRACFB	104753
F-104(CF)	NS	Halifax	ACAM	104783
F-104(CF)	ON-C	CFB Borden	BHT	104792
F-104(CF)	ON-C	Ottaw	CAM	12700
F-104(CF)	Quebec-C	St Jean	CFB	CAF 784
F-104A	CA	Farfield	DA&SM	56-0752
F-104A	CO	CSpri	USAFA	55-2967

Type	State	City	Location	Serial	
F-102A	WI	CDoug	WNGML&M		
F-102A(TF)	AL	Birmingham	SMoF		
F-102A(GF)	CO	Denver	WOTR		
F-102A(TF)	AZ	Tucson	PAM	54-1366	
F-102A(TF)	CA	Lanca	MoFM		
F-102A(TF)	CA	Rosamond	EAFB	54-1353	
F-102A(TF)-35-CO	MI	Belleville	YAF	56-2317, "La Tina"	
F-102A(GTF)	MI	Mt Clemens	SMAM	54-1351	
F-102A(TF)	PA	Annvi	AANG		
F-102A(YF)	NC	Charlotte	CAM	53-1788	
F-102A(YF)	SC	Flore	FA&MM		
F-102A-80-CO	NY	Baldw	CityPark	61515	
F-102A-CO	NE	Ashland	SACM	54-1405	
F-102D	FL	Clear	FMAM		
F-104A	CO	Pueblo	PWAM		
F-104A	DC	Washi	NA&SM		
F-104A	GA	Pooler	MoF	56-0817	FG-817
F-104A-1-LO	IL	Rantoul	OCAM	56-0732	
F-104A	LA	Alexandria	RE	56-0791	
F-104A	OH	Dayton	NMUSAF	56-0754	
F-104A	TX	Abilene	DLAP	56-0748	
F-104A	TX	Addison	CFM	56-0780	
F-104A	TX	Tyler	HAMM		
F-104A(2ea)	CA	Rosamond	EAFB	56-0801	
F-104A(NF)	CA	Rosamond	EAFB	56-0760	
F-104B	CA	McClellan	McCelAFB	57-1303	
F-104B	KS	Hutchinson	C	57-1301	
F-104B	SC	Flore	FA&MM		
F-104C	AZ	Phoen	LAFB	56-0892	
F-104C	AZ	Phoen	PANG	56-0891	
F-104C	CA	Palmdale	PPHP	57-0915	
F-104C	CA	Victorville	GAFB	56-0934	
F-104C	CA	Van Nuys	VNAFB	56-0932	
F-104C	CO	CSpri	EJPSCM	56-0936	
F-104C	CO	Denver	WOTR	56-0910	
F-104C	CT	Winds	NEAM	56-0901	

Type	State	City	Museum	Serial / Notes
F-104C	IL	Chica	MoS&I	
F-104C	KS	Liberal	MAAM	56-0933
F-104C	MI	Kalamazoo	KAHM	56-0898
F-104C	MS	Bilox	KAFB	56-0938
F-104C	NM	Alamo	HAFB	56-0886
F-104C	OH	Dayton	NMUSAF	56-0914
F-104C	SC	McEnt	MEANGB	57-0920, 60920
F-104C	TN	Chatt	CANG	
F-104C	TN	Knoxv	KANG	56-0890 8th FG
F-104C	TX	Whichita Falls	SAFB	56-0912
F-104C	VA	Hampton	VA&SC	57-0916 FG-916
F-104C	WA	Everett	MoF, 56-0934, N56-934, N820NA	
F-104C(TF)	FL	Shalimar	USAFAM	57-1331
F-104D	AZ	Tucson	PAM	57-1323
F-104D	BC-C	Langley	CMoF	
F-104D	CA	Atwater	CAM	57-1312, FG-312
F-104D	CA	Burba	VWF	57-1334
F-104D	CA	LAnge	CMoS&I, 57-1333, 104545, D-MKZ	
F-104D	CA	Redlands	CM	61-0069
F-104D	NJ	Jackson	AP	57-1320
F-104D(CF)	ON-C	Hamilton	CWH	10-4756, Tiger Paint
F-104D(CF)	ON-C	Hamilton	CWH	104641
F-104D(CF)	ON-C	Trenton,	RCAFMM, 10646, Side # 646, 2 Seater	
F-104D(TF)	WI	Oshkosh	EAAAAM	N104JR
F-104D-10	TX	San Antonio	LSAD	57-1319
F-104G	IN	Huntington,	Airport	57-1322,
F-104G	CA	Chino	PoFAM	FX82
F-104G(TF)	CA	Paso Robles	EWM	NASA 824NA
F-104G	NJ	Lumberton	AVM	56-0933, D-8090, FX-81
F-104G	OR	Hillsboro	CAAM	63-12699
F-104G	OR	Hillsboro	CAAM	FX-84, N104PJ
F-104G(TF)	OR	Hillsboro	CAAM	66-5926, N104TF

CF-105 Avro Arrow

Type	State	City	Museum	Serial / Notes
F-105(CF)	ON-C	Campbellford	MMM	181106
F-105(CF)	ON-C	Ottawa	CAM	
F-105(CF) Mk 1 Replica	ON-C	Toronto	TAM	

F-105 Republic Thunderchief

Type	State	City	Museum	Serial / Notes
F-105	AL	Birmingham	SMoF	
F-105B-IRE	AL	Mobile	CityPark	54-0102
F-105	CT	Windsor	ANG	
F-105	MO	Chill	CityPark	
F-105	MS	Jacks	AmLg1	
F-105	NC	Kings	CityPark	
F-105	NC	Wilmi	VFW P2573	
F-105	ND	Fessenden	City Park	
F-105	NM	Roswell	Airport	61-110, TH
F-105	OR	McMinnville	EAM	
F-105	SC	Sumte	SAFB	
F-105	TX	Midland	AAHM	
F-105D	CA	Atwater	CAM	57-837
F-105B	AZ	Grand Canyon	PoFAMGC	
F-105B	CA	Riverside	MFAM	57-5803
F-105B	CT	Winds	NEAM	
F-105B	FL	Clear	FMAM	
F-105B-5-RE	IL	Rantoul	OCAM	54-0104
F-105B	NC	Hickory	HRA	54-0107
F-105B	NJ	Trent	MGANG	
F-105B	NY	Garde	CoAM	5783
F-105B	OH	N Canton	MAP	
F-105B	SC	Ander	ACA	
F-105B	SD	Rapid City	SDA&SM	
F-105B	UT	SaltL	SLANG	
F-105B	WA	Spokane	AF&AM	
F-105B	WI	CDoug	WNGML&M	
F-105B(JF)	TX	San Antonio	LSAD	54-105
F-105D	AL	Montg	MAFB	
F-105D	AZ	Gila	GBAFAF	
F-105D	AZ	Tucson	DMAFB	
F-105D	AZ	Tucson	PAM	61-86
F-105D	CA	Chino	YAM	

Model	State	City	Location	Serial/Notes
F-105D	CA	Farfield	DA&SM	
F-105D	CA	Riverside	MFAM	62-4383
F-105D	CA	Rosamond	EAFB	61-146
F-105D	CA	McClellan	McCelAFB	62-4301
F-105D	CA	San B	NAFB	
F-105D	CA	Victorville	GAFB	
F-105D	CO	CSpri	USAFA	
F-105D(GF)	CO	Denver	WOTR	
F-105D	CT	Winds	BANGB	
F-105D	DC	Washi	AAFB	
F-105D	DC	Washi	BAFB	
F-105D	FL	Shalimar	USAFAM	58-771 JV
F-105D	GA	Pooler	MoF	
F-105D	IL	Sugar Grove	ACM	61-0099
F-105D	IN	Peru	GAFB	61-088
F-105D	KS	Topek	CAM	
F-105D	MD	Andrews	APG	AF 61041
F-105D	VA	Chantily	NASMUVC	
F-105D	MS	Bilox	KAFB	60-535
F-105D	NC	Fayet	PAFB	
F-105D	NC	Goldsboro	SJAFB	61-056, SJ
F-105D	NM	Alamo	HAFB	
F-105D	NM	Albuq	NAM	
F-105D Simulator	NY	Garde	CoAM	
F-105D	OH	Colum	CDCSC	
F-105D	OH	Dayton	NMUSAF	60-504
F-105D	OK	Enid	VAFB	
F-105D	OK	Tinke	TANG	
F-105D	TN	Arnol	AAFS	
F-105D	TX	Abilene	DLAP	59-1738
F-105D	TX	FWort	CAFB	
F-105D	TX	FWort	NASFW JRB	
F-105D	TX	FWort	PMoT	
F-105D	TX	San Antonio	LSAD	62-4387
F-105D	TX	Slaton	TAM	
F-105D	TX	Tyler	HAMM	
F-105D	TX	Whichita Falls	SAFB	
F-105D-5-RE	UT	Ogden	HAFBM	59-1743
F-105D	VA	Hampton	LAFB	
F-105D	VA	Richm	SMAM	
F-105D15	VA	Hampton	APM	61-73
F-105F-1-RE	IL	Rantoul	OCAM, 63-8287, "Root Rat Pak", RK
F-105F	KS	Wichi	K&HAP	62-4253
F-105F	TX	Addison	CFM	
F-105F	TX	Dallas	FoF	63-8343
F-105F	TX	FWort	SAM	
F-105G	CA	Palmdale	PPHP	62-4416
F-105G	CA	Victorville	GAFB	
F-105G	GA	Marie	DAFB	
F-105G	GA	Pooler	MoF	62-4438 HI
F-105G	KS	Liberal	MAAM	
F-105G	LA	Alexandria	EAP	63-296, MD, AD
F-105G	MD	Middle River	GLMAM	64-3899
F-105G	NV	LasVe	NAFB	
F-105G	NY	Scotia	ESAM	62-4444
F-105G	OH	Dayton	NMUSAF	63-8320
F-105G-1-RE	UT	Ogden	HAFBM	62-4440, "Wild Weasel"
F-105G (2 ea)	AZ	Tucson	PAM	62-4427
F-105H	GA	Pooler	MoF	63-8309

F-106 Convair Delta Dart

Model	State	City	Location	Serial/Notes
F-106	AL	Birmingham	SMoF	
F-106	CT	Windsor	ANG	
F-106	FL	Titusville	VAC	
F-106	DE	Dover	DAFB	
F-106	UT	Ogden	DAFB	
F-106 Simulator	DE	Dover	DAFB	
F-106A	AZ	Tucson	PAM	59-3
F-106A	CA	Fresn	FANG	
F-106A	CO	CSpri	EJPSCM	59-0134

207

Model	State	City	Location	Serial/Notes
F-106A	DC	Washi	AAFB	
F-106A	FL	Clearwater	FMAM	
F-106A	FL	Jacksonville	JIA	
F-106A	FL	Panama City	TAFB	70230 13
F-106A	GA	Pooler	MoF	59-145
F-106A	HI	Honolulu	HANG	59-123
F-106A(NF)	MI	Mt Clemens	CityPark	53366
F-106A	MT	Great Falls	GFANG	56-451
F-106A	ND	Minot	MAFB	72492
F-106A	NY	Rome	GAFBM	
F-106A	OH	Dayton	NMUSAF	58-787
F-106A	SC	Charl	CAFB	56-0459
F-106A	WA	Tacoma	MAFB	
F-106A Cockpit	MI	Kalamazoo	KAHM	
F-106B	CA	Chino	YAM	
F-106B	CA	Rosamond	EAFB	
F-106B	NJ	Pomon	ANG	
F-106B	TX	San Antonio	KAFB	72533
F-106B(NF)	VA	Hampton	VA&SC	N816NA, 816

North American — Mach 2 Jet Fighter — 55-5118, Man Sn 212-1, 1st F-107

North American — 55-5119 — Mach 2 Jet Fighter

Let — N2170D

Model	State	City	Location	Serial/Notes
F-107A	AZ	Tucson	PAM	
F-107A	OH	Dayton	NMUSAF	
F-107(LF)	WA	Seattle	MoF	

F-111 General Dynamics Aardvark

Model	State	City	Location	Serial/Notes
F-111	AL	Huntsville	AC	
F-111 Cockpit	CA	Chino	YAM	
F-111	CA	Chino	YAM	
F-111	NM	Santa Fe	SFMA	27FW, #408
F-111	TX	Midland	AAHM	
F-111	TX	Tyler	HAMM	
F-111A	AL	Birmingham	SMoF	
F-111A	CA	Rosamond	EAFB	63-9766
F-111A	IL	Rantoul	OCAM,	63-9767, NA, 474th TacFW
F-111A	NV	Battl	BMAM	66-12
F-111A	OH	Dayton	NMUSAF	67-067
F-111A(FB)	SD	Rapid City	SDA&SM	68-0248
F-111A	TX	Antonio	KAFB	
F-111A	TX	Tyler	HAMM	
F-111A	TX	Whichita Falls	SAFB	
F-111A(FB)	CA	McClellan	McCelAFB	67-159
F-111A(NF)	CA	Rosamond	EAFB	63-9778
F-111A(RF)	ID	Mount	MHAFB	RAAF
F-111E	AZ	Tucson	PAM	63-33
F-111E	FL	Shalimar	USAFAM	68-58 ET
F-111E	GA	Pooler	MoF	68-255
F-111E	UT	Ogden	HAFBM	
F-111F	NM	Clovis	CP	"My Lucky Blonde"
F-111F	NM	Portales	CP	
F-111F	OH	Dayton	NMUSAF	70-2390
F-111F Escape Module	TX	Dallas	FOF	

Model				Serial/Notes
F-111A(EF)	NM	Clovi	CAFB	General Dynamics Raven (ECM)
F-111A(EF)	OH	Dayton	NMUSAF	General Dynamics Raven (ECM) 66-0057
F-116A(CF)	ONT-C	Ottawa	CAM	Canadair
F-117A	NV	LasVe	NAFB	Lockheed Nighthawk
F-117A(YF)	OH	Dayton	NMUSAF	Lockheed Nighthawk 79-10781

F2H McDonnell Banshee

Model	State	City	Location
F2H-2	CA	Miramar	FLAM

F2H (continued)

Model	State	City	Museum	Serial / Notes
F2H-2	TX	C Christi	USS Lexi	
F2H-2N	MO	SLoui	SLAM	
F2H-2P	FL	Pensacola	NMoNA	126673, MW-2, VMJ-1, Photo Recon
F2H-2P	NY	Horseheads	NWM	125690, VFP-61
F2H-3	AB-C	Calga	NMoA	At Naval Museum
F2H-2	NS-C	Shear	CFBS	126464
F2H-3	ON-C	Ottaw	CAM	
F2H-3	VA	VBeac	ONAS	7693, AD 300
F2H-4(F-2D)	FL	Pensacola	NMoNA	126419, 127663

F2G-1D (See F4U)

Model	State	City	Museum	Serial / Notes
F3B	NY	NYC	ISASM	

McDonnell   Demon

F3D(F-10B) Douglas Skynight

Model	State	City	Museum	Serial / Notes
F3D (F-10B)	CA	Rosamond	EAFB	125850
F3D (F-10B)	KS	Topek	CAM	
F3D (F-10B)	NY	NYC	ISASM	
F3D-2(F-10B)	AZ	Tucson	PAM	124629
F3D-2(F-10B)	CA	Miramar	FLAM	L,T VMF(AW)-531
F3D-2(F-10B)	FL	Pensacola	NMoNA	124598
F3D-2(F-10B)	RI	NKing	QAM	124620
F3D-2(F-10B)	VA	Quantico	NMMC	124618

F3F Grumman Flying Barrel

Model	State	City	Museum	Serial / Notes
F3F-2	AZ	Grand Canyon	PoFGCVA	
F3F-2	CA	Carls	CAJM	8F8
F3F-2	CA	San Diego	SDAM	0964
F3F-2	FL	Pensacola	NMoNA	0976, VMF-2, #16
F3F-2	NY	NYC	ISASM	
F3F-2F	SC	Mt Pleasant	PPM	
F3F-2	TX	Galve	LSFM	972, N20RW
F3F-2 (2ea)	CA	Chino	PoFAM	
F3F-3	NY	Garden City	CoAM	

F3H / F.4 / F4B

Model	State	City	Museum	Manufacturer	Nickname	Serial / Notes
F3H	NY	NYC	ISASM	McDonnell	Demon	
F3H	FL	Clearwater	FMAM	McDonnell	Demon	
F3H-2(F-3B)	AZ	Tucson	PAM	McDonnell	Demon	145221
F.4	AL	Gunte	LGARFM	Martinsyde	Buzzard	
F4B-3(P-12E)	NC	Havelock	HTC	Boeing	Biplane	
F4B-4(P-12E)	FL	Pensacola	PSAM	Boeing		
F4B-4(P-12E)	DC	Washi	NA&SM	Boeing		9029, 6-F-1, Felix the Cat Sq

F4D-1(F-6A) Douglas Skyray

Model	State	City	Museum	Serial / Notes
F4D-1(F-6A)	AZ	Tucson	PAM	134748, Man Sn 10342
F4D-1(F-6A)	CO	Pueblo	PW AM	1-34936
F4D-1(F-6A)	CT	Winds	NEAM	134836
F4D-1(F-6A)	FL	Pensacola	NMoNA	134806
F4D-1(F-6A)	MD	Lexin	PNA&EM	
F4D-1(F-6A)	TX	Tyler	HAMM	

F4F-3(FM-2) Grumman Wildcat

Model	State	City	Museum	Serial / Notes
F4F-3A(FM-2)	CA	San Diego	SDAM	11828
F4F-3	FL	Pensacola	NMoNA	4039
F4F-3	FL	Pensacola	NMoNA	3969
F4F-3	FL	Pensacola	NMoNA	3872, 72-F-7
F4F-3	IL	Chicago	O'Hare	12320, Side # F-15

F4F-3A(FM-2)	NY	Garde	CoAM	12297
F4F-3(FM-2)	SC	Mt Pleasant	PPM	3956

FG-1D Goodyear Corsair

FG-1D	CA	Palm Springs	PSAM	92629
FG-1D	CO	Denver	WOTR	92085
FG-1D	CT	Strat	SMA	92460
FG-1D	DC	Washington	NM	92013
FG-1D	FL	Pensacola	NMoNA	92246, N766JD
FG-1D	MI	Kalamazoo	KAHM	92509, 611
FG-1D	MI	Mt Clemens	SMAM	92085, Side # 9
FG-1D	NY	Farmingdale	AAM	67089
FG-1D Fuse	OH	Akron	GWoR	76671
FG-1D	OH	Batavia	TSWM	92132

F2G-1D Super Corsair, ND, Fargo,	FAM	88458, N5588N, #5,
F2G-1 Super Corsair, TX, Galve	LSFM	88457, N5588N

F4U Chance-Vought Corsair

F4U 1/3 Scale	ON-C	Wellington	G	
F4U	CA	Inglewood	PBR	
F4U	CA	Palm Sprg	PSAM	3890, NX62290, 301, S
F4U	DC	Washi	NM	
F4U	FL	Titus	VACM	
F4U	FL	WPalm	Beach	391BG
F4U	ND	Fargo	FAM	
F4U	SC	Mt Pleasant	PPM	88368
F4U	TX	Breckenridge,	BAF,	97302, NX 65HP, VMF(N)-513
F4U	TX	Addison	CFM	
F4U-1A	CA	Chino	PoFAM	17799
F4U-1D	VA	Chantilly	NASMUVC	50375, 56, "Sun Setter"
F4U-1D	VA	Suffolk	FF	
F4U-4	AZ	Tucson	PAM	97349, N22SN
F4U-4	CA	Chino	YAM	97390, N47991, 97390

F5D-1(X-4)	OH	Wapak	NAA&SM	Douglas	Skylancer	142350

F6C (See P-1)

F6C-4 Replica	VA	Quantico	NMMC	Curtiss	Hawk	A-7412

F4F	VA	Triangle	NMMC	12114
F4F-3(FM-2)	HI	Honolulu	PAM	12296

FG-1D	OH	Newbury	WSC	88026
FG-1D	OR	Mc Minnville	EAM	92095, N67HP
FG-1D	TX	Addison	CFM	92399
FG-1D	TX	Lancaster	CAF-DFW	92468, N9964Z
FG-1D	VA	Triangle	NMMC	13486
FG-1D	VA	Suffolk	FF	82640, N46RL, VF-17
FG-1D	WA	Arlington	FHC	88303
FG-1D	WA	Bellevie	AM	88303, N700G
FG-1D	WA	Olympia	OFM	92436, Side # 115
FG-1D	WA	Seattle	MoF	88382

F2G-1 Super Corsair	WA	Seattle, MoF, 88454, NATC 454, NX4324
F2G-2 Super Corsair	OH	Cleveland FCAAM 88463, #74

F4U-4	CA	San Diego	USSM	96885
F4U-4	FL	Pensacola	NMoNA	97142, WR 18, #86
F4U-4	FL	Polk	FoF, 97286, N5215V, "Angel of Okinawa"
F4U-4	NM	St Teresa	WEAM	81698, JM 53
F4U-4	VA	Triangle	NMMC	97369
F4U-4(XF)	WI	Oshkosh	EAAAAM	97259, N6667
F4U-5	CT	Winds	NEAM	80759
F4U-5	IL	Springfield	ACM	124486
F4U-5N	MA	Stow	BCF	124692
F4U-5N	CA	Miramar	FLAM	122189
F4U-5N	IN	Valparaiso	IAM	12368
F4U-5N	KS	Liberal	MAAM	124447
F4U-7	TX	Galve	LSFM	121881, N43RW
F4U-7(AU-1)	OR	Tillamook	TAM	133722
F4U-7(AU-1) Rear Fuse AL, Mobile, BMP, 133704, LO10, VMA-212, "Marines"				

F6F Grumman Hellcat

Model	State	Location	Museum	Registration / Notes
F6F	CA	Point Mugu	PMMP	79063
F6F	FL	Polk City	FoF	43014
F6F	MD	Andrews	APG	77722, 22
F6F	MD	Chantilly	NASMUVC	
F6F	SC	Mt Pleasant	PPM	79593
F6F	WA	Arlington	FHC	79863
F6F-3	CA	San Diego	SDAM	42874, 21
F6F-3	FL	Pensacola	NMoNA	66237, #17
F6F-3	OR	Mc Minnville	EGM	41476
F6F-5 Rep	NY	NYC	ISASM	
F6F-5	CA	Camarillo	CAF-SCW	70222, N1078Z, "Minsi III"
F6F-5	CA	Chino	PoFAM	93879, N4994V, 31
F6F-5	CA	Chino	YAM	78645, N9265A, 78645
F6F-5	CA	Palm Springs	PSAM	94473, NX4964W, #36
F6F-5	CT	Winds	NEAM	79192
F6F-5	FL	Pensacola	NMoNA	94203
F6F-5	NY	Garde	CoAM	94263
F6F-5	RI	NKing	QAM	70185
F6F-5K	MI	Kalamazoo	KAHM	79683, 47-8960, N4PP, 4
F6F-3K	VA	Chantilly	NASMUVC	41834
F6F-5N	TX	Galve	LSFM	94204, N4998V, 32
F7C-1	FL	Pensacola	NMoNA	Curtiss Sea Hawk A-7667

F7F Grumman Tigercat

Model	State	Location	Museum	Registration / Notes
F7F-3E	CA	Rialto	KA	80375
F7F	FL	Polk City	FoF	80404
F7F-3,	CA	Palm Sprg,	PSAM,	45-80412, NX207F, BP", "King of Cats"
F7F-3 (2 ea)	FL	Pensacola	NMoNA	80373, N7654C
F7F-3N	AZ	Tucson	PAM	80410
F7F-3N	CA	Chino	PoFAM	80382
F7F-3P	MI	Kalamazoo	KAHM	80390

F7U-3 Chance-Vought Cutlass

Model	State	Location	Museum	Registration / Notes
F7U-3	CA	Alameda	USSHM	129565
F7U-3	PA	Willow Grove	NVHAA	129642
F7U-3	WA	Everett	MoF	129554
F7U-3M	FL	Pensacola	NMoNA	129655
F8C/K-2	SC	Beauf	MAS	Vought Crusader 146963, DC5, VMF(AW)-122
F8E	CA	Miramar	FLAM	Grumman Crusader

F8F Grumman Bearcat

Model	State	Location	Museum	Registration / Notes
F8F-2	CA	Camarillo	CAF-SCW, 122674, N7825C, 201	

Designation	State	City	Museum	Manufacturer	Name	Serial / Notes
F8F-1	CA	Chino	PoFAM	Grumman	Bearcat	122614, N41089, VF-6A, Tail S, Side # 204
F8F-1 (G-58B)	CA	Palm SPrg	PSAM	Grumman	Bearcat	1262, NL700A, "Bob's Bear"
F8F-2	FL	Pensacola	NMoNA	Grumman	Bearcat	121710, B, 100
F8F-2	VA	Chantilly	NASMUVC	Grumman	Bearcat	121646, "Conquest I"
F8F-1D(XF)	MI	Kalamazoo	KAHM	Grumman	Bearcat	90454, N9G
F8F-2	TX	Galve	LSFM	Grumman	Bearcat	1217761, N68RW
F8U-1(F-8A)	CA	Alameda	USSHM	Vought	Crusader	143703
F8U-1	CA	Chino	PoFAM	Vought	Crusader	16
F8U-1(F-8J)	CA	El Cajon	SDAMGF	Vought	Crusader	
F8U-1	CA	SRosa	PCAM	Vought	Crusader	
F8U-1	FL	Jacksonville	NASJ	Vought	Crusader	14135,1 AD, 201, VF-174
F8U-1	PA	Willow Grove	NVHAA	Vought	Crusader	143806
F8U-1	SC	MtPleasant	PPM	Vought	Crusader	
F8U-1(XF)	WA	Everett	MoF	Vought	Crusader	138899
F8U-1(F-8)	CO	Pueblo	PWAM	Vought	Crusader	145349
F8U-1(F-8)	NV	FAllon	NASF	Vought	Crusader	
F8U-1(F-8A)	AZ	Tucson	PAM	Vought	Crusader	144427, AC, 207, VF-32
F8U-1(F-8A)	TX	FWort	PMoT	Vought	Crusader	
F8U-1(F-8C)	VA	VBeac	ONAS	Vought	Crusader	149150, AD, VF-101
F8U-1(F-8H)	CA	SRosa	PCAM	Vought	Crusader	
F8U-1(F-8H)	KS	Liberal	MAAM	Vought	Crusader	
F8U-1(F-8J)	CA	San Diego	SDAM	Vought	Crusader	150297
F8U-1(F-8J)	HI	Kaneohe	KBMCAS	Vought	Crusader	146973, VMF AW235DB
F8U-1(F-8J)	MI	Kalamazoo	KAHM	Vought	Crusader	150904
F8U-1(F-8K)	CA	Alameda	USSHM	Vought	Crusader	146931
F8U-1(F-8K)	FL	Titusville	VAC	Vought	Crusader	
F8U-1(F-8K)LTV	CT	Winds	NEAM	Vought	Crusader	
F8U-1(F-8L)	CA	China Lake	USNMAT	Vought	Crusader	
F8U-1(RF-8G)	CA	Rosamond	EAFB	Vought	Crusader	
F8U-1(RF-8G)	VA	Chantilly	NASMUVC	Vought	Crusader	
F8U-1P(F-8A)	FL	Pensacola	NMoNA	Vought	Crusader	144347, NP201, VF-24
F8U-1P(F-8G(RF))	AL	Mobile	BMP	Vought	Crusader	146898
F8U-1P(F-8G(RF))	FL	Pensacola	NMoNA	Vought	Crusader	146898
F8U-1P(RF-8G)	CA	Miramar	FLAM	Vought	Crusader	WS, VMF-323, 14467, #21
F8U-1P(F-8G(RF))	VA	Chantilly	NASMUVC	Vought	Crusader	
F9-5	TX	Hawki	RRSA		Sparrowhawk	
F9C-2	FL	Pensacola	NMoNA	Curtiss	Sparrowhawk	9056

Model	State	City	Museum	Mfr	Type	BuNo / Notes
F9C-2	VA	Chantilly	NASMUVC	Curtiss	Sparrowhawk	
F9F	AZ	Mesa	GAM	Grumman	Panther	141675
F9F	FL	Titusville	VAC	Grumman	Panther	
F9F	KS	Topek	CAM	Grumman	Panther	
F9F	MD	Lexington	PRNAM	Grumman	Panther	144276, AD Tail
F9F	MD	Middle River	GLMAM	Grumman	Panther	
F9F	MS	Petal	MWHMM	Grumman	Panther	
F9F	NY	NYC	ISASM	Grumman	Panther	
F9F	NY	Tonaw	CityPark	Grumman	Panther	
F9F	SC	Mt Pleasant	PPM	Grumman	Panther	
F9F	TX	FWort	PMoT	Grumman	Panther	
F9F	WI	Janes	CityPark	Grumman	Panther	
F9F	WI	Janesville	VFW 75	Grumman	Panther	
F9F-2	CA	Chino	YAM	Grumman	Panther	
F9F-2	CT	Winds	NEAM	Grumman	Panther	
F9F-2	FL	Pensacola	NMoNA	Grumman	Panther	123050
F9F-2	PA	Willow Grove	NVHAA	Grumman	Panther	127120, V209, VF-113
F9F-2B	TX	Addison	CFM	Grumman	Panther	N9525A, 123078, A 112, VF-21 From: USS Kearsage, Boxer
F9F-2B	VA	Triangle	NMMC	Grumman	Panther	123526
F9F-2	VA	VBeac	ONAS	Grumman	Panther	123612, AD 200
F9F-5P	AL	Mobile	BMP	Grumman	Panther	126285, F21, "F21"
F9F-4 (2 ea)	AZ	Tucson	PAM	Grumman	Panther	125183
F9F-5	CA	San Diego	SDAM	Grumman	Panther	
F9F-5	FL	Tittusville	VACM	Grumman	Panther	
F9F-5P	CA	Chino	PoFAM	Grumman	Panther	94203
F9F-5P	FL	Pensacola	NMoNA	Grumman	Panther	
F9F-5P	FL	Pensacola	VC	Grumman	Panther	
F9F-5P	MN	Winoma	MCA	Grumman	Panther	125952
F9F-6(TF)	CA	San Diego	SDACM	Grumman	Cougar	
F9F-6	FL	Pensacola	NMoNA	Grumman	Cougar	128109, A, 211, VF-142
F9F-6	MN	Brain	CWCRA	Grumman	Cougar	
F9F-6P	NC	Havelock	HTC	Grumman	Cougar	
F9F-7	NY	Garde	CoAM	Grumman	Cougar	124382
F9F-7	NY	Horsehead	WoE	Grumman	Cougar	53-130802
F9F-8	CO	Pueblo	PWAM	Grumman	Cougar	138876
F9F-8	MD	Lewington	PRNAM	Grumman	Cougar	51-44276, AD 310
F9F-8	WA	Seattle	MoF	Grumman	Cougar	131232

Designation	State	Location	Museum	Manufacturer	Model	Notes
F9F-8(TAF-9J)	AZ	Tucson	PAM	Grumman	Cougar	147397 , 368 141121, 110 144426
F9F-8(TAF-9J)	CA	San Diego	SDACM	Grumman	Cougar	
F9F-8(TAF-9J)	MI	Kalamazoo	AZ	Grumman	Cougar	
F9F-8P	NY	Horsehead	WoE	Grumman	Cougar	144402
F9F-8P	CA	Miramar	FLAM	Grumman	Cougar	TN VMCJ-3
F9F-8T	TX	C Christi	USS Lexi	Grumman	Cougar	
F11A-1	MI	Kalamazoo	AZ	Grumman	Tiger	
F11F	FL	Pensacola	NASP	Grumman	Tiger	1, "Blue Angels"
F11F	FL	Pensacola	PRA	Grumman	Tiger	3, "Blue Angels"
F11F	MI	Ypsilanti	YAF	Grumman	Tiger	
F11F	SC	Flore	FA&MM	Grumman	Tiger	
F11F-1	SC	MtPleasant	PPM	Grumman	Tiger	
F11F-1	AZ	Grand	PoFGCVA	Grumman	Tiger	141868, "Blue Angles #2"
F11F-1	AZ	Tucson	PAM	Grumman	Tiger	141824
F11F-1	KS	Topek	CAM	Grumman	Tiger	5, "Blue Angels"
F11F-1(F-11A)	MI	Kalamazoo	KAHM	Grumman	Tiger	141872
Fa 330	AZ	Tucson	PAM	Focke-Achgelis	Rotor Kite	
Fa 330	VA	Chantilly	NASMUVC	Focke-Achgelis	Rotor Kite	Towed Behind U-Boats
Fa 330A-1	OH	Dayton	NMUSAF	Focke-Achgelis	Sandpiper	
Fairchild 100B	AK	Ancho	AAHM	Fairchild	American Pilgrim	N709Y, "American Pilgrim"
Fairchild F-27A	NV	Las Vegas	LBAHSM	Fairchild	Friendship	Model 27, Sn 48, N753L, "Bonanaza Airlines"
Fairey Battle 1T	ON-C	Ottaw	CAM	Fairey	Battle	R7384
Fairey Firefly Mk.5	ON-C	Hamilton	CWH	Fairey	Firefly	C-GBD6
Fairey Firefly Mk.5	ON-C	Ottawa	CAM	Fairey	Firefly	CDK545
Fairey Firefly Mk.I	NS-C	Shear	CFBS	Fairey	Firefly	
Fairchild XAUM	NY	Garden	CoAM	Fairchild	Petrel	E278
Fairey Swordfish	NS-C	Shear	CFBS	Fairey	Swordfish	
Fairey Swordfish	ON-C	Ottaw	CAM	Fairey	Swordfish	
Fairey Swordfish	ON-C	Ottaw	VWoC	Fairey	Swordfish	
Fairey Swordfish Mk.IV	FL	Polk	FoF	Fairey	Swordfish	
Falck Racer	WI	Oshkosh	EAAAAM	Falck	Racer	
Fanjet Falcon 20	VA	Chantilly	NASMUVH	Dassault	Fanjet Falcon	"Federal Express"
Fantasy 7	ON-C	Ottawa	CAM			
Farley Vincent-Starflight	LA	Patte	WWMAM	Farley	Starflight	
Farman Sport	VA	Chantilly	NASMUVH	Farman	Sport	
FB-5	CA	Chino	PoFAM	Boeing	Model 55	Model 55
FB-5	VA	Chantilly	NASMUVC	Boeing	Model 55	Model 55

Model	State	City	Museum	Manufacturer	Name	Notes
FB-111A	CA	Atwater	CAM	General Dynamics	Aardvark	69-6507
FB-111A	CA	Riverside	MFAM	General Dynamics	Aardvark	68-0245, "Ready Teddy"
FB-111A	LA	Barksdale AFB	BAFB	General Dynamics	Aardvark	SAC Bomber
FB-111A	NE	Ashland	SACM	General Dynamics	Aardvark	68-0267, SAC Bomber
FC-2	DC	Washi	NA&SM	Fairchild		
FC-2	MB-C	Winni	WCAM	Fairchild		
FC-2W-2	ON-C	Ottaw	CAM	Fairchild		NC 6621
FC-2W-2	VA	Sands	VAM	Fairchild		"Stars & Stripes"
FC-2W-2	WI	Oshkosh	EAAAAM	Fairchild		NC 3569
FC-22	CA	San Carlos	HNCAVM	Fairchild		
FC-22	IA	Ottumwa	APM	Fairchild		512, N11649
FC-22-C7B	OR	Hood	WAAAM	Fairchild		
FC-24	CA	Camarillo	CAF-SCW	Fairchild		
FC-24C28C	CA	San Carlos	HNCAVM	Fairchild		
FC-24	CA	Santa Paula	SPAA	Fairchild		
FC-24	PA	Reading	MAAM	Fairchild		
FC-24R	FL	Miami	WOM	Fairchild		
FC-24	NY	Bayport	BA	Fairchild		206, N37161
FC-24W	WA	Seattle	MoF	Fairchild		
FC-24	WA	Vancouver	PAM	Fairchild		

FC-24 (See C-61(UC))

Model	State	City	Museum	Manufacturer	Name	Notes
FC-24-C8F	OH	Dayton	NMUSAF	Fairchild		N16817 For Mil Version See UC-61J
FC-71	AB-C	Wetas	RM	Fairchild	Super 71	USAAF as C-8 or UC-96
FC-71	IA	Ottumwa	APM	Fairchild	Super 71	603, N9726
FC-71	MB-C	Winni	CC	Fairchild		
FC-71(C-8)	MB-C	Winni	WCAM	Fairchild	Super 71	USAAF as C-8 or UC-96
FC-71C	AB-C	Edmonton	AAM	Fairchild	Super 71	17
FC-82A	ON-C	Ottaw	CAM	Fairchild	Packet	CF-AXL
FE-8	DC	Washi	NA&SM	RAF		
FE-8	MD	Suitland	PEGF	RAF		
FE-8	ME	Owls Head	OHTM	RAF		
Ferret Scout Car	ON-C	Oshaw	OAM&IM	Ferret	Scout Car	
FF-1	FL	Pensacola	NMoNA	Grumman	Goblin	9351 5-F-1

FG-1D (See F4U)

Model	State	City	Museum	Manufacturer	Name	Notes
FH-1	DC	Washi	NA&SM	McDonnell	Phantom	
FH-1	FL	Pensacola	NMoNA	McDonnell	Phantom	111793
FH-1	NY	Horseheads	NWM	McDonnell	Phantom	111768, Side #5, Tail MW

FH-1099	CA	San Carlos	HNCAVM	Fairchild-Hiller	CAMEL	LargestJet Helicopter
Fi-103(V-1)	CA	Chino	PoFAM	Fiesler	Flying Bomb	
Fi-103(V-1)	IN	Green	CityPark	Fiesler	Flying Bomb(Buzz)	
Fi-103(V-1)	KS	Hutch	KC&SC	Fiesler	Flying Bomb	
Fi-103(V-1) FZG-76	NS	Halifax	ACAM	Fiesler	Flying Bomb	
Fi-103(V-1)	OH	Dayton	NMUSAF	Fiesler	Flying Bomb	
Fi-103(V-1)	VA	Suffolk	FF	Fiesler	Flying Bomb(Buzz)	
Fi-103(V-1)	VA	Chantilly	NASMUVC	Fiesler	Flying Bomb(Buzz)	
Fi-156	MD	Suitland	PEGF	Fiesler	Storch	"Ms. 500"
Fi-156	NM	St Teresa	WEAM	Fiesler	Storch	
Fi-156	OH	Dayton	NMUSAF	Fiesler	Storch	4389
Fi-156	PA	Philadelphia	CAFDVW	Fiesler	Storch	G4103D
Fi-156A-1	VA	Suffolk	FF	Fiesler	Storch	2631.751
Fi-156C-2	WI	Oshkosh	EAAAAM	Fiesler	Storch	NX464FB
Fiat G.55	VA	Suffolk	FF	Fiat	Pan	MM6244, NC10
Fiat G.91 Pan	WA	Seattle	MoF	Fiat	Pan	19
Fike Model A	OR	Eugen	OAM	Fike	Homebuilt	
Fike Model C	WI	Oshkosh	EAAAAM	Fike	Homebuilt	13390
Fisher Kola 202	KS	Liberal	MAAM	Fisher	Kola	
Fisher F-303	FL	Lakeland	SNFAM	Fisher	Classic	
FJ-1A	CA	Chino	YAM	North American	Fury	
FJ-1	CT	Winds	NEAM	North American	Fury	
FJ-1	FL	Pensacola	NMoNA	North American	Fury	120351, S104
FJ-1	KY	Louisville	CCA	North American	Fury	
FJ-2	CA	Alameda	USSHM	North American	Fury	
FJ-2	FL	Pensacola	NMoNA	North American	Fury	132057
FJ-2	NM	St Teresa	WEAM	North American	Fury	N132023
FJ-2	SC	Mt Pleasant	PPM	North American	Fury	
FJ-3	AL	Everg	MAE	North American	Fury	
FJ-3	CA	Chino	PoFAM	North American	Fury	
FJ-3	CA	Miramar	FLAM	North American	Fury	WS, VMF-323
FJ-3	NC	Hickory	HRA	North American	Fury	
FJ-3	NY	NYC	ISASM	North American	Fury	
FJ-3M	SC	Beauf	MAS	North American	Fury	
FJ-4B	FL	Pensacola	NMoNA	North American	Fury	134841, DN9, VMF-333
FJ-4B	TX	Tyler	HAMM	North American	Fury	N136008
FJ-4B	GA	Cordele	GVMSP	North American	Fury	

Model	State	City	Museum	Manufacturer	Name	Registration
FJ-4B	NY	Buffalo	B&ECNP	North American	Fury	
FJ-4B	NY	Buffalo	City	North American	Fury	
FJ-4B	PA	Willow Grove	NVHAA	North American	Fury	143568
FJ-4B(AF-1E)	AZ	Tucson	PAM	North American	Fury	139531, FU-525
Flaglor Sky Scooter	AZ	Tucson	PAM	Flagor	Sky Scooter	1000, N6WM
Flaggler Scooter	VA	Richmond	VAM	Flaggler	Scooter	
Flagg	MO	Maryland Hts	HARM	Flagg	Biplane	
Fleet	NM	Kirkl	KA	Fleet		
Fleet	TX	Brown	RGVW-CAF	Fleet		N16BR
Fleet	ON-C	Collingwood	CCAF	Fleet	Canuck	48, C-FDPV
Fleet 2	VA	Suffolk	FF	Fleet	Canuck	
Fleet 7C Mk.II	AB-C	Nanto	NLS&AM	Fleet	Fawn	
Fleet 7C	IA	Ottumwa	APM	Fleet	Fawn	
Fleet 7C	ID	Athol	NAM	Fleet	Fawn	
Fleet 7C	PA	Bethel	GAAM	Fleet	Fawn	
Fleet 7C II	ON-C	Hamilton	CWH	Fleet	Fawn	
Fleet 7C II	ON-C	Windsor	CAHS	Fleet	Fawn	
Fleet 21K	ON-C	Hamilton	CWH	Fleet		
Fleet	MB-C	Brandon	CATPM	Fleet		
Fleet 50K Parts	ON-C	Ottaw	CAM	Fleet	Fort	CF-BXP
Fleet 60K	ON-C	Hamilton	CWH	Fleet	Fort	
Fleet 80K	AB-C	Langley	CMoF&T	Fleet	Fort	
Fleet 80K	ON-C	Ottaw	CAM	Fleet	Canuck	CF-EBE
Fleet Biplane (2 ea)	VA	Bealt	FCA	Fleet	Canuck	347
Fleet Model 1	VA	Sandston	VAM	Fleet	Finch	N605M
Fleet Model 2	AZ	Tucson	PAM	Fleet	Finch	N605M
Fleet Model 2	BC-C	Langley	CMoF	Fleet	Finch	542, RCAF4725
Fleet Model 2	BC-C	Sidney	BCAM	Fleet	Finch	CF-AOD, Floats
Fleet Model 2	CA	Santa Maria	SMMoF	Fleet	Finch	
Fleet Model 2	CA	San Diego	SDAM	Fleet	Finch	
Fleet Model 2	NY	Garde	CoAM	Fleet	Finch	
Fleet Model 2	NY	Ghent	POMAM	Fleet	Finch	N648M
Fleet Model 2	OH	Madis	CFR	Fleet	Finch	NC614M
Fleet Model 2	ON-C	Ottaw	CAM	Fleet	Finch	
Fleet Model 2	TX	Brown	CAFRGVW	Fleet	Finch	
Fleet Model 2	WA	Vancouver	PAM	Fleet	Finch	
Fleet Model 16	AB-C	Wetas	RM	Fleet	Finch	

Model	State	City	Museum	Manufacturer	Type	Registration
Fleet Model 16B	NY	Bayport	BA	Fleet	Finch II	
Fleet Model 16B	NY	Rhine	ORA	Fleet	Finch	
Fleet Model 16B	ON-C	Hamilton	CWH	Fleet	Finch	C-FFLA, 4738
Fleet Model 16B	ON-C	Ottaw	CAM	Fleet	Finch	4510
Flight Simulator	BC-C	Langley	CMoF			
Fly Baby 1A	KS	Liberal	MAM		Fly Baby	
Flying Boat	CT	Winds	NEAM			
FM-2(F4F)	CA	Chino	PoF	General Motors	Wildcat	86774
FM-1(XF)(F4F-2)	FL	Titusville	VAC	Grumman	Wildcat	14994
FM-1(F4F)	DC	Washington	NA&SM	General Motors	Wildcat	15392
FM-2(F4F)	CA	Chino	PoF	General Motors	Wildcat	86774
FM-2(F4F)	CA	Chino	YAM	General Motors	Wildcat	86564, N4629V
FM-2(F4F)	CA	Miramar	FLAM	General Motors	Wildcat	
FM-2(F4F-3)	CA	Palm Springs	PSAM	General Motors	Wildcat	55627, F-3, N47201
FM-2(F4F)	CA	San Diego	FLM	General Motors	Wildcat	16278, 7
FM-2(F4F-3)	CT	Windsor Locks	NEAM	Grumman	Wildcat	74120
FM-2(F4F)	FL	Pensacola	NMoVA	General Motors	Wildcat	86747
FM-2(F4F-3)	FL	Pensacola	NMoNA	Grumman	Wildcat	16089
FM-2(F4F)	FL	Polk	FoF	General Motors	Wildcat	86741
FM-2(F4F)	MI	Kalamazoo	KAHM	General Motors	Wildcat	86581
FM-2(F4F)	OR	Tillamook	TAM	General Motors	Wildcat	86754, N58918
FM-2(F4F)	PA	Tough	CFCM	General Motors	Wildcat	47030, N315E, Side # F-13
FM-2(F4F)	TX	Addison	CFM	General Motors	Wildcat	86956, 17
FM-2(F4F-3)	TX	Fredericksburg	NMotPW	Grumman	Wildcat	74161
FM-2(F4F-3)	TX	Galveston	LSFM	Grumman	Wildcat	47160, N551TC
FM-2(F4F-3)	WA	Olympia	OFM	Grumman	Wildcat	86690
FM-2(F4F)	WA	Seattle	MoF	General Motors	Wildcat	74512
FO-141	CA	Riverside	MFAM	Folland	Gnat	E1076, "Green Mountain Boys"
Foose Tigercat	IL	Rantoul	OCAM			
Fokker C.IVa	ME	Owls Head	OHTM	Fokker	C.IVa	
Fokker D.I	TX	Addison	CFM	Fokker	D.VII	
Fokker D.VII	AL	Birmingham	SMoF	Fokker	D.VII	Project
Fokker D.VII	AL	Gunte	LGARFM	Fokker	D.VII	
Fokker D.VII 7/8 Scale	CO	Ft Lupton	VA	Fokker	D.VII	
Fokker D.VII	WA	Seattle	MoF	Fokker	D.VII	N38038
Fokker D.VII	DC	Washi	NA&SM	Fokker	D.VII	

Model	State	City	Organization	Manufacturer	Type	Notes
Fokker D.VII	FL	Orlan	CSS	Fokker	D.VII	
Fokker D.VII	FL	Orlan	OFW	Fokker	D.VII	
Fokker D.VII	FL	Pensacola	NMoNA	Fokker	D.VII	1975, 18
Fokker D.VII	NY	Rhine	ORA	Fokker	D.VII	
Fokker D.VII	NY	River	RE	Fokker	D.VII	
Fokker D.VII	OH	Dayton	NMUSAF	Fokker	D.VII	D7625118
Fokker D.VII	CA	Inglewood	PBR	Fokker	D.VII	
Fokker D.VII	ON-C	Ottaw	CAM	Fokker	D.VII	10347, 18
Fokker D.VII	PQ-C	Knowl	BCHS	Fokker	D.VII	
Fokker D.VII	TX	Kingsbury	VAHF	Fokker	D.VII	Project
Fokker D.VII	AL	Gunte	LGARFM	Fokker	D.VII	N111CV
Fokker D.VIII Replica	AZ	Mesa	CAFAWM	Fokker	D.VIII	Project
Fokker D.VIII Replica	CO	Ft Lupton	VA	Fokker	D.VIII	
Fokker D.VIII	IL	Peoria	WoT	Fokker	D.VIII	
Fokker D.VIII	NY	Rhine	ORA	Fokker	D.VIII	
Fokker D.VIII	TX	Addison	CFM	Fokker	D.VIII	
Fokker D.VIII	TX	Bealt	FCA	Fokker	D.VIII	
Fokker D.VIII	WA	Seattle	MoF	Fokker	D.VIII	NX7557U
Fokker DR.I	AB-C	Calga	AMoC	Fokker	Triplane	Dreidecker
Fokker DR.I	AL	Gunte	LGARFM	Fokker	Triplane	Dreidecker
Fokker DR.I	WA	Seattle	MoF	Fokker	Triplane	535, NX2203
Fokker DR.I	CA	Chino	PoFAM	Fokker	Triplane	Dreidecker
Fokker DR.I Rep	CA	San Diego	SDAM	Fokker	Triplane	Dreidecker
Fokker DR.I	CO	Ft Lupton	VA	Fokker	Triplane	Project
Fokker DR.I	CT	Winds	NEAM	Fokker	Triplane	Dreidecker
Fokker DR.I	FL	Orlan	CSS	Fokker	Triplane	Dreidecker
Fokker DR.I	FL	Orlan	OFW	Fokker	Triplane	Dreidecker
Fokker DR.I	IA	Hampton	DWWIAM	Fokker	Triplane	Dreidecker
Fokker DR.I	ID	Athol	NAM	Fokker	Triplane	Dreidecker
Fokker DR.I	ID	Cadwe	WAM	Fokker	Triplane	Dreidecker
Fokker DR.I	IL	Rantoul	OCM	Fokker	Triplane	Dreidecker
Fokker DR.I	ME	Owls Head	OHTM	Fokker	Triplane	Dreidecker
Fokker DR.I 3/4 Scale	MI	Kalamazoo	KAM	Fokker	Triplane	Dreidecker
Fokker DR.I	NY	EGall	GA	Fokker	Triplane	Dreidecker
Fokker DR.I	NY	Rhine	ORA	Fokker	Triplane	Dreidecker
Fokker DR.I	OH	Dayton	NMUSAF	Fokker	Triplane	Dreidecker, N1387B
Fokker DR.I	OH	Madis	CFR	Fokker	Triplane	Dreidecker

Aircraft	State	City	Museum	Mfr	Type	Notes
Fokker DR.I	OK	Oklahoma	OSM	Fokker	Triplane	Dreidecker
Fokker DR.I	ON-C	Brampton	TGWFM	Fokker	Triplane	Dreidecker
Fokker DR.I	OR	Eugene	OA&SM	Fokker	Triplane	Dreidecker
Fokker DR.I	OR	Mc Minnville	EAM	Fokker	Triplane	Dreidecker
Fokker DR.I	PA	Bethel	GAAM	Fokker	Triplane	Dreidecker Project
Fokker DR.I	TX	Kingsbury	VAHF	Fokker	Triplane	Dreidecker
Fokker DR.I	TX	Midland	AAHM	Fokker	Triplane	Dreidecker
Fokker DR.I	WA	Seattle	Restaura	Fokker	Triplane	Dreidecker, Fl 102/17
Fokker DR.I	WA	Vancouver	Pam	Fokker	Triplane	Dreidecker
Fokker DR.I	WI	Oshkosh	EAAAAM	Fokker	Triplane	Dreidecker, Redfern, N 105RF
Fokker DR.I	WI	Oshkosh	EAAAAM	Fokker	Triplane	Dreidecker, Sorrell, N 4435C
Fokker E.III	AL	Gunte	LGARFM	Fokker	Eindecker	
Fokker E.III	WA	Seattle	MoF	Fokker	Eindecker	208 226, N3363G
Fokker E.III Rep	CA	San Diego	SDAM	Fokker	Eindecker	
Fokker F.VIIA	MI	Dearb	HFM	Fokker	Trimoter	1
Fokker F.XI	MB-C	Winni	WCAM	Fokker	F.XI	
Fokker SU	MB-C	Winni	WCAM	Fokker	Super Universal	
Fokker SU	AB-C	Edmonton	AVM	Fokker	Super Universal	
Fokker SU Frame	AK	Fairbanks	PAM	Fokker	Super Universal	NC 9792
Folkerts Gullwing	WI	Oshkosh	EAAAAM	Folkerts	Gullwing	
Ford 4-AT	CA	MHill	Restaura	Ford	Tri-Motor	
Ford 4-AT-15	MI	Dearb	HFM	Ford	Tri-Motor	NX 4542, Byrd Antarctic Expedition, "Floyd Bennett"

Ford Tri Motor

Model	State	City	Museum		State	City	Museum	Notes
Ford 4-AT-B	OH	Port	IA		MI	Kalamazoo	KAHM	8, N9645
Ford 4-AT-E	WI	Oshkosh	EAAAAM		MN	Blaine	GH	
Ford 5-AT	AK	Ancho	AAHM		NV	L.Veg	MIA	
Ford 5-AT	AZ	Grand	PoFGCVA N414H, "Scenic Airways"		NV	LasVe	MIAHM	
Ford 5-AT			NC 8407 / Wreckage		OR	Mc Minnville	EAM	46, NC7861, 9206
Ford 5-AT(RR-5)	DC	Washi	NA&SM		FL	Pensacola	NMoNA	N9637
Ford 5-AT-B	FL	Polk	FoF		CA	San Diego	SDAM	

Aircraft	State	City	Museum	Mfr	Type	Notes
Ford Flivver	FL	Kissimmee	SNFAM	Ford	Flivver	
Ford Flivver	FL	India	FAHS	Ford	Flivver	
Ford Flivver	MI	Dearb	HFM	Ford	Flivver	268
Ford Flivver	WI	Oshkosh	EAAAAM	Ford	Flivver	268
Formula One Racer	CA	Chino	PoFAM		Racer	
Formula One Racer	WA	Vancouver	PAM		Racer	"Miss Cosmic Wind"
Fouga Magister	FL	Kissimmee	FTW AM			

Model	State	City	Museum	Type / Notes	Registration
Fouga Magister	FL	Miami	WOM		
Fouga Magister	NY	New Windsor	RSAM		
Found FBA-2C	ON-C	Ottaw	CAM	Found FBA-2C	CF-OZV
Fournier RF-4D	WA	Everett	MoF	Fournier Glider	4064, N1700
Fowler-Gage Tractor	VA	Chantilly	NASMUVH	Fowler-Gage Tractor	
Fowler-Gage Tractor	CA	San Carlos	HNCAVM	Fowler-Gage Tractor	
FP-404	NJ	Lumberton	AVM	Fisher Kit Biplane	
FR-1	CA	Chino	PoFAM	Ryan Fireball	
Franklin Sport 90	OR	Hood	WAAAM	Franklin Sport 90	
Frasca IFR Simulator	ON-C	Sault Ste Marie	CBHC	Frasca Simulator	
Froebe Helicopter	MB-C	Winni	WCAM	Froebe Helicopter	
Fulton FA-3	OH	Cleveland	FCAAM	Fulton Airphibian	
Fulton FA-3-101	MD	Suitland	PEGF	Fulton Airphibian	

Funk

Model	State	City	Museum	Notes	Registration
Funk B85C	FL	Kissi	FTWAM		
Funk Model B	SK-C	Moose Jaw	WDM		B85C, CF-HAR
Funk Model B	CA	Oakla	OWAM		
Funk Model B	IA	Ottumwa	APM		60, N24134
Funk Model B	KS	Coffeyville	CAHM	Funk Model B-75	
Funk Model B	KS	Wichita	KAM		
Funk Model B	NY	Rhine	ORA		
Funk Model B	OK	Fredi	AAM		
Funk Model B	WI	Oshkosh	EAAAAM		NC24116
Funk Model B-75	WA	Port Townsend	PTAM		196, N24170

Model	State	City	Museum	Registration
Fw 44	TX	Brown	RGVW-CAF	N 2497
Fw 44-J	AZ	Tucson	PAM	2827 N 133JM

Fw 190 Focke-Wulf

Model	State	City	Museum	Registration
Fw 190A-3	TX	San Antonio	TAM	SN5467, "Yellow 9"
Fw 190A-6	TX	San Antonio	TAM	550470
Fw 190A-8	TX	San Antonio	TAM	SN732183, "Blue 4"
Fw 190A-8	TX	San Antonio	TAM	SN732070
Fw 190A-8	VA	Suffolk	FF	
Fw 190A-8N	VA	Suffolk	FF	
Fw 190D-9	OH	Dayton	NMUSAF	60-1088
Fw 190D-13	AZ	Mesa	GU	
Fw 190F-8	VA	Chantilly	NASMUVC	
Fw 190F-8	FL	Kissimmee	FTWRM	
Fw Ta 152H	MD	Suitland	PEGF	SN931862, "White 1"

Model	State	City	Museum	Type	Registration
G-1B(YG)	CA	Chino	YAM	Kellett Autogyro	37-381
G-1B(YG)	CT	Washi	TFC	Kellett Autogyro	
G-21 (OA-13), (JRF)	CA	Palm Springs	PoFAM	Grumman Goose	
G-21	DC	Washi	NA&SM	Grumman Goose	
G-21	NY	Garde	CoAM	Grumman Goose	1051
G-21	NY	Horsehead	NWM	Grumman Goose	
G-21A	ONT-C	Ottawa	CAM	Grumman Goose	C-FMPG

Designation	State	City	Museum	Manufacturer	Name	Reg.
G-21A	VA	Chantilly	NASMUVC	Grumman	Goose	
G-22	VA	Chantilly	NASMUVC	Grumman	Gulfhawk II	
G-44	AK	Ancho	AAHM	Grumman	Widgeon	
G-44	CA	Chino	YAM	Grumman	Widgeon	
G-63	NY	Garde	CoAM	Grumman	Kitten	NX31808
G4M1	CA	Chino	PoF	Mitsubishi	Betty	
G4M3	MD	Suitland	PEGF	Mitsubishi	Betty	N5516M
GA-22	WI	Oshkosh	EAAAAM	Goodyear	Drake	
GA-36	NY	Niagara Falls	NAM	Cunningham-Hall		
GA-400-R-2J	WI	Oshkosh	EAAAAM	Goodyear	Gismo	N69N
GB Penquin Trainer	WI	Oshkosh	EAAAAM	Gunderson/Burke	Penquin Trainer	N41047
GB-2	FL	Pensacola	NMoNA	Beech	Traveller	23688
Gee Bee R-1	CA	Chino	PoFAM	Grandville Aircraft	GeeBee Racer	
Gee Bee R-1	CT	Winds	NEAM	Grandville Aircraft	GeeBee Racer	711, NR2100
Gee Bee R-1 Model A	CT	Winds	NEAM	Grandville Aircraft	GeeBee Racer	
Gee Bee R-1 Replica	OH	Cleveland	FCAAM	Grandville Aircraft	GeeBee Racer	
Gee Bee R-5 Model E	CT	Winds	NEAM	Grandville Aircraft	GeeBee Racer	
Gee Bee R-6H	MEXI	CLedr	CL	Grandville Aircraft	GeeBee Racer	
GEM X-2	VA	FtEus	USATM	Grandville Aircraft	Little Carrier	M2500

Gemini McDonnell Space Capsule

Designation	State	City	Museum
Gemini	CA	San Diego	SDAM
Gemini	KS	Hutch	KC&SC
Gemini Trainer	KY	Louis	MoH&S
Gemini Mock Up	MI	Kalamazoo	KAM
Gemini	MO	SLoui	MDPR
Gemini	OH	Dayton	NMUSAF
Gemini	OK	Oklahomaoma	OSM
Gemini 11	CA	LAnge	CMoS&I
Gemini Grissom	IN	Mitch	SMSP
Gemini GT-3	NY	NYC	ISASM
Gemini VIII	OH	Wapak	NAA&SM
Gemini XI Mock Up	WA	Seattle	PSC

Designation	State	City	Museum	Manufacturer	Name	Reg.
GH-1	WA	Everett	MoF	Howard	Nightingale	
GH-2	MI	Kalamazoo	KAHM	Howard	Nightingale	32347
GH-2	MI	Ypsilanti	YAF	Howard	Nightingale	
GH-3	TX	C Christi	USS Lexi	Howard	Nightingale	
Gibson Twin	BC-C	Sidne	BCAM	Gibson	Twin	
GK-1	FL	Pensacola	NMoNA	Fairchild		
GK-1	OR	Tillamook	TAM	Fairchild		7033
Glasair	CA	Oakla	OWAM	Hamilton	Glasair	
Glasair II-FT	AL	Birmingham	SMoF	Hamilton	Glasair	

Model	State	City	Museum	Manufacturer	Name	Registration
Glassair Ham-2	WI	Oshkosh	EAAAAM	Hamilton	Glasair	N88TH
Glasflugel BS-1	TX	Dallas	FoF	Glasflugel	Glasair	
Glasair SHA	OR	Mc Minnville	EAM	Hamilton		
Glider	CA	Calis	Nance's		Glider	
Glider	CA	San F	TE		Glider	
Glider 1942	CO	Denve	JWDAS		Glider	
Gliders 6 ea	PA	Water	TGAM		Glider	
Global Flyer	VA	Chantilly	NASMUVH	Virgin	Atlantic	
Globe GC-1B	AR	Fayetteville	AAM	Globe	Swift	
Globe GC-1B	CA	Modesto	HAM	Globe	Swift	
Globe GC-1B	KS	Liberal	MAAM	Globe	Swift	
Globe GC-1B	OK	Fredi	AAM	Globe	Swift	
Globe GC-1B	NY	Bayport	BA	Globe	Swift	
Globe KD2G-2	AZ	Grand Canyon	PoFGCVA	Globe		
Globe KD2G-2	WI	Oshkosh	EAAAAM	Globe		
Go 229	MD	Suitland	PEGF	Gotha		
Goddard Model A	NY	Garde	CoAM	Goddard	Rocket	
Gonzales Biplane	CA	Farfield	DA&SM	Gonzales	Tractor	
Gonzales Biplane	CA	San Carlos	HNCAVM	Gonzales	Tractor	
Goodyear 195	FL	Pensacola	NMoNA	Goodyear	Inflat A-Plane	Model XA029
Goodyear 195	MD	Lexin	PNA&EM	Goodyear	Inflat A-Plane	
Goodyear Blimp K Car	CT	Winds	NEAM	Goodyear	Blimp K Car	
Goodyear Blimp K Car	VA	Chantilly	NASMUVC	Goodyear	Blimp K Car	
Goodyear Gondola	MD	Suitland	PEGF	Goodyear	Gondola	"Pilgram"
Goodyear Racer	NC	Charlotte	CAM	Goodyear	Air Racer	
Gossamer Albatross	VA	Chantilly	NASMUVH	MacReady	Albatross	
Gossamer Albatross II	WA	Seatle	MoF	Gossamer	Albatross II	GA-11
Gossamer Condor	DC	Washi	NA&SM	Gossamery	Condor	
Gostave 21	CT	Bridg	CoveRest	Gostave	Whitehead	
Graflite	WI	Oshkosh	EAAAAM	Kotula-Lundy	Graflite	N780GF

Great Lakes Sport Trainer

Model	State	City	Museum	Registration
Great Lakes 2T-1A	CA	Santa Maria	SMMoF	
Great Lakes 2T-1A	CO	Ft Lupton	VA	Project 252, N11339
Great Lakes 2T-1A	IA	Ottumwa	APM	
Great Lakes 2T-1A	NY	Rhine	ORA	
Great Lakes 2T-1A	OH	Cleveland	FCAAM	#8
Great Lakes 2T-1A	PA	Bethel	GAAM	N75M
Great Lakes 2T-1A	TX	Gilmer	FotP	
Great Lakes 2T-1A-2	AL	Birmi	Southe	
Great Lakes 2T-1AE	CT	Winds	NEAM	461

Aircraft	State	City	Code
Great Lakes 2T-1AE	NM	St Teresa	WEAM
Great Lakes 2T-1AE	WI	Oshkosh	EAAAAM
Great Lakes Special	KS	Ashla	HKAM
Griffon Lionheart	TN	Tullahoma	SFM
Grob 102	VA	Chantilly	NASMUVC
Grob 103	NM	Hobbs	NSF
Groud Trainer	WI	Oshkosh	EAAAAM
Gruneu 2	MB-C	Winni	WCAM
Gruneu B-2	VA	Chantilly	NASMUVC
Grumman AgCat	GA	Woodstock	NGWS
Grumman Echo Cannister	NY	Garde	CoAM
Grumman LM -13	NY	Garde	CoAM
Grumman LRV Molab	NY	Garde	CoAM
Grumman LTA-1	NY	Garde	CoAM
Grunau Baby IIb	MD	Suitland	PEGF
Gulfstream	PA	Hagerstown	HAM
Gulfstream Peregrine	OK	Oklahomaoma	A&SM
Gulfstream Peregrine	OK	Oklahomaoma	OSM
Gulfstream SC	OK	Oklahomaoma	SFG
Guff R/C	MI	Kalamazoo	AM
Gyrodyne 2C	NY	Garde	CoAM
GZ-22	OH	N Canton	MAM
H- 1 Racer Rep	OR	Cottage Grove WT	Hughes
H- 1 DC	Washi	NA&SM	Hughes

Manufacturer	Model	Registration
Great Lakes	Sport Trainer	N3182
Great Lakes	Sport Trainer	N21E
Great Lakes	Special	
Griffon	Aerospace	Lionheart 003, N985CC
Grob	Standard Astir III	
Grob	Glider	
Groud	Trainer	
Grunau	Glider	
Grunau	Baby II	
Grumman	AgCat	
Grumman	Echo Cannister 7	
Grumman	LM Ascent Stage	
Grumman	LRV Mo Lab	
Grumman		
Grunau	Baby IIb	
Gulfstream	Business Jet	
Gulfstream	Peregrine	
Gulfstream	Peregrine	
Gulfstream	Shrike Commander	
Guff	R/C	
Gyrodyne	Gyrodyne 2C	N6594K
	Gondola	
Racer Rep	NX258Y	
Racer	NX258Y	

AH-1 and UH-1 See Addition Listings last pages of book
AH- 1Bell Huey Cobra

Type	State	City	Code	Registration
H- 1 (AH)	AL	Huntsville	AC	
H- 1 (AH)	CA	Miramar	FLAM	
H- 1 (AH)	CA	Riverside	MFAM	
H- 1 (AH)	CA	San Diego	SDAM	
H- 1 (AH)	CT	Windsor Locks	NEAM	70-15981
H- 1 (AH)	FL	St Cloud	VMP	0-17052
H- 1 (AH)	FL	Sykes	BVMC	68-17023,
H- 1 (AH)	FL	Tampa	VMM&P	
H- 1 (AH)	HI	Honolulu	USAM	
H- 1 (AH)	HI	Oahu	USAM	
H- 1 (AH)	IA	Des Moines	ING	0-45454
H- 1 (AH)	IA	Greenfield	IAM	0-21041
H- 1 (AH)	IA	Ida Grove	CMP	
H- 1 (AH)	IN	Anderson	HMAM	
H- 1 (AH)	IN	Auburn	HAM	67-15720
H- 1 (AH)	KS	Pratt	City Display	
H- 1 (AH)	KS	Topeka	MoKNG	
H- 1 (AH)	KY	FKnox	PMoC&A	
H- 1 (AH)	KY	Lexington	AMoK	67-15759
H- 1 (AH)	LA	New Orleans	BC NAS	
H- 1 (AH)	MD	Lexington	USNTPS	0-15645,

Designation	Location	State	Museum	Serial
H-1 (AH)	Mt Clemens	MI	SMAM	67-15675
H-1 (AH)	Monroe	MI	MCVVM	
H-1 (AH)	Shakopee	MN	VMP	
H-1 (AH)	SLoui	MO	SLUPC	
H-1 (AH)	St Joseph	MO	NMHM	68-15200
H-1 (AH)	Springfield	MO	AMMO	
H-1 (AH)	Lexington	NE	HMoMV	79-23234
H-1 (AH)	Rio Grande	NJ	NASWAM	67-15633
H-1 (AH)	Groveport	OH	MMM	67-15480
H-1 (AH)	Citadel	SC	CC	
H-1 (AH)	MtPleasant	SC	PPM	159210
H-1 (AH)	Vancouver	WA	PAM	77-22791
H-1 (AH)	Madison	WI	MTFMDCRA	
H-1 (AH)	Oshkosh	WI	EAAAAM	68-17026
H-1 (AH)	Ft Doouglas	UT	FDMM	
H-1 (AH)Cockpit	WChes	PA	AHM	68-15138
H-1A(AH)	Lumberton	NJ	AVM	
H-1A(AH)	Norwalk	OH	FMoMH	66-00825
H-1F(AH)	Huntsville	AL	RA	
H-1F(AH)	Ozark	AL	AAM	
H-1F(AH)	Yuma	AZ	USAPG	66-15350
H-1F(AH)	Burinlgton	CO	VFW6491	67-15479
H- 1F(AH)	Niagara Falls	NY	NAM	65-09834
H- 1G(AH)	Ozark	AL	USAAM	66-15246
H- 1G(AH)	Hampton	GA	AAHF	
H- 1G(AH)	Collinsville	IL	AM 365	
H- 1G(AH)	Olympia	WA	OFM	
H- 1J(AH)	Miramar	CA	FLAM	
H- 1J(AH)	Bloomington	IL	PAM	15-7771
H- 1J(AH)	Kalamazoo	MI	AM	
H- 1J(AH)	Charlotte	NC	CAM	529616
H- 1J(AH)	Triangle	VA	NMMC	159212
H- 1P(TAH)	Hampton	GA	AAHF	
H- 1S(AH)	N Canton	OH	MAM	70-16084
H- 1S(AH)	Fayet	AR	AAM	70-16050
H- 1S(AH)	Waikiki	HI	FRAM	67-15796
H- 1S(AH)	Wheeler	HI	WAFB	0-15036
H- 1S(AH) 2ea	Wheeler	HI	MAAM	
H- 1S(AH)	Liberal	KS	FRBC	70-16038
H- 1S(AH)	Fall River	MA	AHoFNJ	69-16437
H- 1S(AH)	Teterboro	NJ	AASF	67-15800
H- 1S(AH)	N Canton	OH	QAM	66-15317
H- 1S(AH)	NKing	RI	USS Lexi	
H- 1S(AH)	C Cristi	TX		

HH-1 Bell Huey (Iroquois)

Designation	Location	State	Museum	Serial
H-1 (HH)	Grand Rapids	MI	GFM	
H-1 (HH)	Pampa	TX	PAAF	
H-1H(HH)	Fairbanks	AK	PAM	66- 934
H-1H(HH)	Tucson	AZ	PAM	64-13895
H-1H(HH)	Marys	CA	FWM	
H-1H(HH)	McClellan	CA	McCelAFB	70- 2467, "Huey Slick"
H-1H(HH)	Clear	FL	FMAM	
H-1H(HH)	Eglin	FL	USAFAC	
H-1H(HH)	Linco	IL	HIFM	
H-1H(HH)	Tillamook	OR	TAM	
H-1H(HH)	NKing	RI	QAM	64-13402
H-1H(HH)	Ogden	UT	HAFBM	70-02470
H-1K(HH)	Pensacola	FL	NMoNA	157188, 301, HAL-3
H- 1K(HH)	Olympia	WA	OFM	157842,
H- 1L(TH)	Lexington	MD	PRNAM	
H- 1L(TH)	WChester	PA	AHM	
H- 1L(TH)	Dallas	TX	FoF	157838, N7UW
H- 1 (UH)	Birmingham	AL	SMoF	
H- 1 (UH)	Starke	AL	BMP	
H- 1 (UH)	Tuscalloosa	AL	I-20/59	
H- 1 (UH)	Compton	CA	TAM	66-00765
H- 1 (UH)	Long Beach	CA	HP	66-15028
H- 1 (UH)	Los Alamitos	CA	NAS	
H- 1 (UH)	Paso Robles	CA	EWM	61-3859
H- 1 (UH)	China Lake	CA	USNMAT	
H- 1 (UH)	San Diego	CA	SDACM	60-3614
H- 1 (UH)	Pueblo	CO	PWAM	

Designation	State	City	Org	Serial
H-1 (UH)	DE	Dover	AMCM	
H-1 (UH)	FL	Shalimar	USAFAM	
H-1 (UH)	FL	Tittusville	VACM	
H-1 (UH)	FL	Sykes	MVMC	17 Calvary, H Trp
H-1 (UH)	FL	Tampa	VMM&P	
H-1 (UH)	HI	Oahu	WAFB	
H-1 (UH)	IA	Des Moines	ING	0-38825
H-1 (UH)	IL	Lansing	LVM	
H-1 (UH)	IL	Sugar Grove	ACM	68-16215
H-1 (UH)	IL	Sugar Grove	ACM	68-16265
H-1 (UH)	IN	Mentone	BAM	63-08801
H-1 (UH)	IN	Munster	VMP	
H-1 (UH)	IN	Peru	GAM	68-16256
H-1 (UH)	IN	South Bend	MHP	
H-1 (UH)	KS	Augusta	AAM	
H-1 (UH)	KS	Emporia	VP	
H-1 (UH)	KS	Topeka	MoKNG	64-14001
H-1 (UH)	KS	Topeka	MoKNG	65-09617
H-1 (UH)	KS	Topeka	MoKNG	66-683
H-1 (UH)	KY	FKnox	FC	
H-1 (UH)	KY	Lexington	AMoK	68-16594
H-1 (UH)	KY	Lexington	AMoK	66-1071
H-1 (UH)	MI	Mt Clemens	SMAM	67-17368
H-1 (UH)	MI	Sterling Hts	FHCMP	15719
H-1 (UH)	MO	St joseph	NMHM	66-00551
H-1 (UH)	MN	St Paul	MANG	
H-1 (UH)	MT	Helena	HA	
H-1 (UH)	NV	Fallon	NASF	
H-1 (UH)	NC	Fayetteville	A&SOM	72-21524
H-1 (UH)	NC	Kure	NCMHM	0-16289
H-1 (UH)	NJ	Rio Grande	NASWAM	59462
H-1 (UH)	NE	Lexington	HMoMV	66-15211
H-1 (UH)	NE	Lexington	HMoMV	68-00513
H-1 (UH)	NE	Lexington	HMoMV	68-16329
H-1 (UH)	NY	Glenville	ESAM	65-09435
H-1 (UH)	NY	Niagra Falls	NAM	65-09839
H-1 (GUH)	OH	Dayton	NMUSAF	65-7922
H-1 (UH)	OH	Groveport	MMM	56-17048,
H-1 (UH)	OH	Norwalk	FMoMH	66-00992
H-1 (UH)	SC	Mt Pleasant	PP	
H-1 (UH)	TN	Caryville	I-75&US25W	
H-1 (UH)	TX	FWort	NASFW JRB	
H-1 (UH)	TX	Midland	AAHM	69-15500
H-1 (UH)	TX	Slaton	TAM	
H-1 (UH)	TX	Sweetwater	CP	
H-1 (UH)	WI	Madison	MTFMDCRA	
H-1 (UH)	UT	Bluffdale	CW	
H-1 (UH)	UT	Ft Douglas	FDMM	
H-1 (UH)	UT	West Jordan	NGA	
H-1 1A(UH)	CA	SRosa	PCAM	
H-1 1A(UH)	NC	Fayet	FBADM	59-1711
H-1 1A(UH)	NY	NYC	ISASM	
H-1 1A(UH)	TN	Pigeon Forge	HH	
H-1 1A(UH)	VA	Ft Eustis	USATM	5-1616
H-1 1B(UH)	AL	Ozark	USAAM	60- 3553
H-1 1B(UH)	CT	Strat	NHM	
H-1 1B(UH)	CT	Winds	NEAM	62-12550
H-1 1B(UH)	DC	Washi	AAFB	
H-1 1B(UH)	GA	Hampton	AAHF	
H-1 1B(UH)	IA	SBluf	MAAM	
H-1 1B(UH)	IL	Rantoul	OCAM	61-0686
H-1 1B(UH)	IN	Vince	IMM	
H-1 1B(UH)	KS	Liberal	MAAM	66-01204
H-1 1B(UH)	KY	FKnox	PMoC&A	
H-1 1B(UH)	MI	Battle Creek	BCANG	
H-1 1B(UH)	MO	SLoui	NPRC	
H-1 1B(UH)	OK	FtSil	USAFAM	
H-1 1B(UH)	OK	Oklahomaoma	45IDM	62-4588
H-1 1B(UH)	OH	N Canton	MAM	
H-1 1B(UH)	SC	Columbia	FJM	
H-1 1B(UH)	VA	Eustis	USATM	61-0788
H-1 1B(UH)	WA	Tacom	FL	
H-1 1C(UH)	NY	Horseheads	NWM	69-16723
H-1 1C(UH)	CA	S El Monte	ASMH	

Model	City	State	Location	Serial
H-1D(UH)	Ozark	AL	USAAM	60-6030
H-1D(UH)	San Diego	CA	SDAM	432
H-1D(UH)-BF	Belleville	MI	YAF	66-16006, N5700
H-1D(UH)-BF	Oscoda	MI	YAF	66-16048, N13YA
H-1D(UH)	Seattle	WA	MoF	
H-1E (UH)	Triangle	VA	NMMC	154760
H-1E (UH)	Brist	WI	Museum	
H-1F(UH)	Green	AZ	TMM	
H-1F(UH)	Tucson	AZ	PAM	66-1211
H-1F(UH)	Riverside	CA	MAFB	63-13143
H-1F(UH)	Knob	MO	WAFB	
H-1F(UH)	Great Falls	MT	MAFB	65-956
H-1F(UH)	Grand Forks	ND	GFAFB	
H-1F(UH)	Minot	ND	MAFB	
H-1F(UH)	Albuq	NM	KAFB	
H-1F(UH)	Rapid City	SD	SDA&SM	66-7591
H-1F(UH)	Weirton	WA	City Park	
H-1F(UH)	Cheye	WY	FEWAFB	
H-1F2(UH)	Pooler	GA	MoF	65-7959
H-1H(UH)	Fayet	AR	AAM	70-16050
H-1HA(UH)	Kalaeloa	HI	NAMBB	69-15708
H-1HB(UH)	Wheeler	HI	WAFB	0-15127
H-1M(UH)	Wheeler	HI	WAFB	27548
H-1M(UH)	Hampton	GA	AAHF	
H-1M(UH)	Bloomington	IL	PAM	67-17832
H-1M(UH)	Russell	IL	MMM, 66-01169, "123 AVBN AMDIV"	
H-1M(UH)	Russell	IL	MMM	66-16122
H-1M(UH)	Russell	IL	MMM	65-9534
H-1M(UH)	Fairmount	IN	AMP313	68-16504, 05/19/85
H-1M(UH)	Topek	KS	CAM	TA-897
H-1M(UH)	Cheboygan	MI	VFW	0-15586
H-1M(UH)	Augusta	ME	MANG	63-8809
H-1M(UH)	Bangor	ME	CTM	65-9915
H-1M(UH)	Bangor	ME	MAM	71-20317; 73-21661
H-1M(UH)	Charlotte	NC	CAM	01-3731
H-1M(UH)	McVille	ND	City Park	73-21687
H-1M(UH)	Angel Fire	NM	VVNM	64-13670
H-1H(UH)	Buffalo	NY	B&ECN$SP	63-12982
H-1H(UH)	Horsehead	NY	WoE	65-09589
H-1H(UH)	Horsehead	NY	WoE	66-16200
H-1H(UH)	Horsehead	NY	WoE	66-16906
H-1H(UH)	Norwalk	OH	FMoMH	67-17658
H-1H(UH)	Mc Minnville	OR	EAM	64-13502
H-1H(UH)	Beaver Falls	PA	AHM	
H-1H(UH)	Smethport	PA	AAAM	
H-1H(UH)	NKing	RI	QAM	65-09996
H-1H(UH)	NKing	RI	QAM	64-13492
H-1H(UH)	MtPleasant	SC	PPM	10132
H-1H(UH)	Pigeopn Forge	TN	HH	66-16415, "Trojan Hoss"
H-1H(UH)	San Angelo	TX	VVM	65-09889
H-1H(UH)	San Antonio	TX	TAM	64-13624, 24A
H-1H(UH)	Tyler	TX	HAMM	
H-1H(UH)	W Houston	TX	Airport	
H-1H(UH)	FtEus	VA	USATM	74-22376
H-1H(UH)	Chantilly	VA	NASMUVC	
H-1M (UH)	CPoin	NC	CPMB	
H-1M (UH)	CPoin	NC	CPMB	
H-1M (UH)	Huntsville	AL	RA	
H-1M (UH)	Fayetteville	AR	OMM	
H-1M (UH)	Littl	AR	LRAFB	
H-1M (UH)	Tucson	AZ	PAM	65-9430
H-1M (UH)	Atterbury	IN	CAM&MC	0-15084
H-1M (UH)	Pensacola	FL	VMP	314 HL-3
H-1M (UH)	Hampton	GA	AAHF	
H-1M (UH)	Topek	KS	CAM	
H-1M (UH)	Suitland	MD	PEGF	
H-1M (UH)	Monro	MI	MCVVM	632
H-1M (UH)	Las Cruces	NM	WSMP	
H-1M (UH)	NYC	NY	ISASM	
H-1M (UH)	Scotia	NY	ESAM	65-9435
H-1M (UH)	Fall River	MA	FRBC	66-00609
H-1M (UH)	NKing	RI	QAM	66-15083
H-1M (UH)	MtPleasant	SC	PPM	65-10132
H-1M (UH)	Amari	TX	EFA&SM	

H- 1M(UH)	VA	Hampton	VA&SC	
H- 1P(UH)	FL	FtWal	HF	64-15493
H- 1P(UH)	GA	Pooler	MoF	
H- 1P(UH)	OH	Dayton	NMUSAF	64-15476
H- 1S(UH)	AR	Fayetteville	OMM	
H- 1V(UH)	FL	Tittusville	VACM	
H- 1V(UH)	PA	Willow Grove	NVHAA	68-16614
H- 1V(UH)	VA	Richmond	VAM	

CH-34 Sikorsky Jolly Green Giant

H- 3C(CH)	AZ	Tucson	DMAFB	
H- 3C(CH)	UT	Ogden	HAFBM	
H- 3E(CH)	CA	Chino	YAM	
H- 3E(CH)	CA	Rosamond	EAFB	62-12581
H- 3E(CH)	CA	McClellan	McCelAFB	65-5690
H- 3E(CH)	GA	Pooler	MoF	65-12797
H- 3E(CH)	OH	Dayton	NMUSAF	63- 9676
H- 3E(CH)	OR	Tillamook	EAM	
H- 3E(CH)	NC	Charlotte	CAM	65-12797
H- 3E(CH)	NC	Charlotte	CAM	65-12790

HH-3 Sikorsky Pelican

H- 3F(HH)	SC	Mt Pleasant	PPM	149932, Side 55
H- 3F(HH)(S-61)	IL	Chica	MoS&I	
H- 3F(HH)(S-61)	FL	FtWal	HF	65-12784, AH
H- 3F(HH)(S-61)	AZ	Tucson	PAM	1476
H- 3F(HH)(S-61)	FL	Pensacola	NMoNA	CGNR1486
H- 3F(HH)(S-61)	FL	Clear	FMAM	
H- 3F(HH)(S-61)	PA	WChester	AHM	
H- 3F(HH)(S-61)	WI	Janesville	BHTSAC	
H- 3F(HH)(S-61)	IL	Russell	MMM	1485
H- 3F(HH)(S-61)	IL	Russell	MMM	44043

H-3H(UH)	HI	Kalaeloa	NAMBP	Sikorsky	Sea King	148043
H-3H(UH)	HI	Kalaeloa	NAMBP	Sikorsky	Sea King	152701
H- 3S(OH)	NY	NYC	ISASM	Bell	Souix	
H- 4A(OH)	AL	Ozark	USAAM	Ryan	Jet Ranger	62-4201

H-5 (S-51) Sikorsky Dragonfly

H- 5 (HH)(S-51)	AK	Palme	MOAT&I	
H- 5 (R)	AL	Ozark	USAAM	51-24352
H- 5A(OH)(S-51)	AL	Ozark	USAAM	62-4206
H- 5A(YH)(S-51)	OH	Dayton	NMUSAF	43-46620
H- 5G(S-51)	AZ	Tucson	PAM	48-548, N9845Z
H- 5G(S-51)	NM	Albuq	KAFB	
H- 5H(S-51)	CT	Winds	NEAM	

H- 6A(AH)	NC	Fayetteville	A&SOM	Boeing	Little Bird

OH-6A Hughes Cayuse

H- 6A(OH)	AL	Ozark	USAAM	65-12917
H- 6A(OH)	AL	Birmingham	SMoF	
H- 6A(YO)	AL	Ozark	USAAM	62-4213
H- 6A(OH)	CA	Compton	TAM	67-16091
H- 6A(OH)	CA	Marys	FWM	
H- 6A(OH)	CA	Riverside	MFAM	68-17252
H- 6A(OH)	CO	CO.Sp	FCBA	
H- 6A(OH)	CT	Windsor Locks	NEAM	67-16127
H- 6A(OH)	FL	Tampa	VMM&P	
H- 6A(OH)	GA	Hampton	AAHF	
H- 6A(OH)	KS	Liberal	MAAM	

Designation	State	City	Collection	Notes
H-6A(OH)	KS	Topeka	MoKNG	
H-6A(OH)	LA	Reser	AMHFM	
H-6A(OH)	NJ	Rio Grande	NASWAM	67-16638
H-6A(OH)	NY	Horseheads	NWM	67-16668
H-6A(OH)	NY	Scotia	ESAM	68-17343
H-6A(OH)	OK	Oklahoma	45IDM	
H-6A(OH)	PA	WChes	AHM	
H-6A(OH)	RI	NKing	QAM	67-16570
H-6A(OH)	UT	Ft Douglas	FDMM	
H-6A(OH)	UT	Ogden	HAFBM	
H-6A(OH)	UT	West Jordan	NGA	

H-12 Hiller Raven

Designation	State	City	Collection	Notes
H-12	OK	Lexington	CPT	
H-12(UH)	CO	Denve	JWDAS	
H-12 (UH)	HI	Oahu	WAFB	
H-12 (UH)	IN	Mentone	LDBAM	
H-12 (UH)(U-23)	CA	Chino	PoFAM	
H-12 (UH)(U-23)	MI	Kalamazoo	KAHM	51-4007
H-12A(HTE-1)	FL	Pensacola	NMoNA	41-4017, N3HK, 1
H-12C(UH)	AZ	Tucson	PAM	345, N7725C,
Model 360				
H-12D(UH)(H-23)	PA	WChes	AHM	Model 360
H-12E(UH)	OR	Mc Minnville	EAM	2100, N1H
H-12E(UH)	OR	Mc Minnville	EAM	2049, N5363V
H-12L(UH) Model 360	CA	San Carlos	HNCAVM	

H-13 Bell Sioux

Designation	State	City	Collection	Notes
H-13	AL	Starke	CBM	0-21455
H-13	FL	Kissimmee	AA	N48316
H-13	GA	Hampton	AAHF	
H-13	IN	Mentone	LDBAM	
H-13	KS	Liberal	MAAM	
H-13	NJ	Teter	AHoFNJ	
H-13	SD	Rapid City	SDA&SM	
H-13	WA	Bellingham	HFM	
H-13	IL	Russell	MMM	
H-13 (HTL-2)	MI	Ypsilanti	YAF	Air Ambulance
H-13 (OH)	CA	SanLu	CSLO	
H-13 (OH)	CO	CO.Sp	FCBA	
H-13 (OH)	TX	Midland	AAHM	633EB
H-13A(VH)	CA	Riverside	MFAM	
H-13B(OH)	AL	Ozark	USAAM	48- 827
H-13D(OH)	CA	El Cajon	SDAMGF	
H-13E(HTL-4)	CA	Miramar	FLAM, Air Ambulance	
H-13E(HTL-4)	FL	Pensacola	NMoNA, Air Ambulance, 128911	
H-13E(HTL-4)	VA	Quantico	NMMC, Air Ambulance, 128635	
H-13E(OH)	AL	Ozark	USAAM	51-14193
H-13E(OH)	KY	FKnox	PMoC&A	
H-13E(OH)	NM	Albuq	KAFB	
H-13E(OH)	OK	Oklahoma	45IDM	
H-13E (OH)	OR	Mc Minnville	EAM	
H-13E(OH)	WA	Seattle	MoF	51-14030, N795
H-13G(OH)	NJ	Lexington	NASWAM	
H-13H(VH)	CA	Atwater	CAM	
H-13(UH)	CO	Denve	JWDAS	
H-13J(UH)	OH	Dayton	NMUSAF	57-2728
H-13J(VH)	VA	Chantilly	NASMUVC	"Eisenhower"
H-13M(TH)	GA	Pooler	MoF	142376
H-13M(TH)(HTL-6)	FL	Pensacola	NMoNA	142377, 18
H-13N(TH)(HTL-7)	AZ	Tucson	PAM	145842
H-13P(UH)	GA	Pooler	MoF	143143
H-13S(OH)	NY	NYC	ISASM	
H-13T(TH)	UT	Ogden	HAFBM	67-17053
H-13T(TH)	AL	Ozark	USAAM	67-17024
H-13T(TH)	IL	Linco	HIFM	
H-13T(TH)	TX	Dallas	FoF	67-17059

UH-19 Sikorsky Chickasaw

Designation	State	City	Collection	Notes
H-19 (CH)	CA	Ramona	CR	

Model	State	Location	Museum	Serial / Notes
H-19 (CH)	CA	SanLu	CSLO	
H-19 (CH)	NY	New York	ISASM	
H-19 (CH)	OR	Mc Minnville	EAM	
H-19 (UH)	TX	Slaton	TAM	0-13948
H-19A(UH)	VA	Chantilly	NASMUVC	
H-19B(UH)	AZ	Tucson	PAM	52-7537, N2256G
H-19B(UH)	OH	Dayton	NMUSAF	52-7587, "Whirl-O-Way"
H-19B(UH)	MT	Helena	MHSM	(S-55)
H-19B(UH)-ST	NE	Ashland	SACM	53-4426
H-19D(UH)	VA	FtEus	USATM	56-1550
H-19D(UH)	AL	Ozark	USAAM	55-5239
H-19D(UH)	CA	Ramona	CR	
H-19D(UH)	FL	Tittusville	VACM	
H-19D(HH)	GA	Pooler	MoF	55-3328
H-19D(UH)	ND	Grand Forks	GFAFB	
H-19E(CH)	FL	Pensacola	NMoNA	130151, (HRS-2)
H-19E(CH)	FL	Pensacola	NMoNA	142432, (HRS-3)
H-19F(UH)	NM	Albuq	KAFB	
H-19G(HH)	SC	Flore	FA&MM	(HO4S-1)
H-20 (XH)	OH	Dayton	NMUSAF	
McDonnell				46-689, "Lt Henery"

CH-21 Piasecki Workhorse (Flying Banana)

Model	State	Location	Museum	Serial / Notes
H-21B(UH)	CA	River	MFAM	53-4326
H-21B(CH)	AL	Mobile	BMP	51-15859
H-21B(CH)	CA	Farfield	DA&SM	
H-21B(CH)	CA	Ramona	CR	53-4347
H-21B(CH)	CO	Pueblo	PWAM	52-8685
H-21B(CH)	GA	Pooler	MoF	
H-21B(CH)	NM	Albuq	KAFB	
H-21B(CH)	OH	Dayton	NMUSAF	51-15857,
H-21B(CH)	PA	Readi	MAAM	
H-21B(CH)	SC	Flore	FA&MM	
H-21B(CH)	TX	FWort	PMoT	
H-21B(CH)(PD-22)	WI	Oshkosh	EAAAAM	N57968, 28683
H-21B-PH(CH)	NE	Ashland	SACM	52-8676

CH-21 Piasecki Shawnee

Model	State	Location	Museum	Serial / Notes
H-21C(CH)	CA	Rosamond	EAFB	52-8623
H-21C(CH)	CA	McClellan	McCelAFB	51-15886
H-21C(CH)	CO	Denver	WOTR	
H-21C-VL(CH)	UT	Ogden	HAFBM	56-2142
H-21C(CH)	AL	Ozark	USAAM	
H-21C(CH)	AR	Fayetteville	OMM	
H-21C(CH)	AZ	Tucson	PAM	56-2159
H-21C(CH)	NY	NYC	ISASM	
H-21C(CH)	PA	WChester	AHM	
H-21C(CH)	QB-C	LaBaie	ADM	
H-21C(CH)	RI	N kingston	QAM	
H-21C(CH)	VA	FtEus	USATM	56-2130
H-21C(CH)	WA	Everett	MoF	53-4366, N6797

OH-23 Hiller Raven

Model	State	Location	Museum	Serial / Notes
H-23 (OH)	CA	SanLu	CSLO	
H-23 (OH)	GA	Hampton	AAHF	
H-23 (OH)	LA	New Orleans	JBMM	51-16336
H-23 (OH)	NY	NYC	ISASM	
H-23 (OH)	OR	Mc Minnville	EAM	
H-23 (OH)	AL	Ozark	USAAM	51-3975, G
H-23A(OH)	KS	Topeka	CAM	
H-23B(OH)	CA	Ramona	CR	
H-23B(OH)	CA	San Carlos	HNCAVM	
H-23B(OH)	GA	Hampton	AAHF	
H-23B(OH)	KY	FKnox	PMoC&A	
H-23B(OH)	PA	West Chester	AHM	62-3769
H-23B(OH)	TX	FWort	PMoT	
H-23A(OH)	VA	FtEus	USATM	51-16168
H-23C(OH)	GA	Pooler	MoF	56-421

Model	Manufacturer	Name	State	City	Museum	Serial
H-23C(OH)			OK	Oklahoma	45IDM	55-4124
H-23F(OH)			AL	Ozark	USAAM	62-12508
H-23F(OH)			OK	FtSil	USAFAM	62-3791
H-23G(OH)			CT	Winds	NEAM	
H-23G(OH)			HI	Wheeler	WAFB	64-15245
H-25 (UH)	Piasecki	Army Mule	MI	Kalamazoo	KAHM	
H-25A	Piasecki	Army Mule	AL	Ozark	USAAM	51-16616
H-25A(UH)	Piasecki	Army Mule	VA	FtEus	USATM	130043
H-25C(OH)	Piasecki	Army Mule	GA	Pooler	MoF	
H-26 (XH)	American Helicopter	Jet Jeep	OH	Dayton	NMUSAF	50-1841
H-26A(XH)	American Helicopter	Jet Jeep	AL	Ozark	USAAM	50-1840
H-30(YH)	Jovair	McCulloch	CA	Ramona	CR	
H-32(YH) See HOE						
H-32	Hiller	Hornet	CA	Ramona	CR	
H-34 See S-58						
H-34A(VCH)	Sikorsky	Army One	AL	Ozark	USAAM	56-4320
H-34A(VCH)	Sikorsky	Army One	VA	Quantico	NMMC	147161

H-34 Sikorsky Choctaw

Model	State	City	Museum	Serial
H-34 (CH)	AL	Ozark	USAAM	65-7992
H-34 (CH)	CA	Chino	YAM	
H-34 (CH)	CA	Farfield	DA&SM	
H-34 (CH)	CA	SanLu	CSLO	
H-34 (CH)	MN	Blaine	AWAM	14173
H-34 (CH)	NC	Camp Lejeune	CLVC	
H-34 (CH)	SC	Flore	FA&MM	
H-34A(CH)	AL	Ozark	USAAM	53-4526
H-34C(CH)	NC	Charlotte	CAM	55-4496
H-34C(CH)	VA	FtEus	USATM	57-1725

H-34 Sikorsky Seahorse

Model	State	City	Museum	Serial
H-34	CA	Alameda	USSHM	140136
H-34	CA	Chino	PoFAM	
H-34	CA	Ramona	CR	
H-34	FL	Kissi	FTWAM	
H-34	GA	Calhoun	WAM	
H-34 (HH)	NM	Albuq	KAFB	
H-34 (UH)	NY	NYC	ISASM	
H-34 (UH)	TX	FWort	NASFWJRB	
H-34A	FL	Clear	FMAM	
H-34C(VH)	AZ	Tucson	PAM	57-1684
H-34C(VH)	CA	Rosamond	EAFB	57-1726
H-34D(VH)	VA	Quantico	NMMC	147161
H-34D(HH)(HOK-1)	CA	Miramar	FLAM	
H-34D(LH)	CT	Winds	NEAM	
H-34D(UH)	CA	Miramar	FLAM	YP, HMM-163
H-34D(UH)	VA	Chantilly	NASMUVC	
H-34D(UH)	PA	Readi	MAAM	
H-34D(UH)(HUS-1)	FL	Pensacola	NMoNA	X0, 657, 150227, 1
H-34E(HH)	GA	Pooler	MoF	
H-34G(UH)	CA	Rosamond	EAFB	137856
H-34J(UH)	UT	Ogden	HAFBM	148943
H-34J(UH)	CO	Pueblo	PWAM	

H-34 Sikorsky Seabat

H-34

Model	State	City	Museum	Notes
H-34J(UH)	PA	Willow Grove	NVHAA	145694
H-34J(HH)	AZ	Phoen	LAFB	148963
H-34J(HH)	GA	Pooler	MoF	
H-34(SH)	SC	MtPleasant	PPM	14171
H-34(UH)(SS-1)	CA	San Diego	SDACM	143939

CH-37 (HR2S-1) Sikorsky Mojave

Model	State	City	Museum	Notes
H-37(CH)	FL	Pensacola	NMoNA	145864
H-37B(CH)	AL	Ozark	USAAM	55-644
H-37B(CH)	AZ	Tucson	PAM	56-1005, "Tired Dude"
H-37B(CH)	CA	Ramona	CR	57-1651
H-37B(CH)	VA	FtEus	USATM	

Model	State	City	Museum	Mfr	Notes
H-41A(YH)	AL	Ozark	USAAM	Cessna	
		Seneca			56-4244

HH-43 Kaman Huskie (HOK-1)

Model	State	City	Museum	Notes
H-43 (HH)	CA	Atwater	CAM	
H-43A(HH)	CA	Ramona	CR	62-4513
H-43B(HH)	CT	Winds	NEAM	289
H-43B(HH)	DE	Dover	AMCM	4532
H-43B(HH)	GA	Pooler	MoF	58-1853
H-43B(HH)	NM	Albuq	KAFB	
H-43B(HH)	TX	FWort	PMoT	
H-43B(OH)	UT	Ogden	HAFBM	65-4561
H-43D(OH)	AZ	Tucson	PAM	139974
H-43F(HH)	AZ	Tucson	PAM	62-4531
H-43F(HH)	OH	Dayton	NMUSAF	60-263

H-44 / H-46 / H-47 / H-50 / H-51

Model	State	City	Museum	Mfr	Notes
H-44 (XH)	VA	Chantilly	NASMUVC	Hiller	Commuter
H-44(UH)	CA	San Carlos	HNCAVM	Hiller	Commuter
H-46(CH)	CA	Miramar	FLAM	**Boeing, Seaknight**	
H-46(CH)	CA	San Diego	SDACM	Boeing, Seaknight, 150954	
H-46E(CH)	NC	Charlotte	CAM	Boeing, Seaknight, 153389	
H-46E(CH)	VA	Triangle	NMMC	Boeing, Seaknight, 154824	
H-47 (CH)	CA	SanLu	CSLO	**Boeing-Vertol**	**Chinook**
H-47 (CH)	CO	Pueblo	PWAM	Boeing-Vertol	Chinook, 59-94984
H-47 (CH)	VA	Eustis,	USATM,	Boeing-Vertol	Chinook
H-47A(CH)	AL	Huntsville		Boeing-Vertol	Chinook
H-47A(CH)	AL	Ozark	USAAM	Boeing-Vertol	60-3451 (64-13149) "Easy Money"
H-47(HK)	OK	Tulsa	TA&SC	**Bell**	
H-50A(HH)	SC	MtPleasant	PPM	**Gyrodyne**	**Drone**
H-50C(OH)	CT	Winds	NEAM	Gyrodyne	Drone
H-50C(OH)	GA	Pooler	MoF	Gyrodyne	Drone
H-50C(OH)	MD	Lexington	PRNAM	Gyrodyne, Drone, DS-1679	
H-50C(QH)	NC	Charlotte	CAM	Gyrodyne, Drone, DS-1355	
H-50C(QH)	PA	WChester	AHM	Gyrodyne	Drone
H-51A(XH)	AL	Ozark	USAAM	**Lockheed**	**Rigid Rotor** 61-51262
H-51A(XH)	AL	Ozark	USAAM	Lockheed	**Rigid Rotor** 61-51263

HH-52 Sikorsky Seaguard (Polar Star)

Model	State	City	Museum	Notes
H-52A(HH)	AZ	Tucson	PAM	62-71, N8224Q
H-52A(HH)	CA	Chino	YAM	
H-52A(HH)	CT	Winds	NEAM	1428, Polar Star
H-52A(HH)	FL	Pensacola	NMoNA	CGNR1355
H-52A(HH)	IL	Chica	MoS&I	Polar Star
H-52A(HH)	MI	Mt Clemens	SMAM	1466, Polar Star
H-52A(HH)	NJ	Lexington	NASWAM	
H-52A(HH)	NJ	Teterboro	AHoFNJ	
H-52A(HH)	NY	NYC	ISASM	Polar Star, 1429
H-52A(HH)	PA	Readi	MAAM	Polar Star
H-52A(HH)(S-62)	PA	WChester	AHM	
H-52A(HH)(S-62)	WA	Everett	MoF	CGNR1415

CH-53 Sikorsky Sea Stallion

Designation	State	Museum	Location	Serial
H-53A(CH)	CA	FLAM	Miramar	
H-53A(CH)	FL	NMoNA	Pensacola	151687
H-53A(CH)	HI	NAMBB	Kalaeloa	156974
H-53A(CH)	HI	MB	Kaneohe	
H-53A(CH)	KS	CAM	Topeka	
H-53A(CH)	MD	PRNAM	Lexington	151686
H-53A(CH)	VA	NMMC	Triangle	151692
H-53A(CH)	VA	NASN	Norfolk	158748, 1st MAW ASE
H-53D(RH)	HI	KBMCAS	Kaneohe	158690
H-53D(RH)	NJ	AVM	Lumberton	

CH-54 Sikorsky Skycrane

Designation	State	Museum	Location	Serial
H-54 (CH)	MS	AFM	McLaurin	
H-54 (CH)	NC	CLVC	Camp Lejeune	
H-54 (CH)	WI	Museum	Brist	
H-54 (CH)	IL	MMM	Russell	446, "The Bull Stops Here"
H-54 (CH)	IL	MMM	Russell	486
H-54 (S-64)	OR	EAM	Mc Minnville	
H-54A(CH)	AZ	PAM	Tucson	68-18437, 64039
H-54A(CH)	KS	CAM	Topek	67-14824
H-54A(CH)	VA	USATM	FtEus	64-14203
H-54B(CH)	AL	SMoF	Birmingham	
H-54B(CH)	CT	NEAM	Winds	6-18465
H-54B(CH)	KS	MoKNG	Topeka	
H-54D(CH)	GA	GSMA	Spart	

TH-55 Hughes Osage

Designation	State	Museum	Location	Serial
H-55A(TH)	AL	USAAM	Ozark	
H-55A(TH)	AZ	PAM	Tucson	67-16795
H-55A(TH)	AZ	PAM	Tucson	67-18350
H-55A(TH)	AZ	PAM	Tucson	67-18273
H-55A(TH)	AZ	PAM	Tucson	67-18203
H-55A(TH)	AZ	PAM	Tucson	67-18017
H-55A(TH)	AZ	PAM	Tucson	67-118133
H-55A(TH)	IN	HMAM	Anderson	
H-55A(TH)	PA	AHM	WChester	
H-55A(TH)	OR	EAM	Mc Minnville	38-0002, N79P
H-55A(TH)	VA	USATM	FtEus	67-16944

Designation	State	Museum	Location	Manufacturer / Name	Serial
H-56A(AH)	AL	USAAM	Ozark	Lockheed Cheyenne	66-8830
H-57A(TH)	FL	NMoNA	Pensacola	Bell Sea Ranger	157363 O4-E

OH-58 Bell Kiowa

Designation	State	Museum	Location	Serial
H-58(OH)	FL	VMM&P	Tampa	
H-58(OH)	HI	WAFB	Oahu	
H-58A(OH)	KY	AMoK	Lexington	72-21256
H-58A(OH)	LA	JBMM	New Orleans	70-15426
H-58A(OH)	KS	AAM	Augusta	
H-58(OH)	KS	MoKNG	Topeka	
H-58(OH)	MB-C	WRCAFB	Winnipeg	
H-58(OH)	ON-C	CFB	Kingston	
H-58(OH)	ON-C	CFB	Trenton	136408
H-58(OH)	RI	QAM	NKing	0-15117
H-58(OH)	TX	H10FM	Denton	0-15358
H-58A(OH)	HI	WAFB	Wheeler	70-15258
H-58A(OH)	CA	MAFM	Riverside	
H-58A(OH)	MI	AZ	Kalamazoo	
H-58A(OH)	OK	45IDM	Oklahoma	
H-58A(OH)	OH	MAM	N Canton	69-16153
H-58A(OH)	NC	CAM	Charlotte	71-20516
H-58A(OH)	TN	HH	Pigeon Forge	
H-58A(OH)	TX	NASFW JRB	FWort	

Designation	State	Location	Museum	Manufacturer / Name	Serial
H-61A(YU)	AL	Ozark	USAAM	Boeing-Vertol UTTAS	73-21656

Type	State	City	Museum	Manufacturer	Model	Reg./Notes
H-63 (YAH)	AL	Ozark	USAAM	Bell	Model 409	74-22247, Bell 409
H-64A(AH)	AL	Huntsville	RA	Hughes	Apache	74-22249
H-64A(YAH)	AL	Ozark	USAAM	Hughes	Apache	
H-65 (AH)	KY	FKnox	FC	Hughes		11301
H-113(CH)	ON-C	Ottawa	CAM	Boeing	Labrador	
HA-200A	FL	Titusville	VACM	Hispano	Cairo	
HA-200B	MD	Suitland	PEGF	Hispano	Cairo	
HA-1112	AZ	Grand Canyon	PoFGCVA	Hispano	Buchon	
HA-1112	MB-C	Winni	WCAM	Hispano	Buchon	C.4K 114
HA-1112	ON-C	Ottawa	CAM	Hispano	Buchon	C4K-19
HA-1112	MI	Kalamazoo	KAHM	Hispano	Buchon	N109BF
HA-1112	WI	Oshkosh	EAAAAM	Hispano	Buchon	
Halberstadt	VA	Chantilly	NASMUVC	Halberstadt		
Halberstadt CL.II	OH	Dayton	NMUSAF	Halberstadt		8103
Halberstadt CL-IV	AL	Gunte	LGARFM	Halberstadt		
Halberstadt CL-IV	VA	Suffolk	FF	Halberstadt		
Halberstadt D.III	AL	Gunte	LGARFM	Halberstadt		
Hanson-Meyer Quickie	CT	Winds	NEAM	Hanson-Meyer	Quickie	
Harbinger Sailplane	ON-C	Ottaw	CAM	Harbinger	Sailplane	
Hardly Abelson	WI	Oshlosh	EAAAAM	Hardly	Abelson	
Harlow PJC-2	WI	Oshkosh	EAAAAM	Harlow		
Harrison Mini-Mack	AL	Birmingham	SMoF	Harrison	Mini-Mack	N3947B
Hartman 1910	NE	Minde	HWPV	Hartman		
Hawk	CO	CSpri	EJPSCM			
Hawk 2	WI	Oshkosh	EAAAAM	Haufe Dale	Hawk 2	N18278
Hawk Major M.2.W	WI	Oshkosh	EAAAAM	Miles	Hawk Major	CF-NXT
Hawker FB.1 Sea Hawk	NY	NYC	ISASM	Hawker FB.11	TX	Addison CFM
Hawker FB.1	WI	Oshkosh	EAAAAM N83SH	Hawker FB.11	TX	Breck BAM
Hawker FB.11 Sea Fury	AB-C	Calga	AMoC	Hawker FB.11 Fuse	TN	Memph LS
Hawker FB.11	AB-C	Calga	NMoA	Hawker FB.11	VA	Suffolk FF
Hawker FB.11	WA	Olympia	OFM	Hawker FB.11	WA	Olympia OFM
Hawker FB.11	ON-C	Ottaw	CAM			
Hawker Hind	ON-C	Ottaw	CAM	Hawker	Hind	
Hawker Hunter	CA	Chino	YAM	Hawker Hunter Mk.51	Oshkosh WI	EAAAAM Side # 737
Hawker Hunter Mk.9	ON-C	Trenton	RCAFMM J-4029	Hawker Hunter Mk.58	Grand Canyon AZ	PoFGCA N611JR

Registry listing (aircraft type, state/province, city, museum/collection, and registration):

Type	State	City	Museum	Serial
Hawker Hunter Mk.58A	PA	Reading	MAAM	
Hawker Hurricane				
Hawker Hurricane 5/8 Scale	AB-C	Wetas	RM	RCAF 5418
Hawker Hurricane	AB-C	Edmonton	AAM	
Hawker Hurricane	FL	Polk City	FoF	RCAF 5400
Hawker Hurricane	MB-C	Brandon	CATPM	RCAF 5461
Hawker Hurricane	ON-C	Ottaw	CAM	RCAF 5584
Hawker Hurricane	WA	Arlington	CFM	BM 881
Hawker Hurricane Mk.II	OH	Dayton	NMUSAF	RCAF 5390
Hawker Hurricane Mk.II	VA	Suffolk	FF	RCAF5667, N2549
Hawker Tempest Mk.2	FL	Lakeland	SNF	
Hawker-Siddeley Kestrel	DC	Washi	NA&SM	
HD-1	CA	Chino	PoFAM	
HD-1	FL	Pensacola	NMoNA	
HD-1	NY	Rhine	ORA	
HD-4 Remains	NS-C	Badde	AGBNHP	
He 100	CA	Chino	PoFAM	
He 111/CASA 2.111	WA	Seattle	MoF	
He 111/CASA 2.111D	OH	Dayton	NMUSAF	
He 111/CASA 2.111E	TX	Addison	CFM	
He 162	ON-C	Ottaw	CAM	
He 162A	MD	Suitland	PEGF	
He 162A-1	CA	Chino	PoFAM	
He 219A-3	VA	Chantilly	NASMUVC	
Headwind JD-HW L-7	AR	Little Rock	AEC	
Heath Feather	WI	Oshkosh	EAAAAM	
Heath Center Wing 115	KY	Lexington	AVoK	
Heath LNA-4D	PA	Reading	MAAM	
Heath Parasol				
Heath Parasol	AL	Birmingham	SMF	
Heath Parasol	CT	Winds	NEAM	
Heath Parasol	MI	Kalamazoo	KAHM	
Heath Parasol	NC	Hende	WNCAM	
Heath Parasol	NY	Rhine	ORA	
Heath Parasol	OR	Hood	WAAAM	
Heath Parasol	WA	Seattle	MoF	

Type / Manufacturer	Model	State	City	Museum	Registration
Hawker Hunter Mk.58A Rep		TX	Galve	LSFM	N68RW, CCF-96
Hawker Hurricane Mk.IIB		VA	Chantilly	NASMUVC	LF 686
Hawker Hurricane Mk.IIC		ON-C	Ottawa	VWoC	KZ 321
Hawker Hurricane Mk.IV		CA	Chino	PoFAM	AE 977
Hawker Hurricane Mk.X		AB-C	Calga	AMoC	RCAF 5389
Hawker Hurricane Mk.XIIb		ON-C	Ottawa	VWoC	RCAF 5447
Hawker Hurricane Mk.XII		AB-C	Edmonton	AAM	Replica
Hawker Hurricane Mk.IIB Rep		ON-C	Hamilton	CWH	C-GCWH, P3069,
Hawker	Tempest				
Hawker-Siddeley	Kestral				
Hanriot	Scout				
Hanriot	Scout				A5625
Hanriot	Scout				
Hanriot	Hydrofoil				19
Heinkel					
Heinkel	Dresden				G
Heinkel	Dresden				
Heinkel	Dresden				N99230
Heinkel	Volksjager				120086
Heinkel	Volksjager				
Heinkel	Volksjager				
Heinkel	Uhu				
Headwind	Ultralight				
Heath	Feather				
Heath	Center Wing 115				NR2881
Heath	LNA-4D				
Heath Parasol		WI	Oshkosh	EAAAAM	N88EG
Heath Parasol 5		NE	Minde	HWPV	
Heath Parasol Rep	Parasol	NY	Mayvi	DA	
Heath Super Parasol		FL	Lakel	SFAF	31919
Heath Super Parasol		VA	Sands	VAM	N953M
Heath Super Parasol		WI	Oshkosh	EAAAAM	

Designation	State	Manufacturer	Name	Location	Museum	Serial / Registration
Hegy R.C.H.I.	WI	Hegy		Oshkosh	EAAAAM	N9360, "El Chuparosa"
Helio 1A	MD	Helio	Courier	Suitland	PEGF	Man Sn 9512, N1512H
Helton Lark 95	AZ	Helton	Lark 95	Tucson	PAM	
Henderschott	WI	Henderschott	Monoplane	Oshkosh	EAAAAM	8902
Henderson Highwing	WI	Folkerts	Henderson	Oshkosh	EAAAAM	
Henderson Longster	NY	Henderson	Longster	Mayville	DA	
Henderson Longster	OR	Henderson	Longster	Hood	WAAAM	
Henri Farman III	ME	Henri Farman		Owls Head	OHTM	
Herring-Curtiss	NY	Herring-Curtiss	Golden Glider	Garde	CoAM	Aircraft
High Max	KS		Experimental	Augusta	AAM	
Hill Hummer	WI	Hill	Hummer	Oshkosh	EAAAAM	N90381, "Pete"
Hiller VZ1 1301	CA	Hiller	Flying Platform	San Carlos	HNCAVM	
Hiller Flying Platform	AZ	Hiller	Flying Platform	Tucson	PAM	
Hiller Helicopter	CA	Hiller		Chino	PoFAM	
Hispano-Suiza	NY	Hispano-Suiza		River	TFAC	
Hisso Standard	MO	Hisso	Standard	Maryland Hts	HARM	
HJD-1(X)	MD	McDonnell	Whirlaway	Suitland	PEGF	
HJD-1H(X)	MD	McDonnell	Whirlaway	Suitland	PEGF	
Hild Marshonet No 17	PA	Hild	Marchonet	Reading	MAAM	
H-4	OR	Hughes	Spruce Goose	Mc Minnville	EAM	NX37602
HM-14	WI	Mignet	Flying Flea	Oshkosh	EAAAAM	Pou du Ciel
HM-	FL	Midget	Flying Flea	Lakeland	SNF	
HM-360	WI	Mignet	Flying Flea	Oshkosh	EAAAAM	N360HM
HO-3B(YHO)	AL	Brantley		Ozark	USAAM	58-1496
HO-45	AK	Hamilton	Metalplane	Fairbanks	PAM	NC10002
HO-49	FL			Pensacola	NMoNA	1049
HO-6A(YH)	AL	Hughes	Cayuse	Ozark	USAAM	62-4213
HO3S	VA	Sikorsky	Dragonfly	Triangle	NMMC	124344
HO3S-1(S-51)	NC	Sikorsky	Dragonfly	Charlotte	CAM	125136
HO3S-1(S-51)	OR	Sikorsky	Dragonfly	Mc Minnvile	EAM	
HO3S-1G	AZ	Sikorsky	Dragonfly	Tucson	PAM	CG, 232, N4925E
HO4S (S-55)	FL	Sikorsky	Chickasaw	Pensacola	NMoNA	
HO4S-3	NS-C	Sikorsky	Chickasaw	Shear	CFBS	CGNR1258, 130151
HO4S-3	ON-C	Sikorsky	Chickasaw	Ottaw	CAM	
HO5S-1G(S-52)	FL	Sikorsky	Dragonfly	Pensacola	NMoNA	
HO5S-1G(S-52)	PA	Sikorsky	Dragonfly	W Chester	AHM	
HOE-1(XH06-1)	VA	Hiller	Hornet	Chantilly	NASMUVC	N8003E, 125519

236

Model	State	City	Museum	Manufacturer	Name	Serial / Registration
HOE-1(HJ-1)	CA	San Carlos	HNCAVM	Hiller	Hornet	55-4965, "Sally Rand"
HOE-1(YH-32)	AL	Ozark	USAAM	Hiller	Hornet	55-4969
HOE-1(YH-32)	CA	San Carlos	HNCAVM	Hiller	Hornet	139990
HOE-1(YH-32)	WA	Everett	MoF	Hiller	Hornet	
HOK-1	NC	Charlotte	CAM	Hiller	Hornet	
Homebuilt	AZ	Tucson	PAM		Homebuilt	
Homebuilt	NS-C	Halifax	ACAM		Scamp 1	
Horten Ho II	MD	Suitland	PEGF	Horten	Flying Wing Glider	1, N30154, "Mike"
Horten Ho III	VA	Chantilly	NASMUVC	Horten	Flying Wing Glider	N111PL, "Little Audrey"
Horten Ho III-H	VA	Chantilly	NASMUVC	Horten	Flying Wing Glider	N319Y
Horten Ho IV	CA	Chino	PoFAM	Horten	Flying Wing Glider	N96326
Horten Ho VI	VA	Chantilly	NASMUVC	Horten	Flying Wing Glider	NA337
Hovercraft	NY	River	TFAC	Hovercraft	Hovercraft	
Howard 250	CA	Chino	PoFAM	Howard	Ero	
Howard	WA	Port Townsend	PTAM	Howard	Replica	
Howard Pete	WI	Oshkosh	EAAAAM	Howard	Pete	
HP-10	WI	Oshkosh	EAAAAM	Helisoar	Glider	
HP-18-LK Sailplane	WI	Oshkosh	EAAAAM	Bryan-Harris	Sailplane	
HP-52	ON-C	Trenton	RCAFMM	Handley-Page	Hampden	
HRP-1	CT	Winds	NEAM	Piasecki	Rescuer	37969
HRP-1(X)	MD	Suitland	PEGF	Piasecki	Rescuer	147608
HRP-3	IN	S Bend	JA			127828
HRS-1(S-55)	VA	Triangle	NMMC	Sikorsky	Chickasaw	WW, MALS-16
HRS-3(S-55)	CA	Miramar	FLAM	Sikorsky	Chickasaw	
HS-2L	ON-C	Ottawa	CAM	Curtiss		G-CAAC
HTK-1(K-125)	FL	Pensacola	NMoNA	Kaman		129313
HTK-1	OR	Tillamook	TNAM	Kaman		
HTL-3	OR	Mc Minnville	EAM	Bell	Sioux	
HU-1B	CA	Chino	YAM	Piasecki	Helicopter	147610, 147610

HU-16 Grumman Albatross

Model	State	City	Museum	Manufacturer	Name	Serial / Registration
HU-16	AZ	Tucson	TI		HU-16	2132, N226GR, N115FB,
HU-16	AZ	Tucson	TI		HU-16	51-043, N7049D,
HU-16	AZ	Tucson	WIA		HU-16	USCG 7218, 310
HU-16	CT	New England	NEAM		HU-16	N43GL, 367
HU-16	FL	Lantana			HU-16	
HU-16	ID	Driggs	TAC		HU-16	1906
HU-16	MA	Cape Cod	CGAS		HU-16	USCG 7250, 340
HU-16	NY	Brooklyn	NARF		HU-16	51-067, N3395F
HU-16	NV	Carson City			HU-16	N120FB, MSN 331
HU-16	NV	Carson City			HU-16	N117FB, MSN 461
HU-16	NV	Carson City			HU-16	141278, N20861,
HU-16	VA	VA Beach	MAFB		HU-16	USCG 7209, 282

Model	St	City	Museum	Serial/Reg	Model	St	City	Museum	Serial/Reg
HU-16 (SA-16)	CA	Atwater	CAM		HU-16B	SC	Flore	FA&MM	51-7212, MSN 281
HU-16 (SA-16)	OK	Fredi	AAM		HU-16B	TX	FWort	PMoT	50-17176
HU-16A	CA	SRosa	PCAM		HU-16B-GR	NE	Ashland	SACM	51-0006
HU-16A	NM	Albuq	KAFB	USCG 1280, 302	HU-16E	AL	Mobile	BMP	2129
HU-16A(SA-16)	AZ	Tucson	PAM	51-22, MSN 096	HU-16E	AZ	Phoen	LAFB	
HU-16B	CA	McClellan	McCelAFB	51-7209	HU-16E	CA	Riverside	MFAM	1293, "Cape Cod"
HU-16B	GA	Pooler	MoF	51-7144	HU-16E	CT	Winds	NEAM	
HU-16B	IL	Rantoul	OCAM	51-7200	HU-16E	FL	Pensacola	NMoNA	CGNR7236, 7236
HU-16B	MD	Balti	BANG		HU-16E	NY	NYC	ISASM	
HU-16B	OH	Dayton	NMUSAF	51-5282	HU-16E	TX	Abilene	DLAP	51-7251
Huber 101-1 Aero	WA	Seattle	MoF		Huber	Aero	Peru (IN)	GAM	001
Huff-Daland Duster	AL	Birmi	Southe		Huff-Daland	Duster	New York (NY)	ISASM	
Huff-Daland Duster	VA	Chantilly	NASMUVC		Huff-Daland	Duster	WChes (PA)	AHM	
Hughes Helicopter	IL	Russell	MMM		Hughes	Helicopter	Willow Grove (PA)	NVHAA	
Hughes 269A	TN	Pigeon Forge	HH		Hughes	Helicopter	Ramona (CA)	CR	128517
Hughes 500	OR	Mc Minnville	EAM		Hughes	Helicopter	Liberal (KS)	MAAM	

HUP Piasecki Retriever

Model	St	City	Museum	Serial/Reg	Model	St	City	Museum	Serial/Reg
HUP-1(UH-25)	CA	Alameda	USSHM	124915	HUP-2	MI	Kalamazoo	KAHM	146700, 51-16607
HUP-1	CA	Ramona	CR		HUP-2	ON-C	Ottaw	CAM	51-16623
HUP-1	CT	Winds	NEAM	7228	HUP-2	AZ	Tucson	PAM	147595, 51-16608
HUP-1	FL	Kissi	FTW AM		HUP-2(H-25)	FL	Pensacola	NMoNA	N4953S, 147607
HUP-2(H-25A)	AZ	Tucson	PAM	134434, N8SA	HUP-3				
HUP-2	AZ	Tucson	PAM	N8SA	HUP-3				
HUP-2	CA	Chino	YAM		HUP-3(H-25A)				
HUP-2	CA	Rosamond	EAFB	130059	HUP-3(UH-25C)				
HUP-2	CA	Miramar	FLAM						
Hutter 17	NY	Elmir	NSM		Hutter				W B153624, CF-RCD, 1934
HV2A	MD	Suitland	PEGF		Herrick	Convertaplane			
Hydro-Kite Gallauder	DC	Washi	NA&SM		Gallauder	Hydro-Kite			
Hyper Light Hang Glider	AZ	Tucson	PAM		Hyper Light	Hyper Light			
I-16 Rata	TX	Midland	AAHM	30425	Polikarpov	Rata			
I-16 Rata	VA	Suffolk	FF		Polikarpov	Rata			
I-152	VA	Suffolk	FF	#7	Polikarpov		#7		
I-153	VA	Suffolk	FF		Polikarpov	Rata			

Designation	State	City	Museum	Notes
Icarus Hang Glider	AZ	Tucson	PAM	Icarus; Hang Glider
Icarus I	MD	Suitland	PEGF	Icarus
ICBM	AL	Mobile	BMP	Redstone; Arsenal Redstone
ICBM	OH	Dayton	NMUSAF	Redstone; Hard Mobile Launcher
Ikarus Aero 3A	CA	Oakla	OWAM	Ikarus; Aero
Ikarus Aero 3A	FL	Miami	WOM	Ikarus; Aero
Ikenga 530Z Autogiro	VA	Chantilly	NASMUVH	Gittens; Autogiro
Ilyushin IL-14P	CA	Santa Rosa	PCAM	Ilyushin; Model SO
Ilyushin IL-2m3	MD	Suitland	PEGF	Ilyushin; Shturmovik
Ilyushin	NV	Reno	Steade	Ilyushin; Model SO; 1954
Ingram/Foster Biplane	NM	Albuq	AA	Ingram-Foster; Biplane
Insitu Aerosonde	WA	Seattle	MoF	Insitu; Aerosonde

J-1 Standard

Designation	State	City	Museum	Reg./Notes
J-1	AZ	Grand Canyon	PoFGCVA	
J-1	CA	Chino	YAM	
J-1	CA	San Diego	SDAM	1598, N2826D
J-1	FL	Polk	FoF	
J-1N1	VA	Chantilly	NASMUVC	
J-1	ME	Owls Head	OHTM	
J-1	ND	W Farg	Bonanzav	
J-1	NY	Buffalo	B&ECHM	
J-1	NY	Rhine	ORA	
J-1	OH	Dayton	NMUSAF	1141
J-1	OH	Dayton	NMUSAF	Fabric Covered
J-1	PA	Bethel	GAAM	
J-1	WI	Oshkosh	EAAAAM	N6948
J-2 — McCulloch Super Gyroplane	AZ	Tucson	PAM	Man Sn 019, N4309G
J-2 — McCulloch Super Gyroplane	CA	Ramona	CR	
J-2 — McCulloch Gyro-Plane	KS	Liberal	MAAM	
J-2 — Wizard Ultralight	WA	Seattle	MoF	

J-2 Taylor Cub

Designation	State	City	Museum	Reg./Notes
J-2	CA	Modesto	HAM	
J-2	IA	Greenfield	IAM	
J-2	MD	College Park	CPAM	NC16769
J-2	MD	Hager	HRegAirP	
J-2	NE	Minde	HWPV	
J-2	NY	Niagara Falls	NAM	NC17834
J-2	NY	Rhine	ORA	
J-2	OK	Fredi	AAM	
J-2	OR	Hood	WAAAM	
J-2	PA	Readi	MAAM	
J-2	PA	Lock Haven	PAM	
J-2A	MD	Suitland	PEGF	

Piper Cub

Designation	State	City	Museum	Reg./Notes
J-2	NC	Hende	WNCAM	NC16315
J-2	ND	Minot	DTAM	
J-2	WI	Oshkosh	EAAAAM	
J-3	AL	Birmingham	SMoF	
J-3	AR	Fayet	AAM	Project, NC38668

Model	State	City	Museum	Reg./Notes
J-3	CA	San Diego	SDAM	NC333ED
J-3	CO	Denver	WOTR	
J-3	CO	GJunc	CAF-RMW	N53503
J-3	CT	Winds	NEAM	
J-3	FL	Ameli	IAT	
J-3	FL	Kissi	FTWAM	8375H NC
J-3	FL	Pensacola	NMoNA	
J-3	IA	Greenfield	IAM	
J-3	IN	Auburn	HW	
J-3	MB-C	Brand	CATPM	
J-3	VA	Chantilly	NASMUVC	
J-3	MO	Missoula	MMF	
J-3	NC	Charlotte	CAM	
J-3	ND	Minot	DTAM	
J-3-F-65	ND	Fargo	BUSAHM	
J-3	NM	St Teresa	WEAM	
J-3	NY	Bayport	BA	
J-3	NY	Horsehead	WoE	N33769
J-3	NY	Mayvi	DA	
J-3	NY	Rhine	ORA	
J-3	NY	River	RE	
J-3	NC	Asheboro	PFAC	Flitfire
J-3C-65-8	OH	Dayton	NMUSAF	NC42050
J-3	OR	Hood	WAAAM	4-469, NC22783
J-3	OR	Hood	WAAAM	1st edition
J-3	OR	Hood	WAAAM	Year 1946
J-3	PA	Lock Haven	PAM	CF-LBE
J-3	SK-C	Moose Jaw	WDM	N24935
J-3	TX	Addison	CFM	
J-3	TX	Gilmer	PotP	
J-3	TX	Kingsbury	VAHF	Project
J-3	TX	Ladero	Airport	
J-3	UT	Heber	HVAM	
J-3	VA	Bealt	FCA	
J-3	VA	Richm	SMoV	
J-3	WA	Port Townsend	PTAM	17083, N70109
J-3	WA	Vancouver	PAM	
J-3	WA	Yakima	MMoA	
J-3	WI	Oshkosh	EAAAAM	
J-3 CP-65	OK	Fredi	AAM	
J-3C	CA	Palm Sprg	PSAM	N28118
J-3C	KS	Liberal	MAAM	
J-3C	ME	Owls Head	OHTM	
J-3C	NY	Horsehead	WoE	N25769
J-3C	WA	Seattle	MoF	15641, N88023
J-3C-65	MI	Kalamazoo	KAHM	
J-3C	PA	Harri	SMoP	
J-3C-65	NC	Hende	WNCAM	N3450K
J-3C-65	OR	Mc Minnville	EAM	G-31, N46471
J-3P	OR	Hood	WAAAM	
J-4A Piper Coupe				
J-4A	OK	Fredi	AAM	
J-4A	WI	Oshkosh	EAAAAM	
J-4A	AZ	Tucson	PAM	
J-4B	NY	Horsehead	WoE	4867, N26726
J-4F	KS	Liberal	MAAM	Coupe
J-4F	OK	Fredi	AAM	
J-5 Piper Cruiser				
J-5	GA	Woodstock	AAM	N30340
J-5	GA	Woodstock	AAM	
J-5	GA	Woodstock	AAM	NC38499
J-5	NC	Hende	WNCAM	
J-5	OH	Madis	CFR	
J-5(AE-1)(HE-1)	OR	Hood	WAAM	
J-5	VA	Sands	VAM	
J-5C(AE-1)	TX	San A	ILP&AAM	
J-10-JET	CA	San Carlos	HNCAVM	Model 360
J-29	MD	Suitland	PEGF	Saab, Tunman; Swept Wing Fighter

Type	State / Prov	City	Museum	Manufacturer	Name	Serial / Registration
J-35	GA	Woodstock	AAM	CuMaulaCraftMan		
J1N1-S	MD	Suitland	PEGF	Nakajima	Moonlight	
J2F-6	AK	Ancho	AAHM	Grumman	Duck	
J2F-6	AZ	Grand Canyon	PoFAM	Grumman	Duck	
J2F-6	CA	San Diego	SDAM	Grumman	Duck	N1273N, 33594
J2F-6	FL	Lakeland	SnF	Grumman	Duck	
J2F-6	FL	Pensacola	NMoNA	Grumman	Duck	33581, 149
J2F-6	FL	Polk	FoF	Grumman	Duck	
J2F-6	OR	Tillamook	TAM	Grumman	Duck	N3960C
J2F-6	WI	Oshkosh	EAAAAM	Grumman	Duck	36976
J2M3	CA	Chino	PoFAM	Mitsubishi	Raiden	
J4F-1(G-44A)	FL	Lakeland	SNF	Grumman	Widgeon	1260, N212ST, V 212, Model G-44
J4F-1	FL	Pensacola	NMoNA	Grumman	Widgeon	32976, Model G-44
J4F-2	AZ	Tucson	PAM	Grumman	Widgeon	
J4F-1	ON-C	Hamilton	CWH	Grumman	Widgeon	
J7W1	MD	Suitland	PEGF	Mitsubishi	Kyushu	
J8M1	CA	Chino	PoFAM	Mitsubishi	Shusui	
JC-1	MD	Suitland	PEGF	Chase-Church	Weedhopper	
JC-1	WI	Oshkosh	EAAAAM		Midwing	N9167
JC-24-B	WI	Oshkosh	EAAAAM	Weedhopper	Weedhopper	N1005Z
JN-2D-1	WI	Oshkosh	EAAAAM	Curtiss	Jenny	

JN-4D Curtiss Jenny

Type	State / Prov	City	Museum	Serial / Registration
JN-4D	AB-C	Wetas	RM	
JN-4D	AL	Ozark	USAAM	
JN-4D	CA	Chino	YAM	
JN-4D	CA	Chino	YAM	
JN-4D	CA	Paso Robles	EWM	N1563, D-51
JN-4D	CA	San Diego	SDAM	A-996
JN-4D	CA	San Francisco	CFAMA	N5391, 3826, 38262
JN-4D	CO	Denve	DIA	SC1918, #65
JN-4D	CT	Washi	TFC	
JN-4D	FL	Pensacola	NMoNA	490, A, 995
JN-4D	FL	Polk	FoF	
JN-4D	IL	Chica	MoS&I	
JN-4D	KS	Topek	CAM	N-101JN
JN-4D	MD	College Park	CPAM	
JN-4D	MD	Suitland	PEGF	
JN-4D	ME	Owls Head	OHTM	
JN-4D	MI	Kalamazoo	KAM	(2/3 Scale)
JN-4D	MO	Maryland Hts	HARM	
JN-4D	NE	Minde	HWPV	
JN-4D	NY	Garde	CoAM	1187
JN-4D	NY	Hammond	CM	
JN-4D	NY	Rhine	ORA	
JN-4D	NY	Niagara Falls	NAM	3059
JN-4D	OH	Dayton	NMUSAF	2805
JN-4D	OK	Tulsa	TA	
JN-4D	ON-C	Ottaw	CAM	
JN-4D	OR	Hood	WAAAM	
JN-4D	OR	Mc Minnville	EAM	
JN-4D	PA	Bethel	GAAM	39158

Designation	State	City	Museum	Name	Manufacturer	Serial / Notes
JN-4D	TX	San Antonio	LSAD			
JN-4D	TX	San A	MoFM			
JN-4D	TX	San A	SAMoT			
JN-4D	UT	Ogden	HAFB			
JN-4D	VA	Richmond	VAM			5002, N5001
JN-4HG	VA	Triangle	NMMC			A-4160
JN-4D	WA	Seattle	MoF			
JN-4D	WA	Stevenson	CGIC			
JN-4D	WI	Oshkosh	EAAAAM			N5357
JN-4D	WI	Oshkosh	EAAAAM			2525
JN-6H	MN	Minne	MAGM	Jenny	Curtiss	CF-PFB
Jodel D-9	SK-C	MJaw	WDM		Jodel	N31420
JP-51	OK	Oklahoma	OSM	Sawyer	Pierce	V190, Model G-21A
JRF-3(OA-13), (G-21)	FL	Pensacola	NMoNA	Goose	Grumman	4325, NC16934, 1059
JRS-1 (S-43)	AZ	Tucson	PAM	Cargo Trans	Sikorsky	
JRS-1 (S-43)	MD	Suitland	PEGF	Cargo Trans	Sikorsky	
Ju 52	IL	Chica	CAF-GLW	Aunti Ju	Junkers	T2B 176, N352JU
Ju 52	VA	Chantilly	NASMUVC	Aunti Ju	Junkers	D-ALD4
Ju 52/3M(Sasa 352L)	OH	Dayton	NMUSAF	Aunti Ju	Junkers	T.2B-244
Ju 52/1M	MB-C	Winni	WCAM	Aunti Ju	Junkers	
Ju 87/B (7/8 Scale)	NY	Elmir	CRA	Stuka	Junkers	
Ju 87B	IL	Chica	MoS&I	Stuka	Junkers	
Ju 88D/1	OH	Dayton	NMUSAF	Zerstorer	Junkers	430650
Ju 388L	MD	Suitland	PEGF		Junkers	1945 Recon.
Junkers D.1	AL	Gunte	LGARFM		Junkers	1st All Metal Fighter
Junkers F-13	MB-C	Winni	WCAM		Junkers	
Junkers J1	ON-C	Ottaw	CAM		Junkers	586
Junkers W 34f/fi	ON-C	Ottaw	CAM		Junkers	1934
Junkin Brukner	OH	Troy	WHS	Baby Flying Boat	Junkin Brukner	
K-2	OH	Dayton	NMUSAF	Kellett		2
K-16 V-STOL	CT	Winds	NEAM		Kaman	
K-225	CT	Winds	NEAM		Kaman	
K-47 CAR	VA	Chantilly	NASMUVC	Dirigible		
K-84 Biplane	FL	Pensacola	NMoNA			
KA-4	AK	Palme	MOAT&I	2 Place Glider	Schleicher	
KA-6	NM	Moriarty	SSM	2 Place Glider	Schleicher	
Kaminskas RK3	NM	Moriarty	SSM	Jungster VI	Kaminskas	N8355
Kaminskas RK3	CA	San Diego	SDAM	Jungster III	Kaminskas	N76AQ,"Johnathan Livingston Seagull"
Kamov Ka-26	WI	Oshkosh	EAAAAM	Hoodlum	Kamov	
KAQ-1	CA	Ramona	CR	Drone	Kawasaki	
	CA	Atwater	CAM			

Designation	State	City	Museum	Manufacturer	Name	Notes
Karp Pusher	WI	Oshkosh	EAAAAM	Karp	Pusher	
Kasperwing 180-B	WA	Everett	MoF	Kasperwing		
Kaviler	OK	Oklahoma	A&SM		Kaviler	
KD-1A	CA	Chino	YAM	Kellett	Autogiro	
KD-1A	PA	Readi	MAAM	Kellett	Autogiro	
KD-3G	FL	Pensacola	NMoNA			
Ki-43	OR	Tillamook	TAM	Nakajima	Oscar (Hayabusa)	Peregrine Falcon
Ki-43B	TX	Ft Worth	TAF	Nakajima	Oscar (Hayabusa)	Peregrine Falcon (2ea)
Ki-43B	WA	Seattle	MoF	Nakajima	Oscar (Hayabus)	
Ki-43B	WI	Oshkosh	EAAAAM	Nakajima	Oscar (Hayabusa)	Peregrine Falcon
Ki-45	VA	Chantilly	NASMUVC	Kawasaki	Nick	
Ki-46	MD	Suitland	PEGF	Mitsubishi	Dinah	
Ki-51 Replica	TX	Slaton	TAM	Mitsubishi	Ida	
Ki-61	FL	Polk	FoF	Kawasaki	Tony (Hein)	Army Type 3 Hein
Ki-61	VA	Suffolk	FF	Kawasaki	Tony (Hein)	Army Type 3 Hein
Ki-61 Rep	TX	SMarc	CTWCAF	Kawasaki	Tony (Hein)	
Ki-115	MD	Suitland	PEGF	Nakajima	Tsurugi	Suicide Plane
Kiceniuk Icarus V	WI	Oshkosh	EAAAAM	Kiceniuk	Icarus V	
Kikka	MD	Suitland	PEGF		Kikka	
Kinner Sportster	IA	Ottumwa	APM	Kinner	Sportster	Sportster
Kinner Sportster	B-1	PA	Reading	MAAM	Kinner	
Kit Fox	CO	Denver	WOTR	Denny Aerocraft	Speedster	
Kit Fox Model 1	FL	Lakel	SFAF	Denny Aerocraft	Speedster	N3LB
Knight Twister Imperial	WI	Oshkosh	EAAAAM	Payne	Twister Imperial	N5DF, "White Knight",
KR-21(C-6)	FL	Kissi	FTWAM	Fairchild	Challanger	FC Took Over Kreider-Reisner
KR-21B(C-6)	WI	Oshkosh	EAAAAM	Fairchild	Challanger	N954V
KR-31(C-2)	PA	Hagertstown	HAM	Kreider Reiser	Challanger	
KR-34	FL	Kissi	FTWAM	Kreider Reiser	Challanger	
KR-34C(C-4)	MB-C	Winnipeg	WRCAFB	Fairchild	Challanger	Kreider Reiser Formerly
KR-34C(C-4)	MD	Suitland	PEGF	Fairchild	Challanger	900, C-FADH,
KR-34C(C-4)	ON-C	Sault Ste Marie	CBHC	Fairchild	Challanger	
KR-34C(C-4)	VA	Chantilly	NASMUVH	Fairchild		
Krier Kraft	KS	Ashla	HKAM	Kraft	Kraft	N5400E
Kurir	NY	Horseheads	NWM	Kurir	Kurir	50-133
L-1	TX	FWort	VFM	Piaggio	Royal Gull	
L-1A(O-49)	FL	Polk	FoF	Vultee	Vigilant	
L-1A(O-49)	OH	Dayton	NMUSAF	Vultee	Vigilant	41-19039

L-1A(O-49) — Vultee Vigilant

Type	State	City	Museum
L-1A(O-49)	TX	San A	ILP&AAM

L-2 Taylorcraft Grasshopper

Type	State	City	Museum	Serial
L-2	FL	Kissi	FTWAM	
L-2	KS	New Century	CAF-HoAW	N50573
L-2	KS	New Century	CAF-HoAW	N75891
L-2	NY	Geneseo	1941AG	
L-2	NC	Hendersonville	WNCAM	
L-2	ND	Fargo	FAM	
L-2	OK	Fredi	AAM	
L-2	TX	Brown	CAFRGVW	
L-2	TX	Midland	AAHM	53768
L-2	TX	San A	ILP&AAM	
L-2	WA	Evere	CAF-EW	N53768
L-2	WA	Olympia	OFM	Side # 8B
L-2A	AL	Ozark	USAAM	
L-2A	PA	Tough	CFCM	
L-2A(D)	IA	Ottumwa	APM	
L-2D	OH	N Canton	MAM	
L-2M	AZ	Tucson	PAM	43-26402, N59068
L-2M	CA	McClellan	McCelAFB	43-5745, N53792
L-2M	IL	Springfield	ACM	43-26564
L-2M	GA	Woodstock	NGWS	
L-2M	GA	Woodstock	NGWS	
L-2M	GA	Woodstock	NGWS	
L-2M	KS	Liberal	MAAM	
L-2M	OH	Dayton	NMUSAF	43-26753
L-2M	OR	Hood	WAAAM	
L-2M	TX	San Antonio	TAM	95-04, N47344

L-3 Aeronca Grasshopper

Type	State	City	Museum	Serial
L-3	AR	Fayetteville	OMM	
L-3	AR	Pine Bluff	REAA	
L-3B	MO	SChar	CAF-MW	N36681
L-3B(O-58B)	AZ	PBluf	RWCAF	
L-3B(O-58B)	AZ	Tucson	PAM	43-27206, N46067
L-3B(O-58B)	CA	Shafter	MFAM	
L-3B(O-58B)	CA	SRosa	PCAM	
L-3B(O-58B)	GA	Pooler	MoF	
L-3B(O-58B)	IA	Council Bluffs	GPW	
L-3B(O-58B)	IA	Ottumwa	APM	058B12783, N50334
L-3B(O-58B)	KS	Liberal	MAAM	
L-3B(O-58B)	MO	St Charles	CAFWM	
L-3B(O-58B)	NY	Horseheads	NWM	
L-3B(O-58B)	OH	Dayton	NMUSAF	42-36200
L-3B(O-58B)	OK	Fredi	AAM	
L-3B(O-58B)	TX	Brown	CAFRGVW	
L-3B(O-58B)	TX	Addison	CFM	
L-3B(O-58B)	TX	FWort	VFM	
L-3B(O-58B)	TX	San A	ILP&AAM	
L-3B(O-58B)	WA	Port Townsend	PTAM	058B-7742, N48145; 9223, N47427
L-3B(O-58B)	WA	Seattle	MoF	
L-3E	IA	CBluf	CAF-GPW	N36687
L-3J	TX	Slaton	TAM	

L-4 Piper Grasshopper

Type	State	City	Museum	Serial
L-4	CA	Atwater	CAM	
L-4	CA	Corno	CAF-IES	N35786
L-4	CA	Farfield	DA&SM	
L-4	CO	Denve	JWDAS	
L-4	FL	Polk	FoF	
L-4	IN	Valparaiso	IAM	
L-4	KY	Lexington	AVoK	
L-4Rep	MI	Saginaw	YAF	NC42008
L-4	MN	Minne	MAGM	
L-4	NC	Asheboro	PFAC	
L-4	OK	FtSil	USAFAM	
L-4	TX	Brown	CAFRGVW	
L-4	TX	Burnet	CAFHLS	

Model	State	City	Org	Number
L-4	TX	C Christi	USS Lexi	
L-4	TX	LV	LVAM	
L-4	TX	San A	ILP&AAM	
L-4	TX	Uvalde	AM	
L-4	WA	Vancouver	PAM	
L-4A	OH	Dayton	NMUSAF	42-36790
L-4A	OR	Hood	WAAAM	
L-4B	AL	Ozark	USAAM	43-515
L-4B	FL	Pensacola	NMoNA	
L-4B	GA	Hampton	AAHF	
L-4B	OK	Oklahoma	45IDM	
L-4H	MI	Kalamazoo	KAHM	44-79817
L-4J	FL	Tittusville	VACM	
L-4J	OK	Fredi	AAM	
L-4J	OR	Hood	WAAAM	
L-4J	TX	Addison	CFM	N9073C
L-4J	UT	Ogden	HAM	45-4655

L-5 Stinson Sentinel

Model	State	City	Org	Number
L-5	CA	Chino	YAM	
L-5	CA	El Cajon	CAFFFM	N59AF
L-5	CA	Farfield	DA&SM	
L-5	CA	Riverside	MFAM	63085
L-5	CO	Denve	JWDAS	
L-5	IA	Council Bluffs	GPW	
L-5	KS	Liberal	MAAM	
L-5	LA	New Orleans	DDM	
L-5	VA	Chantilly	NASMUVC	
L-5	NC	Charl	CHAC	
L-5	OH	Colum	CAF-OVW	N5138B
L-5	OH	Dayton	NMUSAF	42-98667
L-5	OK	Fredi	AAM	
L-5	PA	Pitts	CAF-KW	N25818
L-5	SD	Rapid City	SDA&SM	45-35046
L-5	TX	Abile	PSCAF	
L-5	TX	Amarillo	CAFDS	
L-5	TX	Burnet	HLS-CAF	
L-5	TX	Brown	RGVW-CAF	
L-5	TX	Ft Worth	VFM	1039, N68MH
L-5	TX	Galve	LSFM	
L-5	TX	San A	ILP&AAM	
L-5	TX	SMarc	CTWCAF	
L-5	VA	Chesa	CAF-ODS	N61100
L-5	VA	Manas	CAF-NCS	N1156V
L-5	VA	Suffolk	FF	41-7588
L-5A	MN	S St Paul	CAF-SMW	N68591
L-5B	AZ	Tucson	PAM	44-16907, N4981V
L-5E	CA	Atwater	CAM	
L-5E	CA	Okdal	CAF-CCVS	N5625V
L-5E	CA	Paso Robles	EWM	44-17944, N45CV
L-5E-1VW	WI	Oshkosh	EAAAAM	4297
L-5E(OY-2)	OH	Columbus	CAF-OVW,	44-181143, N5138B
L-5G	CA	Chino	PoFAM	
L-5Spatz-55	NS-C	Halifax	ACAM	

L-6 Interstate Cadet

Model	State	City	Org	Number
L-6	AZ	Tucson	PAM	
L-6	KS	Liberal	MAAM	
L-6	OH	Dayton	NMUSAF	43-2680
L-6	OK	Fredi	AAM	N37214
L-6 (S-1B1)	PA	Philadelphia	CAFDVW	43-159, N46336, "Cathy O"
L-6	TX	Brown	CAFRGVW	
L-6	TX	Corpus Christi	CAF-TCW	
L-6	TX	Denton	H10FM	
L-6	TX	San A	ILP&AAM	
L-6(S-1A)	AK	Palme	MOAT&I	1941

Model	State	City	Museum	Reg / Serial
L-9B	PA	Pitts	CAF-KW	
L-13 Convair Scorpion				
L-13	CA	Atwater	CAM	
L-13	AR	Fayetteville	OMM	
L-13	MN	Minne	JJ	
L-13	WA	Bellingham	HFM	
L-13A	CA	Chino	PoFAM	
L-13A	MI	Farfield	YAFNE	
L-13A	NJ	Fairfield	YAM	47-389, N65893
L-13A	NM	St Teresa	WEAM	
L-13B	WA	Seattle	MoF	
L-15(YL)A	AL	Ozark	USAAM	
Scout		Boeing		N26295
Scout				47-429
L-16 Aeronca Chief				
L-16	AR	Fayetteville	AAM	
L-16A	CA	Paso Robles	EWM	47-0787, N82107
L-16	CO	Denve	JWDAS	
L-16	IL	Linco	HIFM	
L-16	NY	Geneseo	1941AG	
L-16	OK	Fredi	AAM	
L-16	TX	Amarillo	CAFDS	
L-17 Ryan Navion				
L-17	AR	Pine Bluff	REAA	
L-17	CO	Denve	JWDAS	
L-17	GA	Hampton	AAHF	
L-17	IL	Linco	HIFM	
L-17	KS	Liberal	MAAM	
L-17	GA	Hampton	AAHF	
L-17	GA	Woodstock	AAM	
L-17	NY	Geneseo	1941AG	
L-17A	AL	Ozark	USAAM	47-1344
L-17A	CA	Paso Robles	EWM	47-1333, N91668
L-17A	OH	Dayton	NMUSAF	47-1347
L-17A	OK	Oklahoma	45IDM	
L-17A	TX	Denton	H10FM	
L-17B	FL	Deland	FW-CAF	
L-17B	OH	N Canton	MAM	
L-17B	TX	Burnet	CAFHLS	NAV-4 1463, N444AC
L-19 Cessna Bird Dog				
L-19	CA	El Cajon	SDAMGF	
L-19	CO	Denve	JWDAS	
L-19	MI	Kalamazoo	AZ	
L-19	MN	Winoma	WTI	N1983AP
L-19	NJ	Lexington	NASWAM	
L-19	NY	River	RE	
L-19	NC	Charlotte	CAM	0-20777, N777VN
L-19	OK	FtSil	USAFAM	
L-19	OK	Oklahoma	45IDM	56-367
L-19	ON-C	Petawawa	CFBPMM	
L-19(O-1G)	AZ	Tucson	DMAFB	
L-19(O-1)	FL	Pensacola	NMoNA	51-14981
L-19(O-2)	WA	Everett	MoF	67-21363
L-19A	AL	Ozark	USAAM	50-1327
L-19A	AL	Ozark	USAAM	51-4943
L-19A	AZ	Grand	PoFGCVA	51-12129
L-19A	GA	Hampton	AAHF	
L-19A	GA	Pooler	MoF	
L-19A	IL	Waukegan	WHM	022677, N677RH
L-19A	KY	FKnox	PMoC&A	
L-19A(O-1)	CA	SanLu	CSLO	
L-19A(O-1)	IN	Crawfordsville	RAM	
L-19A(O-1)	CA	SanLu	CSLO	53-8029

Model	Manufacturer	Type	State	City	Museum	Serial / Registration
L-19A(O-1)			VA	FtEus	USATM	51-12745
L-19A(O-1A)			MD	Suitland	PEGF	
L-19A(O-1E)			FL	FtWal	HF	56-4208
L-19A(O-1E)			GA	Pooler	MoF	51-12857
L-19A-CE			MI	Oscoda	YAM	51-12107, N3302T
L-19A			NC	Asheboro	PFAC	51-11917
L-19A(O-1)			ND	Fargo	FAM	55-4681
L-19A(O-1G)			OH	Dayton	NMUSAF	
L-19D(TL)			AL	Ozark	USAAM	
L-19D			GA	Hampton	AAHF	
L-21 (PA-18)	Piper	Super Cub	CA	Atwater	CAM	
L-21A(TL)(PA-18)	Piper	Super Cub	AL	Ozark	USAAM	51-15782
L-21B(PA-18)	Piper	Super Cub	NY	Geneseo	1941AG	
L-21B(PA-18)	Piper	Super Cub	PA	Beave	AHM	
L-21B(PA-18)	Piper	Super Cub	PA	Readi	MAAM	53-7720, N50084
L-29	Aero	Delfin	FL	Miami	WOM	
L-29	Aero	Delfin	NY	New Windsor	RSAM	
L-29	Aero	Delfin	ND	Minot	DTAM	
L-29	Aero	Delfin	OR	Tillamook	TAM	
L-29	Aero	Delfin	TX	Tyler	HAMM	
L-29C	Aero	Delfin	WI	Amery	AMA	
L-39	Aerovodochody	Albatross	CA	El Cajon	WW	
L-39	Aerovodochody	Albatross	ID	Rexburg	LFM	
L-39	Aerovodochody	Albatross	KS	New Century	CAF-HoAW	
L-39	Aerovodochody	Albatross	MN	Anoka	Airport	N139BH
L-39A	Aerovodochody	Albatross	NY	New Windsor	RSAM	
L-39C	Aerovodochody	Albatross	WA	Bellingham	HFM	
L-049(C-69)	Lockheed	Columbine	WA	Olympia	OFM	931526, N239PW
L-106	Lamson	Alcor Glider	IL	Waukegan	WHM	
L-1649A	Lockheed	Starliner	AZ	Tucson	PAM	42-94549, 48-614, N90831
L-1649A	Lockheed	Starliner	WA	Seattle	MoF	18, N924LR
L-1649A	Lockheed	Starliner	FL	Orlando	OSA	N974R, "Jenny's Star"
L-1649A	Lockheed	Starliner	FL	Polk City	FoF	N8083H, "Jason's Star"
L-450F LTVE	Lockheed	Starliner	ME	Aubur	SLP	N7316C, "Brian's Star"
L-10A	Lockheed	Electra	ME	Aubur	SLP	
L-10A	Lockheed	Electra	TX	FWort	SAM	N3828
L-10A	Lockheed	Electra	CA	Oakla	OWAM	
L-10A	Lockheed	Electra	CT	Winds	NEAM	
	Lockheed	Electra	MB-C	Winni	WCAM	
	Lockheed	Electra	ON-C	Ottaw	CAM	
L-12A	Lockheed	Electra	KY	Lexington	AMoK	1203, N12EJ

Designation	State	Location	Code	Manufacturer	Variant	Reg/Serial
L.12A	ON-C	Ottaw	CAM	Lockheed	Electra	
L.14	CT	Winds	NEAM	Lockheed	Super Electra	
L.18(C-60)	HI	Honolulu	HIA	Lockheed	Lodestar	
L.18(C-60)	TX	Denton	H10FM	Lockheed	Lodestar	
L-24 See U-10						
L.25J	PA	Beave	AHM	British Aircraft	Swallow	
Laird Swallow	KS	Wichi	KAM	Laird	Swallow	
Lancair 200	WI	Oshkosh	EAAAAM	Lancair	Lancair 200	N384L, Neibauer
Lancair 360	OR	Mc Minnville	EAM	Lancair	Lancair 200	
Langley Aerodrome A	MD	Suitland	PEGF	Langley	Aerodrome	
Langley Aerodrome N0. 5	MD	Suitland	PEGF	Langley	Aerodrome	
Langley Aerodrome	VA	Chantilly	NASMUVC	Langley	Aerodrome	
Latter	PA	Tough	CFCM	Latter		
Lazair	FL	Lakel	SFAF	Lazair		
Lazair SS EC Ultralight	MD	Suitland	PEGF	Lazair	Ultralight	49-1949
LC-126	OH	Dayton	NMUSAF	Laird		
LC-DW500	CT	Winds	NEAM	Laird	Super Solution	
LC-DW500	MD	Suitland	PEFG	Laird	Super Solution	
LC-DW500	MI	Dearb	HFM	Laird	Super Solution	
LC-DW500	WI	Oshkosh	EAAAAM	Laird	Super Solution	NR12048
LC-DW500 Fuse	MD	Suitland	PEGF	Laird	Super Solution	
LCVP	LA	New Orleans	DDM	Higgins	Boat	
LCVP	DC	Washington	NM	Higgins	Boat	
Le Rhone	FL	Pensacola	NMoNA	Le Rhone		
Learjet 23 Gates	AR	Fayetteville	AAM			
Learjet 23	AZ	Tucson	PAM			
Learjet 23	CA	Chino	YAM			23-015, N88B
Learjet 23	KS	Wichita	KAM			6
Learjet 23	MD	Chantilly	NASMUVC			
Learjet 23	MI	Kalamazoo	KAHM	Learjet 23		23-083
Learjet 23	VA	Richm	SMoV	Learjet 23		
Learjet 24D	TX	Dallas	FoF	Learjet 24D		N281FP
Learjet 25	AL	Ozark	AA&TC	Learjet 25		
LeBel VTO	CA	Chino	PoFAM	LeBel		
LEM Grumman	NY	NYC	ISASM	Grumman	LEM	
Les Broussard 1956	MI	Hamil	ML	Les Broussard		
Lew Ann Model DD-1	AZ	Grand Canyon	PoFGCVA	Lew Ann	Biplane	N2170D
LF-107 Glider	WA	Everett	MoF	Let	Lunak	001, N626BL
LF-2100	WA	Seattle	MoF	Learfan		

Aircraft	State/Prov	City	Museum	Type	Registration
LF-2100 / Learfan	WI	Oshkosh	EAAAAM		N327ML / N192GP
Lilienthal Glider	CA	San Diego	SDAM	Glider	
Lilienthal Glider	DC	Washi	NA&SM	Glider	
Lilienthal Glider	ME	Owls Head	OHTM	Glider	
Lilienthal Glider	NY	Garde	CoAM	Glider	
Lilienthal Glider	WA	Seattle	MoF	Glider	
Linburgs Monocoupe	MO	SLoui	SLLIA	Monocoupe	
Lincoln Biplane	WI	Oshkosh	EAAAAM	Biplane	
Lincoln Page LP3A	IL	Paris	HAAM		
Lincoln PT-K	WI	Oshkosh	EAAAAM	Biplane	N275N
Lincoln Sport	BC-C	Sidney	BCAM	Sports Biplane	
Lincoln Sport	NS	Halifax	ACAM	Sports Biplane	
Lindsey Model 2	WA	Vancouver	PAM	Monoplane	Restoration Project

Link Trainer

Aircraft	State/Prov	City	Museum	Reg
Link Trainer	AL	Birmingham	SMoF	
Link Trainer	AB-C	Calgary	AMoC	
Link Trainer	AB-C	Nanton	NLSAM	
Link Trainer	AB-C	Wetas	RM	
Link Trainer	AR	Little Rock	AEC	
Link Trainer	AR	Walnut Ridge	WRAFSM	
Link Trainer	CA	Chino	YAM	
Link Trainer	CA	Oakla	OWAM	
Link Trainer	CA	San Diego	SDAM	
Link Trainer	CO	Denver	DIA/UAL	
Link Trainer	DE	Dover	DAFB	
Link Trainer	FL	Tittusville	VACM	
Link Trainer	KS	Liberal	MAAM	
Link Trainer	KY	Lexington	AMoK	
Link Trainer	MI	Kalamazoo	KAHM	
Link Trainer	MI	OScoda	YAF	
Link Trainer	MN	Duluth	CAF-LSS	
Link Trainer	MN	Minneapolis	MSPIA	
Link Trainer	NF-C	Gander	NAAM	11242
Link Trainer	NJ	Milli	MAAFM	
Link Trainer	NJ	Milvi	MAAFM	
Link Trainer	NM	St Teresa	WEAM	
Link Trainer	NS	Halifax	ACAM	
Link Trainer	NY	Binghamton	LFSC	
Link Trainer	NY	Binghamton	BRA	
Link Trainer	NY	Ghent	POMAM	
Link Trainer C-3	OH	N Canton	MAM	
Link Trainer	ON-C	Hamilton	CWHM	
Link Trainer	ON-C	Sault Ste Marie	CBHC	
Link Trainer	OR	Eugen	OAM	
Link Trainer	PA	Bethel	GAAM	
Link Trainer	PA	Lock Haven	PAM	
Link ANT-18	TX	Addison	CFM	
Link ANT-18	CT	Winds	NEAM	
Link Trainer	UT	Ogden	HAM	
Link Trainer Mk.IV	WA	Vancouver	PAM	
Link Trainer Mk.IV	AB-C	Edmonton	AAM	

Aircraft	State	City	Museum	Type	Registration
Lippisch DM-1	MD	Suitland	PEGF	Lippisch	
Little Looper	CA	San Carlos	HNCAVM	Beachy	"Little Looper"
Little Rocket	FL	Lakel	SFAF	Racer	N345JA

Aircraft	State/Prov	City	Museum	Registration
Liverpuffin 11	PA	Tough	CFCM	
LK-10 Glider	CA	Chino	PoFAM	
LNA-40 Super	WI	Oshkosh	EAAAAM	
LNE-1 Pratt-Read Glider				
LNE-1	AL	Birmingham	SMoF	31543, N60432
LNE-1	CA	San Martin	WoHM	
LNE-1	FL	Pensacola	NMoNA	N60745
LNE-1(HH-2D)	FL	Pensacola	NMoNA	149031
LNE-1	KY	Lexington	AMoK	PRG-01-73, N60235
LNE-1 Cockpit	MD	Ft Meade	QM	
LNS-1 Schweizer	FL	Pensacola	NMoNA	
LNS-1 Schweizer	FL	Pensacola	NMoNA	
LNS-1	MI	Kalamazoo	AZ	
Loudenslager Laser 200	VA	Chantilly	NASMUVC	
Lockheed 402-2	NJ	Teter	AHoFNJ	
Lockheed 1329-8	SK-C	Moose Jaw	WDM	
Lockheed Hudson Mk IIIa	NF-C	Gander	NAAM	
Lockheed Mk.6 (Fuse)	NS-C	Halifax	ACAM	
Lockheed Mk.6	SK-C	Moose Jaw	WDM	
Lockheed Q-5	AZ	Grand Canyon	PoFGCVA	
Lockheed Satellite	OH	Dayton	NMUSAF	
Lockheed Sirius 8	DC	Washi	NA&SM	
Lockheed Vega 5				
Lockheed Vega 5	AB-C	Edmonton	AAM	
Lockheed Vega 5	CA	Inglewood	PBR	
Lockheed Vega 5B	KS	Liberal	MAAM	
Lockheed Vega 5C	MI	Dearb	HFM	N965Y
Loehle 5151 Mustang	GA	Woodstock	NGWS	
Lone Star	OK	Oklahoma	OSM	
Long Eze	AZ	Tucson	PAM	
Longster	MI	Kalamazoo	KAHM	
Longwing Eaglerock	AL	Birmingham	SmoF	
Loving's-Love	FL	Lakeland	SNF	
Loving-Wayne WR-1 Love	WI	Oshkosh	EAAAAM	

Aircraft	Type/City	State	Museum	Registration
Liverpuffin	Glider			
Laister-Kauffman	Super			
Heath				N16GR
LNE-1	Elmira	NY	NSM	31561, Sn 57, N5346G
LNE-1	Fargo	ND	BAM	31569, Sn 65, N56660
LNE-1(TG-3A)	Dayton	OH	NMUSAF	42-52988, N69215
LNE-1(TG-3A)	Dayton	OH	NMUSAF	N6513
LNE-1(HH-2D)	Auburn	IN	HW	
LNE-1(X)	Horseheads	NY	NWM	31506, NC4467U
LNE-1(PR-G1)	Everett	WA	MoF	31517, Sn 13, N60353
Schweizer	Glider			S-4385
Schweizer	Glider			04384, #6
Schweizer	Glider			
Loudenslager	Arko Laser			
Lockheed	Bushmaster			N160IL
Lockheed				802
Lockheed	Hudson			41-23631
Lockheed	Hudson			
Lockheed	Hudson			42-47022, FK466
Lockheed	Satellite			
Lockheed	Sirius			
Lockheed Vega 5	Fredi	OK	AAM	
Lockheed Vega 5B	Washi	DC	NA&SM	
Lockheed Vega 5C	Chantilly	VA	NASMUVC	
Lockheed Vega 5C	Oshkosh	WI	EAAAAM	"Winnie Mae" NC105W
Loehle	Mustang Kit			
Lone Star	Helicopter			
Rutan	Long Eze			N82ST
Longster	Homebuilt			
Longwing	Eaglerock			
Loving-Wayne	Love			
Loving-Wayne	Love			N351C

Model	State	City	Museum	Manufacturer	Name	Reg./Notes
LP-3	CA	Chino	YAM	Lincoln	Page	156, N3830
LP-3	OR	Hood	WAAAM	Lincoln	Page	
LST	MI	Muskegon	USS S		Landing Ship Tank	
LTV/E	TX	Dallas	FoF	Greenville	L-450	72-01287
LTV4	OH	Hubbard	WWIIVM		Water Buffalo	D11
LTV4	TX	Frede	NMofPW			
Lunar Excursion Module	OK	Oklahoma	OSM			
Lunar Lander	KS	Hutch	KC&SC		Lunar Module	
Lunar Orbiter	WA	Seattle	PSC			
Lunar Rover	KS	Hutch	KC&SC			
Lusac-11	OH	Dayton	NMUSAF	Packard LePere		SC-42133
Luscombe T-8F	KS	Liberal	MAAM	Luscombe		

Luscombe 8 Silvaire

Model	State	City	Museum	Manufacturer	Name	Reg./Notes
Luscombe 8	MN	Winoma	WTI			NC13308
Luscombe 8A	CA	Chino	PoFAM			Skypal
Luscombe 8A	BC-C	Sidne	BCAM			
Luscombe 8A	KS	Liberal	MAAM			990
Luscombe 8A	ME	Bangor	MAM			
Luscombe 8A	OH	Dayton	NMUSAF			
Luscombe 8A(UC-90)	OH	Madis	CFR			
Luscombe 8A	OK	Fredi	AAM			
Luscombe 8A	TX	Kingsbury	VAHF	Luscombe 8A	Observer	
Luscombe 8A	WA	Port Townsend	PTAM	Luscombe 8A		3675, N77948
Luscombe 8E	GA	Woodstock	AAM	Luscombe 8E		
Luscombe 8E	NY	River	RE	Luscombe 8E		
Luscombe 8F	IA	Ottumwa	APM	Luscombe 8F	Phantom I	6735, N805B
Luscombe 8F	WI	Oshkosh	EAAAAM	Luscombe 8F	Phantom	
Luscombe 8F	OK	Fredi	AAM	Luscombe 8F	Phantom I	NC1025

Model	State	City	Museum	Manufacturer	Name	Reg./Notes
M-1	OH	Dayton	NMUSAF	Ryan	Messenger	68-533
M-1	PA	Bethel	GAAM	Ryan	Messenger	NX2073
M-1	WA	Seattle	MoF	Ryan	Messenger	HN-1, N46853
M-2	VA	Chantilly	NASMUVC	Douglas	Mail Plane	
M-6	NY	Garden	CoAM	Douglas	Nike Hercules	
M-39	CA	Chino	PoFAM	Macchi	Schneider Cup Racer	
M.J.5 Sirocco	WI	Oshkosh	EAAAAM	Jurca	Sirocco	N8038E
M2-F3(HL-10)	DC	Washi	NA&SM	Northrop	Lifting Body	
M6A1	VA	Chantilly	NASMUVC	Aichi	Seiran	
MA14/LJ-5B	VA	Hampton	APM	NA-McDonnell	Spacecraft	
Mace Model III WI	Oshkosh		EAAAAM		Mace	
Mahoney Sorceress	VA	Chantilly	NASMUVC	Mahoney	Sorceress	
Manhigh II Gondola	OH	Dayton	NMUSAF	Manhigh	Gondola II	
Marcoux-Bromberg	CT	Winds	NEAM	Marcoux-Bromberg	Special	
Marske Pioneer II	CA	Santa Martin	WoHAM	Marske	Pioneer II Glider	Year 1985, Flying Wing Glider

Designation	State	Location	Organization	Name	Registration
Marinac Flying Mercury	WI	Oshkosh	EAAAAM	Marinac Flying Mercury	
Martin 162A	MD	Balti	BMoI	Martin 162A	14074, N93204
Martin 2-0-2A	NJ	Teter	AHoFNJ	Martin Martinliner	
Martin 4-0-4 Cockpit	CA	Chino	YAM	Martin Martinliner	
Martin 4-0-4	MD	Middle River	GLMAM	Martin Martinliner	SN 14142, N145S
Martin 4-0-4	MO	Kansas City	AHM	Martin Martinliner	
Martin 4-0-4	MT	Billings		Martin Martinliner	
Martin 4-0-4	PA	Readi	MAAM	Martin Martinliner	"Silver Falcon"
Martin J.V. K-III	MD	Suitland	PEGF	Martin Kitten	
Maupin-Lanteri Black Dia	MD	Suitland	PEGF	Maupin-Lanteri Black Diamond	
Maurice Farman S.11	ON-C	Ottaw	CAM	Maurice Farman	
MB-2 Rep	OH	Dayton	NMUSAF		
MC-4C	AZ	Tucson	PAM	McCulloch Helicopter	133817, N4072K
MC-4C	CA	Chino	YAM	McCulloch Helicopter	3818
MC-12	CA	Chino	PoF	Rombaugh Cricket	N1377L
MC-12	WI	Oshkosh	EAAAAM	Rombaugh Cricket	N1377L
M.C. 200	OH	Dayton	NMUSAF	Macchi Seatta	372, McCulloch
MC-202	DC	Washi	NA&SM	McCulloch	
McAllister Yakima Clipper	WA	Seattle	MoF	McAllister Yalima Clipper	N10655
McCook Wind Tunnel	OH	Dayton	NMUSAF	McCook Wind Tunnel	
McDowall Monoplane	ON-C	Ottaw	CAM	McDowall Monoplane	
McKinney 165	ND	Fargo	BUSAHM		

Me 108 Messerschmitt Taifun

Designation	State	Location	Organization	Registration
Me 108	NM	Hobbs	CAF-NMW	N2231
Me 108	NY	Geneseo	1941AG	N2231
Me-108	TX	Slaton	TAM	
Me-108	VA	Suffolk	FF	
Me 108	WA	Everett	MoF	

Me 109 Messerschmitt GUSTOV

Designation	State	Location	Organization	Name	Registration
Me 109	CA	Inglewood	PBR		
Me 109	FL	FtLau	WJAIS&L		
Me 109	NY	Ghent	POMAM		
Me 109	NY	Shirley	DLIA		
Me 109	OR	Mc Minnville	EAM		
Me 109	TX	Midland	AAHM	Me 109B	109ME
Me 109	KS	Topek	CAM	Me 109 Mock Up	
Me 109	WA	Seattle	MoF	Me 109E-3	186, NX109J
Me 109	OH	Dayton	NMUSAF	Me 109G-5	C.4K-64
Me 109	TX	Addison	CFM	Me 109G	N48157, 14

Me 163 Messerschmitt Komet

Aircraft	State	City	Museum	Aircraft	Note	City	Museum	Serial/Reg
Me 163	GA	Savan	MEHM	Me 163B	CA	Chino	PoFAM	Komet 191095
Me 163B	OH	Dayton	NMUSAF	Me 163B	ON-C	Ottaw	CAM	191916
				Me 163B	OH	Dayton	NMUSAF	Messerschmitt

Aircraft	State	City	Museum	Aircraft	Note	City	Museum	Serial/Reg
Me 208	FL	Tittusville	VACM	Ramier			Messerschmitt	187, Nord 1101
Me 208	NY	Geneseo	1941AG	Ramier			Messerschmitt	
Me-208	VA	Suffolk	FF	Ramier			Messerschmitt	

Me 262 Messerschmitt Stormbird

Aircraft	State	City	Museum	Aircraft	Note	City	Museum	Serial/Reg
Me 262 A	DC	Washi	NA&SM	Me 262 A	WA	Everett	TMP	
Me 262 A	WA	Arlington	FHC	Me 262 A	WA	Everett	TMP	
Me 262 A	WA	Everett	TMP	Me 262A	OH	Dayton	NMUSAF	121442
Me 262 A	WA	Everett	TMP	Me 262B-1A	PA	Willow Grove NVHAA		110639

Aircraft	State	City	Museum	Aircraft	Note	City	Museum	Serial/Reg
Me 410 A-3	MD	Suitland	PEGF	Messerschmitt	Hornisse			
Mead C-III	SK-C	MJaw	WDM	Mead	Glider			
Mead Glider	AB-C	Wetas	RM	Mead	Glider			
Mead Primary Glider	IA	Greenfield	IAM	Mead	Glider			
Mead Primary Glider	NY	Mayvi	DA	Mead	Primary Glider			
Mead Rhon Ranger	CT	Winds	NEAM	Mead	Rhon Ranger			

Mercury Capsule

Aircraft	State	City	Museum	Aircraft	Note	City	Museum	Serial/Reg
Mercury Capsule MR-2	CA	Chino	PoFAM	Mercury Capsule	NY	NYC	ISASM "Aurora 7"	
Mercury Capsule	CA	LAnge	CMoS&I	Mercury Capsule Rep	NC	Charlotte	CAM	
Mercury Capsule	CA	San Diego	SDAM	Mercury Capsule	OH	Colum	CoS&I	
Mercury Capsule	OH	Dayton	NMUSAF	Mercury Capsule Rep	OK	Oklahoma	OSM	
Mercury 7 Capsule	IL	Chicago	MoS&I	Mercury 6 Capsule	TX	Houston	HMoNS	
Mercury 7 Capsule	KS	Hutch	KC&SC	Mercury Capsule Rep	WA	Seattle	MoF	
Mercury Capsule Rep	MO	SLoui	MDPR					

Aircraft	State	City	Museum	Aircraft	Note	City	Museum	Serial/Reg
Mercury Air Shoestring	CA	San Diego	SDAMGF	Mercury	Air Shoestring			N16V
Mercury Chick	NY	Hammond	CM	Mercury	Chick			
Mercury S-1 Racer	NY	Hammond	CM	Mercury	Racer			
Merlin Hang Glider	NY	Garde	CoAM	Merlin	Hang Glider			
Meteor 1919	CA	Oakla	MDoH	Meteor	Meteor			
Meyer Little Toot	TX	Dallas	FoF	Meyers	Little Toot			N217J, "Petit Papillon",
Meyer Little Toot	WI	Oshkosh	EAAAAM	Meyers	Little Toot			N42963
Meyers M-1 Special	WI	Oshkosh	EAAAAM	Meyers	Special			

Meyers OTW					**Meyers OTW**			
Meyers OTW	FL	Pensacola	NMoNA	N26482	Meyers OTW	TX	Kingsbury	VAHF
Meyers OTW	IL	Cahokia	GSLA&SM		Meyers OTW	WA	Vanco	PAM
Meyers OTW	KS	Topek	CAM		Meyers OTW-145	WI	Oshkosh	EAAAAM	N34357
Meyers OTW	OH	Madis	CFR					

Midget Mustang	NC	Charlotte	CAM		Long/Schweizer	Midget Mustang	100001
Midget Mustang	NC	CPoin	CPMB		Long/Schweizer	Midget Mustang	
MiG-3	VA	Suffolk	FF		Mikoyan-Gurevich		

MiG-15 Mikoyan Midget

Model					Model			
MiG-15	AL	Birmingham	SMoF		MiG-15	NV	FAllon	NASF
MiG-15	AZ	Grand	PoFGCVA	1301	MiG-15	NV	Reno	SAFB
MiG-15	CA	Chino	PoFAM	1301	MiG-15	NY	New York	ISASM
MiG-15	CA	Inglewood	PBR		MiG-15	OH	Dayton	NMUSAF	20-15357
MiG-15	CA	Miramar	FLAM		MiG-15	TX	Amirillo	EFA&SM	#509
MiG-15	CA	San Diego	SDAM		MiG-15	TX	San Angelo	GAFB
MiG-15	CA	SRosa	PCAM		MiG-15	ON-C	Ottawa	CAM	316
MiG-15	CT	Winds	NEAM	83277	MiG-15	WA	Seattle	MoF	79
MiG-15	ID	Driggs	TAC	358	MiG-15	WI	Oshkosh	EAAAAM	N15MG
MiG-15	KS	Topek	CAM	B01016, N15YY	MiG-15 (2 Seater)	MN	Minneapolis	MAGM
MiG-15	VA	Chantilly	NASMUVC		MiG-15 (2 Seater)	NM	St Teresa	WEAM	640
MiG-15	MI	Kalamazoo	KAHM	1B-01621	MiG-15bis	AZ	Tucson	PAM	1A-06-038, 822
MiG-15	NJ	Cape May	NASWF	N51MG	MiG-15UTI	AZ	Mesa	CAFAWM	N9012
MiG-15	NJ	Lexington	NASWAM		MiG-15UTI	AZ	Tucson	PAM	38, N38BM
MiG-15	NY	New Windsor	RSAM		MiG-15UTI	OR	Mc Minnville	EAM	IA-242271, NX271JM
					MiG-15UTI/SB	TX	Addison	CFM

MiG-17 Mikoyan Fresco

Model					Model			
MiG-17	AL	Huntsville	AC		MiG-17	NY	New York	IASASM
MiG-17	CA	Chino	PoFAM		MiG-17	OH	Dayton	NMUSAF	799
MiG-17	CA	San Diego	SDAM		MiG-17	OH	N Canton	MAM
MiG-17	FL	Tittusvill	VACM		MiG-17(Lim-5)	TN	Sevierville	TMoA	IC1706
MiG-17	KS	New Century	CAF-HoAW	Ic1717, N1717M	MiG-17(Lim-5R)	TN	Sevierville	TMoA	IC1728
MiG-17	KS	Topek	CAM	611	MiG-17	TX	Addison	CFM
MiG-17	NV	Fallon	NASF		MiG-17	WA	Seattle	MoF	1406016, IFJ-10
MiG-17	NY	New Windsor	RSAM		MiG-17A	GA	Pooler	MoF	54- 713 85
MiG-17	NV	Reno	SAFB		MiG-17F	AZ	Tucson	PAM	1C 1905
MiG-17	NY	Horseheads	NWM		MiG-17F	NY	Scotia	ESAM	605
					MiG-17F	OR	Hillsboro	CAAM	1C1426, N1426D

Type	State	City	Museum	Serial
MiG-17F	RI	NKing	QAM	1F0325
MiG-17F	TX	Tyler	HAMM	
MiG-17F	UT	Ogden	CFM	1C0406
MiG-19	CA	Riverside	MFAM	Mikoyan
MiG-19	CA	Riverside	MFAM	Mikoyan
MiG-19	NV	Reno	SAFB	Mikoyan
MiG-19S	OH	Dayton	NMUSAF	Mikoyan

MiG-21 Mikoyan Fishbed

Type	State	City	Museum	Serial
MiG-21	AZ	Mesa	CAFAWM	507
MiG-21 PFM	AZ	Tucson	PAM	N21MF
MiG-21	AL	Birmingham	SMoF	
MiG-21	CA	Chino	PoFAM	
MiG-21	CA	El Cajon	SDAMGF	
MiG-21F-13	CA	Riverside	MAFM	1101
MiG-21	FL	Kissi	YAF	
MiG-21	FL	Shalimar	USAFAM	85, RED
MiG-21	LA	Barksdale AFB	BAFB	
MiG-21	VA	Chantilly	NASMUVC	
MiG-21PF	MI	Kalamazoo	KAHM	4107
MiG-21F	NE	Ashland	SACM	60-2105
MiG-21	NY	Horseheads	NWM	
MiG-21	NY	New Windsor	RSAM	

MiG-23 Mikoyan Flogger

Type	State	City	Museum	Serial
MiG-23BN	CA	Riverside	MAFM	5744
MiG-23	NV	Fallon	NASF	353
MiG-23	OH	Dayton	NMUSAF	
MiG-25	OH	Dayton	Dayton	
MiG-29	OR	Tillamook	EAM	
MiG-29	TX	San Angelo	GAFB	
MiG-29A	OH	Dayton	NMUSAF	
MiG-29 Flogger D	CA	Chino	YAM	
Mil Helicopters MI-2	CA	Ramona	CR	
Mil Helicopters MI-2	TN	Pigeon Forge	HH	

Type	State	City	Museum	Man Sn
MiG-17PF	AZ	Tucson	PAM	Man Sn 1A06038, 634
MiG-17PF	CA	McClellan	McCelAFB	186
Farmer				0301, A-5(F-9) Fantan, F-6 = China
Farmer				0409
Farmer				
Farmer				TB, 972, A-5(F-9) Fantan, F-6 = China
MiG-21	OH	Dayton	HAFBM	PF 408
MiG-21	OH	Dayton,	NMUSAF, 560-301, "City of Moscow"	
MiG-21	OK	Wetherford	SA&SC	
MiG-21 MF	ON-C	Trenton	RCAFMM	23 45
MiG-21F-13	OR	Hillsboro	CAAM	261109, N6285L
MiG-21	TX	Addison	CFM	
MiG-21F	UT	Ogden	HAFBM	585
MiG-21 PF	WA	Seattle	MoF	TT1697, 4315
MiG-21 PFM	WA	Seattle	MoF	5411
MiG-21(F-7)	WI	Oshkosh	EAAAAM	N21MG
MiG-21F	CA	McClellan	McCelAFB	201
MiG-21PFM	NM	St Teresa	WEAM	
MiG-21PFM	NY	NYC	ISASM	4105
MiG-21PFM	NY	Scotia	ESAM	2406
MiG-21U	TN	Sevierville	TMoA	
MiG-23	QC-C	La Baie	ADM	
MiG-23K	OH	Dayton	NMUSAF	
				2505
Mikoyan				Fulcrum
Mikoyan				Fulcrum
Mikoyan				Fulcrum
Target Drone				
Mil Helicopters				MI-2
Mil Helicopters				MI-2, "Nadine"

Miles Atwood	CA	Chino	PoFAM	Miles Atwood	Air Racer	
Miller S-1 Fly Rod	KS	Liberalal	MAM	Miller	Fly Rod	
Miller Special 1949	CA	Whittier	WM	Miller	Racer	JM-101, Ol' Tiger, N74J
Milliken Special	ME	Owls Head	OHTM	Milliken	Special	
Mini-Cab	WA	Vancouver	PAM			
Mini-500	AR	Fayetteville	AAM		Mini Helicopter	
Minimora	NY	Elmir	NSM	Minimora		56, N16923
Mitchell Wing B-10	AL	Birmi	Southe	Mitchell	Buzzard	Wing Ultralight
Mitchell Wing	OK	Oklahoma	OSM	Mitchell	Buzzard	Wing Ultralight, N579C
Mitchell Wing	PA	Reading	MAAM	Mitchell	Buzzard	Wing Ultralight
Mitchell Wing	ON-C	Ottawa	CAM	Mitchell	Buzzard	Wing Ultralight
MMC-845	CA	Rosamond	EAFB			1454
Monerai S	AL	Birmi	Southe	Monerai	Powered Sailplane	
Monerai S	CT	Winds	NEAM	Monerai	Powered Sailplane	
Mong Sport	IL	Rantoul	OCAM	Mong	Sport	N1174
Mong Sport	OK	Oklahoma	OSM	Mong	Sport	N119F
Mong Sport	WI	Oshkosh	EAAAAM	Mong	Sport	

Moni Motor Glider	CO	Denver	WOTR	N39JG
Moni Motor Glider	FL	Lakel	SFAF	N46431
Moni Motor Glider	KS	Liberal	MAAM	
Moni Motor Glider	VA	Chantilly	NASMUVC	
Moni Motor Glider	TX	Galveston	LSFM	
Moni Motor Glider	WI	Oshkosh	EAAAAM	N153MX
Moni Motor Glider	WI	Oshkosh	EAAAAM	N82MX
Moni Motor Glider	WI	Oshkosh	EAAAAM	N107MX
Monnett Sonerai II	CA	El Cajon	SDAMGF	
Monnett Sonerai II	IN	LaPorte	DPAM	N4ML
Monnett Sonerai II	WI	Oshkosh	EAAAAM	

Monocoupe Special				
Monocoupe	PA	Readi	Restrant	
Monocoupe 70	CA	San Carlos	HNCAVM	
Monocoupe 90	IA	Ottumwa	APM	504, NC170K
Monocoupe 90A	PA	Bethel	GAAM	NC11750
Monocoupe 90A	WI	Oshkosh	EAAAAM	N11783
Monocoupe 110	CA	Oakla	OWAM	
Monocoupe 110	ID	Athol	NAM	
Monocoupe 110	MD	College Park	CPAM	NC 12345
Monocoupe 110	ND	Minot	DTAM	
Monocoupe 110	VA	Chantnilly	NASMUVC	
Monocoupe 110	WI	Oshkosh	EAAAAM	N15E
Monocoupe 110	WI	Oshkosh	EAAAAM	NC533W
Monocoupe 113	NY	Rhine	ORA	
Monocoupe 113	WI	Oshkosh	EAAAAM	N7808

Monoprep	IA	Ottumwa	APM			6077, NC179K
Monte Copter 10	CA	Ramona	CR	Monte	Copter 10	
Monte Copter 12	CA	Ramona	CR	Monte	Copter 12	

N-series naval aircraft (survivors list)

Model	Manufacturer	Name	Serial / Reg	City	State	Museum
N-9H	Burgess	Curtiss	343-A-19	Chantilly	VA	NASMUVC
N1K1	Kawanishi	Rex		Pensacola	FL	NMoNA
N1K1-J	Kawanishi	Rex		Seattle	WA	MoF
N1K1-J	Kawanishi	Rex	343-A-19	Chantilly	VA	NASMUVC
N1K2-J	Kawanishi	George	5312	Pensacola	FL	NMoNA
N1K2-J	Kawanishi	George	A8529	Dayton	OH	NMUSAF
N2C-2	Curtiss	Fledgling		Pensacola	FL	NMoNA

N2S Boeing-Stearman — Kaydet

Model	Serial / Reg	City	State	Museum
N2S		Hendersonville	NC	WNCAM
N2S-2		Fayet	AR	AAM
N2S-2	N5862	Modesto	CA	HAM
N2S-2		Olympia	WA	OFM
N2S-2(PT-17)		Addison	TX	CFM
N2S-3	214	San Diego	CA	SDAM
N2S-3(B75N1)	N1301M, 5414	Palm Springs	CA	PSAM
N2S-3	75-7990, N81235	Pensacola	FL	NMoNA
N2S-3	569, 41	Rexburg	ID	LFM
N2S-3(PT-17)		Glenview	IL	VM
N2S-3	75-4924, N52107 N2S3(B-75N-1)	Waukegan	IL	WHM
N2S-3(PT-17)		Auburn	IN	HW
N2S-3(PT-17)	07190	Horseheads	NY	NWM
N2S-3(PT-17)	15923, N48272	Charlotte	NC	CAM
N2S-3	75-2743	Hampton	VA	VA&SM
N2S-3	N68827	Suffolk	VA	FF
N2S-4(PT-17)	N5258	Vashon	WA	OTA
N2S-5	N5359N	Mesa	AZ	PSAM
N2S-5	43156	Palm Springs	CA	PSAM
N2S-5		Seattle	WA	MoF
N2S-5		Pensacola	FL	NMoNA
N2S-5		Suitland	MD	PEGF
N4S		Chantilly	VA	NASMUVC
		Readi	PA	MAAM
		Hendersonville	NC	WNCAM

N2T / N2Y

Model	Manufacturer	Name	Serial / Reg	City	State	Museum
N2T-1	Timm	Tuter	32478, 312	Pensacola	FL	NMoNA
N2T-1	Timm	Tuter	2951, 32622	Kalamazoo	MI	KAHM
N2Y-1	Consolidated	Fleet I	A8605	Pensacola	FL	NMoNA

N3N Naval Aircraft Factory — Yellow Pearl

Model	Serial / Reg	City	State	Museum
N3N	N45084, 4497	Tucson	AZ	PAM
N3N		Denve	CO	JWDAS
N3N		Driggs	ID	TAC
N3N		Twin	ID	NWWI
N3N		Kalamazoo	MI	KAHM
N3N		Carso	NV	YF
N3N		Hood	OR	WAAAM
N3N		Mt Pleasant	SC	PPM
N3N	2959, 703	C Christi	TX	USS Lexi
N3N	N44741, "The Real Thing", N44757, 2621	Houston	TX	CAF-WHS
N3N-3	2621, N44757, 2621	Chino	CA	YAM
N3N-3	2685, N45265, 2685	Chino	CA	YAM
N3N-3	2804, N45070, 2804	Chino	CA	YAM
N3N-3	2827, N45280, 2827	Chino	CA	YAM
N3N-3	4480, N695M, 4480	Chino	CA	YAM
N3N-3	2693	Pensacola	FL	NMoNA
N3N-3	N6399T, 3046	Pensacola	FL	NMoNA
N3N-3		Ypsilanti	MI	YAF
N3N-3	Side # 46	Maryland Hts	MO	HARM
N3N-3		Readi	PA	MAAM
N3N-3	1974, N3NZ	Galve	TX	LSFM
N3N-3		Chantilly	VA	NASMUVC

Model	State	Location	Museum	Manufacturer	Name/Type	Registration
N9M-B	CA	Chino	PoFAM	Northrop	Flying Wing	004, N9MB
N22S	AZ	Tucson	PAM	A/C Factories	Nomad	Man Sn F163, N6328, VH-HVZ,
NA-64 (*See BT-14*)						
Nagler-Rolz NR 54 V2	VA	Chantilly	NASMUVC	Nagler-Rolz		
Nangchang CJ-6A	CA	Santa Rosa	PCAM			
Nangchang C-5-6A	PA	Beaver Falls	AHM			
NASA Parasev	MD	Suitland	PEGF	NASA	Paresev	B488DS
Navion B	MN	Anoka	Airport	Ryan	Navion	
NB-8G	MO	Maryland Hts	HARM	Nicolas-Beazley	NB-8G	
NC-9-A	FL	Pensacola	NMoNA		Pilgram	Gondola
NE-1(J3C-65)	PA	Readi	MAAM	Piper	Cub	
NE-1(J3C-65)	PA	Readi	MAAM	Piper	Cub	
Nelson Dragonfly	CA	Santa Martin	WoHAM	Nelson	Dragonfly	
Nemesis	VA	Chantilly	NASMUVC	Nemesis		
Nesmith	IA	Ottumwa	APM	Nesmith	Cougar	L-1, N10162
NF-11(TT-20)	CA	Chino	PoFAM	Gloster	Meteor	
NF-11(TT-20)	CA	Rosamond	EAFB	Gloster	Meteor	
Nieuport Bebe						
Nieuport 10	NY	Rhine	ORA			
Nieuport 11 7/8 Scale	CA	Riverside	MAFM			
Nieuport 11	CA	Santa Martin	WoHAM			N1486
Nieuport 11	CA	San Diego	SDAM			N8217V
Nieuport 11	NC	Hende	WNCAM			
Nieuport 11	OK	Oklahoma	OSM			N1504
Nieuport 12	ON-C	Ottaw	CAM			
Nieuport 17	OR	Eugene	OA&SM			
Nieuport 24	VA	Chantilly	NASMUVC			N24RL
Nieuport 24	WA	Seattle	MoF			
Nieuport 24	WI	Oshkosh	EAAAAM			N65113,
Nieuport 27	NY	River	RE			
Nimbus II	KY	Lexington	AMoK	Schemp-Hirth	Nimbus II	N257JB
Nimbus II	WI	Oshkosh	EAAAAM	Schemp-Hirth	Nimbus II	N257JB
Nixon Special	CT	Winds	NEAM	Nixon	Special	
Nord 1002	FL	FtLau	WJAIS&L	Nord	Taifun	
Nord 1002	PA	Readi	MAAM	Nord	Taifun	

Type	State	Location	Museum	Registration
Nieuport 27	WA	Seattle	MoF	N5597M, H
Nieuport 28	AL	Gunte	LGARFM	
Nieuport 28	CA	San Diego	SDAM	N28GH, 6
Nieuport 28	FL	Pensacola	NMoNA	5769, 21
Nieuport 28	IA	Hampton	DWWIAM	
Nieuport 28 Rep	ME	Owls Head	OHTM	N8539
Nieuport 28	OH	Dayton	NMUSAF	
Nieuport 28C-1	ON-C	Brampton	TGWFM	14
Nieuport 28C-1	WA	Seattle	MoF	
Nieuport 17 7/8 Scale	AL	Ozark	USAAM	
	VA	Chantilly	NASMUVC	
	BC-C	Sidne	BCAM	

Designation	State	City	Museum	Mfr	Name	Serial/Reg
Nord 1101	OR	Tillamook	TAM	Nord	Noralpha	N1101M
Nord 1101	PA	Readi	MAAM	Nord	Noralpha	
Nord 3202	CO	Denver	WOTR	Nord	Taifun	"TWA"
Northrop Alhpa 4A	DC	Washi	NA&SM	Northrop	Alpha	
Northrop Delta Fuse	ON-C	Ottaw	CAM	Northrop	Delta	
Northrop Gama	DC	Washi	NA&SM	Northrop	Gama "Polar Star"	
Northrup	IA	Greenfield	IAM	Northrop	Primary GLider	
NR-1W	NY	Bayport	BA	Nicholas-Beazley		
NR-1W	NY	Rhine	ORA	Nicholas-Beazley		
NT-1	FL	Pensacola	NMoNA	New Standard		A8588
NW Porterfield	KS	Liberal	MAAM	Northwest-Porterfield		
O-1E	MN	Blaine	AWAM			

O-2 Cessna Super Skymaster

Designation	State	City	Museum	Serial/Notes
O-2A	AL	Birmingham	SMF	
O-2A	AZ	Tucson	PAM	68-6901, N37581
O-2A	CA	Atwater	CAM	67-21413
O-2A	CA	El Cajon	WW	
O-2A	CA	Farfield	DA&SM	
O-2A	CO	Denver	69thB	
O-2A	CO	Denve	JWDAS	
O-2A	FL	FtWal	HF	67-21368
O-2A	FL	Shalimar	USAFAM	86864
O-2A	HI	Oahu	WAFB	
O-2A	IL	Rantoul	OCAM	67-21411
O-2A	IN	Peru	GAFB	68-6871
O-2A	MD	Suitland	PEGF	
O-2A	MI	Mt Clemens	SMAM	67-21340
O-2A	MN	Blaine	AWAM	
O-2A	NC	Asheboro	PFAC	"Navy"
O-2A	NC	Asheboro	PFAC	"Air Force"
O-2A	OH	Dayton	NMUSAF	67-21331
O-2A	OH	Lockb	RANGB	69-7630
O-2A	OH	N Canton	MAM	
O-2A	RI	NKing	QAM	68-10997
O-2A	SC	Sumte	SAFB	
O-2A	SD	Liberal	MAAM	
O-2A	SD	Rapid City	SDA&SM	
O-2A	TX	Abilene	DLAP	67-21326
O-2A	TX	San Antonio	LSAD	67-21440
O-2A	UT	Ogden	HAFBM	
O-2A	WA	Everett	MoFRC	67-21363, N18BB
O-2A (2 ea)	WI	CDoug	WNGML&M	
O-2A(GO)	GA	Pooler	MoF	68-6894
O-2B	TX	Austi	BAFB	
O-2B	CA	Riverside	MFAM	67-21465
O-2B	IN	Indianapolis	AMHF	"Twigger Happy", 997
O-2B	IN	Indianapolis	AMHF	Project
O-2B	KS	Wichi	KAM	
O-3A(YO)	AZ	Tucson	PAM	69-18006
O-38F	OH	Dayton	NMUSAF	Douglas — 33-324
O-46A	OH	Dayton	NMUSAF	Douglas — 35-179
O-47A	MN	Minne	MAGM	North American — Observation Plane — 38-295
O-47A(RO)	MD	Suitland	PEGF	North American — Observation Plane

Designation	State	City	Museum	Manufacturer	Type	Serial / Notes
O-47B	KS	Topek	CAM	North American	Observation Plane	
O-47B	OH	Dayton	NMUSAF	North American	Observation Plane	39-112
O-52	CA	Chino	YAM	Curtiss	Owl	40-2769, N61241
O-52	OH	Dayton	NMUSAF	Curtiss	Owl	40-2763
O1-A	CO	Denver	69thB	FAC		
OA-1A	OH	Dayton	NMUSAF		Loening	26-431
OA-1A	VA	Chantilly	NASMUVC		Loening	
OA-10A(PBY-5A)	OH	Dayton	NMUSAF	Consolidated	Catalina	44-33879, 46595
OA-12A(J2F-6)	OH	Dayton	NMUSAF	Grumman	Duck	48-563, 33587
Ohm Special Racer	NY	Hammond	CM	Ohm	Special Racer	
Oldfield Special BGL	WI	Oshkosh	EAAAAM	Oldfield	Special BGL	N11311
Olmstead Pusher	MD	Suitland	PEGF	Olmstead	Pusher	
OMAC-1	WA	Seattle	MoF			
OQ-1	CA	San Diego	SDAM	Radioplane	Drone	
OQ-2A	OH	Dayton	NMUSAF	Radioplane	Drone	
OQ-2A	UT	Ogden	HAM	Radioplane	Drone	
OQ-2A	WI	Oshkosh	EAAAAM	Radioplane	Drone	
OQ-3	AZ	Tucson	PAM	Radioplane	Drone	
OQ-A	WI	Oshkosh	EAAAAM	Globe	Drone	26, "Wimpy"
OQ-14	OH	Dayton	NMUSAF		Drone	
OQ-19(MQM-33)	AZ	Tucson	PAM	Northrop	Drone	KD2R-5
OQ-19(MQM-33)	KS	Liberal	MAAM	Northrop	Drone	
OQ-19D	WI	Oshkosh	EAAAAM	Northrop	Drone	
Ornithopter 1510	CA	San Diego	SDAM	Ornithopter		
OS2U	AL	Mobile	BMP	Vought	Kingfisher	BU0951, 60
OS2U	VA	Suffolk	FF	Vought	Kingfisher	Storage in Virginia Beach
OS2U-3	CA	Chino	YAM	Vought-Skirosky	Kingfisher	9643, 9643
OS2U-3	FL	Pensacola	NMoNA	Vought-Skirosky	Kingfisher	7534, 5926
OS2U-3	VA	Chantilly	NASMUVC	Vought-Skirosky	Kingfisher	
OS2U-3	NC	Wilmi	USSNCBC	Vought	Kingfisher	3073

OV-1 Grumman Mohawk

Designation	State	City	Museum	Serial / Notes
OV-1	GA	Dobbi	DAFB	
OV-1	MN	Blaine	AWAM	61-5936
OV-1B	GA	Hampton	AAHF	
OV-1B	NY	Garden City	CoAM	59-2633
OV-1	NY	Horseheads	NWM	62-5856, N6744
OV-1A(JOV)	MN	Blaine	AWAM	62-5856, N6744
OV-1B	MN	Blaine	AWAM	62-5856, N6744
OV-1B (2 ea)	AL	Ozark	USAAM	59-2631
OV-1B	TX	Amarillo	EFA&SM	
OV-1C	AZ	Tucson	PAM	61-2724, "Dirty Dawg"
OV-1C	FL	Clear	FMAM	

OV- 1C(JOV)	MN	Blaine	AWAM	61-2718, N-2036P
OV- 1C	NY	Horseheads	NWM	62-05856
OV- 1D	AZ	FtHua	FH	18930
OV- 1D	CO	Denver	69thB	
OV- 1D	FL	Tittusville	VACM	
OV- 1D	GA	Spart	GSMA	
OV- 1D	MI	Kalamazoo	KAHM	68-16993, 993
OV- 1D	NC	Charlotte	CAM	62-5874, N1171Y
OV- 1D	NC	Charlotte	CAM	62-5890, N1209P
OV- 1D	NJ	Teterboro	AHM	603740
OV- 1D	PA	Beaver Falls	AHM	62-5856, N6744
OV- 1D	IL	Russell	MMM	67-18900, "Valdez II"
OV- 1D	IL	Russell	MMM	68-16992
OV- 1D	IL	Russell	MMM	
OV- 1D	OR	Mc Minnville	EAM	67-18902

OV- 3A(YO)	AL	Ozark	USAAM	Lockheed	Silent One	69-18000

OV-10 Grumman Bronco

OV-10	FL	Esther	HAP	
OV-10	KS	Liberal	MAAM	
OV-10	TX	Ft Worth	VFM	
OV-10 Mock-Up	TX	Ft Worth	VFM	
OV-10A	AZ	Tucson	DMAFB	
OV-10A(NH)	FL	Mary Esther	HF	67-14626
OV-10A	OH	Dayton	NMUSAF	68-3787
OV-10A	UT	Ogden	HAM	67-14675
OV-10D	AZ	Tucson	PAM	155499
OV-10D	CA	Miramar	FLAM	UU, VMO-2

OW-8	IA	Ottumwa	APM	Welch		
OY-1	CA	Miramar	FLAM	Convair	Sentinel	
OY-1	FL	Pensacola	NMoNA	Convair	Sentinel	60645
OY-2	VA	Quantico	NMMC	Convair	Sentinel	120454
P- 1(F6C-1)	FL	Pensacola	NMoNA	Curtiss	Hawk	N6969A
P- 1(F6C-1)	MO	SLoui	SLDPA	Curtiss	Hawk	
P- 1(F6C-4)	VA	Chantilly	NASMUVC	Curtiss	Hawk	
P- 3A	FL	Jacksonville	NASJ	Lockheed	Orion	151374, LQ, 56
P- 3A	FL	Pensacola	NMoNA	Lockheed	Orion	152152, PJ, 1, VP-96
P- 3A	HI	Oahu	BPNAS	Lockheed	Orion	
P- 3A	HI	Kaneohe	KBMCAS	Lockheed	Orion	152169
P- 3A	LA	New Orleans	Belle Chasse NAS	Lockheed	Orion	
P- 3B	MI	Mt Clemens	SMAM	Lockheed	Orion	152748, VP-93
P- 3B	PA	Willow Grove	NVHAA	Lockheed	Orion	154574
P- 6 7/8 Scale	CA	Riverside	MAFM	Curtiss	Hawk	AC 32-240, N90DS
P- 6E(F6C)	OH	Dayton	NMUSAF	Curtiss	Hawk	32-261
P- 6E(F6C)	WI	Oshkosh	EAAAAM	Curtiss	Hawk	NX 606PE
P- 9 Pober Pixie EAA	KS	Liberal	MAAM	Pober	Pixie	
P-10 Cuby	WI	Oshkosh	EAAAAM	Wag-Aero	P-10 Cuby	NC23254, "Lil' Gonk"

P-12 through P-36A (Boeing / Seversky / Curtiss)

Model	Mfr	Name	State	City	Org	Serial / Notes
P-12 (F4B)	Boeing		WA	Seattle	MoF	N872H
P-12E(F4B-4)	Boeing		CA	Chino	PoFAM	
P-12E(F4B-4)	Boeing		OH	Dayton	NMUSAF	
P-26A	Boeing	Peashooter	CA	Chino	PoFAM	31-599
P-26A	Boeing	Peashooter	VA	Chantilly	NASMUVC	Model 266
P-26A Rep	Boeing	Peashooter	OH	Dayton	NMUSAF	33-135
P-35A	Seversky		OH	Dayton	NMUSAF	Model 266
P-35A	Seversky		FL	Miami	WOM	36-404
P-36A	Curtiss	Hawk	OH	Dayton	NMUSAF	38-001

P-38 Lockheed Lightning

Model	State	City	Org	Serial / Notes
P-38	AK	Anchorage	EAFB	42-13400
P-38 Replica	CA	Riverside	P38NA	
P-38	FL	Polk City	FOF	42-26761
P-38	VA	Suffolk	FF	
P-38 Replica	IL	Wheeling	94 Aero Sq	
P-38F-5	CA	Rialto	KA	42-12652, #33, Restoration
P-38J	VA	Chantilly	NASMUVC	42-67762
P-38J 2/3 Rep	MI	Kalamazoo	KAHM	
P-38J-15	CA	Rialto	KA	42-103988, "Jandina III", Restoration
P-38J-20-LO	CA	Chino	PoFAM	44-23314, N29Q, "Porky II"
P-38J-10-LO	UT	Ogden	HAFBM	42-67638, Nose 85
P-38L-5	WI	Superior	RBHC	44-53286, 42-103993, "Marge"
P-38L-5-LO	OR	Tillamook	TAM	44-27083, N38V, "Tangerine"
P-38L-5-LO	OH	Dayton	NMUSAF	44-53232, NX66678
P-38L-5-LO(F-5G)	CA	Chino	YAM	44-27183, N718
P-38L-5-LO(F-5G)	NJ	Trent	MGAFB	44-53015, "Pudgy V"
P-38L-5-LO(F-5G)	NM	St Teresa	WEAM	44-27087, N577JB,
P-38L-5-LO(F-5G)	OR	Mc Minnville	EAM	44-53186, N503MH,
P-38L-5-LO(F-5G)	WI	Oshkosh	EAAAAM	44-53087, N3800L, "Marge"
P-38M-5-LO	WA	Seattle	MoF	44-53097, NL3JB,

P39 Bell Airacobra

Model	State	City	Org	Serial / Notes
P-39	FL	Polk	FoF	42-4312
P-39	VA	Suffolk	FF	Storage in Virginia Beach
P-39	VA	Suffolk	FF	Storage in Virginia Beach
P-39N	PA	Beave	AHM	42-18814
P-39N-0	CA	Chino	YAM	42-8740, N81575
P-39N-5-BE	CA	Chino	PoFAM	42-19027
P-39Q	CA	Riverside	MFAM	42-20000
P-39Q	MI	Kalamazoo	KAHM	44-3908, "Whistlin Britches"
P-39Q-8-DC	NY	Buffalo	B&ECNP	"Snooks 2"
P-39Q	NY	Niagara Falls	NAM	44-2433, "Galloping Gertie"
P-39Q	OH	Dayton	NMUSAF	44-3887
P-39Q	OH	N Canton	MAM	42-19995
P-39Q	TX	SMarc, CTW	CAF, 42-19597, N6968, "Miss Connie"	
P-39Q	VA	Hampton	VA&SC	42-20027

P-40 Curtiss Warhawk

Model	State	City	Org	Serial / Notes
P-40 Mock-Up	Hi	Wheeler	WAFB	41-18P, #155,
P-40 Replica	CA	Inglewood	PBR	
P-40 Replica	Hi	Oahu	WAFB	
P-40D	TX	Hawki	RRSA	
P-40C	FL	Pensacola	NMoNA	AK255
P-40E Fuse	AK	Anchorage	AAHM	
P-40E	CA	Chino	YAM	AK827, N40245
P-40E	CA	San Diego	SDAM	AK979, N40FT
P-40E Rep	CO	CSpri	EJPSCM	
P-40E Mk.1	VA	Chantilly	NASMUVC	41-13574, AK875
P-40E Replica	HI	Honolulu	PAM	

P-40 (continued)

Model	State	City	Museum	Serial / Notes
P-40E	ID	Nampa	WAM	AK933, N94466
P-40E Replica	LA	BRoug	LNWM	Tail # 191, "Joy"
P-40E	ND	Fargo	FAM	AK753
P-40E	NM	St Teresa	WEAM	AL152, N95JB
P-40E	NY	Shirley, WOLI, 15280, N9837A, "Old Exterminator"		
P-40E	ON-C	Ottaw	CAM	AL 135, 1076
P-40E	VA	Suffolk	FF	41-35927
P-40E	VA	Suffolk	FF	41-35918
P-40K	OR	Mc Minnville	EAM	42-9749, FR293
P-40K	GA	Griffin	CHF	42-10083
P-40M	NY	Farmingdale	AAM	43-5795, N1232N,
P-40M	OH	Batavia	TSWM	43-5813
P-40N	CA	Chino	PoFAM	42-105192
P-40N	CA	Chino	PoFAM	42-106101
P-40N	CA	Palm Springs	PSAM	44-7084
P-40N	FL	Polk City	FoF	44-47923
P-40N	GA	Douglas	TW	42-46111
P-40N	ID	Nampa	WAM,	42-106396, N1195N
P-40N	MI	Kalamazoo	KAHM,	44-7619, N222SU
P-40N	NC	Fayet	PAFB	42-105702
P-40N	TX	Addison	CFM	44-7369, 40, 40
P-40N-5-CU	UT	Ogden	HAM	42-105270
P-40N	WA	Seattle	MoF	44-7192, NL10626
P-40N(TP)	CA	Palm Sprg, PSAM, 44-7284, NX999CD, "Miss Josephine"		
P-40N Replica	CA	Riverside	MFAM	
P-40N-5-CU	GA	Pooler	MoF	42-105927

P-47 Republic Thunderbolt

Model	State	City	Museum	Serial / Notes
P-47D 3/8 Scale	WA	Seattle	MoF, 42-8205 N14519, 88, "Big Stud"	
P-47 ½ Scale	AZ	Mesa	CAFAWM	N47DJ
P-47 ½ Scale	AZ	Tucson	PAM	N555TN, Experimental
P-47D Replica	SC	Sumte	SAFB	
P-47	NJ	Millville	MAFM, 45-49192, "No Guts, No Glory"	
P-47	IL	Wheeling	94th Aero Sq	
P-47	FL	Wpalm Beach	391BG	
P-47 5/8 Scale	WA	Seattle	MoF	42-8205
P-47D	CA	Rialto	KA	42-22521, Project
P-47D	CA	Rialto	KA	45-49385, NX47D
P-47D	CA	Palm SPrg	PSAM, 45-49205, NX47RP, "Big Chief"	
P-47D	CT	Winds	NEAM	45-49458, 54, "Norma"
P-47D	IL	Danville	MA	44-90471
P-47D	OH	Dayton	NMUSAF	42-23278
P-47D	FL	Shalimar, USAFAM, 44-89320, "Expected Goose"		
P-47D	MI	Kalamazoo	KAHM	45-49181, N444SU
P-47D-RE	NC	Charlotte	CAM	42-22331
P-47D	TN	Sevierville, TMoA, 44-90460, N9246B, "Hun Hunter XVI"		
P-47D	TN	Sevierville	TMoA	44-90438, NX647D
P-47D-30-RA	UT	Ogden	HAM	44-32798
P-47D	WA	Arlington	FHC	45-49406
P-47D-11-RE	CA	Rialto	KA	42-75284, Project
P-47D-2-RE	CA	Rialto	KA	42-08074, Project
P-47D-30-NA	VA	Chantilly	NASAUH	44-32691 LH-E
P-47D-30	OH	Dayton	NMUSAF	45-49167
P-47G	CA	Chino, PoFAM, 42-25234, "Spirit of Atlantic City NJ"		
P-47M	CA	Chino	YAM	42-27385, N27385
P-47N	NY	Garde	CoAM	44-89444
P-47N	TX	Addison	CFM	45-53436, N47TB
P-47N	TX	Galveston, LSFM, 44-90368, N47DG, "Little Demon"		
P-47N	TX	San Antonio	LSAD	44-89348
P-47N	CO	CSpri	EJPSCM	44-89425

P-51 North American Mustang

Model	State	City	Museum	Serial / Notes
P-51 Replica	GA	Savan	MEHM	
P-51 Replica	IL	Wheeling	94th Aero Sq	
P-51 Replica	MO	Branson	VMM	44-60356
P-51 Replica	OH	Cleve	100thBGR	
P-51 Replica	WI	Madison	MWVM	
P-51 ½ Scale	IN	Auburn	HW	
P-51 Mk IV	ON-C	Ottaw	VWoC	44-73463
P-51	AL	Troy	TMA	44-1757
P-51	OR	Tillamook	TAM	44-14826

Type	State	City	Code	Serial Numbers / Names
P-51(XP)	WI	Oshkosh	EAAAAM	41-038, NX51NA
P-51A	CA	Chino	PoFAM	43- 6251, NX4235Y
P-51A-1	CA	Chino	YAM	43- 6274, N90358, HY
P-51B	ID	Idaho Falls	PM	43-12112
P-51C	FL	Polk City	FoF,	42-103831, "Ina the Macon Bele"
P-51C	ID	Nampa	WAM	42-83878
P-51C	MN	S St Paul,	NASMUVC	CAF-SMW, 42-103645, N215CA, "Gunfighter"
P-51C	VA	Chantilly	NASMUVC	44-10947, "Excalibur III"
P-51D(F)	AL	Mobile	BMP	44-74216, "Derailer"
P-51D	AL	Ozark	USAAM	44-72990
P-51D	CA	Chino,	PoFAM,	45-11582, N5441V, "Spam Cam,
P-51D	CA	Chino,	PoFAM	44-84961, "Wee Willy"
P-51D-10	CA	Chino,	YAM	44-74910, N74920, "Miss Judy"
P-51D	CA	Fresno	FANG	44-73972
P-51D	CA	Palm Springs	PSAM	44-74908
P-51D	CA	Palm Springs,	PSAM,	44-74908, N151BP, "Button Nose"
P-51D	CA	San Diego,	SDAM,	44-73683, N5555D, "Bunny", DGP
P-51D	CA	Shafter,	MFAM,	44-13105, N71FT, "Strega"
P-51D	CA	SRosa,	PCAM	44-84860, "Lady Jo", V-C5 A
P-51D	CO	Lafayette	SoFC	44-63791, N151GP
P-51D	CT	Winds	NEAM	44-72400
P-51D	DC	Washi	NA&SM	44-74939, "Willit Run"
P-51D(TF)	FL	Kissi	S51C	44-84745, "Crazy Horse"
P-51D(TF)	FL	Kissi	S51C	44-74502, "Crazy Horse 2"
P-51D	FL	FtLau	WJAIS&L	44-73518
P-51D	FL, Lakeland,	SNF,	45-11507, NL 921PHO, "Cripes A Mighty 3"
P-51D-11	FL	Shalimar	USAFAM	41-13571
P-51D	GA	Atlanta	CAF DW	44-73843
P-51D	GA	Warner Robbins, MoA,		44-13704, "Ferocious Frankie"
P-51D	IA	Council Bluffs	CAF-GPW,	44-73264, "Gunfighter"
P-51D(F)	ID	Rexburg	LFM	67-22579, N251RM
P-51D	ID	Rexburg	LFM	44-74739, N51RH, "Old Yeller"
P-51D	IL	Danville	MAM	44-73822, "Lil Margaret"
P-51D-25NA	IL	Springfield	ACM	44-73287, N5445V "Worry Bird"
P-51D	IN	Shellersburg	CCA	44-11553, NL-51VF, "Shangrila"
P-51D	IN	Valparaiso	IAM	45-11540, "excalibur"
P-51D	LA,	Barksdale	BAFB,	44-73656, "Moonbeam McSwine"
P-51D	MI	Kalamazoo	KAHM	44-7366, Winter Only
P-51D	MN	Minne	MAGM	68-15795, 489
P-51D	NC	Goldsboro	SJAFB	44-63615
P-51D	ND	Fargo	FAM,	44-74404, "Dazzling Donna"
P-51D	ND	Fargo	FANG	44-74407
P-51D(TF)	NM	St Teresa	WEAM	44-84658, "Friendly Ghost"
P-51D	NY	Shirley	WOLI	44-84453, "Glamorous Gal"
P-51D	OH	Batavia	TSWM	44-73260, "Cincinnati Miss"
P-51D	OH	Dayton	UASM	44-74936, "Shimmy IV"
P-51D	ON-C	Ottaw	CAM	44-73347
P-51D	OR	Mc Minnville	EAM	44-63576, N51DH
P-51D-20-NA	TX	Addison	CFM	44-72339, N251JC, WD-C
P-51D	UT	Ogden	HAFBM	41-13371, "Audrey"
P-51D	VA	Suffolk	FF	44-63507, "Double Trouble Two"
P-51D	WA	Arlington	FHC	44-72364
P-51D-30NT	OK	Bethany,	OMoF,	44-74536, N991R "Miss America" Racer
P-51D-30NT	WA	Bellingham	HFM	44-11525, "Val-Halla"
P-51D	WA	Olympia	OFM	44-73436, "American Beauty"
P-51D(CF)	WA	Seattle	MoF	NL151X, CV-J, "Ho! Hun"
P-51D	WI	CDoug	WNGML&M	44-72989, WIS-NG
P-51D	WI	Charl	CANG	44-72948, "Wham Bam"
P-51D(XP)	WI	Oshkosh	EAAAAM	44-75007, "Paul I"
P-51H-5-NA	WI	Oshkosh	EAAAAM	44-75007, N, "Paul I"
P-51H	IL	Rantoul	OCAM	44- 64265, MASS ANG
P-51K-NT-10	OH, Clevel,	San Antonio	LSAD	44-64376
			FCAAM,	44-12116, "Second Fiddle"

Type	State	City	Code	Manufacturer	Name
P-55(XP)	MI	Kalamazoo	KAHM	Curtiss	Ascender
P-56(XP)	MD	Suitland	PEGF	Northrop	Black Bullet
P-56(XP)	WVA		Northrop	Northrop	Black Bullet
P-59	NE	Minde	HWPV	Bell	Airacomet
P-59(XP)	DC	Washi	NA&SM	Bell	Airacomet

42-78846

P-59 / P-61

Model	State	Location	Code	Mfr	Name	Serial / Notes
P-59A-1	CA	Riverside	MFAM	Bell	Airacomet	44-22614, Side 88
P-59A(YP)	CA	Chino	PoFAM	Bell	Airacomet	
P-59B	CA	Rosamond	EAFB	Bell	Airacomet	44-22633
P-59B	OH	Dayton	NMUSAF	Bell	Airacomet	44-22650
P-61 Nose	MD	Ft Meade	QM	Northrop	Black Widow	42-39445
P-61B-1	PA	Readi	MAAM	Northrop	Black Widow	43-8353, "Moonlight Serenade"
P-61C	OH	Dayton	NMUSAF	Northrop	Black Widow	43-8330
P-61C	VA	Chantilly	NASMUVC	Northrup	Black Widow	

P-63 Bell Kingcobra

Model	State	Location	Code	Serial / Notes
P-63	FL	Lakeland	SNFAM	43-11117
P-63	GA	Atlanta	CAFDW	42-68941
P-63A	CA	Palm SPrg	PSAM	42-68864, NX163BP, "Pretty Polly"
P-63A	ID	Rexburg	LFM	42-6021
P-63A	MD	Suitland	PEGF	42-70255
P-63C	CA	Chino	YAM	42-69080, N94501
P-63E	AZ	Tucson	PAM	43-11727, N9003A
P-63E	OH	Dayton	NMUSAF	43-11728,
P-63E	VA	Suffolk	FF	
P-63G(RP)	TX	San Antonio	LSAD	45-57295

P-75 / P-80 / P-81 / P1Y / P2B

Model	State	Location	Code	Mfr	Name	Serial / Notes
P-75A	OH	Dayton	NMUSAF	Fisher	Eagle	44-44553
P-80(XP)	MI	Kalamazoo	AZ			
P-80(XP)	OH	Dayton	NMUSAF			
P-81(XP)	OH	Dayton	NMUSAF			
P1Y1-C	MD	Suitland	PEGF	Kugisho	Frances (Ginga)	
P2B-1S	CA	Richm	AMS			
P2B-1S	FL	Polk	FoF			

P2V Lockheed Neptune

Model	State	Location	Code	Serial / Notes
P2V	AZ	Tucson	PAM	N14448, 147957
P2V	CA	Mt View	MNAS	
P2V	HI	Kaneohe	MB	
P2V	NY	Brooklyn	NARF	210
P2V-1(P-2)	FL	Pensacola	NMoNA	89082
P2V-1(XP)	FL	Pensacola	NMoNA	
P2V-3	FL	Clear	FMAM	Underwater in Ocean
P2V-5	CO	Pueblo	PW AM	128402
P2V-5	FL	Jacksonville	NASJ	131410, VP-62, #02 LN-4
P2V-5	HI	Kaneohe	KBMCAS	150279, VP-17 / VP-6
P2V-7	ME	Bruns	BNAS	
P2V-7	AZ	Tucson	PAM	135620
P2V-7	NS-C	Greenwood	GMAM	Side # VN101
P2V-7	OR	Tillamook	TAM	
P2V-7	PA	Beave	AHM	
P2V-7(SP-2H)	PA	Readi	MAAM	144683
	FL	Pensacola	NMoNA	141234, PG 6, VP-65

P5M / P6M / P8M

Model	State	Location	Code	Mfr	Serial / Notes
P5M(SP-5B)	FL	Pensacola	NMoNA	Martin	5533, QE, 10, VP-40
P6M (Fuse/Tail)	MD	Middle River	GLMAM	Martin	
P8MU-3	MD	Suitland	PEGF		

Piper

Model	State	City	Museum	Notes
PA-5				
PA-11 Cub Special	FL	Kissi	FTW AM	
PA-11 Cub Special	PA	Lock Haven	PAM	
PA-12 Super Cruiser	CA	Hayward	VAM	
PA-12 Super Cruiser	VA	Chantilly	NASMUVH "City of Washington"	
PA-18	VA	Chantilly	NASMUVH	
PA-20 Pacer	NY	Bayport	BA	
PA-20 Pacer	WI	Oshkosh	EAAAAM	N3762P
PA-22 Tri Pacer	IL	Rantoul	OCAM	N8726C
PA-22 Tri Pacer	IN	LaPorte	LCHSM	N2852Z
PA-22 Tri Pacer	KS	Liberal	MAAM	
PA-22 Tri Pacer	OK	Fredi	AAM	
PA-22 Tri Pacer	TX	Dallas	FoF	
PA-22-125	PA	Readi	MAAM	
PA-22-150	WI	Oshkosh	EAAAAM	
PA-23 Apache	AR	Pine Bluff	REAA	
PA-23 Apache	KS	Liberal	MAAM	
PA-23 Apache	NE	Minde	HWPV	
PA-23 Apache	OK	Fredi	AAM	
PA-23 Apache	VA	Chantilly	NASMUVC	
PA-23(U-11A)(O-1)	AZ	Tucson	PAM	149067, Model 250
PA-23-250 Aztec	CA	Hayward	VAM	
PA-23-250 Aztec	OK	Fredi	AAM	
PA-23-250 Aztec	PA	Readi	MAAM	N14281
PA-24 Commanche	KS	Liberal	MAAM	
PA-28-140	AL	Birmingham	SMoF	
PA-28-140	WI	Oshkosh	EAAAAM	
PA-29 Papoose	PA	Lock Haven	PAM	
PA-34-200 Seneca II	PA	Readi	MAAM	N5297T
PA-38-112 Tomahawk	PA	Readi	MAAM	N382PT
PA-44 Cheyenne II	FL	Dayton	ERAU	
PA-44 Cheyenne II	MN	Winoma	WTI	N23MW
PA-48 Enforcer	CA	Rosamond	EAFB	48-35010 2
PA-48 Enforcer	OH	Dayton	NMUSAF	48-83011

Entry	State	City	Museum	Type	Designation	Serial
Pacific Airwave Kiss 89	AZ	Tucson	PAM	Pacific Airwave	Kiss	Man Sn KM92514
Packard LePere LUSAC	OH	Dayton	NMUSAF	Packard LePere	LUSAC	SC42133
Panavia Tornado	OH	Dayton	NMUSAF	Panavia	Tornado	ZA-374
Paramount Cabinair	FL	Delan	OHA	Paramount	Cabinair	
Paramotor FX-1	NY	Garden	CoAM	Paramotor	FX-1	
Parker JP-001	WI	Oshkosh	EAAAAM	American Special	N113JP	
Parker Sailplane	CA	Santa Maria	SMMoF	Parker	Sailplane	
Parsons Autogyro	PA	WChester	AHM	Parsons	Autogyro	
Passett Ornithopter	NY	Rhine	ORA	Passett	Ornithopter	
Pathefinder	VA	Chantilly	NASMUVC		Pathefinder	
PB2M-1(XP)	BC-C	P.Alb	Spoat Lk	Martin	Mars	
PB4Y-2	CA	Chino	YAM	Consolidated	Privateer	59882
PB4Y-2	FL	Pensacola	NMoNA	Consolidated	Privateer	66261, F 202
PB4Y-2	TX	Galve	LSFM	Consolidated	Privateer	59819, N3739G
PB4Y-2G(P4Y-2G)	MI	Belleville	YAF	Consolidated	Privateer	59876, N6319D
PBM	MD	Balti	BMoI	Martin	Mariner	

PBM

Designation	State	Location	Code	Manufacturer	Name	Reg
PBM	TX	Hawki	RRSA	Martin	Mariner	
PBM-5A	AZ	Tucson	PAM	Martin	Mariner	N3190G 122071

PBY Consolidated Catalina

Designation	State	Location	Code	Reg
PBY	MN	S St Paul	CAF-SMW	
PBY	NC	CPoin	CPMB	
PBY	NY	Brooklyn	NAAM	
PBY	TX	Brown	CAFRGVW	
PBY-5	FL	Pensacola	NMoNA	8317
PBY-5A	AK	Ancho	AAHM	
PBY-5A	CA	Chino	YAM	
PBY-5A	CA	San Diego	SDAM	N5590V 48406
PBY-5A	FL	Jacksonville	NASJ	6582, J1-P 17
PBY-5A	FL	Miami	WOM	
PBY-5A	NF-C	Gander	NAAM	9837
PBY-5A	NM	Albuq	KAFB	
PBY-5A	NS	Halifax	ACAM	BU05021, CF-HFL
PBY-5A	ON-C	Ottaw	CAM	11087
PBY-5A	NF-C	Botwood	CAM	
PBY-5A	OR	Tillamook	TAM	N2172N
PBY-5A	TX	Brown	RGVW-CAF	N68756
PBY-5A	TX	Galve	LSFM	407, N68740
PBY-5A	VA	Suffolk	FF	48294, N9521C, VP-82
PBY-6A	NM	Albuq	KAFB	(OA-10A)
PBY-6A	MN	Duluth	CAF-LSS	N7179Y
PBY-6ACF	MN	S St Paul	CAFSMW	
PBY-6A	MN	Duluth	CAF-LSS	
PBY-6A	NY	Farmingdale	AAM	N324FA

PCA onwards

Designation	State	Location	Code	Manufacturer	Name	Reg
PCA-1A	MD	Suitland	PEGF	Pitcairn	Autogiro	
PCA-1A	PA	WChester	AHM	Pitcairn	Autogiro	NC 2624
PCA-2	ON-C	Ottaw	CAM	Pitcairn	Autogiro	
Pearson-Williams	CA	Chino	PoFAM	Pearson-Williams	W-7 Racer	"Mr Smooth"
Pedal Plane	WI	Oshkosh	EAAAAM	Pedal	Pedal Plane	
Pegasus XL	VA	Chantilly	NASMUVC		Pegasus	
Peel Z-1	CA	Santa Martin	WoHAM	Peel	Glider Boat	15-822, W
Pembroke C.51	NJ	Fairf	YAFDCWA	Hunting-Percival	Pembroke	K66B-4001, N51973
Penaud Planaphore	ME	Owls Head	OHTM	Penaud	Planaphore	
Penguin Ground Trainer	CA	Santa Martin	WoHAM	Penguin	Ground Trainer	
Penguin	KS	Augusta	Aam		Experimental	Aircraft
Pentecost E.III	AZ	Tucson	PAM	Pentercost	Hoppicopter	269
Pentecost E.III	MD	Suitland	PEGF	Pentercost	Hoppicopter	
Pfalz D.III	AL	Gunte	LGARFM	Pfalz		
Pfalz D.III	NV	Carso	YF	Pfalz		
Pfalz D.XII	WA	Seattle	MoF	Pfalz		3498, N43C
Pfalz D.XII	DC	Washi	NA&SM	Pfalz		
Pfalz D.XII	MD	Suitland	PEGF	Pfalz		
PG-1 Explorer	WI	Oshkosh	EAAAAM	Skiier Aquq	Explorer	N6498D, "Bayou Bird"
PG-185	MD	Suitland	PEGF	Nelson	Hummingbird	

Aircraft	Type / Name	State	City	Museum	Registration
PGM-17	Douglas Thor	AZ	Tucson	PAM	
PGM-17A	Douglas Thor	CA	Rosamond	EAFB	
PGM-17	Douglas Thor	OH	Dayton	NMUSAF	
PGM-19	Douglas Jupiter	OH	Dayton	NMUSAF	
Pheasant H-10	Pheasant	WI	Oshkosh	EAAAAM	
Phoenix 6	Phoenix	VA	Chantilly	NASMUVC	NC151N
Phoenix 6-C Hang Glider	Phoenix	KS	Liberal	MAAAM	
PHSC Scout	Piccard Scout	NY	Rhine	ORA	
Piccard Hot Air Balloon	Balloon	AB-C	Edmonton	AAM	
Piel-Emeraude	Piel Emeraude	AL	Birmingham	SMoF	
Piel-Emeraude	Piel Emeraude	FL	Lakeland	SNFAM	
Pietenpol	Pietenpol Aerial	GA	Woodstock	NGWS	

Pietenpol B4A Aircamper

Aircraft	State	City	Museum	Registration
Pietenpol B4A	AB-C	Wetas	RM	
Pietenpol B4A	BC-C	Sidne	BCAM	
Pietenpol B4A	CA	Santa Martin	WoHAM	
Pietenpol B4A	CA	El Cajon	SDAMGF	
Pietenpol B4A	CA	San Carlos	HNCAVM	001, N3133
Pietenpol B4A	CA	San Diego	SDAM	N37680
Pietenpol B4A	FL	Lakeland	SNFAM	
Pietenpol B4A	IA	Ottumwa	AAA	N4716
Pietenpol B4A	IL	Sprin	SA	
Pietenpol B4A	IN	LaPorte	DPAM	
Pietenpol B4A	KS	Liberal	MAAM	
Pietenpol B4A	MN	Minne	MAGM	N2NK
Pietenpol B4A	MN	Fountain	FCM	N1932A
Pietenpol B4A	ND	Fargo	BUSAHM	N12072
Pietenpol B4A	ND	Minot	DTAM	N6262
Pietenpol B4A	NY	Niagara Falls	NAM	NX54N
Pietenpol B4A	NY	Rhine	ORA	410, N86404
Pietenpol B4A	OK	Fredi	AAM	N44162
Pietenpol B4A	PA	Bethel	GAAM	N12937
Pietenpol B4A	PA	Readi	MAAAM	N7533U
Pietenpol B4A	VA	Sands	VAM	
Pietenpol B4A	WI	Fond du Lac	WAM	
Pietenpol B4A	WI	Oshkosh	EAAAAM	
Pietenpol B4A	WI	Oshkosh	EAAAAM	

Aircraft	Type / Name	State	City	Museum	Registration
Pietenpol P-9	Sky Scout	IA	Ottumwa	APM	SC1, N12942
Pietenpol P-9	Sky Scout	OR	Hood	WAAAM	
Pietenpol P-9	Sky Scout	TX	Kingsbury	VAHF	
Pietenpol P-9	Sky Scout	WI	Oshkosh	EAAAAM	N12941
Pigeon Fraser	Pigeon Fraser	NY	Rhine	ORA	
Pilatus P-3	Pilatus	NC	Asheboro	PFAC	
Pioneer Flightstar	Pioneer Flightstar	CT	Winds	NEAM	
Piper Commanche	Piper Commanche	IL	Elliot	CFF	
Piper PT	Piper PT	WI	Oshkosh	EAAAAM	X4300
Piper Vagabond	Piper Vagabond	MO	Maryland Hts	HARM	

Pitcairn AC-35	VA	Chantilly	NASMUVC	Pitcairn		
Pitcairn C-8	MD	Suitland	PEGF	Pitcairn	C-8	
Pitcairn PA-5	VA	Sands	VAM	Pitcairn	Mailwing	9

Pitts Special

Pitts S-1	AL	Birmi	Southe	
Pitts S-1	AZ	Scott	SA	
Pitts S-1	AZ	Tucson	PAM	Man Sn 66, N2RB
Pitts S-1	ND	Fargo	BUSAHM	
Pitts S-1	WI	Oshkosh	EAAAAM	N58J
Pitts S-1	WI	Oshkosh	EAAAAM	NX528
Pitts S-1	WI	Oshkosh	EAAAAM	N442X
Pitts S-1-C	MD	Suitland	PEGF	"Little Stinker"
Pitts S-1-C	NS-C	Halifax	ACAM	
Pitts S-1-C	VA	Hampton	VA&SC	
Pitts S-1-C	WI	Oshkosh	EAAAAM	N66Y
Pitts S-1-S	CA	San Diego	SDAMGF	N4HS
Pitts S-1-S	VA	Chantilly	NASMUVC	"Maryann"
Pitts S-1-S	TX	Addison	CFM	N215JC
Pitts S-1-S	WI	Oshkosh	EAAAAM	N9J
Pitts S-2	WI	Oshkosh	EAAAAM	N22Q, "Big Stinker"
Pitts S-2-A	ON-C	Ottawa	CAM	C-FAMR
Pitts S-2-B	AZ	Grand	PoFGCVA	N25CH, "Double Take"
Pitts S-2-B	OR	Mc Minnville	EAM	5105, N5352E

Pitts P-6	WI	Oshkosh	EAAAAM	Pitts	Special	N58P
Pitts Racer 190	WI	Oshkosh	EAAAAM	Pitts	Racer 190	N8JD, "Little Monster"
PA-18	MI	Dearb	HFM	Pitcairn	Autogiro	
PA-18	NE	Minde	HWPV	Pitcairn	Autogiro	
PA-18	NY	Rhine	ORA	Pitcairn	Autogiro	
PA-18-125	TX	Dallas	FoF	Pitcairn	Autogiro	
PA-39	WI	Oshkosh	EAAAAM	Pitcairn-Larsen	Autogiro	N3908
Pizza Peddler	KS	Augusta	AAM		Hang Glider	
PL-4A	AL	Birmingham	SmoF		PL-4A	
Platt-LePage XR-1	MD	Suitland	PEGF	Platt-LePage		
Player Sportplane	WI	Oshkosh	EAAAAM	Player	Sportplane	N21778
Po-2(U-2)	VA	Suffolk	FF	Polikarpov	Mule	641543, N46GU
Pober Jr. Ace	WI	Oshkosh	EAAAAM	Pober	Junior Ace	NX16PP
Pober P-5 Sport	WI	Oshkosh	EAAAAM	Poberenzy	Sport	N51G
Pober P-9 Pixie EAA	WI	Oshkosh	EAAAAM	Pober	Pixie	N9PH
Pober Super Ace	WI	Oshkosh	EAAAAM	Poberenzy	Super Ace	N113PP
Polan Special	WA	Vancouver	PAM	Polan	Racer	

PQ-14 Culver Cadet

PQ-14 (TD2C-1)	FL	Pensacola	NMoNA	120082
PQ-14 (TD2C-1)	MD	Suitland	PEGF	
PQ-14 (TDC-1)	AZ	Tucson	PAM	44-21819, N1063M
PQ-14 (TDC-1)	CA	Chino	PoFAM	
PQ-14B(TDC-2)	IA	Ottumwa	APM	N-917, N5526ANR-D

Model	State	City	Museum	Manufacturer	Name	Serial / Registration
PQ-14B(TDC-2)	OH	Dayton	NMUSAF			44-6462, TDC-1, 2 PQ-14B(TDC-2)
PQ-14B(TDC-2)	WI	Oshkosh	EAAAAM			N999ML, 68334
Pratt-Read Line-1	CT	Winds	NEAM	Pratt-Read	Line	
PRG-1	ND	Fargo	BUSAHM	Pratt-Reed	Glider	
Primary	NY	Elmir	NSM			
Princeton Air Scooter	MD	Suitland	PEGF	Princeton	Air Scooter	
Princeton Air Cycle	PA	W Chester	AHM	Princeton	Air Cycle	

Provost Jet British Aerospace

Model	State	City	Museum	Manufacturer	Name	Serial / Registration
Provost Jet	FL	Melbourne	FITA	Provost Jet		
Provost Jet	FL	Miami	WOM	Provost Jet		
Provost Jet	NY	New Windsor	RSAM	Provost Jet	Trusty	
Provost Jet	OR	Hillsboro	CAAM	Provost Jet	Trusty	XM357, N27357
Provost Jet	WA	Everett	MoF	Provost Jet	Trusty	NX4107, XW307
PS-2	FL	Pensacola	NMoNA	Franklin		9617
PS-2	MD	Suitland	PEGF	Franklin		"Texaco Eaglet"
PT-6A	CA	Riverside	MFAM	Cunningham-Hall		30-385, "Riverside"
PT-6	CA	S. Monica	MoF	Cunningham-Hall		N1238V, Side # 8
PT-1	CA	San Diego	SDAM	Consolidated	Trusty	"Husky"
PT-1	OH	Dayton	NMUSAF	Consolidated	Trusty	26- 233
PT-1	PA	Lock Haven	PAM	Consol;idated	Trusty	
PT-12	OH	Colum	CoS&I			
PT-13	CA	Oakla	OWAM	Boeing-Stearman	Kaydet	
PT-13	FL	Pompa	PAC	Boeing-Stearman	Kaydet	
PT-13	OK	Oklan	CAF-OW	Boeing-Stearman	Kaydet	N51583
PT-13	OR	Mc Minnville	EAM	Boeing-Stearman	Kaydet	75-5300, n450ur
PT-13	TX	Burnet	CAFHLS	Boeing-Stearman	Kaydet	
PT-13	TX	Odessa	CAFDS	Boeing-Stearman	Kaydet	
PT-13	WA	Bellingham	HFM	Boeing-Stearman	Kaydet	
PT-13A	WA	Seattle	MoF	Boeing-Stearman	Kaydet	75-055, n8fl
PT-13D	CA	Riverside	MAFB	Boeing-Stearman	Kaydet	42-16388
PT-13D(N2S-5)	MI	Kalamazoo	KAHM	Boeing-Stearman	Kaydet	61614
PT-13D	NC	Asheboro	PFAC	Boeing-Stearman	Kaydet	
PT-13D	OH	Dayton	NMUSAF	Boeing-Stearman	Kaydet	42-17800
PT-13D	PA	Readi	MAAM	Boeing-Stearman	Kaydet	
PT-16(YPT)(ST-A)	OH	Dayton	NMUSAF	Ryan		40-44, NC18922

PT-17 Stearman

Model	State	City	Museum
PT-17	AL	Ozark	USAAM
PT-17	AR	Fayet	AAM
PT-17	AZ	Grand Canyon	PoFGCVA

Kaydet (See N2S)

Model	State	City	Operator	Registration / Notes
PT-17	AZ	PBluf	RWCAF	
PT-17	AZ	Tucson	PAM	41-8882
PT-17	AZ	Tucson	PAM	41-869, N58219
PT-17	CA	Atwater	CAM	
PT-17	CA	Chino	PoFAM	
PT-17	CA	Palm SPrg	PSAM	N9955H
PT-17	CA	Shafter	MFAM	
PT-17	CO	Pueblo	PWAM	
PT-17	DE	Dover	DAFB	#13
PT-17	FL	Kissi	FTWAM	
PT-17	FL	Miami	WOM	
PT-17	FL	Titusville	VACM	
PT-17	GA	Pooler	M8AFHM	
PT-17	GA	Woodstock	AAM	
PT-17	GA	Woodstock	NGWS	
PT-17	GA	Woodstock	NGWS	
PT-17	HI	Honolulu	PAM	
PT-17	IN	Crawfordsville	RAM	
PT-17	IN	Valparaiso	IAM	41-8311, "Delta Airlines"
PT-17	KS	Topek	CAM	N-5764,
PT-17	KS	New Century	CAF-HoAW	#34, N234x
PT-17	MA	Stow	BCF	
PT-17	MD	College Park	CPAM	
PT-17	MN	Marshall	RBM	N801RB
PT-17	MN	Marshall	RBM	N802RB
PT-17	MN	Marshall	RBM	N803RB
PT-17	MN	Marshall	RBM	N804RB
PT-17	MN	Marshall	RBM	N805RB
PT-17	MN	Marshall	RBM	N806RB
PT-17	MN	Marshall	RBM	N808RB
PT-17	MO	Missoula	MMF	
PT-17	MS	Petal	MWHMM	N79500
PT-17	NC	Durham	CB	
PT-17	NJ	Lexington	NASWAM	
PT-17	NY	Ghent	POMAM	
PT-17	NY	Horseheads	NWM	07190, N64606
PT-17	NY	Shirley	WOLI	
PT-17	OR	Tillamook	TAM	N65727
PT-17	TX	Bealt	FCA	
PT-17	TX	Ft Wort	VFM	
PT-17	TX	Burnet	CAFHLS	
PT-17	TX	Midland	AAHM	48182
PT-17	TX	SMarc	CTWCAF	
PT-17	TX	San Antonio	TAM	
PT-17A	UT	Ogden	HAFBM	41-25284
PT-17	UT	SLake	CAF-UW	N1387V
PT-17	VA	Bealt	FCA	
PT-17	WA	Vashon	OTA	N68462 (A75N1)
PT-17	ME	Owls Head	OHTM	(B75N1)(N2S-3)
PT-17	OK	Fredi	AAM	42-16365, 365, C302
PT-17D	GA	Pooler	MoF	
PT-18	CA	Palm Springs	PoFAM	Boeing Stearman

PT-19 Fairchild Cornell

Super Kaydet — 41-61042, N1391V

Model	State	City	Operator	Registration / Notes
PT-19	AB-C	Edmonton	AAM	
PT-19	AL	Birmi	SMoF	
PT-19	AZ	PBluf	RWCAF	
PT-19	CA	Farfield	DA&SM	
PT-19	ID	Zellw	BWA	
PT-19	KS	New Century	CAF-HoAW	33, N50303
PT-19	KS	New Century	CAF-HoAW	44
PT-19	MB-C	Brandon	CATPM	
PT-19	ND	Fargo	FAM	N51437,
PT-19	NY	Bayport	BA	
PT-19	OH	N Canton	MAM	
PT-19	OK	Fredi	AAM	
PT-19	SK-C	Moose Jaw	WDM	15307
PT-19	TX	Brown	RGVW-CAF	
PT-19	TX	Burnet	HLSCAF	42-2767, N274351
PT-19	TX	Corsicana	CFHF	
PT-19	TX	Midland	AAHM	49797

Model	State	City	Code	Registration
PT-19	TX	Uvalde	AM	
PT-19	WA	Bellingham	HFM	
PT-19 Cockpit	CA	Chino	PoFAM	
PT-19A	AZ	Tucson	PAM	41-14675, N53963
PT-19A	GA	Pooler	MoF	43-7220
PT-19A	MD	Suitland	PEGF	
PT-19A	MI	Ypsilanti	YAF	
PT-19A	NY	Horseheads	NWM	5203AE, N49830
PT-19A	ND	Fargo	BUSAHM	
PT-19A	OH	Dayton	NMUSAF	43-34023
PT-19A	PA	Toughkenamon	CFCM	42-83641, N51324,
PT-19A	TX	Addison	CFM	N58307, 44 217
PT-19A-AE	MI	Belleville	YAF	43-31550, N9884
PT-19A-FA	KS	Liberal	MAAM	
PT-19B	KS	New Century	CAF-HoAW	AE6103, N50481
PT-19B	WA	Vancouver	PAM	
PT-19B	CA	Riverside	MFAM	43-5598, Side 29
PT-19B	NY	Horseheads	NWM	42-47871, Side # 65
PT-19B (2ea)	PA	Readi	MAAM	40-2594, N119EC, 39
PT-19B	PA	Toughkenamon	CFCM	N60112, Nose # 60
PT-19B(M-62A)	WI	Oshkosh	EAAAAM	43-7240

PT-22 Ryan Recruit

Model	State	City	Code	Registration
PT-21(NR-1)	FL	Pensacola	NMoNA	1541, 49086
PT-22	AK	Fairbanks	PAM	N50880, (ST3KR)
PT-22	AZ	Tucson	PAM	41-15736, N1180C
PT-22	CA	Atwater	CAM	
PT-22	CA	Corno	CAF-IES	N48742
PT-22	CA	Modesto	HAM	
PT-22	CA	Palm Springs	PoFAM	41-15550, N441V
PT-22	CA	San Diego	SDAMGF	1901, N47483
PT-22	CO	Denve	JWDAS	
PT-22	FL	Kissi	FTWAM	
PT-22	FL	Miami	WOM	
PT-22	GA	Pooler	MoF	41-21039, 66
PT-22	IA	Ottumwa	APM	1254, N50644
PT-22	KS	Liberal	MAAM	
PT-22	IL	Paris	HAAM	
PT-22	IL	Springfield	ACM	41-20796, 2005
PT-22	MI	Kalamazoo	KAHM	41-20652
PT-22	OH	Dayton	NMUSAF	41-15721
PT-22	OH	Madis	CFR	
PT-22	OK	Fredi	AAM	
PT-22	OK	Oklahoma	OSM	N53173
PT-22	OR	Hood	WAAAM	
PT-22	TX	Addison	CFM	N46217, 4847AAF
PT-22	TX	Brown	RGVW-CAF	N22AL
PT-22	TX	Dallas	FoF	
PT-22	TX	Ft Worth	VFM	
PT-22	VA	Chantilly	NASMUVC	

PT-23 Fairchild Cornell

Model	State	City	Code	Registration
PT-23	CA	Atwater	CAM	
PT-23	KS	Liberal	MAAM	
PT-23	KS	Wichita	CAF-JW	
PT-23HO	MI	Kalamazoo	KAHM	N64176
PT-23	MN	Blaine	GH	
PT-23	OK	Fredi	AAM	
PT-23	PA	Readi	MAAM	
PT-23	WI	Oshkosh	EAAAAM	
PT-23A	CT	Winds	NEAM	
PT-26	AB-C	Wetas	RM	42-71000
PT-26	AB-C	Nanton	NLS	N6072C
PT-26	AR	PineB	CAF-RW	10530, N127O,
PT-26	AZ	Tucson	PAM	
PT-26	CA	Chino	YAM	
PT-26	CA	Shafter	MFAM	
PT-26	CO	Denve	JWDAS	
PT-26	GA	Atlan	CAF-DW	N26GA
PT-26	IN	India	CAF-IW	N60535
PT-26	NM	Albuq	CAF-LW	N5519N

Model	State	City	Collection	Reg. #		Model / Mfr	State	City / Name	Collection	Reg. #
PT-26	NY	Albion	VAG			PT-26	TX	Amarillo	CAFDS	N940H
PT-26	NY	Bayport	BA			PT-26	TX	Brown	RGVW-CAF	N4732G
PT-26	OH	Dayton	NMUSAF			PT-26	TX	Brown	RGVW-CAF	6072C
PT-26	OK	Fredi	AAM	N2039A		PT-26	TX	Midland	AAHM	10738
PT-26	PA	Readi	MAAM			PT-26B	ON-C	Ottaw	CAM	
PT-26	PA	Toughkenamon	CFCM	N75463, Side # FH950		PT-26B	ON-C	Hamilton	CWH	
PT-27	ON-C	Hamilton	CWH			Boeing-Stearman		RCAF Kaydet		M
Pterodactyl Fledgling	VA	Chantilly	NASMUVC			Manta Products		Fledgling		
Pulsar	KY	Lexington	AmoK			Pulsar		Ultralight		N156KB
PV-2 Piasecki	IN	Indianapolis	AMHF			Piasecki		Harpoon		37396, N2697C
PV-2 Piasecki	VA	Chantilly	NASMUVC			Piasecki		Helicopter		

PV-2 Lockheed Harpoon

Model	State	City	Collection	Reg. #		Model	State	City	Collection	Reg. #
PV-2	VA	Quantico	NMMC	34807		PV-2	SC	N Myrtle Beach	M	
PV-2	AZ	Tucson	PAM	N7255C, 37257		PV-2	TX	SAnto	CAF-YRS	N25YR
PV-2	NM	Las Cruces	SA			PV-2D	TX	C Christi	USS Lexi	
PV-2	OR	Tillamook	TAM			PV-2D	TX	Galve	LSFM	37634, N6655D
PV-2	PA	W Ches	AHM			PV-2D	TX	Midland	AAHM	
						PV-2D	WI	Wauke	CAF/WW	N86493, "Empire Express"
Q-200	FL	Lakel	SFAF			Rutan		Quickie		N150CS
Q-200	VA	Richmond	VAM			Rutan		Quickie		
Q-3A(YQ)	AL	Ozark	USAAM							
Q-4(XQ)	CO	Monte	ALP53			Sikorsky				
Q-4(XQ)	NM	Alamo	CityPark			Sikorsky				
QH-50C	GA	Pooler	MoF			Gyrodyne		Dash Drone		DS-1045
QH-50C	NY	Garde	CoAM			Gyrodyne		Dash Drone		1235
QH-50C	WA	Seattle	MoF			Gyrodyne		Dash Drone		DS-1045
QH-50C/DSN-3	AZ	Tucson	PAM			Gyrodyne		Dash Drone		
QU-22B	OH	Dayton	NMUSAF			Beech		Beech 36		
Quick Kit Seaplane	NY	River	TFAC			Quick		Seaplane		
Quick Monplane	AL	Hunts	AS&RC			Quick		Monoplane		
Quick Silver	CA	San Diego	SDAM			Quick		Silver		Glider 1980
Quick Silver MX	AK	Fairbanks	PAM			Quick		Silver MX		
R-3(M-B)	CT	Winds	NEAM			Keith Rider				

R-4B Sikorsky Hoverfly

Model	State	City	Collection	Reg. #
R-4(XR) Cockpit	PA	W Ches	AHM	346514

R-4C(XR)	VA	Chantilly	NASMUVC	
R-4B	AZ	Tucson	PAM	43-46521
R-4B	CA	Chino	YAM	
R-4B	CT	Winds	NEAM	
R-4B	OH	Dayton	NMUSAF	43-46506

R4D Douglas Skytrooper

R4D	PA	Reading	MAAM	
R4D-5	NY	Horseheads	NWM	39091
R4D-6(DC-3)	CA	Atwater	CAM	90407
R4D-6(DC-3)	PA	Readi	MAAM	26819, N68AH, GB50819, "NATS 1945"
R4D-6(DC-3)	TX	Lancaster	CAF-DFW	50783, N151ZE

R22	VA	Chantilly	NASMUVH	
R44	VA	Chantilly	NASMUVH	
R50-5	AZ	Tucson	PAM	
R50-5	CA	Riverside	MFAM	

RA-5C North American Vigilante

RA-5C	CA	San Diego	SDACM	156641
RA-5C	CO	Pueblo	PWAM	
RA-5C	FL	Pensacola	NMoNA	156624

Rabbit Model A	WI	Oshkosh	EAAAAM	
Rawdon T-1	KS	Wichita	KAM	
Rally 3	KS	Liberal	MAAM	
Ranchero	FL	Lakel	SFAF	

Rand KR-1 Robinson

Rand KR-1 Robinson	AL	Birmingham	SMoF	
Rand KR-1	FL	Lakel	SFAF	N12NS
Rand KR-1	KS	Liberal	MAAM	
Rand KR-1	OK	Fredi	AAM	

Rasor 21	WI	Oshkosh	EAAAAM	
Raven Hang Glider	WI	Oshkosh	EAAAAM	
Raven S-50	AK	Fairbanks	PAM	

R-4B(HNS)	AZ	Tucson	PAM	43-46521
R-4B(HNS)	CA	Chino	YAM	43-46534
R-4B(HNS-1)	FL	Pensacola	NMoNA	104, N75988, 39047
R-4B	ON-C	Ottawa	CAM	43-46565

R4D-6Q(DC-3)	AL	Birmingham	SMoF	
R4D-8(C-117)	CA	Miramar	FLAM	708,MCAS, MCASIWAKUNI
R4D-8(C-117D)	AZ	Tucson	PAM	50826, 43363, 26924
R4D-8(C-117D)	AZ	Tucson	PAM	43-49663
R4D-8(C-117D)	FL	Pensacola	NMoNA	50821, 821

Robinson	Helicopter	
Robinson	Astro Helicopter	G-MURY
Lockheed	Lodestar	12481, N15SA, Model 18
Lockheed	Lodestar	12473

RA-5C	MD	Lexin	PNA&EM	
RA-5C	NV	Fallon	NASF	
RA-5C	NY	NYC	ISASM	
RA-5C(A3J-3)	AZ	Tucson	PAM	149289

Welsh	Rabbit	N3599G
Rawdon	T-1 Ag Plane	
Rally	Ultralight	
Ranchero		N4659S, "Spirit of Ft Myers"

Rand KR-1	WI	Oshkosh	EAAAAM	N1436
Rand Robin KR-2	CA	Santa Maria	SMMoF	
Rand Robin KR-2	IA	SBluf	MAAM	

Rasor		
Raven	Hang Glider	F28AO
Raven	S-50	N24061

RB-1	AZ	Tucson	PAM	Budd	Conestoga	39307, XB-DUZ
RB-1	PA	Pitts	FI	Budd	Conestoga	
RB-1 Racer	MI	Dearb	HFM	Dayton-Wright	Racer	

RC-3 Republic Seabee

RC-3	AL	Birmi	SMoF	
RC-3	BC-C	Sidne	BCAM	
RC-3	Ont-C	Sault Ste Marie	CBHC	822, C-FDKG
RC-3	CA	Modesto	HAM	
RC-3	CA	San Carlos	HNCAVM	N87482
RC-3	CT	Winds	NEAM	
RC-3	FL	KeyWe	HTC&C	N87596
RC-3	MD	Suitland	PEGF	
RC-3	NY	Garde	CoAM	N6461K
RC-3	OR	Tillamook	EAM	
RC-3	PA	Readi	MAAM	

RC-12G	AZ	Ft Huachuca	HMS	Beech	Crazyhorse	80-23372

Rearwin Sportster	WA	Vancouver	PAM	
Rearwin 2000C	TX	Kingsbury	VAHF	Project
Rearwin 7000	IA	Ottumwa	APM	
Rearwin 7000	KS	Liberal	MAAM	NC187
Rearwin 7000	OK	Fredi	AAM	
Rearwin 8135 Cloudster	CA	San Diego	SDAM	N25553
Rearwin 8135	CT	Winds	NEAM	
Rearwin 8135	IA	Ottumwa	APM	832, N25555
Rearwin 8135	NY	River	TFAC	
Rearwin 8135	OR	Hood	WAAAM	
Rearwin 8135	PA	Reading	MAAM	
Rearwin 8135	SD	Liberal	MAAM	
Rearwin Skyranger 175	KS	Liberal	MAAM	
Rearwin Speedster	KS	Wichita	KAM	

Redstone Booster	OH	Dayton	NMUSAF	Redstone	Booster	
Renegade Spirit	MI	Kalamazoo	KAHM	Murphy	Spirit	
Resures 500	WA	Seattle	MoF	Resures	Space Capsule	
Revolution Mini 500	FL	Lakeland	SNF	Revolution	Mini 500	
Revolution Mini 500	TN	Pigeon Forge	HH	Revolution	Mini 500	
Rheintocher	MD	Aberd	APG	Rheintocher		
Rick Jet RJ-4	CA	Chino	PoFAM	Ricj	Jet	
Rider R-4	CA	Chino	PoFAM	Rider	Racer	"Firecracker"
Rider R-8	CA	Chino	PoFAM	Rider	Racer	"8 Ball"
Rigid Midget	NY	Elmir	NSM			1001, N90871
Ritter Special	FL	Lakel	SFAF	Russ Ritter	Ritter Special	N1017Z
Ritz 1983	IA	Ottumwa	APM	Ritz	Pusher	

RLU-1 Breezy	KS	Liberal	MAAM
RLU-1	ND	Minot	DTAM
RLU-1	PA	Bethel	GAAM
RLU-1	OK	Fredi	AAM

RLU-1	WI	Oshkosh	EAAAAM	N59Y			
RLU-1	WI	Oshkosh	EAAAAM	N555JS			
RLU-1	WI	Oshkosh	EAAAAM	N3915			
Rockwell Commander 500S	VA	Chantilly	NASMUVC		North American	Commander 500S	
Rockwell	NY	Garde	CoAM		Rockwell	Command Module 002	
Rockwell HiMat	DC	Washi	NA&SM		Rockwell	HiMat	
Rockwell Ranger 2000	OK	Tulsa	TA&SM		Rockwell	Ranger 2000	
RODA	OR	Mc Minnville	EAM		Homebuilt		
Rogallo Wing	NC	Ralei	NCMoH		Rogallo	Wing	
RON-1(X)	MO	SLoui	NMoT		Gyrodyne	Rotorcycle	
RON-1(YR)	FL	Pensacola	NMoNA		Gyrodyne	Rotorcycle	4013
Rose Parakeet A-1	IA	Ottumwa	APM		Rose	Parakeet A-1	N-13676
Rose Parakeet	PA	Bethel	GAAM		Rose	Parakeet	
Ross Seabird	AL	Birmingham	SMF		Ross	Seabird	
Rotec Rally IIIB	PA	Readi	MAAM		Rotec		
Rotec Rally IIIB	WA	Seattle	MoF		Rotec	Rally IIIB	
Roton	CA	Ramona	CR		Roton		
Rotor Cycle Hiller	MD	Lexin	PNA&EM		Hiller	Rotorcycle	
Rotorway Exec 90	CA	Ramona	CR				
Rotorway Exec 152	AL	Birmingham	SMoF				
Rotorway Exec 152	PA	Readi	MAAM				
Rotorway Exec 152	WI	Oshkosh	EAAAAM	N3WN			
Rotorway Exec 162	TX	Ladero	Airport				
Rotorway Exec 162	WI	Oshkosh	WAM				
Rotorway Scorpion I	CA	Ramona	CR				
Rotorway Scorpion I	PA	WChester	EAAAAM				
Rotorway Scorpion I	TN	Pigeon Forge	HH				
Rotorway Scorpion I	WI	Oshkosh	EAAAAM	N6165			
Rotorway Scorpion 133	AK	Fairbanks	PAM	133			
Rotorway Scorpion 133	CA	Ramona	CR	133			
Rotorway Scorpion II	VA	Chantilly	NASMUVC				
Rotorway Scorpion II	NJ	Teterboro	AHoF&MNJ	N96328			
Rotorway Scorpion II	PA	WChester	AHM				
Rotorway Scorpion II	WA	Seattle	MoF	75RJM, N65229			
Rotorway Scorpion II	WI	Oshkosh	EAAAAM				
RQ-1A	OH	Dayton	NMUSAF		General Atomics	Predator	
RQ-3A	OH	Dayton	NMUSAF		Lockeheed Martin	Dark Star	
RQ-3A	OH	Dayton	NMUSAF		Northrop Grumman	Global Hawk	
RP- 5A Drone	AZ	Grand	PoFAM		Radioplane	Drone	
RP- 54D Drone	CA	Grand Canyon	PoFGCVA		Radioplane	Anti-RadiationMissile	
RP-76B Drone	AZ	Grand Canyon	PoFGCVA		Radioplane	Drone	
RT-14	VA	Chantilly	NASMUVC	Turner	Meteor		

Aircraft	St	City	Collection	Type	St	City	Collection	Reg.
Rumpler Taube	WA	Seattle	MoF	Rumpler / Taube				
Rutan	FL	Tittusville	VACM	Rutan				N309V
Rutan 354	CA	Rosamond	EAFB	Rutan / Model 354				
Rutan Grizzly	WI	Oshkosh	EAAAAM	Rutan / Grizzly				N80RA, "Griz"
Rutan Quickie	AB-C	Calga	AMoC	Rutan / Quickie				
Rutan Quickie	BC-C	Sidney	BCAM	Rutan / Quickie				
Canadian Quickie	BC-C	Langley	CMoF	Rutan / Quickie				
Rutan Quickie	AZ	Tucson	PAM	Rutan Quickie	NF-C	Gander		C-GZGR
Rutan Quickie	CT	Winds	NEAM	Rutan Quickie	ON-C	Ottawa		C-GGLC
Rutan Quickie	FL	Lakel	SFAF	Rutan Quickie	WA	Seattle	MoF	1, n77q
Rutan Quickie	IA	Des M	ISHD	Rutan Quickie	WA	Vancouver	PAM	
Rutan Quickie	KS	Agusta	AAM	Rutan Quickie	WI	Oshkosh	EAAAAM	N2WX
Rutan Quickie	KS	Liberal	MAAM	Rutan Quickie II	CA	Chino	PoFAM	
Rutan Quickie	VA	Chantily	NASMUVC	Rutan Quickie II	MB-C	Winni	WCAM	
Rutan Quickie	OR	Tillamook	TAM	Rutan Quickie Q1	CA	Santa Martin	WoHAM	
Rutan Long-Easy	AZ	Grand Canyon	PoFGCVA	Rutan — Long-Easy				
Rutan Vari-eze	AL	Birmingham	SMoF	Rutan Vari-eze	ND	Minot	DTAM	
Rutan Vari-eze	AK	Fairbanks	PAM	Rutan Vari-eze	OK	Fredi	AAM	
Rutan Vari-eze	CT	Winds	NEAM	Rutan Vari-eze	PA	Readi	MAAM	
Rutan Vari-eze	FL	Lakel	SFAF	Rutan Vari-eze	VA	Hampton	VA&SC	
Rutan Vari-eze	KS	Liberal	MAAM	Rutan Vari-eze	WA	Seattle	MoF	300, n300ez
Rutan Vari-eze	VA	Chantily	NASMUVC	Rutan Vari-eze	WI	Oshkosh	EAAAAM	N7EZ
Rutan Varigiggen	AL	Birmingham	SMoF	Rutan / Varigiggen				
Rutan Varigiggen	FL	Lakel	SFAF	Rutan / Varigiggen				
Rutan Varigiggen	TX	Uvalde	AM	Rutan / Varigiggen				115, n27ms
Rutan Varigiggen	WA	Seattle	MoF	Rutan / Varigiggen				N27VV
Rutan Variviggen 50-160	WI	Oshkosh	EAAAAM	Rutan / Voyager				
Rutan Voyager	DC	Washi	NA&SM	Homebuilt / Monoplane				N32KM
RV-4 Monoplane	AR	Pine Bluff	REAA	Homebuilt / Monoplane				
RV-4 Monoplane	CA	San Diego	SDAM	Homebuilt / Monoplane				
RV-6 Homebuilt	WI	Fond du Lac	WAM	Ryershtahl				
RVFC	NY	Bayport	BA	Ryan / Twin Navion				N5128K
Ryan D-16	AZ	Tucson	PAM					

(Registrations also appearing in the listing: N 80EB, N303Q, N37840.)

Ryan

Model	State/Prov.	City	Code	Reg. / Notes
Ryan D-16	KS	Liberal	MAAM	Twin Navion
Ryan D-16	OK	Fredi	AAM	Twin Navion
Ryan G Drone	CA	El Cajon	SDAMGF	Firebee Drone
Ryan G Drone	SC	FLore	FA&MM	Firebee Drone
Ryan M-1	CA	San Diego	SDAM	
Ryan Navion A	OK	Fredi	AAM	Navion

Ryan NYP, NX-211 "Spirit of St. Louis"

Model	State/Prov.	City	Code	Reg. / Notes
Ryan NYP (Rep)	CA	San Diego	SDAMGF	
Ryan NYP	DC	Washi	NA&SM	
Ryan NYP	IL	Rantoul	OCAM	
Ryan NYP	MI	Dearb	HFM	
Ryan NYP	MN	Bloom	SPMIA	
Ryan NYP	MN	Minne	MSPIA	
Ryan NYP	MO	SLoui	MHM	
Ryan NYP	NY	Garde	CoAM	
Ryan NYP	NY	Rhine	ORA	
Ryan NYP	OK	Weatherford	SA&SC	
Ryan NYP	WI	Oshkosh	EAAAAM	

Model	State/Prov.	City	Code	Reg. / Notes
Ryan SCW-145	WI	Oshkosh	EAAAAM	NC17372
Ryan SCW-147	CA	San Diego	SDAM	
Ryan STA	CA	Hayward	VAM	N14954, Special
Ryan STA	CA	San Diego	SDAM	NC17361, Special
Ryan STA	IA	Ottumwa	APPM	198, N18902, Special
Ryan STA	WA	Vancouver	PAM	Special

S-2 Grumman Tracker

Model	State/Prov.	City	Code	Serial / Notes
S-2	CA	Hemet	HAAB	70
S-2	FL	Kissi	FTW AM	
S-2	HI	Kaneohe	KBMCAS	147870, #22
S-2(CP-121)	MB-C	Winnipeg	WRCAFB	12176, Side # 157
S-2(CP-121)	NS	Halifax	SAM	12187
S-2(CP-121)	ON-C	Ottawa	CAM	136468
S-2(S2F-1)	AZ	Tucson	PAM	
S-2(CS)	ON-C	Toronto	TAMD	148730, AU, 32, VS-27
S-2A	FL	Jacksonville	NASJ	144721
S-2A	MI	Mt Clemens	SMAM	
S-2A	OK	Fredi	AAM	
S-2A(CS2F)	ON-C	Sault Ste Marie	CBHC	577, CF-21
S-2A(S2F-1)	KS	Topek	CAM	486
S-2A(TS)	NY	NYC	ISASM	
S-2B(E-1B)	AZ	Tucson	PAM	147227, "Willie Fudd"
S-2B(E-1B)	CT	Winds	NEAM	147217
S-2B(E-1B)	NY	NYC	ISASM	
S-2B(US-2B)	FL	Pensacola	NMoNA	48146, AE 711, VAW-121
S-2D(US)(E-1B)	CA	Alameda	USSHM	136691
S-2E	CA	Paso Robles	EWM	44-17944, N45CV
S-2E(S2F)	NY	NYC	ISASM	
S-2E(S2F)	MD	Lexin	PNA&EM	
S-2E(S2F)	NY	Garde	CoAM	151664
S-2E(S2F) Fuse	PE-C	Summe	PEIHAS	
S-2E(S2F)	TX	Addison	CFM	Model 131
S-2E(S2F-1)	TN	Memph	LS	
S-2E(S2F-1)	MD	Lexin	PNA&EM	
S-2E(S2F-1)	FL	Pensacola	NMoNA	151647, AW-334, 27, VS-73
S-2E(TS)	KS	Liberal	MAAM	
	OK	Fredi	AAM	
	NY	NYC	ISASM	

S-2 (Grumman Tracker) entries

Type	State	City	Org	Serial / Notes
S-2F(CS2F)	FL	Titusville	VAC	12155
S-2F(CS2F-3)	MB-C	Winnipeg	CFB	
S-2F(CS2F-3)	NS-C	Shear	CFBS	
S-2F(CS2F)	OH	N Canton	MAM	
S-2F(CS2F)	ON-C	CFB Borden	BHT	1506
S-2F(CS2F)	PEI-C	Summerside	CFB	12131
S-2F(US-2A)	AZ	Tucson	PAM	147552, N8225E, "Stoof"
S-2F-1(TS-2A)	AL	Birmingham	SMF	
S-2F1T	AZ	Mesa	MAC	Firefighter
S-2R	AZ	Mesa	MAC	Firefighter

Main list

Type	State	City	Org	Manufacturer	Nickname	Notes
S-3A	CA	San Diego	NINAS	Lockheed	Viking	Tail NH, Side VS29, 700
S-3A(US)	CA	San Diego	SDACM	Lockheed	Viking	
S-3A	FL	Jacksonville	NASJ	Lockheed	Viking	157993, AA, 700, VS-24
S-3B	MI	Kalamazoo	KAM	Lockheed	Viking	Storage
S-4B	NY	Rhine	ORA	Thomas-Morse	Scout	
S-4B(T-4M)	FL	Polk	FoF	Thomas-Morse	Scout	
S-4C	CA	San Diego	SDAM	Thomas-Morse	Tommy	
S-4C	CT	Washi	TFC	Thomas-Morse	Tommy	
S-4C	FL	Pensacola	NMoNA	Thomas-Morse	Tommy	A5858
S-4C	NY	Garde	CoAM	Thomas-Morse	Tommy	38934
S-4C	OH	Dayton	NMUSAF	Thomas-Morse	Tommy	SC-38944
S-4C	VA	Quantico	NNMC	Thomas-Morse	Tommy	NR66Y
S-39	CT	Winds	NEAM	Sikorsky		
S-43	AK	Ancho	AAHM	Sikorsky		
S-51(H-5)	AB-C	Calga	AMoC	Sikorsky	Dragonfly	
S-51(H-5)	CT	Winds	NEAM	Sikorsky	Dragonfly	
S-51(H-5)	ON-C	Hamilton	CWH	Sikorsky	Dragonfly	9601
S-51(H-5)	ON-C	Ottaw	CAM	Sikorsky	Dragonfly	9601
S-51(R-5)	PA	W Ches	AHM	Sikorsky	Dragonfly	
S-55	AB-C	Calga	AMoC	Sikorsky	Chickasaw	
S-55(HO4S-2)	BC-C	Sidney	BCAM	Sikorsky	Chickasaw	RCN
S-55	BC-C	Langley	CMoF	Sikorsky	Chickasaw	53-4414
S-55	FL	Sandf	VAT	Sikorsky	Chickasaw	
S-55	TX	FtBli	TCRM	Sikorsky	Chickasaw	
S-56	NY	Garde	CoAM	Sikorsky		
S-58C(H-34)	TN	Pigeon Forge	HH	Sikorsky	Seabat	NC349N
S-58D	NY	NYC	ISASM	Sikorsky	Seabat	"Charlene"
S-60	CT	Winds	NEAM	Sikorsky		
S-61	MN	Winoma	WTI	Sikorsky		
S-62A	NJ	Teter	AHoFNJ	Sikorsky	Houston	46008, "Disposal"
S-64E	CT	Winds	NEAM	Sikorsky	Skycrane	

Model	State	City	Museum	Builder	Name	Registration
S.P. 3				Pereira	Osprey II	N345JD
SA- 2A	AK	Fairbanks	PAM	Stits	SA-2A	N5K
SA- 3A	WI	Oshkosh	EAAAAM	Stits	Playboy	
SA- 3A	ND	Fargo	BUSAHM	Stits	Playboy	
SA- 8	WI	Oshkosh	EAAAAM	Stits	Skeeto	N8KK
SA- 11A	WI	Oshkosh	EAAAAM	Stits	Playmate	N6048C
SA-100	AL	Birmingham	SMoF	Stolp	Starduster	N9681Z
SA-102-5	KS	Liberal	MAAM		Cavalier	
SA-102-5	OK	Fredi	AAM		Cavalier	
SA-300	MI	Belleville	YAF	Stolp	Starduster Too	SN 001, N693H
SA-300	NV	Carsu	YF	Stolp	Starduster Too	
SA-300	WA	Vanco	PAM	Stolps	Starduster Too	
SA-300	WI	Oshkosh	EAAAAM	Stolp	Starduster Too	N32CH
SA-500L Starlet	WI	Oshkosh	EAAAAM	Stolp	Starlet	N2300
SA-700	WI	Oshkosh	EAAAAM	Hayes-Greffenius	Acroduster-1	
Saturn V Boat Tail	NY	Coron	NYHoS	Saturn	Flying Boat	
Saunders ST-27	MB-C	Winni	WCAM	Saunders	Commuter	
Saunders ST-28	MB-C	Winni	WCAM	Saunders	Commuter	
Saunders ST-28 Sim	ON-C	Sault Ste Marie	CBHM	Saunders	Commuter	009, G-GCML, Restoration
SB2C-3	CA	Chino	ISASM	Curtiss	Helldiver	
SB2C-3 Replica	NY	NYC	ISASM	Curtiss	Helldiver	
SB2C-5	MD	Chantilly	NASMUVC	Curtiss	Helldiver	83479, 212
SB2C-5	TX	Midland	CAF-WTW	Curtiss	Helldiver	

SBD Douglas Dauntless

Model	State	City	Museum	Serial / Registration
SBD Replica	CA	Inglewood	PBR	
SBD-1(A-24)	CA	San Diego	SDACM	42-54643
SBD(A-24)	GA	Atlan	CAF-DW	42-54532, N54532
SBDReplica	HI	Honolulu	PAM	
SBD-2	FL	Pensacola	NMoNA	02106
SBD-3	CA	San Diego	SDACM	06508, 132MSB7
SBD-3	FL	Pensacola	NMoNA	06508, 132MSB7
SBD-3	MI	Kalamazoo	KAHM	06624
SBD-3(A-24)	OR	Tillamook	TAM	42-60817, N5254
SBD-3	TX	C Christi	USS Lexi	06694
SBD-4	CA	Alameda Pt	USSHM	10508
SBD-4	CA	Chino	YAM	10518, N4864J,
SBD-4	CA	San Diego	SDAM	06900, N4522
SBD-4	FL	Pensacola	NMoNA	6833, 25
SBD-5	IL	Chicago	MAP	10575
SBD-5	CA	Chino	PoFAM	28536
SBD-5(A-24)	CA	Palm Sprg	PSAM	36175, B-25
SBD-5	OH	Dayton	NMofUSAF	42-54582
SBD-5(A-24)	SC	MtPleasant	PPM	36173, Side # 2
SBD-5(A-24B)	TX	Galve	LSFM	42-54682, N93RW
SBD-6	DC	Washi	NA&SM	54605

Model	State	City	Museum	Builder	Name	Registration
SBS 2- 8	WI	Oshkosh	EAAAAM	Schweizer	Glider	N10VV

Model	State	City	Museum	Mfr	Type	Notes
Sceptre	WA	Yakima	MmoA	Sceptre	Pusher	Twin Tail Monoplane
Schleiche ASW-12	VA	Hampton	VA&SC	Schleiche	Glider	N491V
Schmitt Commuter	AZ	Grand	PoFGCVA	Schmitt	Helicopter	N17RS
Schulgleiter SG. 38	MD	Suitland	PEGF	Schulgleiter		
Schupal & Nylander	CA	Chino	PoFAM	Schupal-Nylander	Wing	
Schweitzer Secondary	IA	Greenfield	IAM	Schweitzer	Glider	
Schweizer 1-19	OK	Oklahoma	OSM	Schweizer	Glider	
Schweizer 1-23	NY	Niagara Falls	NAM	Schweizer	Glider	
Schweizer 1-26	NM	Hobbs	NSF	Schweizer	Glider	
Schweizer 2-22	MB-C	Winni	WCAM	Schweizer	Glider	
Schweizer 2-22 EK	VA	Chantilly	NASMUVC	Schweizer	Glider	
Schweizer 2-33	NM	Hobbs	NSF	Schweizer	Glider	22-325

Model	State	City	Museum
SE-5A	FL	Orlan	CSS
SE-5A	FL	Orlan	OFW
SE-5A	ID	Athol	NAM
SE-5A	ME	Owls Head	OHTM
SE-5A	NC	Hendersonville	WNCAM
SE-5A	NY	Bayport	BA
SE-5A	NY	Mayville	DA
SE-5A	NY	NYC	ISASM
SE-5A	OH	Dayton	NMUSAF
SE-5A	ON-C	Brampton	TGWFM
SE-5A	TX	Kingsbury	VAHF

SE-5 Royal Aircraft Farnborough

Model	State	City	Museum	Notes
SE-5A	AL	Gunte	LGARFM	
SE-5A 7/8 Scale	ON-C	Brampton	TGWFM	
SE-5A	AL	Ozark	USAAM	
SE-5A Rep	AR	Fayet	AAM	
SE-5A Rep	AZ	Mesa	CARAWM	
SE-5A	WA	Seattle	MoF	
SE-5A	BC-C	Langley	CMoF	002, CF-QGL
SE-5A (American)	CO	Ft Lupton	VA	F-8010, N1917J, 19
SE-5A (British)	CO	Ft Lupton	VA, C.1084, "BABE Cincinnati USA"	
SE-5A	FL	Lakel	SFAF	RAF

Model	State	City	Museum	Type	Notes
Sea-Bee	FL	Key West	CRTC		
Seahawker	WA	Vanco	PAM	Biplane	N87596
Security Airster	CA	Santa Martin	WoHAM	Airster	Year 1939
Sellers Quadroplane	KY	Louis	MoH&S	Quadroplane	
SG-1A	NM	Moriarty	SSM	Boom Glider	

SGC Schweizer Glider

Model	State	City	Museum	Notes	Model	State	City	Museum
SGS 1-19	NY	Elmir	NSM	14, N91806	SGS 2-22EK	MD	Suitland	PEGF
SGS 1-19	NY	Mayvi	DA		SGS 2-32	CA	Calis	CG
SGS 1-26	NY	Elmir	NSM	1, N91889	SGS 2-32	OR	Mc Minnville	EAM
SGS 1-26B	CA	Calis	CG		SGS 2-33	CA	Calis	CG

SH-2 Kaman Sea Sprite

Model	State	City	Museum	Serial / Notes
SH-2	CA	Alameda	USS Hornet	
SH-2F	AL	Mobile	BPM	150181
SH-2F	CA	San Diego	NINAS	
SH-2F	CA	San Diego	SDACM	Nose 33
SH-2F(HH-2D)	VA	Norfo	NNAS, AHM	149029, HT 33, HSL-30
SH-2F	MD	Lexington	PRNAM	161642,
SH-2G	PA	Willow Grove	NVHAA	162576
SH-2G	PA	W Chester		

SH-3 Sikorsky Sea King

Model	State	City	Museum	Serial / Notes
SH-3(HH-52)	AL	Mobile	BMP	1378
SH-3	CA	San Diego	SDACM	149711
SH-3	CA	San Diego	NINAS	Tail HC11, Side 727
SH-3(VH)	CA	Simi Valley	PRL	150611, HMX-1
SH-3	NB	Omaha	FP	
SH-3	NY	Brooklyn	NARF	
SH-3B	FL	Jacksonville	NASJ	9695, HS-7, AR 401, 610
SH-3D(H-3)	FL	Pensacola	NMoNA	150613, 148990, 156484
SH-3H	RI	NKing	QAM	149738

Name	State	City	Museum
SH-34J	CO	Pueblo	PWAM
SH-60B	CA	San Diego	NINAS
Shafor Ganagobie	WI	Oshkosh	EAAAAM
Sherpa C203A MT	Misso	AFDSC	Sherpa
Shober Willie II	KS	Liberal	MAAM
Shober Willie II	OK	Fredi	AAM
Short S-29	NY	Rhine	ORA
Short Skyvan	IL	Cahok	PCUSL
Short Solent Mark 3	CA	Oakla	OWAM
Shultz G-6 CA	Chino	YAM	Schultz
Siemens-Schuckert D.III	NY	Rhine	ORA
Siemens-Schuckert D.IV	AL	Gunte	LGARFM
Siemens-Schuckert D.IV	AZ	Grand	PoFGCVA
Sikorsky	AR	Pocahontas	PMA
Sikorsky	NE	Minde	HWPV
Silver Dart	NY	Hammonds	CM
Silver Dart	ON-C	Ottaw	CAM
Silver Dart	ON-C	Sault Ste Marie	CBHC
Simulator 2B13	FL	Titusville	VAC
Skycat V33	NC	Charlotte	CAM
Skycat	NC	CPoin	CPMB
Skylab Module	FL	Pensacola	NMoNA
Skyseeker C-IFAI	BC-C	Sidney	BCAM
Smith DSA	IA	Ottumwa	APM
Smith DSA	IN	Auburn	HW

Builder	Type	Reg / Notes
Sikorsky	Sea Horse	17217
Sikorsky	Sea Horse	Tail T2, Side HSL 45
Shafor	Ganagobie	N60G
Shober	Willie II	
Shober	Willie II	
Short	Skyvan	
Short	Solent	
Glider	Schultz	
Siemens-Schuckert		
Siemens-Schuckert		
Siemens-Schuckert	Fliegertruppe D IV	N1094G, Replica
Sikorsky		3251
Sikorsky		1944
A.E.A.	Silver Dart	
A.E.A.	Silver Dart	
A.E.A.	Silver Dart	
Navy	Multi Engine	
Hal Fogel	Skycat	
Hal Fogel	Skycat	
Skylab	Command Module 116	
Skyseeker	Ultralight	
Smith	Miniplane	ES-1, N44ES
Smith	Miniplane	

Popular name listing

Aircraft	State	City	Museum	Registration
Smith DSA	OH	Madis	CFR	
Smith DSA	ON-C	Collingwood	CCAF	
Smith DSA	WI	Green	GBPHoF	
Smith DSA-1	WI	Oshkosh	EAAAAM	
Smith Eroplane	IN	FWayn	GFWAM	
Smith H1	OK	Fredi	AAM	
Smyth Playmate	FL	Lakel	SFAF	
Smyth Sidewinder	FL	Lakel	SFAF	
Smyth Sidewinder	WI	Oshkosh	EAAAAM	
SNC-1	FL	Pensacola	NMoNA	
Soko Galeb	IL	Springfield	ACM	
Solar Riser	WI	Oshkosh	EAAAAM	
Solbrig Biplane	IA	Des M	ISHD	
Solitaire Motor-Glider	WI	Oshkosh	EAAAAM	
Sollar Challenger	VA	Richm	SMoV	
Sopwith Camel	AL	Gunte	LGARFM	
Sopwith Camel F.1	AR	Little Rock	AEC	
Sopwith Camel	BC-C	Langley	CMoF	
Sopwith Camel	ID	Athol	NAM	
Sopwith Camel	MI	Kalamazoo	KAHM	
Sopwith Camel	NY	Rhine	ORA	
Sopwith Camel	OH	Dayton	NMUSAF	F6034
Sopwith Dolphin	NY	Rhine	ORA	
Sopwith Pup	AL	Gunte	LGARFM	
Sopwith Pup	FL	Polk	FoF	
Sopwith Pup	IA	Hampton	DWWIAM	
Sopwith Pup	ME	Owls Head	OHTM	
Sopwith Pup	ON-C	DonMi	OSC	
Sopwith Pup	ON-C	Hamilton	CWH	
Sopwith Snipe	MD	Suitland	PEGF	
Sopwith Snipe	ON-C	Ottaw	CAM	
Sopwith Snipe F.1	WA	Seattle	MoF	NX67650
Sopwith 1-Strutter	AL	Gunte	LGARFM	

Manufacturer listing

Manufacturer	Model	State	City	Museum	Registration
Smith	Miniplane	TX	Addison	CFM	N8156
Smith	Miniplane	ON-C	Brampton	TGW FM	NX6330
Smith	Miniplane	ON-C	Ottaw	CAM	A5658
Smith	Miniplane	WA	Seattle	MoF	N358L
Smith	Pusher	FL	Pensacola	NMoNA	N90P
Smith	Termite	OR	Mc Minnville	EAM	
Smyth	Playmate	PA	Beave	AHM	N77JA
Smyth	Sidewinder				N28Z
Smyth	Sidewinder				N55P
Curtiss					
Soko	Galeb				5194
UFM	Solar Riser				23172
Solbrig	Biplane				
Rutan	Solitaire				
	Sollar Challenger				N142SD
Sopwith	Camel				
Sopwith	Camel				
Sopwith	Camel 2F.1				
Sopwith	Camel F.1				
Sopwith	Camel F.1				
Sopwith	Camel F.1				
Sopwith					
Sopwith	Pup	ON-C	Ottaw	CAM	
Sopwith	Pup	ON-C	Toronto	OSC	
Sopwith	Pup	TX	Dalla	FoF	SN:NCH1, N914W
Sopwith	Pup	WA	Seattle	MoF	A 635, NX6018
Sopwith	Pup	WI	Madison	MWVM	
Sopwith	1-Strutter	FL	Polk	FoF	
Sopwith	1-Strutter	ON-C	Brampton	TGW FM	
Sopwith	**Triplane**	AL	Gunte	LGARFM	

Type	State	City	Museum	Model	Registration / Notes
Sopwith Triplane	WA				Ottaw, CAM, N5492
Sopwith Triplane	FL				
Sorta Baby Lakes	AZ	Grand Canyon	PoFGCVA	Sorta	Baby Lakes
Sorrell Bathtub	WA	Seattle	MoF	Sorrell	Bathtub — 1, N5087K
SP-2E	CT	Winds	NEAM	Lockheed	Neptune
SP-2E	NY	NYC	ISASM	Lockheed	Neptune
SP-2H	PA	Readi	MAAM	Lockheed	Neptune — 145915, N45309, VP 67
Space Capsule	NY	NYC	ISASM	GT-3	"Unsinkable Molly Brown"
Space Shuttle	AL	Huntsville	SC	Shuttle	
Space Shuttle	VA	Chantilly	NASMUVC	Space Shuttle	"Enterprise"
Space Shuttle 1/3	CA	Moffe	NASAAVC		
Spacecraft	AL	Hunts	AS&RC		
Spacecraft	CA	San F	TE		
Spacecraft	FL	Cocoa	USAFSM		
Spacecraft	FL	Merri	KSC		
Spacecraft	FL	Orlan	JYM&P		
Spacecraft	MO	SLoui	MP		
Spacecraft (5 ea)	MA	Bosto	MoSP		
Spad VII	AL	Gunte	LGARFM		
Spad VII	CA	Santa Martin	WoHAM		
Spad VII	CO	Ft Lupton	VA		
Spad VII	FL	Polk	FoF		Project
Spad VII	MI	Kalamazoo	KAHM		AS
Spad VII	OH	Dayton	NMUSAF		AS, 94099
Spad VII	ON-C	Ottaw	CAM		
Spad VII	VA	Sands	VAM		9913
Spad VII	WI	Oshkosh	EAAAAM		N9104A
Spad VII.c.1	CA	San Diego	SDAM		5334, S 3
Spad XIII	AL	Gunte	LGARFM		
Spad XIII	AZ	Tucson	PAM		
Spad XIII	CA	Inglewood	PBR		
Spad XIII	DC	Washi	NA&SM		"Smith IV"
Spad XIIIc.1	ME	Owls Head	OHTM		
Spad XIII	NY	Rhine	ORA		
Spad XIII	OH	Dayton	NMUSAF		N2030A
Spad XIII	OR	Tillamook	TAM		
Spad XIII	WA	Seattle	MoF		NX3883F
Spad XVI	VA	Chantilly	NASMUVC		
Spartan C-3	NY	Rhine	ORA	Executive	
Spartan Executive 7W	WI	Oshkosh	EAAAAM	Executive	N13993, "Mrs. Mennon"
Speedbird	IN	Auburn	HW	Speedbird	
Spencer Air Car	AK	Ancho	AAHM	Air Car	N14NX
Spencer Air Car S-14	WI	Oshkosh	EAAAAM	Air Car	N31SA
Spinks Akromaster	WI	Oshkosh	EAAAAM	Akromaster	

Supermarine Spitfire

Model	State	City	Museum	Registration / Notes
Spitfire	LA	New Orleans	DDM	BL370
Spitfire	VA	Suffolk	FF	MJ730, N730MSJ
Spitfire	BC-C	Sidney	BCAM	
Spitfire	WA	Arlington	FHC	AR614
Spitfire Mk.IA	IL	Chica	MoS&I	P9306
Spitfire Mk.II B	ON-C	Ottaw	CAM	NH188
Spitfire Mk.Vc	OH	Dayton	NMUSAF	MA 863
Spitfire Mk.VII	DC	Washi	NA&SM	EN474
Spitfire Mk.VII	ON-C	Ottawa	CWM	P8332
Spitfire Mk.VIII	OR	Tillamook	TAM	MT818, N58JE
Spitfire Mk.IX	CA	Chino	PoF	ML 417
Spitfire Mk.IX	WA	Seattle	MoF	MK923, C8AF-1X-1886, N521R
Spitfire Mk.IXe	CA	Caramillo	CAF-SCW	65-583887, NH749DP
Spitfire Mk.IXe	WI	Oshkosh	EAAAAM	MJ772N62EA
Spitfire Mk.XI	OH	Dayton	NMUSAF	PA908
Spitfire Mk.XIV	CA	Palm Sprg	PSAM	NH904, 65-648206, NX114BP, WZ-P
Spitfire Mk.XIV	OR	Mc Minnville	EAM	TE356
Spitfire Mk.XIV	TX	Galve	LSFM,	TE392, N97RW
Spitfire Mk.XVI	CA	San Diego	SDAM	SL 574
Spitfire Mk.XVI	FL	Polk City	FoF	TE 476
Spitfire Mk.XVI	ON-C	Hamilton	CWHM	TE214
Spitfire Mk.XVI	ON-C	Ottawa	VWoC	SL 721
Spitfire Mk.VIIIc LF	TX	Addison	CFM	MT719, YB-J
Spitfire Parts	SK-C	MJaw	WDM	

Model	State	City	Museum	Notes
Sport Fury	AL	Birmingham	SmoF	Sport Fury Control Wing
Spratt 108 Control Wing	PA	Reading	MAAM	

SR-71 Lockheed Blackbird

SR-71A See Also A-12

Model	State	City	Museum	Serial / Notes
SR-71	LA	Barksdale AFB	BAFB	61-7967
SR-71	CA	Palmd	PAFB	61-7973
SR-71	VA	Chantilly	NASMUVC	61-7972
SR-71	AZ	Tucson	PAM	61-7951
SR-71A	CA	Atwater	CAM	61-7960
SR-71A	CA	Marys	BAFB	61-7963
SR-71A	CA	Riverside	MFAM	61-7975
SR-71A	OR	Mc Minnville	EAM	61-7971
SR-71A	CA	Rosamond	EAFB	67-7980
SR-71A	CA	Rosamond	AFFTCM	61-7955
SR-71A	FL	Shalimar	USAFAM	61-7959
SR-71A	GA	Pooler	MoA	61-7958, "Ichi Ban", 958
SR-71A	KS	Hutch	KC&SC	61-7961
SR-71A	DC	Washington	NASM	61-7962
SR-71A	OH	Dayton	NMUSAF	61-7976
SR-71A	TX	San Antonio	LSAD	61-7979
SR-71A	VA	Sandstrom	VAM	61-7968
SR-71A-LO	WA	Everret	MoF	61-7977
SR-71B	NE	Ashland	SACM	61-7964
SR-71C	MI	Kalamazoo	AZ	61-7956
	UT	Ogden	HAFBM	61-7981

Model	State	City	Museum	Note 1	Note 2	Note 3
Spectrum RX550	ON-C	Ottawa	CAM	Spectrum	Beaver	C-IGOW
ST-34KR	PA	Tough	CFCM	Ryan		
Stahltaube	CA	Santa Martin	WoHAM	Stahltaube	Tiny	
Staib LB-5	KS	Liberal	MAAM	Staib		
Stampe SV4	NY	Rhine	ORA	Stampe		
Stan Hall Cherokee II	CA	Santa Martin	WoHAM	Stan Hall	Sherokee II	Glider
Stan Hall Safari	CA	Santa Martin	WoHAM	Stan Hall	Safari	Powered Glider

Aircraft	State	City	Museum	Notes
Stanley Nomad	VA	Chantilly	NASMUVC	
Stargazer Gondola	OH	Dayton	NMUSAF	
Starr Bumble Bee	AZ	Tucson	PAM	N83WS, Worlds Smallest Aircraft
Stearman				
Stearman	AB-C	Wetas	RM	
Stearman	AR	Pine Bluff	REAA	
Stearman	CA	Hayward	VAM	
Stearman	LA	Patte	WWMAM	"Delta Airlines"
Stearman	ON-C	Trenton	CAHS	
Stearman	MO	Maryland Hts	HARM	
Stearman	NY	Bayport	BA	
Stearman	TX	Ft Worth	VFM	
Stearman	UT	Heber	HVAM	Kaydet
Stearman	WA	Vancouver	PAM	
Stearman 4-CM-1	CA	Hayward	VAM	Bull
Stearman 4-D	CA	Chino	YAM	Bull 4026, N11224
Stearman 4-D	KS	Wichita	KAM	
Stearman 4-E	NV	Carso	YF	Bull
Stearman 4-EM	ON-C	Ottaw	CAM	Bull
Stearman A-75 (8 ea)	VA	Bealt	FCA	
Stearman C-2B	AK	Ancho	AAHM	N5415
Stearman C-3B	WA	Seattle	MoF	166, N7550
Stearman EC 75	OR	Mc Minnville	EAM	
Stearman Fr 24	FL	Arcia	AA Clark	
Stearman 70	OR	Hood	WAAAM	Model 70
Stearman 73 NS-1	KS	Wichita	KAM	
Stearman Super	WI	Oshkosh	EAAAAM	N5051V
Stearman-Hammond Y	MD	Suitland	PEGF	
Stearman-Hammond YS-1CA		San Carlos	HNCAVM	
Steco 1911	MN	St Paul	MA&SM	
Steen Skybolt	KS	Liberal	MAAAM	
Steen Skybolt	NV	Carso	YF	
Steen Skybolt	PA	Reading	MAAAM	
Steen Skybolt	WI	Fond du Lac	WAM	
Stephens Akro	WA	Seattle	MoF	434, N78JN
Stingray Hand Glider	SK-C	Moose Jaw	WDM	
Stinson Voyager				
Stinson 105	ON-C	Collingwood	CCAF	055, Parts: 7102, 7246
Stinson 105	SK-C	MJaw	WDM	CF-SFF
Stinson 108	AB-C	Edmonton	AAM	
Stinson 108	AK	Ancho	AAHM	
Stinson 108	GA	Woodstock	NGWS	
Stinson 108	OH	Madis	CFR	
Stinson 108	WA	Everett	MoF	108-626, N97626
Stinson 108-3	OK	Fredi	AAM	
Stinson SA-10A	AL	Birmingham	SMoF	
Stinson SA-10A	AK	Palme	MOAT&I	
Stinson SA-10A	CA	Santa Martin	WoHAM	
Stinson SA-10A	IA	Ottumwa	APM	7655, N27710
Stinson SA-10A	MB-C	Brand	CATPM	
Stinson SA-10A	MI	Oscoda	YAF	7883, N32235
Stinson SA-10A	NJ	Teter	AHoFNJ	
Stinson SA-10A	OK	Fredi	AAM	
Stinson SA-10A	OK	Oklahoma	OSM	
Stinson SA-10A	WA	Tacoma	MAFB	43-43847

Stinson (cont.)

Aircraft	State/Prov	City	Museum	Notes
Stinson SA-10A(L-9)	KS	Liberal	MAAM	
Stinson 7-B	NV	Carso	YF	
Stinson A Trimotor	AK	Ancho	AAHM	
Stinson A Trimotor	MN	Blaine	GH	
Stinson SM-1 Detroiter	CA	El Cajon	SDAMGF	
Stinson SM-1	CT	Winds	NEAM	
Stinson SM-1	MI	Dearb	HFM	
Stinson SM-1	NE	Minde	HWPV	
Stinson SM-8A Jr	AR	Fayetteville	AAM	
Stinson SM-8A Jr.	IA	Ottumwa	APM	8074, NC-12165
Stinson SM-8A Jr.	FL	Titusville	VACM	
Stinson SR Reliant	CA	Santa Maria	SMMoF	
Stinson SR	NC	Morga	CWCAF	
Stinson SR	ON-C	Ottaw	CAM	
Stinson SR	OR	Hood	WAAAM	
Stinson SR Float Plane	WA	Seattle	MoF	8732, N13477
Stinson SR(AT19)V-77	KS	Liberal	MAAM	
Stinson SR-5 Replica	AL	Birmingham	SMoF	
Stinson SR-5A	ND	Minot	DTAM	
Stinson SR-5E	OR	Eugen	OAM	
Stits DS-1	WI	Oshkosh	EAAAAM	
Stits SA-3A	ON-C	Ottaw	CAM	
Stolp Starduster II	RI	NKing	QAM	
Stolp V Star	WI	Oshkosh	EAAAAM	
Stout Skycar	MD	Suitland	PEGF	
Struchen Helicopter	BC-C	Langley	CMoF	
Stuart M-5	WA	Tili	CMANGP	
Student Prince	WA	Vancouver	PAM	
Su-26M	VA	Chantilly	NASMUVC	
SU-22M4	OH	Dayton	NMUSAF	

Aircraft	Subtype	State/Prov	City	Museum	Notes
Stinson					NC15165, 15, "Pennsylvania Central"
Stinson	Tri-Motor	OR	Mc Minnville	EAM	"Flagship Texas"
Stinson	Trimotor	CA	San Carlos	HNCAVM	
Stinson SM-6000B		WA	Port Townsend	PTAM	4009, NC418M
Stinson SM-7 Jr		WA	Port Townsend	PTAM	4098, NC930W
Stinson SM-8A		WI	Oshkosh	EAAAAM	
Stinson SM-8A Jr.		WI	Oshkosh		NC408Y, "Spirit of EAA"
Stinson SM-8A Jr.		WI	Oshkosh	EAAAAM	N1026
Stinson SR-5JR		AK	Fairbanks	PAM	N13482, "Spirit of Barter Island"
Stinson SR-8		MB-C	Winni	WCAM	
Stinson SR-9FM		AB-C	Edmonton	AAM	5732
Stinson SR-9		ON-C	Sault Ste Marie	CBHC	5702, CF-BGN
Stinson SR-9 CM		AK	Ancho	AAHM	
Stinson SR-9 CM		WI	Oshkosh	EAAAAM	
Stinson SR-10F		DC	Washi	USPM	NC2311, "Human Pick-Up"
Stinson SR-10F		MD	Suitland	PEGF	
Stinson SR-10G		VA	Sandston	VAM	5903
Stits					N4453H, "Baby Bird"
Stits					
Stolp	Starduster II				N100LF
Stolp	V Star				N9LS
Stout	Skycar				
Strechen	Helicopter				
Stuart					
Acft Bldg Corp	Student Prince				"Ladt Summer"
Sukhoi					31203

Model	State	City	Museum	Description	Registration
Sud Aviation SE 210	AZ	Tucson	PAM	Caravelle	N1001U
Sun Standard Hang Glider	MI	Kalamazoo	KAHM	Hang Glider	
Sundancer I Racer	CA	San Diego	SDAM	Racer	N1AE
Super Lancer Hang Glider	FL	Lakeland	SNF	Hang Glider	
Supermarine F.1	NY	NYC	ISASM	Scimitar	
Surca-Tempete Homebuilt	FL	Lakel	SFAF	Homebuilt	
SV-5J	CO	CSpri	USAFA	PRIME	Lifting Body
SV-5J	OH	Dayton	NMUSAF	PRIME	Lifting Body
SVA-9	CT	Washi	TFC	Ansaldo	
Swallow	KS	Wichita	KAM		
Swallow	WA	Seattle	MoF		968, N6070
Swallow Monoplane	NY	Mayville	DA	Monoplane	
Swallow Model 1924	WI	Oshkosh	EAAAAM	Three Seater	N4028
Swallow 1926	NE	Minde	HWPV		
Swallow A	AZ	Tucson	PAM		
Swallow C	KS	Wichita	KAM		
Swallow OX5	ND	Fargo	BUSAHM		
Swallow TP	CA	Chino	YAM		
Swallow TP	CA	San Diego	SDAM	Biplane	
T-1	CA	Chino	PoFAM	Gnat	N8761
T-1	FL	Miami	WOM	Gnat	
T-1	IN	Ft Wayne	Mercury	Gnat	
T-1	KS	Liberal	MAAM	Gnat	

T-2 North American Buckeye

Model	State	City	Museum	Notes
T-2	AR	Fayetteville	OMM	
T-2	DC	Washi	NA&SM	
T-2	IN	Crawfordsville	RAM	
T-2	TX		TAM	47, 5
T-2A	CA	Chino	PoFAM	
T-2A	NC	Charlotte	CAM	148239
T-2B	ID	Driggs	TAC	155226, Side # 300S, Tail B
T-2B	IL	Waukegan	WHM	155235, N27WS
T-2C	AL	Birmingham	SMF	156697
T-2C	CA	San Diego	SDACM	157058
T-2C	FL	Pensacola	NMoNA	
T-2C	TX	Tyler	HAMM	
T-3	CA	San Carlos	HNCAVM	Boeing
T-11	IN	Crawfordsville	RAM	

T-18 Thorp Tiger

Model	State	City	Museum
T-18	CA	El Cajon	SDAMGF
T-18	IA	SBluf	MAAM
T-18	KS	Liberal	MAAM

North American

T-18 *(Homebuilt)*

Type	State	City	Museum/Location	Serial / Notes
T-18	OK	Fredi	AAM	
T-18	TX	Dallas	FoF	
T-18	WA	Seattle	MoF	1093, N1093
T-18	WI	Oshkosh	EAAAM	N455DT, "Victoria 76"

T-28 Trojan

Type	State	City	Museum/Location	Serial / Notes
T-28	AL	Birmingham	SMF	
T-28	CO	Denve	JWDAS	
T-28	DC	Washi	NHND	
T-28	DC	Washington	ANAS	
T-28	FL	Milto	CityPark	
T-28	FL	Tittusville	VACM	
T-28	ID	Driggs	TAC	Cowl # 249, Tail NATC
T-28	IL	Rockf	CRA	
T-28	IN	Crawfordsville	RAM	
T-28	KS	New Century	CAF-HoAW	
T-28	LA	Reser	AMHFM	
T-28	MI	Ypsilanti	YAF	
T-28	MS	Bilox	KAFB	13747
T-28	NC	Charlotte	CAM	138258
T-28	NJ	Lexington	NASWAM	
T-28	NM	St Teresa	WEAM	
T-28	NY	New Windsor	RSAM	
T-28	NV	Carso	YF	
T-28	ON-C	Hamilton	CWH	91679
T-28	PA	Beaver Falls	AHM	
T-28	TX	Big Springs	H25	
T-28	TX	C Christi	NAS	
T-28	TX	FWort	PMoT	
T-28	TX	San Angelo	GAFB	
T-28	TX	Ladero	Airport	
T-28	TX	W Houston	CAF-WH	0-37799
T-28	UT	Heber	HVAM	
T-28	WI	Beloi	BA	
T-28	WI	Boscobel	BA	
T-28A	AL	Ozark	USAAM	51-3612
T-28A	GA	Pooler	MoF	51-3612, "Rocly Yates"
T-28A	IA	Davenport	CAFHSS	N70743
T-28A-NI	MI	Belleville	YAF	50-234, N234NA
T-28A	MI	Kalamazoo	KAHM	51-7700
T-28A	OH	Dayton	NMUSAF	49-1494
T-28A	OK	Enid	VAFB	
T-28A	OK	Fredi	AAM	
T-28A	TX	D Rio	LAFB	
T-28A	TX	San A	RAFB	
T-28A(GT)	TX	San Antonio	San Antonio	LSAD 49-1611
T-28A	WA	Vancouver	PAM	
T-28B	CA	Palm Springs	PSAM	140041, NX28BP
T-28B	CA	Paso Robles	EWM	138303
T-28B	CA	Rosamond	EAFB	137702
T-28B	CA	McClellan	McCelAFB	138327
T-28B	FL	Pensacola	NMoNA	136326, 2W, 341, VT-3
T-28B	IL	Waukegan	WHM	138360, N73MG
T-28B	IN	Valparaiso	IAM	140018
T-28B	NC	Asheboro	CHAC	
T-28B	NC	Charl	CHAC	
T-28B	OH	Dayton	NMUSAF	140048
T-28B	OR	Mc Minnville	EAM	13 8334, N394W
T-28B	TN	Sevierville,	TMoA,	138129, N32257, "Showtime"
T-28B	TX	C Christi	USS Lexi	
T-28B	UT	Ogden	HAFBM	137749
T-28B	UT	Wendover	HWA	"Zorro's Mistress"
T-28C	AL	Everg	MA	
T-28C	AL	Everg	MAE	
T-28C	AZ	Grand Canyon	PoFGCVA	
T-28C	AZ	Tucson	PAM	140481
T-28C	CA	El Cajon	WW	
T-28C	CA	SRosa	PCAM	7696, 2G, 133, VT-2
T-28C	CO	Pueblo	PWAM	140064
T-28C	CT	Winds	NEAM	
T-28C	MA	Fall	USSMM	
T-28C	MI	Belleville	YAF	YAF 140531, N944SD, "Tough Old Bird"
T-28C	TX	Galveston	LSM	

T-28D

Type	State	City	Location	Serial
T-28D	PA	Readi	MAAM	
T-28D (AT-28D-5) VA, Suffolk			FF	1634
T-28D(AT)	FL	FtWal	HF	51-3565, N85227
T-28S	OH	N Canton	MAM	

T-29 — Convair

Type	State	City	Location	Serial
T-29	VT	Burlington	NANG	
T-29 (C-131)	GA	Calhoun	WAM	515145, N1178Q
T-29A(C-131)	NE	Ashland	SACM	50-0190
T-29A(C-131A)	AZ	Tucson	PAM	49-1918
T-29A(C-131A)	GA	Pooler	MoF	49-1938
T-29A(GT)(C-131)	TX	Wichita Falls	SAFB	Convair
T-29B(VT)	AZ	Tucson	PAM	51-7906
T-29B(VT)	TX	San Antonio	LSAD	51-5172
T-29C(C-131)	CA	McClellan	McCelAFB	
T-29C(C-131)	TX	Abilene	DLAP	52-1175
T-29C(C-131)	UT	Ogden	HAFBM	52-1119

T-33 Lockheed Shooting Star

Type	State	City	Location	Serial
T-33	AR	Fayetteville	OMM	
T-33	AZ	Apache Jnct	Airport	53-6008
T-33	CA	Torrance	Airport	
T-33	GA	Griffin	SCA	
T-33	GA	Marietta	NASA	
T-33	IA	SBluf	MAAM	
T-33	IL	Danville	MAM	
T-33	IN	Hobar	DickBoyd	
T-33	LA	Barksdale	BAFB	
T-33	MI	Jackson	EAAC	
T-33	MN	Alexandria	Airport	52-9529
T-33	NC	Hickory	HRA	
T-33	NJ	Lexington	NASWAM	
T-33	ON-C	London	LIA	133422, 420 Sq
T-33	ND	Minot	DTAM	
T-33	ON-C	Grand Bend	PAFM	
T-33	NM	St Teresa	WEAM	
T-33	TX	Big Springs	H25	
T-33	TX	Ft Worth	SAM	
T-33	TX	Tyler	HAMM	
T-33	WA	Seattle	MoF	
T-33	WI	Janesville	BHTSAC	
T-33	WI	Stoughton	VFW	
T-33A	AK	Ancho	EAFB	
T-33A	AK	Ancho	KANGB	
T-33A	AL	Atmor	CityPark	
T-33A (2ea)	AL	Birmingham	SMoF	
T-33A	AL	Flora	CityPark	
T-33A	AL	Mobile	CityPark	
T-33A	AL	Monro	CityPark	
T-33A	AL	Tusca	CityPark	
T-33A	AR	Grave	VWF	
T-33A	AR	Helen	VWF	
T-33A	AR	Littl	LRAFB	51-9080
T-33A	AZ	Gila	GBAFAF	
T-33A	AZ	Grand	PoFGCVA	71-5262
T-33A	AZ	Tucson	PAM	53-6145
T-33A	CA	Atwater	CAM	58-0629
T-33A	CA	Chino	YAM	
T-33A	CA	Shafter	MFAM	
T-33A	CA	Fresn	FANG	
T-33A	CA	Los G	VWF	
T-33A	CA	Mader	VWF	
T-33A	CA	Oakland	CAF-GGW	16581, NX9124ZZ
T-33A	CA	Paso Robles	EWM	52-9769
T-33A	CA	Richm	AMS	
T-33A	CA	Riverside	MFAM	58-0513
T-33A	CA	McClellan	McCelAFB	53-5205
T-33A	CA	Torrence	FAAF	52-9239
T-33A	CO	CSpri	EJPSCM	57-0713
T-33A	CO	Denver	WOTR	
T-33A	CO	Flage	VWF	
T-33A	CT	Winds	NEAM	

State	City	Location	Serial	Type
DE	Dover	AL P-2		T-33A
DE	Dover	DAFB	TR-497	T-33A
FL	Clear	FMAM		T-33A
FL	De Fu	CityPark		T-33A-5-LO
FL	Jacksonville	JIA	35325, 27	T-33A
FL	Lakel	SFAF	58-697	T-33A
FL	Shalimar	USAFAM	53-5947	T-33A
GA	Calhoun	WAM	52-9574, TR-574	T-33A
GA	Corde	CityPark		T-33A
GA	Dougl	CityPark		T-33A
GA	Griff	CityPark		T-33A
GA	Thoma	CityPark		T-33A
GA	Pooler	MoF	52-9633	T-33A
GA	Wayne	ALP120		T-33A
GA	Willa	CityPark		T-33A
HI	Oahu	HAFB		T-33A
IA	Burli	CityPark		T-33A
IA	Cedar Rapids	Vet Mem	53-5916	T-33A
IA	Oelwe	ALP19		T-33A
IA	Sheld	CityPark		T-33A
IA	Sigou	CityPark		T-33A
IA	Burle	CityPark		T-33A
ID	Lewis	CityPark		T-33A
ID	Malad	CityPark		T-33A
ID	Twin	CityPark	35979	T-33A
IL	Bloom	PAM		T-33A
IL	Cahok	PCUSL		T-33A
IL	Centr	CityPark		T-33A
IL	Highl	CityPark		T-33A
IL	Linco	HIFM		T-33A
IL	Pinck	CityPark		T-33A
IL	Quicy	CityPark		T-33A
IL	Rantoul	OCAM	55-9797	T-33A-1-LO
IL	Versa	CityPark		T-33A
IN	Covin	VFWP2395	50-29326	T-33A
IN	Elkhart	NIAM	70688, TCD17	T-33A
IN	Hunti	CityPark		T-33A
IN	Peru	GAFB	52-9563	T-33A
KS	Indep	VFWP1186	0-29632	T-33A
KS	Topek	CAM	53-5998	T-33A
KS	Wichi	K&HAP		T-33A-5-LO
LA	Houma	CityPark		T-33A
LA	Mansf	VFWP4586	34967	T-33A
LA	New Orleans	JBMM		T-33A
LA	Rusto	LTUD305		T-33A
LA	Sprin	CityPark		T-33A
MA	Bourne	HQMMR	14335	T-33A
MA	Otis	OANG		T-33A
MA	Stow	BCF		T-33A
MD	Cumbe	CityPark		T-33A
MD	Middle River	GLMAM	53-5854	T-33A
MD	Pocom	ALP93	52-9650, TR-650	T-33A
MD	Rockv	CityPark		T-33A
MD	Breck	ALP295		T-33A
MI	Calum	CAFS		T-33A
MI	Grayl	ALP106	35073,	T-33A
MI	Hart	City Fog		T-33A
MI	Iron	CityPark		T-33A
MI	Roseb	ALP383		T-33A
MI	Sebew	CityPark	53-6099	T-33A
MI	Mt Clemens	SMAM		T-33A
MI	Ypsilanti	YAF		T-33A
MN	Alber	CityPark		T-33A
MN	Buffalo	CityPark		T-33A
MN	Hecto	CityPark		T-33A
MN	Minne	CityPark		T-33A
MN	Minne	MAGM	52-9806	T-33A
MN	Winoma	WTI	N86905	T-33A
MN	Under	VFW874		T-33A
MO	Carut	CityPark		T-33A
MO	Mount	CityPark		T-33A
MO	Richm	ALP237		T-33A
MO	SLoui	ALP179		T-33A
MO	SLoui	NMoT	52-9446	T-33A

Type	State	City	Location	Serial
T-33A	MO	StCha	CityPark	
T-33A	MS	Bilox	KAFB	58-0567
T-33A	MS	Colum	CityPark	
T-33A	MT	Glasg	CityPark	52-9564
T-33A	MT	Great Falls	CityPark	
T-33A	MT	Great Falls	GFANG	57-0574
T-33A	MT	Great Falls	MAFB	57-0574
T-33A	NC	CPoin	CPMB	
T-33A	NC	Williamngton	VFW 2573	52-9766
T-33A	ND	Dicke	CityPark	
T-33A	ND	Hatto	CityPark	
T-33A	ND	Hillsboro	CityPark	35326
T-33A	ND	Hatto	CityPark	
T-33A	ND	Minot	MAFB	
T-33A	NE	Beatr	CityPark	51-8880
T-33A	NE	Fairb	CityPark	
T-33A	NE	Frank	CityPark	
T-33A	NE	Linco	LANG	52-9264,
T-33A	NM	Clovi	CAFB	
T-33A	NM	Truth	CityPark	
T-33A	NY	Albion	VAG	
T-33A	NM	Truth	CityPark	
T-33A	NY	NYC	ISASM	
T-33A	NY	White Plains	WCA	
T-33A	OH	Brook	CityPark	53-5974
T-33A	OH	Dayton	NMUSAF	51-4120
T-33A(NT)	OH	Dayton	NMUSAF	58-586,
T-33A	OH	Lockb	RANGB	
T-33A	OH	Marie	CityPark	
T-33A	OH	Newar	NAFM	
T-33A	OH	Wadsw	CityPark	
T-33A	OK	Coman	CityPark	
T-33A	OK	Elk C	CityPark	
T-33A	OK	Enid	VAFB	
T-33A	OK	Musko	City	
T-33A	OK	Oklahoma	45IDM	58-0505
T-33A	OK	Oklahoma	A&SM	
T-33A	OK	Oklahoma	OSM	
T-33A	OK	Tinke	TANG	
T-33A	OR	Woodb	CityPark	
T-33A	PA	New K	CityPark	
T-33A	PA	NHunt	VFW P781	
T-33A	PA	Phila	FI	
T-33A	SC	Charl	CAFB	
T-33A	SC	Flore	FA&MM	
T-33A	SC	Harts	CityPark	
T-33A	SC	Huron	VFW P1776	
T-33A	SC	Lake	CityPark	
T-33A	SC	McEnt	MEANGB	
T-33A	SD	Rapid City	SDA&SM	57-0590
T-33A	SD	Sioux	SDANGSF	
T-33A	TN	Johnson City	R/CF	
T-33A	TN	Crossville	CCHS	51-6756, "Miss Netie"
T-33A	TN	Dayton	CityPark	
T-33A	TN	Johns	CityPark	
T-33A	TN	Sevierville	TMoA	53-6069
T-33A	TN	Pulas	CityPark	
T-33A	TX	Abilene	DLAP	51-4300
T-33A	TX	D Rio	CityPark	36124
T-33A	TX	D Rio	LAFB	
T-33A	TX	Eagle	ALP211	
T-33A	TX	Ellin	EANGB	
T-33A	TX	FWort	PMoT	
T-33A	TX	FWort	SAM	
T-33A	TX	Lubbock	LSS	2920, ATC
T-33A	TX	Odessa	CAFDS	
T-33A	TX	Plainview	HCA	16753, TR-753
T-33A	TX	San A	RAFB	
T-33A	TX	Slaton	TAM	52-519
T-33A	TX	Sweet	CityPark	
T-33A	TX	Sweetwater	CP	
T-33A	TX	Texar	CityPark	
T-33A	TX	Whichita Falls	SAFB	
T-33A	UT	Murra	CityPark	

T-33

Type	State/Prov	Location	Org	Serial(s)
T-33A-1-LO	UT	Ogden	HAFBM	51-9271
T-33A	UT	Wendover	HWA	N12422
T-33A	VA	Chantilly	NASMUVH	
T-33A	VA	Hampton	APM	51-9086
T-33A-1	VA	Hampton	APM	52-9734
T-33A	VT	Burli	BANG	
T-33A	WA	Brewster	CityPark	
T-33A	WA	Othel	CityPark	
T-33A	WA	Spokane	CityPark	
T-33A	WA	Spokane	AF&AM	
T-33A	WI	Brill	CityPark	
T-33A	WI	Fall	VFWP2219	
T-33A	WI	Madis	VFWP8483	
T-33A	WI	Milwa	MANG	0-18814
T-33A	WI	Prentice	Vetrans Park	TR476
T-33A	WI	Oshkosh	EAAAAM	51-8627
T-33A	WI	Oshkosh	EAAAAM	53-5250
T-33A	WY	Cheye	WYANG	
T-33A	WY	New R	ALP80	
T-33A	WY	Reeds	ALP199	
T-33A	WY	Sherw	ALP496	
T-33A	WY	Stoug	VFWP328	
T-33A (2 ea)	AL	Selma	CityPark	
T-33A	CA	Chino	PoFAM	
T-33A Last Built	WA	Tacoma	MAFB	58-2106
T-33A(3ea)	CA	Rosamond	EAFB	58-669
T-33A(QT)	TX	Whichita Falls	SAFB	
T-33A-1-LO	MI	Belleville	YAF	51-8786, N6570
T-33A-1-LO	MI	Belleville	YAF	51-17445, N133CK, "Kalitta Bounty Hunter"
T-33A-1-LO	MI	Oscoda	YAF	52-9843, N58417
T-33A-1-LO	WA	Tacom	G Spieth	52-9646
T-33A-5-LO	MI	Oscoda	YAF	53-5948
T-33A-5-LO	MI	Belleville	YAF	53-5484, N1541
T-33A-5-LO	OR	Mc Minnville	EAM	53-5943
T-33A-5-LO	IL	Russell	MMM	0-29141
T-33B	CO	Pueblo	PWAM	137936
T-33B	CT	Winds	NEAM	53-5646
T-33B	IN	Crawfordsville	RAM	
T-33B	NC	CPoin	CPMB	
T-33B	NV	Battl	BMAM	1338064
T-33(TV-1)	NC	Charlotte	CAM	33866

T-33 Lockheed Seastar

Type	State/Prov	Location	Org	Serial(s)
T-33B(TV-2)	NC	Charlotte	CAM	
T-33B(TV-2)	NC	Charlotte	CAM	
T-33B(TV-2)	AZ	Tucson	PAM	53-2704,
T-33B(TV-2)	CA	Chino	PoFAM	
T-33B(TV-2)	CT	Winds	NEAM	138048
T-33B(TV-2)	KS	Wichita	KAM	
T-33B(TV-2)	MI	Kalamazoo	KAHM	53-5696,
T-33B(TV-2)	NY	NYC	ISASM	

T-33(CT) Canadair Silver Star

Type	State/Prov	Location	Org	Serial(s)
T-33(CT)	AB-C	Calga	NMoA	
T-33(CT)	AB-C	Cold Lake	CFB	133181
T-33(CT)	AB-C	Edson	CFB	21506, 21097
T-33AN(CT)	AB-C	Edmonton	AAM	21001
T-33A-5-LO(CT)	AB-C	Leduc	CFB	21518
T-33(CT)	AB-C	Lethbridge	CFB	21578
T-33(CT)	AB-C	Nanton	NLSAM	21272
T-33(CT)	AB-C	St Albert	CFB	Xx271
T-33A(CT)	AB-C	Wetas	RM	
T-33AN(CT)	BC-C	Langley	CMoF	33-4787,
T-33A(CT)	BC-C	Sidney	BCAM	Project
T-33(CT)	MB-C	Gimli	CFB	21239
T-33(CT)	MT	Helena	CoT	
T-33A-5-LO(CT)	NE	Ashland	SACM	61-7964
T-33(CT)	NF-C	Goose Bay	CFB	
T-33(CT)	NS-C	Greenwood	GMAM	133434, 434
T-33A(CT)	NS-C	Greenwood	GMAM	13393

Type	Loc	City	Museum	Serial(s)
T-33(CT)	NS-C	Halifax	ACAM	133174
T-33(CT) Cockpit	NS-C	Halifax	ACAM	133635, 21635
T-33(CT)	ON-C	Barrie	CFB	21100,
T-33(CT)	ON-C	CFB Borden	BHT	21079
T-33(CT)	ON-C	Campbellford	MMM	133303
T-33(CT)	ON-C	Cornwall	RCAFA	21347
T-33(CT)	ON-C	Cornwall	RCAFA	133423
T-33(CT)	ON-C	Dundas	CFB	21123
T-33(CT)	ON-C	Ft Erie	NP	21373,
T-33(CT)	ON-C	Goose Bay	TH	
T-33(CT)	ON-C	Hamilton	HAA	
T-33(CT)	ON-C	Picton	CFB	133238
T-33(CT)	SK-C	Saskatoon	CFB	21630,
T-33(CT)	MB-C	Brandon	BA	21130
T-33(CT)	MB-C	Portage	S	21277
T-33(CT)	MB-C	Winnipeg	WRCAFB	133186
T-33(CT)	MB-C	Winnipeg	WRCAFB	21232,
T-33(CT)	MB-C	Dudas	HAA	
T-33(CT)	MB-C	Winni	WCAM	133401
T-33A(CT)	NS-C	Cornwallis	CFBS	
T-33A(CT)	NS-C	Shear	CFBS	
T-33A(CT)	ON-C	Hamilton	CWH	21275, PP275
T-33A(CT)	ON-C	Ottaw	CAM	21574
T-33A(CT)	SK-C	MJaw	WDM	133275
T-33(CT) Mk III	ON-C	Trenton	RCAFMM	21435,
T-33(CT) Mk 3	TN	Sevierville	TMoA	T33-566, N307FS
T-33(CT) Mk 3	WI	Oshkosh	EAAAAM	N72JR

Beechcraft — Mentor

Type	Loc	City	Museum	Serial(s)
T-34	AR	Fayetteville	AAM	
T-34	AZ	Scott	SA	
T-34	CO	Denve	JWDAS	
T-34	CA	Palm Sprg	PSAM	BG-33, N8662E
T-34	CA	San Diego	SDACM	144071
T-34	NY	New York	ISASM	
T-34	ON-C	Hamilton	CWH	
T-34	TX	Amarillo	CAFDS	
T-34	TX	Galve	LSFM	53-4135, N134
T-34	TX	W Houston	CAF-WH	
T-34(YT)	VA	Suffolk	FF	55-0221, #117
T-34A	CA	Atwater	CAM	50-0735
T-34A	CA	El Cajon	WW	
T-34C	IL	Springfield	ACM	675
T-34A	MI	Kalamazoo	KAHM	140768
T-34A	OH	Dayton	NMUSAF	53-3310
T-34A	TX	San Antonio	LSAD	55-206
T-34B	AL	Birmingham	SMF	
T-34B	CO	Pueblo	PWAM	
T-34B	FL	Pensacola	NMoNA	144040, F-4033
T-34B	GA	Atlan	SW	SW4130, 30
T-34B	IN	Valparaiso	IAM	BG-411
T-34B	OK	Altus	AAFB	
T-34B	TN	Tullahoma	SFM	BG-322, N434RM
T-34B	TX	Abilene	DLAP	140810
T-34B	TX	C Christi	USS Lexi	
T-34B	TX	D Rio	LAFB	
T-34B	TX	San A	RAFB	
T-34C	FL	Whitt	WNAS	

Cessna — Tweedie Bird

Type	Loc	City	Museum	Serial(s)
T-37	CA	Chino	YAM	
T-37 Cockpit	CA	Chino	YAM	
T-37	FL	Clear	FMAM	
T-37	IN	Peru	GAM	
T-37	FL	Tittusville	VACM	
T-37	KS	Liberal	MAAM	
T-37	KS	Wichita	KAM	67-21469
T-37	OK	Tulsa	TA&SC	
T-37	TX	Big Springs	H25	
T-37	TX	Burnet	CAFHLS	
T-37	TX	Denison	PAFBM	

T-37

Type	State	City	Location	Serial
T-37	TX	Waco	WRA	
T-37	UT	Ogden	HAFBM	
T-37A	TX	D Rio	LAFB	
T-37B	AL	Birmingham	SMoF	
T-37B	AZ	Tucson	PAM	57-2267
T-37B	CA	Riverside	MAFM	57-2316
T-37B	CO	Pueblo	PW AM	
T-37B	FL	Clearwater	FMAM	
T-37B	GA	Pooler	MoF	57-2261
T-37B	MI	Battl	BCANG	
T-37B	MS	Colum	CAFB	
T-37B	OH	Dayton	NMUSAF	57-2289
T-37B	TX	Abile	PSCAF	54-2734
T-37B	TX	San A	RAFB	
T-37B	TX	Tyler	HAMM	

T-38 Northrop Talon

Type	State	City	Location	Serial
T-38	AL	SMF	CAJM	
T-38	CA	Carls	CAJM	
T-38	CA	Chino	YAM	
T-38	CA	LAnge	CMoS&I	
T-38	CA	Palmdale	PPHP	63-8182
T-38	IL	Bloom	PAM	60-0549
T-38	IN	Edinburg	VFW 233	00558
T-38	KS	Liberal	MAAM	
T-38	MN	Dulut	CityPark	
T-38	NM	Gallup	GMA10829	
T-38	NY	Moria	AL	
T-38	OK	Weatherford	SA&SC	
T-38A(YT)	SD	Rapid City	SDA&SM	58-1192
T-38	TX	Big Springs	H25	
T-38	TX	Burnet	CAFHLS	
T-38	TX	C Christi	USS Lexi	
T-38	TX	D Rio	LAFB	
T-38A	AL	Montg	MAFB	
T-38A	AZ	Tucson	PAM	61-854
T-38A	CA	Appley Valley	LCfER	60-0591
T-38A	CA	Chino	YAM	
T-38A	CA	Riverside	MFAM	60-0593
T-38A	CA	Rosamond	EAFB	61-810
T-38A	CA	McClellan	McCelAFB	60-551
T-38A	CO	CSpri	USAFA	
T-38A	KS	Hutch	KC&SC	
T-38A	MS	Colum	CAFB	
T-38A	NM	Santa Teresa	WEAM	
T-38A(AT)	OH	Dayton	NMUSAF	63-8172
T-38A	OR	Mc Minnville	EAM	63-8224
T-38A	TX	Abilene	DLAP	60-0592
T-38A	TX	Dallas	FoF	62-3645
T-38A	TX	Whichita Falls	SAFB	
T-38A	UT	Ogden	HAM	61-0824
T-38B	KY	Lexington	AMoK	64-13292

T-39 North American Sabreliner

Type	State	City	Location	Serial
T-39A	AL	Birmingham	SMF	
T-39A	CA	Riverside	MFAM	62-4465
T-39	MO	SLoui	SLUPC	
T-39	MT	Helena	CoT	
T-39 Parts	TX	Ladero	Airport	
T-39A	CA	Farfield	DA&SM	62-4461A
T-39A	GA	Pooler	MoF	
T-39A	OH	Dayton	NMUSAF	62-4478
T-39A	TX	Abilene	DLAP	61-634
T-39A	WI	Milwa	MANG	
T-39A(CT)	AZ	Tucson	PAM	62-4449
T-39A(CT)	CA	Rosamond	EAFB	60-3505
T-39A(CT)	CA	McClellan	McCelAFB	61-660
T-39A(CT)	CA	San B	NAFB	
T-39A(CT)	IL	Sugar Grove	ACM	60-3503
T-39A(CT)	IL	Belle	SAFB	
T-39A(CT)	IL	Cahokia	PCUSL	03504

T-39A-1-NO(CT)	IL	Rantoul	OCAM	62-4494	T-39D	AL	Birmingham	SMoF	
T-39A-1	UT	Ogden	HAFBM	61-0674	T-39D	MD	Lexington	PRNAM	150987
T-39A-NA	NE	Ashland	SACM	62-4487					
T-40	TX	Galveston	LSFM	Turner	TEDDE				59, N585N
T-40	WI	Oshkosh	EAAAAM	Turner	TEDDE				N191T, "Ophelia Bumps"
T-41	FL	Clearwater	FMAM	Cessna	Mescalero				
T-41	IN	Peru	GAFB	Cessna	Mescalero				65-5251
T-41A	OH	Dayton	NMUSAF	Cessna	Mescalero				
T-41B	GA	Hampton	AAHF	Cessna	Mescalero				
T-41B	NC	Asheboro	PFAC	Cessna	Mescalero				
T-46A	CA	Rosamond	EAFB	Fairchild/Republic	Demonstrator				
T-46A	OH	Dayton	NMUSAF	Fairchild/Republic	Demonstrator				84-0493
T-46(NGT)	NY	Garde	CoAM	Fairchild/Republic	Demonstrator				N73RA
T-20	AB-C	Nanton	NLSAM	Cessna	Crane 1				3760-60462
T-50(UC-78)	**Cessna**	**Crane 1 Bamboo Bomber**							
T-50	AB-C	Calga	AMoC		T-50	MB-C	Brandon	CATPM	
T-50	AB-C	Wetas	RM		T-50	MB-C	Winni	WCAM	
T-50	AK	Ancho	AAHM		T-50	OK	Fredi	AAM	
T-50	CA	Shafter	MFAM		T-50	OH	Trotwood	WSS	N1238N
T-50	CA	Chino	YAM	N46617, 5193	T-50	ON-C	Campbellford	MMM	
T-50	FL	Pensacola	NMoNA	N63426, 5515	T-50	ON-C	Ottaw	CAM	8676
T-50(UC-78)	IN	Auburn	HW		T-50 Cockpit	ON-C	Ottaw	CAM	
T-50D	KS	Liberal	MAAM		T-50	SK-C	MJaw	WDM	7829
T-50(UC-78)	KS	Wichita	CAF-J		T-50	TX	Galve	LSFM	6644, N51469
T2C	TX	C Christi	USS Lexi		Seastar		144200		
T2V(T-1A)	AZ	Tucson	PAM	Lockheed	Seastar				
T8P-1	AB-C	Calga	AMoC	Barkley	Grow				
T8P-1	AB-C	Edmonton	AAM	Barkley	Grow				
Tacit Blue	OH	Dayton	NMUSAF	Northrop	Whale		"Tatic Blue",		
Target Drone	NM	St Teresa	WEAM						
Target Drone	NY	Hammond	CM						
Task Silhouette	WA	Seattle	MoF	Task	Silhouette		TR601, N84TR		
Taylor Aerocar	WI	Oshkosh	EAAAAM	Taylor	Aerocar		N4994P		
Taylor Monoplane	AB-C	Langley	CMoF&T	Taylor	Monoplane				

Taylor Monoplane

Type	State	City	Museum	Registration / Notes
Taylor Monoplane	WI	Fond du Lac	WAM	
Taylor Monoplane HB	WI	Oshkosh	WoHAM	Homebuilt, Year 1980
Taylor Titsch	CA	Santa Martin	FTWAM	
Taylor Young	FL	Kissi	APM	
Taylor Young A	IA	Ottumwa	Readi	
Taylor Young Model A	PA		MAAM	Model A

Taylorcraft

Type	State	City	Museum	Registration / Notes
Taylorcraft	MN	Winoma	WTI	N438RM
Taylorcraft A	WA	Vancouver	PAM	
Taylorcraft A	OH	Allia	FBA	
Taylorcraft BC	WA	Everett	MoF	Classic CG398, NC19893
Taylorcraft BC-12D	WI	Oshkosh	EAAAAM	N21292
Taylorcraft BC-12D	AR	Fayetteville	AAM	
Taylorcraft BC-12	IA	Greenfield	IAM	8171, N95871
Taylorcraft BC-12	WA	Seattle	MoF	
Taylorcraft BC-12D	NY	River	RE	N5406E
Taylorcraft BC-12D	NC	Hendersonville	WNCAM	
Taylorcraft BC-12D	PA	Bethel	GAAM	
Taylorcraft BC-65	MD	College Park	CPAM	
Taylorcraft BC-65	NY	Rhine	ORA	
Taylorcraft BC-65	OC-C	Ottawa	CAM	
Taylorcraft Mk.VII	AB-C	Calga	AMoC	Auster

Grumman Avenger

Type	State	City	Museum	Registration
TBF	LA	New Orleans	DDM	
TBF	TX	C Christi	USS Lexi	
TBF-1	CA	Chino	YAM	5997, 5997
TBF-1	MD	Suitland	PEGF	
TBM	AB-C	Wetas	RM	
TBM	AL	Troy	TMA	
TBM	CA	Chino	D Tallichet	53229, N7236C, Parts
TBM	CA	Inglewood	PBR	
TBM	FL	FtLau	WJAIS&L	
TBM	ID	Twin	NWWI	
TBM	MB-C	N Brunswick	NBM	14, C-GLEK
TBM	NM	St Teresa	WEAM	
TBM	NS-C	Shear	CFBS	
TBM	NJ	Lexington	NASWAM	
TBM	NY	E Garden City	CoA	
TBM	TX	Frede	NMofPW	
TBM-3	OH	Batavia	TSWM	69-375
TBM-3	CA	Alameda	UUSHM	
TBM-3	CA	Oakla	OWAM	86123, N6831C, "The Admiral"
TBM-3	CA	Chino	PoF	91264, 69374, NX7835C
TBM-3	CA	San Diego	SDACM	85957
TBM-3	CA	San Diego	SDACM	53503, N53503, #309
TBM-3	CO	GJunc	CAF-RMW	
TBM-3	FL	Deland	DNASM	91598, N9548Z
TBM-3	FL	Miami	WOM	
TBM-3	ID	Rexburg	LFM	
TBM-3	MN	Minne	JJ	R8 123
TBM-3	KS	Liberal	MAAM	
TBM-3	MN	Minne	JJ	
TBM-3	NM	Santa Fe	WoH	
TBM-3	NS-C	Halifax	HAM	53607, C-FPL
TBM-3	OK	Fredi	AAM	
TBM-3	PA	Reading	MAAM	
TBM-3	TX	College Station	GBLM	
TBM-3	TX	Hawki	RRSA	
TBM-3	TX	Midland	AAHM	53353, N5264V, N9593C, 69472
TBM-3E	AZ	Tucson	PAM	53785, NL7075C, VMTB-242
TBM-3E	CA	Palm Springs	PoFAM	91664, SM, VS-27, #01
TBM-3E	CA	Miramar	FLAM	N 6822C, 53593
TBM-3E	FL	Jacksonville	NASJ	
TBM-3E	FL	Pensacola	NMoNA	

Model	City	State	Code	Registration / Notes
TBM-3E	Kalaeloa	HI	NAMBB	85828
TBM-3E	Stow	MA	BCF	91733, N9590Z
TBM-3E	St Charles	MO	CAFWM	
TBM-3E	Asheboro	NC	PFAC	91388, N9564Z
TBM-3E	Boiestown	NB-C	CNBWM	85733, N6824C
TBM-3E	Fredricton	NB-C	FP	85460, C-GFPS, #3
TBM-3E	Fredricton	NB-C	FP	53787, C-GFPT, #10
TBM-3S	Fredricton	NB-C	FP	86180, C-GFPL, #12
TBM-3S	Fredricton	NB-C	FP	53200, C-GLEL,, #13
TBM-3E	Fredricton	NB-C	FP	91426, C-FMUE, #18
TBM-3E	Fredricton	NB-C	FP	53857, CGFPM, #21
TBM-3E	Fredricton	NB-C	FP	86020, C-GFPL, #22
TBM-3E	Fredricton	NB-C	FP	53610, C-FIMR, #23
TBM-3E	Fredricton	NB-C	FP	69323, C-GLEJ, #24
TBM-3E	Garde	NY	CoAM	91586
TBM-3E	Horseheads	NY	NWM	91752, #64, 401SL
TBM-3E	New York	NY	ISASM	85886, N9586Z, "The Cockpit"
TBM-3E	Boiestown	ON-C	CNBWM	C-OLEK, #14
TBM-3E	Beaaverton	OR	PANW	
TBM-3E	Mc Minnville	OR	EAM	91726, N5260V, #32
TBM-3E	Tillamook	OR	TAM	53575, 91726, N6447C
TBM-3E	NKing	RI	QAM	53914
TBM-3E	Mt Pleasant	SC	PPM	
TBM-3E	Sevierville	TN	TMoA	91453, N4170A, VMT232
TBM-3S	C Christi	TX	USS Lexi	
TBM-3E	Addison	TX	CFM	86280, N86280, # 54, ATA
TBM-3E	Galve	TX	LSFM	69329, N700RW
TBM-3E	Suffolk	VA	FF	53454, VS-22/801
TBM-3E	Triangle	VA	NMMC	85890
TBM-3E	Olmypia	WA	OFM	69325, N325GT, Side # T-88
TBM-3S	Dawson Creek	BC-C	Ag Air Inc	91171, C-FBQT

Model	City	State	Code	Manufacturer	Type	Notes
TDD-1	Pensacola	FL	NMoNA	Radioplane	Target Drone	43-2, A
TDD-2(PQ-14A)	Pensacola	FL	NMoNA	Radioplane	Target Drone	120082
TDD-2(PQ-14A)	Suitland	MD	PEGF	Radioplane	Target Drone	
TDR-1	Pensacola	FL	NMoNA			
TDU-25B	Chino	CA	YAM	Hayes Int'l	Tow Target Drone	33529
Teal Ruby Satellite	Dayton	OH	NMUSAF	Teal	Ruby	
Teasdale	Elmir	NY	NSM			
Temple Aero Sportsman	Dallas	TX	FoFM		Temple Aero Corp Sportsma	C-987N, "Texas Temple"
Terrapin	Garde	NY	CoAM	Republic	Terrapin Rocket	
TG-1A	Chantilly	VA	NASMUVC	Frankfort	Cinema B	
TG-1A	Moriarty	NM	SSM	Frankfort	Cinema B	
TG-2(LNS-1)	Riverside	CA	MFAM	Great Lakes	Martin TG-2	N54301
TG-2A	Columbus	IN	ABAM	Great Lakes	Martin TG-2	
TG-2(LNS-1)	Horseheads	NY	NWM	Great Lakes	Martin TG-2	

TG-3A Schweizer Glider

Model	City	State	Code	Registration / Notes
TG-3A	Tucson	AZ	PAM	15, N69064
TG-3A	Tucson	AZ	PAM	32, N63905
TG-3A	Atwater	CA	CAM	
TG-3A	Chino	CA	YAM	
TG-3A	Denve	CO	JWDAS	43, N61279
TG-3A	Elmir	NY	NSM	
TG-3A(LNE-1)	Birmingham	AL	SMF	
TG-3A(LNE-1)	Ghent	NY	POMAM	
TG-3A(LNE-1)	Dayton	OH	NMUSAF	

TG-4A Laister-Kauffman Glider

Aircraft	State	City	Museum	Mfr / Note
TG-4A	AL	Birmingham	SMoF	
TG-4A	CO	Denve	JWDAS	
TG-4A	DE	Dover	AMCM	
TG-6	AZ	Tucson	PAM	Taylorcraft
TG-6A	OR	Hood	WAAAM	Taylorcraft
TG-32	OH	Dayton	NMUSAF	
TGM-13	CO	Flage	VWF	
Thomas Pidgeon	CA	Chino	YAM	Thomas
Thomas Pusher	NY	Rhine	ORA	Thomas
Tilbury Flash	IL	Bloom	McLCHS	Tilbury
Tocan Ultright	AB-C	Edmonton	AAM	Tocan
Trains 6	OH	Dayton	CP	
Trains 60	MO	SLoui	NMoT	
Transporter-Erector	ND	Grand Forks	GFAFB	
Travel Air	CA	Calistoga	CG	Travel Air
Travel Air Texaco Rep	MI	Kalamazoo	KAM	

Travel Air — Mystery Ship

Aircraft	State	City	Museum	Serial / Reg
Travel Air 1000	CA	Lanca	BA	
Travel Air 1000	IL	Chica	MoS&I	
Travel Air 1000	TN	Tullahoma	SMF	1, NC241
Travel Air 2000	KS	Wichita	KAM	
Travel Air 2000	ON-C	Ottaw	CAM	
Travel Air 2000	PA	Bethel	GAAM	
Travel Air 2000	VA	Sands	VAM	721 CAM
Travel Air 2000	WA	Port Townsend	PTAM	645, NC6147
Travel Air 2000	WI	Oshkosh	EAAAAM	N241
Travel Air 4000	AR	Fayetteville	AAM	
Travel Air 4000	CA	Hayward	VAM	
Travel Air 4000(D4D)	KY	Lexington	AMoK	N434N
Triumph	CA	Palmdale	PPHM	Rutan
Troyer VX	PA	Readi	MAAM	Troyer
TS-1	FL	Pensacola	NMoNA	
TS-11	CA	Chino	PoFAM	Polish

(right-hand column entries)

Aircraft	State	City	Museum	Mfr / Serial
TG-4A	GA	Pooler		MoF 42-43740, N43LK
TG-4A	NM	Moriarty	SSM	
TG-4A	OH	Dayton	NMUSAF	
TG-6				Taylorcraft — 42-58662, N59134
Glider				Taylorcraft — 31523
Pidgeon				Thomas — 1
Pusher				Thomas
Flash				Tilbury — NR12931
Ultright				Tocan
Mystery Ship		Mystery Ship		
Travel Air				Travel Air
Travel Air 4000	MO	Maryland Hts	HARM	
Travel Air 4000	NY	Hammondsport	CM	
Travel Air 4000	NY	Ghent	POMAM	
Travel Air 4000	OR	River	TFAC	
Travel Air 4000	OR	Hood	WAAAM	
Travel Air 4000	TN	Tullahoma	SMF	1295, NC367M
Travel Air 4000	WA	Port Townsend	PTAM	850, NC9049
Travel Air 4000	WA	Vancouver	PAM	
Travel Air 4000E	ON-C	Hamilton	CWH	
Travel Air 4000E	WI	Oshkosh	EAAAAM	NC 648H
Travel Air 6000A	TN	Tullahoma	SMF	RB0001, NR614K
Travel Air 6000B	AK	Ancho	AAHM	
Travel Air 6000B	GA	Atlanta	DATHM	6B-2040
Iskra				A 6446

Type	State	City	Collection	Name	Serial(s)
TS-11	MI	Belleville	YAF	Polish / Iskra	1H1019, N101TS
TS-11	TX	Addison	CFM	Polish / Iskra	
TS-11	TX	Tyler	HAMM	Polish / Iskra	
Tu-2	FL	Polk	FoF	Tupolev / Bat	
Tu-2	NM	St Teresa	WEAM	Tupolev / Bat	
TU-6	TX	Ft Worth	SAM	Charic	
U-2	CA	Moffe	NASAAVC		
U-2	VA	Chantilly	NASMUVC		
U-2 Flying Wing	AB-C	Calga	AMoC	Mitchell / Superwing	
U-2 Flying Wing	KS	Coffeyville	CAHM	Mitchell / Flying Wing	

U-2 Lockheed Gray Ghost

Type	State	City	Collection	Serial(s)
U-2A	OH	Dayton	NMUSAF	56-6722
U-2C	AZ	Tucson	DMAFB	
U-2C	DC	Washi	NA&SM	
U-2C	GA	Pooler	MoF	56-6682
U-2C	TX	D Rio	LAFB	
U-2C-LO	NE	Ashland	SACM	56-6701, "Dragon Lady"
U-2CT	CA	Rosamond	EAFB	56-6953
U-2D	CA	Rosamond	EAFB	
U-2R	CA	Marys	BAFB	

U-3A Cessna Blue Canoe

Type	State	City	Collection	Serial(s)
U-3A	AL	Ozark	USAAM	57-5863
U-3A	CA	Atwater	CAM	57-5849
U-3A	CA	Farfield	DA&SM	
U-3A	CO	Denve	JWDAS	
U-3A	CO	Denver	WOTR	
U-3A	IN	Peru	GAFB	57-5922
U-3A	MI	Mt Clemens	SMAM	58-2111
U-3A	OH	Dayton	NMUSAF	58-2124
U-3A	SD	Rapid City	SDA&SM	57-5872
U-3A(L-27A)	UT	Ogden	HAFBM	
U-3A	AZ	Tucson	PAM	58-2107
U-3B9D	GA	Pooler	MoF	60-6052

Type	State	City	Collection	Name	Serial(s)
U-4A	AL	Ozark	USAAM	Aero / Commander	55-4640
U-4B	GA	Pooler	MoF	Aero / Commander	63-7948, N37948
U-4B	OH	Dayton	NMUSAF	Aero / Commander	55-4647
U-505 German	IL	Chica	MoS&I	Submarine / Submarine	
U-8	CO	Denve	JWDAS	Beech / Queen-Air	
U-8	KS	Wichita	KAM	Beech / Queen-Air	
U-8	GA	Hampton	AAHF	Beech / Queen-Air	
U-9A(YU)	AL	Ozark	USAAM	Aero Eng. / Commander	
U-9A	CA	Riverside	MFAM	Aero / Commander	52-6219
U-9A	IL	Russell	MMM	Aero / Commander	52-6218
U-10	CO	Denve	JWDAS	Helio / Courier	
U-10(YU)(YL-24)	AL	Ozark	USAAM	Helio / Courier	52-2540

Model	State	Location	Code	Manufacturer	Type	Serial / Notes
U-10A	FL	FtWal	HF	Helio	Courier	62-3606, AH
U-10D	GA	Pooler	MoF	Helio	Super Courier	63-13096, N87743
U-10D	OH	Dayton	NMUSAF	Helio	Super Courier	66-14360
U-21	CO	Denve	JWDAS	Beech	Ute	
U-21(YU)	AL	Ozark	USAAM	Beech	Ute	63-12902
U-21G	GA	Hampton	AAHF	Beech	Ute	
UFM Easy Riser	WI	Oshkosh	EAAAAM	UFM	Easy Riser	
Ultra-Light	CA	Chino	PoFAM			
Ultimate 100	ON-C	Toronto	TAM	Ultimate	100	
Unident Atec	MN	Winoma	WTI	Unident	Aztec	
Unruh	WI	Oshkosh	EAAAAM	Unruh	Uhruh	N1473V, "Pretty Prairie Special III"
UTVA-66	FL	Titusville	VAC	YUGO	Trainer	
UAV	MD	Lexington	PRNAM	Israeli Aircraft Industry	Pioneer	101
UV-18	CO	Denver	69thB		Twin Turboprop	
V-1 * See Fi-103* Flying Bomb						
V-1	FL	Shalimar	USAFAM	Vultee	Voland	
V-1	MI	Kalamazoo	KAM	Vultee	Voland	
V-1	ON-C	Ottaw	CAM	Vultee	Voland	
V-1(JB-2)	UT	Ogden	HAM	Vultee	Voland	
V-1-A	VA	Sands	VAM	Vultee	Voland	25
V-1(Fi-103)	VA	Suffolk	FF	Vultee	Voland	
V-1(XV)	AL	Ozark	USAAM	McDonnell	Convertiplane	53-4016
V-2	KS	Hutch	KC&SC	Peene Munde	Rocket	
V-2	MD	Aberd	APG	Peene Munde	Rocket	
V-2	NM	Las Cruces	WSMP	Peene Munde	Rocket	
V-2	OK	Oklahoma	OSM	Peene Munde	Rocket	
V-2	OH	Dayton	NMUSAF	Peene Munde	Rocket	
V-3A(XV)	OH	Dayton	NMUSAF	Peene Munde	Rocket	54-148
V-6A(XV)	AL	Ozark	USAAM	Hawker-Siddley	Kestrel	64-19264
V-6A(XV)	OH	Dayton	NMUSAF	Hawker-Siddley	Kestrel	64-18262, NASA 521
V-6A(XV)	VA	Hampton	HAP	Hawker-Siddley	Kestrel	64-18266, NASA 520
V-22 Osprey II	AZ	Tucson	PAM	Pereira	Osprey	105, N17EH, A
V-22 Osprey II	PA	West Chester	AHM	Bell-Boeing	Osprey	
V-22 Osprey II	WI	Oshkosh	EAAAAM	Pereira	Osprey	N346JS
V-101B	AR	Roger				
V-173	MD	Suitland	PEGF	Vought	Flying Pancake	
Valkyrie Hang Glider	VA	Chantilly	NASMUVC		Valkyrie	Hang Glider

Note: "Voland" entries for V-1 listed as "Restoration" for the V-1 (MI, Kalamazoo, KAM).

Aircraft	State	City	Org.	Make / Type	Model	Reg.
Van Dellen LH-2	IA	Ottumwa	APM	Van Dellen		
Vancraft Gyro Copter	OR	Tillamook	TNAM	Vancraft	Gyro Copter	N920SR
Vansgrunsven RV-3	FL	Lakel	SFAF	Vansgrunsven	Homebuilt	
Vansgrunsven RV-3	WI	Oshkosh	EAAAAM	Vansgrunsven	Homebuilt	
Vansgrunsven RV-4	WI	Oshkosh	EAAAAM	Vansgrunsven	Homebuilt	
Vector 27			CMoS&I	Vector		
Velie Model 70	CA	LAnge	CoAM	Velie	Monocoupe	
Veligdans Monerai	NY	Garde	EAAAAM	Veligdans	Monerai Glider	N525S
Venture 200	WI	Oshkosh	EAAAAM	Questair		N62V
Ventuier Airship	NY	Geneseo	1941AG	Ventuier	Airship	
Vertol 44B	CA	Ramona	CR	Vertol		
Verville Sport Trainer	MD	Suitland	PEGF	Verille	Sport	
Vickers Vedette V	MB-C	Winni	WCAM	Vickers	Vedette	
Vickers Viking Mk.IV Rep	AB-C	Edmonton	AAM		Viking Mk.IV	
Vickers Viscount 744	AZ	Tucson	PAM		Viscount 744	40, N22SN
Vickers Viscount	BC-C	Sidney	BCAM	Vickers	Viscount 757	
Vickers Viscount	MB-C	Winni	WCAM	Vickers	Viscount 757	CF-THG, TCA
Vickers Viscount	ON-C	Ottaw	CAM	Vickers	Viscount	
Vickers Viscount	PA	Readi	MAAM	Vickers	Viscount	
Vickers Viscount	WA	Seattle	MoF	Vickers	Viscount 724	
Viking Dragonfly	KS	Liberal	MAAM	Viking	Dragonfly	
Viking Dragonfly	OK	Fredi	AAM	Viking	Dragonfly	
Viking Kittyhawk	CT	Winds	NEAM	Viking	Kittyhawk	
VJ-21	CA	Santa Martin	WoHAM	Volmer-Jensen		
VJ-23	IA	Ottumwa	APM	Volmer-Jensen	Powered Glider	
VJ-24	FL	Lakel	SFAF	Lazair	Ultralight	
Voisin Model 8	DC	Washi	NA&SM	Voisin	Model 8	
Voisin Model 8	MD	Suitland	PEGF	Voisin	Model 8	
Voisin Model 8	NY	NYC	ISASM	Voisin	Model 8	
Voisin Model 8	NY	Rhine	ORA	Voisin	Model 8	
Volscraft	KS	Augusta	AAM	Evans	Experimental Aircraft	
VP-1	AZ	Tucson	PAM	Evans	Volksplane	
VP-1	FL	Kissimmee	SNFAM	Evans	Volksplane	N 47188
VP-1	IA	Ottumwa	APM	Evans	Volksplane	
VP-1	ND	Minot	DTAM	Evans	Volksplane	
VP-1	TX	Galveston	LSFM	Evans	Volksplane	
VP-1A	TX	Galveston	LSFM	Evans	Volksplane	VP-DH1

Type	State	City	Museum	Builder	Name	Serial/Reg
VPS Hu-Go Craft	WI	Oshkosh	EAAAAM	Hugo	VPS Hu-Go Craft	N29H
VS-300A	DC	Washi	NA&SM	Sikorsky	Helicopter	
VS-300A	MI	Dearborn	HFM	Sikorsky		
VS-300A Cockpit	PA	WChester	AHM	Sikorsky		
VS-316(R-4B)	ON-C	Ottaw	CAM	Sikorsky	Hoverfly	43-46565
VS-44A	CT	Windsor Locks	NEAM	Sikorsky	Excambian	
VXT-8 Coleopter	CA	San Carlos	HNCAVM	Hiller	Coleopter	
VZ-2A Vertol	MD	Suitland	PEGF	Boeing	Vertol	56-6941
VZ-3RY	AL	Ozark	USAAM	Ryan	Vertiplane	56-9642
VZ-4-DA Doak	VA	FtEus	USATM		Doak	
VZ-8P	PA	WChes	AHM	Piasecki	Airgeep	58-5511
VZ-8P-2	VA	FtEus	USATM	Piasecki	Airgeep	
VZ-9V	MD	Suitland	PEGF	Avro-Canada	Avrocar	
VZ-ZAP	AL	Ozark	USAAM			
VZ1 Hiller 1031	CA	San Carlos	HNCAVM	Hiller	Flying Platform	
VZ1 Hiller 1031	VA	Chantilly	NASMUVC	Hiller	Flying Platform	

Type	State	City	Museum	Reg/Notes
Waco	AK	Palme	MOAT&I	
Waco	AZ	Scott	SA	
Waco	CA	Calistoga	CG	
Waco	ND	Minot	DTAM	
Waco	NY	Rhine	ORA	
Waco	TX	Houston	1940ATM	
Waco Model F	MO	Maryland Hts	HARM	
Waco 4	OH	Troy	WHS	
Waco 9	ID	Athol	NAM	
Waco 9	MD	Suitland	PEGF	
Waco 9	NY	Rhine	ORA	
Waco 10	CA	San Carlos	HNCAVM	
Waco 10	CA	Santa Martin	WoHAM	
Waco 10	FL	Ameli	IAT	
Waco 10	ON-C	Ottawa	CAM	C-GAFD
Waco 125	MN	Bloom	SPMIA	
Waco 128	MN	Minne	MSPIA	NC 4576, "Northwest Airways"
Waco AQC-6	BC-C	Langley	CMoF	4646, CF-CCW
Waco Arisocraft "W"	OH	Troy	WHS	
Waco ATO	PA	Reading	WAM&ALC	A118
Waco Cabin UIC	MD	Suitland	PEGF	
Waco CTO	OH	Troy	WHS	
Waco CTO	WI	Oshkosh	EAAAAM	NC75527
Waco EQC-6	AB-C	Calga	AMoC	
Waco Glider	MD	Suitland	PEGF	
Waco Glider	OH	Troy	WHS	
Waco INF	BC-C	Langley	CMoF	3324, N6005Y, CF-CJR
Waco INF	MI	Kalamazoo	KAHM	
Waco INF	OR	Hood	WAAM	NC644V
Waco QCF-2	OR	Hood	WAAAM	
Waco GXE 10	OR	Hood	WAAAM	-2
Waco RNF	AZ	Tucson	PAM	3392, NC11206
Waco RNF	WI	Oshkosh	EAAAAM	
Waco Taperwing	ON-C	Ottawa	VWoF	
Waco VPF-7	MI	Kalamazoo	KAM	
Waco UBF-2	ME	Owls Head	OHTM	
Waco UEC	CA	Chino	YAM	
Waco UIC	AB-C	Edmonton	AAM	
Waco UPF-7	AB-C	Wetas	RM	

Aircraft	State	City	Museum	Registration
Waco UPF-7	AZ	Tucson	PAM	
Waco UPF-7	ND	Minot	DTAM	
Waco UPF-7	OH	Troy	WHS	
Waco UPF-7	VA	Bealt	FCA	
Waco UPF-7	WA	Vashon	OTA	N30135
Waco UPF-7	WA	Vashon	OTA	5540, NC30143
Waco YKS	AK	Ancho	AAHM	5871, NC39738
Waco YKS	AL	Birmi	Southe	
Waco YKS-6	WA	Vashon	OTA	NC16241, Trainer
Waco UPF-7	ID	Athol	NAM	
Waco YKS-6	MB-C	Winni	WCAM	
Waco YKS-6	CA	San Diego	SDAM	N48980
Waco YKS-7	WI	Oshkosh	EAAAAM	
Waco YKS-7	OH	Troy	WHS	
Waco YMF	NC	Durham	CB	5644
Waco YPF-7	AL	Birmi	Southe	
Waco YOC	VA	Sands	VAM	4279
Waco YOC	AZ	Tucson	PAM	N16523
Waco ZKS-6				

Aircraft	State	City	Museum	Owner / Builder	Model / Registration
Wag-Aero CUBy	WI	Oshkosh	EAAAAM	Brugioni	CUBy, N1933J
Wallis Model 3	MI	Belleville	YAM	Wallis	Redwing Black Bird, N65022
Warwick W-4	WI	Oshkosh	EAAAAM	Warwick	N4777W, "Hot Canary"
Wasol Racer	WA	Vancouver	PAM	Wasol	Formula 1 Racer, Reno
Waspair Tomcat Tourer		Oshkosh	EAAAAM	EAAAAM	Waspair Tomcat Tourer, "Feeline Fokker IV"
Waterman Aeromobile	MD	Suitland	Chantilly	NASMUVH	Waterman Aeromobile
Waterman Whatsit	MD	Chantilly	PEGF	Waterman	Whatsit
Watkins Skylark	KS	Wichita	KAM	Watkins	Skylark
W D-A	WI	Oshkosh	EAAAAM	Estupinan Hovey	Wing Ding, N6272
W E-1	WI	Oshkosh	EAAAAM	Evans	Volksplane, N6414
Weddell-Williams	LA	Patte	WWMAM	Weddell-Williams	Racer, 44
Weddell-Williams	OH	Cleve	FCAAM	Weddell-Williams	Racer, Model 44
Wee Bee	CA	San Diego	SDAM		Wee Bee
Weedhopper	NE	Minde	HWPV	Gypsy	Weedhopper
Weeks Solution	FL	Polk	FoF	Weeks	Solution
Weeks Special	FL	Polk	FoF	Weeks	Special
Westland Lysander Rep	AB-C	Edmonton	Edmonton	AAM	Westland
Westland Lysander	VA	Chantilly	NASMUVH	Westland	Lysander
Westland Lysander	MB-C	Brand	CATPM	Westland	Lysander
Westland Lysander	TX	Lubbock	SWM	Westland	Lysander
Westland Lysander 2/3 Scale	AB-C	Edmonton	Edmonton	AAM	
Westland Mk.III	BC-C	Langley	CMoF	Westland	McHardy, 1194, RCAF2349
Westland Mk.III	ON-C	Hamilton	CWH	Westland	Lysander, 2361
Westland Mk.III	ON-C	Ottaw	CAM	Westland	Lysander
Whirlwind	NY	Horsehead	WoE		
Whirlwind	NY	River	TFAC		
Whitaker Centerwing	WI	Oshkosh	EAAAAM	EAAAAM	Whitaker Centerwing, N121LW

Aircraft	State	City	Museum	Type	Reg.
White 1912 Monoplane	TX	McAll	McAll	Monoplane	
Wiley Post Biplane	OK	Oklahoma	OSM	White Post Biplane	
Wills Wing XC	ON-C	Ottaw	CAM	Wiley Wing XC	
Windecker Eagle I	MD	Suitland	PEGF	Wills Eagle	
Windstead Special	PA	Bethel	GAAM	Windecker Special	2297
Wiseman-Cooke	DC	Washi	USPM	Windstead	
Wiseman-Cooke	MD	Suitland	PEGF	Wiseman-Cooke	
Wisman-Prescott	KS	Wichita	KAM	Wiseman-Cooke	
Wisman-Prescott	WI	Oshkosh	WRA	Wittman Pusher	N4486E, "Bonzo"
Wittman W	WI	Oshkosh	EAAAAM	Wittman Pusher	
Wittman Buster	DC	Washi	NA&SM	Wittman Midwing	
Wittman DFA	WI	Oshkosh	EAAAAM	Wittman Buster	N1292, "Little Bonzo"
Wittman W-8C	NC	Hendersonville	WNCAM	Wittman Tailwind	
Wittman W-8C	TX	Dallas	FoF	Wittman Tailwind	N5747N
Wittman W-8C	WI	Oshkosh	WRA	Wittman Tailwind	
Wolf Boredom Fighter	MI	Kalamazoo	Kalamazoo	Wolf Boredom (AZ)	
Woodstock Glider	OK	Oklahoma	OSM	Woodstock Glider	N5553V
Woodstock Glider	WI	Fond du Lac	WAM	Woodstock Glider	
Woody Pusher	CO	Denver	WOTR	Woody Pusher	
Woody Pusher	FL	Lakel	SFAF	Woody Pusher	N100FQ
Woolaroc Airplane	OK	Bartl	WM	Woolaroc	NX-869

Aircraft	State	City	Museum
Wright Brothers B	CA	San Carlos	HNCAVM
Wright Brothers B	MD	College Park	CPAM
Wright Brothers B	OH	Dayton	NMUSAF
Wright Brothers B	PA	Phila	FI
Wright EX Vin Fiz	CA	Oakla	OWAM
Wright EX Vin Fiz	CA	San Diego	SDAM
Wright Ex Vin Fiz	DC	Washi	NA
Wright EX Vin Fiz	MA	Stow	BCF
Wright EX Vin Fiz	ME	Owls Head	OHTM
Wright EX Vin Fiz	VA	Suffolk	FF
Wright 1903	NE	Minde	HWPV
Wright Flyer	AL	Birmingham	SMF
Wright Flyer	AR	Little Rock	AEC
Wright Flyer	AZ	Tucson	PAM
Wright Flyer	CA	San Diego	SDAM

Aircraft	State	City	Museum	Reg.
Wright Flyer	CA	Santa Martin	WoHAM	
Wright Flyer	DC	Washi	NA&SM	
Wright Flyer	FL	Dayton	ERAU	
Wright Flyer	FL	Polk	FoF	
Wright Flyer	IL	Rantoul	OCM	
Wright Flyer	IN	Hagerstown	WWBP	
Wright Flyer	MI	Kalamazoo	KAHM	
Wright Flyer	NC	Mante	WBNM	
Wright Flyer	NC	Ralei	NCMoH	
Wright Flyer	NY	Rhine	ORA	
Wright Flyer	OH	Dayton	CP	
Wright Flyer	OH	Dayton	NMUSAF	18731, AK987
Wright Flyer	OH	Miamisburg	WBF	
Wright Flyer	OK	Wetherford	SA&SC	
Wright Flyer	OR	Mc Minnville	EAM	Flyable Replica

Aircraft	State	City	Museum	Manufacturer	Type	Serial
Wright Flyer	TX	Dallas	FoF			
Wright Flyer	WA	Hampton	VA&SM			
Wright Flyer	WA	Vancouver	PAM			
Wright Kitty Hawk	WI	Oshkosh	EAAAAM			
Wright Glider	CA	LAnge	CMoS&I			
Wright Glider	NC	Charlotte	CAM			
Wright Glider	NC	Mante	WBNM			
Wright Glider	NY	Elmir	NSM 5			
WSA-1	WA	Vancouver	PAM			
X-1	CA	Inglewood	PBR	Bell	Research	
X-1	DC	Washi	NA&SM	Bell	Research	"Glamorous Glennis"
X-1B	OH	Dayton	NMUSAF	Bell	Research	48-1385
X-2	CA	Chino	PoFAM			
X-3	OH	Dayton	NMUSAF	Douglas	Stiletto	49-2892
X-4	CA	Rosamond	EAFB	Northrop	Skylancer	
X-4	CO	CSpri	USAFA	Northrop	Skylancer	
X-4	OH	Dayton	NMUSAF	Northrop	Skylancer	46-677
X-4	WVA	Northrop	Northrop	Northrop	Skylancer	
X-5	OH	Dayton	NMUSAF	Bell	Swept Wing	50-1838
X-7	CA	Chino	PoFAM	Lockheed		
X-7	OH	Dayton	NMUSAF	Lockheed		
X-10	OH	Dayton	NMUSAF	North American		
X-13	CA	San Diego	SDAM	Ryan	Vertijet	41619
X-13	OH	Dayton	NMUSAF	Ryan	Vertijet	54-1620
X-15A-1	DC	Washi	NA&SM	North American	Research	56-6671
X-15A-2	AZ	Tucson	PAM	North American		
X-15A-2	OH	Dayton	NMUSAF	North American		
X-17	OH	Dayton	NMUSAF	Lockheed		
X-19	OH	Dayton	NMUSAF			62-12198A
X-21	CA	Rosamond	EAFB			55- 408
X-21	OH	Dayton	NMUSAF	Bell		
X-22	NY	Niagara Falls	NAM	Bell		151521
X-24B(SV-5J)	OH	Dayton	NMUSAF	Martin	Marietta	66-13551
X-25A	CA	Boron	SAM	Bensen	Gyrocopter	
X-25A	GA	Pooler	MoF	Bensen	Gyrocopter	N 61CN
X-25A	OH	Dayton	NMUSAF	Bensen	Gyrocopter	68-10770

Aircraft	State	City	Museum
Wright Glider	NY	Rhine	ORA
Wright Glider	VA	Richm	SMoV
Wright Glider 1900	VA	Sands	VAM
Wright Glider 1901	VA	Sands	VAM
Wright Glider 1902	VA	Sands	VAM
Wright Glider	WA	Seattle	MoF
Wright Aeroboat	OH	Wapak	NAA&SM

Designation	State	Location	Museum	Manufacturer	Name	Serial
X-25B	CA	McClellan	McCelAFB	Lockheed	Quiet One	67-15345
X-26B	AL	Ozark	USAAM	Sopery	Air Skimmer	
X-28	KS	Liberal	MAAM	Pereira	Air Skimmer	
X-28A	MI	Kalamazoo	KAHM	Sopery	Air Skimmer	
X-29	MI	Ypsilanti	YAF	Grumman		
X-29A	DC	Washi	NA&SM	Grumman	Fighter	82-0003
X-32	OH	Dayton	NMUSAF	Boeing	Joint Strike	
X-35	OH	Dayton	NMUSAF	Lockheed Martin	Joint Strike	
X-112	VA	Chantilly	NASMUVC	Lippisch	Aerofoil Boat	N 5961V
XA-6	WI	Oshkosh	EAAAAM	American Helicopter		
XB-25B	CA	Ramona	CR	Bensen	Gyro-Chute	
XC-99	CA	Rosamond	EAFB	Convair		
XC-142A	OH	Dayton	NMUSAF			Tilt Wing 1964
XF-81	OH	Dayton	NMUSAF	Consolidated	Vultee	44-91000
XF-81	OH	Dayton	NMUSAF	Consolidated	Vultee	44-91001
XF15C-1	CT	Winds	NEAM	Curtiss-Wright	Stingaree	01215
XF15C-1	RI	NKing	QAM	Curtiss-Wright	Stingaree	
XF2Y-1	MD	Balti	OMA	Convair	Sea Dart	135764
XF2Y-1	MD	Suitland	PEGF	Convair	Sea Dart	135765
YF2Y-1	PA	Willow Grove	NVHAA	Convair	Sea Dart	135765
XF2Y-1	WA	Seattle	MoF	Convair	Sea Dart	135763
XF2Y-1(SF)	FL	Lakel	SFAF	Convair	Sea Dart	
YF2Y-1	CA	San Diego	SDAM	Convair	Sea Dart	
XFV-1	FL	Lakel	SFAF	Lockheed	Salmon	138657
XFV-1	FL	Pensacola	NMoNA	Lockheed		
XFY-1	MD	Suitland	PEGF	Convair	VTO	31400 N 54205
XJL-1	AZ	Tucson	PAM	Columbia	Columbia	
XO-60	VA	Chantilly	NASMUVC	Kellett	Autogiro	
XR-4	MD	Suitland	PEGF	Kellett	Autogiro	
XRG-65	PA	WChes	AHM	Glaticopter	Helicopter	
XROE	CA	San Carlos	HNCAVM	Goodyear		4004
XROE	MD	Lexington	PRNAM	Goodyear	Inflatoplane	
XROE-1	AL	Ozark	USAAM			
XRON-1	NY	Elmira	B&ECN&SP	Gyrodyne	Rotorcycle	4014
XRON-1	NY	Garde	CoAM	Gyrodyne	Rotorcycle	4012
YRON-1	VA	Quantico	NMMC	Gyrodyne	Rotorcycle	

Conovertiplane

Aircraft	State	Location	Collection	Notes
XV-1	MD	Suitland	PEGF	
XV-15	VA	Chantilly	NASMUVC	

Yak — Yakovlev

Aircraft	State	Location	Collection	Notes
Yak 3	CA	Camarillo	CAF-SCW	On loan
Yak 3	ID	Nampa	WAM	
Yak 3UA	CA	Santa Monica	MoF	NX854DP
Yak 9	WA	Seattle	MoF	
Yak 11 Moose	CA	Chino	PoFAM	
Yak 12	NY	Bayport	BA	
Yak 18 Max	CA	Chino	PoFAM	
Yak 18 Max	MD	Suitland	PEGF	1160314
Yak 18	VA	Suffolk	FF	832604
Yak 50	OR	Mc Minnville	EAM	
Yak 52	CA	Santa Rosa	PCAM	
Yak 52	FL	Miami	WOM	
Yak 52	NY	New Windsor	RSAM	
Yak 55	VA	Suffolk	FF	

Aircraft	State	Location	Collection	Name/Notes	Reg.
YF-22	OH	Dayton	NMUSAF		
Yokosuka P1Y1c	MD	Suitland	PEGF	Yokosuka — Frances	
Youngsters Simulator	KY	Lexington	AmoK	Youngsters — Simulator	
YPT-9B	CA	Chino	YAM		6004 N 795H
YS-11A-600	TX	Ladero	Airport	Nihon	N-173RV
YS-11	IN	Peru	GAM		
Zenair Zenith	MI	Kalamazoo	KAM	Zenair — Zenith	Storage
Zenair Zenith	MO	Maryland Hts	HARM	Zenair — Zenith	
Zenair Zenith	ON-C	Ottawa	CAM	Zenair — Zenith	C-GOVK
Zenair Zenith	ON-C	Toronto	TAM	Zenair — Zenith	
Zephyr Zal	CT	Winds	NEAM	Zephyr — Zal	
Zimmerman	MD	Suitland	PEGF	Zimmerman — Flying Platform	
Zlin 526M	CA	Santa Rosa	PCAM	Zlin	
Zoegling Glider Rep	NM	Moriarty	SSM	Zoegling — Glider	Z-12
Zoegling Glider	SK-C	MJaw	WDM	Zoegling — Glider	141561
ZPG Rudder	FL	Pensacola	NMoNA	ZRG — Rudder	N 111MG
Zugvogel III-B	AZ	Tucson	PAM	Zugvogel	

Armored Vehicles

Personnel Carrier:

Vehicle	State	Location	Collection	Notes	Type
Fort T-16	OH	Norwalk	FmoMH		Armored Personel
Mark VII Ferrett	OH	Norwalk	FmoMH	British	Armored Car
WC-46	TX	Midland	AAHM		Ambulance
M-2A1	CT	Danbury	MMoSNE		Halftrack
M3A	CA	Chino	YAM		Armored Halftrack
M3	AL	Starke	CBM		Half Track

Model	State	Location	Org	Type	Extra
M3	LA	New Orleans	DDM	Half Track	
M4-81	TX	Midland	AAHM	Half Track	
M16	OH	Hubbard	WWIIVM	Half Track	A-27
M-20	CT	Danbury	MmoSNE	Armored Car	
M75 APC	AL	Mobile	BMP	Armored Personel	16196782
M84 APC	NY	Buffalo	B&ECNP	Armored Personel	
M106	CA	Chino	YAM	Mortar Track	
M578	CT	Danbury	MmoSNE	Armored Wrecker	
M113	CA	Chino	YAM	Armored Personel	

Cannons:

Model	State	Location	Org	Type	Extra
25MM	CT	Danbury	MmoSNE	Anti-Tank Gun	
3.7CM	CT	Danbury	MmoSNE	Anti-Tank Gun	
37MM	CT	Danbury	MmoSNE	Anti-Aircraft Gun	
5 Inch	CT	Danbury	MmoSNE	Anti-Aircraft Gun	
5	IL	Edgew	KAALP	Howitzer	
M1	CT	Danbury	MmoSNE	57mm Anti-Tank Gun	
M108	CT	Danbury	MmoSNE	Howitzer	
M110A2	MO	SLoui	NPRC	Howitzer	
M110A2	OH	Groveport	MMM	Howitzer	
M110A2	OH	Hubbard	WWIIVM	Howitzer	
M110A2	TX	Pampa	FM	Howitzer	
M115	IN	Atterbury	CAM&MC	Howitzer	
M1918A3	IN	Atterbury	CAM&MC	Schneider	155mm
M3A1	CT	Danbury	MmoSNE	37mm Anti-Tank Gun	
M5	CT	Danbury	MmoSNE	3 Inch Anti-Tank Gun	
M5	IN	Atterbury	CAM&MC		
M6AZ	IL	Collinsville	AM 365	Howitzer	155mm
M9	IL	Sprin	S.ArmyNG	Howitzer	
WWI Howitzer	IL	Salem		Howitzer	

Tanks:

Type	State	City	Org	Notes
Tank	FL	W palm BEach	S.ArmyNG	391BG
Tank	IL	Sprin	VFW	
Tank	IN	Van Buren	KCH	
Tank M-3A3	IN	Warsaw	City Park	
Tank	NB	Beaver City	MMA	
Tank	TX	Harli	ING	
Tanks	IA	Des Moines	MMM	
Tank M-1A	IL	Russell	YAM	Abrams
Tank M-3	CA	Chino	City Hall	Lee/Grant
Tank M-3	CT	New Milford	PAAM	Lee/Grant
Tank M-3	NJ	Dover	NMofPW	
Tank M-3	TX	Frede		

GPS: N40(08.102), W99(50.025)

6 Different Tanks
In Movie "Curage Under Fire"

M-4 Stuart Sherman Tank

Type	State	City	Org	Notes
Tank M-4	AL	Mobile	BMP	
Tank M-4	AL	Starke	CBM	
Tank M-4	CA	Chino	PoF	D51011
Tank M-4	IN	Scottsburg	INGC	
Tank M-4	IN	Warsaw	Court Hoise	
Tank M-4	LA	Many	VFW	
Tank M-4	ON-C	Oshaw	OAM&IM	
Tank M-4	WI	Appleton	VFW	
Tank M-4	IL	Russell	MMM	
Tank M-4	IL	Russell	MMM	D706
Tank M-4 Turret	TX	Midland	AAHM	70676A,
Tank M-4	IL	Wheat	Cantigny	
Tank M-4A1	IN	Atterbury	CAM&MC	2-2084
Tank M-4A1	IN	Atterbury	CAM&MC	1-2451
Tank M-8	PA	Tough	CFCM	Barlett · Hovercraft
Tank M-18C	MD	Suitland	PEGF	Mooney · Mite
Tank M-19	OH	Hubbard	WW IIVM	Duster
Tank M-24	ON-C	Oshaw	OAM&IM	
Tank M-4A1E8	OH	Hubbard	WWIIVM	
Tank M-4A3(75)	IN	Sunman	AM	
Tank M-4A3	LA	New Orleans	DDM	
Tank M-4A3	CA	S El Monte	ASMH	
Tank M-4A3	OH	Hubbard	WWIIVM	
Tank M-4A3	SC	Citadel	CC	
Tank M-4A3	TX	FtBii	TCRM	
Tank M-4A3E8	IL	Wheaton	FDM	
Tank M-4A3E8	CA	S El Monte	ASMH	
Tank M-5	IL	Wheaton	FDM	
Tank M-5A	IL	Russell	MMM	
Tank M-5A1	OH	Carroll	HAS	C105826
Tank M-7B1	OH	Hubbard	WWIIVM	M5058147 · 105 mm
Tank M-7	IL	Russell	MMM	105 mm

Model	State	City	Code	Maker	Type	Notes
Tank M-26	AL	Mobile	BMP		Pershing	E10609 / Korean
Tank M-31	NJ	Dover	PAAM		Pershing	
Tank M-37	IL	Russell	MMM	Stuart	105 mm	
Tank M-38	IL	Russell	MMM	Stuart	105 mm	
Tank M-38A1	IL	Russell	MMM	Stuart		
Tank M-41	IL	Wheaton	FDM	Walker	Walker Bulldog	254
Tank M-41	IN	Atterbury	CAM&MC	Stuart	Walker Bulldog	38-1-1, 138
Tank M-41	IN	Atterbury	CAM&MC	Stuart	Walker Bulldog	
Tank M-41	IN	Atterbury	CAM&MC	Stuart	Walker Bulldog	
Tank M-41	NY	Buffalo	B&ECNP	Walker	Walker Bulldog	
Tank M-41	WA	Tilli	CMANGP	Walker	Walker Bulldog	
Tank M-41	IL	Russell	MMM	Walker	Walker Bulldog	#26
Tank M-42A1	AL	Mobile	BMP	General Motors	Duster	112L729
Tank M-42 Twin	IN	Atterbury	CAM&MC	General Motors	Duster	
Tank M-42 Twin	NY	NYC	ISASM	General Motors	Duster	
Tank M-42 Twin	OH	Groveport	MMM	General Motors	Duster	40 mm
Tank M-42 Twin	OH	Norwalk	FMoMH	General Motors	Duster	40 mm
Tank M-42 Twin	PA	Smethport	AAAM	General Motors	Duster	40 mm
Tank M-42 Twin	IL	Russell	MMM	General Motors	Duster	40 mm

M-46 Chrysler Patton Tank

Model	State	City	Code	Serial / Notes
Tank M-46	IL	Wheat	Cantigny	J26E4
Tank M-46	IN	Cromw	City	
Tank M-46	IL	Russell	MMM	
Tank M-47	CA	S El Monte	ASMH	
Tank M-47	CT	Danbury	MMoSNE	
Tank M-47	IL	Wheat	FDM	2313
Tank M-47	IN	Atterbury	CAM&MC	A00193, 753710338
Tank M-47	IN	Atterbury	CAM&MC	38-11, 138, K7389955 Ser 4
Tank M-47	OH	Groveport	MMM	331
Tank M-47	IL	Russell	MMM	
Tank M-48	CA	S El Monte	ASMH	
Tank M-48	CT	Danbury	MMoSNE	
Tank M-48	IL	Wheat	FDM	2650
Tank M-48	IN	Jeffersonville	USAR	
Tank M-48	NC	C Lejuene	CL	
Tank M-48A1	AL	Mobile	BMP	8369684
Tank M-48A1	CA	S El Monte	ASMH	
Tank M-48A1	PA	Smethport	AAAM	

Model	State	City	Code	Maker	Notes
Tank M50	IN	Atterbury	CAM&MC	Douglas	OW TOS
Tank M-51	NJ	Dover	PAAM		Six 106mm's

M-60 Chryler Patton Tank

Model	State	City	Code	Notes
Tank M-60	AL	Starke	CBM	
Tank M-60	AL	Tuscalloosa	I-20/59	
Tank M-60	AR	Littl	LRAFB	
Tank M-60	CA	Imperial	PM	
Tank M-60	CT	Danbury	MMoSNE	

Item	State	City	Museum	Note	Designation / Mfr	Type	State 2	City 2	Museum 2	Note 2
Tank M-60	D.C.	Washington	USS&AH		Tank M-60		OH	Norwalk	FMoMH	8208
Tank M-60	IL	Wheaton	FDM		Tank M-60		WI	Appleton	FMoMH	
Tank M-60	IN	Atterbury	CAM&MC	280	Tank M-60A1		AL	Mobile	BMP	
Tank M-60	IN	South Bend	MHP	1201, 105mm	Tank M-60A1		CA	S El Monte	ASMH	
Tank M-60	KS	Emporia	VP		Tank M-60A1		KY	Louisville	KNG	
Tank M-60	KY	Middleboro	LS		Tank M-60A-1		MI	Sterling Hts	FHCMP	
Tank M-60	NY	NYC	ISASM		Tank M-60A-3		TN	Caryville	CP	
Tank M-60	NC	C Lejuene	CL		Tank M-60		IL	Russell	MMM	
Tank M551	CA	S El Monte	ASMH		General Motors	Sheridan				
Tank M551	CT	Danbury	MMoSNE		General Motors	Sheridan				
Tank M551	IL	Wheaton	FDM		General Motors	Sheridan				725
Tank M551A	NC	Charlotte	CAM		General Motors	Sheridan				1447 Airborne
Tank M551A	NC	Fayetteville	A&SOM		General Motors	Sheridan				
Tank MBT-70	CT	Danbury	MMoSNE			Medium Tank				
Tank MK3	TX	Frede	NMofPW							
Tank T-55	AL	Mobile	BMP			Pershing				1184 USATTU
Tank T-26E4	IL	Wheat	FDM							
Tanks	WA	Tacom	FL							
Tanks	VA	Triangle	NMMC							

Missiles

Item	State	City	Museum	Mfr	Type	Note
Missile	AZ	Green	TMM		Missile	
Missile	CA	Point	PMMP		Missile	
Missile	FL	Cocoa	USAFSM		Missile	
Missile	GA	Cochr	CityPark		Missile	
Missile	WA	Tacom	FL		Missile	
Missile Silo	AZ	Green Valley	TMM		Titan II	571-7
Missile Silo	SD	Rapid City	SDA&SM		Minuteman	
ADM-20C	AZ	Tucson	PAM	McDonnell	Quail	
ADM-20C	CA	McClellan	McCelAFB	McDonnell	Quail	
ADM-20C	OH	Dayton	NMUSAF	McDonnell	Quail	
ADM-20C	SD	Rapid City	SDA&SM	McDonnell	Quail	
ADM-20C-40-MC	UT	Ogden	HAM	McDonnell	Quail	
AGM-12	AZ	Tucson	PAM	Maxson	Bullpup	D79
AGM-12C	NY	Garde	CoAM	Maxson	Bullpup	
AGM-22A	NJ	Dover	PAAM			

Designation	State	City	Museum	Manufacturer	Name	Serial
AIM-9J	CA	China Lake	USNMAT	Ford	Sidewinder	71-1812
AIM-9J	GA	Pooler	MoF	Ford	Sidewinder	
AIM-26	UT	Ogden	HAM	Hughes	Falcon	
AIM-26A	GA	Pooler	MoF		Super Falcon	
AIM/RIM-7	NY	Horsehead	WoE		Sparrow	
AIM-54	CA	China Lake	USNMAT	Hughes	Phoenix	
AIM-54	NC	Charlotte	CAM	Hughes	Phoenix	
AIM-120	UT	Ogden	HAM	Hughes	AMRAAM	
AIR-2A	GA	Pooler	MoF	McDonnell/Douglas	Genie	
AIR-2A	UT	Ogden	HAM	McDonnell/Douglas	Genie	
AIR-21	AZ	Tucson	PAM	Douglas	Genie	TE-04813
AQM-34	AZ	Tucson	PAM	Teledyne-Ryan	Compass Dawn	69-6108
AQM-34	CA	Rosamond	EAFB	Ryan	Firebee	
AQM-34	CA	San Diego	SDAM	Ryan	Firebee	
AQM-34L	AZ	Tucson	PAM	Teledyne-Ryan	Compass Bin	69-432
AQM-34L	OH	Dayton	NMUSAF	Teledyne-Ryan	Compass Bin	
AQM-34L	TX	San Antonio	VMP	Teledyne-Ryan	Compass Bin	
AQM-34L	UT	Ogden	HAFBM	Teledyne-Ryan	Compass Bin	Firebee
AQM-34N	OH	Dayton	NMUSAF	Teledyne-Ryan	Compass Bin	74-2147
AQM-34V	GA	Pooler	MoF			
AQM-37A	CA	Chino	YAM	Maxson	Jayhawk Drone	
AQM-37A	FL	Pensacola	NMoNA	Maxson	Jayhawk Drone	
AQM-37A	NY	Garde	CoAM	Maxson	Jayhawk Drone	
AQM-91A	OH	Dayton	NMUSAF	Ryan	Drone	
AQM-91A	SC	FLore	FA&MM	Ryan	Drone	

BQM-34 Ryan Firebee

Designation	State	City	Museum	Manufacturer	Name
BQM-34	OH	Dayton	NMUSAF		
BQM-34A	CA	Rosamond	EAFB		
BQM-34A	FL	Panama City	TAFB		
BQM-34A	FL	Shalimar	USAFAM		
BQM-34F	CA	San Diego	SDAM		
BQM-34F	FL	Panama City	TAFB		
BQM-34F	FL	Shalimar	USAFAM		
BQM-34F	GA	Pooler	MoF		
BQM-34F	OH	Dayton	NMUSAF		
BQM-34S	CA	San Diego	SDAM		
BQM-126A	CA	Chino	YAM	Beechcraft	Target Drone
BGM-109	CA	China Lake	USNMAT	Convair	Tomahawk
BGM-109	CA	San Diego	SDAM	Convair	Tomahawk

Designation	State	City	Museum	Manufacturer	Name	Notes
BGM-109	NJ	Lexington	NASW AM	Convair	Tomahawk	
BGM-109	PA	Phila	FI			
BGM-109A	CA	Simi Valley	RRL	General Dynamics	Gryphon	1 of 8 in the world
BGM-109A	OH	Dayton	NMUSAF	General Dynamics	Gryphon	
BGM-109C	TX	Dallas	FoF	General Dynamics	Gryphon	12436C0001
BGM-109G	AZ	Tucson	PAM	General Dynamics	Gryphon	
BLU-80B	CA	China Lake	USNMAT			
BLU-97	CA	China Lake	USNMAT			
BGM-109G	UT	Ogden	HAM	General Dynamics	Gryphon	280
BQM-34	CA	Chino	YAM		Firebee	
BQM-74	CA	Chino	YAM		Chucker	
BQM-126	CA	Chino	YAM			
CBU Mk 20	UT	Ogden	HAM	Marquardt	Rockeye II	
CBU-59	CA	China Lake	USNMAT	Marquardt	Rockeye	
CBU-72	CA	China Lake	USNMAT	Marquardt	Rockeye	
CGM-13	FL	Panama City	TAFB		Mace	
CGM-13B	FL	Wildwood	ALP-18		Mace	
CGM-13B	GA	Pooler	AFASSOC		Mace	
CGM-13B	OH	Dayton	NMUSAF		Mace	
CGM-16	CA	El Cajon	SDAMGF	General Dynamics / Convair	Atlas ICBM	59-2051
CGM-16	OH	Dayton	NMUSAF	General Dynamics / Convair	Atlas ICBM	
CIM-10A	CO	CO Springs	EJPSCM	Boeing	Bomarc	
CIM-10A	GA	Pooler	MoF	Boeing	Bomarc 59-1953	
CIM-10A	OH	Dayton	NMUSAF	Boeing	Bomarc	
CIM-10A	UT	Ogden	HAM	Boeing	Bomarc	
CIM-10B	VA	Hampton	APM	Boeing	Bomarc	
Drone Missile	IL	Russell	MMM		Drone Missile	
GAM-54	AZ	Grand Canyon	PoFGCVA	Northrop	Crossbow	
GAM-63	CA	Atwater	CAM	McDonnell	Quail	
GAM-63	OK	Midwe	ALP170			
GAM-63(X)	OH	Dayton	NMUSAF	Bell	Rascal	
GAM-67(X)	CA	Banning	Airport		Crossbow	64-2965
GAM-67(X)	WA	Bridg	CityPark			
GAM-72	AL	Montg	GAFB	McDonnell	Quail	
GAM-72	CA	Oakland	WAM	McDonnell	Quail	
GAM-77	CA	Farfield	DA&SM		Hound Dog	
GAM-77	FL	Shalimar	USAFAM		Hound Dog	

Designation	State	City	Museum	Manufacturer	Name	Notes
GBU-8	UT	Ogden	HAM	Rockwell	Paveway II	
GBU-12	UT	Ogden	HAM	Raytheon		
GBU-15	UT	Ogden	HAM	Rockwell	Paveway III	
GBU-24B	UT	Ogden	HAM	Raytheon		
Grumman Rigel	NY	Garde	CoAM	Grumman	Rigel	
Hawk Missile	IL	Russell	MMM		Hawk	
HGM-25A	OH	Dayton	NMUSAF		Titan I	
IM-99	FL	Shalimar	USAFAM	Boeing	Bomarc	
IRBM	TX	Dallas	FoF		Jupiter	
JB-2	AL	Wasilla	MoAT&I	Republic	Loon	
JB-2	CT	Winds	NEAM	Republic	Loon	
JB-2	IL	Milford	LC	Republic	Loon	
JB-2	NY	Garde	CoAM	Republic	Loon	Buzz Bomb
KD2R	AB-C	Langley	CMoF&T	Radioplane	Target Drone	1268
KD2G-2	FL	Pensacola	NMoNA	Globe	Target Drone	
KD6G-2	AZ	Tucson	PAM	Globe	Cardinal Drone	633
KD6G-2	CA	Chino	YAM	Globe	Cardinal Drone	
KDB-1	CA	Chino	YAM	Beech	Firefly Drone	
KDB-1	FL	Pensacola	NMoNA			
Kettering Bug Torpedo	OH	Dayton	NMUSAF	Kettering	Bug Torpedo	
LGM-25C(N-10)	AZ	Tucson	PAM	Martin Marietta	Titan II 60- 8817, 9510003, "Small Paul's Pocket Rocket"	
LGM-25C(N-10)	NY	Coron	NYHoS	Martin Marietta	Titan II	Gemini
LGM-118	OH	Dayton	NMUSAF	Martin Marietta	Peacekeeper	
LGM-118A	UT	Ogden	HAM	Martin Marietta	Peacekeeper	
LGM-30	CA	Riverside	MAFM	Boeing	Minuteman II	
LGM-30	OH	Dayton	NMUSAF	Boeing	Minuteman II	
LGM-30A	OH	Dayton	NMUSAF	Boeing	Minuteman I	
LGM-30G	OH	Dayton	NMUSAF	Boeing	Minuteman III	
LTV	NC	Hickory	HRA			
LTV	OH	Dayton	NMUSAF			
M-41	CA	Chino	YAM		AST	
Maxi-Decoy	CA	Chino	YAM		Redeye	
MGM-1	GA	Hawki	CityPark		Maxi-Decoy	
MGM-5	KS	Topeka	CAM	Firestone Tire-JPL	Corporal M2 From Ft Riley, KS	
MGM-5	VA	Hampton	HAP	Firestone Tire-JPL	Corporal M2	
MGM-5	IL	Russell	MMM	Firestone Tire-JPL	Corporal M2	
MGM-13A	FL	Shalimar	USAFAM	Martin	Mace	

Model	State	City	Facility	Manufacturer	Missile Name	Number
MGM-13B	AR	Pocah	VWF	Martin	Mace	62863
MGM-13B	GA	Calhoun	WAM	Martin	Mace	
MGM-13B	GA	Pooler	I-75 E45	Martin	Mace	58-1465
MGM-13B	GA	Pooler	MoF	Martin	Mace	
MGM-13B	PA	Mildr	ALP452	Martin	Mace	
MGM-18	IL	Russell	MMM		Lacrosse	
MGM-52	IL	Orland Hills	VoOH		Lance	
MGM-109	AZ	Tucson	PAM	General Dynamics	Cruise	
LGM-30A	IL	Rantoul	OCAM		Minuteman	
LGM-30F	AZ	Tucson	PAM		Minuteman	
LGM-30F	ND	Grand Forks	GFAFB		Minuteman	
LGM-30F Trainer	OH	Dayton	NMUSAF		Missile Trainer	
LGM-30F	SD	Rapid City	SDA&SM		Minuteman	
MQM-107	CA	Chino	YAM		Streaker	
MGR1B	IL	Russell	RMM		Honest John	
MGR1B	KS	Topeka	CAM	Douglas	Honest John	49
MGR1B	KS	Topeka	CAM	Douglas	Honest John	68.165
MGR1B	NC	Charlotte	CAM	Douglas	Honest John	54
M139C Launcher	IN	Atterbury	CAM&MC		Honest John	762mm, 22 Miles
XM33 Launcher	IN	Atterbury	CAM&MC		Honest John	762mm, 22 Miles
NIM-3	CO	CSpri	EJPSCM	Western Electric	Nike Ajax	
NIM-3	IL	Russell	MMM		Nike	2105
NIM-3	KS	Topeka	CAm		Nike-Ajax	64.87
NIM-3	KS	Topeka	CAm		Nike-Ajax	
NIM-3	MD	Handc	VFW	Western Electric	Nike Ajax	
NIM-3	SD	Rapid City	SDA&SM	Western Electric	Nike-Ajax	
NIM-3	VA	Hampton	APM	Western Electric	Nike Ajax	
NIM-14	CO	CSpri	EJPSCM	Western Electric	Nike Hercules	
NIM-14	KS	Topeka	CAM	Western Electric	Nike Hercules	64.87
NIM-14	VA	Hampton	APM	Western Electric	Nike Hercules	
NIM-14	WA	Ft.Lewis	Ft.Lewis	Western Electric	Nike Hercules	
Pershing II	VA	Hampton	VA&SM		Pershing II	
Posedon Missile	DC	Washi	NM		Posedon	
Rockets	AL	Hunts	AS&RC			
Rockets	FL	Cocoa	USAFSM			
Rockets	FL	Merri	KSC			
Rockets	MD	Green	NASAGVC			

Name	State	City	Collection	Manufacturer	Type	Notes
Rockets	MI	Jacks	MSCJCC			
Rockets	NM	Las Cruces	WSMP			
Rockets	NM	Roswe	RM&AC			
SA- 3 GOA	NV	Las Vegas	NAFB			
SA- 8	NV	Las Vegas	NAFB			
SAM S-2A	OH	Dayton	NMUSAF	Soviet	Missile Transporter	
SAM S-2A	TX	Paris	FTAM	Soviet	Launch Vehicle	
SAM AT Replica	NY	Garde	CoAM	Sperry	Missile	
SAM M1 Replica	NY	Garde	CoAM	Sperry		
SAM-N-7(SM-2)	NY	Garden	CoAM	Sperry		
SAM-N-8	NC	Surf City	TIM	Bendiz/McDonnell	Terrier	
SAM-N-8	SC	MtPleasant	PPM	Bendiz/McDonnell	Talos	# 114
SICM	OH	Dayton	NMUSAF	Boeing	Talos	
SM-61	CA	Chino	YAM	Standard	Midgetman	
SM-62	OH	Dayton	NMUSAF	Northrop	Snark	
SM-62A(XSM)	UT	Ogden	HAM	Northrop	Snark	53-8183
SM-65	OH	Dayton	NMUSAF	Northrop	Atlas	
SM-68(B-68)	AZ	Tucson	PAM	Martin Marietta	Titan I	4515
SM-68(B-68)	FL	Kissi	HJFPPH	Martin Marietta	Titan I	Lox/Kerosene Fuel
SM-68(B-68)	GA	Corde	I-75 E32	Martin Marietta	Titan I	
SM-68	OH	Dayton	NMUSAF	Northrop	Titan II	N2O4/Aerozine Fuel
SM-68(B-68)	NE	Kimba	CityPark	Martin Marietta	Titan I	
SM-68(B-68)	SC	FLore	FA&MM	Martin Marietta	Titan I	
SM-72	PA	Hagerstown	HAM	Fairchild	Goose	
SM-78(PGM-19)	VA	Hampton	APM	Chrysler	Jupiter	58-5282
Sperry Messenger	OR	Hood	WAAAM	Sperry	Messenger	
SSM-N-8	NC	Charlotte	CAM	Chance-Vought	Regulus 1	
T-72	NV	Las Vegas	NAFB		Missile Launcher	
Talos Rocket	SC	Topsail Beach	TIM			
Tartar	KS	Topeka	CAM		Missile	Navy
Titan II Missile	CA	Paso Robles	EWM		Upper Stage	Titan I
Titan I Missile	OR	Mc Minnville	EGM		Titan I	
Titan I Missile	SD	Rapid City	SDA&SM		Titan I	
TM-61	AZ	Grand Canyon	PoFGCVA	Martin	Missile	
TM-61A	GA	Pooler	MoF	Martin	Matador	52-1891
TM-61A	OH	Dayton	NMUSAF	Martin	Matador	
TM-61C	NC	Charlotte	CAM	Martin	Matador	

Name	State	Location	Code	Manufacturer	Type	Notes
TM-61C	SC	FLore	FA&MM	Martin	Matador	
Torpedo Mk.14	MI	Sterling Hts	FHCMP	US Navy	Torpedo	
UGM-27	CA	China Lake	USNMAT			
YIM-99B	WA	Brews	CityPark			
YCGM-121B	CA	Chino	YAM	Boeing	Brave 200	"Pave Tiger"
YCGM-121B	OH	Dayton	NMUSAF	Boeing	Brave 200	"Seek Spinner"
YCGM	CA	Chino	YAM	Boeing	Brave 300	
YCGM	OK	Oklahoma	OSM	Boeing	Brave 300	
YO3A	CA	San Carlos	HNCAVM	Lockheed	Quiet Star	
YQM-94A RPV	OH	Dayton	NMUSAF	Boeing	Compass Cope B	
YQM-98A Drone	AZ	Tucson	PAM			72- 1872

Naval Ships

Name	State	Location	Code	Manufacturer	Type	Notes
CSS Neuse	NC	Kinston	CSS N&GCM	Confederate Navy	Ironclad Gunboat	"Ram" 1862, 1 of 3 survor out of 22
German Seehund	DC	Washi	NM	German WWII	Submarine	
HMCS Haida	ONT	Hamilton	OP	Vickers Armstrong	Destroyer	Tribal Class, # G63
Japanese Kaiten II	NJ	Hackensack	SMA-NJNM	Japanese WWII	Submarine	
LCVP	LA	New Orleans	DDM	Higgins	Landing Craft	
LCVP	OH	Groveport	MMM	Higgins	Landing Craft	PA 36-7
LST 325	IN	Evansville				
PBR	AL	Mobile	BMP		River Boat	
PBR	IL	Russell	MMM		River Boat	31RP7331
PBR	IL	Russell	MMM		River Boat	NSN 1940000BOAT, Movie "Apocalypse Now"
PBR Mk I	SC	Mt Pleasant	PP		Patrol Boat River	2 at this location
PBR	WI	Pleasant Prairie	BMP		River Boat	
PT-309	TX	Fredericksburg	NmotPW	Higgins	Patrol Boat	
PT-617	MA	Fall	USSMM	Higgins	Patrol Boat	
PTF-17	NY	Buffalo	BECNSP		Patrol Boat Fast	Mark I
Russian Foxtrot Class	CA	Long Beach	TQM	Sudomekh Shipyard	Submarine	b-427, "Scorpion"
Russian Juliett 484	RI	Providence	RSM	Gorky Shipyard	Juliett	K-77
SS American Victory	FL	Tampa	AVMM&MS		Liberty Ship	Built 1968
SS Keewatin	MI	Douglas	KMM		Passenger Steamer	
SS Queen Mary	CA	Long	QM&SG		Ocean Liner	
U-505	IL	Chicago	CS&IM	German	Submarine	U-505
USCG Taney	MD	Baltimore	BMM		Cutter	
USD-4	GA	Agust	FG			
USD-5	GA	Agust	FG			

Ship	State	Location	Code	Type	No.
USF Constitution	MA	Boston	BIH	Frigate	
USF Constellation	MD	Baltimore	AM	Frigate Sister Ship	
USS Airzona	HI	Honolulu		Battleship	BB- 39
USS Alabama	AL	Mobile	BMP	Battleship	BB- 60
USS Becuna	PA	Philadelphia	ISM		
USS Blueback	OR	Portland	OmoS&I	Submarine	SS-581
USS Bowfin	HI	Honolulu	AM	Submarine	SS-287
USS Cassin Young	MA	Boston	USSC	Destroyer	DD-793, DestroyerDD-793
USS Chesapeake	MD	Baltimore	BMM	Lightship	
USS Clamagore	SC	Mt Pleasant	PPM	Submarine	SS-343
USS Cobia	WI	Manit	WMM	Submarine	SS-245
USS Cod	OH	Cleveland	SUSSC	Submarine	SS-224
USS Croaker	NY	Buffalo	B&ECN&SP	Submarine	SSK-246
USS Drum	AL	Mobile	BMP	Submarine	SS-228
USS Fall River	MA	Fall River	BC	Cruiser	
USS Growler	NY	NYC	ISASM	Submarine	SS-215
USS Guadalcanal	NY	NYC	ISASM	Helicopter Carrier	LPH- 7
USS Hazard	NB	Omaha	FP	Mine Sweeper	AM-240
USS Helena Parts	OH	Newcomerstown	NNM		CL50
USS Hornet	CA	Alameda	USSH	Aircraft Carrier	
USS Ingham	SC	Mt Pleasant	PPM	Coast Guard Cutter	35
USS Intelligent Whale	NJ	Sea Grit	NJNGMM	Submarine	
USS Intrepid	NY	NYC	ISASM	Aircraft Carrier	CVA-11
USS Jeremiah O'Brian	CA	SFransico	SF	Liberty Ship	
USS JP Kennedy	MA	Fall	USSMM	Destroyer	DD-850
USS John Brown	MD	Baltimore	PLS	Liberty Ship	
USS Kidd	LA	BRoug	LNWM	Destroyer	DD-661
USS LSM-45	NB	Omaha	FP	Landing Ship	
USS Laffey	SC	Mt Pleasant	PPM	Destroyer	DD-724
USS Lane Victory	CA	San Diego	PPM	Liberty Ship	
USS Lexington	TX	C Christi	USS Lexi	Aircraft Carrier	CV- 16
USS Lionfish	MA	Fall	USSMM	Submarine	SS-298
USS Ling	NJ	Hackensack	SMA-NJNM	Submarine	SS-297
USS Little Rock	NY	Buffalo	B&ECNP	Cruiser	CLG-4
USS Maiale SSB	DC	W ashi	NM	Submarine	
USS Marlin	NB	Omaha	FP	Submarine	SST-2, T-2
USS Massachusetts	MA	Fall	USSMM	Battleship	BB- 59

Ship	State	City	Abbrev.	Note	Type	Designation
USS Misouri	HI	Honolua	AM		Battleship	BB-63
USS New Jersey	NJ	Camden	PSNS		Battleship	BB-62
USS North Carolina	NC	Wilmi	USSNCBC	NY Navy Shipyard	Battleship	BB-55< "Showboat"
USS Olympia	PA	Philadelphia	ISM			
USS Orleck	TX	Orange	STWM		Destroyer	DD-886
USS Pamanito	CA	San Franciso	USSC		Submarine	SS-387
USS Pinato Tower	TX	Frede	NMotPW		Submarine	
USS Radford Parts	OH	Newcomerstown	NNM		Destroyer	DD-446
USS Requin	PA	Pittsburg	CSC		Submarine	SS-481
USS Roncador Tower	CA	San Francisco		MPA	Submarine	SS-301
USS Salem	MA	Quincy	USN&SM		Battleship	CA-139, Flagship, Graf Spee Movie
USS Saratoga	RI	Providence	USSSM		Aircraft Carrier	CV-60
USS Savannah	VA	Newpo				
USS Silversides	MI	Muske	USS SILV		Submarine	SS-236
USS Slater	NY	Albany	USS S		Destroyer	DE-766
USS Sullivans	NY	Buffalo	B&ECNP		Destroyer	DD-537
USS Texas	TX	LaPor	USS Texa		Battleship	BB-35
USS Towers	NB	Omaha	FP		Captains Gig	DDG-9
USS Torsk	MD	Baltimore	BMM		Submarine	
USS Turner Joy	WA	Breme	PSNS		Destroyer	DD-951
USS Turtle	DC	Washi	NM		Submarine	
USS Wisconsin	VA	Norfolk	TBW		Battleship	BB-64
USS Yorktown	SC	Mt Pleasant	PPM		Aircraft Carrier	CV-10

H-1(AH) Bell Huey Cobra

State	City	Organization	Number
AL	Dothan	DAV Chapter #87	71-21014
AL	Dothan	DAV Chapter #87	71-21014
AL	Florence	AL Post #11	67-15803
AL	Huntsville	Vet Mem mus	70-15940
AL	Troy	City of Troy	67-15771
AR	Bull Shoals	VFW Post #1341	66-15343
AR	Fort Smith	Viet Vet Assoc467	67-15469
AR	Wynne	CCVMC	68-17080
AZ	Marana	VFW Post #5990	78-23066
AZ	Three Points	VFW Post #10254	68-17104
CA	Stockton	AL Post #632	70-15987
CA	Susanville	City of Susanville	67-15684
CO	Burlington	VFW Post #6491	67-15479
CO	Kremmling	Town of Kremmling	68-15001
CO	Walsenburg	State Vet Nursing	66-15309
CT	East Hampton	VFW Post #5095	66-15325
CT	Prospect	VFW Post #8075	67-15479
CT	Waterbury	City of Waterbury	70-15986
FL	Deltona	City of Deltona	67-15843
FL	Merritt Island	Vet Mem Cntr	68-17023
FL	New Smyrna	VFW Post #4250	71-21028
GA	Donalsonville	AL Post #157	70-16001
IA	Ida Grove	AL Post #61	
IA	Manchester	VFW Post #6637	67-15717
IA	Parkersburg	AL Post #285	70-16087
IA	Waterloo	AL Post #730	71-21040
IL	Waterloo	Hawkeye College	70-16022
IL	Collinsville	AL Post #365	81-23539
IL	Herrin	VFW Post #1567	68-15143
IL	Highland	VFW Post #5694	71-20987
IL	Island Lake	Village of Isl Lake	67-15736
IL	Washington	Washington Park	70-16045
IN	fishers	AL Post #666	
KS	Atwood	AL Post #46	66-15338
KS	Pratt	City of Pratt	67-15624
KY	Prestonburg,	Kentucky Wing CAP	70-15945
LA	Many	DAV Chapter #21	68-15130
MA	Freetown	VFW Post #6643	79-23240
MA	Worcester	VVA Chapter #554	70-16096
MI	Charlotte	AL Post #42	67-15805
MI	Decatur	VFW Post #6248	68-17070
MI	Monroe	VVA Chapter #142	68-15074
MI	Onondaga	VFW Post #6986	70-16056
MN	Arlington	AL Post #250	68-17042
MN	Fosston	City of Fosston	68-15000
MN	Hill City	City of Hill City	67-15513
MN	Shakopee	City of Shakopee	70-16032
MO	Ellington	VFW Post #6043	68-15018
MO	O'Fallon	VFW Post #5077	68-15204
MO	Saint Joseph	NMHM	68-15200
MO	Springfield	AMMO	70-16086
MO	Springfield	AL Post #639	
MO	St. Louis	VFW Post #3944	70-15944
MO	Warsaw	AL Post #217	66-15306
NC	Marshville	AL Post #440	67-15587
NC	Statesville	AL Post #65	68-17040
ND	Lidgerwood	City of Lidgerwood	67-15769
NE	Gordon	AL Post #34	70-15967
NE	Wakefield	AL Post #81	67-15772
NJ	Clark	AL Post #328	70-16043
NJ	Hamilton	Town of Hamilton	83-24193
NJ	Milltown	AL Post #25	68-17072
NJ	Monroe	Stone Museum	68-15116
NJ	S Plainfield,	Borough of SPlainfield	69-16442
NY	Adams	AL Post #586	71-21033
NY	Bath	VFW Post #1470	68-15086
NY	Campbell	AL Post #1279	67-15668
NY	Eden	AL Post #880	67-15506
NY	Franklinville	VFW Post #9487	78-23097
NY	Hamburg	VFW Post #1419	69-16446
NY	Lowville,	MCL Detachment754	68-17074
NY	Massena	AMVETS Post #4	67-15790
NY	New Hartford	AL Post #1376	68-15110
NY	Parish	AL Post #601	78-23047
NY	Patterson	AL Post #1542	66-15318
NY	SacketsHarb	AL Post #1757	68-15091
NY	Stittville	VFW Post #8259	67-15528
OH	Ellsworth	VFW Post #9571	
OH	Jefferson	VFW Post #3334	67-15450
OH	Pickerington	AL Post #283	71-21009
OH	Sidney,	AMVETS Post 1986	67-15683
OH	Sidney	VFW Post #4239	66-15250
OH	Zanesville	VVA Chapter #42	67-15490
PA	Beaverdale	AL Post #460	68-15085
PA	Butler	County of Butler	68-15057
PA	Carrolltown	VFW Post #506	67-15795
PA	Chambersburg	Guilford Township	67-15663
PA	Du Bois	VFW Post #813	66-15348
PA	Midland	AL Post #8168	71-21031
PA	New Galilee	VFW Post #8106	68-17043
PA	Philipsburg	Mid-State Airport	67-15663
PA	Pleasant Hills	AL Post #712	68-17088
SC	Chesnee	AL Post #48	70-16034
SC	Greer	City of Greer	67-15768
TN	Collegedale	City of Collegedale	67-15642
TN	Crump	City of Crump	70-16053
TN	Louisville	VFW Post #5154	66-15321
TN	Sweetwater	VFW Post #5156	68-17085
TX	Big Spring,	Viet Memorial Commi	68-15054
TX	Hallettsville,	Viet Vet Assoc. #854	67-15479
TX	Hawkins	GHVMA	69-16440
TX	Hubbard	City of Hubbard	68-15179
TX	Killeen	City of Killeen	77-22795
TX	Seadrift	VFW Post #4403	67-15700
UT	Vernal	VFW Post #5560	78-23110
VA	Bristol	City of Bristol	66-15299
VA	Danville,	America Armoured	68-17022
WI	Almond	AL Post #339	68-15169
WI	Bangor	Village of Bangor	67-15824
WI	Black River Falls,	Jackson Par	66-15316
WI	Chippewa Falls,	State of WI	70-15948
WI	Eagle River	AL Post #114	68-15151
WI	Eagle River	AL Post #114	68-15151
WI	Elderon	VFW Post #8068	70-16047
WI	Fond du Lac	AL Post #75	68-17026
WI	Footville	AL Post #237	68-15133
WI	Hurley	VVA Chapter #529	70-15975
WI	Janesville	VFW Post #1621	67-15491
WI	Kendall	AL Post #309	68-17099
WI	Lake Geneva	AL Post #24	71-21044
WI	Lowell	VFW Post #9392	68-15123
WI	LyndonStati	VFW Post #5970	68-15123
WI	Marshfield	AL Post #54	68-15022
WI	Mosinee	VFW Post #8280	68-15152
WI	New Lisbon	AL Post #110	70-16044
WI	North Lake	Town of Merton	68-15106
WI	Pound	Village of Pound	71-21003
WI	PrairieduSac	VFW Post #7694	70-15998
WI	Sparta	AL Post #100	67-15661
WI	Waterford	VFW Post #11038	67-15813
WI	Wild Rose	AL Post #370	66-15302
WV	Weirton	BHCVM	66-15307

UH-1 Bell Huey (Iroquois)

State	City	Organization	Number
AL	Andalusia	Town of Sanford	68-16097
AL	Daleville	City of Daleville	66-16325
AL	Dothan	City of Dothan	65-09643
AL	Elba	City of Elba	66-16877

State	City	Organization	Code
AL	Enterprise	City of Enterprise	65-09747
AL	Eufaula	VFW Post #5850	68-16349
AL	Jacksonvi	AL Post #57	66-16769
AL	Mobile	VVA Chapter #701	69-16730
AL	Monroevill	AL Post #61	66-17052
AL	Ozark	City of Ozark	65-09770
AL	Tuscaloosa	40/8 Voiture#1060	66-16907
AR	Holiday Isl	VFW Post #77	71-20244
AR	Rogers	City of Rogers	67-17416
AR	Springdale	NW Arkansas WWII	65-12882
CA	Santa Barb	Viet Vet Assoc.218	65-10054
CA	Santa Moni	Museum of Flying	66-00765
CA	Susanville	City of Susanville	66-16374
CO	Fruita	City of Fruita	70-16329
DE	New Castle	VVA DE St	60-16227
FL	Hernando	VFW Post #4252	
FL	Inverness	Vet Educational	71-20139
FL	Merritt	Islan Vet Mem	66-16886
FL	Orlando	The Ntl Vet War.	66-16923
GA	Alpharetta	AL Post #201	64-13736
GA	Bainbridge	City of Bainbridge	69-15693
GA	Cairo	VFW Post #8433	70-16406
GA	Chickamau	City of Chickamuga	66-16405
GA	Conyers	AL Post #77	64-13643
GA	Cordele	GA Vet Mem Park	70-16224
GA	Lexington	AL Post #123	66-16992
GA	Tallapoosa	Haralson CntyVet	68-16609
GA	Williamson	City of Williamson	66-16304
IA	Colum Jnct	LA Cnty Area Viet	64-13601
IA	Onawa	City of Onawa	67-17281
ID	Burley	City of Burley	67-17599
IL	Aurora	City of Aurora	65-09819
IL	Canton	City of Canton	66-01039
IL	Dixon	VFW Post #540	71-20066
IL	Oglesby	City of Oglesby	
IL	Pekin	VFW Post #1232	
IL	Quincy	IL Vet Home	66-16683
IL	Washbount	AL Post #661	66-00761
IN	Fairmount	AL Post #313	68-16504
IN	Munster	Town of Munster	67-17288
IN	Orland	AL Post #423	67-17562
IN	Sullivan	VFW Post #2459	66-16665
KS	Emporia	City of Emporia	68-15652
KS	Overbrook	AL Post #239	66-16674
KS	Tonganoxie	VFW Post #9271	67-17267
KY	Flatwoods	Greenup CntyWar	68-16594
LA	Ball	Town of Ball	67-19526
LA	Lafayette	LA Museum Mil	68-16134
LA	Ruston	VFW Post #3615	65-12873
LA	Ville Platte	Viet Vet Asoc 632	65-09775
MA	Beverly	VFW Post #545	65-09560
ME	Millinocket	AL Post #80	64-13678
MI	Adrian	VFW Post #1584	66-17031
MI	Ann Arbor	VFW Post #423	68-15275
MI	Bay City	City of Bay City	70-16358
MI	Cheboygan	VVA Chapter #274	68-15586
MI	Fraser	VFW Post #6691	66-00796
MI	Hermansv	VVA Chapter #571	71-20333
MI	Lapeer	VFW Post #4139	64-13851
MI	Marcellus	VFW Post #4054	67-17514
MI	Monroe	VVA Chapter #142	66-00632
MI	Pontiac	VVA Chapter #133	66-01130
MN	River Roug	City of River Rouge	73-21712
MN	Belle Plaine	City of Belle Plaine	68-15369
MN	Chisholm	AL Post #247	69-15916
MO	Bloomfield	The Stars Stripes	74-22453
MO	Lee's Sumit	VVA Chapter #243	66-00979
MO	Neosho	City of Neosho	68-15533
MO	Saint Joseh	Ntl Military Heritage	62-02113
MO	Saint Joseh	Ntl Military Heritage	66-00551
MO	Springfield	AL Post #639	69-15051
MS	Magee	VFW Post #9122	67-17219
MS	Purvis	County of Lamar	66-16287
MS	Walnut	Town of Walnut	72-21639
MT	Missoula	Rocky Mntn Mus	
NC	Conover	VFW Post #5305	64-13729
NC	Salisbury	VFW Post #3006	6616236
NC	Waynesvile	VFW Post #5202	67-17145
ND	McVille	City of McVilled	73-21687
ND	New Rockd	AL Post #30	67-17500
NE	Omaha	AL Post #374	
NM	Angel Fire	Viet Vet Ntl Mem	64-13670
NV	AmargosaV	VFW Post #6826	66-17004
NV	Winnemuca	Cnty of Humboldt	66-16654
NY	Arcade	VFW Post #374	66-16155
NY	Buffalo	BECNSP	63-12982
NY	Cuba	MilitaryVehicles	70-15815
NY	Dix Hills	AL Post #362	64-13754
NY	East Aurora	VFW Post #8495	67-17798
NY	Fairport	AL Post #409	67-17611
NY	Gowanda	AL Post #79	66-00831
NY	Massena		
NY	NTonwanda	Town of Wheatfield	65-09690
NY	Waterloo	VFW Post #6433	68-16521
OH	Arcanum	VFW Post #4161	65-09888
OH	Batavia	VVA Chapter #649	63-12972
OH	Columbus	Defense Const	69-15939
OH	Harrod	Village of Harrod	65-09587
OH	Holmesville	AL Post #551	70-16349
OH	Medina	VFW Post #5137	70-16428
OH	Newark	Viet Vet Assoc. #55	
OH	Vandalia	VFW Post #9582	65-09696
OH	Washingtvil	VFW Post #5532	68-16610
OK	Cushing	City of Cushing	70-16460
OK	Glencoe	City of Glencoe	66-16135
OK	Roland	AL Post #339	65-09937
OR	Canby	Viet Vet Asoc392	70-16351
PA	Doylestown	VVA Chapter #210	68-15336
PA	Glenside	VVA Chapter #590	65-09897
PA	Greensburg	City of Greensburg	66-01129
PA	Jersey Shor	AL Post #36	66-16014
PA	Milford	AL Post #139	68-15543
PA	New Berlin	AL Post #957	68-15526
PA	NewKensing	VFW Post #92	64-14175
PA	Pottsville	AMVETS Post227	66-16012
PA	Stoystown	AL Post #257	66-16993
PA	Towanda	VFW Post #1568	70-16432
PA	W Brownsvi	AL Post #940	67-17813
PA	White Havn	VFW Post #6615	66-15102
SC	Barnwell	VVA Chapter #828	67-17338
SC	Gaffney	AL Post #109	66-00764
SC	Mount Plea	PPNMM	65-10132
TN	Chattanoog	VVA Chapter #203	64-13786
TN	Dickson	VFW Post #4641	66-00868
TX	Big Spring	Viet Mem	0-61078
TX	Conroe	VVA Chapter #734	67-17456
TX	Eagle Pass	VFW Post #8562	68-16536
TX	Midland	Viet Vet Mem	73-21676
TX	Pampa	Freedom Museum	67-17859
TX	Port Neche	VFW Post #4820	65-10090
TX	Sweetwater	City of Sweetwater	65-10014
VA	South Hill	VFW Post #7166	64-13745
WI	Endeavor	VVA Chapter #659	66-17059
WI	Madison	WI Vet Museum	
WI	River Falls	Viet Vet Asoc331	74-22438
WI	Waupaca	VFW Post #1037	65-09803
WV	Fairmont	VietnamVetMem	66-16109
WY	Casper	VFW Post #9439	69-15660